Virtual Environments for Corporate Education:
Employee Learning and Solutions

William Ritke-Jones
CyberMations Consulting Group, USA

BUSINESS SCIENCE REFERENCE

Hershey · New York

Director of Editorial Content: Kristin Klinger
Director of Book Publications: Julia Mosemann
Acquisitions Editor: Lindsay Johnston
Development Editor: Beth Ardner
Publishing Assistant: Myla Harty
Typesetter: Myla Harty
Production Editor: Jamie Snavely
Cover Design: Lisa Tosheff
Printed at: Yurchak Printing Inc.

Published in the United States of America by
    Business Science Reference (an imprint of IGI Global)
    701 E. Chocolate Avenue
    Hershey PA 17033
    Tel: 717-533-8845
    Fax: 717-533-8661
    E-mail: cust@igi-global.com
    Web site: http://www.igi-global.com/reference

Library of Congress Cataloging-in-Publication Data

Virtual environments for corporate education : employee learning and solutions
/ William Ritke-Jones, editor.
    p. cm.
 Includes bibliographical references and index.
 Summary: "This book should be used by human resource managers, corporate educators, instructional designers, consultants and researchers who want to discover how people use virtual realities for corporate education"--Provided by publisher.
 ISBN 978-1-61520-619-3 (hbk.) -- ISBN 978-1-61520-620-9 (ebook) 1. Virtual reality in management. 2. Employees--Training of. 3. Virtual reality in education. I. Ritke-Jones, William, 1958- II. Title.

HD30.2122.V55 2010
 658.3'124--dc22

2009039913

British Cataloguing in Publication Data
A Cataloguing in Publication record for this book is available from the British Library.

All work contributed to this book is new, previously-unpublished material. The views expressed in this book are those of the authors, but not necessarily of the publisher.

Table of Contents

Section 2
Applications

Section 3
Designs and Measurements

Section 4
Connections

Section 5
Integrated Technologies

Detailed Table of Contents

Section 1
Foundations

Chapter 1

Lea Kuznik, University of Ljubljana, Slovenia

This chapter illustrates how the immersive environment of virtual worlds offers people various intellectual and sensory activities. The chapter argues that human connections can be made in ways that cannot be replicated in the physical world, illustrating the impact of these connections in K-12 learning as well as in corporate education. In the corporate world, the chapter shows, adults can learn and explore in multiple and different ways, thus enhancing their educational experience.

Chapter 2

Mary Rose Grant, Saint Louis University, USA

This chapter defines the characteristics and learning preferences of the adult learner within the parameters of androgogy and argues that because constructivist learning appeals to adult learners, the online environment is well suited to courses concerned with teaching adults. Virtual environments give adult learners the opportunity to apply what they learn immediately. The chapter concludes by recommending instructional design and teaching strategies for adult learners in virtual environments.

Chapter 3

Christopher Keesey, Ohio State University, USA
Sarah "Intellagirl" Smith-Robbins, Indiana University, USA

This chapter describes the first corporate forays into virtual worlds and why they failed. The chapter also illustrates the nature of virtual worlds and provides corporations with a set of questions that they can ask themselves to determine whether a virtual world will meet their training needs.

Chapter 4

This chapter details the history of Web 2.0 and its applications to corporate education. It illustrates how Web 2.0 is being used in the workplace now and considers future developments, including Web 3.0. Using this illustration as a foundation, the chapter then makes training recommendations for future teachers, trainers and administrators.

Section 2
Applications

Chapter 5

This chapter attributes pressures on small businesses and their difficulties in competing with larger businesses to being able to train their workers. The chapter argues that virtual realities can be used to support training in small and medium businesses. Finally, it offers a detailed description of how car mechanics were trained in a virtual reality and discusses future trends.

Chapter 6

This chapter argues that virtual world learning environments should be used to train engineers in the manufacturing sector just as they are in the academic sector. The chapter posits that virtual worlds hold tremendous promise to safely and effectively train engineers in distributed corporations. This training can range from basic skills to expert level training in process planning and simulation without any cost for travel, physical environments, materials, or tools.

This chapter evaluates the attributes of a successful training project that was conducted in Second Life. This project, the Canadian border simulations shows how simulations in Second Life were used to teach port-of-entry interview skills to students. Test scores, motivation and level of engagement increased substantially for students taking the course and resulted in the Canadian Border Services Agency piloting the program with agency recruits. The recruits had results similar to the students.

Section 3
Designs and Measurements

This chapter describes an online competency-based model for teaching adult learners. The chapter expands emergent themes within best practices and identifies competencies for course design, delivery and facilitation of adult centered online learning environments. The chapter then applies this model to train-the-trainer programs for those educators engaged in teaching in online environments, including virtual worlds.

This chapter introduces an assessment rubric for virtual world learning environments developed from proven principles of user experience design, instructional design, interface design, learning theory, technical communication, instructional systems design (ISD), and VIE motivation theory. The authors have coined their system the CIMPLe system because it is a holistic approach that weaves together context, interactivity, motivation, presence, and cognitive load, all necessary ingredients for a successful virtual world learning environment. Course designers can use this system as a checklist for developing courses in virtual worlds.

This chapter illustrates the necessity for promoting digital literacy in future business workers and describes a business-writing course that integrates Second Life. The chapter also offers how such a course could be implemented in a corporate environment so that learners will experience communicating in virtual realities.

Chapter 11

This chapter provides a deep discussion of virtual realities and distance education in corporate environments. Building on other taxonomies of learning as well as social presence theory, collaborative theory and situated learning theory, the authors have developed a taxonomy of learning that should be applied to corporate education in virtual realities. The taxonomy progresses from one-way communication to two-way communication to education co-creation to community building. Using this taxonomy, the chapter makes a convincing argument that the immersive nature of the virtual world can provide rich learning experiences for the corporate learner.

Section 4
Connections

Chapter 12

This chapter argues that transformative learning needs to be accomplished in most diverse teams. It provides a deep explication of transformative learning theory and explains how to promote it through coaching and role-playing. The chapter further describes how a virtual world can provide an effective environment for coaching and role playing where the transformation of distorted assumptions is the learning goal.

Chapter 13

This chapter argues that 3D virtual worlds are the new company water cooler, i.e., the place where people go to connect and socialize. In the virtual world, colleagues all over the globe can come together to forge and maintain relationships. As they do so, a corporate learning community is fostered as ideas are exchanged. The authors explain how to design environments in virtual worlds that will promote the formation of learning communities and illustrate learning communities that they promoted.

Chapter 14

Martha C. Yopp, University of Idaho, USA
Allen Kitchel, University of Idaho, USA

This chapter defines the characteristics of high-functioning teams and explains issues that affect teams functioning in virtual realities. It then identifies best practices that can positively contribute to effective and efficient teamwork. The chapter provides extensive coverage of the concept called "bioteaming," in which the characteristics of nature's most effective teams are applied to teams operating in virtual realities. The chapter finishes by describing effective teams in Second Life and what human resource directors and trainers can learn from these teams.

Chapter 15

K.A. Barrett, Distance Education Consultant, USA
W. Lewis Johnson, Alelo, USA

This chapter uses socio-cultural theory to provide a foundational pedagogy for teaching cross-cultural communication skills in serious games. The chapter provides design scenarios for environments that have as their goal the development of cross-cultural communication skills. Finally, the chapter describes how corporations and organizations are using or have used this method.

Section 5
Integrated Technologies

Chapter 16

Natalie T. Wood, St. Joseph's University, USA
Michael R. Solomon, St. Joseph's University, USA
Greg W. Marshall, Rollins College, USA
Sarah Lincoln, St. Joseph's University, USA

This chapter recommends a hybrid approach to curriculum development for corporate education, especially as the Millennium Generation enters the workforce because this generation has been brought up on digital technologies. It distinguishes between educating and training in the corporate world and discusses how virtual realities can be used for both educating and training. The chapter emphasizes a dichotomy between content and experience-based learning.

Julie Davis, Clarkson University and Texas Tech University, USA
Letitia Harding, University of the Incarnate Word and Texas Tech University, USA
Danna Mascle, Morehead State University and Texas Tech University, USA

This chapter establishes that the distance educator should incorporate both synchronous and asynchronous technology to accommodate all learning styles. The authors use their own experiences as educators and students in a MOO (multi-user doman, object oriented) to make their case. Blending technologies will often ensure that training objectives are met.

Mikail Feituri, Università Telematica Guglielmo Marconi, Italy
Federica Funghi, Università Telematica Guglielmo Marconi, Italy

This chapter discusses the use of intelligent agents (artificial intelligence) in virtual worlds and their application to corporate education. The chapter shows how intelligent agents can be constantly present in the learner's environment, interacting verbally and non-verbally. This interaction makes self-directed learning more interactive, interesting and fun. The chapter also illustrates common techniques to create a society of agents and how to integrate them into the learning environment.

Anna Peachey, Eygus Ltd., UK
David Livingstone, University of the West of Scotland, UK
Sarah Walshe, Open University, UK

This chapter describes cutting-edge technology that mashes Moodle, an open source distance education platform, with Second Life. The chapter first explains a pioneering collaboration between Thomas Reuters and The Centre for Professional Learning and Development at the Open University that developed a 10-week cohort-based course for first line managers using Flash modules. It then proposes that the integration of Second Life would provide a greater immersive experience and details how the mash-up between Moodle and Second Life works. The remainder of the chapter shows how an evaluative tool can be developed for evaluating the introduction of virtual realities into work-place training.

Preface

THE EVOLUTION OF VIRTUAL REALITIES

When many people think of virtual worlds, they think of games such as *World of Warcraft*. Others think of virtual worlds as places where people socialize, gamble, have cybersex or otherwise spend their extra time. Both of these notions about virtual worlds are corrects ones because certainly virtual worlds started as places for people to play, and they still are.

Virtual worlds had their genesis when government scientists who were connected via intranet, the internet still being some years in the future, developed games that they could play with each other while they were at different workstations. Later, influenced by the game *Dungeons and Dragons,* Will Crowther developed a game called *Adventure* with a computer language called *Apranet* in 1975. Roy Trubisaw and Richard Bartle developed the first MUD, muti-user domain, in 1978 (Bartle, n.d.). From there many other MUD's were developed using "telnet," including the once very popular Lambda MOO, created by Pavel Curtis at Stanford University. Lambda MOO (MOO stands for multi-user domain, object oriented) remains in existence and is created entirely with text so that as one moves from place to place, s/he reads descriptions of the space and of the people in that space.

Virtual worlds have changed significantly over the years, changed rather than developed because 3-D worlds limit what can be done in virtual worlds as much as they expand what can be done. For instance, while many wild and interesting things can be created in *Second Life*, the most popular 3-D virtual world, what can be created with pixels still cannot match the creations of a person with a keen imagination and a sharp facility with words. Too, a place like Lambda MOO is truly created collaboratively by all the people who go there and create characters and spaces because everything is connected directly or indirectly. On the other hand, one "sim" may not be connected at all to another sim in *Second Life*, either physically or thematically.

VIRTUAL REALITIES IN CORPORATE EDUCATION

Nonetheless, the evolution of virtual realities has been positive for education in general and corporate education specifically, at least technically. While one might applaud the ease that the newer technology has made connecting people with images, text and audio, creating with words as was done in the earlier MUDS has largely been lost. Yet the ability to connect has been the primary catalyst for corporations and other organizations to begin considering potential uses for virtual realities. Corporations first took notice of Second Life when they thought they could market within Second Life's space, since Second Life supposedly had so many participants and its own economy. To tap into that market, a number of corporations established a presence, spending much money to build spaces and to market. But nobody came. Moreover, the porous firewalls needed for Second Life, the need for high performance computers, the gambling and sex sims right next door and the spotty technical support, in my experience, caused many corporations to abandon Second Life.

Over the past couple of years, corporations have taken another look at virtual realities not because of their potential for marketing but because of their potential for connecting people. Unlike other technologies, a 3-D virtual reality provides the illusion of space and identity, so a virtual world such as Second Life can accommodate a real time meeting with employees all over the globe interacting within the same space. Moreover, since identities can be created in Second Life by buying clothes, skins, shapes, even walks, people can interact with one another through avatars that serve as representations of themselves. This technology has an advantage over technologies such as video or audio conferencing, then, because all participants can be in the same space at the same time, an advantage if the space has been personalized.

Corporations have discovered the training and educational potential of virtual worlds as well as the potential for collaboration. AHG Corporation uses training simulations within Second Life so that people can make "real" mistakes without any real life consequences ("AHG, Inc," 2008). Medical schools and other health care providers simulate emergencies within the virtual world so doctors and nurses can make quick decisions and develop their team skills (Gage, 2009). Northrop Gruman has built a replica of a high-tech bomb disposal system on which it trains people with Second Life, and if they make a mistake, nobody really gets blown up ("Case Study" 2009). Other entities such as the U.S. Military, the Financial Leadership Corporation, and IBM, who has made a large commitment to training in Second Life, have training activities within the virtual world (Hood, 2008).

The ability to connect people and the ability to create simulations has also allowed corporations to train managers, sales staff, even receptionists. The immersive nature of the 3-D virtual world and its ability to provide space also creates enormous possibilities for team training. A number of corporations have started to use this environment for team training, and some consultants have specialized in training teams in the virtual world. Since the technology can bring teams together in one space, cultural contact zones can be created where team members can learn about each other in ways that will help them accomplish their team's mission more effectively.

A FEW OF THE VIRTUAL WORLDS BEING USED WITH THEIR BENEFITS AND DRAWBACKS

Thus far, Second Life has dominated training in virtual worlds, but other worlds are seeking to solve Second Life's issues. For instance, Sun Microsystems has devoted its Wonderland to strictly business applications. Wonderland boasts of a totally immersive experience for participants by employing VOIP (voice over internet protocol) and video and making it easier to use. Another advantage over Second Life, a Wonderland platform can be devoted to a corporation's server, solving security issues. Wonderland lacks, however, the enormous identity creation capacity of Second Life as well as the capacity for creating personalized spaces, an important point because teams work better in spaces that they can claim as their own. Also, rather than having employees create identities, Wonderland allows for people to connect directly to a LinkedIn, Facebook or Human Resources profile. While this capacity provides a deeper portrait of employees, it disallows anonymity, useful for learning projects such as transformative learning that I discuss in one of this volume's chapters. On the other hand, my personal experience and the research of others suggests that anonymity and the creation of avatars that may not even resemble a human may cause people to dehumanize the other's avatar and may promote anti-social behavior.

As Sun continues in its development, it may address issues such as these and others that have applications to education, but thus far they have asked for much input from programmers but not much from educators. To develop this technology for corporate education, Sun should seek the collaboration of educators, not just programmers. Otherwise, the tool may become just another gadget, something to play with rather than work with.

Other technologies such as Forterra Olive offer more flexibility than Second Life for the corporate user who wants to load a virtual reality onto the corporation's server, but it seems only capable of giving corporations another meeting venue, and with software such as Webex available, one wonders why this software would be used. The demonstration video on its website illustrates how it can be used for PowerPoint presentations, and it likely has chat and VOIP capabilities, but I saw no mention of it. It may have more potential, but since it will not download onto a MacIntosh, I could not fully test it.

Also geared exclusively to the corporate user, Qwaq Forums offers more versatility in identity creation, but not much more. Upon entering the forum, one is provided with a character that looks much like the old Gumby cartoon character, but one can download a personal picture to act as Gumby's head. Also, it does not seem to offer the opportunity for a group to create its own space, one of which the group can take ownership. Nevertheless, because a corporation can buy the software and load it directly onto their server, it provides greater security than Second Life. The issue of being "griefed" or of other avatars sexually harassing employees or of sensitive employees accidentally running into sexually themed sims does not exist.

Still in the alpha stage of development, Open Simulator claims that one has the flexibility to create identity in the same way as one can in Second Life. A group can also, apparently, create its own space. If this virtual reality has the same features as Second Life, simulations for skills training can be accomplished in it as well as team training and transformative learning, a shortcoming of the other virtual worlds at which I looked because their avatars could not be "animated." For skills training, avatars that can perform actions are essential, so if this technology can accomplish this feat, it will answer some significant training needs.

Another great plus for this Open Simulator, an intranet can be created for it so that it operates on a private grid. At this stage of its development, I could not download the software; thus I could not test it. However, if its claims are true, then perhaps this technology has successfully addressed Second Life's issues while retaining its benefits. I hope that in further developing this technology, the developers will seek collaboration with corporate educators and consultants.

Virtual realities cannot answer every training need of the networked corporation. Other technologies should be used in complement to virtual realities in order to fill the toolbox of the educator or consultant. Issues with Second Life such as the technical issues as well as the social focus of the environment make Second Life, perhaps, not the best tool for the educator's toolbox.

HOW TO USE THIS BOOK

This book should be used by human resource managers, corporate educators, instructional designers, consultants and researchers who want to discover how people have used virtual realities for corporate education and who want to talk to other educators about how they might be used. Further, I hope that virtual world designers and programmers will use this book to discover how educators have used and want to use this technology. This book strives to lay a strong theoretical background for the use of virtual realities in corporate education, but it focuses on practical application. Divided into five sections, it provides a foundation for education in virtual worlds in the section titled, "Foundations," a section that displays actual educational events in virtual worlds titled, "Applications," a section that outlines approaches to designing and measuring virtual world education titled, "Designs and Measurements," a section that focuses on team training titled, "Connections," and finally a vital section titled, "Integrated Technologies" that illustrates how various technologies can be integrated with virtual realities in order to provide the most effective learning environment.

Virtual realities give the educator another tool to use in the design, development and implementation of educational programs. We must always remember, however, that the tool must fit the job and that we must never become so enamored of the tool that we lose sight of the job we need to do. In other words, the educational need should drive the development of the technology; we should not force our educational needs into a tool just because it exists. With that in mind, we should know when to use virtual realities, when to use other high technology tools, and when to use a chalkboard.

REFERENCES

"AHG, Inc." (2008). Retrieved July 30, 2009 from http://www.crmbyweb.com/

Bartle,R.(n.d.).Summary MUD history. In *Living internet*. Retrieved July 30, 2009 from http://www.livinginternet.com/d/di_major.htm

"Case Study: Northorp Grumman." (2009, May). In *Second life*. Retrieved July 28, 2009 from http://work.secondlife.com/successstories/case/ngc/

Gage, D. (2009, July 21). Second life trains first responders. *InformationWeek: The Business Value of Technology*. Retrieved August 2, 2009 from http://www.informationweek.com/news/personal_tech/virtualworlds/showArticle.jhtml?articleID=218501620

Hood, T. (2008, Aug 8). A second life for training. Retrieved August 2, 2009 from http://www.fastcompany.com/blog/tom-hood/toms-fastcpa-thoughts/second-life-training

Section 1
Foundations

Chapter 1
Using Virtual Worlds for Learning

Lea Kuznik
University of Ljubljana, Slovenia

ABSTRACT

Virtual worlds for adults (e.g. Second Life), youth (e.g. Habbo) and children (e.g. Whyville) have a great potential for learning and teaching practices for enriching wider public and engendering collective experience and collaboration. Informal learning environments such as virtual worlds offer people various intellectual and sensory activities or »peak« experiences, according to Gogala. Virtual worlds promote social interaction and offer visitors an opportunity for various interactive activities which can sometimes not be realized in real life corporate learning and training which is one of the major concerns for large companies. Adults can explore and learn in a different way and from a different perspective. Virtual worlds represent a new medium that allows people to connect in new virtual ways and offer new challenges in the corporate educational field.

INTRODUCTION

Emerging technologies such as virtual worlds, serious games, wikis and social networking sites have been heralded as technologies that are powerful enough to transform learning and teaching. When we think of learning, school comes to mind first. However, many people, especially the disadvantaged, do not achieve their full potential through traditional educational approaches for a variety of reasons. A lot of valuable learning also takes place outside school, often facilitated by digital technologies, for example, through online games. Mobile technologies and internet can provide access to rich digital media content and facilitate communication with others both local and remote to provide powerful learning experiences that go well beyond the traditional classroom.

Due to new technologies new approaches to learning become possible, diversifying the range of learning experiences available, and thereby engaging with people who have not achieved their

DOI: 10.4018/978-1-61520-619-3.ch001

full potential with more traditional approaches. Many new approaches to learning and teaching are facilitated by new technologies. In addition to the real world, online world contains a whole range of virtual worlds in which we can live our second (virtual) life. Although virtual worlds for adults, youth and children differ according to their content, they offer an opportunity to learn in a virtual learning environment and have great potential for learning activities.

Virtual worlds are persistent virtual environments in which people experience others as being there with them - and where they can interact with them. How does education keep up with virtual worlds and leisure trends? Virtual worlds are attracting interest from different organizations and companies as platforms for learning. Also known as immersive environments, these systems can provide significant advantages over other learning strategies. Virtual worlds are also creating opportunities for activities, which can not be realized in real life corporate education. Above all, adults can explore things and learn in a different way and from a different perspective. On this basis the paper focuses on some of the possibilities and opportunities posed by adapting virtual worlds for educational use in corporations. It is important to create an environment which would enable people to construct their knowledge on their own or through interaction with peers, objects, learning games, simulations and other activities.

THE CONCEPT OF EXPERIENTIAL PEDAGOGY

When designing corporate learning activities in virtual learning environments we have to take into account some of the following theorists of learning: Dewey (1963) and his concept of experiential learning, Piaget's (1990) theory of construction of knowledge, Kolb's (1984) theory of experiential learning as a constant cyclic process and Gardner's

(1991) theory of multiple intelligences. Moreover, we should also consider Vygotsky's (1978) theory which emphasizes the social component of learning, Gogala's (2005) idea of experiential pedagogy and the flow concept proposed by Csikszentmihalyi (2002).

A recent pedagogic concept which is important for designing interactive learning environments is the idea of experiential pedagogy proposed by Slovene pedagogue Stanko Gogala (2005). He claims that a successful development of someone's personality requires experience - emotional exchange, a feeling that in a suitable situation enables us to become aware of the problem and work to benefit from its dismissal. However, in order to do this, we have to design encouraging environments and assure diverse experiences, considering interests of adults or children involved and offering possibility of choice in which adults or children become involved in interactions with different objects, materials, peers... An adult or a child is encouraged to get involved in a certain exciting activity that drags him into a circle of intense experiencing and unconventional establishment of social relations. The main factor of the experiential pedagogy is the intense situation in which a person experiences an exciting event and engages in relationships with other persons and creates a more cohesive social connection and forms of person's active collaboration. And according to his/her own interests, needs, learning style helps to construct active learning environment, including different activities and social relations.

»To experience something« in the full sense of the word is not the same as »to have an experience of« something. Gogala therefore distinguishes superficial experience and peak experience. Psychology talks about superficial experiences that we call ideas, images, thoughts, emotions, and strivings. Richness of superficial experiences is enormous. The concept of peak experience, however, implies deeper mental actions as e.g. deep astonishment, experience of beautiful or suffering. We gain education via superficial experiences, whereas the upbringing is an ability to experience different cultural values growing in our psyche after we have experienced something (Gogala, 2005). Gogala views the peak experience as the very psychological base. Peak experiences are experiences that a person gains through active collaboration and encounters them in active learning environments in different interactions with materials and peers, through which a person accesses findings in explorations of the world, with his/her own actions. We can say that peak experiences are permanent collaborative interactions during which an adult or a child constructs his/her own knowledge (Kuznik 2007).

FLOW EXPERIENCES IN VIRTUAL LEARNING ENVIRONMENTS

Positive psychology is the scientific study of human happiness. The history of psychology as a science shows that the field has been primarily dedicated to addressing mental illness rather than mental wellness:

Flow is the mental state of operation in which the person is fully immersed in what he or she is doing by a feeling of energized focus, full involvement, and success in the process of the activity (Csikszentmihalyi, 1990). Flow is experienced when perceived opportunities for action are in balance with the actor's perceived skills. Adapted from Csikszentmihalyi (2002, 1997) retaining the essential insight that perceived challenges and skills must be relative to a person's own average levels. The conditions of flow include: perceived challenges, or opportunities for action that stretch existing skills; a sense that one is engaging challenges at a level appropriate to one's capacities and clear proximal goals and immediate feedback about the progress that is being made (Csikszentmihalyi, 2002).

Flow principles have been translated into practice in a variety of contexts. Two types of intervention can be distinguished: those seeking to shape activity structures and environments so that they foster flow or obstruct it less and those attempting to assist individuals in finding flow. Several art museums, including the Getty museum in Los Angeles, have incorporated flow principles during their design of exhibits and buildings (Csikszentmihalyi, 2002). Educational settings present an opportunity to apply the results of flow research most directly. Educational game designers in virtual worlds also benefit from integration of flow principles into game play design.

In virtual worlds flow can be fostered by influencing both environment and individual. Visitors have many opportunities to actively choose and engage in activities related to their own interests and then pursue these activities without imposed demands or pacing. People select activities that challenge and stretch them. They also indentify new challenges as their capacities grow (Csikszentmihalyi, 1997). Games, sports, and other flow activities provide goal and feedback structures that make flow more likely. A given individual can find flow in almost every activity, however – working a cash register, building a house or driving a car. Similarly, under certain conditions and depending on individual's history with the activity, almost any pursuit – a museum visit, a round of golf, a game of chess – can bore or create anxiety. It is the subjective challenges and subjective skills, not objective ones, that influence the quality of a person's experience (Csikszentmihalyi, 2002).

Csikszentmihalyi developed a series of theories to help people get into their flow state. Since then, these theories have been applied to various fields for designing better human interactive experiences, e.g. games. In order to maintain a person's flow experience, the activity needs to reach a balance between the challenges of the activity and the abilities of the participant. If the challenge is higher than the ability, the activity becomes overwhelming and generates anxiety. If the challenge is lower than the ability, it provokes boredom. Fortunately, human beings have tolerance, there is a fuzzy safe zone where the activity is not too challenging or too boring, and psychic entropies like anxiety and boredom would not occur (Csikszentmihalyi, 1990).

The description of flow is identical to what a player experiences when totally immersed in a game. During this experience, the player loses track of time and forgets all external pressures. It is obvious that gamers value games based on whether or not those games can provide flow experiences (Holt, 2000). Games and simulations involve people in collaborative learning and are among the most widespread ways of learning in virtual worlds. They are increasingly important in helping the corporate world to manage change because they create a shared language and stories, push people to the limits of their capabilities, help organizations to sustain their focus on key issues and address complex subjects.

VIRTUAL WORLDS TODAY

Virtual worlds are persistent virtual environments that allow for interaction through which people experience others as being there with them (Schroeder, 2006). These interactive online three-dimensional virtual environments are possible to visit 24 hours a day, 7 days a week (Castronova, 2005). Virtual worlds are designed for different age groups, children, youth and adults, and separated in terms of content. Some of them emphasize education (Whyville), while others focus on role play (Gaia), fashion (Stardoll), music (vSide), sports, television, movies and books (Virtual MTV), toys and games from the real world (Barbie Girls), casual games (Club Penguin), socializing (Habbo), creating the content of the virtual world (Second Life).

In all virtual worlds the player is physically represented by his/her virtual person – avatar, whose appearance is chosen by the player alone. Avatars can be people (Second Life, There, Whyville), house pets (Webkinz), fantasy creatures (Funkeytown), animals (Club Penguin), monsters (Moshi Monster)... Their appearance is chosen and changed by each player alone (e.g. color and length of hair, clothes, shoes, equipment...).

The following graphs represent currently most popular virtual worlds for children, youth and adults that have millions of registered accounts since the year of launch.

The most popular virtual world at the moment among children is virtual world called Neopets with 45 millions of users, launched in 1999, followed by Poptropica with 20 millions, launched

Figure 1. The most popular virtual worlds for children under 12 years old

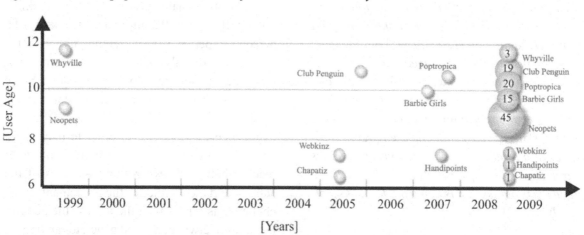

Figure 2. The most popular virtual worlds for children and youth from 12 to 20 years old

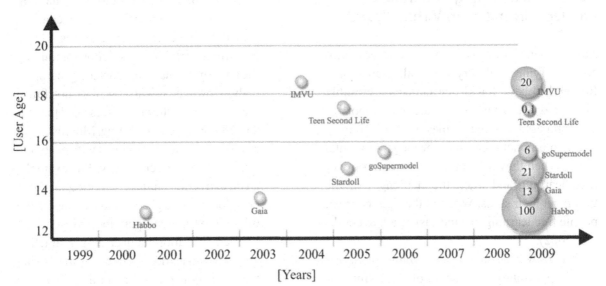

in 2007 and Club Penguin with 19 millions of registered accounts, launched in 2005.

The most popular virtual world at the moment among youth is Habbo with 100 millions registered accounts that was launched in 2000, followed by Stardoll with 21 millions launched in 2005 and IMVU with 20 millions registered accounts, launched in 2004.

The most popular virtual world at the moment among adults is Second Life with 15 millions registered accounts that was launched in 2003, followed by Virtual MTV with 3 millions launched in 2006 and there with 2 millions registered accounts, launched in 2005.

Figure 3. The most popular virtual worlds for adults

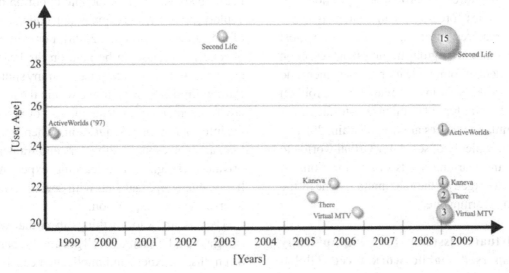

Corporate Learning Possibilities and Opportunities in Virtual Worlds

Most human learning is self-motivated, emotionally satisfying, and very personally rewarding. Researches have found that humans are highly motivated to learn when they are in a supportive environment, engaged in meaningful activities, freed from anxiety, fear, and other negative mental states, when they have choices and control over their learning and when the challenges of the task meet their skills. When in the right context, people find learning fun and easy (Falk & Dierking, 2002).

Virtual worlds provide a new range of educational opportunity. The nature of these environments is generative, allowing users not only to navigate and interact with a pre-existing three-dimensional environment, but also to extend that environment by creating objects of their own. These objects can be seen and used by others. Although the user is ultimately constrained by the technologies driving the virtual world, each virtual world offers a set of tools for recreating real world objects and experiences and for expanding these objects and experiences as far as the imagination and technology can reach.

Corporate learning and training is one of the major concerns for large companies with high rate of work force turnaround and rotation. For example, sales forces and call center operators training requires substantial budget. The most complex training is a group training that focuses on development of communication, management and leadership skills during a collaborative problem solving. For this type of training face-to-face business simulation games are used (Swain, 2001).

There is plenty of scope for virtual worlds to manage the learning needs of organizations. It can be leveraged to the maximum extent in the following learning areas:

1. **Virtual classroom for geographically dispersed mobile work force**: Global organizations have employees that are dispersed geographically. These employees often have common learning needs. E-learning certainly is a solution for training the employees that are dispersed geographically. However e-learning does not fulfill the needs when the employees need to learn something by experimenting. Moreover employees often need to interact with peers and trainers in an effective way. For example, an oil extraction engineer working for Oil & Gas Company might want to learn about the oil well extraction operations by getting a live demonstration about drilling. Extraction engineer can learn effectively by discussing the extraction procedure in a virtual well with a fellow engineer or a trainer in virtual worlds.

Classes in virtual worlds offer opportunities for visualization, simulation, enhanced social networks, and shared learning experiences. Some people learn best by listening to the course content, others by seeing and visualizing the content in context, and the rest by using a hands-on approach to demonstrate course competencies. In virtual worlds, we can leverage a mix of content and activity to support all learners: auditory, visual, and kinesthetic. Virtual worlds support these different learning styles and give people opportunities to explore, discover, and express their understanding of the subject (Calongne, 2008). For example in Second Life class can be held on the beach, in another country, in outer space, or in any simulated setting. Employees can move within the learning environment, communicate via text or voice, offer information or ask questions whenever they like, and correspond with peers and trainers via private messaging. The learning experience is lively, engaging, and rich with social networks, interaction, and expression.

Users share a lot of things in virtual worlds using avatar. This removes all geographic barriers. Strengths, weakness and intellectual capabilities of employees can be very easily judged by the trainer and peers using avatar based interaction in virtual worlds. This can help the trainer provide the training material matching the learning needs of an individual.

Naturally, the tool's capabilities do not guarantee a great learning experience. The success of a course depends on effective course design, delivery, and assessment. Course designers, instructors, and IT professionals are challenged to create stimulating content, deliver it reliably, and ensure a stable virtual world learning environment.

2. **Simulation of new concepts and processes**: Organizations generally use road shows, e-learning, audios, videos, newsletters to educate employees about new processes, tools and products. However a live simulation where employee can actually experience the new product or tool is required in some circumstances to remove employee inertia and convince users about the capability of a new product. As an example employees of an automobile manufacturing company might need a new component for auto manufacturing process. By simulating the component for automobile manufacturing in a virtual world, employees can get a complete experience of using the component and understand the component completely.

3. **New hire introduction**: Large numbers of new employees are frequently »digital natives« who have grown up with 3-D games and will appreciate a company that »gets it«. They might have some experiences with virtual worlds and other 3-D environments. In addition, new hires are equipped with brand new computers, which run the virtual world without hangups. We can send new employees through a time machine in Second Life to see the company's storied history or have them walk around 3-D models of factory floors, call centers and offices around the world facilities they might never get to experience first-hand during their career at the company, walk around and fly around 3-D models of the company's products and meet with other young people who are about to start at the company (Gronstedt, 2008).

4. **Sales training**: Sales training and product roll-outs are other common virtual world applications. Companies will role-play sales skills, show models of new products, host guest speakers. Sales reps are typically geographically dispersed, motivated to learn and eager to socialize with colleagues. One example is training a salesperson for selling complex pharmaceutical products. A scenario for training pharmaceutical sales force personnel would include a virtual hospital world, which would allow the salesperson to emulate navigating the front desk, talking with the receptionists, dropping off samples, having discussions with doctors, and several other points. This kind of scenario can be used for business training in the other industries:

   ◦ For selling complex goods (selling cars, broker dealers, investment management, etc.).
   ◦ Call center operators training for complicated call situations.
   ◦ Financial manager training for decision making in investment/risk management and analysis in combination with standard simulation.
   ◦ Training for lawyers in courtroom scenarios.

Another training scenario may assume that students' roles are equally important. For example, training of management or leadership skills can use a scenario of a military mission or an exploration expedition with a group of people, when the formal leader is absent (get killed or wounded at the beginning of the scenario) (Nebolsky, Yee, Petrushin & Gershman, 2003).

5. **Avatar-based marketing**: Global companies such as Adidas, Apple, IBM, Toyota and the news agency Reuters are just a few of the companies who have moved into virtual worlds, especially in Second Life. Adidas even sell some of their clothes and shoes through Second Life and Toyota use Second Life as a showroom for some of their cars. Reuters has a news reporter on one of the Second Life islands with the sole task of reporting news and events that take place on the island to other residents (Terdiman, 2006). Inevitably, companies see the potential in Second Life, especially from a marketing point of view. Marketing in socially interactive 3D-worlds such as in Second Life has even gone so far that the phenomenon has got its own name: avatar-based marketing. The phenomenon is about that the avatar carries the organizations message. The avatar-based marketing is about targeting avatars created by the users psyche to make them consume the products (Harvard Business Review, 2006). As Bonita Stewart, in charge of the interactive marketing of Daimler Chrysler states: »When marketing online, you want sustained engagement with the brand rather than just a click-through to a purchase or product information. Avatars create an opportunity for just this type of engagement« (Harvard Business Review, 2006).

The above learning areas clearly demonstrate a learning need of organizations that can only be fulfilled by virtual worlds.

The emergence of virtual worlds in pedagogical contexts tries to combine avatar-based interaction without losing out on the flexibility benefits traditional distance learning offers. For example, using Second Life for educational purposes is a relatively new phenomenon. Yet, it has received its share of publicity in the media with newspapers, network channels and websites flooding the matter with articles, insights and attention.

Second Life is used as a platform for education and interactive experiences by many institutions, such as colleges, universities, libraries, government entities and corporates. There are over one hundred regions used for educational purposes covering different subjects. Educators use it for classes, research, learning and projects with their students, bringing a new dimension to learning. A series of educational institutions such as Harvard University have started to realize the pedagogical potential in Second Life and now offer online courses in this virtual reality world. Universities either rent or build their own islands in order to ensure privacy, and then set up virtual lectures in which teachers and students can communicate in real time using instant chatting or microphones. Harvard University, one of the universities that perhaps have gone the furthest when it comes to bringing education into the virtual world, now offer law courses to geographically dispersed students from all over the world (Harvard Business Review, 2006). There are also many companies in Second Life today which are putting their message out there, establishing their brands and identities, and learning to engage users with their products and ideas. However, it's suitability as a pedagogical tool has yet to be assessed to a greater extent, mainly due to its novelty.

Although Second Life is currently the most popular virtual world it does not necessarily need to be the most suitable for different companies. Compared to the other virtual worlds, Second Life has the advantage of offering a relatively easy way of designing buildings, changing avatar appearance and interaction between its citizens. Some setbacks it has compared to the other worlds are that it is perceived to be much slower. Opportunities within Second Life are perceived to be that a new type of online learning could be conducted.

Using a virtual world environment for training can dramatically decrease the cost and improve the availability of training that requires significant person-to-person interaction. The virtual world can simulate a business environment visually, while using live remote people to deliver the lessons. The virtual world does this by representing real life interactions through avatar character visualization coupled with telephone driven voice conversations. This simulates the level of quality of interaction of the face-to-face training environment without having to bring people to the same location. Additionally, training can be spread out throughout a long period of time. Instead of a focused week of training, employees could take training at regularly scheduled times with the trainers being paid by the amount of time they log into the system to support the virtual sessions. This shifts training from a "once and done" mentality to an ongoing channel for continuous skills development. For example, if a sales person wants to try a new strategy or technique on a customer, they can practice in advance in the virtual world before attempting the task in the real world (Nebolsky, Yee, Petrushin & Gershman, 2003).

All these different possibilities for learning in virtual worlds can be organized in a framework or a model. We can use this framework to identify learning activities in our content area and connect these activities to potential applications of virtual worlds. Basically, both virtual life and real life consist of people and objects, and these can interact in three possible combinations: person-person, person-object and object-object interaction (Antonacci & Modaress, 2005). Many opportunities for learning can be categorized into these three interaction combinations.

First possibility is person-person interaction, e.g. virtual classroom or role play. According to a scenario a person accepts the chosen role in a certain realistic situation (assuming a role of a salesperson, takes suitable products, talks with the receptionists, drops off samples, has discussions with doctors, does something, solves something...). Characteristics of person-person interaction are solving problems, group task involvement, exchange of opinions concerning certain theme, common creation... Emphasis

is on the social interaction. Various games and events such as interviews, lectures, belong here as well.

In person-object interaction adults also learn how to interact with objects. This includes designing and building their own 3D objects, exploring objects by using them, organizing, dismantling and assembling objects which is how they get information concerning these objects. Adults can learn how to use the selected object, build a house, design jewellery, clothes, cars... We can present a problem scenario in order for adults to create their own virtual solutions. Different simulations involving persons also belong here.

In object-object interaction adults learn how objects interact with other objects. We can use virtual worlds to illustrate and explain physical and procedural processes. For example, different simulations of cultural and natural phenomena, like a volcanic eruption, how mountains are formed when two tectonic plates collide, how hazardous chemicals get into our water supply, and how a car is built in an assembly line. An adult can change different variables and influence the process with a purpose of understanding the processes or natural and cultural phenomena better.

Virtual worlds create opportunities for activities which cannot be realized in real life education. Above all, adults can explore things and educational content in a different way and from a different perspective: they can fly, float above an object, sit on it, create his/her own, change it, jump onto or into it, break it, tie it up and explore it in a way that is not possible in real life education. They can change the size of objects - make them bigger or smaller. Because of better conditions for exploration they can enlarge objects which are tiny in real life and the other way around. Virtual worlds also enable adults to exchange opinions with other residents of the virtual world, to communicate with people from all over the world, to reach the unreachable location (e.g. flying with spacecraft to the outer space), projection of films, slides, streaming videos.

CONCLUSION

The capacity to learn (not just in virtual worlds) is always dependent upon prior knowledge and experience as well as upon interest, motivation, and expectations. What might someone learn by changing their race or even being an animal or a fantasy creature in virtual world? What might people with physical disabilities do in virtual world which would be difficult or impossible for them in real life? Despite the open possibilities virtual worlds provide, we still remain a little bit constrained by our own real life experiences and expectations.

However, virtual worlds can introduce quality virtual learning environments with lots of flow experiences and following characteristics. First of all, virtual worlds are accessible to all regardless of geographic location. By visual representation of people around us, voice communication and fully navigable and interactive 3D environment virtual worlds enable people from all over the world to feel as if they are all present in the same place together. Social experience and social collaboration with other people is the primary value of virtual worlds. Virtual worlds enable equal conditions for learning also for people with special needs, physical restraints or the handicapped. In virtual worlds individuals can express their interests, ideas and challenges. They express themselves via the character of avatar, conversations and gestures.

So what does this mean for corporate education? Virtual worlds extend our audience to an international level, gets the users involved in the social aspects of the internet, appeals to gamer cultures, allows user generated content (creative writing, visual art, short films...), enables collaboration, allows wandering, linking, searching activities that promote discovery, compelling technical features, enables capabilities to interface with external data sources, rich media content support and up-to-date hardware capabilities (Rothfarb & Doherty, 2007). One of the best uses of virtual worlds today are virtual events that reach people around the world. Events can allow different people to attend the same event in person and virtually. Recently, more and more emphasis is being placed on the role of information technologies in education of adults, youth and children. Virtual worlds develop technological savvy, offer experiential learning as well as foster global relationships and civic responsibility.

Virtual worlds provide learning organizations a powerful, unique ability to engage and empower employees in ways that accommodate their digital lifestyles, adapt to their individual learning needs and encourage collaboration. It is revolutionary, but it's not an overnight revolution. For now, the virtual worlds can be perplexing and intimidating. It is a lot like the WorldWideWeb in 1993-94: clunky and slow, but we could all see the potential. Most companies are not clamoring for a place in virtual worlds yet as the notion is still new and the learning benefits are still emerging. But dismissing the importance of Web 3D technologies that millions are already using in learning strategy would be like dismissing the Internet in 1994 (Gronstedt, 2008).

Fundamentally, virtual worlds represent a new medium that allows people to connect in new virtual ways. An international research and analytic company Gartner Group claims that by the end of 2011, 80% of active internet users will have a »second life« in one of virtual worlds. Moreover, they predict that by the end of 2012, 3-D will become a standard practice for education and training (Gartner, 2007). There are some people that are even predicting that virtual worlds will redefine the Internet. It would be far too simple to say that the Metaverse will consist of Linden Lab's virtual world with maps or Google's mirror world with avatars. What's coming is a larger digital environment combining elements of all these technologies – a 3-D Internet (Mitham, 2008). It is not yet possible to switch avatars from one to another virtual world although it had already happened once accidentally (avatar from Second Life has emerged in There). Nevertheless, Google is already developing a project of universal avatars that will move through different virtual worlds (Lohr, 2008). The audience is there. The tools are available. The content is waiting. It is up to us to take the next step.

REFERENCES

Andersen, A., Hristov, E., & Karimi, H. (2008). *Second Life - New Opportunity for Higher Educational Institutions*. Bachelor Thesis, Business Administration, Jönköping University, Sweden.

Antonacci, D., & Modaress, N. (2008). Envisioning the Educational Possibilities of User-Created Virtual Worlds. *AACE Journal, 16*(2), 115–126.

Calongne, C. M. (2008). Educational Frontiers: Learning in a Virtual World. *Educause Review Magazine, 43*(5), September/October.

Castronova, E. (2005). *Synthetic Worlds: The Business and Culture of Online Games*. Chicago, IL: University of Chicago Press Publisher.

Csikszentmihalyi, M. (1990). *Flow: The Psychology of Optimal Experience*. New York: Harper and Row.

Csikszentmihalyi, M. (1997). *Finding flow*. New York: Basic.

Dewey, J. (1963). *Experience and Education*. New York: Collier Books.

Edwards, S. E., & Schaller, D. T. (2007). The Name of the Game: Museums and Digital Learning Games. In Din, H., & Hecht, P. (Eds.), *The Digital Museum: A Think Guide* (pp. 62–68). Washington, DC: American Association of Museums.

Falk, J. H., & Dierking, L. D. (2002). *Lessons Without Limit, How Free-Chioce Learning is Transforming Education*. Walnut Creek, CA: AltaMira Press.

Gardner, H. (1991). *The Unschooled Mind: How Children Think And How Schools Should Teach*. New York: Basic Books.

Gartner Inc. (2007). Retrieved November 29, 2007, from http://www.gartner.com/it/page.jsp?id=503861

Gogala, S. (2005). Chosen Pedagogic Essays. Ljubljana, Slovenia: Drustvo 2000.

Gronstedt, A. (2008). Making Learning Fun and Social. *E-learning Magazine*. Retrived May 10, 2009 from www.gronstedtgroup.com/pdf/ELearningMagazine.pdf

Holt, R. (2000). *Examining Video Game Immersion as a Flow State*. Bachelor Thesis, Department of Psychology, Brock University, Canada.

Kolb, D. (1984). *Experimental Learning (Experience as The Source of Learning and Development)*. Upper Saddle River, NJ: Prentice-Hall.

Kuznik, L. (2007). *Interactive Learning Environments and Children's Museums - Theoretical Model and It's Planning*. Unpublished Doctoral Dissertation, University of Ljubljana, Slovenia.

Lohr, S. (2008). Free the Avatars. *The New York Times*. Retrieved October 15, 2008 from http://www.nytimes.com

Malone, T. W., & Lepper, M. R. (1987). Making Learning Fun: A Taxonomy of Intrinsic Motivations for Learning . In Snow, R. E., & Farr, M. J. (Eds.), *Aptitude, Learning and Instruction III: Conative and Affective Process Analyses* (pp. 223–250). Hillsdale, NJ: Lawrence Erlbaum Associates.

Mitham, N. (2008, April). *Virtual Worlds by The Numbers: Today and The Future*. Paper presented on Virtual Worlds Expo 2008, New York.

Nakamura, J., & Csikszentmihalyi, M. (2002). The concept of flow . In Snyder, C. R., & Lopez, S. J. (Eds.), *Handbook of Positive Psychology* (pp. 89–105). Cambridge, UK: Oxford University Press.

Nebolsky, C., Yee, N. K., Petrushin, V. A., & Gershman, A. V. (2003). Corporate Training in Virtual Worlds. In *The 3rd International Conference on Advanced Learning Technologies,* (pp. 412-420). Riga, Latvia: IEEE Computer Society Press.

Piaget, J., & Inhelder, B. (1990). Psychology of Children. Novi Sad, Serbia: Dobra vest.

Review, H. B. online version. (2006). *Avatar - based marketing*. Retrieved April 12, 2009 from http://harvardbusinessonline.hbsp.harvard.edu/hbsp/hbr/articles/article.jsp?articleID=R0606B

Rothfarb, J. R., & Doherty, P. (2007). Creating Museum Content and Community in Second Life . In Trant, J., & Bearman, D. (Eds.), *Museums and the Web 2007*. Toronto, Canada: Archives & Museum Informatics.

Schroeder, R. (2006). Being There and the Future of Connected Presence. *Journal of Teleoperators and Virtual Environments*, *15*(4), 438–454. doi:10.1162/pres.15.4.438

Swain, J. J. (2001). Power Tools for Visualization and Decision - Making. ORMS Today. Retrieved May 7, 2009, from http://www.lionhrtpub.com/orms/surveys/Simulation/Simulation.html

Terdiman, D. (2006). Newsmaker: Reuters' Second Life Reporter Talks Shop. Retrieved April 5, 2009 from http://www.news.com/Reuters-Second-Life-reporter-talks-shop/2008-1043_3-6129335.html

Vygotsky, L. S. (1977). Thinking and Talking. Belgrade, Serbia: Nolit.

KEY TERMS AND DEFINITIONS

Avatar: A computer user's representation of himself/herself or alter ego, whether in the form of a three-dimensional model used in computer games. It is an "object" representing the embodiment of the user.

Experiential Learning: The process of making meaning from direct experience. Experiential learning focuses on the learning process for the individual (unlike experiential education, which focuses on the transactive process between teacher and learner). An example of experiential learning is going to the zoo and learning through observation and interaction with the zoo environment, as opposed to reading about animals from a book. Thus, one makes discoveries and experiments with knowledge firsthand, instead of hearing or reading about others' experiences.

Flow: The mental state of operation in which the person is fully immersed in what he or she is doing by a feeling of energized focus, full involvement, and success in the process of the activity.

Interaction: A kind of action that occurs as two or more objects have an effect upon one another.

Peak Experiences: Experiences that a child or an adult gains through active collaboration and encounters them in active learning environments in different interactions with materials and peers, through which a child or an adult accesses findings in explorations of the world, with his/her own actions. In general, permanent collaborative interactions during which an adult or a child constructs his/her own knowledge.

Second Life: 3-D virtual world imagined and created by its residents. Residents can explore, socialize, participate in individual or group activities, create and trade virtual property and services with one another, or travel throughout the world.

Virtual Learning Environment: A software system designed to support teaching and learning in an educational setting. It works over the Internet and provides a collection of tools such as those for assessment, communication, uploading of content, return of students' work, peer assessment, administration of student groups, collecting and organizing student grades, questionnaires, tracking tools, etc. New features in these systems include wikis, blogs, RSS and 3D virtual learning spaces.

Virtual World: A computer-based simulated environment intended for its users to inhabit and interact via avatars.

Chapter 2
Application of Adult Learning Theory in Distance Learning

Mary Rose Grant
Saint Louis University, USA

ABSTRACT

Adult learning theory suggests that adults need to perceive the relevance and purpose of learning in order to learn most effectively. Grounded in the notion that adults frame their own learning objectives, are self-directed and active participants in their learning, require constructive feedback and want opportunities to practice new skills, online and virtual learning environments are well suited for adult learners and are directly based on adult learning principles. Virtual environments provide opportunities for adults to construct learning based on what they already know and apply what they are learning in the instructional setting. An online instructor is an adult learning expert. Using adult and constructivist learning theories and current knowledge about web-based andragogy, this chapter will focus on the characteristics and learning preferences of adult-learners in virtual learning environments and recommend instructional design and teaching strategies to encourage behaviors that influence student engagement, retention and learning.

INTRODUCTION

Adult learning and constructivist learning theories, as applied to web-based learning, provide the framework for benchmarking best practices in online learning (Burge, 1988; Diaz and Bontenbal, 2001; Grant & Thornton, 2007). Moore and Kearsley (1996) wrote that the more one understands andrag-

ogy and the assumptions of adult learning, the better one will understand the nature of distance learning and hence, the advantage of learning technologies. Consequently, various adult learning theories and philosophies have influenced the development of best practices on virtual teaching: Knowles' (1980) assumptions of adult learners, Dewey's (1938) thoughts on experience and education, Candy's (1989; 1991) work on constructivist thought and self-directed learning, Jarvis' (1987) social context

DOI: 10.4018/978-1-61520-619-3.ch002

in adult learning, Friere's (1986) "cycle of action and reflection", described as "praxis", and Roger's (1967) acceptance and respect for the learner. These theories are integral to the development of effective virtual learning environment for adults. New knowledge about generational learning styles is expanding what we know about adult and generative learning, bringing necessary and added dimensions to virtual teaching and learning environments.

As online course designers and developers recognize the application of these and other theories, they can construct learning objects and virtual environments that are comprehensive and specific to adult learning. The line between teaching and facilitating is blurred when the student becomes the focus of the learning space. Meeting the adult-learner where they are in their learning process is key to effective teaching and the point where learning begins. The place where facilitation and connectivity meet is the online, virtual learning community. Adult learning theories that inform best practices of online teaching, course design, delivery and management expand the connectivity and interconnectivity of virtual learning environments.

This chapter will describe adult learning theories and their implications for distance learning. Principles of adult learning will be examined for application in design, delivery and management of web-based instruction. The focus will be on learning how to create relevant and meaningful learning environments to engage and retain online adult learners. Recommendations for adaptability in different virtual learning environments are proposed.

The first section provides a theoretical background of adult learning to describe web-based andragogy. The second section reviews current research on adult online learning and summarizes characteristics of online adult learners and learning preferences. The third section describes online instructional processes which cut across generational lines. The final section discusses the

implications for practice and future development of instruction in alternate virtual environments. This chapter provides insights into teaching adults online that can be used by corporate trainers and facilitators to plan and implement successful virtual training and development programs which satisfy and address the needs of a multigenerational and diverse workforce.

BACKGROUND

Adult Learning Theories

Some adult learning theories, more than others, seem to lend themselves to virtual learning environments where adult learner needs and learning preferences are considered. The profile of a distance learning student parallels that of the adult learner, the older student who usually works outside of the home, is married with a family and takes courses on a part-time basis to enhance their personal and professional lives. In order to provide these students educational experiences that will be beneficial in both work and life arenas and to promote lifelong learning, it is important to understand how and why adults learn. In the field of adult education, Malcolm Knowles is well know for his use of the term andragogy, defined as "the art and science of teaching adults", to describe a set of assumptions about the characteristics of adult learners. The adult learning principles, developed by Knowles (1980), posits that adults are internally motivated and self-directed individuals who prefer to participate actively and take responsibility for their own learning. Since adult learners have garnered a myriad of life experiences, they want to be able to use these experiences and be recognized for their contributions. In addition, learning must be relevant and practical with applicable outside of the classroom (e.g. the workplace). Adult learners usually have specific goals in mind when they enroll in a course, and they appreciate organization and structure in course management as well as clearly defined expectations and requirements for successful course completion. Adult learners may not be interested in taking courses for the sole sake of learning but to attain goals that are tangible (e.g. career advancement and employability skills). Finally, adult learners demand and require respect; they bring life and work experiences to the classroom and want to have some control over their own learning experience.

Knowles' theory of andragogy borrows ideas from psychologists from two opposing therapeutic positions, humanist and behavioralist (Smith, 1999). His concept of andragogy, as a learner-centered approach to teaching, was influenced by Carl Rogers, a clinical psychologist in the 1970's, who espoused a humanistic approach to learning, which is facilitative rather than directive (St. Clare, 2003). The behavioral influence comes from Maslow and his Hierarchy of Human needs that suggest reinforcement as a teaching approach (Smith, 1999; 2002). Knowles was also influenced by Freire's concepts of action and reflection, but downplayed the radical context of adult education as social reform (Spencer, 1998). Dewey's ideas on education and experience most influenced Knowles' notion of effective teaching being active not passive (Knowles, 1980). With these influences, Knowles was able to bring about a shift in adult education in the 1970's from a behavioral, teacher-directed, content-driven approach to a more facilitative and student-centered model.

Knowles' attempt to differentiate between the processes of pedagogy and andragogy and to argue andragogy as a theory of adult learning was scrutinized when first proposed and continues to be questioned and criticized by contemporary educators as having little empirical or theoretical basis for critical analysis (Brookfield 1992). Critics of Knowles write that his work as a theory of learning provides little insight into the how and why of adult learning other than prescribing a list of assumptions about learners and offering guidelines for practice (Davenport, 1993; Pratt,

1993; Tennant, 1996). It is rooted in the perspectives of adult education in the mid-1960's rather than grounded in a conceptual framework for broader settings and times. Brookfield (1992) argues against an adult learning theory that excludes the variables of culture, ethnicity, personality and political ethos to present chronological age as the defining element for how learning occurs and is experienced. Given the diversity of learners in today's society more theoretically applicable and inclusive approaches to adult education are needed. Transformative, experiential, and constructivist learning, as well as contemporary learning theories such as "communities of practice" and "connectivism" make more sense for framing andragogy as the e-pedagogy in virtual learning environments (Kolb,1984; Mezirow, 1991; Siemans, 2005; Tisdell,1998; Wenger, 1998).

Another learning theory that supports online learning for adults is constructivism. This theory asserts that knowledge is constructed based on previous experience (Spigner-Littles & Anderson, 1999). The emphasis on experience and subjective reality is consistent with the needs of adult learners. These learners connect new learning to previous experiences, and acquire knowledge actively and internally rather than externally or passively as transmitted by an instructor. Adult learners, with life experience find it difficult to accept learning that is not authentic or experiential. It is difficult to change misperceptions or pre-conceived ideas and beliefs when new concepts are only transmitted through passive lecture with no interaction between instructor and student. Adult learners are more likely to replace old beliefs when they are allowed to construct or generate new knowledge on their own (Merriam & Caffarella, 1999).

Generative learning is very similar to the constructivist model in that students are connecting new concepts with stored knowledge as well as experiences to generate deeper knowledge. The generative process gives students an opportunity to mentally interact with concepts and ideas to create personal understanding and meaning for the subject (Wittrock, 1974; 1990). This is an active learning process. Therefore, courses are more effective when the instructor facilitates rather than directs student learning (Merriam & Caffarella, 1999; Spigner-Littles & Anderson, 1999). The online learning environment gives adult learners an opportunity to take on a more active role in the learning process and to "interact" with course materials and with the virtual environment itself, building conduits between different parts of the environment to construct deeper understanding and knowledge (Wonacott, 2000).

Social constructivism is a variation on the constructivist learning theory and focuses on the social nature of learning. Culture, language and the context of learning is important. Learning takes place, concepts and understandings are mastered with the assistance and in collaboration with instructors and peers. Social constructivism was developed by post-revolutionary Soviet psychologist, Les Vygotsky. He argued that learning was not simply the assimilation and accommodation of new knowledge, but a process by which learners were integrated into a learning community (Vygotsky, 1978). In this theory, learning is a social phenomena and knowledge is co-constructed. The motivation to learn is both intrinsic and extrinsic, in the sense that learning is motivated by rewards from the learning community and dependent on the learner's internal drive to promote the learning process. Both constructivism and social constructivism require learners to be active participants in the learning process, to develop collaborative learning skills and to see individual learning in relationship to a community of learners.

These theories become more critical with technology advancements in education and in e-learning, particularly when designing instructional environments for adult learners. As the environments in which learning takes place are changing, so are the methods of teaching and learning. With modifications, the tenets of andragogy and adult learning theory are still relevant and provide a foundation for e-pedagogy. The nature of the

virtual learning space is dynamic, inclusive and effective. These technology-enhanced spaces tap into the constructivist theories where adult learners actively construct knowledge and generate learning that is authentic and relevant (Jonassen et al., 1993). It is important to see how these adult learning and constructivist theories are combined to provide an environment where learning is social and collaborative, reflective and applicable as well as culturally sensitive and viable. In terms of the nature of the instructional process, there is a convergence of pedagogy and andragogy in the virtual environment and learning becomes ageless. The mature learner enters and re-enters education with expectations of flexibility, application and recognition for experience, while the newer generation of learners wants immediate access to information and views knowledge as a task to complete rather than a process to value. Instructors must be able to recognize, appreciate and accommodate the variety of "generational" learners crowding into virtual learning spaces and be ready to facilitate different needs and preferences for being there.

Today's students are increasingly more diverse than ever before. Incoming undergraduates are in many cases more technologically proficient than their instructors with 80% reporting that they have a computer by the time they reach college. With the majority of these students having already "surfed" the Internet for homework purposes (78%) and two-thirds having used e-mail, they are approaching college courses already experienced in Web technologies (NCES, 2005). Undergraduates also appear to be more non-traditional than in years past with 43% being 24 or older. The majority of these older undergraduates also report being employed (82%) and as a result, are approaching college with responsibilities above and beyond what they encounter in their classrooms.

Today's workforce is also more diverse than ever before with three, and sometimes four, generations working along side of each other. Baby boomers make up 40 percent of the workforce;

Generation X, 36 percent, the Millennial or Generation Y, 16 percent and growing, while the Traditionalists, a shrinking group, born between 1922 and 1945, make up the remaining 8 percent (Lancaster & Stillman, 2003). The number of females, as well as minorities, is also changing the face of the workplace in certain sectors, with a predicted 8 percent growth of women in the workforce over the next 10 years as compared with 5 percent growth of men (Shipman & Kay, 2009). Hence, the demands and challenges management faces in developing and retaining such a diverse group of adult workers is increasing. The practical significance of understanding adult learning theory across generations is most important when moving from traditional to web-based modes of training. As employees today are less bound by brick and mortar work environments, so too should they be less bound by traditional training environments. Offering web-based programs that match individual needs and are convenient and flexible, necessitates a closer look at how adults live and learn. Internal and external pressures to provide and expand distance learning options while maintaining an effective and productive workforce falls on management and those who oversee training and professional development.

The swing from traditional to online learning environments has prompted more interest in assessing the quality of instruction and instructional design, as well as identifying various practices for achieving student learning. Examining the instructional practices of facilitators, and analyzing instructor-student interactions within the learning environment, can be positive predictors of student learning and program satisfaction. A study to identify best practices in design, implementation and assessment of online instruction for adult learners and recommend applications of these practices in different venues to capitalize on the potential of web-based instruction and promote positive learning outcomes was presented. Adult learning and constructivist learning theories, as applied to web-based education, provide the framework for benchmarking these practices (Berge, 1988; Diaz and Bontenbal, 2001).

Our challenge, then, as corporations and those who manage corporate education and training, as well as well as instructors and facilitators, is to develop teaching and learning strategies for virtual learning environments that will capitalize on generational learning styles, maximizing strengths and minimizing weaknesses. The bottom-line for management is immediate return on training which provides specific skill development "just-in-time" and "on demand" that matches individual and corporate goals.

At least four different generations are present in the workforce and in educational settings. In academic and corporate learning environments, corporate management, administrators, instructors and learners themselves, can benefit from awareness and identification of generational learning styles. Demographers have defined these groups on the basis of birth rate. The groupings are also based on shared experiences, perceptions and attitudes that are loosely linked to when they were born. But since generations can span 20 years or more based on birth rate, there will be people at either end of the generation who have different experiences and therefore different world views. For instance, learners in the Baby Boomer generation, born between 1946 and 1964, require and respond to different teaching strategies than do those in Generation X, born between 1965 and 1980, based on different learning preferences, as well as life experiences. Most current adult learners, particularly in online environments, are Generation X'ers, while many of the faculty are Baby Boomers (Coates, 2006). Research regarding learning preferences of Generation X'ers supports the theories of adult learning and constructivism (Coates, 2006). For instance, members of Generation X value efficiency and tend to be independent. They want to know what their options are and what is expected of them upfront. "Generation X'ers" also value visual presentations and technology. This assessment suggests that this group of individuals is able to accept, appreciate, and be successful in virtual learning environments. However, the millennial, or Generation Y, group of students, born between 1981 and 2000, is fast approaching adult learner status and, in a few years, will replace the Gen X'ers as the group most represented in today's academic or corporate online and virtual learning environments (Oblinger, 2003). The challenges educational and corporations face include how to provide meaningful and authentic learning experiences in virtual environments and how to engage and teach adult learners effectively across generational lines. Research shows that most instructors have not had formal training as online facilitators or preparation to engage different generational learners (Moore et. al., 2005). Accommodating generational learning styles is relatively new, many instructors still teach the way they were taught, a style more conducive to the Baby Boomer than to the Gen X or Gen Y learner (Bates, 2005; Oblinger, 2003). The design and delivery of courses and the roles that instructors play in engaging and retaining new generations of learners is paramount to the success of the student, the course, and the organization. Research suggests bridging the generation gap with an understanding of learning preferences, including those described in adult learning and constructivist learning approaches (Skiba & Barton, 2006).

Certainly the field of adult learning theory warrants further scholarly research. Sound instructional design in distance education will depend on a clear understanding of what affects adult learning. Integrating adult learning theory into the course design, instructional strategies and materials, as well as the management and delivery system will provide a framework for the virtual learning environment, enhance teaching effectiveness and improve student learning. Studies have chronicled the advantages of integrating adult learning theory in virtual learning environments and reported that effective methodologies for adult learning are the same needed for technology-based learning environments (Fidishun, 2000; Grant & Thornton, 2007; Lacefield, 1999; Olka, 2005).

Applications of Adult Learning Theories in Online and Virtual Environment

Knowles' concepts on adult learning, as well as those of other theorists, are open to wide interpretation and scrutiny. However, as a guide to teaching adult learners, Knowles' basic set of assumptions provides a strong starting point for the instructional process and best practices in distance and virtual learning environments. Characteristics of distance learners mirror many of those described by Knowles for adult learners. These characteristics include being self-directed, internally motivated, self-sufficient, self-disciplined, purpose-oriented, practical, and learner-centered, but are not limited to or defined by chronological age, social group, culture, ethnicity or gender (Grant & Thornton, 2007; Nah, 1999; Robertson, 2002). Whether these characteristics are all present at the time an adult learner enters the virtual learning environment or are a result of it, is a question to explore.

INTEGRATING ANDRAGOGY AND TECHNOLOGY: A CASE STUDY

Accepting that adult students come into the virtual learning environment with the characteristics and learning preferences described by Knowles and other researchers in the field, the author designed and taught an online introductory biology course for adult learners using these characteristics and learning preferences as the pedagogical framework. This course was included in a case study and pilot to determine whether the online environment would be an option for delivering education to adult learners and whether the integration of adult learning principles with technology resulted in instructional strategies that were satisfactory, interesting and meaningful for adult learners. The information gathered was compiled in a progress report for institutional administrators and decision makers.

To develop a pedagogical framework in which course content could be designed and delivered, each adult learning principle, as represented in Knowles list of assumptions was examined and analyzed. Implications for instructional design, course development and delivery, and applications in online learning environments that cross generational lines are presented.

Assumption: Adult Learners are Self-Directed

This assumption implies that the learning environment be learner-centered as opposed to teacher-directed and that students will take responsibility for their own learning and the path it takes. The virtual learning environment is learner- centered and lends itself to self-directedness because of the nature of the environment itself. However, because of its very nature of random access and information overload, it requires more expertise and discipline than most students have to create a learning experience that is both meaningful and deep. It is not feasible to expect student to control the learning environment online without structure and facilitation. Self-directed learning has little to do with chronological age or maturing of the learner. The younger generations of learners, Gen X and Gen Y, are more adept at being self-directed in online environments because of their familiarity with and ability to "surf" the Internet for information that is instant and current.

Implication for Instructional Design, Course Development and Delivery

The virtual learning environment evolves into a learner-centered environment as students become the driving force for the learning. This, however,

can only take place within a framework designed to facilitate this type of learning. Realizing that not all adult learners are self-directed at the onset of the learning experience, the instructional design of the course should provide the framework for the learning process with structures and guidelines for completion of activities, submission of assignments and assessment of learning outcomes. Adults do not like or have time for ambiguity. They want specific directions, deadlines and timelines for task completion. This is particularly true for Baby boomer learners. Generation X and Generation Y learners, however, want the direction without being micromanaged. The most important element of the course, the course syllabus, provides course goals and learning objectives, as well as course requirements and expectations that guide the student towards self-directedness.

When an online course provides a solid framework, students can use the technology and the virtual environment as a springboard to self-directed paths of inquiry and discovery. The technology itself provides students with a variety of environments and resources for expanding learning in content and in context. The Internet serves as a perfect mechanism for exploration through random, branching, multimodal forms of information, accommodating a variety of learning preferences and interests.

An instructor can create learning activities that allow choice of topic and level of participation for independent and interdependent learners. With choices, students have opportunities to move ahead or return to learning modules when needed. In this regard, online learning is recursive learning and offers students the opportunity to access course content and resource materials at any time, in any place and at any pace during the course of the learning experience.

In the course designed for this case study, websites and web links to additional resources were provided for every topic in the course. Weekly web-searches for topics related to the course material were assigned and each student was expected to share their discoveries with all members of the class. Web links and web quests expanded the content material and enhanced interest and personal meaning for the students. Course topics expanded with web searches, take students away from the confines of content to discover broader perspectives in context of student interest for deeper understanding. This technique is particularly useful for Generation Y learners. The Gen Y learner's desire for immersion in virtual contexts prompts the need for additional opportunities to explore course topics in other venues. As a result these learners find more learning taking place outside than in the online classroom.

Using inquiry methodology, students in this same course, identified and analyzed current media articles on weekly course topics to assess their value and contributions to established bodies of scientific knowledge. These flexible routes through the course material give students, not so much control as creation of their own learning environment. In essence, to facilitate learning in a virtual environment, in any discipline, is to challenge the learner to discover new ways of thinking about learning and themselves as learners. Active learning techniques, rather than passive lecture engage students across generational lines in the learning process they co-create.

Assumption: Adult Learners are Purpose-Oriented

This assumption implies that adult learners have a goal in mind when enrolling in a particular program or course. These goals may be personal or professional, but essentially involve learning how to cope more effectively in different real life situations. Adults look for programs and courses that will help them reach their goals. Adults come to the educational environment when they are ready to learn and apply learning to developmental tasks outside of the educational setting. The readiness to

learn is a significant factor influencing academic achievement (Gibbons & Wentworth, 2001). From the experience of the author, most adult learners come into the educational system with a particular goal in mind, but often fail to make the connections between courses needed to synthesize the learning experience. Sometimes their need to know gets in the way of knowing.

Implication for Instructional Design, Course Development and Delivery

To engage adult students in the first weeks of the online course, opportunities are provided to introduce themselves, discuss their expectations for the course and provide some background on their prior knowledge and experiences. The course syllabus provides course goals and clear learning objectives that are aligned with assignments and assessment for expected student learning outcomes that hopefully match students goals. Active and experiential learning techniques allow students the opportunity to test out real-life problem solving skills. Online projects, web quests, games and simulations can be designed to relate real-life tasks and problems to learning objectives so that students can practice high-level problem solving skills in different situations and environments.

In the online course developed for this study, students were asked to use the scientific method to design a process for solving a problem observed in their community or work place. In another activity, they were given an opportunity to explore a web-based virtual simulation of a living cell to explain the mechanisms of cancer on the processes of cell division. In addition, authentic case studies and metaphors were used to help students connect tenets of biology and science concepts for application in real world settings and contemporary situations. Students also had an opportunity to choose a topic of personal interest and write about it using the concepts and theories learned.

Assumption: Adult Learners Are Internally Motivated

This assumption implies that the motivation to learn is internally as opposed to externally driven. Adults are motivated in different ways for different reasons. Internal motivation to learn may be prompted by self-esteem, social status, or the satisfaction that comes with enhanced knowledge. External motivators may include career or academic advancement as well as improved financial and economic status. Internal and external motivators change through developmental stages and are present across generational lines.

Implication for Instructional Design, Course Development and Delivery

To motivate and encourage students, challenge them to do their best by communicating high expectations in the syllabus and throughout the course. Provide directions, timelines and deadlines along with learning objectives for each weekly learning module. Creating an open atmosphere through discussion posts and chats with students will put students at ease and engage students encountering online learning for the first time. Incorporate rubrics and netiquette guidelines that communicate expectations of respect for other students and the instructor. The enormous amount of work in an online course should convey high expectations for student self-directed learning.

To encourage improvement, provide students with prompt feedback and return work with clear instructions for improvement. This is desired by all generational learning styles. After the first two weeks of grades on discussion or quizzes, students have an indication of the quality of work expected. It is important to create challenging and authentic learning experiences that require higher levels of analysis and critical thinking. Facilitators and students must be willing to take academic risks and explore alternative methods for problem solving and engaging in academic discourse.

Using web-based learning objects and assigning students roles in virtual worlds increases student interaction with learning materials and with other students. Examples of exemplary work should be recognized and praised often in discussion forums and e-mail exchanges. The course designed for this study assessed learning with online tests that challenged and encouraged students' best work. The tests were not timed, but given over a 4 day period with the expectation that students would find the right answers with the text and the entire Internet as resources. The expectation is that the student would answer every question correctly and earn a 100% on the test.

Assumption: Adult Learners are Practical

This assumption implies that adults want learning to apply in real life. Adult learners want to understand the usefulness of the information and knowledge gained. This is particularly true of the Baby Boomer and Generation X learners. They come to the learning environment ready to develop increased competence in social and professional roles. Their orientation to learning is problem-centered, rather than subject centered. However, for the newest generation of adult learner, Gen Y, the orientation to learning is "me" or now-centered…what will it do for me…what will I get out of this learning now.

Implication for Instructional Design, Course Development and Delivery

Online exercises, web quests, virtual world simulations, virtual labs and field trips and case studies provide students an opportunity to use concepts and theories, in real life situations with people in their own families, communities and work settings. An example of an interdisciplinary web quest, used in the case study online course, provided students on opportunity to use theoretical ethics, concepts of leadership and knowledge of human ecology to explore human hunger in a designated community and propose a recommended course of action to community officials. Students refined the problem through interviews with people involved in the community, searched the Internet for similar situations in communities with similar demographics and wrote a proposal to brief city officials on their findings. The students explored a real problem, with real people and completed the task of finding a real solution. The problem-solving task was integral to the learning environment. The task, not the process drove the learning experience. Embedding service learning projects into online learning environments can result in similar experiences for students who want to be able to use and see the fruits of their learning in service to others. Generation Y learners are particularly interested in service and learning experiences that incorporate the service component.

Assumption: Adult Learners need Relevancy

This assumption implies that adults must see a reason for the learning and that it be related to something familiar to them and relevant in their personal lives. This need for relevancy crosses generational learning styles with younger generation Y asking "why" the loudest. Learners want courses that offer immediate and tangible value to their life circumstances. Education and training are too expensive and time consuming for anything less. It is about putting content into context and allowing flexibility in course design for learners to explore issues important to them.

Implication for Instructional Design, Course Development and Delivery

For the online instructional designer and facilitator it is important to communicate relevancy and avoid information that is superfluous or involves busy work or rote memorization. Students want to make the best use of their learning experience.

They need to justify the effort. Baby boomers may be interested in the learning process, but Gen X'ers and Gen Y'ers are looking for outcomes.

When designing courses for an online environment, the designer and facilitator should create content, assignments and assessments that cut across generational lines and accommodate different learner needs for input and relevant work. The course syllabus and each weekly learning module should state the objectives of the course and outline the content, course requirements and expected outcomes. Learning what the student expects from the course helps match student expectations with course learning objectives. In the author's biology course, online learning activities and assignments are aligned with learning objectives and assessments, which are immediately applicable to real problems in authentic situations. Activities and assignments were designed to explore current and pressing issues, fostering active engagement and soliciting student input. One cannot study and understand the tenets of biology without looking at them in the immediate context of present world conditions, i.e. the tenets of structure and function, as well as evolution, can be better understood in context as applied to diseases such as AIDS and Cancer.

The delivery and presentation formats in this course were purposefully designed to be different from traditional courses. Lectures were minimal and interactive with embedded web-resources and links to active learning experience such as simulations and games set in virtual programs that mimic real life. Podcasts from professionals in science and related fields were incorporated to ensure that student understood the relevancy of the course content and its real–world application. Web quests and the use of online media, government and other websites, enriched the learning with examples of real world problems and contemporary issues that students can relate to the course and that illustrate relevancy in the theories and concepts under study.

Each week students were asked to identify a real-life problem in a media article or on a website, on a topic related to the course and then asked to discuss with other students the people affected and how they were able to solve the problem or cope with its effects. The problem-solving approach engages the student with the subject material and with other students and fosters connectivity when defining problems, asking questions and finding solutions. To some extent this gives the student some ability to control the learning environment and discover a more personal and meaningful path through the learning. When students can bring real life problems into the learning environment they have an opportunity to practice the skills needed to address similar situations in their own lives or at their jobs.

Assumption: Adult Learners Have Myriad Life Experiences

This assumption implies that adult learners have a repertoire of life experience and prior knowledge from which to draw upon to make connections and construct new knowledge. Adults bring a diversity of backgrounds, lifestyles and work experiences to the learning environment. Adults want to be able to use this knowledge and experience and be recognized for contributing their expertise and perspectives to the learning environment. This is particularly true for the Baby Boomer generation.

Implication for Instructional Design, Course Development and Delivery

The virtual learning environment provides many opportunities to design web-based activities, case studies, and group projects where students can use prior knowledge, past experiences, and different perspectives as a basis of learning. Providing opportunities for students to draw connections between the learning environment and the real world is generative. Collaborative learning ex-

periences also give students a chance to explore multiple perspectives and ways others construct and generate new knowledge. Baby Boomers and Generation Y learners like the collaborative nature of group projects. Baby Boomers like to discuss their experiences, while the generation Y learner likes to build social networks and create new experiences in a social context.

Students construct and create new knowledge when they have the opportunity to relate new subject material to something they already know. Simple teaching methods like discussion and role-playing within a web quest give students a chance to pull from their rich resource of experiences, to problem-solve and to collaborate in a learning community. Activities that promote connectivity among students and between students and the facilitator, build community. The egalitarian environment of online learning, where formal concepts and theories intersect with experiences and insights, encourages open dialogue for critical discourse. An example of how ideas and experiences are shared through an online course, in this case, biology, is to structure groups around a contemporary environmental issue. Ask each group to take a side on the issue, research the issue, and then argue for the other side. This problem-based learning assignment uses reverse debate as a technique to encourage critical thinking, and promote learning from different perspectives. Generation Y will excel in learning environments that incorporate problem-solving, web quests, games and simulation.

Reflective exercises, i.e. journaling, encourage and require students to reassess prior assumptions, bias, habits, and move towards new understandings. In terms of transformative learning (Mezirow, 1991) critical reflection is transforming when it leads to reevaluation of prior learning and learning patterns to the creation of new meaning and deeper understanding. Reflective writing and journaling is more suitable for Baby boomer and Generation X than Generation Y learners.

Assumption: Adult Learners want Respect

This assumption implies that adult learners, with their wealth of life experience, should be shown respect, be treated as equals and be allowed to express themselves freely in the learning environment. In actuality, all students have the right to be treated equitably with respect and be free to voice opinions in any learning environment. The "whole person" concept is embedded in distance learning as is the learner-centered approach. That all persons are entitled to respect is based on the fact that they are human, have human dignity and deserve respect for that fact alone and not on what the learner has or has not done in the past.

Implication for Instructional Design, Course Development and Delivery

One way to recognize and respect the diversity of learners in virtual learning environments today and in the future, is for designers and facilitators to use a variety of teaching and assessment techniques to accommodate and assess the different learning styles and preferences that accompany diversity. The author varies the text and fonts in online course earning modules, and varies presentation formats with PowerPoint, images, video and audio. The learning environment expands as web links and websites are added. These techniques encourage self-directed paths through the course material and through the Internet helping students maintain motivation. Generation Y learners are particularly motivated with this methodology. Being multitaskers, Gen Y'ers, do well at parallel processing of information. They have the ability to get information quickly from several sources and move from one bit of information to another as quickly as they can in the virtual learning space, while, simultaneously, talking on an Iphone and riding the bus. As visual learners, they experience learning through Internet web images and video,

as well as audio, rather than reading through heavy print and text materials.

Online formats provide a democratization of the learning environment and an even playing field for multiple perspectives and more diverse thinking. Opportunities for peer review expose more points of view. It is important that facilitators encourage student use of their diverse experiences and backgrounds in responding to questions in discussion, while at the same time, keeping the discussions fair and unbiased. Providing guidelines and netiquette for online discussions is important.

Another way to demonstrate respect in the learning environment is to by responding to students as individuals, using their name and often using their own words in responses. Responding appropriately and without public criticism is important in modeling respect. These simple techniques demonstrate listening and foster integrous and respectful behavior.

THE CASE STUDY

The integration of adult learning, as well as constructivist theory and generational learning preferences provided the theoretical background and conceptual framework for developing the online biology course mentioned above as well as three other, theology, philosophy and history, courses. These four courses were offered in an online format for the first time in 2003 in an established adult credit education program at a medium sized private academic institution in the U.S. This pilot for online courses was launched in response to a feasibility study completed in the adult unit, which identified needs and advantages of distance-learning formats for adult learners. The online courses were selected, designed and developed, using principles of adult learning, to enhance the learning experience, expand access to courses, and provide options for educational opportunities for adult students, while sustaining learning outcomes consistent with those in the face-to-face course. Using this pilot as a case study, descriptions and interpretations of students about the learning experience provided an understanding of what influences and motivates adults in virtual learning environments. In addition, formative and summative evaluations were designed and used to assess several aspects of online courses, including use of technology, delivery strategies, learning outcomes, learner attitudes toward distance learning, and learner satisfaction. Based on critical analysis of information acquired from the course evaluations, areas of improvement and implications for designers and facilitators of future virtual learning environments were identified.

Learner Demographics

Forty-nine of the 52 students enrolled in the four classes (theology, philosophy, biology and English), completed the mid-course formative survey. Of these, 61% were female, 53% were between 22 and 33 years of age, 25% were between 34-43 years old and 22% were between 44-55years old. The overwhelming majority, 46 (94%), held full-time jobs (40 hours per week or more), while the remaining 3 (6%) worked half time or more (20 – 35 hours per week). These demographics were consistent for adult learners and what was expected for distance learners (Grant &Thornton, 2007).

Learner Motivations and Influences

In the mid-course survey we asked the students several questions about why they chose to take courses online. Forty-eight (98%) had taken some college courses, but only 19 (39%) had taken online courses. When we asked them why they chose to take a course online, the most common reasons had to do with the inherent flexibility of this option: 32 (65%) liked the convenience of not having to travel to class; 33 (67%) felt that

online courses fit their lifestyle, work, or family schedules; and 31 (63%) liked the flexibility of working at their own pace. Other reasons reported for choosing courses online included: 8 (16%) had taken online courses before and liked the format; only 12 (25%) thought it would be less difficult and time consuming than face-to-face courses; and 15 (31%) felt that online courses allowed them to take more courses in the same term.

Student Comments from the Mid-Course Survey Included

What they liked most about the online class:

- *Convenience, ability to jump online at any time*
- *More comfort in discussions than traditional classes*
- *Taking tests at my own pace*
- *Ability to designate time to read and respond to course assignments*
- *The learner-centered nature of the online course*
- *Websites that were assigned readings*
- *Not having to travel to the city for class*
- *I do not have to be in class 4 hours twice a week*
- *I liked being able to speak freely. I am not sure that I would have spoken as freely as I did if I were in class, particularly on this subject matter*
- *I like having the ability to express myself through writing using the discussion board. It allowed me to fully plan, modify, and evaluate my thoughts without interruption or time constraints*

What they liked least about the online class:

- *I missed the interaction with other people in the classroom setting*
- *Assignment downloads take a long time with my dial-up connection*

- *The inability to use nonverbal communication when discussing controversial subjects*
- *The significant increase in readings, websites, etc.*
- *More time consuming to prepare for any discussion responses and take tests*

What they learned about themselves as a distance learner:

- *To manage my time, I am less self-disciplined and organized than I had hoped*
- *I need to stay focused*
- *It takes a lot of discipline to keep up with the coursework during the week*
- *I can do independent study with no problem. I am more disciplined than I thought*
- *I need to set time aside each week the same way that I do for a grounded course*
- *I do have the discipline to perform well in an unstructured time frame, and I love the flexibility to spend time with my family and go to school*
- *I am able to adapt to different class formats*
- *I must study more on my own to make up for no class lectures*
- *I can learn just as much online as in a class format*
- *I am better in the classroom*
- *I have good time management skills*
- *I realized that I am a better student when I am allowed more freedom in regards to time frames*

Students Who Dropped the Online Course

Fifteen of the 21 students (71%) who dropped the online course, either before the class started or after the 2nd, 5th, or 6th weeks, completed the first 17 questions of the mid-term course evaluation, which included general enrollment information and student demographics as well as reasons for dropping the course. Female dropouts (11) outnumbered the male dropouts (4) by 2.75:1 in the online courses. The numbers of freshmen, sophomores and seniors who dropped the course were equally represented with 4 students in each group, while there were 3 juniors. Fourteen students (93%), who dropped, worked 40 or more hours per week.

When asked why they choose an online course, 9 (60%) of students who dropped responded that they liked the convenience of not having to travel to class. Two students (13%) thought that the class would be less difficult and two others (13%) said that the online format better fit their lifestyle. Only 2 students (13%) had taken other online courses while 13 students (87%) indicated that they had not taken an online course before. However, the majority of responders (87%) had taken other college colleges.

Reasons for dropping the online course before the first week of class varied among the 15 student responders. Four students (27%) decided not to take the course after reviewing the syllabus. Two students (13%) just decided not to take the course, as did two others when they discovered they did not have the necessary hardware and software required to complete the course. Thirteen students, who dropped in the first week, enrolled in a face-to-face class. Six students dropped after the first week. When asked if they would consider taking an online course in the future, all 15 students who dropped said yes.

Learner Satisfaction

Thirty-three of the 52 students (64%) remaining in one of the four online courses completed end of course evaluations, using the same 22 item form that is used for all traditional on ground courses with three questions slightly altered to adjust to the online versus the face-to-face format.

Descriptive statistics were used to generate means for the questions and compared to the means of the same instructor taught face-to-face course. No significant differences were found using a T-Test. In general the online students were as satisfied with the presentation of subject matter, course materials and the instructor as students were who took the course from the same instructor on ground.

When queried about the average number of hours per week spent in studying for the online course, the reported range of hours spent studying in any one of the four courses was 8 to 17, an average of 7 hours per week. A range of 2 to 9 hours per week, an average of 5 hours, was spent studying by students in a similar on ground course taught by the same instructor.

When asked about the grade the student expected to receive in the online course more students reported B's and C's than students who answered the same question in the comparable on ground course. More students expected an A grade in the on ground version of the course.

One section of the end of course evaluation queried students about what they liked or disliked about the class and asked for additional comments. Students said:

- *The online discussion is a great tool.*
- *Online syllabus listed all weekly assignments, easy to follow and very helpful.*
- *Interacted more than I typically do.*
- *I enjoyed the online experience; please offer more online courses.*
- *I would take another online course; the experience was far superior to a telecourse*
- *Amazing how alive the Internet became.*
- *It was amazing to see people commenting online; almost like we were in class together.*
- *I learned so much.*
- *I like the online format and would take more online classes*
- *This was a wonderful class; please continue the online classes.*

- *I did appreciate the online course because with my work schedule, more convenient and time...encourage you to offer more.*
- *I initially thought the online class would work for me. I found myself missing the interaction in a classroom, and having to organize my work offline before going online took a lot of time.*
- *Workload was heavy, lots of reading.*
- *Course work was excessive, but I learned a lot.*
- *Too many discussion topics*
- *Online is just not for me.*
- *I loved this online class*
- *Loved the class, loved the format*
- *Please continue to expand the online courses*
- *It was a good class to start with at the school*
- *I had trouble with computer access with quizzes, but called information technology and received assistance.*
- *Course material and text were clear, concise and easy to follow*
- *This was my first online experience and I enjoyed it.*
- *Online classes have their good points and bad points.*
- *I have learned a lot from this course and instructor. I would like to take another online class with this instructor; she is very good!*
- *I loved the online class.*

Conclusions from the Case Study

The majority of adult students (82%) who completed one of the four pilot online courses were satisfied with their online experience in meeting their expectations for learning, course goals and objectives were clear and course content organized. The courses were reported (100%) to be interesting and user friendly. Students (72%)

seemed to enjoy the online course as much or more than a face to face course and perceived to learn as much as or more than they would have in a comparable on ground class. With regard to course grades, students expected to earn less A's in the online courses than in the face-to-face courses. Since online courses are notorious for attrition, we wanted to know and understand why students dropped the online courses and if the reasons were any different from the usual reasons for dropping out. Students who dropped the course dropped for multiple reasons including, not having the finances or being too busy with a new home or a new job, in other words, life, to take the course. Several commented that they were intimidated by the course requirements as stated in the syllabus and that it was too much work and too demanding, more than what is expected in an on ground class. As much as we wanted to offer adult online learning experiences, we were pleased that students thought the courses would be rigorous. The syllabi obviously clarified expectations and clearly represented the course goals and learning objectives as challenging.

Overall students (100%) were able to communicate easily with the instructor as well as other students in the class. They (94%) found the discussions valuable and the feedback helpful in understanding course material.

Online courses seem to demand more time than face-to-face classes. Students reported that they spent more time studying for the online course (eight or more hours per week) than a comparable face-to-face class (five hours per week), but 91% found it to be a more efficient use of their time. Even though some of the students found the course workload to be excessive and the course work, prep time and reading assignments heavy, the majority (91%) would consider taking another online course, as well as recommend the online course to other students.

Comments from students about the online learning environment itself reinforced the fact that online learning environments provide a bet-

ter fit with their busy lifestyles. Students said that the rigors of the online learning environment required more time for study, but appreciated the additional time to process, reflect and respond. Students also remarked about the self-directed focus of the learning environment.

Remarks about their self-concept as distance learners included thoughts of being more confident as self-directed learners after the experience, as well as improved self-discipline, time-management skills and writing abilities, and enhanced critical thinking skills upon completion of the online course. Additional comments were made about the increased freedom of expression in the online learning environment. Finally, most students stated that they had the prerequisite technology skills to successfully navigate through the course.

Recommendations from the Case Study

The following recommendations, informed by the interpretations and evaluations of this case study and pilot, for designing and facilitating future online courses for this particular adult education program were made:

- Develop and provide guidelines to clearly define the process and procedures for online course development and delivery, using various adult learning theories and generational learning preferences.
- Establish a process for designing online learning environments integrating adult learning principles with appropriate web-based technologies.
- Provide ongoing pedagogical support and professional technical training to instructors and facilitators who develop and teach in online environment.
- Establish a mechanism to review online learning environments before and during delivery to ensure academic rigor, student/

facilitator connectivity and technological appropriateness.

• Institutionalize the online process to provide continuing resources and support for management and enhancement.

These recommendations became the foundation upon which policies and procedures for offering and delivering online education in this particular adult education program were built. The lessons and findings, as well as these recommendations, are certainly generalizable for broader use in other distance learning environments and for other learners as demonstrated in many formal studies on distance learning (Diaz & Cartnal, 1999; Grant & Thornton, 2007; Newlin & Wang, 2002). The virtual learning environment is adaptable and appropriate for different learners across generational lifestyles and learning preferences. E-pedagogy is essentially andragogy with modification, and with the appropriate use of technology, can and will accommodate the diversity of learners in virtual learning environments today, as well as in the future

FUTURE TRENDS

There is an extensive number of online and virtual learning opportunities available to adult learners that offer a wide range of flexibility in programs and services. Institutions using virtual learning environments are continually expanding these environments to meet the needs of learners and keep ahead of the competition for adult learners. At present these characteristics, as well as what we know about adult learning preferences, inform the way we design and facilitate learning in virtual environments. In the future, as the characteristics, learning preferences and motivation of adult learners change, so must the learning structures and functions of virtual environments. Different student attributes, reflecting the values and behaviors of a new generation of adult learner, will

have a profound effect on academic institutions and corporate educational systems.

In the workplace the same phenomena is taking place. Today there are four different generations entering and re-entering the workplace. All will participate in some type of professional training or organizational development. As lifelong learners this may be continuous throughout their tenure of employment and to be vested with the company. A new generation of workers is entering the workforce and the demand for training and development to meet the needs and learning preferences of this new cadre of employees will have a profound effect on industry and business organizations. In today's economy, company and corporate training and development departments are investing in less manpower and physical space and investing in more technology and virtual learning options. Following the lead of many institutions of higher education, corporations are embracing e-learning as their sole method of delivering professional development and training. The integration of adult learning principles and generational learning preferences with technology in these settings will help companies create comprehensive learning environments and effective learning experiences for employees.

As our society continues to evolve culturally with technology driving the change, institutions and corporations must take the lead and become change agents for the fundamental shift from consumption of information to its creation, i.e. Wikipedia, from being place holders of seat time to 3D explorers of virtual worlds, and from "sitting" in closed virtual learning environments to "flying" in spaces without physical or temporal boundaries, i.e. Second Life. The very nature of e-learning is changing fast enough to require a new e-pedagogy, one that accommodates the digital learner, where, for them, information is searched rather than memorized, found on Google rather than in the library and where learning is authentic and experiential rather than contrived. This new e-pedagogy sounds strikingly familiar and remarkably similar to what we have described when integrating adult learning principles with technology. As the learners change so has teaching and learning. Similarly, as the tools and technology have changed and continue to change, so must teaching techniques and learning methods …this is as true for e-pedagogy as it is for adult learning. E-educators are realizing now what adult educators discovered nearly 40 years ago. Education is about ideas to be discussed, not facts to be memorized. Passive transfer of information will not encourage creation of knowledge or connectivity between the student and the subject matter or the student and other learners. Creative thinking and self-directed learning can only be cultivated in learning environments using authentic experiences and assessments in social context. Adult learning principles are grounded in collaboration and communication, hallmarks of e-learning. As business institutions and corporations position themselves in a knowledge-based economy, they will look to higher education for direction in developing accessible and flexible learning experiences to educate a workforce that is capable of working collaboratively for social development, environmental health and economic growth.

Dynamic e-learning experiences result when technology and andragogy intersect in the virtual learning environment and are built on adult learning, as well as constructivist and transformation, theories. For generational learners in academic or corporate arenas, virtual learning environments provide connections for continual learning, encourage diversity and expression of thought, and promote reflection and internalization for personal meaning. The learning opportunities afforded by new technologies and new virtual learning spaces are changing the nature of teaching and learning as we know it, how and where it is delivered, as well as the nature of the learners themselves. New online landscapes for new generations, in both academic and work settings, will revolutionize 21st century education, training and development.

Further studies on the integration of adult learning principles and web-based technology will enhance and improve virtual learning environments, provide a foundation for developing new virtual worlds of learning and increase access to future adult learners across generations and global economies.

CONCLUSION

Historically, distance learning, particularly in online and virtual environments, has been directed to non-traditional adult learners wanting access to education which was convenient and flexible in order to accommodate busy lifestyles and work schedules (Charp, 2000). After reviewing the literature on adult learning theories, the integration of distance learning technology and andragogy is not only complementary but advantageous and necessary as well. The profile of the adult learner and the virtual learner are similar, as are many of their expectations for learning and instruction in both the traditional and the virtual learning environments.

Virtual learning environments provide greater access to education with increased opportunities for relevant and authentic learning. In terms of academic results, virtual environments are effective learning spaces where learners have greater control over the learning materials and more interactivity with the content, the instructor and other students. In terms of pedagogy, virtual learning is forcing instructors to rethink the learning process and to think differently about themselves as educators and about students as learners. In terms of content, in the information rich environment of the Internet, learners become conduits for information and creators of content, while facilitator becomes their guides to selecting and using these resources. In terms of context, as new technologies emerge and become more mobile, virtual learning environments, transcending geographic boundaries, become more inclusive and learning becomes more contextual transforming time, space and location.

Creating effective virtual learning environments in the workplace that accommodate the way adults live and learn has far reaching implications in terms of a competitive advantage for recruiting and retaining the best and brightest talent. As the nature of work becomes more fluid and more virtual and new workers become more focused on getting results than putting time in at the office, the nature of training and development must become more fluid and more virtual, as well as more focused on applicable learning than on "seat time". In practice, the virtual learning environment becomes a compelling business strategy. Corporations who provide opportunities for growth and development that is flexible and convenient in the long term will see increased productivity and profits.

The effectiveness of teaching and learning in virtual environments, in academic and corporate arenas, is realized. However, the scope of possibilities for delivery, beyond the Internet, is far from being realized and demands the need for critical analysis and careful planning. Solid pedagogical concepts and methodologies cannot be sacrificed for networks and nodes. Technologies will continue to evolve as will pedagogical approaches, and concerns about one trumping the other will keep the players in higher education and industry in the game watching for what constitutes a winning hand for adult virtual learners of the future.

REFERENCES

Bates, A. W. (2005). *Technology, E-Learning and Distance Education*. London: Routledge.

Brookfield, S. D. (1992). Developing criteria for formal theory building in adult education. Adult Ed. 42(2), 79-93.

Burge, L. (1988). Beyond andragogy: Some explorations for distance learning design. *Journal of Distance Education, 3*(1), 5-23.

Candy, P. C. (1989). Constructivism and the study of self-direction in adult learning. *Studies in the Education of Adults, 21,* 95-116.

Candy, P. C. (1991). *Self-direction for lifelong learning*. San Francisco: Jossey-Bass.

Charp, S. (2000). Distance education. *T.H.E. Journal, 27*(9), 10-12.

Coates, J. (2006). Generational Learning Styles. River Falls, WI: LERN books.

Davenport, J. (1993). Is there any way out of the andragogy mess? In Thorpe, M., Edwards, R., & Hanson, A. (Eds.), *Culture and Processes of Adult Learning*. London: Routledge.

Dewey, J. (1938). *Experience and education*. New York: Collier Books.

Diaz, D., & Cartnal, R. (1999). Student learning styles in two classes. *College Teaching, 47*(4), 130-141. doi:10.1080/87567559909595802

Diaz, D. P., & Bontenbal, K. F. (2001, August). Learner Preferences: Developing a learner-centered Environment in the Online or Mediated Classroom. *Ed at a Distance Magazine and Ed Journal, 14*(80), 1-8.

Fidishun, D. (2000). Andragogy and Technology: Integrating Adult Learning Theory as We Teach with Technology. *Middle Tennessee State University, Instructional Technology Conference Proceedings*.

Freire, P. (1986). *Pedagogy of the Oppressed*. New York: Continuum.

Gibbons, H., & Wentworth, G. (2001). Andrological and pedagogical training differences for online instructors. *Online Journal of Distance Learning Administration, 4*(3), 1-5.

Grant, M. R., & Thornton, H. R. (2007). Best practices in undergraduate adult-centered online learning: Mechanisms for course design and delivery. *MERLOT Journal of Online Learning and Teaching, 3*(4), 346-456.

Jarvis, P. (1987). *Adult Learning in the Social Context*. London: Croom Helm.

Jonassen, D., Mayes, T., & McAleese, R. (1993). A Manifesto for a Constructivist Approach to Technology in Higher Education . In Duffy, T., Jonassen, D., & Lowyck, J. (Eds.), *Designing constructivist learning environments*. Heidelberg, FRG: Springer-Verlag.

Knowles, M. (1980). *The modern practice of adult education* (2nd ed.). New York: Cambridge Books.

Kolb, D. A. (1984). *Experiential Learning*. Englewood Cliffs, NJ: Prentice Hall.

Lacefield, R. (1999). *Adult Education in Practice: Teaching Methods and Course Structure*. Tripod Education Tipsheets.

Lancaster, C., & Stillman, D. (2003). *When Generations Collide: Who they are, Why they collide, How to Solve the Generational Puzzle at Work*. New York: HarperCollins.

Merriam, S. B., & Caffarella, R. S. (1999). *Learning in Adulthood*. San Francisco: Jossey-Bass.

Mezirow, J. (1991). *Transformative Dimensions of Adult Learning*. San Francisco: Jossey Bass.

Moore, A. H., Moore, J. F., & Fowler, S. B. (2005). Faculty Development for the Net Generation. In Oblinger & Oblinger, (Eds.), *Educating the Net Generation*. Retrieved November 28, 2008 from http://www.educause.edu/PreparingtheAcademyofTodayfortheLearnerofTomorrow/6062

Moore, M. G., & Kearsley, G. (1996). *Distance education: A systems view*. Belmont, CA: Wadsworth.

Nah, Y. (1999). Can a self-director learner be independent, autonomous and interdependent: Implications for practice. *Adult Learning, 1*(1), 18–25.

National Center for Education Statistics. (2005). *Projections of education statistics to 2014 (NCES 2005-074)*. Washington, DC: U.S. Government Printing Office.

Newlin, M., & Wang, A. (2002). Integrating technology and pedagogy: Web instruction and seven principles of undergraduate education. *Teaching of Psychology, 29*(4), 325–330. doi:10.1207/S15328023TOP2904_15

Oblinger, D. G. (2003). Boomers, Gen-X'ers, and Millennials: Understanding the 'New Students. *EDUCAUSE Review, 38*(4), 37–47.

Olka, K. (2007). Technical Communicators as Teachers: Creating E-Learning that Matters. *Intercom, 24*(4).

Pratt, D. (1993). Andragogy after twenty-five years. In *An Update on Adult Learning Theory* . *New Directions for Adult and Continuing Education, 57*, 15–24. doi:10.1002/ace.36719935704

Robertson, D (2002). *Andragogy in color*. US Department of Education, ERIC document Reproduction Service No.EADU 9020.

Rogers, C. (1967). The facilitation of significant learning. In L. Siegel, (Ed). Instructions: Some Contemporary Viewpoints, (pp. 37-54). San Francisco, CA: Chandler.

Shipman, C., & Kay, K. (2009). *Womenomics: Write Your Own Rules for Success*. New York: HarperCollins.

Siemans, G. (2005). *Connectivisim: Learning as Network Creation*. Retrieved November 28, from http://elearnspace.org/Articles/networks.htm

Skiba, D. J., & Barton, A. J. (2006). Adapting your teaching to accommodate the net generation of learners. *Online Journal of Issues in Nursing, 11*(2), 15.

Smith, M. K. (1999). *Andragogy, the encyclopedia of informal education.* Retrieved April 30, 2008 from, http://www.infed.org/lifelonglearning/b-andra.htm

Smith, M. K. (2002). Malcolm Knowles, informal adult education, self-direction and andragogy. *The encyclopedia of informal education.* Retrieved April 30, 2008 from http://www.infed.org/thinkers/et-knowl.htm

Spencer, B. (1998). *The purposes of adult education.* Toronto: Thompson Educational Publishing, Inc. *Spingner-Littles, D & Anderson, C.E. (1999). Constructivism: A paradigm for older learners. Educational Gerontology, 25*(3), 203–209.

St. Clair, R. (2003). Myths and realities, andragogy revisited: theory for the 21st Century? *Clearinghouse on Adult Career and Vocational Education.* ERIC document Reproduction Service No. ED 99-CO-0013.

Tennant, M. (1996). *Psychology and adult learning.* London: Routledge.

Tisdell, E., J. (1993). Feminism and adult learning: power, pedagogy and praxis. *New Directions for Adult and Continuing Education, 7,* 91–103. doi:10.1002/ace.36719935711

Vygotsky, L. (1978). *Mind in Society: The development of higher psychological processes.* Cambridge, MA: Harvard University Press.

Wenger, E. (l998). *Communities of Practice, Learning and Identity.* New York: Cambridge University Press.

Wittrock, M. C. (1974). A generative model of mathematics learning. *Journal for Research in Mathematics Education, 5*(4), 181–196. doi:10.2307/748845

Wittrock, M. C. (1990). Generative processes of comprehension. *Educational Psychologist, 24*(4), 345–376. doi:10.1207/s15326985ep2404_2

Wonacott, M. E. (2000). Web-Based Training and Constructivism. In Brief: Fact Facts for Policy and Practice No. 2. Columbus, OH: National Dissemination Center for Career and Technical Education, the Ohio State University (ED 447 257).

KEY TERMS AND DEFINITIONS

Adult Learners: A non-traditional aged student, 24 or older, who usually works part or full time, has a family, and returns, or enrolls for the first time, in an educational program for career advancement or personal enrichment.

Adult Learning Theories: Theoretical concepts and schema, based on critical analysis, about how and why adults learn, process information and gain knowledge.

Distance Learning: Refers to a system of delivering education that doesn't require the student and the instructor to be in the same place at the same time.

Constructivism: An active learning process of constructing knowledge based on what is already known or experienced by the individual.

Social Constructivism: A variation on constructivist theory that includes constructing new knowledge in a social context, emphasizing the collaboration and the community.

Experiential Learning: An adult learning theory that espouses significant experiences or personal involvement as the learning venue.

Generative Learning: Similar to constructivist theory in that students make connections between stored information, experiences and new information to generate deeper learning.

Generational Learning Styles: Learning preferences based on generational life styles and experiences. A generation is a cohort of people generally spanning about 20 years that share common characteristics, values, and notable events.

Lifelong Learning: The continuous process of inquiry and discovery to enhance knowledge and skills, enrich experiences, gain meaning and enjoy the process as well as the goals relative to where one is in life.

Virtual Learning Environment: An environment created with specific software structures, technologies, and learning objects, where instructional content is delivered, without the physical presence of the instructor and student at a specified time or in a designated place.

Chapter 3

Engagement, Immersion, and Learning Cultures:
Project Planning and Decision Making for Virtual World Training Programs

Christopher Keesey
Ohio University, USA

Sarah Smith-Robbins
Indiana University, USA

ABSTRACT

The decision to use a virtual world for training and development is a potentially treacherous one. Legal issues, adoption barriers, a pedagogical design complexities often inhibit true engagement and adoption. Strategic planning is required for every step from the choice of a virtual world to instruction design and user adoption. In this chapter, Keesey and Smith-Robbins offer guide to avoiding common pitfalls while suggesting a plan for maximum training benefit in virtual world implementations. Included are considerations about sound pedagogical practices, advice regarding the assessment of a corporate culture's ability to engage in a virtual world, as well as recommendations for alleviating common fears and concerns. Special attention is paid to the complexities of virtual world cultures as they interact with organizational cultures. Finally, the authors offer a rubric to aid training designers evaluate whether a virtual world is the right choice for their organization through a series of question and adoption concerns.

THE CHALLENGE OF VIRTUAL WORLD VENTURES

The metaverse is littered with the corpses of failed corporate forays into developing virtual world presence. From late 2006 to the present, companies such as Coke, Reebok, Adidas and many others launched spectacular three-dimensional failures.

These environments appeared to have little beyond a simple presence or conglomeration of slick modern structures, lacking adequate planning for how such a world could provide real Return on Investment (ROI) beyond an initial flurry of wild eyed journalists racing to be the first the report the official announcement of web 2.5, 3.0, 3.5 or whatever new marketing moniker had just been devised. Many of these industry players were guilty of the same

DOI: 10.4018/978-1-61520-619-3.ch003

offenses that were committed only 10 years ago during the height of the Internet bubble. Remember the rush of the wind generated by the stampede of anyone even capable of plopping a sub-par and sub-planned website onto the internet in 1997? Remember the subsequent bubble burst short years later following that wind of folly?

Indeed, recent Gartner research statistics show that nine out of ten business ventures into virtual worlds will fail. Many virtual world naysayers are quick to utilize research data like this in support of a presupposed incompatibility between industry and virtual world technologies. Ultimately these failures were the result of one or a combination of missteps all leading down the same path of lack of proper research, knowledge, information and planning for proper implementation of a virtual world for adding value in the enterprise.

Yet, regardless of the failure rates thus far by business in virtual worlds, Gartner Research also estimates that an over-riding majority of companies will utilize a virtual world within their enterprise by the year 2012. Therefore, the challenge for businesses today is to first identify if a virtual world can offer the kind of value add to justify the investment. Second, if it is determined that there are business functions/processes where a virtual world can increase efficiencies, shave costs, or provide value added, then the company must identify proper planning points to ensure that the initiative will not only succeed but also be continually supported by and provide support back into the enterprise.

THE BEST CORPORATE TRAINING PROGRAMS FOCUS ON THE END-USER

Corporate training programs are one component of organizational management that could stand to benefit from properly planned utilization of virtual world technology. For example, one of the authors can remember back to 2001 and their first forced entry into a corporate LMS. Not only was completion of the training program required for retaining one's job, but it was thought that the program would teach participants how to perform required job functions more effectively and efficiently. At the time, the whole experience was abdominally boring, merely consisting of page-turners and test-taking. That experience in 2001 was not designed for the learner. It was designed for the training managers and for human resources. While it did a great job of collecting data that could subsequently be utilized by trainers and managers, it did a horrible job of training this author or any other associate of the company because it wasn't designed for the end-user or learner.

Since that time, traditional corporate learning experiences across many companies have greatly improved, as training managers and corporate instructional designers conceived and implemented far more engaging, learner-center approaches to employee training. However, many of the early corporate builds in virtual worlds still lack the same consideration of the end-user. They seemed to have been implemented with little end-user focus at their mission core and in-such served no purpose, added no value, and ultimately ended up as visually pleasing ghost-towns. Imagine designing a feature-rich enterprise software application without first engaging in a host of ethnographic studies of your end-user or of how the potential software could add efficiency to their individual process and subsequent company process.

Training initiatives deserve and are most often implemented following similar study of the user, in this case the learner. We study outputs and outcomes to identify training or knowledge gaps or processes where training could close said gaps and add efficiency and value. In the case of a virtual world training experience the scope of research should be even more complete. Ideally, study of the users would happen over multiple levels including training needs assessments and user/training interface study. Additionally, with existing virtual worlds that have existing cultures and norms an additional ethnographic study and intimate knowledge of the world within which you will be delivering the learning experience is critical.

VIRTUAL WORLDS & CULTURAL SENSITIVITIES

Simply from a cultural integration standpoint, moving an organization or a company into an existing virtual world platform has a few similarities to that of moving a company, organization or for that matter an individual into a foreign country. There is more to it than simply plopping structures, machines, processes and yourself into your new location and resuming operations as you did in other contexts. Rather, there are multiple layers to this cultural integration, all of which begin with doing a substantial amount of research just as you would before leaving for a foreign country. Additionally, you will have an entirely different set of cultural considerations depending on the mission of your virtual world presence, the public visibility, and the level of openness and outward faces.

Marketers learned some tough lessons early on about the perception of their brands during the early rush to enter Second Life. They quickly learned the difference in the perception of their brands within virtual world from the more traditional channels both online and offline. (http://www.websitemagazine.com/content/blogs/posts/articles/second_life_metaverse.aspx) Something as simple as a highway billboard or a webpage banner advertisement – items that are a part of the normal landscape in our online and offline everyday lives – are wildly out of place in a virtual world environment. They're the equivalent of a real life elevator having a "Teleport" button.

There are practical reasons for this. Virtual world users are not slow moving sightseers. They are flying and teleporting from place to place, hungry for interaction with other avatars. Buying

is happening, but it is often for the sake of supplementing a social collaboration experience and not simply for the sake of buying something. (http://www.kzero.co.uk/blog/?p=854) This is a different mode of consumption than that of an individual stuck in a traffic jam on their way home from work to watch television, in which case evoking thoughts of a bigger, better television via a billboard would be more fitting. When organizations attempt to employ virtual worlds in a manner that ignore these cultural sensitivities, the inhabitant community may respond. Indeed, transgressions against the unique ethnographic realities of these spaces has led to amusing stories of marketers having their billboards buried by virtual world residents under virtual forests or graffiti. The take away here is that regardless of your mission, an out-of-place, and non-relevant presence within the virtual world culture is quickly identified by residents and often rebelled against – either within the virtual world itself or in subsequent postings across other web 2.0 channels, such as blogs, Facebook or Twitter.

Therefore, learning designers can themselves learn a great deal from the early forays by marketers into Second Life and other platforms. Substantial research and exploration of cultural intricacies during the definition of your project will greatly increase your chances of positively impacting both your organization and the world of which you will become a part. If you are utilizing a consumer focused platform such as Second Life or Active Worlds, don't limit yourself to simply reading and exploring the greater environment. Explore the potential "settlement" location for your organization. Introduce yourself to your potential neighbors and acquaint yourself with their activities, goals and traffic. This advice is already understood within a real life context (for example, you probably do not want to move your fortune 500 or university training environment next door to a region of strip bars); the same rules apply in the metaverse.

Furthermore, in devising a setting for your organization's virtual presence, you can seek a location offering neighbors that may positively supplement the learner experience by providing greater occasion for extended community opportunities. For example, imagine locating your company's supply chain orientation simulation next to a group of your suppliers in the same virtual environment; this could allow for collaboration and discussion that may improve the efficiencies of all those involved.

This idea of community – which is not a new concept in learning circles – is one that must be greatly considered. In an ideal world, learning does not happen in a vacuum regardless of the medium of delivery. The question for those implementing a virtual worlds solution is how much of the community building opportunities of any particular virtual world culture will you leverage, what parts of that virtual world culture will be a benefit to your learning outcomes and what parts will be a hindrance. Further, in answering these questions, it is quite important to keep in mind the interactive nature of your company's learning community: is it primarily asynchronous or synchronous?

KNOWING AND BUILDING ON THE STRENGTHS OF VIRTUAL WORLDS

Virtual Worlds are Social

For example, let's say your organization is currently sustaining learning communities across multiple time-zones via discussion threads, wikis or other shared documents. If you wanted to consider moving these activities into a virtual world, there would be a number of technological and community-based concerns to keep in mind. First, virtual world culture is at its most vigorous and vibrant when residents are being actively social. Virtual worlds, specifically those directed at the consumer such as Second Life or Active Worlds ARE social networking applications. Many virtual worlds have individual profiles, buddy lists, online status and a variety of other features to enable social

activities. Further, they add the "world" element to social networking that allows for play amongst residents. Let's not forget that while virtual worlds are not games, they are a distant cousin and were born with similar DNA. Play is an important part of collaboration and social interaction.

Second, most virtual world residents are not in the world to read large swaths of text and will generally avoid reading large documents for a variety of reasons, one of the most important being related to readability and usability. Outside of the dialogue text from an active conversation, reading content or discussion threads is more preferable in a readable window as opposed to on the face of a three-dimensional structures.

Therefore, if document sharing and collaboration are a large part of your training activities you will want to select a virtual world platform that is best suited for this purpose. Platforms such as QWAK and OLIVE by Forterra Systems Inc. are currently better suited to facilitate document collaboration naively or through third party plug-ins. Second Life is not strong with document collaboration and large quantities of text. However, Second Life, when teamed with your LMS can be quite effective.

Virtual Worlds are Active

Some very effective learning experiences can be delivered in the LMS with learners being sent out to participate in unique, value adding activities. These activities may include items such as self-paced games or process simulations to help explain simple global concepts, all of which can be built to supplement current outcomes addressed through your LMS. In turn, such activities may then drive more detailed discussion and application to your organization within the established learning community environment.

Additionally, if your game or process simulation is not ripe with enterprise secrets, it may provide a great opportunity to involve the greater community of the virtual world in which your organization is based. Such opportunity will drive positive brand extension around the value that you have added to the community at large. Indeed, nothing will get blogged and Tweeted faster by virtual world residents than "I just had a great experience today."

Further, as experiences go, no experience is quite as popular to virtual world residents as the event. In fact, this element of virtual worlds is so popular that "Event Planning" is listed as one of six skills that Second Life residents publicize in their personal profiles. Entire companies are built and seeing profits from planning, organizing and delivering events for other companies within virtual worlds. Moreover, established real world companies can are also beginning to reap the cost benefits of virtual world meeting and conferences: IBM's Academy of Technology recently saved $320,000 by holding an event in Second Life. The figure was reached by cutting $250,000 in travel costs and a further $150,000 in productivity gains. (http://www.virtualworldsnews.com/2009/02/ibm-saves-320000-with-second-life-meeting. html, n.d.) Bottom line: Events can substantially add value for customers, employees, and organizations as a whole.

Considerations for the Synchronous Learning Community

Alternatively, if your organization's learning communities are based from synchronous activities and collaboration (whether online or offline), you should plan an initial deployment that builds on your existing model and uses the strengths of the virtual world, namely the playfulness of the culture.

Virtual Worlds are Playful

One interesting training example that has been fairly seamlessly moved from the synchronous classroom environment to the synchronous virtual world environment is the Six Sigma Catapult experience. Initially, the catapult experience was delivered around synchronous classroom discussions for identifying critical variables that will maximize the distance traveled by the loaded projectile.(http://www.pscoe.gov.sg/repository/open/2/522/Training.htm, n.d.) The outcomes are then tied to greater six sigma concepts for improvement in product development. In this example, we see how virtual worlds can provide a wonderful framework where a playful activity fits and allows for distributed delivery. Subsequently, it can be argued that the exercise takes on an even more engaging tone as individuals launch their co-worker's avatars hundreds of meters into the air to howling laughter, a feat that is not a healthy option for the real classroom.

Virtual Communities Carry Real Expectations

Beyond the preparation for how your learning experience will fit your organizational culture and visa versa one of the greater considerations is preparing learners and instructors for how they will fit as individuals into the culture. Again, the similarities of preparing for travel and integration into the culture of a foreign country are loosely applicable. A good or bad experience traveling abroad can often be tied to the preparedness of the individual for the unique cultural norms of the culture within which they will be spending time. Poor preparation can leave the traveler feeling isolated, alone and out of place. However, proper planning can help travelers prepare mentally for confronting any cultural differences, allowing them to instead focus on more rewarding activities, such as collaboration with and learning from the people of the other culture.

Just as when traveling abroad, instructors and learners must prepare for cultural expectations such as dress and language, both verbal and non-verbal. Though it may seem superficial to the new virtual world resident ("newbie") to have to consider the appearance of their avatar, such a consideration is really no different than considering what to wear to a meeting in the real world; there is a cultural context in which appearance carries meaning.

Avatars adorned in the stock clothing and hair who have taken no time to personalize their avatar will be subject to certain assumptions by other avatars, be they founded or not. Resident avatars will speak differently to those assumed to be newbies. They may even avoid such persons altogether if time is of the essence and an unsolicited training session in virtual world etiquette is not in the cards for the day. Is this really any different than entering a boardroom of upper-level executives for a strategy meeting in your jeans and tee-shirt having not washed or styled your hair that morning? Assumptions will be made, right or wrong.

Virtual World Etiquette Requires a New Skill Set

Overall, virtual environments are hyper-friendly and are, at their core, social environments. Be prepared to for people to say "hi" and to address you by avatar name. Often new residents are taken aback by this and act as they might on the streets when approached by a stranger. These are two of many intricacies of living and working in the virtual world. The most successful organizations prepare their employees for the intricacies of virtual world collaboration through substantial cultural orientation experiences.

One of the best examples of systematic preparation for most effective virtual world outcomes is implemented by World2Worlds, an event planning and coordination company that has worked with multiple organizations on virtual world roll-outs and virtual world events. World2Worlds habitually schedules a barrage of orientation meetings that first get new residents comfortable with often complex interface controls, then further hones their communication abilities, and then finally steers residents to options for avatar customization. All

this is done to prevent cognitive overload when the user attends a virtual event, training session other experience, allowing him to focus on the intended target outcomes.

It is highly encouraged that any company moving into virtual world delivery of training or other collaboration has a scheduled "train of adoption" where a group of experienced early adopters are leading trainers and subsequently, trainers are leading learners through the intricacies of becoming experienced residents. Much like traveling abroad, it is so much more enjoyable to initially walk the streets of a foreign environment with someone familiar with the landscape and cultural considerations to show you the ropes. To reiterate, each virtual world platform is a unique culture inhabited by equally unique residents. They have unique cultural mores that are partly driven by features and abilities given by the coding authority and partly as the outcome of residents developing certain collectively accepted rules that enhance the efficiency and enjoyment of life in that particular world. If this culture is the pallet or shell for a learning experience then lacking intimate knowledge of your shell will surely doom the experience to failure.

Is There a Virtual World Platform that Fits Your Organization?

The ideas extolled above emphasize the key point that not all virtual worlds are created equally. Indeed, one virtual world platform could be of greater fit your needs than another. Though, sometimes the answer might be to use no virtual world at all. Be honest with yourself and don't roll-out a platform just for the sake of rolling out a platform. As you survey your own corporate culture, the pedagogies utilized by your trainers, your security considerations, your budget and a host of other concerns, you will then want to match these factors with the most applicable virtual world platform for your unique requirements.

First, take a realistic look at your organization's culture and ask some simple questions:

Is your Current Technologically-Mediated Learning Initiatives Embraced and Utilized?

If you are offering a strong set of online training environments that are underutilized as is, what would a virtual world change? If buy-in is a problem for an already strong set of tools, odds are that a virtual world is not going to change things.

Does your Organization have the Bandwidth to Support on Boarding Employees to a Virtual World Training Platform?

If you are already struggling to support learners technically in existing LMS platforms or simulations, a virtual world is not going to make this job any easier and will most likely take far greater amounts of support time. Not all industries are ripe with teams of millennials who are ready and willing to ramp up quickly into a 3D environment. If your teams have already demonstrated apprehension and difficulty with more typical technically-mediated initiatives, you might want to realistically consider whether a virtual world is a viable option.

It is also worth noting that a team of young millennials can be as apprehensive to embrace and buy into a virtual world as any other group but for different reasons. It is not uncommon to hear a group of young students state, "It's OK, but it's not World of Warcraft." Many millennial learners place much higher expectations on their 3D environments as many of them have spent far greater amounts of time in environments of similar aesthetics. Dr. Rod Riegel of Illinois State University embraced the expectations of millennial learners by completely delivering his undergraduate course in Social Foundations of Education within the popular massively multiplayer online roleplaying game Everquest II. This is truly an extreme example of embracing your culture of learners, but may nonetheless prelude an interesting and effective future trend.

What is your Threshold for Influence from the Existing Virtual World Platform Culture?

Second Life, the most popular of the consumer focused virtual worlds, does contain the settings to secure areas from outside avatars. Likewise, communication via voice and text can also be contained privately via groups. That said, these settings are only as good as locking the doors to a classroom with windows. The culture is right outside the window. At Ohio University, regardless of security settings in a particular area, students were still able to see and be distracted by a visit from the now infamous flying phalluses.

Second Life is, at its core, a consumer application and as such has a wide and complex culture, as has been discussed. If your threshold of influence from the existing culture is low and the tools inside Second Life are not robust enough to tune out the cultural noise, there are platforms that have been designed specifically with industry in mind.

OLIVE by Forterra Sytems Inc. is one such tool. OLIVE is seeing wider adoption and was most recently adopted by Accenture and Affiliated Computer Services amongst others as the platform of choice. Protosphere is another platform to consider and was developed specifically with a focus on training and learning in mind. More recently Nortel launched their browser-embedded web.alive platform that is billed as "Network secured virtual world platform for collaboration, assisted E-Commerce and virtual learning & training applications." These tools do however come with a higher initial price tag than Second Life, Active Worlds or other consumer focused virtual world applications.

Another promising development that is currently in beta at the time of this chapter's release is 3D integration into Lotus Sametime. The 3D capabilities would extend the current integration of IM, email, telephony and web conferences and add the capability for participants to quickly jump into a virtual world space should the immersive and persistent quality of virtual world collaboration be a desired form of collaboration for expanding on an idea. Lotus Sametime 3D would allow employees to quickly jump in and jump out of the virtual world around specific tasks or concepts, requiring very little in terms of integration into any existing virtual world culture. It also comes with a price tag and will still require you to have an existing virtual world environment in place. Lotus Sametime 3D has currently been tested with Second Life, Open Sim and Forterra.

In terms of an achievable ramp-up for establishing and orienting your culture in a virtual world, Second Life still provides a wonderfully rich environment where organizations can affordably develop training tools and competencies for virtual world delivery. Organizations can take advantage of the openness of the community and relative ease of creating assets to transform content for real impact in a 3D environment. Then, once the virtual world solution achieves initially planned outcomes, greater adoption, greater funding and is holding more enterprise assets, it might be time to seek a more extensive and walled environment.

What are your Internal Policies for Securing the Information you will have in your Virtual World Spaces?

Some organizations may require a more secure option from the onset for any hope of buy-in from IT departments. Likewise, you might be training around sensitive enterprise information that would require more formidable security. Should a completely walled solution on local severs be required there are open source options that are becoming more and more viable for a contained and controlled virtual world solution.

Three such solutions are Open Simulator, Project Wonderland and The Second Life Enterprise Beta. The most promising Open Simulator distribution is realXtend. The purported strength of the realXtend platform is its goal of global standardization and interconnectedness amongst virtual world platforms. Project Wonderland is a toolkit by Sun Microsystems that would enable your developers to create your own enterprise's 3D virtual world. The Second Life Enterprise Beta enables a secure and flexible workspace behind an organization's firewall.

The key word related to both realXtend and Project Wonderland is "developers." You will need people to develop and support any kind of platform that you plan to build on your own servers behind your firewall. Though this may seem like an obstacle at present, these kinds of self-contained solutions will become more and more attractive as these technologies advance and the value-add of virtual worlds for the enterprise are continually documented. The Second Life Enterprise Beta is more of an out-of-the-box solution for securing virtual collaboration. The Second Life documentation states that the installation and setup will take a network administrator thirty minutes. Eventually an architecture of an intra-virtual world and an inter-virtual world – and travel between the two – will more closely resemble the current intranet/internet relationship.

Meanwhile, platforms such as the consumer versions of Second Life or Active Worlds are viable environments for acclimating an organization to the unique culture of immersive virtual environments and offering an introduction to what does and does not work well. The key is to continually keep your feet wet and roll with the very rapid changes in the space, so that – as platforms continue to rapidly develop, change, merge, and become more interoperable and more ubiquitous – your organization is continually well footed to utilize the virtual world for increasing efficiencies where applicable.

Another failure point that is currently more prevalent in the world of higher education is the sudden lack of pedagogical focus when crafting virtual world learning experiences. Where many of the early corporate failures were built around a marketing or customer communication function, most higher education initiatives where built around the hope of enhancing student learning experiences. Many educators made the mistake of throwing current e-learning or face-to-face learning experiences blindly into the virtual world without deciding which experiences or parts of experiences are more or less suitable for a virtual world. Each virtual world has strengths and weaknesses in light of human-computer interface, as well as in capability as an adequate delivery platform. Identifying these strengths and weaknesses is key to supporting learning outcomes with valuable activities that can drive inquiry and ultimate transfer. Indeed, there is only one thing worse than a page-turner: a page-turner delivered in a virtual world.

Examples of How Not to Employ a Virtual World Solution

Considering such mistakes in application, as well as the defining characteristics of virtual worlds discussed earlier, we can identify some examples of how your organization should not employ these environments.

Using Monologic or Inactive Pedagogy

Listening to a talk head is boring no matter what the medium. We've all sat through lectures that were less than engaging. On the flip side, most of us have sat listening to engaging ideas wishing desperately that we would be allowed to contribute and have a conversation rather than merely listen passively. Using a virtual world for employee development, training, and community building requires a new approach to what "learning" looks like. We've all heard about the old "sage on the stage" model of learning and most of us have grim memories of experiences where we were expected to somehow magically absorb information presented to us in some flat, boring form. Learning in a virtual world not only gives

us ways to go against the boring grain but may also occasionally make these old methods nearly impossible. Give a long lecture in Second Life, for example, and even the most intriguing speaker may look out on an audience of slumped avatars who are listening but not engaged.

The virtual worlds we refer to in this chapter are largely constructed for facilitating social activities. They're 3D social networks of people with similar interests. If training is to be successful in these spaces then it has to built around social practices. After all, we all learn better when we're given the opportunity to discuss what we're learning, mull it over, pull it apart, and bounce ideas off of peers. This can only happen when learning is social. It may be hard to imagine a class where everyone can talk at the same time, get up and fly around, or pan their avatar's camera around to inspect another person or just to watch a sunset. This description might sound like a course that's out of control but in fact it's rather normal for people using virtual worlds. Rather than sitting in a virtual auditorium listening to a lecture (which is probably better done in Breeze or another teleconferencing, webinar product), successful virtual learning allows participants to...well, participate! Passive learning just doesn't cut it in a world where every user has the same ability to create content and to engage one another.

Know that you may need to think way outside the box to make learning in a virtual world work in your institution. However, you can also be confident that, if you're successful, you will have ditched all the elements of professional development that have given "training days" their horrible reputation.

Jumping in because Everyone Else is doing it

Adapting your training to fit within a social virtual world is no easy feat. The training, developing new courses and methods, engaging an internal community to make it work...

these are not projects you want to take on if your reason for jumping into a virtual world is "other people are doing it." Virtual worlds are a fairly hot topic. Over 5,000 educators subscribe to the Second Life mailing list but that doesn't mean that every university or every CLO should jump in too. The PR blitz around companies experimenting in virtual worlds has almost completely passed as these spaces become more mainstream. Don't let your CEO convince you that moving your training into a virtual world will be a good external marketing move. It won't. Frankly, enough companies have already done it to render such a move no longer newsworthy. On the other hand, doing it really well might get you some exposure. But this still isn't the best use of your time if your only goal is to get attention. There are certainly better ways to do it.

We don't mean to dissuade you from jumping in. It's just that, if you're to be really successful, you'll need to have realistic goals that suit your needs, your people, and the tool you choose to use. Besides, it's far too common that the brave soul willing to develop a new program is the one who gets the blame if it fails, even when other factors are to blame. Don't let your marketing department turn you into a patsy for PR. Know that you have solid justification for adopting a new tool such as a virtual world. Be ready to justify it in detail and to define what success will be for the project.

THE FALL-OUT OF FAILED APPROACHES: HOW BEST TO INTRODUCE THE IDEA OF A VIRTUAL WORLD SOLUTION

Ineffective introductions of virtual worlds as training spaces can have broad negative effects among a training population and in the organization in general. Such projects are still seen, unfortunately, as risky and experimental so their failure typically means that future efforts will meet increased resistance. But the negatives don't end there.

Once participants are convinced to give such a new approach to training a try, they've begun to invest trust in the trainer beyond simply being willing to learn. Often, the experience of becoming acclimated to a world such as Second Life involves a certain degree of vulnerability as participants learn through awkward circumstances such as flying into buildings or adjusting their avatar's appearance. Once participants have committed to this kind of risk taking, a failure in the actual training experience itself can be destructive not only to that particular training effort but to future training efforts and to the relationship participants have with the trainer. Be as transparent as possible in introducing such a new approach. Including participants in the experimental nature of the training can help them to share the excitement and be more invested in the success of the program.

It should also be noted that, in many cases, virtual world training efforts require a larger investment of time and money than recycling previously used approaches. And again, because using a virtual world is typically seen as risky rather than mainstream, the funds used to support such a project can easily be seen as a waste of money in a more negative way than "successful" but ineffective traditional methods. It's important to explain to those who control budgets that an effort to develop virtual world training accomplishes many tasks at once, including training programs, introduction of new technology, research and development, and marketing efforts (for the attention that many organizations receive for using such a novel approach).

Unfortunately, in many organizations, the outcomes of traditional approaches to training aren't measured with the same standards that a new approach might be. Classroom lectures and self-paced slideshows are well understood and can be extremely ineffective but they are familiar. Therefore, while the outcomes of these approaches might be inferior to a well-run virtual training program, the failure of a more traditional approach usually doesn't draw much attention. Fail at something new and you'll have all eyes on you.

THE BIG QUESTION: ARE VIRTUAL WORLDS RIGHT FOR YOUR ORGANIZATION?

So, if the risk is so high, why would anyone want to try his or her hand at developing virtual world training methods? How can you know beforehand that you've made the right choice when you choose to utilize virtual spaces for training?

Have you Adequately Identified the Need?

You'll need to if you're to get good adoption. First, be sure you've adequately identified the training need and that you'll get good adoption within the organization. Making a few asynchronous training modules available online requires little commitment. If no one takes advantage of them then there isn't much lost. However, if you invest in developing an interactive training experience in a virtual space then you will have put in much more time and effort. Be sure that you've selected a topic that has high interest in your organization. Make the decision to participate an easy one. Students taking the class should clearly understand that there are clear benefits to the program. You may even need to sweeten the deal by stressing that learning the virtual world's tools may be beneficial after the training is over.

Be Sure It's Not Just What You Want to do But What's Best for the Learners

Next, ask yourself the tough question: Is using a virtual world what is best for my learners or is it just interesting to me? It's easy as a trainer to be seduced by something that looks so different from the modes of delivery that you use every day (you can only make so many PowerPoints before you bore even yourself!). Using a virtual space can seem attractive merely for the novelty of them. It's also seductive to think that mastering such a new approach might get you more approbations as a trainer. However, if an experimental approach is antithetical to the culture of your learners (technology novices for example), you'll need to acknowledge that even though you may have a brilliant idea for training, it might not suit your audience.

What Haven't You Been Able to Accomplish in Other Tools; with Other Methods?

As always, pedagogy should come before technology and learning goals should come before delivery method. Perhaps you're trying to improve the results you get with another delivery method or accomplish a kind of training that you haven't been able to deliver with the available tools. Regardless of the perceived need that drives you to consider virtual worlds for training, be sure that the time and effort are worth it and that there isn't an easier to use tool that would allow you to deliver the training with a less steep learning curve. This will also help you make the case for a virtual world application. If you're truly able to do something unique and compelling then gaining buy in should be much easier.

Do you have Adequate Resources for Ensuring Long-Term Success?

Finally, every corporate virtual world roll-out requires ongoing support in a variety of different domains depending on the over-riding mission of the virtual worlds strategy. For a roll-out focused on training function a business will want to vigilantly plan on having processes in place for initial support and training of users, technical support, internal evangelization and sales of the training efforts and ongoing content or learning experience creation, to name just a few. Virtual worlds, like most good web 2.0 applications, are successfully used and populated by users if the users perceive that "this is where the party is at." If you don't provide compelling reasons for your associates to come, learn, and share knowledge, the virtual world real estate will sit barren. If you actively work to populate your virtual world learning space with appropriate and dynamic learning activities and purposes for collaboration, you create motivated learners.

There are also technology-related thresholds for adoption. We've worked with innumerable companies that are excited about using a virtual world until they realize that the standard issue computers in their office don't have the processing power or graphics capabilities to even run the software. Is it worth it to replace the computers of everyone on the team? Perhaps your remote learners are on limited bandwidth and can't get enough connection speed to adequately participate in the training. Is the program worth it to them to upgrade their internet connections or change locations? You may also need a team of people who can support the application and answer questions around the clock if you're an international organization. Most virtual worlds platforms still have severely lacking customer service, so it you may require having an internal resource available to answer common questions or troubleshoot problems that participants encounter.

Virtual communities take more than one evangelist to get started and stay in growth mode.

Most successful projects have a project manager who is assisted by community managers – who help users and trouble shoot problems – as well as event planners – who work through the details of hosting an event and making sure that everyone can participate as expected. Additionally, you may also need to enlist subject matter experts who can help construct courses and experiences on desired topics. Such subject matter experts may be well versed in their topic area, but not in the virtual world platform, and thus may require significant training or support as well. It takes a village to create a community.

SO YOU'VE DECIDED; NOW WHAT?

Virtual world applications require as much planning as traditional approaches if not more so. When you begin to draft your plan you're doing more than just rationalizing the learning goals; you're likely drafting a long term plan for a robust learning community which should be at least somewhat self-sustaining after a time. Knowing what this community will look like, how it will function, and why people should want to engage in it will go a long way toward success.

Spelling Out the Goals

Ask yourself these questions:

- What is the desired outcome?
- How long will it take to achieve it?
- Is the outcome worth the time it will take?

If you hope to develop a long-lived presence in a virtual world, in which many programs will occur and an organizational community will form, it won't happen overnight. Like any culture, it will have to develop over time and be nurtured and encouraged. You can't, for example, build an island in Second Life and expect a community to form on its own. If your goal is to create a learning community you'll need to host events, offer training, and provide incentives. It may take months for enough participants to adopt the tools to really see things happening. Can you wait this long? What are your metrics for success? How will you gather the information necessary to know that the community is growing as you'd expect?

Sharing the Plan & Getting Buy in

A learning community requires, well, a community! Not just a few avid participants but many. To turn hesitant experimenters into excited evangelists may take significant effort and hand holding. You may want to schedule regular training and information sessions to invite people to become involved. Provide them with as much support as you can until they feel comfortable. Once they're well acquainted, these first converts will become your first line of evangelists and make the process much more scalable, especially in a large organization. And bear in mind that people learn in different ways. You may need to make videos and handouts or offer one-on-one training. Be flexible and try to meet the needs of those willing to become involved.

Promise, Tool, Bargain: Spelling out the Plan

Broad adoption may be a long time in the making and you may encounter snags along the way. This doesn't mean that you should give up. Find out why the community fails to grow, or why participants fail to learn, and then be ready to try again. We find Clay Shirky's model of the "Promise, Tool, and Bargain" from his book Here Comes Everybody very useful.

- **Promise**: What users are told that they will get out of the project. This is the compelling "sell" that motivates participants to be willing to give it a try.

- **Tool**: The tool that will allow participants to accomplish what they need to accomplish in order to fulfill the Promise.
- **Bargain**: An explicit description of what users will have to do to gain what is promised.

First, you'll need to acknowledge that everyone may not be as excited as you are. They'll need to be motivated to participate. Be clear about the benefits of the community or program. Give them as many reasons as you can to say 'yes.' When we fail at creating compelling promises it usually means that we haven't thought enough about the benefits to the users, that we haven't anticipated and met their needs well enough. Keep in mind that groups of people in your organization may need different promises to compel them to become involved. Whatever you do, don't present the project as being frivolous or just experimental. Don't make excuses that will make it easy for participants to say no.

Second, be sure that you understand the tool well enough to train others to use it and to solve common problems. Hesitant participants will need to feel that you're in control of the space and can keep them safe and focused. If you, for example, choose a virtual world platform that is unstable and crashes often, then users will see that as an easy reason not to participate.

Finally, be transparent and honest about what the participants will need to do to get the most benefit from the program. If being a passive, quiet user will leave them wondering why they've come, then be sure to tell them in advance that you'll expect them to contribute in explicit ways. If you expect them to learn a bit on their own or to experiment with the tool, then tell them that and offer whatever support that they might need. If they fail to do so it will be easy for you to identify the points of failure that will need to be addressed in order to get the community rolling again. If they aren't willing to fulfill their part of the bargain then you should go back to the promise and make it more compelling.

Last, but not least, know that training in virtual worlds and building community is something that you're never finished with. Like a garden, a community requires constant attention and nurturing. You'll need ongoing programming and support to keep the project going and growing. This is no small task. Nonetheless, provided that it is given the proper consideration, preparation, and resources, a virtual world solution may offer an invaluable new opportunity for your training program.

REFERENCES

http://www.kzero.co.uk/blog/?p=854, (n.d.).

http://www.pscoe.gov.sg/repository/open/2/522/Training.htm, (n.d.).

http://www.virtualworldsnews.com/2009/02/ibm-saves-320000-with-second-life-meeting.html, (n.d.).

http://www.websitemagazine.com/content/blogs/posts/articles/second_life_metaverse.aspx (n.d.).

Shirky, C. (2008). *Here Comes Everybody*. New York: Penguin Press.

KEY TERMS AND DEFINITIONS

Learning Community: A group of people who are actively engaged in cooperative learning whether formal or informal.

Metaverse: Originally coined by Neal Stephenson in Snow Crash (1992), the term has come to be used as a description of al of virtual worlds and the reality and culture they represent.

Pedagogy: The art and science of teaching.

Return on Investment (ROI): A term commonly used in business to describe the quantifiable financial returns on a business effort.

Virtual World: A synchronous, persistent network of people, represented by avatars, facilitated by computers.

Chapter 4

Workplace Use of Web 2.0 Communication Tools and its Implications for Training of Future Communication Professionals

Pavel Zemliansky
James Madison University, USA

ABSTRACT

Traditional instructional models in web design and web communication have, until recently, leaned towards seeing websites primarily as vehicles for information distribution from one centralized source, like a company or organization, to a mass audience. Consequently, training in web communication and design has often been limited to those types of websites. However, with the advent of phenomenon known variously as "web 2.0," or "social web" several years ago and and increasing use of web 2.0 tools in the workplace, this type of training may not be enough for future communicators and designers. This chapter investigates the extent and purposes with which web 2.0 and social media communication tools are being used in the corporate and other workplace settings. Based on this analysis, a set of recommendations for teachers, trainers, and administrators is offered.

INTRODUCTION

Perhaps the best-known explanation of the term "web 2.0" is the one by Tim O'Reilly, of O'Reilly Media (O'Reilly 2005). O'Reilly describes web 2.0 as a "set of principles" which, briefly described, denote the shift from the Internet as a one-way conduit of information from content writers and designers on one end to users on the other, to a more user-centered Internet. Among O'Reilly's principles are the ideas of the Internet as a "platform," users controlling "their own data," "architecture of participation," and so on (O-Reilly 2005). Practical manifestations of web 2.0 familiar to most users nowadays are blogs, wikis, social networks podcasts, and so on. All these applications make the publishing and sharing of content easier for non-experts.

DOI: 10.4018/978-1-61520-619-3.ch004

Several years into the history of web 2.0, which is also variously known as the "read/write web," or the "social web," some skeptics challenge the fact of its existence, dismissing the term as "marketing hype." Hype or not, it is hard to deny that in recent years, the nature of the "Internet experience" has changed. Therefore, in this chapter, I will treat the expression "web 2.0" as a key operational term which is useful for describing the contemporary users' experience on the web.

During the web 1.0 era, users went to the Internet mainly for information. With the development of web 2.0 communication and collaboration tools, many users who used to passively find and consume information also became co-creators of that information.

During the web 1.0 era, all Internet users were, more or less, neatly divided into content creators and content consumers. The creators were typically computer programmers and other technically minded individuals who had access to expensive hardware and special skills in HTML coding. That access and those skills allowed them to create, host, and disseminate web content. The main vehicle for such content were various personal and organizational websites, usually coded in HTML, whose purpose was the publication and dissemination of information.

By early to mid-1990s, such major industry players as Yahoo! (http://www.yahoo.com), Lycos (http://lycos.com), and, later, Google (http://www.google.com), began offering web authoring and publishing tools which allowed non-experts to design and publish web sites relatively easily. Amateur web designers from the 1990s and early 2000s will remember Lycos's Angelfire, and, or recently discontinued Google's Page Creator.

In addition to being free, those services offered multitudes of Internet users an easy way to design and publish websites that combined text with images and hyperlinks. They democratized the Internet as a publishing and information exchange space, diminishing the barrier between the coding and design experts on the one hand and lay users.

These services also took part in another important change in the Internet experience. Users now did not have to code a site on a desktop computer and then upload files to a web server. Instead, they worked in the window of an Internet browser. Much of the design process boiled down to making choices from a list of templates and page layouts. Publishing a website was literally done with the push of a button. While this approach to designing web pages continues to have very significant limitations, it allowed literally millions of people to join the formerly exclusive group of Internet content creators.

The purpose of most of those amateur-made websites was distribution of information, about oneself, one's family, or one's organization. Simultaneously, Angelfire, Google's Page Creator, and other similar services facilitated the inclusion of discussion forums and other elements of interactivity into web sites. While those interactive elements did not afford the level of user participation allowed just a few years later by web 2.0 applications, their availability to the average user marked a significant shift in the Internet experience. The web was becoming not only a place where information was published. Now, users could interact with one another more easily.

Web 2.0 applications eroded the barrier between creators and consumers of the Internet further. While it is still the case that an average user is probably not capable of programming and deploying sophisticated web 2.0 social and business applications, web 2.0 made the creation and posting of multimedia content to the Internet much easier. Substantial portions of a web designer's and communicator's work have moved from the individual's desktop and into the web "cloud." Such skills as HTML and XML coding, the knowledge of software tools like Dreamweaver, Photoshop, and others, as well as principles of document and graphic design will never lose their relevance. At the same time, changes in the nature web communication may necessitate adjustments in the training of future communication professionals.

Such adjustments may include a revision of the software tool set that is taught to current students of technical communication and web design. But it is also possible that these adjustments may need to go deeper and include ways in which communication and design professionals see their professional role and the skill sets they possess.

In this chapter, I investigate the extent to which web 2.0 communication and collaboration tools are being used in the workplace and the purposes for which they are being used. I accomplish this task by reviewing available literature on the subject. Based on this analysis, I develop a series of recommendations for teachers of web communication and web design courses as well as for administrators of technical communication programs.

BACKGROUND: LITERATURE REVIEW

In this section, I review literature dedicated to the use web 2.0 communication and collaboration tools in the workplace. Such a review is necessary for the understanding of the changing nature of technical communicators' work and the implications of web 2.0 for the training of technical communicators. My purpose in this section of the chapter is to determine and explain the main trends in the workplace use of web 2.0.

Symbolic-Analytic Work

The changes brought about by web 2.0 to the work of web communicators and designers go much deeper than new skill sets and the ability to operate with new software. These changes are connected to deep transformations in the 21st century economy that shape the work of communicators and designers.

One such change is the rise of the "Symbolic-Analytic Worker" (Reich, 1991, p. 225). Symbolic analysts manipulate symbols and "reduce reality to a set of manageable symbols" (Reich 1991,

225). Reich writes: "As the value placed on new designs and concepts continues to grown relative to the value placed on standards products, the demand for symbolic analysis will continue to surge" (Reich, 1991, p. 225).

Other authors applied Reich's ideas to the field of technical communication. Johnson-Eilola calls for a shift in the way we see the work of a technical communicator. (Johnson-Eilola, 2004, pp. 180-181). Johnson-Eilola considers technical communicators Symbolic-Analytic Workers. "Symbolic-Analytic Work offers a potential common ground between the broad, conceptual and social issues frequently espoused by academics and the pragmatic, functional concerns of practitioners." (Johnson-Eilola, 2004, p. 189). Johnson-Eilola names "building metaknowledge, network knowledge, and self-reflective processes as one of key projects in technical communication education." (Johnson-Eilola, 2004, p. 189). The profession of technical communication must "think about new formations for knowledge that rely on network organization, metaknowledge, and metawork that act at a level above current knowledge structures." (Johnson-Eilola 2004, p. 189).

Together with Symbolic-Analytic Work, another important fundamental change in the post-industrial economy affecting the work of technical communicators and web designers is the notion of collaborative economy advanded by Don Tapscott and Anthony D. Williams in their book *Wikinomics: How Mass Collaboration Changes Everything*. (Tapscott & Williams, 2006). In the book, Tapscott and Williams describe and theorize about case studies in industrial and business "crowdsourcing." (Tapscott & Williams, 2006)

Web 2.0 Tools in Business

IT and networking needs of companies and other large organizations are quite different from those millions of individual users or even small professional groups that have fully embraced web

2.0 technologies. These large organizations also face different challenges and liabilities related to security and stability of web applications used by their employees. These factors many be the reason for which the business world appears to be adopting web 2.0 tools a little more slowly than other user groups.

A good way to describe the state of adoption of web 2.0 by businesses and other organizations is with the phrase "cautious enthusiasm." While there has been considerable interest in web 2.0 tools for business purposes in recent years, the level of adoption of those tools by enterprise users is not nearly as high as that of non-business users. Literature dedicated to enterprise use of web 2.0 communication technologies seems to often send conflicting messages about both the scope of this technology's use and the ways in which it is being used.

IT managers and other decision makers within corporations and other large organizations seem to understand the potential of web 2.0 tools while at the same time being cautious about implementing those tools. At the heart of this uncertainty lie two issues. The first one is whether companies should keep the traditional division between their intranets and the "open" Internet. And the second one is whether the traditional role of IT departments should be revised to include not only watching over the security of companies' internal networks, but also training and encouragement of employees to use the computing tools available outside of that network for work purposes, including the communication and collaboration tools of web 2.0. The level of adoption of web 2.0 tools and ways in which they are used in the workplace depend on how those questions are answered in each organization's individual case.

Koplowitz and Young (2007) suggest that businesses are slow and cautious in adopting web 2.0 communication technologies. (Koplowitz and Young, 2007) The report surveys 749 IT managers of companies with 500 or more employees. According to the report, 64% of IT departments

had no intention to invest in wikis in 2008, with 8% of those respondents not even familiar with wiki technology. In addition, in 2007, 69% of IT departments had no intention of investing in blog technology while 66% had no interest in Real Simple Syndication (RSS). (Koplowitz and Young, 2007).

On the other hand, 12% of the companies surveyed for the report deployed internal company wikis for various collaborative information management and writing projects, as well as to collect information from their customers. According to the survey, most companies reported that while they did not deploy web 2.0 technologies, they saw value in those technologies. (Koplowitz and Young, 2007)

Another report, entitled "Harnessing Web 2.0: Enterprise Strategies for Living on the Web" paints a different picture. (Neal, 2007). In the report, Neal presents a case study of the use of the "open web" by the British Petroleum corporation (BP). According to Neal's account, BP made a dramatic shift (for most of the business world, anyway) from building "IT castles" and separating its computing environment from the rest of the world's to trusting employees more in managing their computing environments. The report states:

Although the idea of 'Living on the Web' has gained considerable support within BP, especially among business executives, there are still instances where IT's first reaction is to control, not support or teach the users. It is a reflexive reaction born of years running IT that way. When he sees examples of this attitude in meetings, Jim Ginsburgh, VP of Enterprise Architecture, says, "We trust these people with multimillion-dollar drilling platforms. Why won't we trust them with a PC?" (Neal, 2007).

While not discussing web 2.0 communication and collaboration tools directly, this passage represents a potentially important shift in the way in which large companies may begin to see the role of IT departments. It may symbolize the increased role of IT professionals in empowering employees to use new computing tools rather than primarily policing against misuse of those tools. In the age of the "fragmented" internet when users have access to a slew of free or low-cost communication tools which can easily be combined for a given project, such a shift in the role of IT professionals within organizations might mean an increased use of those tools in the future.

Monitoring the use of web-based communication tools by employees appears to remain an important part of many IT departments' mission. According to the report "The Collaborative Internet: Usage Trends, End User Attitudes and IT Impact," between 23% and 28%, of the companies that participated in the survey monitored their employees' use of web 2.0 applications. (NewDilligence). The amount of monitoring varied according to the size of the company. Medium-sized companies of one thousand to five thousand employees monitored the least and large companies, with over five thousand employees, monitored the most. The rates of monitoring of web 2.0 tool by employees are relatively low, compared to up to 84% of companies monitoring their employees' use of e-mail and up to 72% monitoring web browsing. (NewDilligence).

There may be an inherent conflict between the traditional role of IT departments and the influences of web 2.0 on workplace computing and communication. Traditionally, IT professionals have been charged with safeguarding and protecting a company's computing and technological environment against outsiders. On the other hand, because most popular web 2.0 communication tools, such as wikis, blogs, and so on, are hosted online, rather than on users' own computers, they may be inviting the kinds of openness in communication and in exchange of information that this traditional model of IT is not yet capable of supporting. For those companies that are, in principle, interested in exploring web 2.0 communication and collaboration tools, but are afraid

of outsider penetration of their IT environment, hosting those tools on company servers may be a viable solution.

When it comes to which web 2.0 communication tools are the most popular in the workplace, wikis appear to hold the lead. Companies and organizations use wikis as knowledge-base platform for employees, platform for writing collaboration, and even as platforms (Marketing Executives Research Group, 2008) for technical support. The report "Beyond Wikipedia: Wikis as Workplace Tools" states that, "according to a November 2008 report by Marketing Executives Networking Group (Marketing Executives Research Group, 2008), one quarter of US executives are currently using wikis in their marketing efforts." (Marketing Executives Research Group, 2008). Among the companies that actively use wikis for business purposes are Ford, Motorola, and British Telecom whose "more than 16000 staff [employ wikis] to write software, map mobile base phone base stations, and initiate branding campaigns. In fact, virtually every new project produces a wiki" (Marketing Executives Research Group, 2008).

The report attributes the popularity of wikis among corporate employees to the ease with which they allow exchange of information in today's globalized world. The authors of the report predict further integration of web 2.0 communication tools into the business environment (Marketing Executives Research Group, 2008).

Typical examples of workplace wiki use include internal communications and collaborative projects within a company or organization, communication between the company and its clients. In some instances, companies use wikis to create technical support systems, both for their employees and for their clients. (Chau & Maurer, 2005). According to the case study, organization-wide wikis are useful for the support of "not only structured, but also unstructured knowledge representation" (Chau and Maurer 2005, pp. 185-186). Company wikis can be useful not only because they allow employees to assemble knowledge in one location online, but also because they encourage collaboration and communication among staff members. (Chau and Maurer 2005, pp. 185-186).

Among the more "exotic" types of web 2.0 technologies used for corporate work are 3D virtual environments, or virtual worlds, such as Second Life. Their discussion in professional literature is rather limited, but what is available appears to be marked with a heathy dose of skepticism about the true potential of these tools for corporate communication and training.

The opinion on the userfulness of Second Life, which is by far the best developed and most popular virtual world, for corporate work, is split, with some authors believing in its potential and others doubting it. In a case study entitled "Virtual worlds and learning: using Second Life at Duke Corporate Education" and published by Chartered Institute of Personnel and Development, the use of Second Life by Duke University's Corporate Education division is described. The authors of the case study note that Duke's experience with Second Life was successful, allowing to bring trainees dispersed around the world together in one place, albeit it a virtual one (The Chartered Institute of Personnel and Development, 2007).

On the other hand, Gina Minks of the EMC Corporation, writing in an entry on her blog entitled "Can Second Life be used as a reliable Corporate Training Tool?" claims that Second Life is not a suitable tool for corporate education, primarily because of the issues with IT support of Second Life. Minks recounts several experiences using Second Life for corporate education and comes to the conclusion that "until there is a cleaner way to securely connect to SL, and until it becomes a bit less resource intensive, I don't see what is gained by this environment over other forms of training that we already deliver." (Minks, 2008)

Minks' concerns appear to be indicative of the problems which proponents of a wider introduction of web 2.0 in corporate work face. Old habits of corporate IT departments appear to be the main obstacle to a wider adoption of

web 2.0 tools. Speaking at the 2007 Office 2.0 conference, Adam Carson of Morgan Stanley said that, when he proposed using web 2.0 tools, the firm's 10000-strong IT department "didn't get it." According to Carson, "This was all new to them. They had just been stuck in the world of enterprise IT." (Havenstein, 2007)

If adoption of web 2.0 tools in corporate environments is an uphill battle in most cases, then it stands to reason that some corporate trainers may be unwilling to spend much time and energy preparing their employees to understand and use those tools. Instead, they may prefer to stick with the traditional applications and tools which, in addition to being time-tested and familiar, are supported by their firm's IT department.

Web 2.0 Tools in Science and Education

Scientists and educators offer several interesting applications for web 2.0 communication and collaboration tools. The article "Bringing Web 2.0 to Bioinformatics," proposes a web 2.0-based system of collecting, systematizing, and distributing results of biological research. (Zhang, 2008). Zhang et al. argue that the traditional paradigm in bioinformatics information collection has been through one centralized database. This "web 1.0" approach to data collection and distribution is not viable since centralized databases hosting large amounts of information are costly to maintain and require frequent updating. The authors state:

"In bioinformatics, the sword of Damocles hangs over every Web 1.0 database/web server, due to the threat of loss of financial support. With centralized updating of content, even a minor gap in funding support may hamstring and doom even an otherwise cutting-edge Web 1.0 database, largely because in the Web 1.0 model, users are allowed only to retrieve information, but not to update it" (Zhang, 2008, p. 4).

To meet this challenge, Zhang et al. propose a social network-like system for collecting, organizing and redistributing of scientific information. Within their model, "people with similar research interests are linked together an communications among people increase, which makes knowledge discovery possible through collaboration and collective intelligence" (Zhang, 2008, p. 5). While the article does not actually describe specific communication tools through which the participants of this system would achieve their goals, the authors use such phrases as "users add value," "community enhancement," and "collaboration and collective intelligence" to describe the proposed set-up. (Zhang, 2008, p. 5). This is a radical departure from the web 1.0 model of information storage and retrieval. In the web 1.0 model, users interact exclusively with the server (database) while in the proposed web 2.0-based model, they also interact with other users.

Educators at various levels have used a variety of web 2.0 communication, collaboration, and learning tools for a long time. In education, we see perhaps the largest variety in the kinds of web 2.0 tools being used. This variety may well exist due to the considerable freedom which educators, especially in higher education and especially compared to their counterparts in business organizations, to choose and deploy the tools that suit their pedagogical goals. Notable web 2.0 projects in the area of education include iTunes U, a repository of educational podcasts, numerous educational channels and videos on Youtube (www.youtube.com), and Wikibooks (www.wikibooks.org), a collection of collaboratively written and free textbooks.

Like in the business sector, in education, wikis have been the web 2.0 tool of choice for collaborative learning. Many educational institutions now host their own wiki platforms. In addition, several robust wiki services are available to educators on the "open" Internet free of charge. For example, PBWiki (www.pbwiki.com) has reached out to educators with free webinars and other resources

in an attempt to position itself as the wiki for educators. Other popular open Internet wiki platforms used by educators include Wetpaint (www.wetpaint.com), and Wikispaces (www.wikispaces.com). All these wiki providers have invested considerable effort in designing intuitive interfaces allowing users to create rich multimedia content with little to no technical expertise.

In addition to participating in wiki-based projects, students at various levels, create podcasts, blogs, communicate via social networks, and use other web 2.0 learning tools. But it is wikis that appear to be the most actively discussed and theorized web 2.0 communication and learning tool in literature about education.

"Concepts for Extending Wiki Systems to Supplement Collaborative Learning," examines the issue of designing an effective educational wiki. (Reinhold, 2006) Noting that using wikis in the classroom "is not a particularly new idea," Reinhold and Abawi state that "it is not only the course, the classroom, and the participant that can adapt to the technology used. Conversely, the wiki itself can be modified to better suit the didactic scenario." (Reinhold, 2006, p. 756). This article is important because, unlike most educational literature on the use of wikis, it discusses not only wiki assignment design or assessment practices, (although Reinhold and Abawi do that, too) but focuses on wiki design as an e-learning platform.

The article describes three specific courses using wikis. In the first course, students use a wiki in a sociology and political course to "write about and discuss topics of sociological relevance." (Reinhold, 2006, p. 756). In the second one, students in a theology course created a wiki "a quality-assured multimedia dictionary for terms relevant in Religious Education." (Reinhold, 2006, p. 756). The students in the third course were asked to answer specific questions about media and society in a wiki. (Reinhold, 2006, p. 756).

Reinhold and Abawi analyzed the texts written in wikis by all three groups and concluded that, in order to create a successful learning tool, a wiki designer must consider "Workflow and Motivation, Structure and Content, Visualization, Orientation and Navigation, as well as Integration." (Reinhold, 2006, p. 766). In other words, Reinhold and Abawi see students who use wikis not only as learners who seek information, but as users looking for a complete and fulfilling user experience. Such an approach to design is very much in tune with the rest of the "web 2.0 design philosophy" which emphasizes the role of the user as an interactive participant of the communication and collaboration process.

In all the cases of web 2.0 tool implementation reviewed so far, designers and users of those tools have worked to increase inclusion and participation by users. Even those companies and organizations whose IT departments worry about web 2.0 tools disrupting their usual IT flow, wikis and other such tools are usually deployed with the purpose of increasing staff communication and participation. The emphasis is placed on inclusion and involvement of users. This is not surprising given web 2.0's focus on "the wisdom of crowds" in content creation and distribution.

In a significant break with web 2.0's tendency to include as many users as possible, the educational social bookmarking service Brainify (www.brainify.com) attempts to build an exclusive system separated from the rest of the Internet. Brainify's founder Murray Goldberg, who had also developed the course management system WebCT explains the service in this way:

... the heart of Brainify is all about social bookmarking of web sites useful in an academic setting. All the applicable web 2.0 things are there – bookmarking, rating, tagging, commenting, etc. Imagine coming to the site and being able to find, for example, what the community feels are the best web sites to help you understand recursive descent compilers at the intermediate level

(or anything else). I would love to have that kind of information at my fingertips. (http://brainify. blogspot.com).

Godberg's idea is to create a social bookmarking system that contains only academic resources and is immune, or almost immune, from the questionable-quality resources so often found on the Internet. Brainfy will only accept members with college e-mail addresses. While the idea of an "academic" social bookmarking system will certainly attract the attention of some people, it has already been criticized by several academics. For example, a story about Brainify in *The Chronicle of Higher Education*, cites university professors who criticize Godlberg's creation on the grounds of its exclusivity. (Shieh, 2009, 1) According to those critics, social bookmarking services "derive their power from the size of their networks. Whether users create collaborative lists of bookmarks or pool research with colleagues, having as many users as possible—whether or not they are interested in higher education—increases the amount of input a user gets" (Shieh, 2009, 1).

Surveying the use of web 2.0 communication and collaboration tools by scientists and educators, it is clear that this group of users is concerned with different issues from the issues that worry business users. While businesses are often concerned with the potential threat to their computer networks' security that such tools as blogs, wikis, social networks, and others pose, users in science and education seem more concerned with issues of design of web 2.0 communication environments, ways of ensuring credibility of information being exchanged, and ensuring a high level of user involvement.

Web 2.0 Tools in the Government and Non-Profit Sectors

The government and non-profit sectors have tried to integrate web 2.0 tools in their work for a while now. One of the most high-profile examples which received a lot of press recently has been the work of the Chief Technology Officer of Washington, DC Vivek Kundra. As the nation's capital's CTO, Kundra switched 38000 of the District's employees from Microsoft Office to Google Apps. Explaining his decision, Kundra said:

"When I moved to Washington, I had more computing power on my laptop at the local coffee shop than the average police officer or teacher. We looked at the cloud computing model and the consumer space. Compared with the cost of owning infrastructure, it's far cheaper." (Towns, 2008 1).

No doubt, Kundra's ability to harness web 2.0 technology contributed to his appintment, by President Obama, to the post of the first ever Chief Technology Officer of the federal government. (Hart, 2009). Of course, Obama's own election campaign used blogs, social networks, and other web 2.0 tools to a great effect.

Looking at other cases of web 2.0 deployment and use in the government and non-profit sectors, a couple of examples stand out. The report "Web 2.0 in Government: Why and How?," authored by David Osimo for the Joint Research Centre of the European Commission outlines ways in which government bodies might implement web 2.0 communication technologies. (Osimo, 2008). The report uses a combination of surveys and case studies to answer the following questions:

- "Are web 2.0 applications relevant for the government context?
- If they are, in what way is web 2.0 likely to have an impact on government?
- How significant could this impact be?
- How are web 2.0 applications implemented in the government context? (Osimo, 2008, p. 7).

The study found that, so far, web 2.0 applications have played a key role in increasing political participation by citizens while also helping government agencies to provide better and more timely services. According to the report, web 2.0 tools have also had a positive effect on office knowledge management processes, inter-office collaboration, and even regulation and law enforcement (Osimo, 2008, p. 7). The report mentions "a more active user role" as one of the key changes that web 2.0 has brought to government operations. (Osimo, 2008, p. 8). It also concludes that web 2.0 in government will work best if challenges of transparency and making public data readily available to citizens are met. A crucial factor in the successful deployment and use of web 2.0 by government bodies is the creation of an atmosphere of trust between the government and its citizens. (Osimo, 2008, pp. 9-10)

As with other instances of web 2.0 application deployment and use that have beem analyzed so far in this chapter, Osima's report clearly states that the success of government's web 2.0 efforts depends on transparency, honesty, and user involvement. Government agency websites then become not vehicles for one-way information distribution to the masses, but communication and interaction hubs.

Here in the United States, an interesting example of web 2.0 elements implementation is the official website for the state of Delaware (www.delaware.gov). Search terms used by the site's visitors are added to the tag cloud that is prominently displayed at the center of the page and anchors the "one-click" search tool. In addition, the website offers subscriptions to several Real Simple Syndication (RSS) feeds and podcasts. (The State of Delaware, 2009)

Non-profit organizations are using web 2.0 applications to stay in touch with the people they serve as well as to raise funds for their work. One of the most remarkable uses of web 2.0 communication and interaction technologies is by the organization InSTEDD, which stands for Innovative Support for Emergencies, Diseases, and Distasters (www.instedd.org). As Figure 1

Figure 1. Screenshot of the website of InSTEDD

illustrates, InSTEDD not only uses a variety of web 2.0 technologies, but makes those technologies central to its mission.

At the center of InSTEDD's philosophy is the notion of collaboration:

"Effective collaboration requires that responders establish a reliable flow of timely, accurate and complete information. Yet the information technologies required often fail in the difficult environments where humanitarian organizations work. We'd probably all agree that today's public health and relief workers ought to have access to the best possible information whenever they need it, including satellite imagery, sensor data, media reports and all the rich resources of the World Wide Web." (InSTEDD, 2008).

Citing the communication difficulties during disaster relief efforts as a "major obstacle to effective humanitarian action," InSTEDD has developed and used a series of web 2.0 applications to improve such communication. (InSTEDD, 2008).

Perhaps the most innovative of these tools is called Geochat and is designed to let "team members interact to maintain shared geospatial awareness of who is doing what where -- over

any device, on any platform, over any network. GeoChat allows you and your team to stay in touch one another in a variety of ways: over SMS, over email, and on the surface of a map in a web browser." (InStedd Geochat, 2008). The tool is illustrated in Figure 2.

Since people in a disaster area are unlikely to have access to the web or even a computer, the ability to use Geochat over a cell phone network is particularly important. InSTEDD's website mentions that Geochat which is "nearing public Beta release" has recently been tested during a public health emergency situation in Cambodia, but the results of this test are not mentioned or discussed on the organization's website. (InStedd Geochat, 2008).

The review of literature I have presented so far suggests two important conclusions. Communicators and web designers cannot ignore the penetration of web 2.0 communication and collaboration tools and applications into the workplace. Although this penetration is uneven and is sometimes hampered by institutional and technological obstacles, it is safe to assume that, as these obstacles are being overcome, professionals who know how to design, deploy, and use these tools with be in high demand. This means that in order to be competitive in this kind of workplace,

Figure 2. Geochat

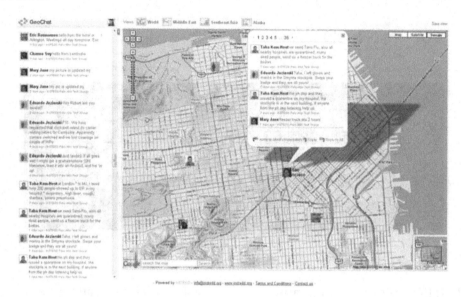

people who study technical communication and web design need to be taught about designing, deploying, and using web 2.0 applications. In the next section of the chapter, I develop a set of recommendations designed to help teachers and trainers of technical communicators and web designers achieve that goal.

IMPLICATIONS FOR TRAINING OF FUTURE TECHNICAL COMMUNICATORS AND WEB DESIGNERS

As the review of literature above demonstrates, profound changes in the nature and functions of the Internet have taken place in recent years. To respond to those changes and to adjust the training of future technical communicators and web designers, teachers and program administrators will find the theoretical model of "total user experience" design proposed by James Zappen and his colleagues in several recently published works (Zappen & Geisler, 2009; Zappen, Harrison, Watson, 2008). The main thrust of these works is that, as the user experience on the Internet has

changed with the advent of web 2.0 technologies, so should the way in which web design and web communication are taught to students. (Zappen & Geisler, 2009).

In "A New Paradigm for Designing E-Government: Web 2.0 and Experience Design," Zappen et al. write that "traditional concepts of information design have their origin in the transition form system-centered to user-centered approaches to system development" (Zappen, et al., 2008, p. 18). In large part of web 2.0, "information design is currently experiencing a transformation from its traditional emphasis upon system performance and the user satisfaction…to a greater emphasis upon the quality of the user's engagement with the system" (Zappen & Geisler, 2009, 7).

As a result, traditional measurements of success in web design, such as usability parameters that focus on the transparency and ease of use of a system may not be suitable for the web 2.0 environment (Zappen & Geisler, 2009, 7-8). Instead, Zappen and his co-authors argue that teaching web design should focus on designing "experience as user engagement" (2009, 8). While this new requirement is not contradictory to ensuring the usability of a system in the traditional sense, this new notion of web design pays attention not only on the quality of the users' interaction with a computer system or website (web 1.0 paradigm), but on the quality of the interactions among users, which are mediated by computer technology (web 2.0 model). At the heart of this interaction is collaboration among users, and one of the tasks of a web designer is the design of a web environment that is conducive to such collaboration (Zappen & Geisler, 2009, 9-12). Zappen and Geisler propose calling the teaching of such web design skills not training in technical communication, but training in tech-mediated communication (2009, 14).

The practical steps in the training of future technical communicators and web designers to meet the challenges of the changing Internet should proceed on two levels. The first level would consist of the adjustments to the course content and assignments within specific technical communication and web design courses. The second level would comprise curricular and philosophical changes and updates within programs, academic departments, and other entities that prepare technical communicators and web designers for the workplace. These two types of activities should proceed in a coordinated fashion because classroom-level reforms will take place more easily if the instructors who undertake them receive concrete support from administrators.

Changes at the Level of Pedagogy and Course Content

Classroom-level changes in technical communication and web design instruction, oriented towards meeting the challenges of the web 2.0-based workplace, could proceed in the following three directions.

- New conceptual knowledge and new understanding of the role of technical communicators and web designers. A useful first step in this direction would be an emphasis on the symbolic-analytic and collaborative

nature of the work done by technical communicators and web designers in the modern workplace. Traditionally, technical communicators and web designers have been seen as "service" professionals who work with messages and texts created by someone else. While this kind of work is not going away completely because of web 2.0, as the review of literature in this chapter demonstrates, future communicators and designers are likely to have to engage in other kinds of tasks which this traditional view of the field simply does not take into account. This kind of theoretical and conceptual coursework will help students to see the work they do in a new light.

- Critical meta-study and reflection on the use of web 2.0 applications, communication, collaboration, and design tools, both in the workplace and by non-professionals on the Internet. The purpose of such work is to equip students with a contextualized understanding of computer-mediated communication in general and web 2.0-mediated communication in particular. Topics of inquiry in this area may include established and emerging models and methods of usability testing and interaction design, and so on. Students may be asked to conduct various meta-analyses of existing web 2.0 communication environments as well as designing their own web 2.0 applications, for specific purposes and audiences. Subject for analysis and reflection may include effective blogs, wikis, social networks, peer-to-peer systems, and so on. Teachers and trainers should make a conscious effort in drawing the learners' attention in the key differences and similarities between these web 2.0 systems and more web 1.0-oriented websites and other online artifacts. In analyzing both kinds of systems, students should be asked to evaluate and question the roles of both designers and users within a given interaction and the decisions being made by both groups. Such critical assessment of web 2.0 systems should not be limited to professional contexts, however, especially in the case of college and university courses and programs in technical and scientific communication and web design. It is impossible to know which area the students will work, and developing metaknowledge about principles of designing web 2.0 environments in various contexts will help the students adjust to specific workplace situations and contexts later in their careers. In addition, students and trainees may be able to acquire more specialized knowledge about the functioning of web 2.0 environments in a specific professional or academic field via internships, thesis or practicum projects, or apprenticeships.

- New software tools and skills should be taught alongside established ones. For example, proficiency in HTML, CSS, and XML is a widely accepted necessity for technical communicators, and so is the knowledge the programs included in Adobe's Creative Suite. However, alongside these skills, students should be taught Asynchronous JavaScript and XML (AJAX) which is the programming backbone of web 2.0 applications. More attention should be given to training in the use and design of content management systems (CMS), including such open-source CMS as Drupal (www.drupal.org), Moodle (www.moodle.org), and others. Both proprietary and open source content management systems are widely used by companies and organizations for project and workflow management, so having CMS proficiency will increase the students' competitiveness in the 21st century workplace. Instruction in web 2.0–oriented web design should go beyond efficiency, aesthetics, and ease

of system use to include "experience as user engagement" (Zappen et al. 2009, 8). Alongside learning practical skills, students should be made aware of the impact of specific software, programming, and formatting choices on the success or failure of the user-engagement designs they attempt to build.

Programmatic Changes

In order for the classroom-level changes to take place and succeed, academic and professional training programs and departments need to adjust as well. Here, I also see three directions along which changes are warranted.

- Technical communication programs need to make sure that their curricula and course offerings are up to date. Programs of study need reflect the current state of the field and of the workplace in which their graduates will function. Steps in this direction should include regular program assessments and revisions, hiring of new faculty with appropriate expertise, and encouraging their faculty members to pursue professional development opportunities.
- Assessment of student achievement needs to reflect the new realities of in technical communication and web design. Students in technical communication programs are routinely accessed via portfolios that include both print-based and electronic pieces. If programs include training in web 2.0 communication and design, and I hope to have made a case in this chapter that they should, then the contents of student portfolios need to reflect that emphasis. In addition to designing static websites and other electronic artifacts, students should be asked to submit web 2.0 oriented designs and products. The Research Assessment Project sponsored by The Council for Programs in

Technical and Scientific Communication will be a useful aid for programs wishing to implement better assessment methods. (Council for Programs in Technical and Scientific Communication, 2008)

- Programs and departments should actively seek professional partnerships with businesses, government agencies, non-profits, and other organizations that would allow their students to receive hand-on training in web 2.0 communication and design. Such partnerships can come in the form of internships, practicum and other projects, during students would be able to work on web 2.0 communication and design tasks.

Overall, the training of future technical communicators and web designers needs to embrace the idea of web 2.0 more. Training in metaknowledge and skills that are specific to designing the web "experience as user engagement" (Zappen et al., 2009) should move center stage in the curricula of technical communication programs. Together with traditional programming, design, and usability skills, these new competencies will allow the graduates of these programs to be more competitive in the 21st century workplace.

But what should employers of technical communicators do when considering an application from a candidate who is not well versed in web 2.0? The answer to this question depends on the kind of work that candidate will be doing should he or she be hired, the kinds of software tools that the hiring organization uses, and on whether this organization is interested in expanding into the world of web 2.0. For example, at the time of the writing of this chapter, I was coordinating the internships of a group of graduate students in technical and scientific communication. Some of these students wrote in their internship reports that they had to work with web 2.0 tools at least occasionally. These tools were primarily enterprise wikis. On the other hand, some of the interns reported doing most of their work using Microsoft

Office, Adobe Creative Suite and other similar tools. In many case, these interns were not even required to work online, with the exception of e-mailing the final drafts of the reports they had written to their supervisors. In many cases, fairly "traditional" writing and editing skills served those interns just fine. At the same time, organizations interested in exploring web 2.0 tools and using them, at least in the near future, should consider hiring communicators with web 2.0 expertise if those candidates meet all other requirements.

FUTURE TRENDS

The stage of the development of the Internet when websites were one-way conduits of information is long gone. Instead, web 2.0 communication and collaboration technologies have put the user into the center of web communication and web design. In the future, businesses and other large organizations will reduce their caution towards the web 2.0 "cloud" and begin using these tools more actively. This change will be guided not only by a growing understanding by IT managers and other administrators that, in order to be competitive in the 21st century marketplace, they need to use web 2.0 communication tools and train their employees in their utilization. It is likely to also be aided by an increased quality of those tools themselves. For example, any outstanding security and stability issues will have to be addressed if large-scale use of blogs, wikis, and social networks by companies and other organizations were to become a reality.

As my review of literature suggests, educators and scientists appear to be somewhat ahead of business people in their adoption of web 2.0 technologies. In the near future, we will probably observe further evidence of this trend in the education and science sectors. Educational and research institutions are probably able to adopt web 2.0 tools faster than businesses because their members typically have to cut through less red tape to adopt those tools. IT departments of colleges and universities will probably continue to provide a high degree of standardization for their faculty and students by purchasing licenses for course management systems like Blackboard and maintaining their e-mail services in-house rather than outsourcing them to external providers. However, early adopters in those organizations will encounter very few real obstacles to using external web 2.0 tools for communication and collaboration.

Governments and non-profit bodies will probably continue to adopt web 2.0 technologies widely. The single most important factor driving this trend may be the desire to cut IT costs, given that, at least now, most web 2.0 communication and collaboration services are offered either free of charge or significantly more cheaply than commercial enterprise solutions. In addition, a major challenge of both effective government and an effective non-profit organization remains engagement with their constituents. Most of those constituents are likely to use web 2.0 technologies for communication and collaboration. It stands to reason, then, that governments and non-profits will want to tap into that use to establish more effective lines of communication with their audiences. The highly effective use of blogs, social networks, and other web 2.0 tools during the 2008 US presidential election season is an example of that trend.

In order to keep their graduates competitive in the 21st century workplace, programs in technical communication and web design will need to keep up with these trends. In the next few years, we are likely to see significant revisions of courses and curricula with more attention being paid to web 2.0 communication and design principles. These changes will take time due to the somewhat slow nature of curricular approval in most educational institutions. Therefore, it is likely that many of these changes will begin taking place at grassroots levels, with individual faculty members making

revisions to existing courses and pedagogies and then these changes percolating up through the system and becoming institutionalized.

The next challenge for all types of workplace users as well as for programs preparing technical communicators and web designers will be adopting their work for the emerging paradigm of web 3.0 or "semantic web." Thec definition of the phrase "semantic web" has remained elusive, and even Sir Tim Berners-Lee, the inventor of the World Wide Web and currently the director of the World Wide Web Consortium, which is one of the leading think tanks behind the development of web 3.0, cannot come up with an all-encompassing definition of semantic web. In an interview with Paul Miller, Berners-Lee describes web 3.0 in the following terms:

"Web 2.0 is a stovepipe system. It's a set of stovepipes where each site has got its data and it's not sharing it. What people are sometimes calling a Web 3.0 vision where you've got lots of different data out there on the Web and you've got lots of different applications, but they're independent. A given application can use different data. An application can run on a desktop or in my browser, it's my agent. It can access all the data, which I can use and everything's much more seamless and much more powerful because you get this integration. The same application has access to data from all over the place." (Miller, 2008)

Other definitions and explanations of this nascent iteration of the web suggest that web 3.0 will make data "smarter" by allowing computers to "understand" meanings of terms, search parameters, and so on. Hence its name "semantic web."

The CEO of Salesforce.com Marc Benioff seems to build on Berners-Lee's explanation when he states that,

"The new rallying cry of Web 3.0 is that anyone can innovate, anywhere. Code is written, collabo-

rated on, debugged, tested, deployed, and run in the cloud. When innovation is untethered from the time and capital constraints of infrastructure, it can truly flourish." (Benioff, 2008)

Existing definitions of web 3.0 may be incomplete and fragmentary, but if these predictions about the next iteration of the web come true, they would mean a further blurring of the line between users and developers, with, ostensibly, programming tools becoming more accessible to more people. This, of course, would not mean that every Internet user will become an expert coder. Nor would it mean that professional technical communicators and web designers will not require special skills to distinguish themselves from the amateur developers. However, the nature of the skills that would separate the professionals from the amateurs and allow those professionals to compete in the modern marketplace will change even compared to the skills necessary for the web 2.0 era, let alone those used in the web 1.0 years. Moreover, such changes would be further evidence of the viability of the notions of Symbolic-Analytic Work and wikinomics (Reich, 1991; Tapscott and Williams, 2006).

CONCLUSION

In order to stay competitive and prepare students for the 21st century workplace, technical communication programs need to pay attention to the changes in web-based communication and web design brought about by web 2.0. Based on the ever-increasing use of web 2.0 communication and collaboration technologies by businesses, scientific communities, educators, governments, non-profits, and other types of professional organizations, proficiency in web 2.0 and social media will be required of any technical communicator hoping to join those organizations. With the beginning of the development of web 3.0 applications,

technical communication programs need to look forward and prepare for more changes in the skill sets required of their graduates in the future.

REFERENCES

Benioff, M. (2008, August 1). *Welcome to Web 3.0: Now Your Other Computer is a Data Center*. Retrieved March 16, 2009, from TechcrunchIT http://www.techcrunchit.com/2008/08/01/welcome-to-web-30-now-your-other-computer-is-a-data-center/

Chau, T. (2005). A Case Study of Wiki-Based Experience Repository at a Medium-sized Software Company. In *Proceedings of the 3rd international conference on Knowledge capture* (pp. 185-186). Banff, Canada: International Conference On Knowledge Capture.

Council for Programs in Technical and Scientific Communication. (2008). *Research Assessment Project*. Retrieved 3 16, 2009, from Council for Programs in Technical and Scientific Communication: http://www.cptsc.org/research-assess.html

Hart, K. (2009, March 5). D.C. Tech Chief Tapped for White House Slot. *The Washington Post*. Retrieved March 16, 2009, from http://www.washingtonpost.com/wp-dyn/content/article/2009/03/05/AR2009030501060.html

Havenstein, H. (2007, September 7). IT is a Key Barrier to Corporate Web 2.0 Adoption, Users Say. *Computerworld*. Retrieved July 16, 2009, from http://www.computerworld.com/s/article/9034898/IT_is_a_key_barrier_to_corporate_Web_2.0_adoption_users_say

InSTEDD. (2008). *InStedd*. Retrieved 3 16, 2009, from InStedd: Innovative Support to Emergencies, Diseases, and Disasters http://www.instedd.org

InStedd Geochat. (2008). *InStedd Geochat*. Retrieved 3 16, 2009, http://www.instedd.org/geochat

Johnson-Eilola, J. (2004). Relocating the Value of Work: Technical Communication in a Post-Industrial Age . In Selber, J. J.-E. (Ed.), *Central Works in Technical Communication* (pp. 175–194). New York: Oxford University Press.

Koplowitz, R. (2007). *Web 2.0 Social Computing Dresses Up For Business*. Cambridge, MA: Forrester.

Lycos. (2009, March). *Lycos*. Retrieved March 2009, from Lycos: http://lycos.com

Marketing Executives Research Group. (2008). *Beyond Wikipedia: Wikis as Workplace Tools*. New York: E-Marketer.

Miller, P. (2008, February 26). *Sir Tim Berners-Lee: Semantic Web is Open for Business*. Retrieved July 19, 2009, from ZDNet: http://blogs.zdnet.com/semantic-web/?p=105

Minks, G. (2008, September 15). *Can Second Life be used as a reliable Corporate Training Tool?* Retrieved July 18, 2009, from Adventures in Corporate Education: http://gminks.edublogs.org/2008/09/15/can-second-life-be-used-as-a-reliable-corporate-training-tool/

Neal, D. (2007). *Harnessing Web 2.0: Enterprise Strategies for Living on the Web. Leading Edge Forum Executive Programme*. Falls Church, VA: Computer Sciences Corporation.

NewDilligence. *The Collaborative Internet: Usage Trends, End User Attitudes and IT Impact*. San Francisco: NewDilligence.

O'Reilly, T. (2005, September 30). *What is Web 2.0: Design Patterns and Business Models for the Next Generation of Software*. Retrieved March 8, 2009, from O'Reilly Media http://www.oreillynet.com/pub/a/oreilly/tim/news/2005/09/30/what-is-web-20.html

Osimo, D. (2008). *Web 2.0 in Government: Why and How?* Seville, Spain: Joint Research Centre of the European Commission.

Reich, R. (1991). *The Work of Nations: Preparing Ourselves for 21st Century Capitalism*. New York: A.A. Knopf.

Reinhold, S. D. (2006). Concepts for Extending Wiki Systems tov extend collaborative learning . In *Z. e. Pan, Edutainment 2006* (pp. 755–767). Berlin: Springer-Verlag.

Shieh, D. (2009, January 26). 'Social Bookmarking' Site for Higher Education Makes Debut. *The Chronicle of Higher Education*. Retrieved March 16, 2009, from http://chronicle.com/free/2009/01/10124n.htm

Tapscott, D., & Williams, A. (2006). *Wikinomics: How Mass Collaboration Changes Everything*. New York: Portfolio.

The Chartered Institute of Personnel and Development. (2007, July 1). *Virtual worlds and learning: using Second Life at Duke Corporate Education*. The Chartered Institute of Personnel and Development. Retrieved July 18, 2009, from http://www.cipd.co.uk/helpingpeoplelearn/_Teedce.htm

The State of Delaware. (2009, January 21). *State of Delaware: The Official website of the first state*. Retrieved March 16, 2009, from State of Delaware: The Official website of the first state http://www.delaware.gov

Towns, S. (2008, July 9). *Vivek Kundra, CTO of Washington, D.C., Focuses on Project Management*. Retrieved March 16, 2009, from Public CIO http://www.govtech.com/pcio/articles/375806

Yahoo. (2009, March). *Yahoo!* Retrieved March 2009, from Yahoo!: http://www.yahoo.com

Youtube. (2009, 3 16). Retrieved 3 16, 2009, from Youtube: http://www.youtube.com

Zappen, J., & Geisler, C. (2009). Designing the Total User Experience: Implications for Research and Program Development. *Programmatic Perspectives, 1*(1), 3–28.

Zappen, J., Harrison, T. M., & Watson, D. (2008). A New Paradigm for Designing E-Government: Web 2.0 and Experience design. *The Proceedings of the 9th Annual International Digital Government Research Conference* (pp. 17-27). Montreal, Canada: 9th Annual International Digital Government Research Conference.

Zhang, Z. C.-H. (2008). Bringing web 2.0 to bioinformatics. *Briefings in Bioinformatics*, *10*(1), 1–10. doi:10.1093/bib/bbn041

Section 2
Applications

Chapter 5
Desktop Virtual Reality Applications for Training Personnel of Small Businesses

Miguel A. Garcia-Ruiz
University of Colima, Mexico

Arthur Edwards
University of Colima, Mexico

Raul Aquino-Santos
University of Colima, Mexico

Samir El-Seoud
Princess Sumaya University for Technology, Jordan

Miguel Vargas Martin
University of Ontario Institute of Technology, Canada

ABSTRACT

Small and medium-sized businesses (SMBs) in most world economies suffer from a series of intense economic pressures from local, regional and international markets. Although these problems are micro-economic to the small and medium-sized business, they are directly related to macro economic factors, particularly in the case of labor. One of the main pressures small and medium-sized businesses suffer from is the lack of worker technical skills. Past research has consistently shown that virtual reality (VR) can be effective for supporting competency-based training skills. The objective of this chapter is to provide an overview on how virtual reality can be used to support technical training in SMBs, including the use of Second Life and DIVE VR platforms. This chapter describes a desktop VR Application for training car mechanics from a small business and highlights advantages and challenges of desktop virtual reality for technical training. Finally, future trends related to the use of VR in training are discussed.

DOI: 10.4018/978-1-61520-691-3.ch005

INTRODUCTION

Small and medium-sized businesses, or SMBs, comprise more than 90% of the firms operating in most world economies. These businesses play a critical role in the economic activity of their respective countries in almost all productive sectors and contribute to the majority of employment and the gross domestic product (GDP). As the U.S. Census Bureau points out (U.S. Census, 2007), small and medium-sized businesses have fewer than 100 and 500 employees, respectively. Similarly, the European Union establishes that small businesses have fewer than 50 employees, and medium businesses have no more than 250 employees (European Commission, 2003).

However, SMBs worldwide suffer intense economic pressures from local markets as well as competition among regional and global competitors. In addition, a number of problems associated with a lack of skills affect the productivity and ultimate survival of SMBs. According to Hamburg and Engert (2007), SMB employees often lack necessary skills to remain competitive in national and international markets. Moreover, SMBs need to develop core competencies to succeed, such as technical topics, including information technology (IT) competencies (Mascarenhas et al. 1998; Tapias Garcia, 2005).

Small businesses need to define skills and core competencies, since they are a basis for marketing, and for making operational decisions. If a business plans to grow, it needs to develop existing core competencies and expand them. If a SMB does something very well and remains focused on it by means of adequate training, it will have a competitive advantage and tend to become a leader in the specific business field (Srivastava, 2005). There is no question that the development of core competencies can be achieved with the support of technology.

Past research shows that computer and Internet-based specialized instruction (e-learning) is an effective way to deliver training courses. Recently, technologies like virtual reality and 3D graphical models displayed on Web pages have been effectively researched and employed for technical training (Gerbaud & Arnaldi, 2008). Virtual reality, or VR (Burdea & Coiffet, 2004; Sherman & Craig, 2003), today, is one of the new frontiers in training and education, both of which extend to the workplace. Some of the advantages of using virtual reality in training and education include first-person experience, active trainee participation in the learning process, multimodal learning (the use of multiple human senses to perceive information), ease of communication between trainees and instructors by decreasing anxiety, lowering of social barriers in a collaborative virtual environment (Youngblut, 1998), as well as enhancing trainee perception and analysis of 3D graphical models and other types of technical information (Dede et al., 1996; Roussos et al., 1997), among others (Cao et al. 2008).

The objective of this chapter is to provide an overview of desktop virtual reality and how it can be used to support technical training in SMBs. This chapter also highlights advantages and challenges of virtual reality for training. In addition, two important, economical and widely used programs for developing and displaying desktop virtual environments are also analyzed for their potential use in training.

Section background describes an overview of technology applied for training personnel in SMBs.

Section Virtual Reality Technology outlines a general description of research and applications carried out with virtual reality (and what it is not) and its classifications.

Section Second Life refers to a description of this virtual environment and current Second Life applications for education and training.

Section DIVE and Other VR Platforms covers a general description of distributed interactive virtual environment (DIVE), an open source program for developing collaborative virtual environments.

Section A VR Application for Training Car Mechanics describes a virtual reality application, and results of its usability study, to train car mechanics needing to learn about an automobile part in a small car repair garage.

Section A Comparison of Second Life and DIVE provides a comparative analysis of the technical advantages and challenges of Second Life and DIVE.

Section Future Trends offers a vision of future research and virtual reality applications applied to training, and what needs to be explored with regards to training and augmented reality.

Section Conclusion focuses on the applications of open source software and desktop virtual reality hardware to SMBs for training.

BACKGROUND

How to best teach the knowledge, skills and competencies necessary for persons to join the workforce and productively contribute to the production of wealth of businesses is the subject of much debate. One general consensus among companies, however, is that training personnel should be carried out quickly, efficiently and inexpensively. The two most common strategies to train personnel are before they enter the workplace, an approach commonly used to train first-time employees, or on-the-job training, for employees who require honing their skills or learning new competencies. These two paradigms of training personnel are becoming more and more relevant as the present worldwide economic crisis forces an almost unprecedented percentage of the workforce to seek new employment opportunities and acquire new skills and competencies and obliges companies to modernize their systems of production and reconsider models of competitiveness. Training personnel is particularly important for small and medium businesses (SMBs) who chronically suffer from a fluid workforce that often does not possess the skills necessary to optimally contribute to the business (Mullins et al., 2007).

The U.S. Small Business Administration (SBA, 2008) currently classifies a business or firm with less than 500 employees as small. The relevance of this chapter is that even though the contributions of SMBs are extremely important, their special concerns are rarely studied in academic and professional journals (Schleich et al., 1990). This is particularly surprising when the importance of SMBs is considered in the context of overall economic welfare. As many as five of every six pay checks in America come from firms with less than 1000 employees and close to 70% of these people work in companies with fewer than 100 employees (Carnevale, 1991).

In a longitudinal study, The United States Department of Labor (USDL, 2008) interviewed 9,964 men and women in 1979 when they were between the ages of 14 and 22. This study, which covers more than a quarter century, interviewed these respondents biannually. The most recent results reported in June, 2008, reveal the following:

- Individuals born between 1957 and 1964 held an average of 11 jobs between the ages of 18 and 42.
- As the baby boomers became older (38-42), the number of jobs they held during this four-year period average almost 2, a very significant number.
- In the 38-42 year-old age group, 31% left their jobs in less than a year and 65% in fewer than 5 years.
- Inflation-adjusted earnings increased most rapidly (7%) for younger workers between 18 and 22 years of age primarily because they worked at entry-level jobs. Earning growth slowed to 3.1% and 1.4% in the 33 to 37-year olds and 38 to 42 year-olds, respectively.

These statistics lead to some very significant conclusions:

- Mobility is great among all age groups, although it is greatest among younger workers because salary differences between entry level or minimum salary jobs and more stable long-term jobs provides sufficient financial incentives to improve earnings.
- As workers become older, they tend to become more stable enjoy smaller salary increases as they reach the top of their pay schedules. However, these adults still change jobs at a very significant pace.
- The fluidity of the workforce requires businesses have well-established strategies to accommodate the constant entrance and exit of its workforce.
- Small and Medium businesses are no exception to these statistics. In fact, because of the small number of employees working for them, they are more susceptible to production problems due to labor considerations.

In the last quarter century of the 20th century, computer technology became more widespread in business and industry. However, due to the costs and lack of know how, much of the early computer technology did not "tickle down" to SMBs. The sometimes prohibitive costs of hardware, software, licences, and training made it difficult for small businesses to enjoy the benefits of computer technology. Although the use of information technology (IT) is growing in SMBs, its use still pales in comparison with IT use in large companies, depending, in part, on the location, size, and nature of the business (Alexander, 1993).

Small and middle sized businesses are largely reluctant to accept new technologies because of: "internal uncertainty, bad experience with previous implementations, lack of honest, reliable partners / media consultants, inadequate hardware infrastructure and, of course, price."

For these reasons, particularly in Europe, there is always a considerable delay before companies take "the decision" to use newly available technologies. On average, it takes about 3 years to reach any next particular level in state-of-the-art technologies. The main task is, in a sense, to "cut the coat to fit the cloth," which in this particular case means adapting (online) applications to the equipment and knowledge level of a "normal," technically untrained user who probably does not even possess an up-to-date internet browser. It is cost effectiveness and the overall benefit to a company which ultimately determines how quickly or whether, if at all, a new technology will be incorporated. The challenge over the next few years will be how to deliver affordable, intuitive and easy computer and communications solutions to the workplace (Wierzbicki & Margolf, 2002).

Prashant et al. (1999) discuss two major variables concerning how IT is accepted in SMBs, including the following:

- Business factors:
  - **Type of business**: Retailers and wholesalers appear to be the most "sophisticated" users and there appears to be significant differences between the manufacturing and service sectors.
  - **Business size**: Investment in technologies is less "risky" in larger businesses.
  - **Profitability**: How much the system costs and how much will it maximize profits.
  - **Location**: How close the business is to competent technical support.
- Owner characteristics:
  - **Age**: Older users tend to be less knowledgeable and more distrustful of technology.
  - **Race**: There appear to be differences in how technology is perceived due

to socioeconomic and educational considerations.

- ○ **Education**: Persons with university degrees graduate with greater computer skills and tend to accept IT much quicker than homologues who have not acquired basic computer competencies.
- ○ **Computing skills**: The greater the owner's computer skills, the more like he/she is likely to introduce computers to the workforce.

The concept of training, particularly in the case of SMBs, has greatly evolved over the last 30 years. The first training courses were knowledge based, stimulus-response programs because of the limited processing power and limitations related to programming languages. However, since the 1990's considerable attention has been given to virtual reality (VR), primarily because it can provide "real-life" experiences in simulators that integrally engages its users (Vince, 2004). According to Rogers' (1969) experiential learning theory, learning should be significant and best takes place when the subject matter is relevant to the personal interests and needs of the student, the learning experience is non-threatening, and self initiated learning is the learning that tends to be more permanent.

According to Knowles' (1975, 1984) Theory of Andragogy, adults need to be actively involved the planning and evaluation of their instruction. This suggests that IT experts need to collaborate with the actual workers to design learning environments to suit their needs. Furthermore, Knowles maintains that instruction should be task-oriented and learning activities need to be contextualized according to the task that is to be performed. Lastly, Knowles maintains that adults are most interested in learning what is immediately relevant to the job and that adult learning needs to be centered more on problem solving than acquiring knowledge.

Finally, according to Cross (1981), who echoes the views of Knowles (1975, 1984) and Rogers (1969), adult learning programs need to capitalize on the actual experiences of the learner, should move from simple to more complex tasks and skills, adult learning programs should adapt to the cognitive differences of adults and that adults should be given as much choice as possible in how learning programs are organized.

Immersive VR technology has excellent potential to contribute to adult learning and training in the workplace (Bricken & Byrne, 1992). However, fully immersive VR technology still remains far too expensive for small and medium size businesses and is generally used in high-end simulators for government (NASA, military and the airline industry) or educational (language learning, medicine, engineering, physics, and chemistry). Fully immersing learners is motivating and encourages them to participate as persons interacting in a space that can suspend physical and temporal restrictions that would otherwise be imposed on them. According to (Yahava et al., 2004), a person's willingness to either live a real-life situation or an environment that supersedes the laws of physics, provides a presence that significantly contributes to perseverance.

VIRTUAL REALITY TECHNOLOGY

Virtual reality (VR) is a computer-based technology capable of generating a 3D space (also called virtual environment), has three main characteristics: It is multi-sensorial, interactive and integrally engages its users with the psychological effect of immersion (Burdea & Coiffet, 2004;). However, virtual reality must comply with the three characteristics, otherwise it is just a 3D graphical simulation shown on a computer screen (Sherman & Craig, 2003).

VR is classified according to the level of immersion (the subjective perception of being present in a virtual environment) it provides. Semi-immersive (or desktop) VR usually employs a typical desktop or laptop computer and

Figure 1. A basic desktop (semi-immersive) VR system

its monitor to watch the virtual environment and interact with it, using either a conventional mouse or keyboard, and listening to sounds from the virtual environment using a couple of speakers or headphones. In a more sophisticated desktop VR, however, the user may also wear 3D glasses (such as anaglyphs or shutter glasses) to watch the 3D environment in stereo using stereoscopic projections. These types of projections may support 3D model visualizations and enhance immersion, although non-stereoscopic visualization provides a certain degree of effective immersion. Figure 1 shows a basic desktop VR system configuration without the 3D glasses.

In fully-immersive VR environments, though, users watch the virtual environment that is projected in a VR helmet, manipulates virtual objects and navigates through the virtual environment using special data gloves with sensors, while listening to sounds through high fidelity headphones (Burdea & Coiffet, 2004). Although immersive VR offers a greater immersion effect than the desktop VR, both are effective in educational settings. The difference is that the equipment used for fully-immersive VR simulators is very expensive, complex to maintain, and requires specially trained professionals to employ and adapt them in educational or training settings. For these reasons, fully-immersive equipment

cannot be bought, employed and maintained by many SMBs. Figure 2 depicts a fully-immersive VR system.

Both desktop and fully-immersive virtual reality has been used by large industries to train their personnel. In an early study, Adams (1996) describes an informal study carried out by a large pager maker and a consultancy business from the US about training employees to supervise a pager production line. A production line was recreated in a desktop and effects of the fully-immersive virtual environment were reported. Results showed that trainees who used VR committed fewer errors and understood the process faster than personnel who used real equipment for their training. Recent VR applications include employee training to operate mining equipment (van Wick and de Villiers, 2008) and the widespread use of virtual reality simulators to train medical personnel (Alverson et al., 2005), among others.

A late nineties report on virtual reality applications in education (Youngblut, 1998) highlighted that desktop virtual reality can provide cost-effective and adequate technological support for education and training. The same report pointed out (almost a decade ago) that desktop VR is a

Figure 2. A fully-immersive virtual reality system

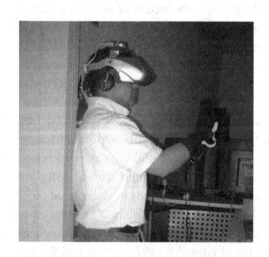

mature technology that can make use of the latest personal computers. In addition, it is likely that according to current unstable world economies, the development of fully-immersive virtual reality applications for training will decrease, at least for SMBs that have greater difficulty acquiring such equipment. There is relatively little literature on desktop VR applied to SMBs, despite how it can complement or enhance technical training.

A number of research institutions around the world have developed and tested networked collaborative virtual environments for education and training since the early nineties. Collaborative VR is a shared virtual environment using a local network or the Internet, where its users interact to work, learn, train, and perform other activities together (Benford et al., 2001). Until recently, however, there was insufficient computer and network power or adequate coding-decoding algorithms (codecs) to carry out smooth communications and immersion of participants in CVREs. Consequently, the result has been a trade-off between realism and speed (due to latency), as well as limited modality interactions that have focused almost exclusively on the exchange of visual and auditory information (Gutierrez, Vexo & Thalmann, 2004; Chan & Lau, 2004).

SECOND LIFE

Second Life (SL) is an online virtual world where millions of Internet users are registered and presently contribute by developing and uploading graphical objects, buildings, etc. Its users can interact as virtual personifications called avatars, and they can communicate using text messages and their voice, using voice over IP (VoIP). Its web page is http://secondlife.com. In general, users can personalize Second Life graphics and many of its features. For example, users can change their avatar's garment to use ''designer'' clothes, as well as trade and sell goods and services using Second Life's own money, called Linden Dol-

lars. The ability to personalize the Second Life environment is compelling and fun. There are two versions of Second Life, one for adults and one for users under 18 years of age, called Teen Second Life. An entire SL virtual environment is called a "metaverse." The metaverse contains "islands" that can be purchased and owned for a fee from Linden Labs (the business that created Second Life) or from other SL residents. Once users purchase an island, they can opt for using their islands for whatever purpose they desire. Second Life applications are mainly for entertainment, but they have potential educational potential. Education and general training are not opposed to providing fun and entertainment. For instance, in foreign language learning, fun and humor are ways to lower the "Affective Filter." By lowering the affective filter to learning, one also lowers anxiety and other negative feelings towards a learning experience (Krashen, 1982, 1988). There are already a number of educational islands that are owned by universities and private firms around the world, where courses are being taught. In addition, some educational institutions provide virtual facilities to their students, such as virtual classrooms, laboratories, and libraries (Gollub, 2007). Second Life also contains virtual museums that can be used in educational activities, too.

Consistent with Stephen Krashen's ((Krashen, 1982, 1988) hypothesis about the affective filter and language learning, there are presently important educational institutions offering second language learning (LL2) classes in Second Life, such as the internationally recognized Instituto Cervantes of Spain. This institution also has a virtual library containing books in Spanish, as well as Spanish memorabilia and a virtual expo hall. Its website is: http://secondlife.cervantes.es/ (in Spanish). Moreover, recent research points out that health institutions have studied Second Life for training personnel.

However, there are few reported cases in the literature about using SL specifically for training. For example, according to Gronstedt (2007), large IT companies such as IBM, Intel, Dell, and others, are investing in the development of virtual islands, offering courses and technical training in Second Life for their employees, although reported studies about SL applications in training still need to be published. Some people involved in these companies helped create SL islands and predictions are that the number of users will grow steadily, especially users from emerging economies like Brazil, India, and China (Gronstedt, 2007).

It appears that one secondary benefit of using collaborative VR like Second Life is to help reduce fuel costs of students and teachers in distance education programs, as they can avoid commuting to and from school every day (Theil, 2008). Other important benefits include quality of life concerns of people who can train at home or at more convenient hours and at lower costs for the SMBs, who can train employees to perform specific tasks at home, thus reducing training time and the risk of damaging actual equipment or risking harm to their employees.

Nevertheless, in order to run smoothly, Second Life requires a considerable amount of computer resources, such as an efficient video graphics card, a large RAM memory, and a reliable Internet connection with large bandwidth, from 1.544 to 6 Mbps. According to SL's web page, it needs a cable or DSL connection for accessing the Internet, and warns that "Second Life is not compatible with dial-up internet, satellite internet, and some wireless internet services." These requirements are strict, since we have collaboratively tested SL with very modest success on a local network connected to the Internet through fiber optics and with about 500kbps at the time of testing. It was not possible to run SL with slower Internet connections or with computers with less than 1Gb video RAM. A possible way to improve access to Second Life metaverse is to arrange a guaranteed Service Level Agreement (SLA) with the Internet service provider, or to increase the bandwidth

connection, although these can be costly solutions for smaller businesses.

Although the network requirements of Second Life to efficiently run over Internet connection is with cable or DSL, we believe that SL may run with IEEE 802.11g wireless networks for a small group of users accessing the network at the same time. However, we recommend using SL over WiMAX (Worldwide Interoperability For Microwave Access) technology, already available in some cities around the world. WiMAX is a recently created wireless communication medium to provide up to 72 Mbit/s symmetric broadband speed, suitable for multimedia and other types of data, based on the broadband wireless access IEEE 802.16 standard (Kumar, 2008).

An important problem with collaborative VR environments like Second Life is that users get frustrated when the local network or the Internet access is slow, greatly affecting VE visualization, sound perception and user communication in the shared virtual environment due to increased latency. This also has been noted in other collaborative VR studies (Fraser et al., 2000). In addition, increased latency will almost certainly hinder user performance, affecting completion of training objectives in future VR applications. One of the main causes of slow collaborative VE access is network delay that is caused by the way VR information (in the form of packets) is delivered onto a local network or over the Internet, and how that information is processed at each computer connected to that network (Gutwin et al., 2004). Network delay also produces latency in collaborative virtual environments, which can be defined as the period of time required to update and display the shared virtual environment for all the users. Network delay can greatly affect group interaction and the sense of immersion the virtual environment produces (Burdea & Coiffet, 2004).

Figure 3 shows one engineering student (from a group of five) collaborating in Second Life to test technical aspects in an informal usability exercise that helped us measure the network speed and other

Figure 3. A student testing the usability of Second Life

network characteristics. The desktop computers they used have one Mb of RAM, with video cards of 128 Mb of graphics memory. The used local network is composed of a 100 Mbps switch with approx. 500 kbps of Internet connection.

Although registering in Second Life is free at the moment, its users have to pay fees for entering and using some SL islands. It is worth trying a third-party Second Life viewer (client) called Onrez (http://viewer.onrez.com/). Onrez runs somewhat faster than the viewer developed by Linden Labs. There are other third-party companies and research groups that have developed Second Life viewers, available from: http://wiki. secondlife.com/wiki/Alternate_viewers.

DIVE AND OTHER VR PLATFORMS

There are alternatives to Second Life that may run with fewer computing requirements, and as stand-alone VE, such as DIVE (Distributed Interactive Virtual Environment), an open source program for collaborative VR developed by the Swedish Institute of Computer Science (Carlsson & Hagsan, 1993). Its web page is: http://www. sics.se/dive. Steed and Frecon (2005) describe DIVE as a peer-to-peer collaborative virtual

environment that allows the virtual environment sharing between various participants in real time, where they can effectively communicate among themselves through voice-over IP (VoIP), gestures, and text messaging. Similar to Second Life, DIVE allows collision detection programming of virtual objects to enhance VE realism. Moreover, Steed and Frecon (2005) point out that DIVE does not intended to produce photorealistic environments representing the real world, because it has been found that well-programmed virtual objects and avatar behaviors are more important than their photorealistic appearance to obtain realistic and convincing virtual environments, thus enhancing immersion (Freeman et al., 2003). DIVE also provides realistic spatialized (3D) sound capability. DIVE has been used mainly for research, and there have been a number of studies about using desktop VR and DIVE for education and training (Garcia-Ruiz et al., 2008; Garcia-Ruiz & Alvarez-Cardenas, 2005; Cervantes-Medina, 2004).

Other open source programs include VR Juggler, created by Iowa State University's Virtual Reality Applications Center in the United States. An alternative to virtual environments for training is VRML, which stands for Virtual Reality Modeling Language, one of the first standardized languages for using 3D virtual environments on the Internet. There are a number of open source and commercial VRML navigators and 3D graphics modelers (the programs for making virtual environments and its contents) that have been effectively used for training stand-alone users, because VRML itself does not work collaboratively, although a new version of VRML, called X3D, will have this capability. For a description of X3D see: http://www.web3d.org/x3d/. Table 1 shows a partial and non-exhaustive list of the aforementioned VR programs that allow collaborative applications.

It is also possible to use programming libraries, application programming interfaces (APIs), and graphics engines to create video games, commer-

Table 1. A list of programs used for collaborative VR

Program name	URL	¿Open source or commercial?
Distributed Interactive Virtual Environment (DIVE)	http://www.sics.se/dive	Open source
VR Juggler	http://www.vrjuggler.org	Open source
Second Life	http://secondlife.com	Open source/commercial
X3D programming language viewers/ authoring tools	http://www.web3d.org/x3d/content/examples/X3dResources. html#Applications	Open source
Avango	http://www.avango.org	Open source
World2World	http://www.sense8.com	Commercial
Flatland	Http://www.flatland.com	?

cially available or as open source. A Wikipedia page shows a comprehensive list these engines: http://en.wikipedia.org/wiki/List_of_game_engines. A 3D API for Java language called Java3D has been successfully used over the past ten years for creating virtual environments, mainly for research applications.

Past research has found that if educational technology has a high degree of usability, it will support learning and training more effectively, and will improve student motivation about its use (Zaharias, 2004; Zaharias, 2006; MacFarlane et al., 2005). The International Organization For Standardization (ISO) defines usability as "The extent to which a product can be used by specified users to achieve specified goals with effectiveness, efficiency, and satisfaction in a specified context of use" (ISO 9241-11, 1998). In addition, researchers have studied virtual environment usability for more that a decade, demonstrating that usable virtual environments lead to better user acceptance and user interactions in a virtual environment (Kaur et al., 1998). For instance, virtual reality medical simulators that have been improved in their usability and positively support skill transfer in medical training (Alverson et al., 2005). Van Wyck and de Villiers (2008) also point out that it is important to take into account the context of use when designing usable virtual environments for training, especially if person-

nel will be trained to operate in hazardous areas such as mining.

A DESKTOP VR APPLICATION FOR TRAINING CAR MECHANICS

We devised a virtual reality environment with the objective to support training mechanics in assembling a car distributor (Garcia-Ruiz & Alvarez-Cardenas, 2005). For some mechanics, this engine part is often difficult to check and assemble, and printed instructions are not clear enough for them. To see how useful DIVE or SL could be for training mechanics, we carried out a preliminary usability test of the virtual environment with the virtual distributor. DIVE was used because it is easy to handle in a basic laptop computer, which requires less bandwidth. However, the results of this study are valid for Second Life because it can produce exactly the same virtual object that was used in this study.

Materials

We used Distributed Interactive Virtual Environments (DIVE) to show the virtual environment, and an AC3D graphics modeller to develop the 3D model of the distributor. Its web page is: http://www.inivis.com/. The 3D models created with

Figure 4. A photo of the original car engine distributor and the created 3D model

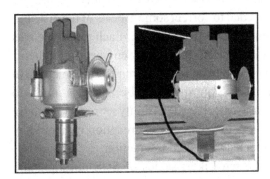

the latest AC3D version can be exported to DIVE format. Figure 4 shows the engine distributor used as a reference to create a 3d model. To the right is a representation of the virtual model used in the study. The virtual environment development was part of an engineering thesis project from our University (Esqueda-Machiche, 2005).

The virtual environment was developed following Fencott´s (2005) methodology, which is intended to obtain a usable virtual reality interface. This methodology is also suitable for integrating multimedia elements, such as 3D graphics, sounds, and images. The design objective was to develop the virtual environment and to set up DIVE navigation controls as simple as possible. In order to improve the VE, there various prototypes of the virtual environment were developed before the usability test was carried out. The various prototypes were used to make correction to the 3D model and the VE. The virtual environment contained two versions of the virtual distributor: One version can self-assemble for demonstration purposes. This version also showed an image of the distributor manual. The other one can be assembled manually, using the navigation controls of DIVE, the computer keyboard and mouse. A distinctive sound was heard when each piece was assembled in its correct place, working as task feedback.

A demographics questionnaire with items about age, previous computing experience, etc., was applied as pretest. The System Usability Scale (SUS) questionnaire (Brooke, 1996) was applied as post test. It is a widely accepted as a valid usability questionnaire. The SUS consists of ten Likert-style scales, with five descriptors (1=Strongly disagree, 5=Strongly agree) to assess general usability of a computer system interface and its human-computer interaction, including computer interfaces for industrial applications. With the SUS questionnaire it is possible to calculate a general usability score, on a scale from 0 (very poor usability) to 100 (excellent usability).

Participants

Five mechanics from a local car and motorcycle repair garage (an SMB) tested the virtual environment. In a demographics questionnaire applied before the test, the mechanics reported that they had very little computing experience, with an average of age of forty-two years. However, the mechanics reported they had played video games occasionally and for a limited period during their adolescent years.

The test was carried out at the mechanics garage to ensure that they would feel comfortable in their natural place of work. We thought that if we did the usability test in an artificial environment like a computer room, this might cause additional stress that would affect their performance. This also ensured ecological validity to the test.

Procedure

Before the test started, each mechanic had allotted 10 minutes to try out the navigation controls and to familiarize with the virtual environment. The mechanics' tasks in the virtual environment were to watch how the virtual distributor was self assembled, and after that, each mechanic tried to assemble it manually using the computer keyboard and the mouse. There was unlimited time to perform this task.

Figure 5. A mechanic interacting with the virtual engine distributor

Figure 5 shows one of the five mechanics who tested the virtual environment in DIVE, using a laptop computer in his repair garage. In addition, it was important to show them that computer technology could be practical tool in their workplace.

USABILITY TEST RESULTS

All the mechanics completed the test and averaged 40 minutes of interaction with the application. At the end of the test, each mechanic filled a SUS questionnaire. The score average of the five mechanics was 77.5, indicating that the virtual distributor VE rated well with them as far as usability is concerned. Although the number of mechanics that participated in the usability test seems low, it is possible to detect about 75% of the usability problems of a computer interface with just five users (Nielsen and Landauer, 1993). This by no means limits the number of usability tests that have to be done to obtain a completely usable and fully-fledged virtual environment for training. Most of the time, it is necessary to carry out various usability tests in an iterative fashion, as well as other complementary methods, which are not within the scope of this chapter. In our case, we had to develop three VE prototypes because we needed to correct some aspects of the distributor model and from the VE. Each prototype was previously tested with some engineering students and people from our research team. We chose to use the SUS questionnaire because it is simple to fill-in, to calculate the usability scores, and because it covers the subjective perception of about any system usability and interaction.

The ten Likert scales of SUS questionnaire (Brooke, 1996) are:

1. I think that I would like to use this system frequently.
2. I found the system unnecessarily complex.
3. I thought the system was easy to use.
4. I think that I would need the support of a technical person to be able to use this system.
5. I found the various functions in this system were well integrated.
6. I thought there was too much inconsistency in this system.
7. I would imagine that most people would learn to use this system very quickly.
8. I found the system very cumbersome to use.
9. I felt very confident using the system.
10. I needed to learn a lot of things before I could get going with this system.

Figure 6 describes a summary of the ten Likert scales that mechanics marked in the SUS questionnaire.

In an interview done after the test, all the mechanics agreed that the virtual environment helped them to visualize the assembling process of the distributor, and they also agreed that the VE would serve to visualize the assembling of practically any auto part, especially for brand new parts they are unfamiliar with. Interestingly, after the usability test one of the mechanics suggested that the virtual environment used in the usability tryout may also

Figure 6. Average results of each Likert scale (1=Strongly disagree, 5=Strongly agree) from SUS questionnaire applied to the five mechanics

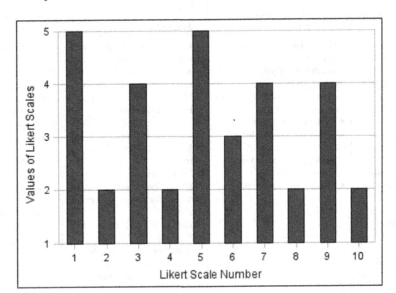

be useful to show engine parts to customers at auto parts store desks. The test also showed that having a laptop with the virtual environment in the car repair garage is an unobtrusive and practical way for the mechanics to get technical training. There are cost-effective and fast usability methods that are intended to improve a computer interface, including virtual environments, such as the SUS questionnaire method used in this test.

In summary, the following shows the findings from the usability test with the five mechanics, where the three main usability aspects were covered (computer interface efficacy, efficiency and user satisfaction):

- **Efficacy and usefulness**: The mechanics truly believed that the virtual environment would help them very much in their work.
- **Good level of acceptance and user satisfaction:** The mechanics agreed that they would use the VE frequently, and were pleased of the VE design (colors, and other features).
- **Good virtual environment general efficiency**: The mechanics learned to use the

virtual environment rapidly and were not confused with the virtual environment navigation controls.

It is important to note that the "novelty effect" may have influenced the test results, and it is necessary to run more usability tests with the virtual environment, especially with more participants, to confirm the findings, as well as longitudinal usability and learning studies with desktop VR are needed.

A COMPARISON OF SECOND LIFE AND DIVE

According to the usability tests we have done on DIVE and SL, and looking at the literature review on both, we have made a technical comparison of both VR programs. Table 2 summarizes a number of advantages and challenges of each program. Both programs are intended for general applications, where DIVE has been used mainly and largely for more than a decade on research, including VR research applications on education and training. Second Life has been initially ori-

Table 2. Advantages and challenges of Second Life and DIVE

Second Life		DIVE	
Advantages	**Challenges**	**Advantages**	**Challenges**
• User registration at no cost. • SL viewer (client) is open source. • Variety of third-party viewers have been developed. • Compelling graphics and sound effects. • Variety of options for menu interaction and navigation. • Easy to install. • Binary (executable) versions available for various operating systems. • Excellent for collaborative applications on the Internet (with adequate access and bandwidth). • Program updated regularly. • Chat, gestural and voice over IP (VoIP) communication possible among users. • Extensive support and documentation from Linden Labs and from the Internet community.	• Needs efficient Internet access (>500Kbps). • Needs certain types of robust graphics cards. • Most educational applications can be used for a fee. • Difficult to program. • Do not run yet on a local network as stand alone*. • Difficult to manage voice (VoIP) interactions. • Server is not configurable.	• Users do not need to register. • Open source (free for non-commercial applications). • Compelling sound effects. • Good for collaborative training in a local network. • Excellent for training with stand-alone applications. • Easy to program and configure. • Easy to install. • Binary (executable) versions available for various operating systems. • Easy to insert 3D models in a virtual world. • Server easily configurable. • Chat, gestural and voice over IP (VoIP) communication possible among users.	• Not efficient with complex 3D graphical models. • Not efficient with high resolution textures (images embedded in the virtual environment). • Unstable when used collaboratively for Internet access. • Avatar graphics need improvement. • Few documentation and manuals available. • Program not updated regularly. • Limited support from its creators and from the Internet community.

*Linden Lab announced in the Virtual Worlds London Conference held on October 2008 that this company is developing a stand-alone SL version (Linden, 2009). It will run on a local server and on a local area network (LAN), which currently is in the development stage and is expected to be released to the general public in the summer of 2009. It seems that this stand-alone version will only be commercially available only, and will be intended mainly to support business organizations, education, and training.

entated to edutainment applications, with recent applications in education and training. Recent research in these fields is beginning and the initial results are promising.

The main technical differences between DIVE and SL are the network performance and the minimum hardware requirements. DIVE currently can run on both slow and fast networks, using the Internet for collaborative applications and as stand alone in a local network, requiring almost any type of recent personal computers, whereas SL works smoothly only on fast networks, fast Internet access, and on fast computers with certain types of graphics cards. However, the graphic aesthetic appearance of SL's virtual worlds and their contents is superior to DIVE's.

It is important to note that there are differences about VR adoption between SMBs and large com-

panies. According to past literature on technology use in SMBs (Wierzbicki & Margolf, 2002) among others, it appears that the main difference regarding whether or not small businesses adopt VR is its cost-effectiveness. Large companies, however, tend to purchase more expensive fully-immersive VR equipment, and pay sometimes extremely high maintenance costs.

FUTURE TRENDS

We foresee that in the future, expensive simulators and fully-immersive virtual reality will continue to be used by the military, large companies and by very specialized training programs that require hands-on skills. However, for the foreseeable future, semi-immersive (desktop) VR technology that use fewer resources and can be programmed by people with fewer computer programming skills, will have a growing demand in both education, training and different government and economic sectors, particularly those who do not have the resources to purchase, maintain and optimally exploit traditional fully-immersive systems. Some of the latter VR programs will be used by SMBs operating in developing countries with limited Internet access as well.

Another issue that will be worth investigating in the future is how workers actually adopt to VR technology in SMBs. Although there are extensive studies in the literature about technology adoption in general, for example see Norman (1998), it could be interesting to see whether the learning curve, integration, acceptance, likeness, adaptation, motivation, and other issues change over time and among SMBs, as well as for larger companies.

To improve the effectiveness of VR for training, it will be necessary to carry out more research on developing more easily usable VR training platforms. One of the key challenges will be to design and adapt VR hardware and software that will support full accomplishment of training objectives. This can be done by developing easy to use, unobtrusive, pleasurable, and efficient VR applications that employ software engineering methodologies in the design and application of VR for training (Tromp et al., 2003; Stanney, 2002).

Augmented reality (AR) technology is a step beyond desktop virtual reality. It will have a significant impact on training procedural skills in many applications. AR is the combination of computer-generated data in three dimensions (computer graphics) and real-world data (Azuma, 2001), complementing human information processing and cognition in training (Neumann and Majoros, 1998). One of its main characteristics is that it is interactive and functions in real time. This technology has been successfully used by the military to train soldiers and pilots (Brown et al.,

2006), and research is currently underway on how to better use desktop AR to train people in other applications. Recent developments include cost-effective and portable AR devices, for example, see Olwal & Hollerel (2005). Facilitating acquisition of specialized technical skills in SMBs by using AR will need to be explored.

CONCLUSION

In conclusion, the objective of this chapter was to depict an overview on how virtual reality can be used to support technical training in SMBs, including the use of Second Life and DIVE virtual reality software platforms. We also showed similarities and differences between a commercial (SL) and open source (DIVE) typical VR platforms, both of which are programmable and support participant collaboration and are suitable for training applications. The chapter also described a desktop VR Application for training car mechanics from a small business. According to recent research and developments in the area of virtual reality training and education, it appears that open source software will have an important role in developing and applying virtual environments for training personnel in SMBs, due mainly to economic and technical reasons. Key factors for small and medium-size businesses to adopt desktop (semi-immersive) VR technology include efficient virtual reality interfaces, adequate use of computer resources (including a reliable network and Internet access) and user satisfaction. Thus, there must be a balance between graphics realism and hardware/software efficiency in collaborative virtual environments for training. VR can be successfully used for training purposes, provided that skill transfer support is adequately and systematically carried out with VR, taking into account both technological and social aspects. Virtual reality technology should be just a medium to support training and not an end in itself, therefore its usability should be high enough to avoid hindering training objectives.

ACKNOWLEDGMENT

This research is supported in part by the national council of science and technology (CONACYT) of Mexico.

REFERENCES

Adams, N. (1996). *A study of the effectiveness of using virtual reality to orient line workers in a manufacturing environment.* Unpublished Masters of Arts Thesis, De Paul University, School for New Learning, Chicago, IL.

Alexander, G. O. (1993). Computing practices in small Arkansas manufacturing. *Arkansas Business and Economic Review, 26*(2), 20–26.

Alverson, D. C., Saiki, S. M., Caudell, T. P., & Summers, K. L. (2005). Distributed immersive virtual reality simulation development for medical education. *J Int Am Med Sci Educ, 15*, 19–30.

Azuma, R. T. (2001). Augmented reality: Approaches and technical challenges. In Barfield, W., & Caudell, T. (Eds.), *Fundamentals of Wearable Computers and Augmented Reality* (pp. 27–63). Mahwah, NJ: Lawrence Erlbaum Associates.

Benford, S., Greenhalgh, C., Rodden, T., & Pycock, J. (2001). Collaborative virtual environments. *Communications of the ACM, 44*(7), 79–85. doi:10.1145/379300.379322

Bricken, M., & Byrne, C. (1992). *Summer students in virtual reality: A pilot study on educational applications of VR technology. Technical Report.* Seattle: University of Washington, Human Interface Technology Laboratory.

Brooke, J. (1996). SUS: A "quick and dirty" usability scale . In Jordan, P. W., Thomas, B., Weerdmeester, B. A., & McClelland, A. L. (Eds.), *Usability Evaluation in Industry.* London: Taylor and Francis.

Brown, D. G., Coyne, J. T., & Stripling, R. (2006). Augmented reality for urban skills training. In *Proceedings of the IEEE Conference on Virtual Reality* (March 25 - 29, 2006), (pp. 249-252). Washington, DC: IEEE Computer Society.

Burdea, G., & Coiffet, P. (2003). *Virtual reality technology* (2nd ed.). New York: John Wiley and Sons.

Cao, J., Crews, J. M., Lin, M., Burgoon, J. K., & Nunamaker, J. F. (2008). An empirical investigation of virtual interaction in supporting learning. *SIGMIS Database, 39*(3), 51–68. doi:10.1145/1390673.1390680

Carlsson, C., & Hagsand, D. (1993). DIVE - multiuser virtual reality system. *VRAIS '93, IEEE Virtual Reality Annual international Symposium.*

Carnevale, A. P. (1991). *America and the new economy: How new competitive standards are radically changing American workplaces.* San Francisco: Jossey-Bass, Inc.

Census, U. S. (2008). *Small and medium-sized businesses.* U.S. Census Bureau. Retrieved October 13, 2008, from http://www.census.gov/epcd/www/smallbus.html

Cervantes Medina, L. (2004). *Application of a collaborative virtual reality tool and 3D models adaptation to support medical diagnosis of bone injuries.* Unpublished thesis, M.S. Telematics, School of Telematics, University of Colima, Mexico.

Chan, K. K. P., & Lau, R. W. H. (2004). Distributed sound rendering for interactive virtual environments. *IEEE International Conference on Multimedia and Expo,* (pp. 1823-1826).

Cross, K. P. (1981). *Adults as learners.* San Francisco, CA: Jossey.Bass.

Dede, C. J., Salzman, M., & Bowen Loftin, R. (1996). The development of a virtual world for learning newtonian mechanics. In Multimedia, Hypermedia, and Virtual Reality Models, Systems, and Applications, (LNCS). Heidelberg, Germany: Springer Berlin.

Esqueda-Machiche, G. (2005). *Development of a collaborative virtual reality environment to teach an engine part assembling (in Spanish)*. Unpublished thesis, College of Telematics, University of Colima, Mexico.

European Commission (2003). The new SME definition. User guide and model declaration. *Commission Recommendation 2003/361/EC* as published in the Official Journal of the European Union L 124, p. 36 of 20 May 2003.

Fencott, C. (2005). A methodology of design for virtual environments . In Sanchez-Segura, M. I. (Ed.), *Developing Future Interactive Systems*. Hershey, PA: IGI Global Publishing.

Fraser, M., Glover, T., Vaghi, I., Benford, S., Greenhalgh, C., Hindmarsh, J., & Heath, C. (2000). Revealing the realities of collaborative virtual reality. In E. Churchill & M. Reddy, (Eds.) *Proceedings of the Third international Conference on Collaborative Virtual Environments,* San Francisco, CA, (pp. 29-37). New York: ACM.

Freeman, D., Slater, M., Bebbington, P., Garety, P. A., Kuipers, E., & Fowler, D. (2003). Can virtual reality be used to investigate persecutory ideation? *The Journal of Nervous and Mental Disease, 191*(8). doi:10.1097/01.nmd.0000082212.83842. fe

Garcia-Ruiz, M. A., & Alvarez-Cardenas, O. (2005). Application of virtual reality in collaborative Work of small and medium businesses (in Spanish). In *Sixth International Congress of Computer Science*, Colima Institute of Technology, Colima, Mexico.

Garcia-Ruiz, M. A., Edwards, A., Aquino-Santos, R., & El-Seoud, S. A. (2008). Collaborating and learning a second language in a Wireless Virtual Reality Environment. *IJMLO Int. J. Mobile Learning and Organisation, 2*(4), 369–377. doi:10.1504/IJMLO.2008.020689

Gerbaud, S., & Arnaldi, B. (2008). Scenario sharing in a collaborative virtual environment for training. In *Proceeding of the 2008 ACM symposium on virtual reality software and technology,* (pp. 109-112).

Gronstedt, A. (2007). Second Life produces real training results. *T + D Magazine*, August.

Gutierrez, M., Vexo, F., & Thalmann, D. (2004). The mobile animator: interactive character animation in collaborative virtual environment. In Proceedings of Virtual Reality conference, (pp. 125-284).

Gutwin, C., Benford, S., Dyck, J., Fraser, M., Vaghi, I., & Greenhalgh, C. (2004). Revealing delay in collaborative environments. In *Proceedings of the SIGCHI Conference on Human Factors in Computing Systems,* Vienna, Austria, April 24 - 29, *CHI '04* (pp. 503-510). New York: ACM.

Hamburg, I., & Engert, S. (2007). Competency-based training in SMEs: The role of e-learning and e-competence. *Paper presented at Web-based Education (WBE 2007)*, Chamonix, France.

ISO 9241-11 (1998). Ergonomic requirements for office work with visual display terminals (VDTs) – Part 11: Guidance on Usability. *International Organization for Standardization*.

Kaur, K., Sutcliffe, A., & Maiden, N. (1998). Improving interaction with virtual environments. In proceedings of IEEE Colloquium on The 3D Interface for the Information Worker (Digest No. 1998/437), London.

Knowles, M. (1975). *Self-directed learning*. Chicago: Follet.

Knowles, M. (1984). *The adult learner: A neglected species* (3rd ed.). Houston, TX: Gulf Publishing.

Krashen, S. D. (1982). *Principles and practices in second language acquisition.* New York: Prentice-Hall, Prentice Hall International.

Krashen, S. D. (1988). *Second language acquisition and second language learning.* New York: Prentice-Hall.

Kumar, A. (2008). *Mobile broadcasting with WiMAX: Principles, technology, and applications.* Boston: Focal Press.

Linden, A. (2009). *Second life lives behind a firewall.* Retrieved May 31, 2009, from https://blogs.secondlife.com/community/workinginworld/blog/2009/04/01/second-life-lives-behind-a-firewall

MacFarlane, S., Sim, G., & Horton, M. (2005). Assessing usability and fun in educational software. In *Proceedings of the Conference on interaction Design and Children IDC '05*, Boulder, CO.

Mascarenhas, B., Baveja, A., & Jamil, M. (1998). Dynamics of core competencies in leading multinational companies. *California Management Review, 40*(4), 117–132.

Mullins, R., Duan, Y., Hamblin, D., Burrell, P., Jin, H., Jerzy, G., Ewa, Z., Billewicz, A. (2007). A web based intelligent training system for SMEs. *Electronic Journal of e-Learning, 5*(1), 39 – 48.

Neumann, U., & Majoros, A. (1998). Cognitive, performance, and systems issues for augmented reality applications in manufacturing and maintenance. In *Proceedings of Virtual Reality Annual International Symposium (VRAIS)*, (pp. pp 4-11). Washington, DC: IEEE.

Nielsen, J., & Landauer, T. K. (1993). A mathematical model of the finding of usability problems. In *Proceedings of ACM INTERCHI '93 Conference,* (pp. 206-213), Amsterdam, The Netherlands, Norman, D. (1998). *The invisible computer.* Cambridge, MA: The MIT Press.

Olwal, A., & Hollerer, T. (2005). POLAR: Portable, optical see-through, low-cost augmented reality. In *Proceedings of VRST 2005 (ACM Symposium on Virtual Reality and Software Technology),* Monterey, CA, Nov 7-9, (pp. 227-230).

Prashant, C., Palvia, A., Shailendra, C., Palviab, P. C., & Palvia, S. C. (1999). An examination of the IT satisfaction of small-business users. *Information & Management, 35*, 127–137. doi:10.1016/S0378-7206(98)00086-X

Rogers, C. R. (1969). *Freedom to learn.* Columbus, OH: Merrill.

Roussos, M., Johnson, A. E., Leigh, J., Barnes, C. R., Vasilakis, C. A., & Moher, T. G. (1997). The NICE project: Narrative, immersive, constructionist/collaborative environments for learning in virtual reality. In *Proceedings of ED-MEDIA/ED-TELECOM,* (pp. 917-922).

SBA. (2008). *Bureau of Labor Statistics. Technical report.* Washington, D.C.: United States Department of Labor.

Schleich, J.F., Corney, W.J., Boe, W.J. (1990). Microcomputer implementation in small business: Current status and success factors. *Journal of Microcomputer System Management,* 2 - 10.

Sherman, W. R., & Craig, A. B. (2003). *Understanding virtual reality.* San Francisco, CA: Morgan Kauffman.

Shneiderman, B., & Plaisant, C. (2004). *Designing the user interface: Strategies for effective human-computer interaction* (4th ed.). Boston: Addison-Wesley.

Srivastava, S. C. (2005). Managing core competence of the organization. *Vikalpa . The Journal for Decision Makers, 30*(4), 49–63.

Stanney, K. M. (Ed.). (2002). *Handbook of virtual environments: Design, implementation, and applications*. Mahwah, NJ: Lawrence Erlbaum.

Steed, A., & Frecon, E. (2005). Construction of collaborative virtual environments . In Sanchez-Segura, M. (Ed.), *Developing Future Interactive Systems*. Hershey, PA: Idea Group.

Tapias Garcia, H. (2005). Technological capacities: A strategic element of competency. In Spanish. Revista Facultad de Ingenieria de la Universidad de Antioquia, 033.

Theil, S. (2008). Tune in tomorrow. *Newsweek*, August 18-25 issue.

Tromp, J. G., Steed, A., & Wilson, J. R. (2003). Systematic usability evaluation and design issues for collaborative virtual environments. *Presence (Cambridge, Mass.), 12*(3). doi:10.1162/105474603765879512

USDL. (2008, June). *News, Bureau of Labor Statistics.*United States Department of Labor, Washington, D.C. Retrieved February 15, 2008, from http://www.bls.gov/news.release/pdf.nlsoy.pdf van Wyck, E., de Villiers, R. (2008). Usability Context Analysis for Virtual Reality Training in South African Mines. In *Proceedings of SAICSIT*, Wilderness, South Africa. New York: ACM.

Vince, J. (2004). *Introduction to virtual reality*. London: Springer.

Wierzbicki, I., & Margolf, K. (2002). Affordable Virtual Reality Content as a Marketing Instrument in Small and Middle businesses. In *proceedings of EUROPRIX, The Scholars Conference.*

Yahaya, R. A., Euler, T., & Godat, M. (2004). Enhancement of learning in decision making and negotiation within virtual reality environment . In McWilliam, E., Danby, S., & Knight, J. (Eds.), *Performing educational research: Theories, methods and practices*. Queensland, Australia: Postpressed Flaxton.

Youngblut, C. (1998). *Educational uses of virtual reality technology. Technical report, IDA Document D-2128*. Alexandria, VA: Institute for Defense Analyses.

Zaharias, P.A. (2004). Usability and e-learning: The road towards integration. *eLearn Magazine*, (6).

Zaharias, P.A. (2006). Usability evaluation method for e-learning: Focus on motivation and learning. In *Proceedings of CHI 2006*, Montreal, Canada. New York: ACM.

KEY TERMS AND DEFINITIONS

Collaborative Virtual Reality: A shared virtual environment using a local network or the Internet, where its users interact to work, learn, train, and perform other activities together.

Competency: The sum of knowledge, skills and characteristics that allow a person to perform an action successfully.

Human-Computer Interaction (HCI): Discipline concerned with the design, evaluation and implementation of easy-to-use, productive, safe and interactive computer interfaces for human use, and the study of its context of use.

Network Latency: Network delay, consisting of how much time it takes for a data packet to get from one designated point to another in a computer network.

Second Life: A networked virtual reality environment shared by millions of registered users, using the Internet as a communication medium.

Service Level Agreement (SLA): a negotiated agreement between a customer and an Internet service provider to guarantee a minimum of bandwidth provided, quality of service (QoS), etc.

Small And Medium-Sized Businesses (SMB): A type of business with less than 500 employees.

Usability: Measurement of the ease of use of a computer interface, based mainly on its efficiency, efficacy, and pleasantness of use.

Virtual Environment: A computer-generated 3D space (also called virtual world or metaverse) where 3D graphical objects and sounds reside. Its user is represented by an avatar (a graphical personification) and can interact with the virtual objects and its environment.

Virtual Reality: Computer technology capable of generating a three-dimensional space called virtual environment, which is highly user interactive, multimodal, and immersive.

Chapter 6
Virtual Learning Environments for Manufacturing

Hamed F. Manesh
Eastern Mediterranean University, Turkey

Dirk Schaefer
Georgia Institute of Technology, USA

ABSTRACT

Since the advent of globalization, the manufacturing industry has been subject to continuous pressure of competition. Products have to be developed faster than before, with equivalent or higher quality, and at significantly lower cost. Whilst modern manufacturing systems provide the technological edge to meet these challenges, one tends to forget that education and training of the workforce also has to be kept up-to-date. Only a workforce that is familiar with the latest advancements in the manufacturing sector and well trained in the use of state-of-the-art technology and tools will be able to effectively face the competition. Although fundamental education and training may have been provided by the academic sector, employees need to continue developing their professional skills and competencies throughout their entire professional life. One potential approach to education and training of engineers in the manufacturing sector is the utilization of Virtual Learning Environments (VLEs). Such VLEs are currently widely used for fundamental engineering education in academia, but they also hold a huge potential for successful deployment in distributed corporate settings. Manufacturing-related VLEs may provide employees at all sites of a company across the globe with an affordable and safe environment for education and training, ranging from the fundamentals of modern manufacturing to expert level training in manufacturing process planning and simulation, without any need for, or cost of, physical equipment, materials, tools or travel. In this chapter the authors discuss how Virtual Learning Environments (VLEs) for manufacturing-related education and training can be utilized in the corporate sector.

DOI: 10.4018/978-1-61520-619-3.ch006

INTRODUCTION

In his bestselling book *The World is Flat* author Thomas L. Friedman (Friedman, 2006) points out that *"Globalization has collapsed time and distance and raised the notion that someone anywhere on earth can do your job, more cheaply"*. This certainly applies to the manufacturing industry, which is increasingly becoming a commodity. In recent years the manufacturing industry has been strongly impacted by globalization, which has resulted in increased global competition. This manufacturing competition has acted as a driving force for the application of new, related technologies in industry. In order to sustain their competitiveness, companies need to be able to adapt quickly to rapidly changing conditions of both the market and their competitors at reduced cost and at least equivalent or better quality.

While modern manufacturing systems may provide the technological means to face the above challenges, one also needs to bear in mind that the workforce which utilizes these systems has to keep up with the latest advances through education and training. Current students, i.e., the workforce of tomorrow, usually receive fundamental manufacturing-related education and basic training through engineering degree programs. For more senior employees this education and training often has to be acquired through participation in continuous professional development programs. What is missing today is an effective means to provide employees of manufacturing companies with continuous education and training opportunities on-the-job, within their corporations, and around the globe. An interesting question to explore with regard to manufacturing-related education and training is: *"Where are we now, and where are we heading?"*

While some universities may be able to expose their students to the latest manufacturing systems and technologies, others may not be that fortunate, due to lack of financial resources. For the latter, alternative avenues for providing their students with equivalent education and training have to be developed. A potential response to this call is the adoption of advanced computer technology to facilitate the provision of flexible manufacturing-related education and training programs. To date many studies have shown that the use of computers for teaching and training purposes is feasible and rapidly becoming an integral part of the general learning process. It has also been confirmed that recent advances in information and communications technologies have positively influenced and changed the economics of engineering education (Hashemipour et al., 2009). These advances can be exploited as a powerful vehicle for educators to develop IT-enabled learning environments for manufacturing that utilize simulation, automated data acquisition, remote control of instruments, rapid data analysis, and video presentations. Computer applications related to simulating manufacturing processes have shaped a field which is currently known as Virtual Manufacturing (VM).

An additional Computer Science field that increasingly plays an important role in Virtual Manufacturing, as well as associated educational activities, is Virtual Reality (VR). VR environments are synthetic environments, which provide a sense of reality and an impression of 'being there'. They have been increasingly employed in various design and manufacturing applications, including computer-aided design (CAD), telerobotics, assembly planning, and manufacturing system visualization and simulation. VR shows great potential for analyzing and investigating manufacturing processes prior to producing any physical artifacts. As a result, such environments help reduce operational expenses through reducing the number of physical prototypes and mistakes made. With regard to training the manufacturing work force, many studies have emphasized the potential of VR technology for education and training purposes. Empirical data has been collected on the relative success of VR in terms of instructional effectiveness, as well as the transfer of skills to the real world (Hashemipour et al., 2009). The utilization of Virtual Learning Environments (VLEs) in manufacturing is considered to be one of the most promising ways of providing a safe, cost-effective, and flexible environment for training and education in manufacturing.

Although such VLEs are more common, and more widely used, for fundamental engineering education in academia, they also have a huge potential for successful deployment in distributed corporate settings. Through such VLEs employees at all sites of a company across the world may be provided with an affordable and safe environment for education and training, ranging from the fundamentals of modern manufacturing to expert level training in manufacturing process planning and simulation, without any need for physical equipment, materials, tools, or travel. However, as discussed earlier, such Virtual Learning Environments for Manufacturing are currently more predominant in academic settings and not yet readily available for industrial settings. Hence much remains to be done to replicate their successful implementation and utilization in the arena of corporate education.

This chapter presents a review of the current state of, and developments in, both virtual manufacturing and associated Virtual Learning Environments for manufacturing-related education and training. In addition to technological realization aspects, infrastructure and equipment, the authors focus on educational paradigms and instructional techniques required to implement and utilize such Virtual Learning Environments both effectively and efficiently. Key differences between academic and corporate settings are discussed, and guidelines for the development and implementation of Virtual Learning Environments for manufacturing-related education and training in distributed corporate settings are proposed.

VIRTUAL REALITY AND VIRTUAL ENVIRONMENT

It is difficult to define the term Virtual Reality (VR) in a precise manner because it is often used in different contexts. A very general definition was given by Aukstakalnis and Blatner (1992): "Virtual Reality is a way for humans to visualize, manipulate and interact with computers and extremely complex data." However, many other definitions can be found in literature, for example, Manetta and Blade (1995) define VR as: "A computer system used to create an artificial world in which the user has the impression of being in that world and with the ability to navigate through the world and manipulate objects in the world". Similarly, Sherman and Judkins (1992) offer: "VR allows you to explore a computer generated world by actually being in it."

In this chapter we leverage the above definitions of VR and define a Virtual Environment (VE) as "a computer graphic system that allows a user to act in a synthetic, computer generated interactive 3D world". In other words, a simple VE is a computer system, which generates a virtual 3D environment with which a user can interact and receive real-time feedback (Normand et al., 1999). In contrast to conventional visualization systems, a VE is an interactive virtual image displayed in such a way that a user may become an active part of a rendered scene. Most VR/VE system configurations fall into three main categories and each category can be ranked by the sense of immersion, or degree of presence, it provides. These categories are: fully-immersive system, semi-immersive projection system and non-immersive (desktop) systems (Mujber et al., 2004). A comparison is presented in Table 1.

Fully-immersive VR systems provide a feeling of depth which is mainly created by techniques such

Table 1. Types of VR Systems (adapted from Mujber et al., 2004)

VR System	Fully Immersive VR	Semi-Immersive VR	Non-Immersive VR
Input Devices	Data Gloves and Voice Commands	Joystick, Spaceballs, Data Gloves	Mouse, Keyboard, Joystick, Spaceball
Output Devices	Head Mounted Display, CAVE	Large Screen Monitor or Projection Systems	Standard Monitor
Resolution	Low-Medium	High	High
Sense on Immersion	High	Medium-High	Low
Interaction	High	Medium	Low
Cost	Very Expensive	Expensive	Lowest

as head mounted display (HMD), Stereoscope Projection and Retinal Projection. In recent years advancements in computer technology and animated Computer Aided Design (CAD) have made it possible for VR technology to be ported down to personal computer platforms as semi-immersive and non-immersive (Desktop-VR) systems and hence provide the possibility of harnessing immersive and interactive environments (Figure 1).

A 3D virtual world can be displayed on a conventional desktop monitor, without use of any specialized movement tracking equipment, through desktop-based virtual reality systems. For instance, many modern computer games, using various triggers, responsive characters and other such interactive devices, make the user feel as if they were in the virtual world. A common criticism of this form of immersion is that there is no sense of peripheral vision, limiting the user's ability to know what is happing around them (Methods of virtual reality, 2008). The operator may interact with the virtual world through a mouse, keyboard or three-dimensional (3D) trackers.

Desktop VR systems play an increasingly important role in the commercial world, offering an affordable solution that displays a virtual

Figure 1. A desktop VR system

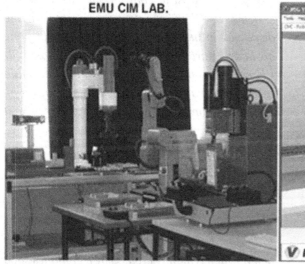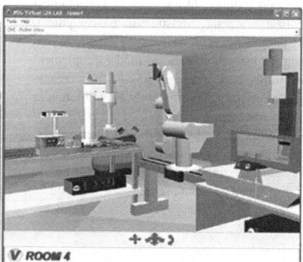

environment on a conventional desktop PC in a non-immersive manner (Rooks, 1999). In many cases Desktop-VR is replacing traditional techniques of communicating and presenting due to its low cost and portability. In addition, Desktop VR allows for providing the user with interactive, real-time, three-dimensional visualization of almost any environment or scenario (Tait, 1998). As the technologies to support VR evolve, VE applications become literally unlimited and the benefits of VR are widely recognized by scientists and engineers working in many different fields, including natural sciences, surgery, architectural modeling and engineering, as well as training and education. It is considered that VR will help to reshape the interface between humans and information technology by offering new ways for the communication of information, the visualization of processes and the creative expression of ideas.

VIRTUAL ENVIRONMENTS IN EDUCATION

"Understanding focuses on application and knowledge-in-action offers the best potential for knowledge transfer, the creative application of knowledge, and the construction of new knowledge" (Chee, 2001).

In some areas of education, such as in engineering, it is often desirable for students and trainees to obtain a great deal of practice, which results in a robust understanding of the subject matter. Unfortunately, this is not always possible due to lack of resources in terms of up-to-date equipment, laboratory space, personnel, and maintenance. As stated previously, one potential approach to improving experience-based education is through the utilization of so-called Virtual Environments (VEs). Studies have emphasized the great potential of VEs for use in education and training at all the levels, for example Tan and Francis (1997)

showed that it is possible to use VEs as a training tool, especially in the use of complicated and potentially dangerous equipment.

Ong and Mannan (2004) state that VR interfaces have the potential to complement existing approaches in education. VEs simultaneously provide learners with 3D visualization, multiple perspectives and frames-of-reference and visual and audio feedback. Put simply, careful design and implementation of VR applications can create a profound sense of motivation and concentration resulting in a deep insight into, and mastery of, complex materials. While such VEs are more common and more widely used, for fundamental engineering education in academia, they also have a huge potential for successful deployment in distributed corporate settings. In this way employees at all sites of a company across the world may be provided with an affordable and safe environment for education and training, ranging from the fundamentals of modern manufacturing to expert level training in manufacturing process planning and simulation, without any need for physical equipment, materials, tools, or travel.

The growing literature on VE-based education shows that its exploitation in a wide variety of fields is a very promising approach in terms of both effectiveness and the reduction of costs. Many successful implementations of VEs in education and training have been reported. El-Mounayri et al. (2005) summarized some of the recent VE-based training and education activities as follows: "*Training for operation of engineering facilities, CNC manufacturing machines, vehicle driving, piloting, traffic and flight control, maintenance simulators, medical procedures training, and military operations training.*"

Advantages of virtual environments in education include:

- Provision of a safe and flexible learning and teaching environment.
- A sense of 'being there', so that trainees are free to develop solutions to 'what if?' scenarios.

- Opportunities to experience operating complex and expensive equipment in a safe and cost-effective way.
- Increased productivity in learning by higher retention and quicker comprehension.
- Opportunities for intuitive learning by doing.
- Fewer restrictions in the number of trainees.
- Less geographic and language barriers in the case of distance learning.

VIRTUAL MANUFACTURING ENVIRONMENTS

In recent years competition has acted as a driving force for the application of new technologies in the manufacturing industry. Successful companies must be able to adapt quickly to rapidly changing conditions of both the market and their competitors within a shorter lead time and at a lower cost.

As a result, there is an increased need for educators to incorporate the latest manufacturing-related approaches, processes and tools into their programs. Graduating engineers and other participating trainees entering the work force must be aware of the latest advancements in the field and trained in using the latest tools in order to help their companies face the global competition and sustain their competitiveness.

The term Virtual Manufacturing (or VM) is now widely used in literature. From the early 1990s, in part through the *U.S. Department of Defense Virtual Manufacturing Initiative* (U.S. Department of Defense, 2008), support has been delivered to develop virtual manufacturing terms and concepts. For the first half of the 1990s only a small number of major enterprises and a few academic research groups were actively involved in the field of virtual manufacturing (Banerjee and Zetu, 2001). Recently the use of virtual manufacturing has become increasingly prevalent, and a considerable volume of research has been carried

out on both the concept and construction of virtual manufacturing. This has become possible due to significant advances in computer and information technology, and has increased awareness of the great potential of virtual manufacturing.

So how can VM be defined? In simple terms, the word *virtual* refers to a concept applied in many fields and is defined as *"that which is not real but may display the full qualities of the real"*. The term *manufacturing* refers to all activities and processes involved in industrial product development. VM is often referred to as *"a computer system which is capable of using information technology to generate information about the state and behavior of a manufacturing process that can be observed in a real world manufacturing environment"* (Banerjee and Zetu, 2001), (Lee et al., 2001), (Iwata et al., 1997). A VM system provides a means of designing and evaluating manufacturing processes on-screen before actual facilities or products are constructed. In other words, VM is understood to be an integrated computer-based model which produces comprehensive information in order to analyze and understand real manufacturing system behavior. Onosato et al. (1993) and Lee et al. (2001) have described VM as a concept of simulating manufacturing processes with computers where operations can be evaluated before being implemented into the real world.

Similarly, Marinov (2000) has proposed a definition based on Norbert Wiener's virtual manufacturing black box; the box contains the abstract prototypes of manufacturing models and the procedure of model exploitation is known as a computer simulation. Modeling and simulation are considered to be vital elements for virtual manufacturing. In recent years, with the emergence of Virtual Reality (VR) technology, many researchers have presented VM in association with VR, therefore an interesting question to ask would be: *"Is virtual reality a must in virtual manufacturing?"*. While Chetan et al. (1996) describe virtual manufacturing as a research area that aims to exploit Virtual Reality technology to

Figure 2. Virtual manufacturing

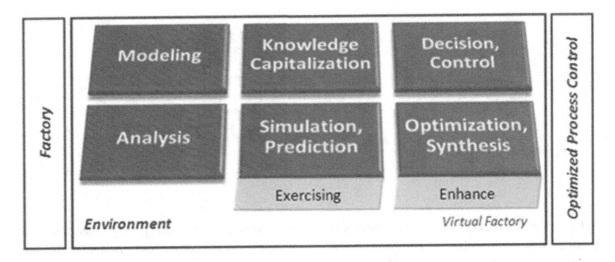

integrate the design sub-functions such as drafting, finite element analysis and prototyping with all the functions within a manufacturing enterprise, Lin et al. (1997) and Marinov (2000) consider VR only as a tool for visualization, which reinforces the graphical user interfaces for VM.

Clearly many approaches have been used for defining the virtual manufacturing concept. Amongst these an often referenced approach has been proposed by the Institute for Systems Research, University of Maryland, and is discussed in (Saadoun et al., 1999), (The Virtual Manufacturing User Workshop, 1994), and (Depince et al., 2004). According to these sources, virtual manufacturing is "*an integrated, synthetic manufacturing environment exercised to enhance all levels of decision and control*" (Figure 2).

To summarize, from all of the above approaches it can be concluded that VM is "*a knowledge and computer-based system technology that integrates the entire information of manufacturing processes, activities, and functions involved throughout the Product Life Cycle associated with virtual models and simulations instead of real facilities and manufacturing activities*".

A major outcome of virtual manufacturing is a Virtual Factory (VF). Again, many definitions and

research directions have been proposed by academics and manufacturing experts. For example, Jain et al. (2001) have developed a basic virtual model of a semi-conductor factory, demonstrating its functions in the design, installation and operation stages. The virtual factory integrates the simulation models of major sub-systems at all levels of hierarchy thus providing a vehicle for validation of integration.

Lin and Fu (2001) have proposed a virtual factory wherein a VR prototyping test bed allows the design of a detailed model to support system operations. The major goal of their prototype virtual factory is to define an operating procedure to capture the requirements of manufacturing engineers. A method for constructing large, rapid and complex virtual manufacturing environments has been developed by Xu et al. (2000), which provides the data link and user controls to enable streamlined data transfer between the virtual environments. Iqbal and Hashmi (2001) have developed a 3D virtual environment for design and analysis of a factory layout by applying problem-solving techniques. In their virtual factory approach, alternative layouts were compared and a new aisle system was introduced. Another factory layout planning problem has been studied

Figure 3. General scope of virtual manufacturing

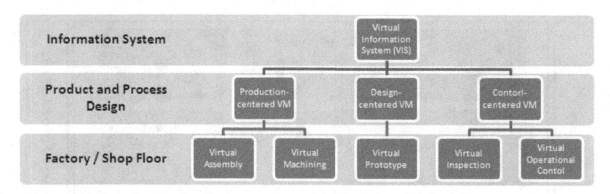

by Kroves and Loftus (2000): an immersive VR interface was used in order to compare an immersive system with a monitor-based VR system for manufacturing workspace analysis. Wiendhal and Fiebig (2003) have also reported a virtual factory approach for modeling and cooperative planning of factories and production systems. They describe a digital factory for planning the manufacturing operations and processes for an industrial case study.

In summary, a Virtual Factory can be defined as "*a complex computer based simulation system that provides the manufacturing system designer all the resources and tasks necessary to achieve the optimized operation of designing, producing and delivering a product*" (Banerjee and Zetu, 2001).

THE SCOPE OF A VIRTUAL MANUFACTURING SYSTEM

The concept of virtual manufacturing can encompass the entire enterprise hierarchy. From the definition of Onosato and Iwata (1993), each manufacturing system comprises two sub-systems: a real information system and a physical system. Whilst the real information system is associated with the entire system's architecture, manufacturing information activities and decision making within cost, weight,

investment, timing and quality constraint, the physical system comprises important units such as resources, machines, and parts. The scope of virtual manufacturing systems (VMS) can be subdivided into three levels (Figure 3): the information system, product and process design, and factory/shop floor.

In VM systems the simulation of the real information system, also called virtual information system, provides the necessary control commands for the virtual physical system (Lee et al., 2001, Iwata et al., 1997, Iwata et al., 1995). At virtual information system level the functional architecture of the manufacturing system is modeled, and covers all aspects directly related to the manufacturing of products. The product and process level of VM systems can be decomposed into design-centered, production-centered, and control-centered (Virtual Manufacturing User Workshop, 1994):

- Design-centered VM makes use of manufacturing-based simulations of different virtual designs to production prototypes in order to provide comparative information about the new product to the designer for use in optimizing the product design process.
- Production-centered VM uses simulation capability to simulate the activities in process development and alternative process plans. It aims to optimize the

manufacturing process by evaluating and validating the production plan, new processes and paradigms.

- Control-centered VM make use of VM technology to control models and actual processes, aiming to optimize the actual production cycle.

At the lowest level, virtual manufacturing includes not only modeling the items and facilities used for executing physical manufacturing activities, but also the simulation of their function throughout manufacturing processes such as Virtual Assembly, Virtual Machining, Virtual Prototyping, Virtual Inspection, and Virtual Operational Control (Lee et al., 2001). These simulated processes are developed independently from the other components of the virtual manufacturing system and possess individual interfaces to interact with.

VIRTUAL MANUFACTURING SYSTEM INFRASTRUCTURES

A Virtual Manufacturing System can be defined as a *"computer-based simulation of the entire manufacturing activities and processes"*. According to this definition, two core infrastructures of VMSs are *modeling,* which encompasses specifying what to model and at what level of abstraction, and *simulation,* which is the procedure of the model exploitation and provides manufacturing process attributes with certain degrees of accuracy and precision. Furthermore, Depince and Chablat (2004) have outlined the following infrastructures for comprehensive virtual manufacturing systems:

- **Manufacturing characterization**: includes capturing, measuring and analyzing the parameters that may affect material transformation during manufacturing.
- **Modeling and representation technologies**: different kinds of models for

representation, abstraction, standardization, multi-use, etc. are the major outcomes of such technologies. The same protocol and standard need to be created for manufacturing-related technologies to represent all the types of information associated with the process and product design in such a way that the information can be shared between all software applications, for example, knowledge-based systems, object-oriented, feature-based model, etc.

- **Visualization, environment construction technologies**: with recent advancements in computer graphics, the exploitation of Virtual Reality technology is more prevalent. The representation of information and manufacturing processes can be visualized in greater detail by the user in a way that is interactive and comprehensible.
- **Verification, validation and measurement**: all the results and decisions provided by virtual manufacturing systems need to be verified and validated.
- **Multi discipline optimization**: VM and simulation are used in combination with "traditional" manufacturing research.

VIRTUAL MANUFACTURING ENVIRONMENT APPLICATIONS

As discussed above, in virtual manufacturing the simulation environment created by computers is an artificial environment reflecting real physical objects and dynamic behavior. Advances in virtual reality technology have made it feasible to directly utilize VR for the modeling and realization of Virtual Manufacturing Environments. The use of virtual environments in simulating manufacturing environments gives engineers or trainers the opportunity to play a pro-active role in identifying flaws and optimizing any aspect of manufacturing-related processes and activities. The features of virtual environments provide an important foundation of virtual manufacturing. Virtual Manufacturing Environment systems can be used in a wide variety of manufacturing systems contexts and have often been classified into several categories:

Product Design – 3D product design: For engineers who are involved in product design it is desirable to visualize the performance and the analysis of the design process throughout the development cycle. Virtual Environments provide the synthetic and expandable Virtual Manufacturing Environments for the designers in the conceptual design stage of a new product without the actual testing of the physical product. At this stage the functional experimentation of mechanical features can be performed to evaluate the conceptual design and any modifications can be made as required by the customers (Iqbal and Hashmi, 2001).

Product Design - Virtual Prototyping: Virtual prototyping is another application of VM in the product development design context. It provides the designer with important features of a product, which can be used before building the physical prototype, to prove design alternatives, to carry out engineering analysis, manufacturing planning, support management decisions, and to obtain feedback on a new product from prospective customers (Iqbal and Hashmi, 2001). In other words, virtual prototyping leads not only to the reduction in the fabrication of physical prototypes and product cost and time, but also supports product design presentation through qualitative simulation and analysis (Weyrish and Drew, 1999).

Process and Production Planning: The potential of VM in process and production planning has been outlined by many researchers. Schaefer et al. (2001) state that optimal planning of a manufacturing system can be obtained by providing all those people involved in the planning process with a visual environment in which to monitor and compare the factors that may result in inadequate outcomes. Such a visual comparison can be performed based on the human experiences and

leads to rapid start-up of production and robust manufacturing processes.

In addition, VM has been found useful by academic researchers and industry specialists for Computer Aided Process Planning (CAPP). For example, a VR-based CAPP system developed by Peng et al. (2000) allows users to create a 3D model of components from an original design, simulate the machining process based on exiting NC code and pass the code to NC machines in the real world to create the real part. Thus any inconsistency in material and information flow can be detected and solved before being employed in practical manufacturing, which prevents costly mistakes (Maropoulos, 2003; Mujber et al., 2003).

Factory layout operation: *Virtual Machining* comprises of a virtual machining process and a virtual machining operation, and mainly involves cutting processes such as turning, drilling, milling, grinding, etc. In virtual machining, material removal processes and the relative motion between tool and work piece are simulated, and all the factors affecting machining setup time and processing time, quality and costs are studied. As a result, the feasibility of designed parts and selected processes for machining can be evaluated (Lee et al., 2001).

Virtual Assembly: Assembly is one of the most important stages in product development. In virtual assembly, the entire design and planning of the assembly process can be simulated in a 3D environment. Thus the assembly operation is verified and potential difficulties encountered in manufacturing are identified. Virtual assembly can benefit the manufacturer by saving time and costs in real production. Choi et al, (2002) suggest that virtual assembly can influence the efficacy of assembly, i.e., assembly methods, assembly sequence, and assembly time.

Virtual Inspection: Product inspection and measuring, specifically in machining operations, are time-consuming and require expensive physical experimentation. Virtual inspection is used to simulate both the inspection process and the

Figure 4. VR factory layout operations

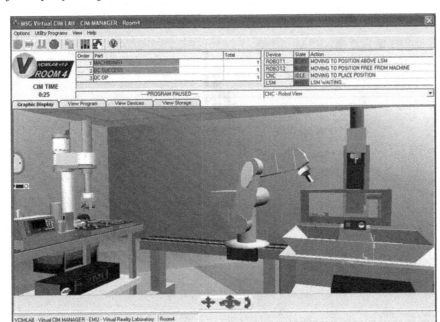

physical and mechanical equipment. Yao et al. (2002) developed a test-bed in a 3-D environment for predicting surface roughness in virtual measuring and the topography of the machined surface of the virtual workspace.

Virtual Operational Control: Material and information flow play an important role in the manufacturing system. Manesh et al. (2007) and Bal et al. (2008) developed a VMS based on a virtual environment for simulation of manufacturing material and information flow, which facilitated the simulation of the manufacturing activities in a more efficient and cost effective way, both prior to, and sometimes in parallel with, manufacturing operations in the real enterprise.

Virtual Agile Manufacturing: Bal et al. (2008) presented a Virtual Reality-based methodology for design of holonic-agile manufacturing systems. Their methodology uses VR for modeling, simulation and monitoring holonic manufacturing control systems and their operation. This allows users to interact intuitively with the manufacturing environments and its objects as if they were real, by immersing them in a highly realistic 3D

environment. As in the earlier step of developing and implementing the VR-based holonic design and operations of agile manufacturing systems, the concept and technologies were validated; the original objective was achieved, thus leading to further development and application.

Virtual Material Handling System: The application of a material-handling system (MHS) in a manufacturing environment aims to optimize productivity and improve equipment utilization and ergonomics. A virtual MHS enables the system designer to compare alternative material handling designs through a 3D environment in order to reduce the cost and increase the scalability and reliability of the system. It can also help the designer to identify and solve potential problems during design and operation to confirm the system model before constructing the actual enterprise. Furthermore, virtual material handling is widely exploited in controlling material handling systems such as Automated Guided Vehicles (AGVs). Wei and Chen (2002) have developed a virtual reality-based tele-autonomous for AGV path guidance. They have applied virtual reality

Figure 5. Virtual operational control

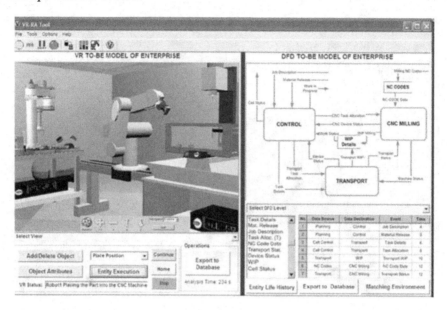

technology to establish a VR-based guidance system. In the developed system, AGV can be controlled through a more realistic and interactive 3-D environment by the operator. It was reported that this method provides better AGV guidance with less error.

VIRTUAL MANUFACTURING ENVIRONMENTS IN EDUCATION AND TRAINING

The efficient use of human skills, knowledge and experience is the major power of modern enabling technologies of agile manufacturing. A manufacturing enterprise needs skilled, cooperative and motivated people in order to achieve its goals. The participation of people throughout the enterprise in planning, designing and implementing new technologies and systems is the essential success factor. Hence, in the development of an agile manufacturing system, technical systems need to be designed not just to meet economic and technical goals, but also to satisfy organizational and human skills, judgment, creativity, knowledge,

and ingenuity, and to make full use of modern computer-based technologies.

Flexible Manufacturing Systems (FMS), automation equipment, robotic manufacturing lines, programmable systems such as Computer Numerical Control (CNC) machines and Automated Guided Vehicles (AGVs) are examples of systems that fit into the category of modern and computer-based technologies which improve manufacturing agility. However, the technologies that make these systems agile consist of highly expensive and complex systems, which involve potentially dangerous machinery and robots. Companies incur high costs in order to train their work force to use such systems and equipment.

In manufacturing education it is often desirable for engineers, technicians and even line managers to gain more practical experience in handling modern equipment and productions systems. However, it is time-consuming to learn how to use the fine controls of the equipment, as well as how to implement new manufacturing systems. Trainees have to be supervised while operating manufacturing equipment to avoid potentially expensive damage and large amounts of money have to be invested to experience different production and manufacturing activities. To date many studies have shown that the use of computers in teaching and laboratory work is feasible, and has changed the economy of manufacturing education (Koh et al., 2002). It also has a positive impact on student motivation and appears to have similar educational effectiveness to 'hands-on' training.

The utilization of Virtual Environments in manufacturing education (Virtual Manufacturing Learning Environments) has been emphasized by many researchers, e.g., Youngblut (1997), Francis and Tan (1999). It has been shown that people can indeed learn to perform certain tasks such as console operation from virtual environments and that knowledge and skills acquired through a VR simulation can be effectively applied in the real world (Koh et al., 2002).

Virtual Reality in instruction utilizes computer models in order to simulate the behavior of a manufacturing system or process (Avouris et al., 2001). In this way it is possible to repeat an operation many times, comparing the findings with model-based values. In general, one can expect that the use of VE and other types of educational software in manufacturing training will provide a sufficient degree of interaction with the trainees. Their use also improves the overall quality of manufacturing-related education and offers a number of important advantages in terms of pedagogical value:

- Trainees devote their time to useful discussion and observations, have the opportunity to analyze results, repeat experiments, compare results with theory, etc.
- Trainees concentrate on understanding fundamental concepts and not performing tedious writing.
- Drilling can be enabled at any time without supplementary effort by the instructers.
- Minimization of failures due to incorrect parameters.
- Trainees can gain experience in manufacturing activities that usually require hours

or days to complete within a few hours or even minutes.

- Pace and complexity of education can be adjusted to suit individual experience.
- Any number of trainees can practice and be trained at any time.
- Trainees can be provided with a virtual tour, guidance, and assistance during the training.
- New possibilities for continuous education, distance learning, and collaboration with other industries in training (Avouris et al., 2001, El-Mounayri and Aw, 2005, Sunrise, 2008).

The various applications of Virtual Environments in manufacturing which were outlined in the previous section can be effectively utilized in manufacturing education. One of its most important applications is for training in operating manufacturing equipment such as machining equipment and robots. It is generally accepted that training on real machines includes disadvantages such as:

- High costs because of system down times.
- Fixed site for the training.
- Hazards for trainees and instructors.

CNC machines are one of the most widely used pieces of machining equipment in the manufacturing industry. Due to their high cost and complexity it is often difficult for companies to keep up with the rapid developments in equipment. The same applies to training of the workforce. Traditionally, the user needs to work through operation manuals and then follow the instructions to practice and learn how to use the equipment. The user may also ask an experienced worker for help, however lengthy explanations are time consuming and ineffective. A new user may make many mistakes while operating the real machine in the initial stage of familiarization. In addition, limited availability of facilities and personnel can make

Figure 6. Virtual robot control

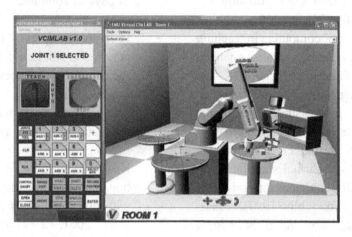

it difficult to train large numbers of trainees for any given machine.

Taking all these problems into account there is an increasing desire to adopt a new education paradigm know as Virtual Reality Based Training and Education in order to make training safer, more economic and effective. Users acquire the same experience and basic operational knowledge using VR-based training for CNC machines as they would using the actual machine. More importantly, it will be safer and more economic to practice on a virtual CNC machine rather than on the real machine.

The use of robots is another manufacturing equipment operation which is categorized as being potentially dangerous, as well as expensive if damaged. In addition, robots are time consuming and difficult to use, and trainees have to be supervised when operating such machinery. To overcome these problems, virtual robots are widely used in education and training for programming and operation purposes. The user can write an off-line task program and then use the virtual robot for teaching trainees to control of its movement in a virtual environment, as well as storing the robot positions into its memory.

Manufacturing systems are complex. In order to design an effective and efficient system, manufacturing system requirement analysis and information modeling are required. Therefore, a *user concept diagram* which contains icons rather than data flow bubbles or boxes for representing the actual physical system is proposed. Billo et al. (1994) state that most trainees, and even users, find diagrams too abstract to understand the system, and difficult to modify and apply to another manufacturing system. A virtual environment constitutes an effective communication means since it is constructed from images which correspond to their real counterparts. Hashemipour et al. (2009) reported that the VE assists the trainees in the modeling and analyzing of the relationship between the material and information flows. Virtual reality-based requirement analysis promotes modeling and understanding of complex systems and reduces the costs and time involved at this stage by producing precise and accurate specification requirements for plans and designs for manufacturing systems. In addition, it allows the users to interact intuitively with the virtual environment and its objects as if they were real, by immersing them in a highly realistic 3D environment.

Inspection is one of the major factors that affects the quality of the finished product. In *virtual inspection* the trainee engineer can practice all the inspection procedures, operations and skills in a completely safe and interactive 3D environment.

In *virtual assembly environments* engineers and trainees are to be trained to investigate the feasibility of different assembly processes based on certain production constraints. Such training enables engineers to optimize the assembly process in response to the rapid change of product types and markets.

In summary, virtual environments provide excellent training opportunities for manufacturing by allowing each employee full access to the entire facility. The virtual environment enables trainees to practice new and existing tasks in a safe, controlled environment. They will be able to see how a product takes shape as it moves through the manufacturing systems, which result in more effective training (Wang and Li, 2004).

KEY DIFFERENCES BETWEEN HIGHER EDUCATION AND CORPORATE EDUCATION

It is widely accepted that each society's broad mission is to provide a skilled work force so that it can build and maintain the productivity of any given industry. Higher education and corporate education are recognized to have an important role in achieving this mission and are equally important to society.

Higher and corporate education are related by different pursuits. Both deliver knowledge and concepts specific to their respective sectors. Higher education encourages analytical thinking which contributes to contribute to the professional and intellectual development of the student. Corporate education delivers practical knowledge, skills and techniques. Many studies have shown that the higher education sector requires up-to-date resources, together with rapid technological advancements, in order to meet the needs of the labor market and industry for high-level user skills (Hashemipour, 2009). In order to fulfill such requirements, higher education needs a major investment in terms of capital and manpower; unfortunately, a shortage of resources could undermine the facilitation of a quality learning environment.

Although some higher education institutions have adopted new educational resources, such as VLEs, to cope with rapid technological changes and to provide students with opportunities to use the latest equipment and technologies during their university education, there is still a gap between industry needs and higher education's output. This is due to the fact that educational institutions are usually more concerned with meeting the requirements of the university with regard to curriculum design and academic content of courses rather than industrial needs.

For the corporate sector to achieve growth, innovation and sustained competitiveness, learning is the most fundamental of the dynamic capabilities (Teece et al., 1997). An essential distinction needs to be made between aspects of learning for an individual in the corporate sector and an individual in the higher education sector. Relentless competitive pressure makes the corporate sector increase the productivity of all resources in the short term, and may be emphasizing short-term needs which could be at different levels, or in different geographic places. However, an individual in the higher education sector may spend several years acquiring knowledge which may no longer be relevant in the future. In other words, change demands continuous development of an individual's knowledge beyond higher education.

The importance of investment in corporate education is justified by a number of studies, e.g., (Paton et al., 2005, Becker, 1964). Major outcomes of corporate education are:

- Boosting individual job performance.
- Providing competent employees at low cost.
- A growing link between business performance and workforce skills.
- Providing advice and assistance to the industry on skill development.

- Meeting the demands of both the market and specific technologies.

SYNERGY BETWEEN VIRTUAL LEARNING ENVIRONMENT AND CORPORATE EDUCATION

Over the past decade, the rapid developments and growth of Information Technology (IT) have exposed a new paradigm for educational technology research and development in a wide range of subject areas and at all levels. Exploiting information and computer technology as teaching and learning tools provides such a learning environment. The so-called Virtual Learning Environment (VLE) overcomes the limits of space and time in knowledge delivery and utilization, along with allowing trainees to determine their own learning path and pace. Studies have shown that VLEs offer a number of advantages over traditional teaching environment in terms of knowledge acquisition, convenience and flexibility (Carrillo, 2004).

VLEs are simply defined as "*computer-based environments that are relatively open systems*" (Wooldridge, 1999). They are capable of supplementing traditional face-to-face teaching methods and normally work over the Internet. A significant body of literature demonstrates how VLEs can be an effective means of enhancing, motivating and stimulating the trainee's understanding of learning material, as well as reducing educational cost (Xa et al., Pan et al., 2006).

Despite all the VLE advantages, it is not always effective and sometimes fails to meet the learning objectives. Xa et al. (2006) reported insufficient interactivity and dynamism as one of its major limitations. One potential approach to overcome these limitations is the utilization of Virtual Reality (VR) technology. VR interfaces are capable of being used to complement existing VLE approaches in education (Pan et al., 2006). Recent advances in computer technology, networking, and advent

of the World-Wide-Web allows Web-based distributed Virtual Environments to be created that are available from any Internet-enabled computer. Distributed Virtual Environments have been used in a wide variety of educational settings of different types.

Integrating VLE with Virtual Environments provides an immersive, interactive and flexible Virtual Learning Environment where learners, especially distributed ones, can share information and form the environment according to their needs (Prasolova-Førland, 2008). Such educational environments can actively involve the trainee in the learning process, which in turn facilitates deep learning, improves learning quality and reduces educational costs.

Though lacking immersion factor, the power of VLEs in the global learning market is demonstrated by a report from Ambient Insight (2007). In 2007 the approximate value of the global market for E-learning products and services (VLEs) was $17 billion. This total is forecasted to rise to $50 billion by 2010, which implies that the market will expand in the near future by applying VR/VE potential into VLE (Pan et al., 2006).

With rapid globalization the emerging technologies are currently being developed faster, as well as more efficiently and at lower cost, in places beyond their origin. One consequence is that many industries, in particular manufacturing industries, are not only outsourcing manufacturing, but also research and development sections. This course of action is resulting in the need to keep their workforce both familiar with the latest manufacturing-related technologies and trained in utilizing state-of-the-art equipment. This implies that access to education is crucial for the success of manufacturing industries.

The authors propose a system architecture for corporate manufacturing education utilizing virtual reality technology to assist learners in improving individual skills or collaborate with other learners through a realistic virtual environment for

Figure 7. Proposed VLE/VE system architecture

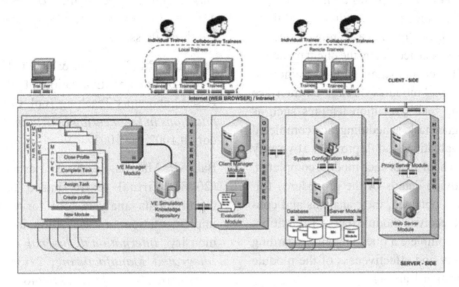

the realization of the VLE/VE system. A Modular Client/Server approach has been chosen, which provides the the following features:

- Multi-user and multi-screen is inherent to the client/server approach.
- Discrete event simulators are easily compatible.
- The modular structure of the system allows the trainers and trainees to alternate the training material configuration and input parameters to contribute to the design of further practice.
- Modules can take advantage of the distributed nature of a client-server environment.
- All modules can be categorized as either independent or collaborative.
- Develops clients' understanding of their working practice either individually or in a group.

An overall architecture of a VLE/VE system is shown in Figure 7.

The Client-side refers to operations which are performed by clients. In the proposed system, the client is categorized into 'trainer' and 'trainees'.

All the operations such as processing, storage of data from clients, managing, reconfiguring, etc. are performed by the server side. The server side includes the VE-server, Output-sever, HTTP-Server, Database-Server, and system configuration module.

VE-server: the VE-manager is the central component of the VE-server. Its main task is to coordinate the work of different VE modules. The VE-manager collects the information from all modules and corresponding clients and stores this in a VE simulation knowledge repository.

HTTP-server: is responsible for accepting requests from clients through web browsers and establishing the safe communication between server-side and client-side by proxy server and web server modules.

System configuration module: allows clients to access each module through different work stations and reconfigures the whole system after new modules have been added or modified by defining a set of configurations in a file.

Database server module: stores all information regarding clients and system settings, and also manages access to all shared data in the program.

Output-server*:* comprises a client manager and evaluation modules. Scheduling, defining the level of difficulty and assigning a client's relationship are carried out by the client manager. In addition, the client manager allows trainees to dynamically load modules through an interface by specifying their execution features such as profile, assigned task, scheduling, and completed tasks. The Evaluation Module provides a two-way feedback mechanism for each module completed. Trainees provide details of the procedures followed, results obtained, their analysis and conclusions and receive a module report. In addition, trainees can complete a questionnaire regarding bugs, usability and effectiveness of the module materials for their learning.

CONCLUSION

The focus of this chapter is the use of Virtual Learning Environments as an important and strategic means to facilitate future corporate education initiatives. VLEs are one of the most promising methods of delivering safe, cost-effective, convenient and flexible learning to supplement traditional teaching and offer an effective means of enhancing the learning process.

A review of existing virtual technologies is provided and a number of VE applications in manufacturing-related education and training have been highlighted. Guidelines for the development and implementation of such a system in distributed corporate settings have been proposed.

REFERENCES

Ambient (2007). *Ambient insight event: the hottest learning technologies for 2007 Jan 18, 2007.* Retrieved from www.ambientinsight.com

Aukstakalnis, S., & Blatner, D. (1992). *Silicon Mirage: The Art and Science of Virtual Reality.* Peach Pit Press.

Avouris, N. M., Tselios, N., & Tatakis, E. C. (2001). Development and Evaluation of a Computer-Based Laboratory Teaching Tool. *Computer Applications in Engineering Education, 9*(1), 8–19. doi:10.1002/cae.1001

Bal, M., Manesh, H. F., & Hashemipour, M. (2008). Virtual reality-based information requirements analysis tool for CIM system implementation: a case study in die-casting industry. *International Journal of Computer Integrated Manufacturing, 21*(3), 231–244. doi:10.1080/09511920701216246

Banerjee, P., & Zetu, D. (2001). *Virtual manufacturing.* Chichester, UK: John Wiley and sons.

Becker, G. S. (1964). *Human Capital.* Chicago: University of Chicago Press.

Billo, R. E., Rucker, R., & Paul, B. K. (1994). Three rapid and effective requirements definition modeling tools: evolving technology for manufacturing system investigations. *International Journal of Computer Integrated Manufacturing, 7*(3), 186–199. doi:10.1080/09511929408944608

Carrillo, C. I. P. d. (2004). *Intelligent Agents to Improve Adaptively in a Web-based Learning Environment.* Spain: Doctoral, University of Girona.

Chee, Y. S. (2001). Invited talk. *International Symposium on Virtual Education 2001*, Busan, South Korea, (pp. 43–54). Symposium Organizing Committee, Dongseo University.

Chetan, S., Vazquez, M., & Chen, F. (1996). Virtual Manufacturing: An Overview. *Computers & Industrial Engineering, 31*(1-2), 79–82. doi:10.1016/0360-8352(96)00083-6

Choi, A. C. K., Chan, D. S. K., & Yuen, A. M. F. (2002). Application of Virtual Assembly Tools for Improving Product Design. *International Journal of Advanced Manufacturing Technology, 19*, 377–383. doi:10.1007/s001700200027

Depince, P., & Chablat, D. (2004). Tools for improving Design and Production . In *CIRP International Design Seminar*. Cairo, Egypt: Virtual Manufacturing.

El-Mounayri, H., Aw, D., Wasfy, T., & Wasfy, A. (2005). *Virtual manufacturing for training and education*. American Society for Engineering Education (ASEE) Conference.

Francis, G.A., & Tan, H.S. (1999). Virtual reality as a training instrument. *The TEMASEK journal, 7*, 4-15.

Friedman, T. L. (2006). The World Is Flat [Updated and Expanded]: A Brief History of the Twenty-first Century. New York: Farrar, Straus and Giroux.

Hashemipour, M., Manesh, H. F., & Bal, M. (in press). A modular virtual reality system for engineering laboratory education. *Computer Applications in Engineering Education*.

Iqbal, M., & Hashmi, M. S. J. (2001). Design and analysis of a virtual factory layout. *Journal of Materials Processing Technology, 118*, 403–410. doi:10.1016/S0924-0136(01)00908-6

Iwata, K., Onosato, M., Keramoto, K., & Osaki, S. (1997). Virtual manufacturing systems as advanced information infrastructure for integrated manufacturing resources and activities. *Ann. CIRP, 46*(1), 335–338. doi:10.1016/S0007-8506(07)60837-3

Iwata, K., Onosato, M., Teramoto, K., & Osaki, S. A. (1995). Modeling and Simulation Architecture for Virtual Manufacturing System. *Annals CIRP, 44*, 399–402. doi:10.1016/S0007-8506(07)62350-6

Jain, S., Choong, N. F., Aye, K. M., & Luo, M. (2001). Virtual Factory: An Integrated Approach to Manufacturing Systems Modeling. *International Journal of Operations & Production Management, 21*(5-6), 594–608. doi:10.1108/01443570110390354

Koh, S. H., Zhou, H., Tan, H. S., & Tan, K. C. (2002). Virtual Environments for Manufacturing & Training (VEMAT). *Distance Learning and the Internet: Human Capacity Development (DLI 2002) Canberra and Sydney Conference. Association of Pacific Rim Universities (APRU)*. Singapore.

Korves, B., & Loftus, M. (2000). Designing an Immersive Virtual Reality Interface for layout Planning. *Journal of Materials Processing Technology, 107*, 425–430. doi:10.1016/S0924-0136(00)00717-2

Lee, G. B., Cheung, f., & Li, J. G. (2001). Application of virtual manufacturing in material processing. *Journal of Materials Processing Technology, 113*, 416–423. doi:10.1016/S0924-0136(01)00668-9

Lin, E., Minis, I., Nau, D. S., & Regli, W. C. (1997). *The institute for System Research*. CIM Lab, University of Maryland.

Lin, M.-H., & Fu, L.-C. (2001). A Virtual Factory Based Approach to On-line Simulation and Scheduling for an FMS and a Case Study. *Journal of Intelligent Manufacturing, 12*(3), 269–279. doi:10.1023/A:1011201009821

Manesh, H. F., & Hashemipour, M. (2007). A New Software Development Tools with Virtual Reality for Computer Integra ted Manufacturing Requirements Analysis. *Journal of Passenger Cars Mechanical Systems-SAE Transaction*, 908-917.

Manetta, C., & Blade, R. (1995). Glossary of virtual reality terminology. *International Journal of Virtual Reality, 1*(2), 35–39.

Marinov, V. (2000). *What Virtual Manufacturing is? Part II: The Space of Virtual Manufacturing.* Turkey: Bosphorus University.

Maropoulos, P. G. (2003). Digital Enterprise Technology. *International Journal of Computer Integrated Manufacturing, 16*(7-8), 465–466. doi:10.1080/0951192031000115778

Methods of virtual reality. (2008). Wikipedia. Retrieved February 10, 2008, from http://en.wikipedia.org/wiki/Methods_of_virtual_reality

Mujber, T. S., Szecsi, T., & Hashmi, M. S. J. (2004). Virtual reality applications in manufacturing process simulation. *Journal of Materials Processing Technology, 155/156,* 1834–1838. doi:10.1016/j.jmatprotec.2004.04.401

Normand, V., Babski, C., Benford, S., Bullock, A., Carion, S., & Farcet, N. (1999). The COVEN project: exploring applicative, technical and usage dimensions of collaborative virtual environments. *Presence (Cambridge, Mass.), 8*(2), 218–236. doi:10.1162/105474699566189

Ong, S. K., & Mannan, M. A. (2004). Virtual reality simulations and animations in a web-based interactive manufacturing engineering module. *Computers & Education, 43*(4), 361–382.

Onosato, M., & Iwata, K. (1993). Development of a Virtual Manufacturing System by Integrating Product Models and Factory Models. *Annals of the CIRP, 42*(1), 475–478. doi:10.1016/S0007-8506(07)62489-5

Pan, Z., Cheok, A. D., Yang, H., Zhu, J., & Shi, J. (2006). Virtual reality and mixed reality for virtual learning environments. *Computers & Graphics, 1*(30), 20–28. doi:10.1016/j.cag.2005.10.004

Paton, R., Peters, G., Storey, J., & Taylor, S. (2005b). *Handbook of Corporate University Development: Managing Strategic Learning Initiatives in Public and Private Domains.* London: Gower.

Peng, Q., Hall, F. R., & Lister, P. M. (2000). Application and evaluation of VR-based CAPP system. *Journal of Materials Processing Technology, 107*(1-3), 153–159. doi:10.1016/S0924-0136(00)00677-4

Prasolova-Førland, E. (2008). Analyzing place metaphors in 3D educational collaborative virtual environments. *Computers in Human Behavior, 24,* 185–204. doi:10.1016/j.chb.2007.01.009

Rooks, B. (1999). The reality of virtual reality. *Assembly Automation, 19*(3), 203–208. doi:10.1108/01445159910280065

Saadoun, M., & Sandoval, V. (1999). *Virtual Manufacturing and its implication, Virtual reality and Prototyping.* France: Laval.

Schaefer, D., Borgmann, C., & Scheffter, D. (2001). *Factory Planning and the Potential of Virtual Reality.*

Sherman, B., & Judkins, P. (1992). *Glimpses of Heaven, Visions of Hell: Virtual Reality and its implications.* London: Hodder and Stoughton.

Sunrise. (2008). *Sunrise Company.* Retrieved from http://www.sunrisevr.com

Tait, A. (1998). *Dimension International Desktop Virtual Reality.* IEEE Colloquium Series.

Tan, s., & Francis, G. A. (1997). *Virtual reality as a training instrument, THEC project.* Temasek Polytechnic.

Teece, D. J., Pisano, G., & Shuen, A. (1997). Dynamic capabilities and strategic management. *Strategic Management Journal, 18*(7), 509–533. doi:10.1002/(SICI)1097-0266(199708)18:7<509::AID-SMJ882>3.0.CO;2-Z

US Department of Defense. (2008). Retrieved from http://www.defenselink.mil

Virtual Manufacturing User Workshop. (1994, 12-13 July). Technical report, Lawrence Associates Inc.

Wang, Q. H., & Li., J. R. (2004). A desktop VR prototype for industrial training applications. *Virtual reality, 7*(43-4), 187-197.

Wei, C., & Chen, S. (2002). VR-based teleautonomous system for AGV path guidance. In *Seventh International conference on control, automation, robotics and vision (ICARCV'02)*, Singapore.

Weyrish, M., & Drew, P. (1999). An interactive environment for virtual manufacturing: the virtual workbench. *Computers in Industry, 38*, 5–15. doi:10.1016/S0166-3615(98)00104-3

Wiendahl, H. P., & Fiebig, T. H. (2003). Virtual factory design: A new tool for a co-operative planning approach. *International Journal of Computer Integrated Manufacturing, 16*(7-8), 535–540. doi:10.1080/0951192031000115868

Wooldridge, M. (1999). Intelligent agents . In Weiss, G. (Ed.), *Multiagent Systems* (pp. 25–77). London: The MIT Press.

Xa, D., & Wang, H. (2006). Intelligent agent supported personalization for virtual learning environments. *Decision Support Systems, 42*, 825–843. doi:10.1016/j.dss.2005.05.033

Xu, Z. J., Zhao, Z. X., & Baines, R. W. (2000). Constructing Virtual Environments for Manufacturing Simulation. *International Journal of Production Research, 38*(17), 4171–4191. doi:10.1080/00207540050205000

Yao, Y., Li, J., Lee, W. B., Cheung, C. F., & Yuan, Z. (2002). VMMC: a test-bed for machining. *Computers in Industry, 47*, 255–268. doi:10.1016/S0166-3615(01)00153-1

Youngblut, C., (1997). Educational uses of Virtual reality technology. *VR in the schools, 3*(1), 1-4.

KEY TERMS AND DEFINITIONS

Virtual Reality: "Virtual Reality is a way for humans to visualize, manipulate and interact with computers and extremely complex data." (Aukstakalnis and Blatner, 1992). "A computer system used to create an artificial world in which the user has the impression of being in that world and with the ability to navigate through the world and manipulate objects in the world" (Manetta and Blade, 1995).

Virtual Environment: A computer graphic system that allows a user to act in a synthetic, computer generated interactive 3D world.

Virtual Manufacturing: "A computer system which is capable of using information technology to generate information about the state and behavior of a manufacturing process that can be observed in a real world manufacturing environment" (Banerjee and Zetu, 2001), (Lee et al., 2001), (Iwata et al., 1997). "An integrated, synthetic manufacturing environment exercised to enhance all levels of decision and control" (Saadoun et al., 1999; Virtual Manufacturing User Workshop, 1994; and (Depince et al., 2004). A knowledge and computer based system technology that integrates the entire information of manufacturing processes, activities, and functions involved throughout the Product Life Cycle associated with virtual models and simulations instead of real facilities and manufacturing activities".

Virtual Factory: A Virtual Factory can be defined as "*a complex computer based simulation system that provides the manufacturing system designer all the resources and tasks necessary to achieve the optimized operation of designing, producing and delivering a product*" (Banerjee and Zetu, 2001).u

Chapter 7
Applied Training in Virtual Environments

Ken Hudson
Loyalist College, Canada

ABSTRACT

Virtual worlds hold enormous promise for corporate education and training. From distributed collaboration that facilitates participation at a distance, to allowing trainees to experience dangerous situations first-hand without threat to personal safety, virtual worlds are a solution that offers benefits for a multitude of applications. While related to videogames, virtual worlds have different parameters of interaction that make them useful for specific location or open-ended instructional exchanges. Research suggests that participants identify quickly with roles and situations they encounter in virtual environments, that they experience virtual interactions as real events, and that those experiences carry over into real life. This paper will evaluate the attributes of a successful applied training project, the Canadian border simulation at Loyalist College, conducted in the virtual world Second Life. This simulated border crossing is used to teach port of entry interview skills to students at the college, whose test scores, engagement level, and motivation have increased substantially by utilizing this training environment. The positive results of this training experience led the Canadian Border Services Agency (CBSA) to pilot the border environment for agency recruits, with comparable results. By analyzing the various elements of this simulation, and examining the process with which it was used in the classroom, a set of best practices emerge that have wide applicability to corporate training.

INTRODUCTION

The game is a proven powerful agent for bringing real life problems into an instructional situation. When games are translated into graphical or online environments, their potency for engaging users is multiplied. However, for most organizations, the costs necessary to create or customize a videogame environment to suit their corporate contexts, makes them inaccessible for the average training situation. With the advent of "desktop virtual worlds" like Second Life, a complex toolset for custom

DOI: 10.4018/978-1-61520-619-3.ch007

instructional experiences is now widely available (Hudson, Wood, Wetsch, & Solomon, 2009).

Virtual worlds emerge from the traditions of online gaming, and are directly related to themed worlds like World of Warcraft, as well as more traditional videogames. However, virtual worlds have different parameters of interaction. While most videogames and online worlds focus the user within a specific themed context, with appropriate goals and tasks, virtual worlds have the flexibility to adapt to whatever environment the user wishes, making them ideal platforms to design open-ended instructional content.

Hundreds of organizations and institutions are exploring these platforms to determine how they may be applied within their local training context, so it is crucial to understand how these environments effect learning, so as to engage these dynamic tools on the basis of their strengths for transferring information and experience. Current research suggests that people feel present both with the environment and with one another in virtual worlds. They identify readily with their avatars, and they are guided in their behavior by the avatar's appearance. Participants experience and remember their encounters in virtual worlds as if they happened in real life, and they organically adopt skills and attitudes from the virtual into their real lives.

As a basis for corporate training, virtual worlds hook participants directly into a complex set of behavioral expectations that can be used to reinforce post-training workplace requirements. One example of how role-play instruction has been transformed by the use of virtual worlds is the Canadian border simulation at Loyalist College. Using Second Life, the college created a fully functioning border crossing to train students on primary port of entry interview techniques.

Participants in this experience reported high sense of being present at an actual border crossing. They were able to master complex mandatory processes quickly by enacting the role in this realistic environment. Most importantly, this mastery persisted past the experience and directly impacted positive test results that underscore the possibilities using virtual worlds for corporate training.

Virtual worlds alone will not transform corporate education. Virtual worlds are new and with great promise, but also present innumerable ways which can bog down learning, and add unnecessary complexity. By examining the attributes of virtual worlds and current research for virtual interactions, we will understand the potency of these environments for applied learning constructs, and a set of best practices will emerge that will act as a guide to evaluating potential virtual world learning initiatives.

ONLINE GAMES AND VIRTUAL WORLDS

Online gaming is a powerful force in our culture. Once just an add-on to videogames, most gaming platforms have migrated the game experience into online communities. As such, while considered a sub-set of virtual worlds (Schroeder, 2008), online games have blurred the distinction between game and virtual worlds; they are a transitional phase toward full virtual world platforms with gaming as a part of them.

Video gaming is deeply involving for the participants. There is both the immediate involvement of the puzzle of the game, the identification with the protagonist, all the way up to communal involvement of social guilds within many online games such as World of Warcraft. As gaming combines with social networking trends there are immediate points of contact between the two mediums, and examples from each may inform an analysis of the other.

Online gaming and virtual worlds share similar technology, interface, and narratives. Structurally, they also each share both diegetic (story elements) and non-diegetic (interface) elements (Galloway 2006). The online game brings players together around a task or a puzzle. There is a right way and a wrong way. The player will not be able to advance without completing the task. The task is encoded into the game play. Players interact in an open-ended manner around the game objectives, and they are able to evoke, in some cases, creative solutions. In other cases, the game play or relationship around it serves a social purpose, and can distract away from the game task. "To play a game means to play the code of the game. To win means to know the system" (Wark, 2007, p.30).

With virtual worlds the opportunity exists for participants to converge around environments and situations, in addition to tasks and puzzles. The development of online environments has moved from games (defined) to virtual worlds (open-ended), with virtual worlds allowing for a broader range of actions and activities.

The key distinction between online gaming and virtual environments is the ability to customize the environment to any learning context. This ability to conform the virtual environment gives an advantage to the serious possibilities for training within a virtual world. The ability to have fully interactive live experiences distinguishes virtual worlds from online games, where the action is to a large part already determined.

Both online games and virtual worlds allow users to collaborate around the game play and to foster relationships within the game that persist outside of the game context. Online games with diverse content from World of Warcraft to America's Army engage users in activities and tasks that foster positive instructional paradigms, applicable within many training contexts.

Each of these online environments, while involving and entertaining, also invariably teach the participants encoded response patterns that have an impact on real life. This involving capacity, our own inclination for imitation, and the repetition within these games, imprint our minds with a range of learned constructs. Teamwork, communication, problem solving, and strategizing all

evolve from collective play within theses online spaces, and regardless of the content of the game, we learn from them.

When we play games, we are able to learn a multitude of skills. Those skills, however, are developed around a fictional context. When we connect the player/learners real life context with the environment of the virtual world or game, then we have a fusion of intent and activity that leads to impressive results. In controlled situations like corporate training or higher education, should provide a vast opportunity to harness this organic situation to specific instructional contexts.

Two examples of the instructional player engagement in online gaming are America's Army (AA) and Counter-Strike Source (CS:S). Both games are from the military first-person shooter genre, and both games involve online participants is a series of tasks which, while fictional, foster important behavioral objectives that are analogous to many corporate training contexts. America's Army instruction in orientation to the army, while success in Counter-Strike Source depends on strategy and teamwork.

The setting of CS:S pits two teams, terrorists and counter-terrorists against one another on a series of maps each with its own objective. CS:S engages users in short missions that require effective strategy, communication, and teamwork to be orchestrated immediately. There is a time limit, and there is no middle ground between victory and defeat.

While the game encourages creative thinking and the marshalling of a strategy for these short missions, the nature of the game play ensures the context is not transcended. There is no higher motive in CS:S, it is black or white. However it does demonstrate the engagement of users in indirect skill acquisition within virtual environments.

On the other hand, America's Army has a much broader instructional perspective. Originally developed as a recruiting tool for the U.S. Army, America's Army's game play brings participants from the first day of basic training through to active duty. The online component of the game allows players to graduate from boot camp into virtual communities of play. More than a game, America's Army is an information tool and a communication medium. Users are not learning how to be a soldier; players are introduced to the content and process of a soldier's education.

That being said, it is important not to underestimate the instructional effects of immersive environments. Recently an America's Army player, having proceeded through the various aspects of a soldier's experience, applied what he had learned within the game, to a real world event. The North Carolina man witnessed an accident and was able to provide first aid as a result of what he had learned during medic training playing America's Army. "I have received no prior medical training and can honestly say that because of the training and presentations within America's Army, I was able to help and possibly save the injured men" (Cavalli, 2008, p.1).

The skills or process that the player learned within the gaming context were clear and repeatable enough to save a person's life. He affected a real world solution based on a virtual experience by simply imitating the procedures he had learned within the game. It is also important to note that the veracity of the America's Army content actually taught the player the correct solution and procedure, rather than a fictional one. The player's identification with the content was real enough transfer to physical action.

In many respects, the type of training that is inherent in Counter Strike Source: teamwork, strategy, communication, execution, are analogous to many types of effective virtual world training constructs. AA and CS:S are similar in their learning structure to the border simulation. Players adopt a role (solider), they are acquainted with environment, and they are given tests to accomplish. In both cases this can be done with other people in an online gaming situation. The difference is the openness, the customizability, and the free-will that the participant may exert on the situation, as well as the freedom of their role-play partner, who does not follow any predictable, scripted patterns.

The learning context of online gaming environments, while instructive, does not have a general value to corporate training in any direct manner. It is true that most games played with others generate group behavior dynamics, including leadership skills, although they may be difficult to harness to any constructive or specific learning outcome. Mostly social contact and interaction within traditional online games focuses on game play only. Without any higher objectives, we get lost in our games (Toro-Troconis, M., Mellstrom, U., Partridge, M., Meeran, K., Barrett, M., & Higham, J., 2008).

THEORETICAL FRAMEWORK

The movement from online games to virtual environments heralds a new era in online immersive instructional approaches. While the study of how people learn within gaming and virtual worlds is relatively new, some important findings exists that underscore the strong identification participants feel within virtual worlds, how they react to their avatars, and to other people present.

Certain attributes of virtual worlds make them ideally suited for applied learning experiences. The "Proteus Effect" observes that "people infer their expected behaviors and attitudes from observing their avatar's appearance" and that "behavioral changes stemming from the virtual environment transferred to subsequent face to face interactions" (Yee, Balienson, Dicheneaut, 2009).

The perspective in virtual worlds, which is largely third person point of view, allows users to see themselves in the role of the exercise (Yee & Balienson, in press) (Lim & Reeves, 2005). Watching oneself enact a role in a virtual environment has a profound effect on the user for they both identify with the avatar and they see it as an example, outside of themselves. Participants within virtual worlds modify their attitudes by observing their own behavior (Yee, Baljenson, Dicheneaut, 2009). This unique perspective in online environments affords learners not only a first-hand experience, but also a vicarious one (Bandura, 2001).

Virtual worlds allow participants to customize their look of their avatars to replicate physical appearances. There is a deep connection between the look of the avatar and the impact on the virtual experience. As identification increases with an avatar that resembles the participant, so does the retention of learned behaviors when participants identify more strongly with their avatars. (Fox & Baljenson, 2009). "Role- play and identification with virtual avatars are central to learning in immersive worlds."(De Freitas, 2006, p.53)

Identification with the virtual environment itself is known as presence, and with other participants within virtual worlds, co-presence. Presence "has been linked to knowledge transfer, where skills or knowledge gained in a virtual environment can be successfully transferred to the real world, as well as possible enhancement of learning and performance" (Casanueva & Blake, 2000, p.1). The potency of the environment "creates the feel of real and establishes a sense of presence, a sense of being rather than merely thinking" (Lauria, 2000, p.3).

Other modes of understanding the rapid skills adoption in virtual environments include mirror neurons and the chameleon effect. As children we imitate what we see and hear. "Through mirror neurons we absorb culture without explicitly being taught it. We are hard-wired for imitation;" and furthermore, "because mirror neurons let us grasp the minds of others through direct simulation rather than conceptual reasoning, videogames are the perfect medium for teaching through feeling, not thinking" (Barry 2009, p.4). The same is true of the chameleon effect, where a perception of a behavior increases the likelihood of adopting that behavior. (Chartrand & Bargh, 1999)

LOYALIST COLLEGE BORDER SIMULATION

Overview

As part of the Justice Studies program at Loyalist, border interview skills training for students incorporated field placement at working port of entry. Since 9-11, such placement has been impossible due to heightened security restrictions. To fill this gap in the learning experience, traditional in-class role-plays were employed with only marginal results. The availability of virtual worlds technology allowed a working simulated environment to be employed to replace the previously successful field placement component. The founding idea was to utilize both the immersive quality of the experience in virtual worlds combined with the complexity of more real to life situations, and to be able to manage those experiences as a component of in-class instruction.

Over the course of two years, the border simulation at Loyalist College gave students a realistic experience of staffing a border crossing by using the virtual world platform Second Life to simulate the border screening process. Initially intended to augment skills training in the area of mandatory screening questions, the experience, in fact, developed into a much more holistic experience of the border services officer role. Once present in the environment, students directed the learning through extensive experientially related questions. Additional components of the border officer role were added, including secondary inspection, immigration inspection, and an additional airport border environment.

Process

The border simulation at Loyalist College is fully integrated within classroom instruction. Students are not required to engage with Second Life outside of class, and all aspects of registration and training are handled in-person. Each student

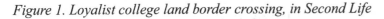

Figure 1. Loyalist college land border crossing, in Second Life

registers an avatar, and is given a modest time frame to customize its appearance, followed by a focused training workshop that teaches the various interface components required to participate. This training is rigid in it's attention to only those skills required to allow the student to participate, in this case, basic movement, voice communication, and camera controls.

In the pilot year of the project, students were not introduced to Second Life prior to their training. Students are now introduced to the environment in the form of early term demonstration and report exercises that utilize the crossing to depict key aspects of the job function. This familiarity leads to mid-term hands-on exploration and avatar creation.

Participants are able to customize their individual avatar so that it "feels" like their selves, while, perhaps appearing quite different than the real life student. It is believed that by allowing students to invest themselves in their active agents in the simulation, that the process of identification with the scenarios will be heightened, leading to greater engagement and knowledge transfer (Casanueva & Blake, 2000).

There was an observable transformation in the student's real life behavior once their avatars wore the border officer uniform. The change was almost instantaneous from the moment they observed their avatars in the job role. Classroom noise and chatter diminished, and the students were poised to begin the exercise. "They became what they beheld" (Carpenter, 1972).

Simulation process was the same as earlier class. The class would gather in a common lab with students each taking turns staffing the port of entry. Travelers, who are separated physically from the students would cross the border, answering the mandatory questions, providing identification, and also imbibing the role-play with a variety of distinctive characteristics from extreme emotional states, to stories that did not make sense, the travelers provided the range of examples the students would encounter in the course of performing this job function.

In the Loyalist College border simulation, after each student had a chance to run several travelers, there was a class wide discussion to make observations and critique the border service officer (BSO). The value of these debrief for reinforcing

Figure 2. Loyalist college students wearing border officer uniform

the experience for the BSO, these were rich and flowing discussions where peripheral issues, best practices, and legal contexts were framed and understood. The discussions were a very valuable learning aspect of the entire simulation.

Additionally, the follow-up group was introduced to a variety of analogous environments as part of their training in the border operations. An airport border station was added to the land crossing, and used as a point of comparison for procedural elements. Also, more immigration related embedded learning objectives were folded into the role-play scenario, and an immigration station within the border was used to expand the range of the students' experience, but within the same time frame as the pilot example. It seems in virtual worlds, there is a hunger for a variety of experiences, and while concern with over pacing the students was considered, instructors allowed the pace of the student comprehension to be followed with more topics of relevance.

CBSA Pilot

During the development of the border simulation, training officers from CBSA became aware of the project and expressed interest in attending a live demonstration live via Second Life. The students at Loyalist College interviewed dozens of travelers for the viewers, while the agencies represented watched, and eventually joined in both roles.

Following the demonstration, CBSA and Loyalist College met to discuss a partnership to explore the value to the agency of this training medium. Loyalist College would provide the agency with access to the border assets and environment, and CBSA would pilot the simulation with new recruits and report on the experience.

While the Loyalist College border simulation was run as part of classroom instruction, the CBSA pilot would test the validity of the simulation for distributed learners:

179 CBSA recruits in a single intake were offered access to the virtual border on a voluntary basis during their online training preceding a pass/fail residential training program in Rigaud, Quebec. A series of scenarios were developed for use by learners to integrate the content of the four-week online training materials. The scenarios required learners to ask mandatory questions, consider policies and procedures they had just learned online, ask additional probing questions, and make a release or refer to secondary inspection decision based on interview with "virtual" traveler, played by a CBSA instructor." (Hudson & Nowosielski, 2009)

Results

For Loyalist College, the follow-up to the pilot was important to confirm that consistently successful results were to be achieved with the border simulation. The initial pilot group had achieved a final grade for interview skills of 86%, a full 28%

higher than the previous class who did not have access to the simulation, and relied on in-class role-play to learn interview techniques. (Hudson & deGast-Kennedy, 2009) The follow-up group achieved a standing 9% greater still, for a final grade of 95%, confirming for Loyalist College that the simulation is a meaningful contribution to the curriculum.

The results for the initial CBSA pilot were consistent with the dramatic rise in grades at Loyalist:

Recruits who were able to complete simulations in Second Life performed 39% better at their testing milestones than those who did not complete their practice sessions. Participants who completed simulations reported low level of fear/hesitation in using SL, were highly positive about the use of SL as a learning tool, and reported greater confidence and increased learning. 37/179 could not use because of technological barriers. (Hudson & Nowosielski, 2009)

Having been piloted in both a distance learning and blended in-person situation, the experience of live role-play interview training improves confidence and accelerates learning and skills retention. While there are many difficulties with distance learning and virtual worlds at the moment, and it was believed that the in-class experience augmented the first-hand learning, it is clear there is a potent learning experience in either case.

Analysis

The border simulation is a very successful project, and there is great confidence on the part of those involved that the open-ended nature of the interchanges within the virtual world have contributed to its overall success. While not the only precipitating factor, this open-ended approach, combined with the sensory stimulus of the environment, and the identification with avatar and role, were all factors that precipitated this success.

Virtual environments and experiences can be evaluated based on the following attributes of personal presence:

1. The sense of "being there" in the virtual environment as compared to being in a place in the real world.
2. The extent to which there were times when the virtual environment become the reality.
3. The extent to which the participant's memory of the virtual environment is similar to their normal memory of a place. (Casanueva & Blake, 2000, P.3)

For the students participating in the border simulation, the following are identified as elements that directly contribute to the learning process:

1. The participants were active in the virtual worlds not just passive observers while functioning with the environment, but fully engaged in the process of interviewing travelers.
2. The participants were able to witness themselves embodying the role of the border officer framed within a powerful context. They both felt themselves to be in the role, and saw themselves as that role, for a potent double perspective on the exercise.
3. The students participated as a collective, with the group observation component having as much impact as the hands-on participant. They acted as a mirroring collective, reflecting on the role and on the content of each crossing as a group.
4. Each student turn as border officer was followed by an immediate debriefing, which allowed for questioning, critique, and a range of relevant discussion around issues discovered through the role-play.

The group as a whole witnessed and discussed each border-crossing scenario, providing immediate feedback for the individual student BSO. These "after action reviews" (AAR) are the hallmark of successful retention and understanding in virtually mediated simulation. (Bonk & Dennen, 2005, De Freitas 2006, De Freitas & Oliver 2006). These AAR also involved the classmates in a process of identification with their peer and with the process as a whole:

In educational contexts, there is a need not only to enter the 'other world' of the game or simulation, but also to be critical about that process in order to support reflective processes of learning as distinct from mere immersion into a virtual space. This 'double' identification approach to the game may in part explain why the use of 'other worlds' can indeed accelerate learning, allowing the learner to at once participate with the 'world' and to reflect upon their relationship when viewed from outside of it, reinforcing learning through empathy or 'being there', whilst allowing sufficient space for reflection. (De Freitas & Oliver 2006, p.255)

The confidence, motivation, and competency levels of the second group were more impressive than the original pilot group. Partly this may be attributed to the confidence of the instructors and facilitators, who had already demonstrated the effectiveness of the simulation. As a result, there was less skepticism and pushback from this group than the pilot case (Hudson & deGast-Kennedy 2009), and therefore the simulation experience was expanded to include more elements.

It is likely without the availability of the affordable virtual world toolset that Second Life offers, Loyalist College not have ventured into virtual environments as a context for applied learning at this time. This does not make Second Life the only choice for this style of applied learning experience. So, while these experiences were held in Second Life and Loyalist College continues to foster its presence within that community, there is also a firm belief that the pedagogy developed within this virtual space will be applicable to any virtual environment that may follow.

Best Practices

The application of virtual worlds to instructional contexts is a new and exciting enterprise. There is much ground to be covered, the landscape is changing constantly with the advent of new technologies, and the limited results around performance enhancement using virtual environments makes them a tantalizing new form to explore. While at this stage in the development of this training approach there can be no definitive guide to all possible uses, the success of the border simulation may offer some sense of which projects might be suited to a blended virtual world experience.

These are some basic recommendations for evaluating virtual world applied learning projects:

- Evaluate project based on accessibility and meaning of real world context.
- Environments that are inaccessible otherwise have immediate benefit from virtual worlds.
- Is the learner role readily enacted within a virtual world; is the work role social?
- Start with a small, manageable project that has simple learning outcomes.
- Focus the activity within a single environment or setting.
- Begin with in-class experience prior to attempt a distance learning initiative.
- Choose skills and situations where learners benefit from rehearsal.
- Adapt as required: Virtual worlds allow for rapid changes in environments.

FUTURE TRENDS

While the Loyalist College border simulation leveraged the in-class possibilities within virtual worlds, the true revolution for these environments

Figure 3. Loyalist airport border crossing

is in the area of distributed learning, where participants may engage with learning activities from any location. Virtual worlds allow people to feel present in a specific environment and co-present with the other participants, no matter where they may be located physically. When it matures, this will be a valuable tool for corporate training. However, as we have seen from the CBSA pilot, the general accessibility to virtual worlds that would enable this step is not quite there.

Virtual worlds have the potential to become ubiquitous training environments for applied learning, and they are already being put to work in top level training programs, such as military and law enforcement. In the very near future, these environments will revolutionize training approaches for average organizations to leverage role and sector specific engaging instructional environments quickly and affordable.

As well, as technology advances, the ability to accurately mime human behavior with a realistic interface will retrieve the kinesthetic aspect of learning into virtual worlds. These interfaces will allow trainees to accurately utilize physical movements and objects with real world results from within the virtual environment, in a way analogous to the use of computers and robots for surgery at a distance, or the way the astronauts use a robotic arm to accomplish work outside the space station.

CONCLUSION

Marshall McLuhan says that, "environments are not just containers, but are processes that change the content totally" (McLuhan & Zingrone, 1995, p.275). This statement is true both of videogames and of virtual environments. In online games, action and behavior is determined by the code and story of the game play, including the context. In virtual worlds, this holds true as well, however it is the individual participants who are both defining the environment, and the style of action that the experience may take on.

Virtual worlds demonstrate an increase in skills retention and recall, more successful testing performance, and an accelerated learning process. Within any organizational training context, such improvement in speed and accuracy is sure to yield enormous costs savings, with some sectors having the most to gain both in terms of applicability of virtual worlds, and also in long-term cost savings.

For corporate education the opportunity both improve results and decrease costs is very real. For example, the average cost to train an employee in the United States is $1,500. When that employee is in a government, law, or border enforcement position, the costs balloon to approximately ten times that. According to statistics from 2006, the average cost train a new border patrol agent in the United States was $14,700, which is consistent with other forms of enforcement training. (Stana, 2008. P.3)

With thousands of new recruits within these sectors each year, the potential savings in training costs is millions of dollars. This, of course, does not even begin to account for the improved performance and motivational aspects of virtual world training. While the amount of savings to be achieved will differ for each context, the potential for virtual worlds to enhance applied training positively in multiple respects is both dramatic and attainable.

For learning to occur in a virtual world there must be first and foremost an experience of the individual learner being present within the constructed environment. The way that this engagement occurs is a complex of influences make the participant feel as if they are actually there. Some of the elements that lead to learner/avatar identification include avatar customization, proper understanding of the reasons for utilizing virtual environments (learning objectives), a sense of meaningful coincidence with the context (as in the border simulation).

Virtual worlds are naturally engaging experiences, and therefore hold great promise as learning tools for augmenting the classroom reality for trainees. They offer advantages for procedural, interpretive, and communication instruction, and they provide a rigorous platform for trainees to rehearse their job function in a realistic setting, allowing them to amalgamate skills into a single learned process.

REFERENCES

Army, U. S. America's Army. (2003). [Multiple platforms] Montreuil-Sous-Bois. France: Ubisoft.

Bandura, A. (2001). Social cognitive theory of mass communication . In Bryant, J., & Zillman, D. (Eds.), *Media effects: Advances in theory and research* (2nd ed., pp. 121–153). Hillsdale, NJ: Lawrence Erblbaum.

Barry, A. (in press). *Mirror neurons: How we become what we see.*

Bonk, C., & Dennen, V. (2005). Massive multiplayer online gaming: A research framework for military training and education. Office of the Under Secretary of Defense (Personnel and Readiness), Readiness and Training Directorate, Advanced Distributed Learning Initiative, Washington, D.C.

Carpenter, E. (1970). *They became what they beheld.* New York: E.P. Dutton.

Casanueva, J., & Blake, E. (2000). *The effects of avatars on co-presence in a collaborative virtual environment.* Rondebosch, South Africa: University of Cape Town, Collaborative Visual Computing Laboratory, Department of Computer Science.

Cavalli, E. (2008). Man imitates America's Army, saves lives. *Wired.com.* Retrieved November 26, 2008, from http://blog.wired.com/games/2008/01/americas-army-t.html

Chartrand, T., & Bargh, J. (1999). The chameleon effect: The perception-behavior link and social interaction. *Journal of Personality and Social Psychology, 76*(6), 893–910. doi:10.1037/0022-3514.76.6.893

De Freitas, S. (2006). Learning in immersive worlds: A review of game-based learning. *Joint Information Systems Committee (JISC) e-Learning Programme.*

De Freitas, S., & Oliver, M. (2006). How can exploratory learning with games and simulations within the curriculum be most effectively evaluated. *Computers & Education*, 46.

Entertainment, B. (2004). *World of Warcraft*. Irvine, CA: Blizzard Entertainment.

Foster, A. L. (2008). What happens in a virtual world has a real-world impact, a scholar finds. *Chronicle of higher education, April 4, 2008*. Retrieved April 21, 2008, from http://chronicle. com/free/v54/i30/30a01402.htm

Fox, J., & Bailenson, J. (2009). Virtual self-modeling: The effects of vicarious reinforcement and identification on exercise behaviors. *Media Psychology*, *12*, 1–25. doi:10.1080/15213260802669474

Galloway, A. R. (2006). *Gaming: Essays on algorithmic culture*. Minneapolis: University of Minnesota Press.

Hudson, K., & deGast-Kennedy, K. (2009). Canadian border simulation at Loyalist College. *Journal of Virtual Worlds Research*, *2*(1).

Hudson, K., & Nowosielski, L. (2009, April). *Canadian border simulation*. Poster session presented at the Federal Consortium on Virtual Worlds Conference, National Defense University, Washington, DC.

Hudson, K., Wood, N., Wetsch, L., & Solomon, M. (2009). From interactive to immersive: Advertising education takes a virtual leap of faith. *Journal of advertising education, 13*(1).

Lauria, R. (2000). Understanding the tactile nature of electric sensibility in virtual environments. *Spark Online,* 15. Retrieved March 9, 2009 from http://www.spark-online.com/december00/print-friendly/lauria.htm

Lim, S., & Reeves, B. (2006, June 16). *Being in the game: Effects of avatar choice and point of view on arousal responses during play*. Paper presented at the annual meeting of the International Communication Association, Dresden International Congress Centre, Dresden, Germany.

McLuhan, E., & Zingrone, F. (Eds.). (1995). *The essential McLuhan*. Toronto: Anansi Press.

Scroeder, R. (2008). Defining virtual worlds and virtual environments. *Journal of Virtual Worlds Research*, *1*(1).

Stana, R. (2008). Border patrol: Costs and challenges related to training new agents. *Testimony before the subcommittee on management, investigations, and oversight, Committee on Homeland Security, House of Representatives*. Retrieved from http://www.gao.gov/cgi-bin/getrpt?GAO-07-997T

Toro-Troconis, M., Mellstrom, U., Partridge, M., Meeran, K., Barrett, M., & Higham, J. (2008). Designing game-based learning activities for virtual patients in Second Life. *Journal of cyber therapy & rehabilitation, 1*(3).

Valve Corporation. (2004). *Counter-Strike Source*. Bellevue, WA: Valve. [Microsoft Windows]

Wark, M. (2007). *Gamer theory*. Cambridge, MA: Harvard University Press.

Yee, N., & Bailenson, J. (in press). The difference between being and seeing: The relative contribution of self perception and priming to behavioral changes via digital self-representation. *Media Psychology*.

Yee, N., Bailenson, J., & Ducheneaut, N. (2009). The proteus effect: Implications of transformed digital self-representation on online and offline behavior. *Communication Research*, *36*(3), 285–311. doi:10.1177/0093650208330254

KEY TERMS AND DEFINITIONS

Virtual Environment: 3D game-like space that allows for interaction with multiple avatars and environments. Also allows for extensive customization.

Online Games: Also known as massive multi-player online games, are game spaces where distributed players converge for play along defined themes.

Identification: The psychological process of seeing oneself embodied by a game or virtual world character, or avatar.

Role-Play: Instructional experience where participants adopt specific job-related functions and practice life-like scenarios as a form of job function rehearsal.

Presence: The visceral experience within a virtual mediated environment that registers as "being there".

Co-Presence: The visceral experience of sharing mutual space within a virtual mediated environment that registers as "being there with others".

Primary Interview Process: The mandatory interview questions asked by border service officers to determine eligibility to enter the country.

Section 3
Designs and Measurements

Chapter 8
Train the Trainer:
A Competency–Based Model for Teaching in Virtual Environments

Mary Rose Grant
Saint Louis University, USA

ABSTRACT

This chapter describes an online competency-based model for teaching adult learners in virtual environments. This model, informed by prior studies for online teaching, expands emergent themes within best practices and identifies competencies for course design, delivery and management of adult-centered online learning environments. The use of part-time instructors, in academic and corporate settings, to facilitate learning in virtual environments requires formal processes to develop web-based teaching skills that meet the needs and expectations of a multigenerational mix of online adult-learners. The competency-based model uses a generative approach to developing instructors as adult learners and builds on adult and constructivist learning theories. The model provides opportunities to improve web-based teaching skills and encourage behaviors that influence student engagement, retention and learning. This chapter guides the reader through a step-by-step process of understanding competencies needed to facilitate virtual learning with suggestions for implementation and practice in corporate settings.

INTRODUCTION

The significant increase in the number of adults enrolled in online courses (NCES, 2005; Sloan, 2005) and programs in academic and corporate settings necessitates a closer look at how effective teaching and learning can maximize the value and benefits of distance learning for adult learners,

instructors, organizations and business. The swing from traditional to online learning environments has prompted more interest in assessing the quality of instruction and instructional design to meet the needs of a diverse population of learners. The virtual environment, which provides flexibility and convenience, seems more conducive to learning for adults in both academic and corporate settings. The online format itself accommodates the characteristics and learning styles of adults in allowing self-paced and

DOI: 10.4018/978-1-61520-619-3.ch008

self-directed learning that is authentic and relevant to real life situations and job roles. The mastery of competencies for teaching online requires an understanding of the adult learner and integration of adult learning theory with technical elements of course design, delivery and management to create virtual learning environments and learning experiences that meet student expectations for personal growth and professional development, as well as organizational needs for skilled and informed employees. The business case for distance learning is strategic in terms of cost-effectiveness, productivity and profit. Web-based training allows for custom training and can be used modularly to focus on specific skills as needed. Virtual learning changes the way corporate training and professional development is delivered and accessed and the way information is managed and disseminated (Rosenberg, 2001).

Instructional practices within virtual environments and analysis of instructor-student interactions, as well as alignment of learning objectives with organizational goals, can yield positive predictors of student learning and program success. In the business world, the Internet creates with the organization a learning culture that expands and encourages the generation and sharing of knowledge for the future. To meet the learning demands of the employee and the performance needs of the organization, management must continually assess the role of virtual learning and support the case for expanding its development and use. Companies like, AT&T, Anderson Consulting, Dell Computer, IBM., Lucent Technologies and Merrill Lynch, just to name a few, moved to Web-based training and online learning in an attempt to reinvent their training and development programs and increase the value-added scalability of instruction and application in the workplace (Rosenberg, 2001).

Despite the proliferation of online courses and programs, there are few studies on what constitutes effective teaching in virtual environments (Grant & Thornton, 2007; Newlin & Wang, 2002). A common mistake online course developers and instructors make is trying to emulate traditional classrooms or training with technology mediated interactions without the benefit of good pedagogy. A study, utilizing Chickering and Ehrmann (1996) "Seven Principles of Good Practice in Undergraduate Education" as applied to online pedagogy, identified and analyzed best practices used by online instructors, which clarified the skills, knowledge and characteristics needed to effectively facilitate learning in a virtual environment (Grant & Thornton, 2007). Competencies most relevant to instructional design, course development, delivery and evaluation were identified, and with best practices, informed and shaped the competency-based model presented in this chapter. Integrating adult learning theory and generational characteristics and learning styles, expand this model's use with today's adult learner. This competency-based model provides opportunities to acquire knowledge, master skills and practice techniques to improve online teaching and encourage behaviors that influence adult student engagement, retention and learning. Recommendations for implementation and adaptability of the model to different institutional and corporate structures and instructor needs are proposed.

The first section will provide background for the development of the competency model. The second section summarizes the characteristics of instructors as adult learners and considers the implications of adult and constructivist learning theories in online learning. The third section describes seven competencies for teaching online, which, when mastered and applied, cut across a matrix of identified best practices and themes. The fourth section presents the process of validating the competency model and outlines the online training course in which the model is taught. The final section discusses the implications for practice and future development of online instruction for academia and business.

BACKGROUND

As higher education moves courses and degree programs online and corporations offer training and development in virtual environments, the demand for quality instruction and instructional design in these environments increases. The shift away from traditional classroom and training settings prompts a look at the competencies necessary for effective instruction online. The tools and technology for teaching and learning have changed, so the methods for teaching and learning must change as well. New criteria for effective teaching in virtual learning environments, where technology and pedagogy intersect, must be developed and new knowledge, skills and behaviors taught and learned in order to maintain quality and integrity in these new learning environments.

While some research reports that the factors that influence good pedagogy are universal across learning environments and generations of learners (Wilkes & Burnham, 1991), others suggest that moving into a virtual learning environment requires a different mindset about teaching and requires the acquisition of teaching strategies beyond those needed in traditional learning environments (Bates, 2000; Palloff & Pratt, 2001). The skills needed to design a course for the virtual environment are not intuitive for most instructors and must be acquired through specific training (Palloff & Pratt, 2001). Teaching in virtual environments needs competence in technological and organizational aspects of course delivery and management as well (Grant & Thornton, 2007). Spector and Anderson (2000) reported that the integration of technology and learning methodologies varies between traditional and virtual learning environments, but that the demands for technology and associated skills in online environments are greater and require specific training and development for instructors in these environments. Weigel (2000) suggests that training be focused on how to use the Internet in

ways that enrich the learning experience rather than only as the medium in which it is delivered. Other studies concur and suggest that competencies unique to virtual teaching are essential for successful instruction online (Collison et al., 2000; Kearsley, 2000; Rosenburg, 2001).

Phipps and Merisotis (2000) identified strategies used by leading academic institutions in distance education emphasizing technology skills to develop, deliver and evaluate online courses that ensure quality outcomes for students and for faculty facilitating web-based learning. In their final analysis, Phipps and Merisotis (2000) identified 24 benchmarks in seven categories: institutional support, course development, teaching/learning, course structure, student support, faculty support, and evaluation and assessment, considered essential to ensuring excellence in web-based distance education.

The concept of using competency models grew out of the work of David McClelland, a Harvard psychology professor in the 1970's. His ideas on competency testing grew into an action model used by business organizations to make decisions about hiring, training, promotion and other human resource issues. Most competency-based models developed today still use McClelland's process to first determine what leads to outstanding results, then to identify top performers and find out what they do to achieve these results (Lucia & Lepsinger, 1999).

In 2005, Smith, published a complex list of 51 competencies needed to teach online and outlined a training program for faculty. He compiled his list of 51 competencies from the suggested teaching strategies and methods for course design and online delivery of learning of other researchers. Based on his review, he grouped these competencies according to whether they were essential prior to, during or after teaching the online course. This grouping was an attempt to integrate these competencies. Smith (2005) also proposed a hybrid training program for new online instructors encompassing these 51 competencies. He suggested that the program include initial and ongoing phases, as well as components for mentoring, in terms of a support forum facilitated by a seasoned online instructor, and assessment of effectiveness in terms of comments from students, instructors and mentors.

In 2007, Varvel proposed a competency model around a flexible design which would constitute an ongoing process, open for revision as needed to accommodate changes in technologies, curriculum, and faculty and student characteristics. His list of 247 competencies was derived from numerous sources, including student course evaluations and instructor surveys, interviews and discussions. These competencies were organized into five categories reflecting the functions and abilities of an online facilitator in administrative, personal, technological, pedagogical and social roles (Varvel, 2007).

A study, utilizing Chickering and Ehrmann (1996) "Seven Principles of Good Practice in Undergraduate Education", examined benefits and outcomes of distance education for adults, identified best practices in design, implementation and evaluation of virtual learning environments. Faculty teaching online courses were asked how they applied best practices in their courses. Quantitative and qualitative methods used in the study uncovered themes and patterns within the best practices for teaching and learning that provided a framework for producing quality instruction for adults in online environments. The results of that study shaped a model of online faculty development that identified behaviors within those themes, manifested in competencies for online teaching (Grant & Thornton, 2007).

This approach builds on McClelland's concept and work for competency modeling. The process was to identify best practices in online teaching, and then ask successful online instructors to report specific behaviors that demonstrated those best practices in their courses. Using a grounded approach, competencies were identified and organized into a model to describe the attributes of an effective online instructor. Seven core competencies were identified in: online format, online pedagogy, course content, instructional design, course management, use of technology, and quality assurance (Grant & Thornton, 2007).

The identification and development of competencies led to the construction of a formal training process for online instructors. An online course was designed to present the competency model and teach the skills, knowledge and attitudes required for competent online instruction, as well as provide examples for application and opportunities for practice. Validation of the competency model was the last step in the process. Behaviors, manifested in the competencies within the model, were correlated with peer and student evaluations of online teaching effectiveness, abilities, skills and knowledge. Competencies were tested and refine in focus groups with seasoned online instructors (Grant & Thornton, 2007).

The competency-based model and online teaching course are open to continuous review and assessment by instructors, peers and mentors. Modifications and revisions are easily made when warranted as necessary for future development needs. Online environments for learning are dynamic and, as new technologies emerge and pedagogies are re-thought, competencies must be dynamic and relevant to the context of the virtual environment and in meeting the standard and necessary skills expected in the online community of practitioners.

The competency-based model also integrates faculty characteristics and patterns of instruction with adult and constructivist learning theories. Additionally a generative approach to developing faculty, as adult learners, builds on active learning, robust feedback, practice, and prior knowledge and encourages further inquiry.

FACULTY INSTRUCTORS AS ADULT LEARNERS

Adult learning and constructivist learning theories, as applied to web-based learning, provide the theoretical framework for the competency-based model and for the design and content of the online teaching course which presents the best practices and competencies outlined in the model. Theories of influence include: Knowles' (1980) assumptions of adult learners, Dewey's (1938) thoughts on experience and education, and Candy's (1991) work on constructivist and self directed learning, as well as contemporary concepts of connectivism and community of practice (Siemans, 2005; Wenger, 1998). Understanding these principles of adult learning and the tenets of andragogy enhance the understanding of e-pedagogy and the nature of virtual learning technologies and environments (Moore & Kearsley, 1996; Grant & Dickson, 2008).

Characteristics of adult learners versus those of traditional learners have been extensively studied (Fidishun, 2000; Flint & Associates, 1999; Knowles, 1980; Merriam & Caffarella, 1999). Adult learners are self-directed, purpose-oriented and practical; they want respect and an educational experience that is relevant and builds upon prior life experience. Traditional learners are more subject-oriented, dependent on the knowledge and experience of the instructor and less willing to construct their own knowledge or create their own learning experience. Faculty, as adult learners, knows what they need to learn and want to learn it for specific purposes and in a timely manner. As adult learners, faculty take responsibility for their own learning and are independent and self-directed. Also, like adult learners, instructors want to be able to use their (teaching) experience and be respected for their expertise.

Adult learning is about transformation, change. Change in how one views the world and oneself in that world. Lifelong learning, another name for adult learning, contributes to society, as well as the growth and development of the individual, enhancing the quality of life and work. Online and virtual learning environments are well suited for adult learners and are directly based on adult learner characteristics and learning principles. Distance learning provides opportunities for adults to construct learning based on what they already know and apply what they are learning in the instructional setting in other roles. An online instructor is an adult learning expert. In an online learning environment, as the one developed for the competency-based model presented, experienced online faculty co-created and identified the content of the online teaching course, defined the standards of practice and provided input for application of the competencies. Instructors set the standard of excellence for fellow instructors and instruction with an opening for personal goal setting and self-assessment. Instructors, as adult learners, are intrinsically motivated to increase skills and competencies that are relevant to their work and effectiveness on the job.

The more institutions and corporate training departments understand the adult learner and the assumptions of adult learning, the better they will understand the nature of distance learning and the importance of providing effective professional development programs for online trainers and instructors that are built on adult learning principles. Distance learning programs are only as successful as the learning outcomes produced. For e-learning to thrive in adult higher education or corporate arenas, administrators and managers must encourage the creation of virtual learning environments that recognize and support instructors as adult learners.

In such training courses, faculty and instructors have an opportunity to actively progress through course material connecting what they bring from past experiences and construct new strategies for teaching online. Instructors, as adult learners, should be able to apply and reflect on the course content, share their thoughts with peers, and form new meanings in a real world context. Professional development that applies adult learning principles in a social context to foster a community of learners, that benefit from the ideals of e-pedagogy and social constructivism in a safe instructional environment, using discussion and discourse as mechanisms of collaboration and community development, exemplifies the methodology to be used as instructors develop their own online courses (Grant & Dickson, 2008; Palloff & Pratt, 2001; Varvel, 2007).

A COMPETENCY-BASED MODEL

A competency–based model identifies and describes the skills and abilities, knowledge and characteristics and attitudes and personality needed to effectively perform the duties of a particular task, in this case, online instruction (Lucia & Lepsinger, 1999). These abilities, knowledge and skills are acquired through learning and experience and manifested in behaviors that lead to effective performance that can be measured against a standard. A competency model not only defines the competencies necessary, but provides examples of effectiveness and opportunities for practice and application in authentic teaching situations.

Additional purposes for developing and implementing a competency-based model include, for instructors, a professional development plan with attainable goals that can be reached over time to enhance skills and provide documentation of mastery for future teaching experiences. For the institution or organization, the competency model is integral to a professional development program that promotes quality of instruction with criteria that specifies the level of competency needed to meet expectations of excellence for potential students and future instructors. Overall, a competency-based model promotes the quality of instruction and the quality of virtual programs, and provides the institution with a tangible means to describe mastery and someone who has mas-

tered the competencies delineated as exemplary for teaching online. A competency model for instruction should not be a list of requirements used in hiring or retaining instructors, but rather expectations or goals that help instructors enhance their skills to become effective online instructors, as well as provide guidance and a better understanding of their roles.

Other models can be found for developing online instruction and instructors. With the continuing interest in online learning, there exists a plethora of teaching and training models, courses and programs, books, workshops and websites available for developing courses and improving teaching effectiveness. Most were developed in university IT and teaching centers. Many come out of corporate training departments and commercial publishing companies. Some are informational, some instructional, but few are focused on the mastery of competencies or development of specific skills needed to design and deliver instruction online (Rosenberg, 2001). Few are based on empirical research or best practices (Grant & Thornton, 2007). Many popular "how- to" books on web-based learning present a compilation of techniques that use multimedia and technology without the benefit of understanding the pedagogical element necessary in virtual learning environments. Web-based training (WBT) has been largely accepted in the United States and elsewhere as the new corporate model for training and development. There are several how to training manuals on the market that assist in the overall training of WBT instructors in web design and integration of multi-media into virtual learning environments (Hall, 1997; Horton, 2000). However, there are few formal training models or manuals that focus on skill development for online instruction and mastery of competencies needed for both design and facilitation (Lucia & Lepsinger, 1999).

A competency-based approach expands the "how to" of skill development with the "why" for understanding and future access. Mastery of competencies requires an understanding and application of knowledge to the real world. Implementation of an online competency-based program must be strategic and integrated with the vision and mission of the organization. To be successful, the online training program must have the support of administration and management. Competency-based training is a better business strategy than knowledge acquisition or training alone (Rosenberg, 2001).

A competency-based training program should be as efficient as it is effective, with a reasonable number of competencies taught, mastered and practiced in a timely manner. When the number of competencies becomes unyielding, models becomes complicated and difficult to implement (Phipps & Merisotis, 2000; Smith, 2005; Varvel, 2007). Too many competencies become overwhelming and confusing for designers and instructors. This presents a problem for institutions and organizations in recruiting and retaining instructors in professional development or training programs. When designing and implementing a competency-based program, institutions and business should organize competencies in a systematic manner, around both foundational and functional skills. Rodolfa (2005) provides a clear and concise definition of foundational competences and functional skills associated with each. The core competencies represent foundational knowledge and attitudes, while functional competencies represent the demonstrated behaviors, tasks and roles that reflect an understanding of the foundational competencies. Smith (2005) grouped his 51 competencies according to whether they were to be used prior, during or after completion of the course, and, as Varvel (2007) pointed out, these categories were limited and did not support any competency that was not strictly instructional. The primary organization of Phipps and Merisotis (2000) 24 benchmarks was purely functional, while Varvel's (2007) 274 competencies were both functional and role oriented.

The seven core competencies presented in this model were organized into categories based on the

data collected on best practices and demonstrated behaviors of online instructors. These competencies are foundational and encompass a wide range of functional skills within each. Functional skills are expected and preferred, but are not absolutely necessary for core competency mastery. Similar functional skills are demonstrated in each core competencies and reinforce the interrelatedness of best practices with competencies necessary for effective online instruction. Mastery of all of the functional skills in each core competencies is not necessary for successful teaching practice. Depending on the skill, the need for learning, relevance and individual preference, competencies may be mixed and matched in combinations needed for a particular instructional context. Functional skills evolve as new technologies and teaching strategies emerge.

The competency model presented here is generative and scaffolded; each of the seven core competencies builds on the other. They serve as the foundation for the tasks competent online instructors will perform. The more competencies one has, the more effective the instruction, and the more positive the learning experience for the student. In agreement with Varvel (2007), the value of competency models is in helping instructors and facilitators make the best use of the competencies they do possess and to develop the ones that are lacking. In business terms, this training model helps to fill the skill gaps so that the instructor can return to training others and apply what was learned as quickly as possible.

METHOD OF MODEL DEVELOPMENT

The first step in developing a competency-based model is to start with a good definition of competence. According to Spector and la Teja (2001), competence is a state of being well qualified to do a certain job and a competency is a way that competence is demonstrated in a relevant community of practitioners. This definition, expanded to competence in online teaching, demands clarity on what is being measured and evaluated. The skills needed to effectively teach online are competencies that can be measured against well-accepted standards for online teaching and be correlated with top performers in the field. A good competency-based model describes a set of skills that are fluid with ever changing technologies and demands for innovative e-pedagogy and can be adapted to meet the needs of the institution or business.

In an earlier study, seasoned online instructors were queried about their best practices using an instrument based on Chickering and Erhmann's article, "Implementing the seven principles: Technology as lever", (1996) and adapted from a survey by the TLT Group. For the development of a competency-based model for online teaching, data collection from the best practices survey, faculty interviews and focus groups, was focused on identifying specific skills, knowledge and behaviors could be acquired through training, effort and practice (Grant & Thornton, 2007).

Patterns and themes emerged within the best practices for instructional design, teaching effectiveness and course management. Competencies needed to implement best practices in virtual environments came out of the emergent themes. From these competencies, seven core competencies were defined as necessary and relevant for anyone facilitating learning in a virtual environment. Mastery of these competencies provides the skills, knowledge and understanding needed to apply best practices for course design, online instruction, and course management. The model was developed to define necessary competencies and to provide examples of authentic teaching experiences that demonstrate application. The competency-based model is grounded in adult and constructivist learning theory and is incorporated in an online training program for full and part-time instructors (Grant & Thornton, 2007).

METHOD OF MODEL DELIVERY

The model is designed to be delivered in a course, a series of workshops, independent study, or whatever best fits the needs of the institution or organization. An asynchronous online course was designed and implemented to present the model and facilitate competency mastery. This format is convenient and accessible for both full time and part time instructors. Online delivery, through Blackboard CE, in this case, provides an opportunity for the instructor to sit in the "seat" as a student and experience learning from the student perspective and to gain insights into the challenges that usually accompany a first time online experience. The course content page, homepage, has a "Getting Started" link that introduces the course and the facilitator and provides information to assist the "student" in navigating the course. Linked to the homepage are separate folders containing learning modules about online teaching and learning, about each of the seven best practices, and about each of the seven core competencies. A course evaluation is also included and linked on the homepage. The discussion forum, announcements, e-mail and course web links are available in the course tools. Upon completion of the course the instructor will be able to use this course as the model to design, manage and facilitate an online course or build a web-based module to augment a tradition classroom or training session.

This competency-based model for skill development uses a learner-centered approach, the hallmark of adult learning and constructivist theories. The competencies for virtual teaching are presented in an asynchronous training course delivered online for convenient access. The model builds on the innate talents and knowledge instructors bring to the course. Instructors, as virtual adult learners, apply what they know about teaching and are presented opportunities to construct and practice new strategies and methods for teaching in the virtual learning environment. The online teaching course, gives instructors opportunities to reflect, exchange ideas, discuss teaching and learning experiences with peers, practice new skills and contribute content to the learning materials. Consequently, the model is tailored to meet the needs of the instructor as an adult learner. The learning is relevant and transformative in altering how instructors think about teaching and about themselves as educators. Old beliefs and teaching styles are reexamined to accommodate new strategies and beliefs about the learning environment. Furthermore, the online delivery of the model itself promotes recursive and reflective learning which extends the instructor's teaching and social presence from the confines of the online course to additional virtual environments, i.e., Second Life and other Web 2.0 technologies.

The course includes learning objectives for each learning module in which a core competency is presented, along with practice quizzes, time allocations for completion of the module and a discussion forum for questions or sharing ideas and experiences. Within the module, functional competencies, skills related to the core competency, are presented with examples for implementation. Screen shots of exemplary courses demonstrating the use of competency skills, as well as web links and web sites are included to expand the content presented in each module. The "student" instructor is given opportunities to apply the learning to an actual course and submit their work for peer review. This course serves as a model, easily adapted for use in their own online courses, and as a learning experience transferable to future students.

In addition, studies report that instructors who garner the skills to successfully teach online increase their teaching effectiveness in traditional settings as well. Effective online instructors generally become better on ground facilitators (Grant & Thornton, 2007)

THE CORE COMPETENCIES TAUGHT IN THE ONLINE TEACHING COURSE

Seven core competencies, identified within the three emergent themes from the study of the best practices for online learning are presented in seven learning modules in the online teaching course. Best practices are identified as: encouraging communication, student cooperation, active learning, prompt feedback, time-on–task high expectations, and respect. The three emergent themes encompass: course design, instructor effectiveness and course management (Grant & Thornton, 2007).

Theme 1: Course Design

To master the elements of course design, instructors must understand the online environment, Competency # 1, in which they will develop, Competency #3, and deliver their course content, and understand online pedagogy, Competency #2, in order to incorporate it into their teaching philosophy and style.

Core Competency 1: Understand the Online Format

This involves understanding the very nature of the medium in which instruction and learning takes place. The virtual learning environment, when utilized to the fullest extent, becomes a vast space for exploration and discovery. It is not confined by time or place. The time commitment for instructors and learners can be immense if not recognized or understood. Expectations for the amount of time and effort spent online and offline in preparation for course delivery and learning should be clear. Adult learners expect learning to be in their own time and appreciate knowing what their time commitments will be. They also want clear directions as well as timelines and deadlines.

Course content in the online environment expands through the vast resources of the Internet. Instructors must develop skills to critically analyze and teach students how to discriminate between too much information and too little context. In mastering the first competency, the instructor can make the online environment make sense for the online learner. To do this effectively, the instructor must understand the use and limitations of the course learning management system (LMS). In this competency, technical knowledge, not technological expertise, is required in terms of assisting the future student in navigating and accessing the online environment and system support when needed.

Mastering this competency requires belief in the process of learning online and confidence that critical thinking, student connections, self-directed learning, and a sense of community can take place. Instructors who master this competency will understand the elements of teaching and social presence in the virtual environment. A teaching presence is a component of the course design and organization, including the facilitation of discussion, direct instruction, personalized feedback and content delivery. The competent instructor understands the notion of teaching presence and realizes that the student is not to be left to fend on his own. The instructor is always overseeing without micromanaging the student learning process. Students want to know that the instructor is available online, reading discussion posts, providing timely feedback and keeping students on tract and on task. A social presence is a component of the affective interactions that an online instructor in a learner-centered, social learning environment is expected to possess. The competent instructor understands the concept of social presence and realizes that the student wants to know that there is a real person online who has a personality and cares about the student.

This competency is illustrated in the instructor's ability to "humanize" the course and engage the student. The instructor's tone, use of stories, humor, and graphics and images incorporated into the content modules, will encourage contact and dialogue. Adult learners want respect and to know that they matter to the instructor. They want an instructor who is approachable and encourages communication and feedback.

Best practices in online learning integrated with mastery of this competency include communication skills, i.e., use of e-mail, introductions, announcements, discussion, as well as a well written syllabus that clarifies expectations for success and time-on-task.

Core Competency 2: Understand Online Pedagogy

This competency cuts across all seven best practices. It involves aspects of design and implementation of instruction.

Two concepts, connectivity and interactivity, in online teaching environments go beyond the pedagogy necessary in the traditional classroom. In order for meaningful learning to be constructed and confirmed, the instructor, the student and the course content must connect in ways that allow dynamic interaction among all three via facilitated dialogue, collaboration and feedback. This integration is only as effective as the quality of the connections and interactions achieved. The most important role of an online instructor is to ensure that dynamic interaction and participation take place in an online course (Kearsley, 2000). In order for this to happen, the competent instructor will design activities and learning experiences that result in connecting students with course content and with each other, as well as with the instructor.

Connectivity is another word for engagement. Learning is a collaborative process and is enhanced by meaningful insights from several perspectives. In an online course, students should become responsible for generating and sharing knowledge. The shift in responsibility from instructor-centered to student-centered learning requires the online instructor to develop and use instructional strategies that support connectivity and interaction and the development of self-directedness.

Interactivity is learner-driven and is the force behind the learning process and student learning outcomes. Online learning is not passive learning where the learner relies solely on the instructor to provide content. It is not a lecture-oriented course in which interaction only takes place between the student and the content or the student and the instructor. Adult students learn best in an active and experiential learning environment where opportunities for collaboration and connections are promoted.

Mastery of this competency is illustrated in learning modules that invite and encourage student interaction in a non-threatening and open environment. The initial use of opinion questions in a discussion forum provides learners an opportunity to practice responding in the written format and encourages student dialogue, as well as peer review and feedback. Creating authentic learning activities, i.e., case studies, connects students with the content and encourages inquiry and discovery. Designing group projects, e. g., web quests, fosters collaboration and promotes a climate for interactivity and integration.

Core Competency 3: Understand Course Content Development

Developing an outline for course content requires that the instructor be the content expert, have mastery of the subject matter and know what he/she wants the students to know about that subject matter. The best practices that cut across this competency are, encouraging contact and time-on-task and communicating high expectations.

The online course discusses three components of course development that must be addressed in putting an online course together:

1. What do I want the students to know… what are the expected student learning outcomes?
2. What learning activities must I provide for that learning to take place?
3. How will I assess that the learning actually happened?

By understanding the online format and online pedagogy, the competent instructor will be able to move forward with developing a course outline and course content with these three components guiding the process.

In addition to determining and planning course content and materials, the competent instructor must consider who the online learner is and what they bring to the learning experience. Knowing the student audience is important in determining: course outcomes, learning objectives and activities, as well as course expectations and assessments for learning. In the case of adult learners, they bring certain characteristics to the online learning environment that must be considered: real-life experience with varied learning styles, desire for meaningful learning and real world application, desire for active learning and control of their own learning process. The competent instructor understands the needs and experiences of the adult learner in order to create a course and learning experience that meets those needs and expectations.

Building the course outline entails constructing the entire course at one time. The course is "front loaded"; the preparation for the class is done up front before the course is delivered online. Every required week of instruction is outlined and developed with learning objectives, assignments, and assessments, each with timelines and deadlines for submission, before the course goes "live" online. The competent instructor is able to develop an overall plan for the course whose outline can be modified as needed.

Mastery of this competency is illustrated in actively building a course outline, during the training course, starting with identified outcomes and continuing with assignments and assessments that align with learning objectives. This competency learning module includes information and examples of how to write learning objectives that, for instance, develop cognitive skills using Bloom's Taxonomy. It also provides exercises to teach students how to navigate the Internet. Different types of learning activities, assignments and assessments are explored in the module and a variety of websites and links are presented that provides example for implementation.

A syllabus is the detailed contract that the instructor writes about learning goals and objectives, as well as expectations for student learning and achievement in the course. The competent instructor will be able to write a course syllabus which tells the student what they will learn, what activities will be performed for learning to take place and how the instructor and learner will determine whether that learning took place. The competent instructor chronicles all components of the course in the syllabus providing detailed information about the instructor's availability, instructions for assignment completion and submission, guidelines for assessments and rubrics, policies for participation, academic integrity and grading, and technical support information. The syllabus is written with the adult learner in mind in terms of clarifying expectations, timelines and deadlines. Examples of exemplary syllabi are presented and a sample template for building a comprehensive syllabus is included.

After mastery of competency in building a course outline and writing a syllabus, the instructor will be able to demonstrate specific behaviors that incorporate best practices in communication, time on task and expectations.

Theme 2: Instructional Effectiveness

To facilitate and maintain instructional effectiveness, instructors must master the task of designing, Competency #4, a course which incorporates web-based instructional design elements and maximizes the use of the Internet, as well as master the components of the course Learning Management System, Competency #5, to help students navigate the course successfully.

Core Competency 4: Understand Instructional Design

This core competency cuts across the best practices of encouraging cooperation, active learning and respect for diversity, respectively. This core competency encompasses several functional auxiliary competencies, skills and behaviors involving actual design, implementation of instruction and student assessment. Core and auxiliary competencies may vary between institutions and disciplines. Hence, to understand instructional design, is to understand that there is no "one size fits all" model for instructional design.

With this in mind, the competent instructor must understand and consider the environment in which the learning will take place. Depending on the learning activities, that environment could be in a website, the Learning Management System, or another site that expands outside of the virtual environment, e. g., web quests, virtual worlds, Web 2.0, etc. The design of the course must maximize the learning environment beyond traditional means while focusing on the content of the subject material. The online audience must be considered as well, and the competent instructional designer will have a guiding theory or concept of the teaching and learning process. For instance, with adult learners, one aspect of learning is based on the constructivist perspective, where new knowledge is constructed by the learner in relationship to prior understanding and knowing. Understanding adult learning principles is important to design and intrinsic to delivery of an online program.

Mastery of this competency entails understanding the elements of instructional design that foster the involvement of the learner in the learning process by developing and using interactive learning activities, i.e., web quests, audio and visual resources, interactive web sites, discussion groups, debates, simulations and role play. This competency learning module also demonstrates skills needed for incorporating authentic assessments in the course that enable students to construct responses and demonstrate problem-solving and critical thinking skills.

The learning module for this competency provides an opportunity to learn how to effectively present course content in a manageable format by modeling "chunking". "Chunking" material into interactive lessons, containing no more than two or three main points, makes reading and processing information online more efficient. Also, examples of templates for design layout, in terms of font size, color, graphics and images, that complements different learning styles, are presented. In addition, balancing course activities for both groups and individuals is demonstrated. With mastery of this module, the competent instructor learns that lecture online is not the same as lecture in the traditional setting; that an interactive conversational approach, using appropriate humor and anecdotes, is more effective than a passive subject-centered approach.

Core Competency 5: Demonstrate Course Management

Understanding course management is essential in operating efficiently and effectively within the online format of the course. Logistics and procedures as well as personal concern for the students in the course are essential to course and student success. Managing the amount of material, inputs and outputs, must be budgeted in the timeframe in which the course is offered. In building the structure of the online course it is essential that the instructor understands and is familiar with the infrastructure, the course learning management system (LMS), in which the course will be housed and delivered. Knowledge of the

course learning management system (LMS) facilitates the organization of information and the use of technology in both accessing and delivering the course content. Managing student learning within the course requires attention to processes and procedures for all course deliverables. The competent instructor knows that organization and communication are the keys to successful course management and navigation.

The competent instructor knows how to effectively use the course learning management system (LMS) and how to help students understand and use course tools. Building a learning community is essential and takes time upfront. The course must have built-in mechanisms for engaging students with the content, other students and the instructor. Providing repositories for e-mail and questions, assignments, assessments, and grade reports make managing the course and engaging adult learners more fluid.

Mastery of this competency is demonstrated in the organization of the course beginning with the ability to access LMS training and support by the instructor and the student. The online module serves as a model for organization and use of the course tools which when achieved builds a community of learners who can communicate with each other and access and share information and knowledge. The online instructor learns how to facilitate discussions, set expectations for timely feedback, keep students on task and help them manage their time. This is accomplished by providing clear directions with timelines and deadlines in the syllabus, discussion forum, announcements and elsewhere in the course for completion and submission of assignments and assessments, as well as links to additional resources, i.e., web links to the library, journals, institution homepage and others, and by maintaining a course calendar. Garnering these skills cuts across the best practices involving communication, feedback, time-on-task, and communicating high expectations.

Theme 3: Course Management Using Appropriate Technology

Instructors must be able to manage the course, to master and practice the use of appropriate technology to meet course goals and improve student learning outcomes, Competency #6. This involves developing the skills to evaluate functionality and usability of the web and course delivery system. Finally, faculty must learn to identify and practice methods of quality assurance and develop attitudes that respect the evaluation process, Competency # 7.

Core Competency 6: Demonstrate Use of Technology

Good organization can help ensure that certain standards for the design and delivery of courses are met (Phipps & Merisotis, 2000). By increasing the attention given to the organization of the materials, the instructor can better gauge and communicate the level of student support or motivation needed, as well as the technologies that should be used in the course (Phipps & Merisotis, 2000).

This competency involves integrating technology into the course. The dependence on the use of technology as well as its proper function in an online course requires that the instructor and students have at least a minimum amount of technology literacy. The competent instructor should have a willingness to experiment with the technology and have some knowledge of what to do when it doesn't function properly or at least where to go to get expert assistance in solving problems.

The competent instructor understands the concepts of functionality and usability in terms of technology. He/she starts with learning what can be done within the LMS and the capabilities, functions and limitations of the course tools. The LMS provides a template for designing the course and provides standardization of usability and functionality from course to course. To further enhance functionality and usability, learning content and course materials are arranged in self-contained modules that have a consistent look and presentation. This is helpful to students for navigating through the content and the LMS. Students should be able to interact with content and technology simultaneously as do faculty, hence completing the cycle where technology and pedagogy come together to achieve teaching and learning.

Mastery of this competency is demonstrated in understanding the concepts of functionality and usability of the LMS. This competency learning module provides examples of appropriate technology integration with different elements of a course, including use of graphics, font, format and color to accommodate a variety of learning styles. The online instructor learns how to use the LMS course tools effectively, how to incorporate technology that enhances pedagogy and how to navigate the Internet to maximize teaching and learning. Instructors are provided examples and taught how to incorporate multi- media, i.e., games, simulations, podcasts, blogs, wikis and audio/ video resources, to enhance course design and teaching effectiveness and to expand learning. Achieving this competency keeps the learning environment manageable for new adult online learners who don't have room for ambiguity while juggling their personal and work lives at the same time. Demonstrating this competency democratizes the learning environment and recognizes the diversity of life experience adult learners bring into the learning process. This competency cuts across the best practices of communication and respect for diversity.

Core Competency 7: Develop Quality Assurance

This competency involves all aspects of evaluation and utilization of mechanisms to ensure quality in course design, delivery and management. The competent instructor will be able to create standards of performance to teach and deliver the course and to set policies for student participation, academic integrity and netiquette. The competent instructor will communicate expectations and provide mechanisms for feedback through a variety of evaluation techniques that respect the diversity of the learning environment.

Mastery of this competency is illustrated in examples of course design that incorporate standards of excellence for students and instructors, including guidelines for conduct and feedback. Instructors are provided examples and opportunities to create rubrics for course assignments and discussion forums, as well as difference types of instruments for mid-course and end of course evaluations. This competency assists the instructor in maintaining a quality learning environment and experience, cutting across the best practices of communication, cooperation, feedback, respect for diversity and communication of high expectations. In setting standards and providing rubrics, the instructor accommodates the adult learner's need for purpose and relevancy.

These seven core competencies, identified as essential for effectively teaching in a virtual environment, can be used to build a course and deliver online learning in either an academic or corporate setting. The utilization of an online training course to systematically present the competencies seems more reasonable and manageable than mechanisms presented in other competency models (Smith, 2005; Varvel, 2007).

These competencies and their associated skills are manifested in some combination in the behaviors of online instructors recognized for excellence in course design, instruction and course management. When an instructor masters a core competency, combinations of associated skills accompany that mastery. Whether all associated skills are exemplary or essential for effective teaching remains to be determined. To test and refine associated skills and validate core competencies a validation process was set in place.

VALIDATION OF COMPETENCIES

Interviews and focus groups were conducted with online instructors of adult learners to determine how well instructors currently teaching online feel that the competencies reflect the skills, abilities, knowledge and characteristics necessary to effectively teach in a virtual environment. These data were collected to determine face validity, that is, whether the core competencies described in the model make sense to those teaching online. It was also important in these query sessions that emphasis be put on specific behaviors within each competency. This was done by asking for behavioral examples of how instructors perform in each of the competency areas. For example: "What does an instructor need to do to demonstrate that they have mastered the online format?" In this case, the model was validated as a predictor of successful performance, that is, the competencies are demonstrated by exemplary and competent online instructors.

Instructors replied to a set of questions focused on what competencies are needed to teach effectively in the online environment and on what behaviors demonstrate the acquisition of these competencies. Common themes were identified through the analyzed responses. Most instructors believed that some technology literacy is essential in order to manage the course in the course learning management system (LMS) and to help students navigate through the course. Competency in course management skills was cited as crucial because adult learners, in particular, expect structure and predictability. Students have to know what they must do in order to succeed. Many instructors specifically mentioned the need to understand online format and online pedagogy, and that these competencies, needed to teach online, were different from those needed to teach in a traditional setting.

Knowledge of the Internet and how to use the web creatively was clearly noted as a competency to master before developing or teaching a course online. In terms of the Internet, many instructors said that helping students develop critical reading and thinking skills was important when doing research online and weeding through the vast amount of information available. Another common thread running through instructor responses entailed behaviors that demonstrated good communication skills, to engage students, to build a community of learners, and to provide feedback.

The participants in the study confirmed the face validity for the core competencies, understanding online format, understanding pedagogy and ability to manage the course, as essential to the success of the online learning experience. In addition, the appropriate use and practice of technology to deliver content and expand learning was confirmed as critical factors for success in the virtual learning environment. Skills in course design, content development and evaluation were repeatedly mentioned as competencies that seemed to make sense for teaching online and for integrating best practices.

To validate competencies as predictors of successful teaching online, exemplary instructors reported the following behaviors most often demonstrated in each core competency. These behaviors are examples of how the competency is practiced, and can be implemented in any online course or web-based learning program for academic or corporate use:

Competency 1: Understand Online Format

a. Use Internet: incorporate Web quests and virtual tours; add web links to sites to expand content.
b. Use the LMS to communicate with students: e-mail, discussion forums, chats, announcements.
c. Communicate expectations of time commitment for assignment completion: specify time lines in the learning module for completion of each reading task, project, quiz or exam.

Competency 2: Understand Online Pedagogy

a. Engage students: ask for introductions and use ice breakers.
b. Communicate expectations: learning objectives for the course in the syllabus and at the beginning of each learning module.
c. Maintain social presence: use student and instructor photos, tell personal stories, use conversational tone in lectures, discussion forum and e-mail.
d. Make announcements to keep students informed: announce the start of a new week, remind students of deadlines and tests.
e. Use e-mail: send messages to the entire class weekly for feedback … "how's it going?"
f. Facilitate discussion forums and chat: without micromanaging the discussion, keep students on task.
g. Provide personalized feedback…use the student's name and respond in his words.
h. Assign group projects: i.e., a web quest or case stud.
i. Assign peer review of writing assignments.
j. Use journaling: ask students to reflect on learning every week in writing.

Competency 3: Develop Course Content

a. Communicate course objectives: in the syllabus
b. Provide clear directions: in the syllabus, in the learning module, with the assignment
c. Explain grading system in the syllabus.
d. Explain course policies, academic integrity, and participation policy in the syllabus

Competency 4: Understand Instructional Design

a. Use learning modules: no more than 2 to 3 main points in a learning module. When one learning module has several parts, each part has a separate page. Learners should not scroll more than 1 or 2 pages.

b. "Chunk" course material: present main points in short sentences and paragraphs; use bullets and images.

c. Vary assignments and assessments: use different mechanisms to accommodate different learning styles … i. e., multiple choice and essay tests.

d. Vary use of fonts, color, images: accommodate different learning styles. Make use of white space.

e. Provide online glossaries and dictionaries: Add web links on the homepage and in the LMS weblink tool to dictionaries and content specific glossary of terms.

Competency 5: Demonstrate Course Management

a. Use assignment drop box to provide a repository for course work.

b. Use templates to design each module so that they have a consistent look, i. e., Part 1: directions, learning objectives, assignments and assessment for each module on one page; next Part 2: the topic presentation.

c. Use course tools: the discussion, calendar, assignment box, etc., but only display and use those tools that are appropriate for the learning experience in that course.

d. Use online testing; design tests for use in the testing tool. It is more convenient and efficient that using e-mail and attachments.

e. Repeat directions in several places; the mantra for online learning is repeat…repeat…repeat…everywhere.

f. Clarify timelines and deadlines.

Competency 6: Practice Use of Technology

a. Use video and images: add images and links to videos in the learning modules and on Power Point slides.

b. Use audio, Podcasts: link Podcasts to learning modules and introductions. Add audio to Power Point slides.

c. Use Power Point: create your own or use those from publishers and link them to the homepage and learning modules.

d. Provide resources for LMS support: add e-mail and phone numbers to IT and LMS support in the syllabus and on the course homepage and web link tool.

Competency 7: Develop Quality Assurances

a. Provide feedback: Use grade book, e-mail and discussion forum.

b. Provide and use rubrics: rubrics can be used for assignments and for discussion forums.

c. Provide mid-course and end of course evaluations: encourage feedback, build or link to evaluations in the test tool or homepage.

d. Open course for review: provide access to peers and supervisors for review and feedback.

The behaviors demonstrated in these core competencies cross cut the seven best practices in online education for student engagement, cooperation among students, active learning, feedback, time on task, expectations and respect for differences. How each competency is implemented in practice can serve as an example and be incorporated into any online course, web-based module or program using the competency model.

These instructors were also asked how competencies are best acquired, whether by way of formal training, experience, collaborative reflection and discussion, or some combination thereof. Most responded that a combination of training and experience provided the skill sets they acquired to teach effectively online, with strong consensus that experience was the best teacher in testing and refining online performance.

It is recommended that the model be circulated to a wider audience to test the likelihood all core and associated skills have been captured, not just those articulated in these interviews. Also, moving to a larger audience may uncover demographic or functional differences in the applicability of the model across disciplines, institutions, organizations, and student populations. Competencies may be different for different factions of faculty and learners, as well as other stakeholders. The more people involved in reviewing the competencies, the more buy in from those who will benefit most from the implementation of the model. Additional insights will expand the model's use and relevancy in different contexts.

IMPLEMENTATION OF THE ONLINE TEACHING COURSE

Implementation is always easier when there is support of those responsible for applying the model and those who will be affected by it. The competency model would have little value to instructors or organizations unless there was a means of applying it. The model is implemented through an online teaching course. When implementing the online course, an androgogical approach should be taken in presenting the competency model, providing instructors a flexible, convenient way to learn with time to process each competency, and then apply best practices as appropriate to their own course and instructional goals. The online course should provide a comfortable environment that promotes active participation and draws out the prior experiences of the learner. By using adult learning principles, institutions and corporations

can plan and implement an online teaching course that will provide instructors opportunities to assess their understanding and mastery of competencies through integrated feedback mechanisms and a process of online peer review.

The instructional design and delivery of content used in the online teaching course presented can serve as a model for implementation of similar train the trainer programs in academic or corporate settings. The course begins with a general introduction to the benefits of teaching and learning online and addresses expectations for instructors and students. The basic concepts of online instruction, stressing the principles of good undergraduate education, with emphasis on adult learners in the online environment, are described. The goals of the course include the review of the seven best practices for online teaching, identification of themes within these practices, and mastery of competencies to implement the practices.

The best practices are presented in the online training course in individual learning modules which include examples of each from exemplary online instructors. Opportunities for discussing practices and applications are provided in the course discussion forum. The seven core competencies identified under the three broader themes of course design, instruction and management, are also presented in seven individual learning modules. Each of the seven learning modules expands the core competencies with detailed illustrations, examples and practice activities matching competencies with online teaching best practices. The examples are specific to skills described, yet applicable in a variety of settings. As instructors move from one competency module to another they are able to discuss their experience and share ideas with other instructors in the online discussion forum. The discussion forum becomes a means of peer review and support as well.

No matter where the online teaching course is implemented, on completion, competent instructors will have an understanding of online formats and pedagogy and an appreciation for the critical balance between student, instructor, and content interactions needed to maintain an effective learner-centered environment. They will also have a better understanding of the course management system and the features that augment learning. Finally, the competent instructor will be able to develop, design, organize, and effectively instruct and deliver an online course, while also integrating online teaching strategies and best practices.

The online course is designed and serves as a model that can be adapted to any discipline or to any training modality. The learning modules are informational and instructional providing content knowledge and learning activities for practice and implementation. This teaching course can be adapted to meet specific institutional or organizational goals for training online instructors. Using the instructional design of this course, an organization can reinvent the way it delivers effective online training, centered on knowledge acquisition, skill mastery and application through practice. The value to business of this or any online learning program is in its cost effectiveness, benefits to the company, i.e., enhanced skills, improved performance and service, as well as availability to all and speed of application to impact production and profits (Rosenberg, 2001).

FUTURE TRENDS

The current interest in developing competency-based models comes full circle back to business and industry (Spector & la Teja, 2001). With the wave of corporate professional development and training courses offered in virtual environments comes the concern for quality and instructional effectiveness, as in higher education. The use of new technologies and delivery venues necessitates the proper preparation and training of online facilitators. The construction of competencies essential for online instruction leads to new professional development programs and formal credentialing for online facilitators.

What organizations must consider in developing future training models is to ask for whom the model is being developed and how will it be used. Recent studies suggest that some situations call for a move away from standards and recommend that competencies take into account the social context of the facilitator and how those competencies will be used in those contexts, for instance with clients and customers, as well as other members of the workplace (Guasch, et al., 2008). They recommend a socially situated competency, in which the facilitators themselves determine and shape the competencies required to perform effectively, hence taking into account the social nature of competency. This is in consistent with the application of adult learning theory in the both the development and delivery of competency-based models. The constant evolution of information and expansion of communication technologies requires a continuous process of refining competencies and demands a commitment to lifelong professional development. A competency-based model that is grounded in adult and constructivist learning theories, favoring active and authentic learning in context, is most suitable for professional development and training of online instructors.

Competency models must assist online instructors in becoming both managers and facilitators of the learning process. As discussed, the literature contains examples of competencies unique to managing and teaching in virtual environments (Smith, 2005; Varvel, 2007). However, there are few that consider the nature or the multiple dimensions of the virtual environment in the process of understanding the shifts in learning that occurs with e-pedagogy. Future studies must investigate these shifts and identify affective as well as instructional practices that stimulate learning in adult students. Future models must construct competencies that meet the demand for the type of skills, knowledge and characteristics needed to teach new generations of adult learners in formats that expand virtual environments to mobile ones, including Web 2.0 technologies.

A competency-based model for online teaching can be adapted for use in any institution willing to provide support and funding to implement the model. It seems a small price to pay to create effective online training and develop qualified instructors, who in the long term lead learning communities in application of competencies. Implementation of a competency- based training program, in concert with business models, needs a set of behaviors that describe what the competencies look like in practice, a process to determine to what extent competencies are currently being used and by whom, awareness that training exists to learn and develop competencies, and an evaluation or follow-up mechanism to ensure that skill gaps are closed (Lucia & Lepsinger, 2001). Finally, as institutions and organizations become more vested in virtual education and demand standards of excellence in delivering online learning, it seems reasonable to expect that recognition for competent online teaching be tied to compensation and promotion.

CONCLUSION

Essentially, this competency-based model, with measurable objectives, criteria and processes for evaluation, is designed as a professional development program for online instructors that can be implemented in multiple settings and situations. The competency-based approach starts with a systematic and collective consensus of what the online instructor needs to know that is valid and important for teaching effectively online. It also introduces mechanisms that encourage understanding and mastery that will flourish and endure throughout future instructional and organizational roles. People who develop and use a competency once are likely to use it again and, having tried it in one situation, will most likely try it again in a different situation (Lucia & Lepsinger, 1999).

This competency model focuses on the instructor as an adult learner, integrating principles of adult learning and teaching strategies into the design and delivery of the model through an online teaching course. Instructors in the course come to recognize the cross cutting nature of competencies with best practices and construct applications of these practices, which in turn creates relevancy for instructors. This model sets the standard for excellence in online instruction that is comprehensive and specific to self-directed adult learning. The experienced change in teaching practice with competency mastery leads to a transformation in teaching and learning.

Teaching online becomes transformative when the assumptions about face to face communication are overcome and student engagement and learning are expanded through a different learning space. The line between teaching and facilitating is blurred when the learner becomes the focus of the learning space. The competent instructor realizes that meeting students where they are in their learning process is essential to effective teaching and the point where learning begins. The seven core competencies of online teaching mastered through this model integrate the elements of course design, delivery and management and remain informed by interactions that are purposeful and acknowledge the contributions of the learner. Using this model, instructors recognize experiences, goals and expectations of different adult learners, then, adapt teaching styles, customize learning modules, tailor assignments and assessments, integrate new technology with best practices for generational learning styles, value individual qualities regardless of generational differences, and find the right balance between pedagogy and technology.

This particular competency-based model represents a new paradigm shift for professional development, which emphasizes the positive role that competencies play in preparing instructors for new virtual learning environments. The interest in the development of competencies for distance learning is evidence that there may be a shift to a "culture of competence" in professional online training in the future.

REFERENCES

Bates, A. W. (2000). *Managing technological change: Strategies for college and university leaders*. San Francisco: Jossey-Bass.

Candy, P. C. (1991). *Self-direction for lifelong learning*. San Francisco: Jossey-Bass.

Chickering, A., & Ehrmann, S. C. (1996). Implementing the seven principles: Technology as lever . *AAHE Bulletin, 49*(2), 3–6.

Collison, G., Elbaum, B., Haavind, S., & Tinker, R. (2000). *Facilitating online learning: Effective strategies for moderators*. Madison, WI: Atwood Publishing.

Dewey, J. (1938). *Experience and education*. New York: Collier Books.

Epstein, R. M., & Hundert, E. M. (2002). Defining and assessing professional competence. *Journal of the American Medical Association, 287*, 226–235. doi:10.1001/jama.287.2.226

Fidishun, D. (2000). Andragogy and Technology: Integrating Adult Learning Theory as We Teach with Technology. In *Proceedings Middle Tennessee State University Instructional Technology Conference*.

Flint, T. (1999). *Best Practices in Adult Learning: A CAEL/APQC Benchmarking Study*. New York: Forbes Custom Publishing.

Grant, M. R., & Dickson, V. J. (2008). Matrix on Virtual Teaching: a Competency-based Model for Faculty Development. In *Adult Education Research, (AERC), Conference Proceedings*, University of Missouri St. Louis, St. Louis, Missouri.

Grant, M. R., & Thornton, H. R. (2007). Best practices in undergraduate adult-centered online learning: Mechanisms for course design and delivery. *MERLOT Journal of Online Learning and Teaching, 3*(4), 346–456.

Guasch, T., Espasa, A., & Alvarez, I. M. (2008). A trans-national study of Teachers' ICT competencies in online learning environments in Higher Education . In *How do we learn? Where do we learn?* Lisboa: EDEN.

Kaslow, N. J., Borden, K. A., Collins, F. L. Jr, Forrest, L., Illfelder-Kaye, J., Nelson, P., & Rallo, J. S. (2004). Competencies Conference: Future Directions in Education and Credentialing in Professional Psychology. *Journal of Clinical Psychology, 60*, 699–712. doi:10.1002/jclp.20016

Kearsley, G. (2000). *Online education: Learning and teaching in cyberspace*. Belmont, CA: Wadsworth.

Kerka, S. (1998). *Competency-based education and training: Myths and realities*. ERIC/ACVE. Retrieved March 06, 2009, from http://www.calpro-online.org/eric/textonly/docgen.asp?tbl=mr&ID=65

Knowles, M. (1980). *The modern practice of adult education* (2nd ed.). New York: Cambridge Books.

Lawler, P. A., & King, K. P. (2000). *Planning for effective faculty development: Using adult learning strategies*. Malabar, FL: Krieger Pub Co.

Lucia, A. D., & Lepinsinger, R. (1999). *The art and science of competency models*. San Francisco, CA: Jossey-Bass/Pfeiffer.

Merriam, S. B., & Caffarella, R. S. (1999). *Learning in adulthood* (2nd ed.). San Francisco: Jossey-Bass.

Moore, M. G., & Kearsley, G. (1996). *Distance education: A systems view*. Belmont, CA: Wadsworth.

National Center for Education Statistics. (2005). *Projections of education statistics to 2014 (NCES 2005-074)*. Washington, DC: U.S. Government Printing Office.

Newlin, M., & Wang, A. (2002). Integrating technology and pedagogy: Web instruction and seven principles of undergraduate education. *Teaching of Psychology, 29*(4), 325–330. doi:10.1207/S15328023TOP2904_15

Palloff, R. M., & Pratt, K. (2001). *Lessons from the cyberspace classroom: The realities of online teaching.* San Francisco: Jossey-Bass.

Parry, S. R. (•••). (1996). The Quest for Competencies. *Training (New York, N.Y.),* (July): 48–56.

Phipps, R., & Merisotis, J. (2000). *Quality on the line: Benchmarks for success in Internet-based distance education.* Washington, DC: The Institute for Higher Education Policy. Retrieved July 2, 2003, from http://www.ihep.com/Pubs/PDF/Quality.pdf

Rodolfa, E. R., Bent, R. J., Eisman, E., Nelson, P. D., Rehm, L., & Ritchie, P. (2005). A cube model for competency development: Implications for psychology educators and regulators. *Professional Psychology, Research and Practice, 36,* 347–354. doi:10.1037/0735-7028.36.4.347

Rosenberg, M. J. (2001). *E-learning: Strategies for delivering knowledge in the digital age.* New York: McGraw Hill.

Siemans, G. (2005). *Connectivisim: Learning as Network Creation.* Retrieved November 28, from, http://elearnspace.org/Articles/networks.htm

Sloan Consortium. (2005). *Growing by degrees: Online education in the United States.* Retrieved January 10, 2007 from, http://www.sloan-c.org/resources/growing_by_degrees.pdf

Smith, T. C. (2005). Fifty one competencies for online instruction. *The Journal of Online Educators, 2*(2), 1–18.

Spector, J. M., & Anderson, T. M. (Eds.). (2000). *Integrated and holistic perspectives on learning, instruction and technology: Understanding complexity.* Dordrecht: Kluwer Academic Press.

Spector, J. M., & de la Teja, I. (2001) Competencies for Online Teaching. *Eric Digest.* Retrieved March 01, 2009 from, http://ericit.org/digests/EDO-IR-2001-09.shtml

Varvel, V. E. (2007). Master Online Teacher Competencies. *Online Journal of Distance Learning Administration, 10*(1). Retrieved on March 3, 2009 from http://www.westga.edu/%7Edistance/ojdla/spring101/varvel101.htm

Weigel, V. (2000). E-15earning and the tradeoff between richness and reach in higher education. *Change, 33*(5), 10–15. doi:10.1080/00091380009605735

Wenger, E. (1998). *Communities of Practice, Learning and Identity.* New York: Cambridge University Press

Wilkes, C. W., & Burnham, B. R. (1991). Adult learner motivations and electronics distance education. *American Journal of Distance Education, 5*(1), 43–50. doi:10.1080/08923649109526731

KEY TERMS AND DEFINITIONS

Best Practices: In online education, refers to widely accepted and researched techniques and methods that consistently produce effective and efficient online course design, delivery and instruction.

Competency-based model: A scheme for developing a set of skills, knowledge and attitudes particular to a community of practice that enables a person to perform at the level of excellence expected in that profession or field of practice.

Faculty Development: A comprehensive program designed to provide opportunities for professional, personal, organizational and instructional development to full and part-time faculty.

Distance Education: Refers to a system of delivering education that doesn't require the student and the instructor to be in the same place at the same time.

Adult Learning Theory: Theoretical concepts and schema, based on critical analysis, about how and why adults learn, process information and gain knowledge

Constructivism: An active learning process of constructing knowledge based on what is already known or experienced by the individual.

Connectivity: Connectivity is the process in online environments to engage student and instructor, to facilitate interactions between instructor and student, between student and course material, between student and other students and with the real world outside the course.

Learning Organization: An organization that embraces learning at all levels of its culture that is aligned with strategic business goals, focused on competencies and promotes lifelong learning.

E-pedagogy: The process and practice of teaching in a virtual learning environment using web-based technologies.

Web 2.0: New developments on the Internet that facilitate participation and collaboration on the Web to create content and control data (e. g., YouTube and Wikipedia), to select specific information (e. g., RSS), to expand services, share ideas and connect with others in social networks, (e. g., Facebook).

Chapter 9

Assessing 3D Virtual World Learning Environments with the CIMPLe System:
A Multidisciplinary Evaluation Rubric[1]

Sean D. Williams
Clemson University, USA

Deborah M. Switzer
Clemson University, USA

ABSTRACT

This chapter introduces an assessment rubric for virtual world learning environments (VWLEs) built from proven principles of user experience design, instructional design, interface design, learning theory, technical communication, instructional systems design (ISD), and VIE motivation theory. Titled the "CIMPLe System," this rubric captures the ways that context, interactivity, motivation, presence, and cognitive load weave together to form a successful VWLE. The CIMPLe System offers an advance in how educators can assess the quality and predict the success of the VWLEs that they build. The holistic approach achieved in the CIMPLe System arises from the multidisciplinary approach represented in the tool. As designers consider what to build into the environment, they can refer to the CIMPLe System as a checklist to ensure that the environment meets the needs that the cross-disciplinary theory suggests are necessary.

INTRODUCTION

Although the idea of virtual environments in education might seem radical, it is not new; rather, programs such as Quest Atlantis (Indiana University), River City (Harvard University) and SciCentr (Cornell Theory Center) have been in use for more than ten years. Research from these programs suggests

that students exhibit gains in engagement, efficacy and achievement (Barab, et al, 2005; Ketelhut, et al, 2006). Additionally, a recent study (Hansen *et al*, 2004) noted that students actively involved in three-dimensional construction of computational models had a more sophisticated understanding of dynamic spatial relationships than students in a traditional classroom environment. Other studies (e.g., Kim, 2006) suggest a statistically significant effect of 3-D virtual environments on

DOI: 10.4018/978-1-61520-619-3.ch009

both achievement and on developing a positive attitude toward science.

Finally, Jones (2004) proposed that multi-user, 3-D, online learning environments demonstrate numerous important educational benefits such as engaged immersion, situated learning, multi-modal communications, breakdown of socio-cultural barriers, bridging the digital divide, problem solving, and the ability to create empathy and understanding for complex systems. Other advantages of virtual environments for learning include the ability to provide experiences that may not be available in real life, the ability to analyze phenomena from different points of view to gain deeper understanding, and the ability to work with virtual companions distributed over different geographical locations (Chittaro and Ranon, 2007).

Why do learners respond so well to virtual environments? In the late 1990s, researchers began hypothesizing, for example, that the level of presence in a virtual world—the feeling of being somewhere else—as well as the level of immersion—the feeling of interacting directly with the environment—account for the success of instructional virtual worlds (Witmer & Singer 1998). More recent studies investigate other aspects of successful virtual worlds for instructional contexts, including the role of social facilitation, or the degree to which having others "present" impacts performance (Park & Catrambone, 2007); (Bronack, Cheney, Riedl, & Tashner, 2008); the role of place metaphors in guiding action (Prasolova-Forland, 2008) and the complementary concerns of cognitive load and system adaptivity (Scheiter & Gerjets, 2007); (Kalyuga, 2007).

While these and many other studies analyze 3D virtual worlds from the perspective of one discipline or another and offer recommendations about building these worlds from those perspectives, none of these studies have proposed a multidisciplinary method of evaluating the success of a virtual world learning environment (*VWLE*) that considers the complex interactions of context,

interactivity, motivation, presence and cognitive load. Virtual worlds require simultaneous attention to a number of factors to ensure that they are successful and when we add the complications of instructional purposes, the range of considerations expands even further. Consequently, many of the approaches that focus on a single aspect of a virtual world, such as presence or interactivity, gloss over the complexity that these environments require. ***To begin moving instructional designers, trainers, and researchers toward a more complex understanding of assessing these environments, this chapter introduces an assessment rubric for virtual world learning environments built from proven principles of user experience design, instructional design, interface design, learning theory, technical communication, instructional systems design (ISD), and VIE motivation theory.*** We have titled this rubric the "CIMPLe System" since it captures the ways that context, interactivity, motivation, presence, and cognitive load weave together to form a successful virtual world learning environment.

To arrive at the CIMPLe System rubric, the chapter first positions the rubric within the larger, more general context of instructional design theory. As a field, instructional design encompasses the requirements for building successful learning experiences regardless of the medium where those experiences appear. Therefore, we begin the discussion of instructional design by situating our chapter within the ADDIE framework (Gagne, Wager, Golas, Keller, & Russell, 2005)—a generally accepted instructional design method—and specifically within the "design" phase. The chapter then combines this framework with the principles of "user experience design" to demonstrate the three necessary parts of experience: attraction, engagement, and conclusion (Shedroff, 2001). The majority of the chapter develops this framework, offering theoretical principles on what constitutes successful attractions, engagements, and conclusions within a learning context. Within this discussion, engagement—the most sophisticated component of the actual experience—assumes the bulk of the discussion. Finally, after theorizing the nature of a learning experience, we present the fully-developed CIMPLe System, a multidisciplinary rubric for analyzing virtual world learning environments.

BACKGROUND: INSTRUCTIONAL DESIGN

Given all of the benefits that VWLEs can provide, but also given the relative complexity of implementing successful multimodal VWLEs, instructional designers need a complex, multidisciplinary frame that encompasses the entire process of designing an instructional element regardless of the medium (e.g.classroom, online, 3D virtual world). Although there are many instructional design models we could adopt that would meet the complex needs of VWLEs, we situate the CIMPLe System within the ADDIE model (Gagne, Wager, Golas, Keller, & Russell, 2005) because the system is complete, yet not overly complicated. ADDIE orders the elements of instructional design into five stages: analysis, design, development, implementation, and evaluation.

The *analysis stage* consists of activities that determine the context in which the instruction will take place—the pre-existing conditions that must be considered in order to design the most appropriate and effective instructional element. In this stage, the designer determines what needs are driving the creation of the instruction and these needs lead to the delineation of the goals of the instruction, with consideration given to the cognitive, behavioral, and attitudinal changes desired. In addition, designers must determine what prior knowledge and skills the learners will have when they begin the instruction. Finally, designers determine the time available for instruction.

The *design stage* is where the instruction unit is built. This begins with designers determining what learning objectives will address which in-structional goals. From these objectives, a list of topics to cover is made, with an approximation of the time each topic will take. Designers then sequence the topics, with consideration given to the prior knowledge determined during the analysis stage. The topics are fully expanded, and mapped to the original learning objectives and activities are added to reinforce the learning. Finally, points for assessment are inserted, both those that inform the direction and progress of the instruction as well as those that assess the final achievement of the learning objectives.

The *development stage* includes those activities that will refine the instructional element. In this stage the materials are used with a group that represents the target audience. From the information gleaned from this initial use, designers revise the materials. Also in this stage, designers develop any required teacher materials and/or user manuals.

The *implementation stage* occurs when the instructional element is marketed and distributed. The target population is advised of the opportunity and resources are made available for solving any problems or confusions that arise as the instruction proceeds.

Finally, data gathered in the *evaluation stage* are used to fine-tune the instructional element. Evaluators compare the learning outcomes to the goals and objectives of the instructional element and plans are devised for ongoing revision and maintenance.

Understanding all stages of the ADDIE model are important for the quality of the instructional element because any element that is developed without reference to the entire system will likely be far less successful than one that was systematically constructed. While we recognize that following the entire ADDIE model produces the best products, space limitations prevent us from fully exploring how to develop elements for virtual worlds against this model. Instead, as a sort of "quick start," the CIMPLe System presented in this chapter focuses mostly on the design phase of the process, outlining the characteristics of a successful VWLE. Even though the tool primarily focuses on the design phase and using the tool as a heuristic, it can nonetheless inform the development stage and the evaluation stage as a lens through which designers might assess their learning environments after they have been built.

EXPANDING THE VIEW OF THE DESIGN PHASE

As noted above, our chapter focuses on the "design" phase of the process for creating instructional materials because creating an optimal experience can occur only if designers begin with a solid process that is both well-theorized and reproducible. As noted user experience designer Nathan Shedroff argues, "the elements that contribute to superior experiences are knowable and reproducible, which makes them designable" (Shedroff, 2001). Shedroff himself suggests many of these elements (which we'll take up later) but chief among them is the overall structure of the optimal user experience, an experience that progresses from *attraction* to *engagement* to *conclusion*.

Attraction represents the reasons a participant would begin an experience. Sometimes the attraction derives from necessity—we have to go the grocery store in order to buy food or a teacher tells students that they must do an exercise. Preferably, though, attraction is intrinsic, where learners choose to undertake the experience because they are drawn to it by their senses—it sounded interesting—or because they have an intellectual attraction—they wanted to learn about something—or because of an emotional appeal—it looks fun. Regardless of the specific reason for the attraction, each experience must draw learners into the experience, setting the context for how and why learners would want to engage with the experience. Attraction gets learners "in the door," so to speak.

Engagement represents the primary focus of the experience. After learners begin the experience, their interest must be maintained by challenging them in interesting ways, motivating them to continue exploring and solving problems of personal relevance, and providing them with feedback so that they can measure their progress. The engagement must also strike a balance between challenge and reward, taking care not to overload learners with complexity but must provide enough ambiguity to encourage continuing engagement. Finally, the engagement must enable social interaction where learners can reveal their image of "self" to others, learn about others' views of the problems and environment, and build shared meanings with colleagues. Engagement keeps learners "in the house," in other words.

Conclusion represents the moment when learners feel that they have completed the goal. Successful conclusions enable learners to see the experience in a larger context, where the meaning of the experience extends into future experiences as learners look back and learn lessons that they can apply in future settings. Good conclusions also bring closure to an experience, confirming that what the participant set out to learn or accomplish has in fact been learned or accomplished. In Shedroff's terms, the conclusion presents learners with awareness that they have internalized the experience and can now count it as "wisdom" applicable across multiple settings, enabling learners to see themselves as more complex.

Engagement is chief among these components of the successful experience because learners spend the majority of their time with the engagement. The majority of our chapter, therefore, focuses on designing the characteristics of engagement, although our theoretical frame includes attraction and conclusions as well. Figure 1 visually represents the nested theoretical frames operating in our chapter as instructional design and user experience design merge into a single approach for designing virtual world learning environments.

Figure 1. The nested framework of the CIMPLe system

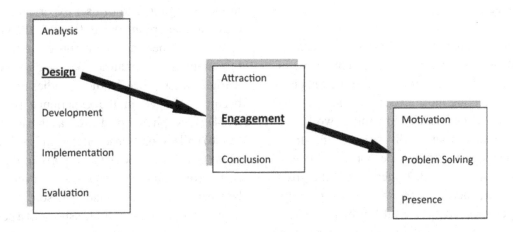

THEORETICAL FRAME FOR THE CIMPLE SYSTEM

As we introduced above, designing a 3-D virtual world learning experience—or really any experience—proceeds from attraction to engagement to conclusion. Each of these categories, though, contains several concerns that instructional designers must recognize as they build a world. These elements of successful design also lead to categories for evaluating the effectiveness of a 3-D virtual world learning environment.In what follows, we discuss the three major stages of an experience—attraction, engagement and conclusion—and within each of these stages outline the multiple concerns that must be considered within that stage. From these concerns, we derive the categories that we compile into the complete evaluation rubric presented later in the chapter.

Attraction: Inspiring Learners to Begin the Experience

Imagine it's about seven p.m. on a spring evening and you and a couple friends are walking down a city street where cafes and restaurants have opened their doors to allow the aromas of their cooking to waft into the street. One particular restaurant catches your attention because the aromas carry spices you can't quite place, and so you glance over the menu posted in the window. You see that the meals are priced reasonably and that the restaurant offers an interesting variety of dishes you've never heard of, let alone eaten. Your group enters, a host seats your group, you order drinks, and then settle in to study the menu more closely. Music, maybe it's Ethiopian, plays in the background as servers weave effortlessly among tables carefully set with small oil lamps and silverware, speaking with smiles to customers in an accent you can't quite identify. Your group agrees on some appetizers and then orders the next time your server comes by your table.

This scenario metaphorically represents what happens in any context where learners are enticed to begin an experience. The learners have a need—they are hungry and need to eat—and following the enticing aromas, they are drawn into a particular experience—the restaurant—where they hope that their needs will be met. The environment of the restaurant also attracts their interest, with its oil lamps and hint of foreign culture. The scenario, then, demonstrates the two key features of an attraction: clear goals and contextual factors.

Clear Goals

In order for people to be attracted to an experience, they must be at least moderately aware of their needs and the experience must present clear steps for meeting those needs. Learners usually have a set of schemas for how things work, and if the initial encounter diverges too far from the schema, learners will be confused at best and frustrated at worst. Either way, if the goals aren't clear, then learners will disengage from the experience. Richard Saul Wurman, "father" of the field of information design, summarizes this idea in *Information Anxiety 2*, arguing that experiences must contain, among other things, a purpose, objectives, core steps, and periodic feedback (Wurman, 2000). In Wurman's terms, *purpose* is the overarching goal, why somebody is doing something, to fulfill hunger in our case. *Objectives* represent the ways people meet that purpose, in this case to eat. The *core steps* present the procedure, the small steps along the way to achieving the objectives, so entering the restaurant, being seated, ordering drinks, studying the menu, and ordering meals in our example. Finally, *feedback* alerts learners whether or not they are doing things correctly (a concept we'll discuss in detail later). Each of these steps represents a match between the learners' goals and the experience's goals: the learners' expectations have been met upon the initial encounter and so they continue with the experience.

Context Factors

However, in addition to the cognitive aspects of attraction where the experience initially meets the learners' goals and needs, the context itself attracts learners. First, as information processing theory teaches us, attractions must surprise us, must present us with something unique or out

of place, something that dazzles us with bright colors and interesting sounds. These are called orienting stimuli (Howes, 1990). Several scholars in the emerging field of user experience design make similar arguments, noting that the visceral level of an experience represents one of the most important aspects of attracting—and retaining— learners' attention as learners' bodies and senses become engaged in the experience (Norman, 2004). This "physio-pleasure," as Patrick Jordan (2000) calls it, or "sensorial design" as Shedroff (2001) calls it, is not just a property of the experience (or product); it represents an interaction between an experience and a person, where the experience engages multiple aspects of a person's body or senses. We build, in other words, this type of physio-pleasure by immersing learners in an environment with fantastic features, things that they wouldn't experience otherwise (Screven, 2000). Referencing our opening scenario, recall that the initial attraction was spices that the group couldn't quite identify and menu items that they hadn't eaten. Upon entering the restaurant, the environment itself pleased the group, with its smiling staff and oil lamps. These aspects contribute to a richness of the environment (Witmer & Singer, 1998) that bears a relationship to reality because the concept of eating at a foreign restaurant is a common schema, yet the experience also presents a certain lack of realism because of the novelty.

In addition to these visceral aspects, information designers frequently talk about the usability of the environment. In other words, the experience must work. If the experience initially promises to meet the needs of learners and draws them in with seductive sensorial input but then fails to deliver on the practical promises that the sensorial design only hinted toward, learners will immediately end the experience, either literally by discontinuing their work within the system, or figuratively by allowing their attention to wander elsewhere. Norman (2004) calls this the "behavioral level" of a product or experience because at this level, learners are concerned with how well a thing works. If, for example, the staff had not been attentive in our scenario, the experience would have failed on practical grounds: the group members are hungry and want to eat and that major objective has not been realized. Additionally, the aspects of an experience must complement each other such that the system has a certain holistic integrity (Prasolova-Forland, 2008). The oil lamps provide "foreign atmosphere" (visceral level) but they also provide light (behavioral level); the wait staff speaks with accents (visceral level) but clearly interacts well in your native language (behavioral). Finally, the experience allows multiple ways to interact, yet constrains those possibilities within a closed system (Gasperini, 2000). In other words, the experience allows the participants multiple opportunities for realizing their goal of eating through the different menu items, yet the menu isn't limitless. Similarly, in a VWLE learners need the opportunity to explore possibilities, but should be limited to only a finite number of possibilities.

Evaluation Rubric Items

Designers of virtual world learning environments must attend carefully to the attractions they build by integrating methods that confirm learners' goals are being met and by constructing a context that maintains interest. Without this clear evidence that the experience and the participant share goals, a learner has no reason to continue the interaction. Why work through a system if the system isn't going to meet your needs? Second, meeting learners' instrumental goals represents just half of the picture because the system must engage learners' bodies and emotions to attract them in the first place. As Norman (2004) writes, "Attractive things work better." And attractive things work better both to attract learners in the first place and to maintain that interest throughout the engagement.

Based on these concepts of attraction, the following rubric items emerge:

- Promises a novel or unique experience
- Experience follows predictable schemas
- Attracts through initial sensorial pleasures
- Technologies and functions operate appropriately
- Presents multiple ways for learners to interact with the environment that correlate with the environment's metaphorical/cognitive scheme.

Engagement: Immersing Learners in the Experience

Learners spend the majority of their time occupied in the actual task of learning, engaged in the experience itself, in other words. After learners have been attracted to an experience, several factors must be present to maintain the learners' interest. *motivation* is foremost among these considerations because learning will not take place if learners feel no need to continue, whether that motivation is extrinsic or intrinsic. Learners must also be engaged with *problem solving* in ways that lead to learning. Without seeing the actual rewards of their activity in terms of increased knowledge—and being made aware through feedback that they are, in fact, learning—learners will direct their attention toward other tasks that they feel are more rewarding. Therefore, learners must be consistently aware of their progress toward learning objectives as they learn but not in such a way that it causes cognitive overload. Finally, successful engagements rely on genuine interaction among learners that constructs a sense of community, even if that community is temporary. This synchronous *presence*, more than any other characteristic, distinguishes learning in 3-D virtual worlds from other virtual learning environments since the presence of avatars makes learners feel like others are "there."

In what follows, we discuss each of these concepts in more detail and present the evaluation rubric items that emerge from each of these three essential areas: motivation, learning and problem solving, and social presence.

Motivation

Learning rarely takes place in the absence of motivation to learn. Motivation is the focus of time and effort toward performing a specific behavior. It is possible for this motivation to be intrinsic—to come from learners' personal interests and goals—but most instructional situations rely on extrinsic motivation, where the characteristics of the instruction entice learners to spend their time and effort on the task. VIE Theory (Green, 1992) provides a powerful theory for conceptualizing the complexities associated with motivation by decomposing motivation into three essential elements: *V*alance, *I*nstrumentality, and *E*xpectancy.

One concern that occurs across all three characteristics of VIE theory is the result learners expect to achieve by performing the activity. The goal can be simple and short-term: if I do this, I expect to feel joy. Alternatively, the goal can be complex and long-term: if I do this, I will be more likely to get a job promotion next year. Learners must be aware of the goals toward which their behavior is directed for motivation to occur. Motivation in learning, therefore, can only be reviewed in reference to a particular goal, whether that goal is extrinsic or intrinsic. This mirrors the concept of optimal experience called "Flow" (Csikszentmihalyi, 1990) in which individuals voluntarily participate in activities that stretch their capacities as they attempt to accomplish something difficult because they believe that activity is worthwhile.

Valance, the first characteristic associated with this type of optimal experience, represents the value associated with the behavior. This value can come from the behavior itself—the activity is fun or interesting by itself—or it can come from the value of the goals associated with the behavior. Valance is additive—the more learners enjoy the situation, the more it piques their interest or satisfies their curiosity, the more goals they associate with the task, and consequently, the higher the overall valance for the behavior will be. Because each individual will perceive the valance of a situation differently based on personal values and interests, designers of virtual world learning environments must provide multiple sources of valence by anticipating what goals individual learners might have, both intrinsic and extrinsic. Without meeting these goals—without providing the necessary conditions for valence—VIE Theory states that there will be no motivation.

Instrumentality represents the strength of a connection learners perceive between the behavior and its associated goal. If learners do not see the utility of the behavior at moving them toward a goal, then there will be no instrumentality. Providing an articulated, written contract delineating the behavior-consequence connection often proves to be a good way to increase the perceived probability that the behavior will lead to the goal. In other words, if learners know upon entering an activity how particular actions lead to particular goals—the rules of the game, so to speak—the learners are more likely to feel a higher sense of instrumentality. Within the conceptualizations of both VIE Theory and Flow, this goal-directed, rule-bound system enables the learners to gather regular feedback on their progress toward the goal which increases the instrumentality present in the experience. Unless a system contains boundaries and unless learners receive commentary upon their progress toward goals within those boundaries, they will not develop a sense that they have made progress toward achieving those goals. Therefore, the concept of instrumentality requires that a VWLE provide opportunities for learners to review their progress at consistent intervals based upon their performance against a set of expectations established by the experience itself. Without these items, instrumentality does not exist and where there is no instrumentality, there will be no motivation.

Expectancy provides the final conceptual thread in VIE theory and measures learners' confidence in their ability to perform a behavior successfully. In order to have this confidence, learners must believe that they possess the knowledge, skills, and resources necessary to perform the behavior. To adopt an example from the concept of Flow, if a certain person believes that they can play tennis well, they are more likely to engage in the activity (Csikszenthihalyi, 1990). However, the tennis player must also feel that the experience challenges their skills, although not too much, so that the experience matches—or perhaps slightly exceeds—their skill level. In this case, the tennis player's game improves as the quality of the competition increases. In terms of a VWLE, learners must believe that they possess skills adequate to cope with the task at hand. Conversely, the tasks must continue to challenge the learners to retain their engagement (we'll discuss more on this topic below in the section on problem solving and cognitive load) and not be so easy to accomplish that learners' confidence levels remain static in spite of accomplishing the goal. Some ways to increase expectancy include building on the learners' past successes on similar tasks, observing others being successful at the task, observing that others believe you can be successful at the task, and receiving constructive feedback on your behavior. Like the other features of VIE Theory, expectancy is a necessary condition for motivation. If learners are not confident that they will eventually succeed in the tasks or behaviors, then there will be no motivation.

The discussion above has hinted at a subtle, but extremely important, component of VIE Theory: its multiplicative nature. If any of the three terms, valence, instrumentality, or expectancy, equals zero then no motivation will be present. One single zero cancels whatever gains might exist in the other terms. However, as the quantity of any of the three items increases, the overall motivation increases. Consequently, having some success in each term becomes necessary for a virtual world learning environment and having great success in any one term creates profound impacts across the entire system.

Based on the elements of motivation discussed here, the following rubric items emerge:

- Provides resources to build learners' confidence with tasks
- Provides feedback to learners' actions
- Checks on learner perceptions of goals as achievable
- Checks that the learner values the goals
- Checks on learner perceptions that the environment provides necessary resources.

Learning and Problem Solving

Learning means storing, or encoding, new information into long-term memory in such a way that learners can retrieve the information for later use. Information Processing Theory (IPT) offers a model that incorporates much of the research about this process of moving information from our experiences to long-term memory. IPT organizes the learning process into a chronological structure that includes sensory input and the sensory registers, attention and perception, working memory, and encoding into long-term memory. This process mirrors the "data to wisdom" transfer where learners first interact with unstructured information known as *data*, then construct some order for that data transforming it into *information*, then relate that information to a context of use transforming it into knowledge. The final step moves knowledge from a single context of use to broader, cross-context understanding where learners view the knowledge in flexible ways that transforms it into *wisdom* since the knowledge has been internalized as a general principle for understanding the world (Shedroff, 2001). Schematically, the transformation looks like this:

Data→Information→Knowledge→Wisdom.

Combining Information Processing Theory (IPT) with the data to wisdom transfer, we begin to see how the process of learning and problem solving works. Specifically, we have five senses (seeing, hearing, touching, smelling, and tasting) that continually pull data into the sensory registers. Although the registers will hold a lot of data, they do so for a very short period of time (a matter of a few seconds, at best), and so the processes of attention and perception are critical to understanding how data continues through the system to become information. Attention represents the stage in the process, then, where we notice specific data in the sensory registers and then begin to organize it into meaningful structures. Attention is a learning bottleneck, because although there are huge amounts of data in the registers, we can attend to only a few pieces at a time as we attempt to transform it into information. Expectations and prior experiences participate in giving meaning to the data at this stage, essentially determining how we process what we are seeing and hearing. Each participant comes to our VWLE, that is, with a unique set of knowledge and experiences, and therefore a potentially different perception of the information there. That is why it is important to test regularly that the VWLE participant is processing their experience in the same way that designers intend. Once perceived, the new information continues to the working memory as it moves from information to knowledge.

In the working memory, learners transform information into knowledge by giving it conscious consideration. We commonly understand this stage as thinking, problem solving, and decision making. The working memory adds to the processing bottleneck because it is a very small space and this small "processing capability"—what the working memory can consider at any one time—is referred to as cognitive load (Sweller, 1988). There are three types of cognitive load (CL): extrinsic, intrinsic, and germane. Extrinsic CL includes information that takes up space in the working memory, but is not necessary for the task at hand. For example, consider a conversation you are having with a person you have just met in which you are hearing several new facts and are trying to determine which facts might be false. *Extrinsic Cl* would be the part of working memory that holds the person's name as you converse with the person. Although their name is held in working memory, it probably is not necessary for solving the prob-

lem of sorting fact from fiction. *Intrinsic Cl*, by comparison, includes all the useful facts and tools that can be used to solve the problem at hand. In the conversation example, intrinsic information would be the facts that have come up during the conversation that you are attempting to sort. In order to complete the task, all of these facts must be held in working memory. Finally, *germane CL* results from actually doing the processing required by the problem. In the conversation example, germane CL would consist of comparing and contrasting the facts from the conversation to uncover the false statement.

These three types of CL vie for working memory space at the same time as learners attempt to transform information into knowledge. Efficient use of working memory requires that potential extrinsic CL be ignored, and intrinsic CL be practiced until it can be stored in long term memory to the point of automaticity (retrievable with little effort), leaving a maximum amount of working memory available for germane CL. In a VWLE, this means that learners need to be trained to ignore potentially useless information such as the complex visual architecture of spaces, and that they need to practice skills like manipulating virtual objects and avatars. Once learners can operate in the environment with little conscious effort, a maximum amount of working memory space can be used for processing relevant information and solving problems.

The final stage of the transformation moves knowledge to wisdom as learners permanently store information in long-term memory—the core of learning. Research tells us much about how to enhance the encoding process (e.g. Baddeley, 1990) and this research leads to specific design strategies for 3-D virtual world learning environments. We know, for example, that when information is presented both visually and verbally, learners are more likely to retain and understand the material. This concept, called "media redundancy" (Markel, 1998), suggests that the visual texture of a VWLE should be supplemented by corollary verbal exercises since the combination enables learning greater than either individual part. Additionally, VWLEs favor problem-based learning where learners engage in real tasks that require manipulating objects and navigating within the environment (Prasolova-Forland, 2008). Many tactics for building problem-based learning into VWLEs come to us from the field of Museology, where researchers have demonstrated the success of these tactics:

- Incorporating leading questions in verbal displays
- Including animated and simulated processes
- Noting contradictions between presentations or objects
- Allowing learners to act on the environment to see cause/effect relationships
- Reporting findings to colleagues (Screven, 2000).

Encoding knowledge as wisdom is also enhanced when learners make meaningful connections to prior knowledge. This elaboration of knowledge enables learners to construct a type of cross-context understanding by building flexible networks of knowledge that bend and morph as new knowledge joins that knowledge already present in long-term memory. This prior knowledge, then, serves as a hook for incoming information because it allows learners to understand the new knowledge in context of existing knowledge. We should attempt, in other words, to see things in the next larger context—to consider a chair in a room, a room in a house, a house on a block—and connecting new knowledge with existing knowledge enables learners to achieve this vision, a state we previously referred to as "wisdom" (Wurman, 2000); (Shedroff, 2001).

The transformation to wisdom, though, is only complete when learners become aware of their own learning. This concept, called metacognitive skill, allows learners to see their own learning in terms of larger contexts and applications, making the learning more meaningful to them. And as we know from VIE Theory, when learners know the learning objectives, and those objectives meet instrumental goals, motivation to learn increases. The increased motivation leads to becoming a more sophisticated learner, which itself increases expectancy—the belief in ability to accomplish tasks. Consequently, knowing how to learn—learning metacognitive skills—empowers learners to regulate their learning and take ownership of the learning tasks. The more metacognitively sophisticated a learner can become, the more they can automate learning and problem solving strategies, leaving more room for germane tasks.

As Information Processing Theory and user experience design show us, learning occurs when learners move information from their experiences to long-term memory. This transformation of data to wisdom enables learners to begin reflecting on learning itself, to build metacognitive skills where they can think about their own thinking in a context larger than the individual experience. We also know that learning is constrained by the concept of cognitive load at each stage of the process and that certain learning strategies, like simulations and reporting to colleagues, enhance the encoding of experiences.

Based on the combination of these theories, the following rubric items emerge:

- Provides supplemental instruction for gaps in prior knowledge
- Makes learners aware of the learning goals
- Organizes information according to a consistent scheme
- Presents context that aids in remembering key information
- Challenges learners through problems or puzzles to solve
- Articulates strategies for learning the information

- Uses modalities (verbal, visual, sound) that do not require simultaneous attention.

Presence

The concept of "presence" represents the key differentiator between 3-D virtual world environments and other types of online environments (Bronack, Cheney, Riedl, & Tashner, 2008). Presence can be compared to the idea of immersion that many researchers have discussed over the last 20 years or so where learners "perceive that they are interacting directly with an [online] environment" (Witmer & Singer, 1998), although VWLEs add the component of people interacting with other people through avatars. Consequently, while the prior descriptions of immersion for web-based virtual environments still pertain, the newer, interactive 3-D environments require a more complex understanding than environments where a single individual interacts with an environment, for example in a flight simulator. Heeter conceptualized this broader definition even before the massive deployment of virtual worlds that we currently experience by proposing that presence within virtual worlds contains three components: environmental presence, personal presence, and social presence. We address each of these in turn below (Heeter, 1992).

Environmental presence relates to the ways that a system enables learners to interact with each other by building those functions into the system components itself (Heeter, 1992). For example, the environment must create opportunities for learners to share their thoughts through chat or voice—to leave traces, that is, of human activity within the system. We can further refine this concept by dividing interactivity into six separate types of functions that include

- *Feedback* where the system or individuals acknowledge that others have initiated action;

- *Control* where the learners are able to act on the environment and leave traces of their actions for others to see;
- *Productivity* where learners can utilize the system and interactions with others to solve real problems;
- *Communications* where the system enables bi-directional communication between individuals and between the system and learners;
- *Adaptively* where the system "learns" on its own about participant needs and changes to better suit those needs (Shedroff, 2001).

Each of these six components contributes to the environmental presence that a VWLE demonstrates and when they combine with compelling metaphors of location (Prasolova-Forland, 2008), learners understand exactly what is possible within the environment.

Research on *personal presence*, the second presence concept, possesses a long history in computer science, human factors and instructional technology (Heeter, 1992). Often thought of as "immersion," personal presence refers to a participant's sense of "being there" in the virtual environment, or the degree to which learners forget that they are interacting with something artificial. In detailed studies of personal presence conducted for the U.S. Army, Witmer and Singer (1998) discovered that four factors contribute to the success of these artificial worlds:

Control factors: or the naturalness of activity within the environment;

Sensory factors: or the environmental richness present through multiple interaction modalities like visual and aural;

Distraction factors: or the degree to which the interface forces itself in front of learners or uses novelty to divert attention from the interface;

Realism factors: or the correspondence between the artificial world and the lived world.

These factors certainly weave closely together with environmental presence components. However, the personal presence components focus on individual learners' sense of being "there" rather than the functionality of the environment. The difference, then, rests on the distinction between form—personal presence—and function—environmental presence.

The third presence factor, *social presence*, represents the key distinguishing feature of 3-D virtual worlds. While most online environments can build environmental and personal presence to lesser or greater degrees, the real sense of sharing an environment with other people in real time is felt most strongly in 3-D VWLEs. Learners feel a significant difference between working synchronously with an avatar that lets learners "see" their collaborators and working synchronously with others through Skype or IM (Bronack, Cheney, Riedl, & Tashner, 2008). The idea that learners can see collaborators causes learners to make a metaphorical jump to the real world where people can only be in one place at a time. In other words, if you're here with me now, then you can't be somewhere else at the same time—you are present with me. In addition to this sense of being able to see those we interact with, avatars enable certain non-verbal cues that approximate physical presence between real people which further strengthens the sense of social presence. For example, avatars enable learners to approximate cues such as gaze, gestures and proximity (Bailenson, 2006). Bronack et. al. (2008) expand on this notion, offering these components of social presence:

Personal space: where avatars' positions indicate their involvement with one another;

Appearance: where the way an avatar is presented reflects, in theory, an aspect of a person's identity (whether real or experimental);

Modeling behavior: where real world nonverbal cues such as eye contact or expressions are purposely used to engage others;

Emotional impact: where avatars can imitate real expressions and articulate feelings beyond simply saying or typing the corresponding emotions.

In all of these cases, the ultimate purpose is to lead learners to feel like they are interacting with other real people rather than just computer-generated "bots." Everybody knows when it's just a bot—like on the telephone voice response systems so common today—even when those bots are good. However, social presence aims to present the real person behind the avatar to other real people represented by avatars in real time because research shows that the more human-like our interactions with computers become, the more engaging learners find those experiences to be (Andre, Rist, & Muller, 1999).

Building environments based on the notion of presence will significantly enhance the outcomes because "the factors that appear to affect presence are known to enhance learning and performance" (Witmer & Singer, 1998). Classroom teachers certainly know that better physical environments, better-structured activities, and genuine interaction all lead to positive learning outcomes. Three-dimensional virtual environments for learning present many of the same opportunities as face-to-face learning when these environments are conceived well.

Based on the discussion of presence in 3-D VWLEs, the following rubric items emerge:

- Uses multiple modalities (verbal, visual, sound)
- Adapts to learner activity
- Employs compelling metaphors to create an environment with fantastic features
- Reflects some correspondence to the real world
- Uses avatars to establish presence of others
- Enables communication in real time
- Allows learners to alter or add to the environment to enhance its meaning

- Enables learners to collaborate
- Enables learners to personalize an avatar.

Summary of Engagement Items

Clearly, the engagement aspect of a 3-D virtual world built for learning should occupy the most time for an evaluator since the learners themselves spend the majority of their time in the actual engagement. Returning to our restaurant metaphor, compare the amount of time that you might spend actually IN a restaurant compared to the amount of time that you might spend ENTERING the restaurant and initiating the dining experience. Attraction certainly bleeds over into engagement, particularly in a well-designed experience, but the engagement components nonetheless comprise the major part of a learning experience. Similarly, the components of the engagement blur into one another as *motivation* factors blend with *learning and problem solving* since learning usually only occurs if people maintain their motivation to learn by remaining challenged but are not overburdened by the *cognitive load* of the challenges. *Presence* factors lean into motivation because as learners begin to feel immersed in an environment by interacting with others and realizing that their actions have an impact on the VWLE, motivation increases. Social presence also leads to effective learning and problem solving because one of the most effective methods of learning—one facilitated particularly well by 3-D virtual worlds—is collaborative work on real problems. Successful engagement in a learning experience, then, becomes circular as *motivation* leads to *learning*, and *problem-based learning* comes from *presence*, but *presence* leads to *motivation*: it's a large interdependent ecology of concerns.

In summary, these three components characterize a successful engagement, the major part of a learning environment:

- Motivation
- Learning and problem solving;
- Presence

CONCLUSION: EXITING THE EXPERIENCE

Let's return for a moment to our restaurant fable. Your group was attracted to the restaurant, was engaged in dining at the restaurant, and now you've had dessert and coffee and have motioned for the server to bring the check. The check arrives, your group pays, rises from the table, and you exit to the street chatting about the good food and how you'd like to come back another time. The experience has concluded.

Conceptually, learning experiences should follow the same pattern. Learners should know when they have accomplished what they set out to learn; they should be able to exit the experience confident with their new knowledge; and they should be able to reflect on their knowledge and its applications for the future. If the conclusion doesn't satisfy learners, the future implications of the experience will be unclear and rather than feeling satisfied or pleased with the experience, learners might feel dissonance or confusion. In either case, as Norman (2003) reminds us, the negative emotions dampen retention. In other words, without a successful conclusion, learning might not have taken place at all.

A conclusion to an experience, therefore, has at least three components that designers must enable.

An announcement of the exit: The end of an experience must be clear to those within it so that learners know that they have just a little time to explore any areas that remain (Siegel, 1997). Learners shouldn't be rushed out, but they should have a limited opportunity to explore things that interest them. Within a VWLE, this means that connections to the "outside" should be clearly marked, either by geographical features such as doors or by instructors (perhaps bots) who are present in the environment. However, because virtual learning environments are often self-directed, the exit should also be a station where learners are questioned about the experience and their learning outcomes because quite possibly the learners wouldn't be aware that they've "seen" everything they need to.

A request for something from the learners: In our restaurant example, we might be tempted to see the check as the request for something and indeed it is. However, the check really serves more as the signal of the ending rather than a request. A more appropriate example would be completing a card to evaluate the dining experience. And in VWLEs we can do exactly the same thing: ask learners to complete assessment tasks to gauge their learning (Screven, 2000). What better way to confirm that learners have, in fact, accomplished their goals than to allow a test or survey or final activity to confirm that the learners have achieved something? As implied above in the discussion of the announcement, the exit serves also as a checkpoint, a spot where learners can confirm that they have accomplished their goals and the goals of the learning activity.

An opportunity to reflect on the experience in a larger context: Metacognition requires that learners become aware of their learning and place that learning into a new, more broadly applicable, schema. Just as your dinner companions reflected on their experience in relationship to other dining experiences, virtual environments should encourage learners to place any particular experience within a larger context of related activities (Wurman, 2000). Recalling our discussion of the data to wisdom transformation, the final transformation occurs only when learners can broadly apply what they've learned in novel contexts. In VWLEs this means that learners should be given opportunities within the system to reflect on their learning, quite possibly leaving "traces" of their learning for others in the future. These traces, then, become part of the environment, enhancing the sense of

presence for future learners while enabling present learners with an opportunity to reflect.

Based on these concepts related to conclusions, the following rubric items emerge:

- Provides feedback to learners' actions
- Enables learners to assess their learning
- Enables learners to reflect
- Enables learners to leave traces of their understanding of their experiences
- Signals the conclusion/exit.

THE COMPLETE EVALUATION RUBRIC

Attraction, Engagement Conclusion: these items represent the key features of an experience and when placed within the ADDIE instructional design frame, we see that designers of 3-D virtual world learning environments must understand not just experience design, not just instructional design, and not just learning theory. Rather, a successful 3-D virtual world for instruction must combine features of all these components. Drawing on the principles that we've outlined so far, we offer below the compiled evaluation rubric for assessing a virtual world learning environment.

The rubric presented below distills the concepts presented above in the more complex theoretical frame into twenty-eight key components. We have dubbed this approach the "CIMPLe System" (pronounced "simple") because we have grouped items according to our fundamental categories: Context, Interactivity, Motivation, Presence, and cognitive Load. The "e" stands for "evaluator." The CIMPLe System arranges the evaluation items in a slightly different order than they are presented above in the theoretical discussion to enable users of the tool to more readily remember the key parts of an effective virtual world learning environment by using the acronym for the key parts—context, interactivity, motivation, presence, and load. Finally, in

Appendix A, we provide a reproducible version of the instrument that individuals can actually use to assess VWLEs.

Context, Interactivity, Motivation, Presenceand Load Evaluator (CIMPLe)

Context: Factors that characterize the "physical" construction and function of the environment:

C1. Attracts through initial sensorial pleasures.

C2. Promises a novel or unique experience

C3. Employs compelling metaphors to create an environment with fantastic features.

C4. Uses multiple modalities (verbal, visual, etc.) that do not require simultaneous attention.

C5. Technologies and functions operate appropriately

C6. Signals the conclusion/exit.

Interactivity: Factors that characterize the ways that learners affect the environment and other learners within the environment:

I1. Presents multiple ways for learners to interact with the environment that are consistent with the environment's scheme.

I2. Enables learners to collaborate.

I3. Challenges learners through problems or puzzles to solve.

I4. Allows learners to alter or add to the environment to enhance its meaning.

I5. Enables learners to leave traces of their understanding of their experiences.

Motivation Factors that impact learners' desire to achieve the goals built into the environment:

M1. Makes learners aware of the learning goals.

M2. Checks that the learner values the goals.

M3. Checks on learner perceptions of goals as achievable.

M4. Checks on learner perceptions that the environment provides necessary resources.

M5. Provides resources to build learners' confidence with tasks.

M6. Provides feedback to learners' actions.

Presence: Factors that give learners a sense of immersion in the environment:

P1. Enables learners to personalize an avatar.

P2. Uses avatars to establish presence of others.

P3. Enables communication in real time.

P4. Adapts to learner activity.

P5. Reflects some correspondence to the real world.

Load: Factors that help the environment strike a balance between cognitive overload and challenging tasks that increase learning:

L1. Organizes information according to a consistent scheme.

L2. Experience follows predictable schemas.

L3. Provides supplemental instruction for gaps in prior knowledge.

L4. Presents context that aids in remembering key information.

L5. Articulates strategies for learning the information.

L6. Enables learners to reflect on their learning.

CONCLUSION

The CIMPLe System presented in this chapter offers an advance in how educators can assess the quality of the virtual world learning environments that they build. Most prior literature on 3D virtual worlds focuses on a single aspect represented in the CIMPLe framework as researchers have discussed, for example, the importance of the context, interactive features, or presence. Instead, the CIMPLe framework combines multiple concerns present in virtual worlds into a single, sophisticated system that demonstrates concerns for the interactions among the various components of a virtual world. In other words, this short tool based on relatively complex theories enables instructional designers to begin thinking holistically about their constructions rather than compartmentalizing the components of a successful virtual world learning environment

The holistic approach to evaluating VWLEs achieved in the CIMPLe System arises from the thoroughly multidisciplinary approach represented in the tool's theoretical backing. Research in user experience design, instructional design, interface design, learning and motivation theory, technical communication—to name the most dominant traditions—combine in the CIMPLe System to present evaluators with a perspective that works across different types of virtual environments. Our concern here has been primarily with 3D worlds, but the CIMPLe System could be used across a variety of virtual learning environments, whether they are three-dimensional or not, because of the system's cross-disciplinary nature.

Finally, one limitation of the approach presented here, of course, is that it cannot measure or suggest content or goals. Instead, the CIMPLe System suggests generic types of activities or categories of features that must be present in a successful virtual world learning environment. For this reason, we want to draw attention, once again, to the importance of positioning the evaluation offered by the CIMPLe System into a larger instructional design framework that includes all five stages of the ADDIE paradigm: analysis, design, development, implementation, and evaluation. The CIMPLe System fits primarily within the "design" phase because at this stage instructional designers can use the rubric as a heuristic for building the type of environment that will succeed. In other words, as they consider what to build into the environment, designers can refer to the CIMPLe System as a sort of best practices checklist to ensure that the environment meets the needs that the cross-disciplinary theory suggests are necessary. What the rubric cannot do, however, is suggest content or learning goals.

That must be left to the individual designer and specific learning situation.

A second limitation arises because the CIMPLe System has only recently been introduced and no research record exists to validate the construct. However, since the CIMPLe System combines components of approaches that other researchers have already validated such as the ADDIE framework, the system has a strong theoretical grounding that we believe will most likely prove valid in future case studies. That is not to suggest that specific items on the rubric might not be modified or that new items won't be added. It is to say, though, that we believe the primary conceptual structure of the system—context, interactivity, motivation, presence, and load—will withstand empirical validation. Indeed, a case study that uses the system for a cohort of teachers designing materials for seventh graders is underway as this chapter goes to press.

Even with these limitations, the CIMPLe System can be used to diagnose usability issues and suggest why an environment might be successful or why it might fail. For example, at the evaluation stage—the final stage of the ADDIE paradigm—designers can determine how successfully the VWLE employs interactive features. Perhaps those interactive features appear but maybe they don't seem to enable learners to grasp the concepts appropriately. The CIMPLe model tells us that we need to have these interactive features and what they should look like in the abstract, so designers can go back and revisit whether or not those interactive features actually are the best ones to achieve the learning goals. The fact that the interactive features must be present doesn't change; the way those features are enacted in the system might need to change. Perhaps future case studies that investigate VWLEs built according to the CIMPLe System will point us toward the most effective ways to implement such features.

We hope that instructional designers will take away some practical guidelines for developing virtual world learning environments from our chapter. The practical guidelines found in the

CIMPLe System evolve from a substantial, cross-disciplinary theoretical approach and we hope that these discussions proved useful for demonstrating the genesis of the CIMPLe System. We also hope that researchers will interrogate the system and that those investigations will combine with feedback from instructional designers so that the CIMPLe System can continue to evolve and be refined into an exceptional tool for assessing virtual worlds designed for instruction.

REFERENCES

Andre, E., Rist, T., & Muller, J. (1999). Employing AI Methods to Control the Behavior of Animated Interface Agents. *Applied Artificial Intellilgence*, (415-48).

Baddeley, A. (1990). *Human Memory: Theory and Practice* (Rev. Ed.). New York: Allyn and Bacon.

Bailenson, J. N. (2006). Transformed Social Interaction in Collaborative Virtual Environments . In Humphreys, L., & Messaris, P. (Eds.), *Digital Media: Transformations in Human Communication* (pp. 255–26). New York: Peter Lang.

Barab, S., Thomas, M., Dodge, T., Carteaux, R., & Tuzun, H. (2005). Making learning fun: Quest Atlantis: A game without guns. *Educational Technology Research and Development*, *53*(1), 86–107. doi:10.1007/BF02504859

Bronack, S. C., Cheney, A. L., Riedl, R. E., & Tashner, J. H. (2008). Designing Virtual Worlds to Facilitate Meaningful Communication. *Technical Communication*, (261-69).

Chittaro, L., & Ranon, R. (2007). Web3-D technologies in learning, education and training: Motivations, issues, opportunities. *Computers & Education*, (49): 3–18. doi:10.1016/j.compedu.2005.06.002

Csikszenthihalyi, M. (1990). *Flow: The Psychology of Optimal Experience*. New York: Harper Perennial.

Dickey, M. D. (2005). Three-dimensional virtual worlds and distance learning: Two case studies of Active Worlds as a medium for distance education. *British Journal of Educational Technology*, *36*(3), 439–451. doi:10.1111/j.1467-8535.2005.00477.x

Gagne, R. M., Wager, W. W., Golas, K. C., Keller, J. M., & Russell, J. D. (2005). *Principles of instructional design* (5th ed.). Belmont, CA: Wadsworth/Thomson Learning.

Gasperini, J. (2000). The Role of Ambiguity in Multimedia Experience . In Jacobson, R. (Ed.), *Information Design* (pp. 301–316). Cambridge, MA: MIT Press.

Green, T. B. (1992). *Performance and MotivationStrategies for Today's Workforce: A Guide to Expectancy Theory Applications*. London: Quorum Books.

Hansen, J. A., & Barnett, M., MaKinster, J. G., & Keating, T. (2004). The impact of three-dimensional computational modeling on student understanding of astronomy concepts: a qualitative analysis. *International Journal of Science Education*, *26*(13), 1555–1575. doi:10.1080/09500690420001673766

Heeter, C. (1992). The Subjective Experience of Presence. In Presence: Teleoperators and Virtual Environments (pp. 262–271). Being There. Presence

Howes, M. (1990). *The Psychology of Human Cognition: Mainstream and Genevan Traditions*. New York: Pergamon Press.

Jones, J. G. (2004). 3-D on-line distributed learning environments: An old concept with a new twist. In R. Ferdig & C. Crawford (Eds.), *Proceedings of the Society for Information Technology and Teacher Education International Conference,* (pp. 507-512), Atlanta, GA.

Jordan, P. W. (2000). *Designing Pleasurable Products*. New York: Taylor and Francis.

Kalyuga, S. (2007). Enhancing Instructional Efficiency of Interactive E-learning Environments: A Cognitive Load Perspective. *Educational Psychology Review*, 387–399. doi:10.1007/s10648-007-9051-6

Ketelhut, D. J., Dede, C., Clarke, J., & Nelson, B. (2006). *A multi-user virtual environment for building higher order inquiry skills in science.* Paper presented at the American Educational Research Association, San Francisco, CA.

Kim, P. (2006). Effects of 3-D virtual reality of plate tectonics on fifth grade students' achievement and attitude toward science. *Interactive Learning Environments*, *14*(1), 25–34. doi:10.1080/10494820600697687

Markel, M. (1998). Testing visual-based modules for teaching writing. *Technical Communication*, (47-76).

Norman, D. A. (2004). *Emotional Design: Why We Love (or hate) Everyday Things*. New York: Basic Books.

Park, S., & Catrambone, R. (2007). Social Facilitation Effects of Virtual Humans. *Human Factors: The Journal of the Human Factors and Ergonomics Society*, 1054-1060.

Prasolova-Forland, E. (2008). Analyzing Place Metaphors in 3D Educational Collaborative Virtual Environments. *Computers in Human Behavior*, 185–204. doi:10.1016/j.chb.2007.01.009

Scheiter, K., & Gerjets, P. (2007). Learner Control in Hypermedia Environments. *Educational Psychology Review*, 285–307. doi:10.1007/s10648-007-9046-3

Screven, C. (2000). Information Design in Informal Settings: Museums and Other Public Spaces . In Jacobson, R. (Ed.), *Information Design* (pp. 131–192). Cambridge, MA: MIT Press.

Shedroff, N. (2001). *Experience Design 1*. Indianapolis, IN: New Riders.

Siegel, D. (1997). *Creating Killer Websites: The Art of Third Generation Site Design*. Indianapolis, IN: Hayden Books.

Sweller, J. (1988). Cognitive load during problem solving: Effects on learning. *Cognitive Science*, 257–285.

Winn, W. (1993). *A conceptual basis for educational applications of virtual reality*. Human Interface Technology Laboratory, University of Washington. Retrieved September 28, 2007, from http://www.hitl.washington.edu/publications/r-93-9/

Witmer, B. G., & Singer, M. J. (1998). Measuring Presence in Virtual Environments: A Presence Questionnaire. *Presence (Cambridge, Mass.)*, 225–240. doi:10.1162/105474698565686

Wurman, R. S. (2000). Information Anxiety 2, (2nd Ed.). Indianapolis, IN: Que.

KEY TERMS AND DEFINITIONS

Virtual World Learning Environments: Electronic learning spaces, usually available through the Internet, that use computers to simulate aspects of the real world with the intention of teaching users some particular topic or content.

Context: The factors that characterize the way a virtual experience operates, including the experience's construction and functionality.

Interactivity: The factors that characterize ways that individuals can affect the environment or other participants within the environment including the opportunity to provide feedback, control the experience, produce something, or have the system adapt to their individual needs.

Motivation: The set of characteristics—valence, instrumentality and expectancy—that helps learners to maintain interest in learning activities, to succeed at learning, and to assess their degree of gain.

Presence: This often refers to the level of immersion that a person feels when the participate in a virtual experience. Presence consists of environmental presence that enables interaction with the system; personal presence that gauges the level of immersion a person feels; and social presence or the degree to which one can interact with others synchronously.

Cognitive Load: The processing capability individuals possess as they consider information in the environment, the relevance of that information, and the application of the information to problems they attempt to solve.

User Experience Design: A method of planning, designing, building, implementing and testing products with a focus on the user's complete experience. The approach is used for computer-based products such as websites, but also for product design of items such as phones.

Attraction: In user experience design, this represents the reasons that a person might begin particular experience. Reasons for undertaking the experience are either intrinsic or evolve from the user's own needs, or extrinsic in which case the user must be meet

Engagement: In user experience design, this represents the major portion of an experience, the thing that a user seeks in the experience. The engagement occupies the bulk of the time a user maintains contact with a particular experience.

Conclusion: In user experience design, the actions that signal the end of the experience or when the end is announced, assess participants' opinions or learning, and provides an opportunity for learners to reflect on the experience.

Data to Wisdom Transfer: This means moving receiving information, processing that information according to its usefulness for solving problems, and ultimately storing that solution in long term memory as a schema for future use in a novel context.

Problem-Based Learning: Experiences that place learners in situations where they have to think through concepts and apply them to solve meaningful problems rather than reciting information from memory.

ENDNOTE

[1] We'd like to express our thanks to the Carolina Virtual Worlds Consortium (CVWC) and the National Science Foundation for supporting the research and instructional activities from which this chapter has evolved.

APPENDIX A: THE CIMPLE SYSTEM FOR REPRODUCTION AND USE

Table 1.Context

	C=Complete	I=In Process	A=Absent
Attracts through initial sensorial pleasures.			
Promises a novel or unique experience.			
Employs compelling metaphors to create an environment with fantastic features.			
Uses multiple modalities (verbal, visual, etc.) that do not require simultaneous attention.			
Technologies and functions operate appropriately.			
Signals the conclusion/exit.			

Table 2. Interactivity

	C=Complete	I=In Process	A=Absent
Presents multiple ways for learners to interact with the environment that are consistent with the environment's scheme.			
Enables learners to collaborate			
Challenges learners through problems or puzzles to solve			
Allows learners to alter or add to the environment to enhance its meaning.			
Enables learners to leave traces of their understanding of their experiences			

Table 3. Motivation

	C=Complete	I=In Process	A=Absent
Makes learners aware of the learning goals.			
Checks that the learner values the goals.			
Checks on learner perceptions of goals as achievable.			
Checks on learner perceptions that the environment provides necessary resources.			
Provides resources to build learners' confidence with tasks.			
Provides feedback to learners' actions.			

Table 4. Presence

	C=Complete	I=In Process	A=Absent
Enables learners to personalize an avatar.			
Uses avatars to establish presence of others.			
Enables learners to communicate in real time.			
Adapts to learner activity.			
Reflects some correspondence to the real world.			

Table 5. Load

	C=Complete	I=In Process	A=Absent
Organizes information according to a consistent scheme.			
Experience follows predictable schemas.			
Provides supplemental instruction for gaps in prior knowledge.			
Presents context that aids in remembering key information.			
Articulates strategies for learning the information.			
Enables learners to reflect on their learning.			

Chapter 10
Developing Digital Literacies in Second Life:
Bringing Second Life to Business Writing Pedagogy and Corporate Training

Dirk Remley
Kent State University, USA

ABSTRACT

The proliferation of virtual environments and their use in business and industry begs the question of where in higher education and corporate training various literacies associated with these digital environments, such as using the technology and critically examining its affordances and constraints in applications, can occur. The author argues that such literacy training can occur in business writing courses as well as in corporate training environments that engage students and trainees in situated learning experiences. This chapter describes an instructional approach that integrates Second Life in a business writing course, which could also be applied in corporate training; and it reports on survey research related to student perceptions of their learning experience with that pedagogy. The discussion also includes how the instruction can be implemented in a corporate training environment to give employees experience using and critiquing business applications in Second Life. Generally, students perceive that Second Life is appropriate to include in business writing pedagogy because it is relevant to their career development as more companies use it in their operations. Implications of this study include identifying activities to help train students with virtual environments that they may experience in workplaces after graduation and offering activities that can be used by corporate trainers to help those already in workplaces develop these situated digital literacies.

INTRODUCTION

Video games have proliferated throughout popular culture, as pre-teens and teens adapt to new video technologies. Educators have adopted a fresh perspective on pedagogy that integrates students' familiarity with video game technologies. People in their twenties and thirties also have become gamers outside and within workplace settings. A number of companies are using video game technologies in

DOI: 10.4018/978-1-61520-691-3.ch010

training new employees or training employees for new tasks. James Gee (2007) observes that airlines and the United States' military uses simulators to train pilots, and Newitz (2006) acknowledges that American Express and Intel are using Second Life for training as well. With these technologies and their proliferation in workplace settings comes the need for new, digital literacy skills. Graduating college students who are entering the job market need to have these digital literacy skills in order for them to be able to be productive on the job in using and evaluating business applications of virtual environments.

Lankshear and Knobel (2005) assess the dimensions of digital literacy and ways for educators to become "digitally literate insiders" that are able to assess the many forms of this new literacy and the socio-cultural impact of the practice of particular digital literacies within learning environments. This literacy also extends to workplace environments that integrate virtual applications. To Lankshear and Knobel, digital literacy in its various dimensions is best represented or considered "as a shorthand for the myriad social practices and conceptions of engaging in meaning making mediated by texts that are produced, received distributed, exchanged etc., via digital codification" (p.9). Researchers and educators revise their assumptions about the forms and delivery of a text as they study and try to understand how, within multiple digital literacies, "the ways skills and techniques are acquired and become practiced and fluent within the context to participating in the social practices of a digital literacy" (p.21). This understanding can help educators and trainers develop classroom and training pedagogies that optimize learning of digital literacy skills.

Among the new literacies included in this scope are 3-D gaming and non-gaming environments. Second Life is an example of non-gaming 3-D environments. Gee (2007) acknowledges thirty six principles of learning and literacy that gaming environments facilitate. These include situated group learning and engagement with multiple

modalities of communication. He also suggests that such learning can be part of what Peter Senge (2006) calls the "learning organization," encouraging continuous learning and innovation. In the 21st century economy, Senge argues the need for employees to develop five particular disciplinary talents: self-awareness, mental mapping abilities, group learning, systems thinking and shared vision. All of these disciplines are entailed within learning environments that engage virtual environments such as Second Life.

The need for these new literacies and disciplines begs the questions, "Where can these new literacies and disciplinary skills be developed within academic and workplace programs, and how?" In this chapter, I argue that such digital literacy instruction can occur within writing pedagogy in higher education and with contextualized, situated training projects within business and industry. Further, I offer a description of a certain teaching approach that integrates these principles associated with virtual environments and findings of survey research associated with this approach. I describe two particular activities: The collaborative report assignment on which I report is an example of a problem-based learning activity, while the interview activity is an example of situated practice. Then I report on results of empirical research I conducted on students' perceptions of their learning experience with these activities.

BACKGROUND

While the term "business writing" tends to generate images of documents that integrate tables and charts, letters and memos, several studies call attention to the increasingly multimodal nature of writing (Selfe, 2004; Kress and Van Leeuwen, 2001; New London Group, 1996; Witte, 1992). Increasingly, writing is defined beyond the traditional perception of print-linguistic, text-based forms of composition; forms of representation occur through audio, embodied practices, and visio-spatial elements. So, writing coursework in higher education is taking on development of skills associated with these forms of representation. Writing instruction occurs in higher education, and it also occurs in corporate settings. According to Applebaum (2008), companies "spend billions of dollars on writing instruction each year"(v). This instruction involves learning not only basic mechanical skills but also use of various forms of representation to optimize communication, including digitally mediated communication. Virtual environments engage all of these forms of representation as people interact on islands in Second Life, mixing visual, audio and print-linguistic text communication.

Kinneavy (1986) and Vygotsky (1978) encourage the use of realistic situations to help students learn the kinds of activities they may experience in their life. Kinneavy encourages instruction to assimilate as closely as possible realistic situations so that learners can learn how to perform in similar, real situations. Providing situated learning applications encourages trainees and students to think about the process they used to arrive at a given outcome and to evaluate toward improving performance in the future. Further, Arnheim (1969) argues that the much meaning-making occurs through the use of visuals cues in the world around us. The closer a learning activity comes to giving us practice with a situation that we may encounter in reality the more it facilitates situated learning; we are able to apply what we learned in that experience to actual, real problems much more readily because there is an immediate connection between the learning experience and reality.

The kind of learning espoused by Kinneavy, Gee and Vygotsky has come to be known as problem-based learning (PBL) in educational settings, and it is also referred to as a simulation in education and corporate settings. An individual or a group is given a problematic scenario and tasked with resolving that situation. Chodos, Naeimi and Stroulia (2009) describe it thusly,

The term simulation-based training refers to a collection of training methods, all of which aim at bridging the gap between classroom knowledge and actual practice, by placing the learner in realistic situations in the context of which he/she has to bring to bear his/her knowledge (of facts, tasks and procedures, and collaboration strategies) to solve a problem. (5)

By experiencing the processes of addressing the problem and challenges associated with identifying potential resolutions, learners come to understand through practice how they can do certain tasks within real settings. Educators and trainers have increased their use of virtual environments for learning experiences and simulations. Chodos, Naeimi and Stroulia state that, "recent developments in software, multiplayer games, the internet and virtual reality have created richer, more life-like learning experiences for more learners" (4).

Finally, studies document the enhanced learning that one experiences in group environments (Vygotsky, 1978; and Inhelder and Piaget, 1958). There is a synergistic effect when we are part of a group environment; the participants share their unique perspectives to enhance ways that we perceive a given situation and solutions to a problem that we cannot consider as well on our own. Problem-based or simulation-based learning experiences that occur in group settings provide opportunities for participants to engage in team-based development that is part of the learning organization (Senge, 2006).

Such instruction can occur not only in higher education settings but also in corporate training. Zimmer (2006) acknowledges that Thompson Netg offers training on its own island in Second Life. Many companies have developed training islands in Second Life. These include IBM and Cisco, too. Such development indicates corporate interest in using the environment for training purposes; however, trainees need to understand the interface before they can learn a given task in that environment (Gee, 2007 and 2009). AHG's Website reports benefits of using simulations in Second Life for training:

Perhaps the most important and strongest feature of Second Life is the ability to create training simulations. They can target both "soft skills" (teamwork, leadership, sales, etc.), and technical skills (equipment training, technical support and others). Simulations can be used by a group of participants from different locations. Moreover, participants can later review their actions step by step, critique their actions and learn from their mistakes.

AHG reports that a single simulation experience can include participants from multiple sites as well.

In addition to simulations, companies are using Second Life to facilitate interviewing and recruitment. New graduates, consequently, need to be able to understand how to use Second Life tools to participate effectively in an interview. Athevaley (2007) reports that, "on Second Life, job seekers who are less tech-savvy are finding they can wind up shooting themselves in their virtual feet. When they start, some people have a hard time designing and controlling their avatars"(parag. 4). Engaging students in interview simulations in Second Life while they are upperclassmen can help them prepare for the job market.

Lankshear and Knobel call for research in New Literacies in educational settings (p. 45). They state that such research should include descriptive, analytic and critical accounts of new literacies. Descriptive research describes practices, while analytic research offers a tool by which to analyze the literacies associated with the technology, and critical research encourages reflective evaluation of new literacies in "efficacious learning" (pp. 45-48). The pedagogy detailed here is an attempt at all three forms of research: It encourages examination of actual practices associated with SL, it presents data related to student perceptions of their learning relative to survey research as well as reflections of those students. This research is relevant to understanding ways to address the multi-modal pedagogies emerging today toward preparing college students for workplace composing literacies. Much professional writing occurs in collaborative settings, and some organizations are using virtual reality systems to facilitate group meetings.

THE PEDAGOGY

In this section I describe some preliminary activities that the instructor used to orient students to SL, as well as learning goals for the collaborative report assignment and the interviewing activity associated with the SL-pedagogy. The pedagogy includes three different phases of Second Life involvement: orientation, long-term situated immersion and short-term contextualized practice. The next three sections detail each phase.

Introduction to SL and SL Projects

As the instructor, I acknowledged that two projects—one an assignment and the other an activity—would be involved in the course. I conveyed that the purpose of the assignment was to engage students in a form of critical study of technology that they may be asked to use or consider using in a workplace. This critical study would entail research in world and externally, in the form of readings about SL and its applications. I positioned myself as one who is acquainted with SL and has an understanding of a number of applications, but who is SL-neutral relative to its potential uses in business and industry.

First Application Exposure

Because SL was a new technology, I gave students an initial viewing of SL. I logged into SL and manipulated my avatar around a single island.

Students saw the interface and I narrated as I manipulated my avatar to walk, run, sit and make various gestures. Students also viewed a student-created machinima video.

Readings

I also provided students with readings about how companies use SL in operations; the list of articles describing this use continues to grow. This information was to help students see potential uses, and to help them understand the relevance of Second Life in their education. When students understand that potential employers are using a certain technology, they are more attentive to learning its nuances.

Orientation

As the collaborative report assignment approached, I showed students how to access the SL account site and create an account. Upon receiving account activation notice, students went to an orientation island and performed the tasks associated with orientation. I provided a week of class time (three hours) to this orientation experience. In the first semester, Second Life facilitated an 'orientation island' experience that engaged new users in specific tasks that helped them understand how to manipulate their avatar and how to move about islands and communicate with others. This experience was less structured in the second semester. In each semester, I helped some students who had difficulty with some tasks, and I asked students to practice certain tasks in particular. These included chatting and moving about an island. Once students completed the initial orientation, they were allowed access to and directed to a single island. I then showed students how to create a landmark at a given island and how to teleport to other islands.

SL Collaborative Report Assignment

Shortly after these activities, I introduced students to an assignment in which they would address a particular manufacturing company's consideration of using SL in its operations. Students developed their own groupings of three to five (3-5) students each. In most cases students paired up with others and then grouped between those pairings on their own, while in other cases the instructor placed students in pairs and groups. The most common group size was four (4), with two 3-person groups and one 5-person group involved. The assignment is detailed in Remley (2010); but, generally, the scenario involves a technology-related company considering using SL for various operations. Different groups were assigned different tasks to consider: Using SL for employee or retailer training, using SL for marketing functions like retailer communications and advertising, and developing a business plan for a certain product. The genres included feasibility analysis and proposals as well as business plans.

I provided students with some reading materials regarding how companies are using SL for different operations and also how some companies are abandoning SL after experimenting with it. I compiled these from Web sources and cited them. I acknowledged, further, that students would be expected to pursue additional research of similar sources in addition to 'field trips' to different islands to see how companies have developed their islands and how they are using them. Such observation challenges students to consider rhetoric of space. Students may address questions such as: How are buildings positioned? What size are they? How does their position and size affect navigation around the island? How do they (position and size) affect the visitor's general experience of the island? Were any avatars representing employees present, and if so, how did they represent the company?

The amount of information available for this research differed from one semester of the study to the next (more articles about how companies use SL were available to student in the second semester of the study, and there were more islands for those students to visit), but the nature of it is consistent across time.

I pointed out that many companies use SL, but that many that have experimented with it have since reduced their involvement or abandoned it entirely. Students understood that the purpose of the assignment was to consider the affordances and constraints of SL for certain business functions, and to give students experience in collaborative writing associated with a particular kind of document and that would assimilate a real setting.

Interviewing Activity

After a lecture about preparing job application materials and preparing for interviews, I paired students up randomly, and they returned to the institution's island in SL to engage in a first interview experience there. Students learned that job fairs occur in SL and some employers conduct interviews in SL. The stated goal of this activity was to give students experience in communicating electronically in a specific task associated with acquiring a job. While SL accommodates audio, the classroom facilities used did not have this equipment; so, students had to rely on their Instant Messaging (IMing)/texting skills.

I encouraged students to consider their dress as well as the positioning of their avatar relative to people involved in the interview. Such consideration challenges students to observe physical rhetorical attributes of the experience. Even though interlocutors are IMing or texting each other, when a physical presence exists, one must also consider nonverbal attributes such as the positioning of the interlocutors as well as gestures.

SL EMPIRICAL STUDY

Method

Research in instructional practices often uses designs that involve classroom experiments and students' reactions to that experience (Barnett, 1991; Barger-Anderson, Domaracki, Kearney-Vakulick, and Kubina, 2004; and Lang, 2009). Barger-Anderson et al observe that "single-case experimental designs are becoming more popular and acceptable ways to conduct classroom-based research. Single-case designs can also be beneficial when conducting literacy research" (217). Such studies are beneficial because they may be replicable and show causal relationships; though, they are not without validity issues. As I describe the method I used for this research, I will call attention to certain items that could affect results.

With Institutional Review Board approval, I invited students in five sections of a junior-level business writing course to participate in a study of students' reactions to the aforementioned pedagogy that integrated SL into it. The course is required of all students majoring in a College of Business Administration program. Each section of the class is capped at twenty (20) students. Students received course credit for participating.

While all students in each of the sections involved would do work with SL as part of the coursework, those who volunteered to participate would submit additional materials that those who did not participate did not submit; and I, as the researcher, would have access to certain work that these participants did as part of the course activities and assignments for this research. The additional work consisted of the completion of a questionnaire and submission of a reflective essay. A total of seventy-five (75) students participated in the study. Table 1 lists demographic information about these seventy-five students.

Most students fell within the traditional college-age range of 18-22, had considerable computer experience including gaming, and al-

Table 1. Demographic information

Variable	Highest frequency (percentage)	Second Highest frequency (percentage)
Age (yrs)	18-22 (78.7%)	23-27 (18.7%)
Gender	Male (62.7%)	Female (37.3%)
Previous Computer Experience	All listed (68%)	Primary (text-production tools such as word-processing, email, IM, and discussion board) and gaming (21.3%)
Previous SL experience	None (94.7%)	Less than one month (2.7%)

most none had any experience with Second Life prior to enrolling in the class. This is important to consider, because it means that, in spite of their general experience with gaming, this course represented their first exposure to this particular environment.

I conducted this research during a two semester period, with two sections of students involved in the first semester of the study and three sections involved in the second semester. Though the study involves two different semesters, I tried to present consistent information about Second Life as well as the research project and assignments across time. This attempted to reduce the effect that time would have on the validity of the study results.

Students who enrolled in the particular sections did so not knowing that they would be using Second Life or that they would be asked to participate in a research study. While the sampling represents a convenience sampling, I attempted to include attributes of a randomized sample by ensuring that different class time periods were represented as well. The five sections involved include classes that occurred at different times of the day: One section started at 7:45am, two began at 11am, one began at 1:10pm, and another began at 2:15pm.

Empirical Analysis Tools

Near the end of the semester, I gave participating students a questionnaire (Appendix A). I tabulated survey responses in SPSS version 12.0, and performing descriptive as well as inferential statistical

tests there as well. Of descriptive statistics, the frequency of responses is reported here. Responses are of nominal or interval scale. For measures of association between variables, Chi Square is the primary two-way measure used for nominal data, and ANOVA is used for tests of associations between interval data (Likert items). The Likert items were coded as 1=strongly agree-5=strongly disagree for all Likert-related questions. One way ANOVA is used to measure associations between nominal and interval data (Dinov, 2007). Eta^2 values are included as measures of effect size. To ascertain any time-related dynamics, the semester in which the student took the course was coded and included in the analysis.

Further, while most of the questions in the questionnaire were closed-ended, two were open-ended. As students provided new responses to the open-ended questions each was coded numerically and with a verbal categorical descriptor. As certain responses assimilated existing categories, those were collapsed into the existing categories. For the most liked attribute question (question 33): categories that emerged were: 1) it was neat to experience new media, 2) it was fun generally, 3) it seemed relevant to my potential career. The categories describing the least liked item (question 34) the categories that emerged were: 1) lack of relevance, 2) technical problems/crashes, 3) took too long to do things, 4) I don't like gaming, 5) too hard, 6) there wasn't enough time provided to do things, 7) economics associated with it (costs money to be able to buy or build), 8) few people use it, and 9) I prefer face-to-face communication.

Table 2. Frequency of likert item responses (n=75)

Variable	Strongly agree Or Agree	Neither Agree nor Disagree	Disagree or Strongly Disagree
Learning objectives were clear	61.3%	25.3%	13.4%
Good order	76%	18.7%	5.3%
Enough time	82.7%	8%	9.3%
Appropriate activities	69.3%	18.7%	12%
Career relevance	57.3%	28%	14.6%
Relation to writing	28%	32%	40%
Would use SL or collaborative writing	37.3%	28	34.7%

Comments like, "It was difficult to navigate from island to island," or "it was difficult to maneuver my avatar," were coded with "too hard"

Additionally, participating students composed a reflective essay in which they responded to certain prompts (Appendix C) which acted as a heuristic to facilitate reflection and response. The frequency of certain comments was coded and is reported here.

RESULTS

Survey

While the survey asked questions regarding several different attributes of the students' experience with SL, including their use of specific communication tools available, I report only those that address their reaction to the pedagogy itself here.

Several variables were measured relative to their frequency of occurrence and potential associations between variables. A breakdown of the frequency distribution is provided in Table 2:

Generally, students perceived that the objectives were clear, the activities were presented in a good order, they were given enough time to do each activity, and the activities were appropriate. However, students perceived that including SL as a pedagogical tool in a business writing course had little relation to writing. Perceptions of using SL to facilitate collaborative writing generally were mixed.

Also, the top three frequencies for "most interesting activity," "most beneficial activity," "what I liked most about using SL," and "what I liked least about using SL" are presented in Table 3:

Generally, students found the collaborative writing and interviewing activities most interesting and beneficial. That they were able to use the

Table 3. Frequency of categorical variables

Variable	Most Interesting Activity	Most Beneficial Activity	Like Most about SL in class	Like Least about SL in class
Highest frequency (%)	Collaborative Writing Assignment (45.3%)	Collaborative Writing Assignment (52.7%)	New Media (52.8%)	Too Hard (29.4%)
Second Highest Frequency (%)	Interviewing (38.7%)	Interviewing (28%)	Fun (27.8%)	Technical Problems (25%)
Third Highest Frequency (%)	Orientation (14.7%)	Orientation (13.3%)	Relevant (19.4%)	Relevance (20.6%)

new media environment of SL in class was what most liked about the experience. Students also liked that it was a fun experience and it seemed relevant to what they would do in their career. Students perceived SL to be difficult to maneuver/use, but they also articulated frustration with the technical support issues associated with using SL. That almost as many liked using it because of its perceived relevance as those who disliked it for its perceived irrelevance begs explanation. Analysis of the student reflective essays will shed some light on this relationship. Some perceived that using SL was irrelevant, though most of these, based on the reflective essays, attached this irrelevance to its use in business operations more than to its use in the business writing course.

A one-way analysis of variance found significant differences at the .05 level among the means of the following variables: Gaming attitude and found SL interesting (F(4, 70)= .900, p=.003; Eta^2=.198); Clear learning objectives and activities were appropriate (F(4, 70)=9.563, p=.000; Eta^2=.353); Clear learning objectives and relevance to career (F(4, 70)=5.137; p=.001; Eta^2=.227); Clear learning objectives and relation to writing (F(4, 70)=2.73; p=.036; Eta^2=.135); and Semester and liked least (F(9, 67)= .44, p=.020; Eta^2=.275). Descriptive statistics for these are in Appendix B.

Relative to the association between "Gaming attitude" and "found SL interesting," the results suggest that the more favorable one's attitude toward gaming, the more one found SL interesting. Also, the more favorable one's attitude toward gaming, the more likely one is to think that the activities were appropriate. It also appears that the more students understood the learning objectives, the more likely they were to perceive that the activities were appropriate, SL's relevance to their career, and its inclusion in a writing class. Also, it is evident that the association between "Semester" and "like-least" shows that the students who took the course in the study's first semester, wherein the course was conducted mostly in a classroom

that was less able to support the SL software, were more greatly affected by the technical difficulties (12 out of 27 responses); while more students who took it in the second semester of the study, wherein the course was conducted in the classroom that could better support the software, identified difficulty with the environment (too hard)-- (15 out of 41) or its perceived lack of relevance (11 out of 41).

Finally, there were no significant associations for semester and any other variable analyzed; these include: gaming attitude, most interesting/least interesting activity, like most, activities appropriate, enough time, good order, relation to writing, career relevance. There were no significant associations for any other variables measured. This suggests independence among a great majority of the different variables. One may conclude that students' perceptions of these other variables were not influenced by any other attribute.

Reflections

Students articulated a variety of positions in the reflective essay. The prompt for the essay is available in Appendix C, but generally, students were asked to consider their experience and comment about what they thought was most interesting and least interesting about using SL in a business writing class. Students were asked if they thought it was appropriate to use SL in a writing class and if they responded to that item, to describe what they thought was appropriate kinds of items to discuss in a business writing class (content).

Some students, like this student, expressed satisfaction with SL's inclusion in a business writing course given that digital media are very much a part of today's business world, indicating its relevance:

...In a business writing class I expected to continuously write memos, professional emails and resumes; so that we would become more familiar with the language and formats. With today's younger population always being online and on the phone, text messaging and IMing, I think everyone should have to take a class like this. Everyone going into the business should have the basic knowledge of how to set up a memo, proposal and cover letter/ resume.

After spending a semester learning about the Second Life network, I feel that it was a good idea to discuss and learn about it in the classroom. Learning this in a business class was a very smart idea, being that it could be potentially used in a business setting; for conferences, interviews, networking with new/ prospective employers and/ or even networking with others in the same and different careers.

My experience with Second Life was a very positive one. It was entertaining and informative. Second Life is not only a game it is the place where business can sell their goods and services to its residents. I got to learn about the new technologies that companies are using, while seeing how they operate on a day-to-basis. Anyone could teleport to a companies island, if it wasn't locked, and go to an information area and find out about companies, inquire information or even mingle with employees or other who are also interested. I got to experience this when I was one of Nissan's islands.

Working on the collaborative report with my group really taught me a lot about the social network and how elaborate SL really is: millions of residents are in the SL businesses can use this virtual world as a new business opportunity. By selling their products and also they can test or promote such as brand marketing, holding events, training and simulations. In SL there are some manufactures and brands such as Microsoft, Adidas and much more. These businesses were not specially founded for SL but they involved themselves into this virtual world.

From the survey, it was clear that some students perceived that SL was irrelevant to a business writing course and/or to their career. Most of these, based on the reflective essays, attached this irrelevance to its use in business operations more than to its use in the business writing course. However, those who indicated its irrelevance to a business writing course also indicated what they felt would be appropriate content for a business writing course. Its perceived irrelevance in both the course and career is represented most vividly by this student:

...The purpose of a business writing course is to teach students how to write effective, correctly constructed business documents. This seems to indicate that a curriculum which focuses directly on writing would be more appropriate as a means of instructing students on the contents of the course. By utilizing a textbook which provides instructions on how to properly format and write various business documents and assigning students to produce their own versions of these documents as homework, the course material may be thoroughly and effectively taught. It seems logical that business writing courses would primarily focus on writing business documents that are widely used in business and professional settings.

Second Life does not play an integral part in the business and professional writing of a majority of the professional business institutions. Currently, only a minority of businesses utilize the program, and those that have implemented Second Life employ it as more of a PR and Marketing strategy than a means of conducting actual day-to-day business. Organizations are far from moving to a model in which a majority of their business operations are conducted wholly in the virtual world. Second Life is primarily an entertainment-based program; it does not have adequate security to allow for sensitive information to be safely communicated through the program. It is very useful for creating media buzz, but the likelihood that it will be viewed as a legitimate alternative to real-world operations is doubtful—virtual activities are much slower, more cumbersome, and less detailed than real world operations. It is not an efficient means of doing things. If many people jump on the Second Life bandwagon, the companies who got on Second Life first may profit—and PR buzz is certainly beneficial, however, it is difficult to take seriously a program that is so similar to gaming and sports nudity clubs and adult entertainment centers which sell various types of phalluses and male genitals.

As with others who acknowledged a similar perception, the student argues that a business writing course should develop writing skills, which are traditionally represented in standard kinds of business-related documents, and that integrating SL into the course detracted from that goal. The only assignment that integrated SL involved using it to facilitate a scenario from which groups researched information about and generated an analysis of its potential use in business operations that they presented in formal types of documents found in business settings—feasibility studies, proposals and business plans.

Other students, though, expressed a middle ground between irrelevance and relevance, suggesting more focus on what they perceive to be more relevant forms of business writing, such as resume-writing:

...The implementation of SL within the course material is a good idea. This allows students to see what current businesses are doing within the program and also allows an in depth study of a business source. Potential employers may be advertising, meeting, or conducting other activities within SL. Taking a look at these will allow students to get a better understanding of the current industries. The amount of time spent on this research should probably be reduced. I felt as though the main focus throughout this course was SL. There are other areas which needed more attention, such as resume writing.

Overall, my Second Life experience proved to be positive. There is a great deal of opportunity presented with the use of this source. I would recommend exploring the virtual world to many incoming business students. This will provide a better understanding of some actual businesses and some of their goals and everyday activities.

Of the interviewing activity, one student wrote,

The most interesting thing we did in Second Life for me was the interviewing process. I found it helpful to hold the mock interviews because one day there is a good possibility that instead of going to a job interview you will conduct it through Second Life. I do not know if I would feel comfortable being interviewed in Second Life if I did not know anything about it or how it worked. This was a positive experience for me because I felt that I could possibly use the interview skills again.

However, the same student acknowledged that she was not excited about SL as a useful technology. The student states,

For a lot of people Second Life may be too technologically advanced and intimidating. Although I felt the interview process taught me useful information the rest of the time I felt like I was not doing much. I do not think that in a business situation I would be able to achieve my greatest potential through a virtual reality.

These reflections convey how students perceive SL as a pedagogical tool within this particular business writing pedagogy. From the survey results and these essays it is clear that most students found SL to be useful in the course; while some struggled with various attributes of it, ranging from maneuvering with and through it to not understanding its relevance to a business writing course. However, those who struggled with its inclusion in the business writing course have a certain perception of what ought to be included in such a course; these notions are traditional notions of business writing.

Student Reports

The learning goals, as stated above, include engaging students in analyses of affordances and constraints of the SL environment. These analyses are expressed in the reports students prepared in response to the collaborative writing assignment.

The reports generated by the groups provide evidence of digital literacy development through the application of critical thinking skills and the actual presentation of the analysis. This evidence comes in the analysis of affordances and constraints of SL for use within this context that groups report. Those groups that report on SL's feasibility consider how SL can help the company accomplish a given task, while also deliberating on how it may limit the ability to do other tasks. Groups that include island designs consider the rhetorical uses of space within SL as afforded and constrained by the technology. Groups tasked with developing a business plan or proposal must consider how affordances overcome certain constraints. Through the experience, participants come to understand that SL can or cannot be used for a specific business context.

While most groups reported potential uses, they did so with the integration of potential drawbacks to implementing SL in the given situation. Evidence of analyses based on island visits is shown with this passage from a student report on the potential for using SL for training and customer service (pseudonyms are used for the company names).

...X-Team is among one of the companies researched for examples of effective training and customer service programs that EFG can learn from. X-Team is a subsidiary of the Y Company that assist customers by offering various computer-

related services and accessories for residential commercial clients. Their island on Second Life provides a number of services that could be used to assist customers in the installation process. The island is frequented by customer service representatives who are on call via a paging station. Downloadable text files and videos also provide customers with assistance and advice. "Tunnels" facilitate navigation throughout the island and allow customers to quickly travel to various locations. There is also a recruitment station located within the island for prospective employees to get information about working for the X-Team. All of these ideas could be used on an EFG island to assist customers with the installation of audgets.

Firm is one of the most well known and respected technology firms in the world. Firm's Second Life Island contains many concepts that could be employed on an island created by EFG to assist customers with installation. Upon entrance to the island users are greeted by a schedule detailing the day's events. A bulletin board provides links to Firm websites explaining installation and use of their products and another bulletin board provides an area where users can post thoughts and ideas relating to Firm. Games are set up throughout the island providing customers with troubleshooting tips. There are classes dealing with the efficient use of Firm products and services are taught throughout the day by Firm employees. Users can view videos that instruct on how to use Firm products more efficiently. Firm's Second Life Island contains many ideas that can be utilized by EFG in the creation of a Second Life island.

This group further considers potential uses of SL for EFG's specific situation (see Appendix D for excerpted portion of the report).

IMPLICATIONS

Education

Working in groups, participants in this pedagogy are exposed to a variety of perspectives that enhance the overall learning experience. Applying any digital literacy skills they had prior to using SL and sharing those skills with others in the group, participants learn additional digital literacy skills within the particular virtual environment. This group experience, combined with a situated, contextualized project also enables learners to apply creative skills and prior knowledge to addressing a given practical situation.

Participants' perceived skill development is evidenced in the survey and reflective essay, and their actual skill development is evidenced in the reports they generate and their reflection in the way they present information. Further, writing courses are charged, generally, with teaching students rhetorical skills in addition to literacy skills. Training that involves rhetorical analysis can also facilitate rhetorical education. Among the rhetorical skills developed within this design are an understanding of the rhetoric of space and body.

As students visit different islands they observe how buildings and other objects are positioned around the island and relative to each other. If several buildings are positioned close together, it may discourage exploration around the island and make accessing information challenging generally because such positioning makes maneuvering difficult. Kress and Van Leeuwen have observed that the easier it is to navigate a website, the better the site experience becomes for the user; the same philosophy can apply to use of space on islands in SL. The easier it is for one to move about a given island, the more inviting the island may appear.

In terms of applying this understanding to practice; as one designs an island, she must consider how the user will perceive the experience. Kress

(2004) acknowledges that the reading experience will affect how a digitally constructed composition, like an island, is designed. A company can think about the kind of experience it wants a user to have on its island and design the space according to that desired effect.

In face-to-face (f2f) interviews, participants read each other's gestures and body positioning to perceive non-verbal elements of communication. Within computer-mediated communication, however, the gestural/nonverbal focus tends to be on the use of emoticons to reflect one's paralinguistic effects. Within SL, because there is a combination of CMC and body, one might position himself a certain way relative to others while expressing a message textually. The body position and/or gestures associated with the message may confuse the receiver or the receiver may come to understand that the sender is not considering his own physical attributes associated with the message.

Because SL facilitates a combination of CMC and f2f paralinguistic dynamics, interlocutors must be more sensitive to how they use their avatar within certain communication settings such as an interview, where certain behaviors may be read certain ways. Jeff Barr (2006) has observed that professional presentations that integrate SL require presenters to be able to synchronize gestures with textual messages. Barr suggested developing a short list of gestures that can be easily called upon. While the audio capabilities of SL reduce the challenge for this synchronicity, presenters still must know how to engage their avatar's gestures with any verbal communication.

An item that needs to be mentioned, though should be commonplace by now in terms of digital literacies, is the inconvenience associated with crashes or technology-related downtime. The pedagogy reported here was initiated in a classroom facility that could not support Second Life software without crashing after approximately ten minutes of use. The classes were moved to another classroom that could support the software better. However, Linden Labs updates the software periodically, and this can cause some downtime as well. On more than one occasion, when SL activities were planned, the class could not login to SL because of updating problems. When planning SL-related activities, one should be aware of the support needed to be able to run SL and of any scheduled software updates.

Finally, an issue that presently exists in writing scholarship is the debate concerning definitions of "writing." Many in other disciplines perceive that writing instruction ought to revolve around improving students' mechanical skills—spelling, grammar and punctuation; and showing students how to format a professional document; what writing scholars consider to be "traditional" or "formalistic" definitions. Writing scholars have moved to definitions of writing that include new media forms of composing, including creating Web pages, audio and visual products that integrate interactive or dynamic, moving features. The debate of what writing instruction ought to include is evidenced here as well. While the pedagogy integrates a number of activities espoused in pedagogical scholarship of writing studies, forty percent of the students surveyed saw no relationship between the activities and writing, and at least three students articulated this lack of relationship in their reflective essay. The confused perception of what constitutes writing and what ought to be included in a writing course is evidenced with the frequency breakdown for "relationship to writing" wherein the mean response was just a little to the disagree side of "neither agree or disagree" ("strongly agree'=1, "strongly disagree"=5, "neither agree nor disagree"=3; and mean frequency = 3.16).

Corporate Training

Corporate trainers can integrate several of the elements from this instructional approach, including the orientation and group report writing activities. Again, the instruction shows learners how to maneuver their avatar and navigate from island to island in Second Life. This instruction and practice encourages learners to visit islands and tour them to see what designs and objects other companies use and how they make products and services available to visitors and facilitate purchases. As participants practice orientation activities, they come to develop a form of digital literacy—how to use a given tool functionally.

The report project encourages learners to assess as a team what a given company can and cannot do with Second Life, facilitating immediate application in a corporate setting. A company that already has a presence in Second Life can apply a real situation they are experiencing toward solving a problem. A company not yet in Second Life can use it to pursue assessment of how it might use Second Life to facilitate purchase of product and/or services. One team might consider developing a Second Life business plan for certain products or services, while another team might research the viability of using Second Life for customer service or business-to-business communications.

As noted above, there are certain technology-related requirements built into the use of Second Life; so, companies can also use the activity to assess costs and potential benefits associated with establishing a Second Life presence.

CONCLUSION

When students and trainees engage in situated problem-based projects they can acquire particular skills required in today's global economic environment. Virtual environments like Second Life engage visual literacy dynamics and encourage learners to practice those literacies within social environments in which it is practiced regularly as well as develop skills associated with workplace-specific practices.

While some students perceived the use of SL in a business writing course to be inappropriate, most felt that it was appropriate and a valuable experience to helping them understand one form of new media that they may encounter in the workplace. As long as students are shown how companies use SL through readings or island visits, they can be motivated to learn more about it and practice it. Even though almost none of the students had ever experienced SL before enrolling in the class, most found the experience valuable and were able to critically assess its use in a particular business situation.

This study focused on student perceptions of their learning with SL as a pedagogical tool. Future studies in the use of digital environments within pedagogy and training should examine how certain technologies facilitate or constrain certain kinds of learning relative to actual performance. Also, studies can examine how access to technology and technological support affect pedagogy and training with certain technologies. As I mention above, there was limited support for audio capabilities available in SL; so, students were not able to use that tool. Yet the availability of audio tools—microphones and speakers—may make using gesturing abilities of SL easier; students would not need to try to coordinate, synchronize what they say with a gesture.

Nota bene: The development of the pedagogy and the study reported here were supported through funding from the Moulton Scholarship program at Kent State University.

REFERENCES

Applebaum, J. (2008). *10 Steps to Successful Business Writing*. Alexandria, VA: ASTD Press.

Athavaley, A. (2007). A job interview you don't have to show up for: Microsoft, Verizon, others use virtual worlds to recruit: dressing avatars for success. *Wall Street Journal*. Retrieved May 7, 2009 from http://online.wsj.com/article/SB118229876637841321.html

Barger-Anderson, R., Domaracki, J. W., Kearney-Vakulick, N., & Kubina, R. M. Jr. (2004). Multiple baseline designs: The use of a single-case experimental design in literacy research. *Reading Improvement, 41*, 217–226.

Barnett, R. H. (1991). Bringing realism to the classroom: an experimental design project for a lecture setting. *Frontiers in Education Conference, 1991, Twenty-First Annual Conference, 'Engineering Education in a New World Order,' Proceedings*, September 21-24, (pp. 639-641).

Barr, J. (2006). *Amazon Web Services Presentation In Second Life*. Retrieved September 6, 2007 from http://www.jeff-barr.com/?p=571

Becker, L. A. (1999, October 5). *Crosstabs: Measures for nominal data*. Retrieved April 22, 2008 from http://web.uccs.edu/lbecker/SPSS/ctabs1.htm

Carter, M. (2007). Ways of knowing, doing and writing in the disciplines. *College Composition and Communication, 58*, 385–418.

Chodos, D., Naeimi, P., & Stroulia, E. (2009, April). An integrated framework for simulation-based training on video and in a virtual world. *Journal of Virtual Worlds Research, 2*(1).

Dickey, M. D. (2005). Brave New (Interactive) Worlds: A Review of the Design Affordances and Constraints of Two 3D Virtual Worlds as Interactive Learning Environments. *Interactive Learning Environments, 13*, 121–137. doi:10.1080/10494820500173714

Dinov, I. (2007). *Choosing the right test*. Retrieved December 4, 2008, from http://www.socr.ucla.edu/Applets.dir/ChoiceOfTest.html

Fogg, B. J. (2003). *Persuasive technology: Using computers to change what we think and do*. Amsterdam: Morgan Kaufmann Publishers.

Gee, J. P. (2007). *What Video Games Have to Teach Us about Learning and Literacy*. New York: Palgrave.

Gee, J. P. (2009, April). Games, learning, and 21st century survival skills. *Journal of Virtual Worlds Research, 2*(1).

Inc, A. H. G. (2008). *Second Life Training Simulations*. Retrieved May 7, 2009 from http://second-life-e-learning.ahg.com/second_life_training_simulations.htm

Inhelder, B., & Piaget, J. (1958). *The Growth of Logical Thinking from Childhood to Adolescence*. New York: Basic Books. doi:10.1037/10034-000

Kinneavy, J. L. (1986). Kairos: A neglected concept in classical rhetoric. In Stephenson, H. (Ed.), *Forecasting opportunity: Kairos, production and writing*. Lanham, MD: UP of America.

Kress, G. (2004). *Literacy in the New Media Age*. London: Routledge.

Kress, G., & Van Leeuwen, T. (2001). *Multimodal Discourse: The Modes and Media of contemporary communication*. New York: Hodder Arnold.

Lang, J. M. (2009). When published research on teaching doesn't help you, why not use your own classroom as a laboratory? *Chronicle of Higher Education (March)*. Retrieved May 7, 2009 from http://chronicle.com/jobs/news/2009/03/2009033101c.htm

Lankshear, C., & Knobel, M. (2005). *Digital literacies: policy, pedagogy and research considerations for education*. Paper presented at Opening Plenary Address: ITU Conference, Oslo, Norway, October 20, 2005. Retrieved from http://www.geocities.com/c.lankshear/Oslo.pdf

Lanshear, C., & Knobel, M. (2004). *New Literacies: Changing Knowledge and Classroom Learning*. Berkshire, UK: Open University Press.

Malaby, T. M. (2007). Contriving constraints: The gameness of Second Life and the persistence of scarcity. *Innovations: Technology, Governance, Globalization, 2*(3), 62–67. doi:10.1162/itgg.2007.2.3.62

New London Group. (1996). A pedagogy of multiliteracies: Designing social futures. *Harvard Educational Review, 66*, 60–92.

Newitz, A. (2007). Your Second Life is Ready. *Popsci.com*. Retrieved May 6, 2009 from http://www.popsci.com/scitech/article/2006-09/your-second-life-ready

Norman, D. A. (2002). *The design of everyday things*. New York: Basic Books.

Remley, D. (2010). *Second Life literacies: Critiquing writing technologies of Second Life*. Computers and Composition Online.

Selfe, C. (2004). Toward a new media text: Taking up the challenges of visual literacy. In Wysocki, A. F., Johnson-Eilola, J., Selfe, C., & Sirc, G. (Eds.), *Writing New Media: Theory and Applications for Expanding the Teaching of Composition* (pp. 67–110). Logan, UT: Utah State Press.

Senge, P. (2006). *The Fifth Discipline*. New York: Doubleday.

Witte, S. P. (1992). Context, text, intertext: Toward a constructivist semiotic of writing. *Written Communication, 9*, 237–308. doi:10.1177/0741088392009002003

Zimmer, L. (2006). Thomson NetG Second Life Corporate Training Campus. *Business Communicators of Second Life*. Retrieved May 6, 2009 from http://freshtakes.typepad.com/sl_communicators/2006/09/thomson_netg_se.html

KEY TERMS AND DEFINITIONS

Affordances: As applied to technology, any activities or tasks that the particular tool enables a user to perform relative to the technology's capabilities or the user's perception of the tool's capabilities.

Computer-Supported Collaborative Writing: any writing activity that includes multiple authors working toward composing a text using computer applications, ranging from word processors to e-mail and online collaboration tools like wikis, in their writing process.

Constraints: As applied to technology, any activities or tasks a tool does not permit a user to perform, whether it be a perceived limitation or actual limitation.

Digital Literacy: The ability to read, compose and critique compositions that integrate digital forms of media.

Multi-Modal: integrating more than one mode of representation from amongst this general list: print-linguistic text, audio, visuals, gestural

New Media: any media that integrate digital forms of representation, such as audio, images and print-linguistic text Online.

Problem-Based Learning: learning activities that simulate real situations, giving learners the opportunity to experience problem-solving and decision-making in a particular context.

APPENDIX A

Questionnaire (learning-related questions provided)

Writing in Second Life

Student Feedback

Course: 30063

Please respond to the following questions as accurately as you perceive.

I) Demographic Information

1) Gender: F M

2) Age: 18-22 23-27 28-32 33-37 over 37

3) I am taking this class to satisfy (please mark one):

a. An LER requirement

b. A major requirement

c. A minor requirement

d. An elective requirement

e. Other

4) Previous writing experiences with computers (mark all that you have used):

a. Word processing

b. E-mail

c. IM

d. Discussion board/list servs

e. Database

f. Spreadsheet

g. Gaming

5) Experience with Second Life prior to this class

a. None

b. Less than 1 month

c. Between 1 and 2 months

d. More than 2 months

6) Describe any experiences with Second Life you had prior to this class.

II) Attitudes towards gaming (please mark response that most accurately or closely reflects your perception)

7) I enjoy playing computer games

a. Strongly agree

b. Agree

c. Neither agree nor disagree

d. Disagree

e. Strongly disagree

8) I am able to learn computer applications fairly easily

a. Strongly agree

b. Agree

c. Neither agree nor disagree

d. Disagree

e. Strongly disagree

9) I found Second Life to be an interesting learning environment

a. Strongly agree

b. Agree

c. Neither agree nor disagree

d. Disagree

e. Strongly disagree

III)Perception of Learning in Second Life

10) The learning objectives of each activity in Second Life were clear to me:

a. Strongly agree

b. Agree

c. Neither agree nor disagree

d. Disagree

e. Strongly disagree

11) I think the order in which we did activities facilitated learning in the Second Life environment:

a. Strongly agree

b. Agree

c. Neither agree nor disagree

d. Disagree

e. Strongly disagree

12) I think we had enough time with each application/activity in order to learn a given task.

a. Strongly agree

b. Agree

c. Neither agree nor disagree

d. Disagree

e. Strongly disagree

13) The activities we did were appropriate for this course's general expectations

a. Strongly agree

b. Agree

c. Neither agree nor disagree

d. Disagree

e. Strongly disagree

14) I understand how what I learned in Second Life within the expectations of this course could benefit me in my career.

a. Strongly agree

b. Agree

c. Neither agree nor disagree

d. Disagree

e. Strongly disagree

15) I learned a lot about professional writing applications in my experience with Second Life in this course:

a. Strongly agree

b. Agree

c. Neither agree nor disagree

d. Disagree

e. Strongly disagree

16) What do you feel was the most interesting activity?

a. Orientation

b. Collaborative writing

c. Presentation

d. Interviewing

IV) Perceptions of effect of using Second Life for specific activities on learning

17) Which activity do you feel most benefited you?

a) Orientation

b) Collaborative writing

c) Presentation

d) Interviewing

18) Which activity do you feel least benefited you?

a) Orientation

b) Collaborative writing

c) Presentation

d) Interviewing

VII) General reaction to using Second Life in a Business Writing course

32) What did you like most, generally, about your experience in Second Life?

33) What did you like least about your experience with Second Life?

Appendix B

Descriptive Statistics

Table B-1. Gaming attitude and found SL interesting

gamingattitude		Slinteresting
strongly agree	Mean	2.2667
	N	15
Agree	Mean	2.7391
	N	23
NA/D	Mean	2.1500
	N	20
disagree	Mean	2.8333
	N	12
strongly disagree	Mean	3.8000
	N	5
Total	Mean	2.5733
	N	75

Table B-2. Clear learning objectives and other variables

learningobjectsclear		activitesappropriate	careerrelevance	relationtowriting
strongly agree	Mean	1.5000	3.0000	3.5000
	N	4	4	4
	Std. Deviation	1.00000	1.41421	1.00000
Agree	Mean	2.1429	2.3810	2.9524
	N	42	42	42
	Std. Deviation	.75131	.79487	1.03482
NA/D	Mean	2.5789	2.4737	3.1579
	N	19	19	19
	Std. Deviation	.76853	.96427	.89834
Disagree	Mean	2.1429	2.5714	3.5714
	N	7	7	7
	Std. Deviation	.69007	.78680	.78680
strongly disagree	Mean	4.6667	4.6667	4.6667
	N	3	3	3
	Std. Deviation	.57735	.57735	.57735
Total	Mean	2.3200	2.5467	3.1600
	N	75	75	75
	Std. Deviation	.91769	.96273	1.01396

Table B-3. Semester and liked least

Semester	Mean	N
sp08	3.2963	27
fall08	4.0732	41
Total	3.7647	68

Appendix C

Reflective Writing Prompts

If you are participating in the SL research study, please write a 2-3 page essay reflecting on your learning experience with the Second Life applications: These applications included orientation, the collaborative report and the interviewing activity.

This essay is NOT graded; I will use it to understand students' learning experiences with Second Life in business writing classes.

Please submit the essay as an attachment to this 'assignment'.

Among some things to think about as you reflect on your learning with SL:

1) What did you understand the purpose of our use of SL in a business writing class to be (that is, why do you think we used it in a business writing class)?

2) What do you think is appropriate content for a business writing class (what kinds of things should students learn in a business writing class)?

3) What positive experiences did you have with the activities in terms of learning how companies use it in business communications?

4) What are some negative learning experiences you had with the activities?

5) What technological issues affected your experience (e.g.: crashes; slow connection)?

6) Do you perceive including SL in business writing classes to be of value? Why, why not?

7) Would you have wanted to use it in more/fewer activities/assignments in class?

8) In what activities would you think it would be useful for learning business writing, if any?

You do not need to respond to all of these items, but use this list to guide what kinds of information you might include.

Appendix D

Excerpted Student report

Ideas for EFG's Island Development

Avatars will travel to EFG Island for many reasons. Many will seek guidance and assistance in the installation process of audgets. One tool that EFG will employ to assist newly arriving avatars is a 3-D interactive map indicating the avatar's location. This map will give avatars a better idea of what's located on the island and how to travel there... Avatars scan map keys and find their destination by connecting a number with its assigned location. The main source of transit will be a system of tunnels that allow avatars to "fly" to their destination. A 3-D map may be somewhat difficult to construct, but the benefits received by customers outweigh the time and money spent to build it. These devices will allow avatars to efficiently navigate the island…

EFG Island will also provide numerous text and video files that assist in the audget installation process. A text file containing common questions and answers regarding the installation of audgets will be available for download to avatars as well as an installation manual available for download. Instructional videos detailing the installation process will also be on hand for viewing and downloading on EFG Island. Text files will assist customers in resolving common installation difficulties, and video files will provide a visual step-by-step guide through the installation process. These files will not assist customers with more complex problems installing audgets. This creates a need for on-island customer service representatives. Customer service avatars/representatives will be on hand to support customers experiencing more complex issues regarding the installation process. While it may prove difficult to find employees that are qualified enough to assist customers in the installation process, an on-island hiring station will assist in the recruitment/interview process for prospective customer service avatars. Issues of increased costs may arise but improved customer service will in turn lead to higher customer satisfaction and more returning business.

Customers will be able to exchange opinions and advice with one another through the use of an interactive bulletin board. This will present EFG Island with a medium in which customers can assist each other without relying on customer service representatives. This will help to limit customer service costs and will allow EFG to monitor and detect frequent problems that customers are experiencing. Negative feedback should be looked upon as constructive criticism for EFG. While some customers may post erroneous information on the bulletin board, a monitoring system will be in place to detect and eliminate such postings.

Chapter 11
Facilitating a Hierarchy of Engagement:
Corporate Education in Virtual Worlds

Paul R. Messinger
University of Alberta, Canada

Xin Ge
University of Northern British Columbia, Canada

Glenn E. Mayhew
Aoyama Gakuin University, Japan

Run Niu
Webster University, USA

Eleni Stroulia
University of Alberta, Canada

ABSTRACT

Virtual worlds, where many people can interact simultaneously within the same three-dimensional environment, are productive enabling environments for corporate education. In this chapter, the authors propose a hierarchy of four types of educational engagement, at successively deeper levels of interaction. The authors then show that virtual worlds can be useful platforms for distance corporate education because they can be used to promote engagement at all four levels of the proposed hierarchy. By linking their hierarchy with existing learning theories, they argue that the effectiveness of corporate education can be successfully carried out by using virtual worlds. They also provide an overview of the historical development of virtual worlds, the development of distance education, and a description of technological, institutional, and research challenges needed to be met for distance corporate education to realize its potential.

DOI: 10.4018/978-1-61520-619-3.ch011

INTRODUCTION

Virtual worlds open up fruitful applications in distance corporate education because they promote multifaceted forms of distance interaction between the instructor and students and among students. The rich and diverse forms of personal and group interactions supported by virtual worlds go beyond one-way and two-way communication, prevalent in instructional videos or facilitated by videoconferencing, to also promote education co-creation and community building.

In this chapter, we propose a hierarchy of engagement in education consisting of four elements, and we discuss how virtualization technologies and virtual worlds provide a space in which distance corporate education can promote education at all four levels of this hierarchy. Section 2 of this chapter provides a background on the development of virtual environments, the history of distance learning, and relevant theories of education. Section 3 develops our proposed hierarchy of engagement and describes how virtual worlds enable engagement at all levels in this hierarchy. Section 4 addresses educational topics that are pertinent to virtual worlds education, including the influence of avatar mediation on learning and communication behavior (from a student's perspective) and instructional issues arising in these worlds (from an instructor's perspective). Section 5 concludes by indicating future technological, institutional, and research issues that will need to be resolved as we continue to leverage virtualization technologies and virtual worlds for corporate education.

BACKGROUND

We begin with a brief background about the emergence of virtual environments, the history of distance learning and corporate training, and a review of education theories related to distance learning.

Emergence of Virtual Environments. Virtual worlds represent a blending of two generations of gaming elements, developed over the past 35 years, with online social networking features. Understanding this progression provides perspective on virtualization functionalities that can be applied for education.

The first generation of video games dates back to the earliest coin-operated video games (e.g., *PONG* in 1972) which added real-time video interactivity to elements of earlier strategic or thematic role-playing games. Such interactivity enhanced reflexes and provided excitement. In 1986, video games were brought into the home with console system technology, such as the Nintendo Entertainment System released across the U.S. (previously released as Famicom in Japan), featuring popular characters like Mario, Donkey Kong, Zelda, and Popeye (Herman et al., 2008). Many of these games were initially for a single player, but multiplayer console system games followed, first with the *MIDI Maze* for the Atari ST in 1987. In these games, players compete or fight against each other (modern forms, such as the Nintendo Wii system, include dynamic user interfaces for various physical games and electronic sports). Similar games subsequently came to be run from LAN (Local Area Network) systems, which permitted everyone's characters on the system to interact with each other. For example, in *Maze War*, a "first-person shooter" game first developed by high school students in a program sponsored by NASA's Ames Research Center, users were represented as eyeballs hunting each other through a maze using only lines to give perspective to the 3D graphics. It was developed into a networked version (via serial cable) when one of the creators went on to college at MIT, and later was playable over the ARPAnet, the precursor to the Internet (see Jansz & Martens, 2005, for related LAN games). Subsequently, *Neverwinter Nights* and *Dungeons and Dragons* were introduced by America Online in 1991, which were early multiplayer games with a graphical user interface (GUI) for the personal computer. A key element of all games in this generation was that players operated characters that interacted with other characters or with the environment in the game, and this element is carried into virtual worlds and has an important impact on the potentialities of the medium for education.

A second generation of video games can be linked with the emergence of the personal computer and Internet technology (after Tim Berners Lee of CERN made his World Wide Web software available for free download in 1992). Releases of the PlayStation 2 and Microsoft Xbox offered gamers the ability to connect to the Internet and play against and talk with other gamers. This completely redefined what types of games would be popular in the home. With a network of users able to join in on a game, the landscape of video games became much more expansive, not only geographically, but also in terms of the nature of the social interaction they enabled. A few particularly important developments in Internet-based multiplayer games were *Quake*, a 1996 game that was the first in which players could exchange their own creations, *Grand Theft Auto*, the first to allow players to explore a world instead of moving through it in a linear fashion, and *The Sims*, a PC game later available for online play in which most of the content was user-created. Finally, *World of Warcraft* demonstrates how quickly a massively multiplayer online role-playing game (MMORPG) can grow, having gained over 11.5 million active users as of December 2008 since its beta release in March 2004 (Blizzard Entertainment, 2008; Murray, 2005). According to mmorpgchart.com, there were over 16 million active MMORPG subscriptions at the end of 2008. In this generation of games, remote access by many players, user generation and exchange of content (in some games, with well-defined currency and exchange systems), and flexibility and independence of movement (and even of user objectives) became standard – these are features that are shared with

virtual worlds and influence the latter's application for education.

Although not gaming, *per se*, social networking sites have also influenced the development of virtual worlds. Beginning with SixDegrees.com in 1997, social networking sites such as MySpace and Facebook have proliferated quickly (see Boyd & Ellison, 2007 for an overview). In addition, shared video materials have been facilitated by YouTube. The primary elements required for social networking are some sort of (asynchronous or synchronous) communication mechanism (e.g., comment boards, chat, instant messages, blogs or live voice chat) and the ability to identify who is speaking (e.g., user names that are permanently assigned). Given the ability to communicate, networks of participants naturally arose. Social networking sites also added two more common elements: the ability to create a user profile with information about oneself that is accessible to other users, and a "friend list" that allows the definition of a set of users that one trusts and with whom one wants to remain in contact. Those on the friend list are often given access to more information, the ability to know each other's online status, notices of updated profile information, etc. Social networking sites exist for those who share a common interest or hobby, geographical location or other demographic attribute (e.g., sites created specifically for children or teens), or for professional networking. One study of college students in 2006 found Facebook to be tied with beer for popularity and second only to the iPod (FOX News, 2006). Mobile phone handset manufacturers, seeing the growth of social networking site access from handsets (15% of the 25 million U.S. users of smart phones use them to access social networking sights almost every day) are adding social networking site access capabilities to phones that lack normal smart-phone features in an attempt to bring in more mainstream customers. Overall, virtual worlds have come to include many of these social networking features, particularly various similar communication mechanisms (e.g., chat, text messaging, live voice chat), user profile information and news, and lists of friends (and interest group memberships) that constitute extensive networks.

Virtual worlds have grown to incorporate many elements first introduced in video gaming and social networking. Although virtual worlds vary greatly in purpose, type or location of world, users, interaction patterns, and business models, they share a number of the above-described elements: (1) people represent themselves with avatars, (2) people are free to move about and act as they please, and (3) people communicate and exchange content in various ways.

First, the most basic element of virtual worlds is that the users are represented by customizable 3D anthropomorphic digital representations of themselves, called avatars. The term "avatar" derives from the Sanskrit word "avatara," which means "incarnation," and in the context of virtual worlds, the term denotes a graphical object corresponding to the user's virtual body in the world.[1] Users can generally choose the avatar's sex, basic shape, hair, etc., with very detailed customization possible in many of the worlds. They can dress the avatar in clothing that they choose. In many worlds the avatar does not even need to be human: it can be an animal, mythical creature, cloud of mist, point of light, or anything else imaginable, but the large majority of users in most worlds use human-looking avatars. The incredible freedom to very effectively project almost any image of oneself to the world is an important part of the popularity of virtual worlds. This image may reflect the user's real life appearance, personality, etc. or it can be something entirely different. The key is that the representation is rich and meaningful. And the more engaging the setting and believable the characters, the more meaningful the user's interaction is with a particular world.

Second, a key element in most virtual worlds is the ability to explore and move within the world. Avatars can generally walk or run, and in some worlds they can even fly. Vehicles may be available, or – the ultimate convenience – avatars can teleport from one place to another place. The experience of interaction in the virtual world can also be heightened as avatars gain the ability to interact with objects. These objects can be anything, including animal and plant life, structures, and vehicles. Objects and avatars can be scripted to move in certain ways, with some worlds allowing programmed movement that can be quite subtle and life-like. Several worlds also employ sophisticated physics engines, which consist of software that replicate gravity, etc. Scripted movement can also be interactive, animations being chosen from a heads-up display (HUD) on the screen, for example. The content can be supplied by professional content creators or can be developed by the users themselves, possibly in collaboration with others. In many worlds, the content can be bought and sold in a virtual economy, complete with an in-world monetary system, that may be tightly controlled by the company running the virtual world or that may be quite open with anyone able to convert in-world currency for U.S. dollars (and by extensions, Euros, Yen, etc.).

Third, in-world collaboration, of course, would not be possible without communication and exchange. As suggested by virtual worlds' roots in social networking, interaction with others is absolutely essential. Text communication is common, and some worlds allow for voice communication. Generally, either public or private conversations are possible. The one extremely important element of communication missing in most worlds is "body language," those elements of meaning that we take from being able to actually see the person as he or she talks. As mentioned above, avatars can be scripted to move in lifelike ways, so that communication within the world becomes much more than just text or even voice chat. Still, this does not have all of the richness of the actual human body language, but enhanced gesturing enabled by new sensor applications is becoming more possible.

Overall, virtual worlds are playing an increasingly important role in the lives of many people (Messinger et al., 2008). According to one estimate, 20 to 30 million people regularly participated in virtual worlds in 2006, spending an average of almost twenty-two hours per week within these spaces (Balkin & Noveck, 2006). A market research company goes on to suggest that "by the end of 2011, 80 percent of active Internet users (and Fortune 500 enterprises) will have a 'second life'" (i.e., an avatar or presence in a virtual community like Second Life; Gartner, 2007). Some authors even suggest that virtual worlds will become as important to companies in five years as the Web is now (Driver et al., 2008). For those who participate in them, the names of these worlds are household words, including (adult worlds such as) Second Life, World of Warcraft, Kaneva, Entropia Universe; (children's worlds such as) Webkinz, Neopets, Club Penguin, Habbo, Whyville, TyGirlz, and RuneScape; (community-specific worlds such as) Cyworld, HiPiHi; (media-focused worlds such as) vSide; (and educational worlds such as) ActiveWorlds, there.com, and Forterra Systems. Indeed, virtual worlds are believed to have implications that go beyond how we play, to also include how we work and learn (Balkin & Noveck, 2006; Bartle, 2006); and many activities in virtual worlds are growing in the realms of education and culture.

Concerning education, well over 150 universities now have a presence in Second Life, and a number of universities conduct classes and other educational activities (Graves, 2008). Business, public organizations, and cultural groups are using the environment for conferencing, public meetings, delivering informational services, performances, and exhibits. Given this burgeoning activity, it is timely for us to understand the implications of virtual worlds and virtualization technologies for distance corporate education.

Distance Learning and Corporate Education. In order to put into perspective the potentialities of virtual worlds for corporate education, we begin by providing background about distance learning and its relationship with corporate education.

Distance learning can be traced to the mid 1800's in Europe (Moore, 1990). In the U.S., it was advocated by a Boston-based group, "The Society to Encourage Studies at Home," founded in 1873 by Anna Eliot Ticknor. The concept was popular and the society had gained about 10,000 students within its first 24 years (Watkins, 1991). Academic degrees for students completing the required correspondence courses were first offered by Chautauqua College of Liberal Arts (1883-1891, as authorized by the state of New York).

As distance learning grew, institutions worked to better meet the needs of their students. Faculty traveled to hold classes off campus (Moore, 1990). As technology for both live distance connections (e.g., telephones, television) and recording (e.g., audiotape, videotape) developed, it was incorporated into distance education (Meyer, 2002). In the 1980s, satellite telecommunications became popular for broadcasting lectures to off-campus locations. Microwave-based interactive video emerged in the late 1980s and was later replaced by land-based technologies (Chaney, 2004). The broad adoption of personal computers and the subsequent development of the World Wide Web, however, have taken interactive educational technology to a new level. Institutions of higher education offering distance education courses increased from 33 percent in fall 1995 to 44 percent in academic year 1997-98 (the statistics from this point come from Meyer 2002). Among public institutions, the numbers were even higher, with distance education courses offered by 72 percent of two-year and 79 percent of four-year institutions. The same period saw a doubling in the number of degree or certificate programs (860 to 1520), courses (25,730 to 52,270), and enrollment (753,640 to 1.6 million). By 1997-98, 60 percent of institutions used the Internet for distance education. What would have earlier required dedicated communication lines and very expensive specialized equipment, generally set up in dedicated distance learning or teleconferencing facilities, can currently be accomplished with much less expensive software and hardware. Indeed, for small groups or for personal video chat, all that one needs are video chat software, available for free from many social networking sites, and an inexpensive webcam and headset.

Overall, there are five characteristics of distance learning (also known as correspondence study, home study, independent study, external study, distance instruction, distance teaching, distance education, etc.) pointed out by Keegan (1996): (a) the learner is in a remote location relative to the teacher, (b) an educational organization influences the planning and preparation of materials and provides support services, (c) course content is provided in technical media – print, audio, video, or computer – that coordinate the activities of the teacher and learner, (d) two-way communication is available so that the student may benefit from or even initiate dialogue, and (e) learners are generally taught as individuals rather than groups, except for occasional larger group meetings either face-to-face or at a distance (Chaney, 2004; Holmberg, 2003; Keegan, 1996, p. 50).

In the past several decades, distance learning has become a primary format of corporate training. The classroom programs have been blended with or substituted by various forms of technology-supported distance learning with a goal of increasing reach and reducing cost (e.g., CD ROMs, VideoDisks, VHS tapes, Video Broadcasts, online corporate universities, and other web-based programs). Often corporate training is in groups at a remote location. Compared to general-purpose distance education, corporate training has different needs – more situation-specific training and often geared toward practical skill development. Corporate clients often ask for things that are much more specific and corporate trainees may bristle at presentations of theories out of context of application.

Corporate training is particularly suited to virtual worlds, because corporate learners respond well to, and often expect, interactive educational formats. General education can be done in one-way communication modes, such as PowerPoint presentations in lecture formats. By contrast, corporate training often is more effective when learners are put in situational learning environments insofar as possible (e.g., business negotiations, client consulting, or customer conflict resolving). And virtual worlds can be used to enable situational training even when participants are interacting with each other remotely.

Review of Learning Theories Related to Corporate Education. Prior to presenting our hierarchy of engagement for learning, we consider related extant hierarchy of objectives models for learning. In particular, hierarchy of objectives models describe different objectives (or cognitive attainments) associated with the process of individual learning. According to these models, one must master a lower level of objective before one can move on to achieve the next level of objective. The most influential formulations of the hierarchy of objective model include the following. (1) Bloom et al.'s original taxonomy identifies six levels of cognitive objectives, ordered from simple to complex (and from concrete to abstract): knowledge, comprehension, application, analysis, synthesis, and evaluation (1956). (2) Anderson et al.'s revision of Bloom et al's taxonomy describes six classes or stages: remember, understand, apply, analyze, evaluate, and create (2001). Compared to Bloom et al.'s original work, the names of the objectives have changed from nouns to verbs. In addition, the revised framework elaborates on the "subject matter" of knowledge and classifies it into four types: factual knowledge, conceptual knowledge, procedural knowledge, and metacognitive knowledge (i.e., knowledge of cognition in general and awareness of one's own cognitive process). (3) Krathwohl, Bloom and Masia's (1964) taxonomy recognizes five hierarchical stages of learning: receiving (i.e., awareness of the ideas being taught), responding (i.e., showing some level of commitment to the education), valuing (the ideas being taught), organization (i.e., relating and harmonizing the ideas to the value system already held), and characterization by value (i.e., acting consistently with the value being taught). At the highest stage of learning, the ideas being taught have been completely internalized by the learner. Overall, the conceptual framework advanced in this chapter differs from the above theories. But there is a relation, perhaps a correspondence, whereby at each successively deeper stage of engagement that we will describe in our hierarchy, corresponding higher educational objectives in these above hierarchies will be obtained.

We also acknowledge existing learning theories as background for our proposed hierarchy of engagement for learning framework. These include social presence theory, collaborative learning theory, and situated learning theory. We briefly discuss these theories below.

(1) **Social Presence Theory**. Social presence theory is the foundation for many theories on the effects of new media. The basic idea is that the effectiveness of communication through a medium is principally determined by the degree of social presence (i.e., a person's sense of awareness of the presence of the other party in a communication interaction) that the medium affords to its users (Short, Williams & Christie, 1976). According to this theory, increased sense of presence leads to better interpersonal involvement. In addition, Short et al. rank face-to-face communication highest on a continuum of social presence, whereas written, text-based communication the lowest. As virtual worlds bypass many technical limitations of remote communications and bring back certain elements of face-to-face communication through the use of avatars in an immersive 3D virtual environment, we expect that virtual worlds significantly increase learners' sense of synchronous presence of facilitators and other learners, and thus intensify two-way communications in corporate education.

(2) **Collaborative Learning Theory.** The term collaborative learning refers to an instruction approach that involves collaborative effort among students or between students and teachers to achieve educational goals. It emphasizes the importance of collaboration and sharing learning responsibilities and experiences, rather than considering the learners as competitors against each other, or viewing the teachers as unilaterally controlling the learning process. The effects of collaborative learning have been widely investigated. Abundant literature has recorded that, for primary, secondary, and undergraduate education, collaborative leaning methods can produce desirable effects compared to individual learning, such as increasing learner interest, improving information retention, and enhancing critical thinking (e.g., Gokhale, 1995; Johnson & Johnson, 1986). Other desirable implications of collaborative learning include (a) positive interdependence among participants, (b) high levels of interaction among participants, preferably face-to-face, (c) individual accountability, (d) enhancement of participants' interpersonal skills, and (e) learning to communicate about group processes (Johnson & Johnson, 1993). Compared to traditional school-based education, corporate training puts more emphasis on active involvement of the employees/learners and on teamwork within the workforce. Employees need to perform critical thinking, solve problems, and make decisions as a team. Indeed, the development of professional practices and skills through collaborative learning is one of the primary goals of corporate training. Consequently, corporate training actively engages employees/learners with peers and facilitators to co-create an educational experience through collaborative learning. Since virtual worlds create an enriched sense of immersion in virtual scenario-specific

environments, with animated visual projection of participants interacting with each other, these worlds enable companies to better carry out collaborative learning by involving learners in the process of education co-creation.

(3) **Situated Learning Theory**. Situated learning theory recognizes the fact that knowledge is situated within a community of practice rather than existing in isolation, and therefore emphasizes the importance of learners' interaction with the community that embodies certain beliefs and skills to be acquired. In particular, it is noted that unintentional learning (versus deliberate learning, such as learning through classroom instruction) can take place when novices or newcomers in various occupational groups become engaged with a community of practice through a process referred to as "legitimate peripheral participation" (Lave & Wenger, 1991). Participation can take a form of seeking membership of the community, living in the world, interacting with other members, taking apprenticeship, etc. (Wenger, 1998). Participation is legitimate in a sense that all parties in the community accept the newcomers as members of the community. Finally, participation of the newcomers is peripheral because the newcomers start by performing peripheral or less important tasks in the community. In sum, situated learning theory suggests that engaging learners with a community enhances the effectiveness of the learning process. When companies use virtual worlds to facilitate corporate education, employees, learners, and facilitators can easily build and maintain communities around certain themes or practices in virtual worlds, both as part of the training programs, and as an on-going platform for information sharing after classes are over. This kind of engagement with a community is conducive to corporate education.

HIERARCHY OF ENGAGEMENT AND CORPORATE TRAINING

We now propose a hierarchy of engagement for corporate training and describe how virtual worlds facilitate all levels of this hierarchy. The purpose of our hierarchy is to reframe past taxonomies of learning in a form that is more directly reflective of the stages of engagement that are done using interactive electronic media. With the aid of this hierarchy, one can classify the extent to which different educational endeavors utilize the various levels of engagement in this hierarchy. In principle, we suggest that maintaining a balance among these forms is particularly desirable – the basic information can be stated in the lower levels, but practice, correction, and reinforcement leading to deeper levels of mastery and utilization of concepts are attained at the higher levels. Technology plays a key role in our hierarchy of engagement, as movement from one level to the next, particularly in distance settings, becomes more difficult without technology to facilitate the various types of interaction. Figure 1 shows a progression of four stages of engagement in education.

According to this hierarchy, the education process includes (1) one-way communication, (2) two-way communication, (3) education co-creation, and (4) community building. The activities of the learner correspondingly include (1) receiving and beginning to retain information, (2) assimilating (or accommodating) the information and skill development, (3) applying the information to practical contexts to generate value for the company and other employees, and (4) interacting with other employees in a process of ongoing learning. Traditional distance learning is most suited to one-way communication, and the Internet constitutes an improved vehicle for students' engagement in enhanced asynchronous communication. The thesis of this chapter is that 3D virtual worlds go a step further by promoting a synchronous avatar-based social computing context for deeper educational engagement at all four levels of the proposed hierarchy.

Figure 1. Hierarchy of engagement

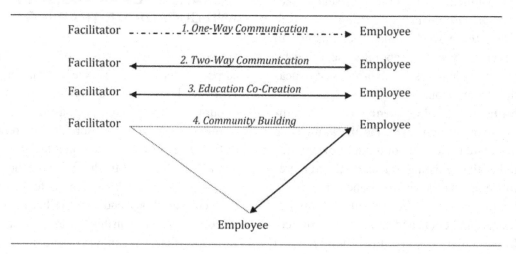

We propose a progression of learning forms with increasing levels of engagement, as shown in Figure 2. One-way communication facilitates simple knowledge transfer. This is mostly new knowledge that fits into people's existing informational structures (or schemata, in the language of Piaget). That is, people's basic understanding of the world is not changed, but they are given new information to place within their existing cognitive structures. Two-way communication facilitates people learning new cognitive structures and developing new skills. To internalize such knowledge, it is necessary for learners to try out new skills or cognitive structures on new examples and to obtain feedback from the instructor and other learners. For skill development, which requires a cognitive step from passively knowing a set of principles to seeing how to apply them in context, it is helpful for learners to try out new practices in hypothetical learning situations and to receive feedback from the instructor and other learners. Education co-creation goes a step further in the interactive process by having learners try out new practices in their actual work settings. In this context, the educators or facilitators essentially act as expert consultants to the learners, providing feedback on the suitability of the learners planned

or past activities. Community building goes to the next step where employees begin to interact with each other on an ongoing basis (possibly using virtual environments as a communication medium, if convenient), to help one another continue to learn and enhance productive effort with the company. Thus, the outcome of learning progresses, along this hierarchy from simple knowledge transfer, to learners benefiting from new ways of thinking (cognitive structures) and skill development, and, finally, to learners developing an enhanced set of values that better promote ongoing learning and productivity.

Overall, past forms of asynchronous distance learning mostly promoted knowledge transfer. The richer forms of synchronous communications in virtual worlds better facilitate two-way communication, and educational co-creation. With time, community building on these virtual platforms permits the educational activity to take on a life of its own as employees utilize the environments for ongoing dialog. Some of these ideas are summarized in Table 1, wherein we see a progression from (a) asynchronous to synchronous communication, (b) instructor-learner communications to learner-learner communications, (c) abstract knowledge (possibly with scenario-based examples) to

Figure 2. Learning progression in the hierarchy

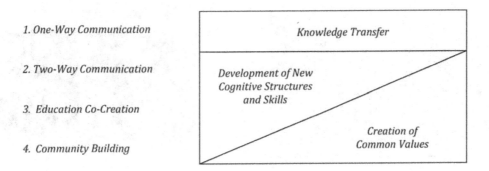

1. *One-Way Communication*

2. *Two-Way Communication*

3. *Education Co-Creation*

4. *Community Building*

Knowledge Transfer

Development of New Cognitive Structures and Skills

Creation of Common Values

collaboration on real problems, and, finally, (d) interaction occurring primarily during classroom time to interaction occurring any time.

The stages of interaction in the hierarchy are described in detail as follows.

One-Way Communication. The lowest level of education consists of simple one-way information transfer from the instructor to the learner. Such communication, which is as old as writing, is what many might first think of about distance education, with knowledge being passed from teachers to students either through a live, remote connection, or in a prerecorded lecture or text.

The advantage of one-way communication is that the cost per participant can become trivial as the number of participants rises. A disadvantage of one-way communication is that it is very limited in terms of its ability to reach higher levels of

educational objectives. For example, this type of communication is unlikely to advance educational attainment beyond knowledge and comprehension in Bloom et al.'s taxonomy (1956), or beyond remember and understand in Anderson et al.'s taxonomy (2001).

The Internet has been very useful for one-way communications, using web-based modules, assignments, quizzes and exams. This is supplemented with communication with instructors through email. This is an efficient way to disseminate knowledge to motivated students. The nuances of how to learn are harder to transfer in this way, but assistance from a real instructor via email can fill this gap.

In virtual worlds, one-way communication involves asynchronous provision of information very much like other distance education. This in-

Table 1. The nature of interaction along the hierarchy

	Interactivity	Who speaks	Domain	Timing
One-Way Communication	Asynchronous	Teacher	Set Examples	Class time and studying time
Two-Way Communication	Synchronous (or Asynchronous)	Instructor and Learner	Scenario-based	Class time and office hours
Education Co-Creation	Synchronous (or Asynchronous)	Instructor and Learner	Real-collaboration	Class time and office hours
Community Building	Synchronous (or Asynchronous)	Many Learners	Real-collaboration	Any time

Figure 3. Outdoor classroom and interactive 3D tutorial

cludes multiple media provision (primarily video and audio) of such information formats as printed handouts of lectures and supporting material and downloadable articles and lectures (see Figure 3, left panel; Edwards, 2006). This may also permit learners to make queries of pre-programmed informational sources or to manipulate 3D objects, or possibly the use of automated bots or simulators (see Figure 3, right panel).

Overall, virtual worlds can perform one-way communication in much the same ways as traditional distance learning and the Internet. The 3D medium may also permit some forms of more vivid delivery of one-way communications, which can be a benefit for certain domains of instruction. Generally, while all forms of one-way communication are low-cost, they are mostly limited to lower-level educational objectives.

Activeworlds, Inc. is an example of a virtual-world service provider that helps companies to deliver corporate education. In addition to hosting a large open virtual world of its own (AlphaWorld), its services facilitate various forms of advanced one-way communication, as well as other communication forms more elevated in the hierarchy. The company offers a quick entry into the use of virtual worlds, hosting client-specific virtual worlds on its servers and licensing its technology to clients who want an independent hardware solution. Those virtual worlds come equipped

with Office documents display tools and a library of models and textures (which facilitate one-way communication). They also support VoIP, building tools, and standard modeling program formats for creating custom objects (facilitating two-way communication). As of our writing, the company claims among their licensees many fortune 500 organizations and well over 250 schools and universities.

Two-Way Communication. The next level of education consists of information exchange between the instructor and students to facilitate learning and new skill development. A traditional form of two-way communication involves classroom settings in which participants are geographically collocated and communication is synchronous. Early forms of distance education involved asynchronous two-way communication (with written or phone feedback). The Internet led to substantial growth in electronic asynchronous two-way communication through on-line learning forums and sites. With the aid of new technologies, two-way communication at a distance has increasingly allowed us to return to situations where the instructor and learners are temporally collocated (in 3D or 2D virtual spaces) with synchronous (i.e., live) interaction.

The main advantage of this level of engagement is that it allows the instructor and learners to jointly explore the content at deeper levels, matching the level of learners' interests and knowledge (often in real-time). Two types of such deeper interaction include "Q&A" sessions and scenario-based skill development. First, concerning two-way communication, real-time queries can help avoid gaps in an instructor's presentation. They also provide the instructor with the opportunity of elaborating on a topic in which a sizable group of learners shows interest. Perhaps, more importantly, providing students with chances to ask questions and obtain answers can greatly assist students in forming new internal models of particular subject matter, with students checking their perceptions through directed trial and error. Second, concerning scenario-based skill development, two-way communication can permit students to run through particular preplanned learning scenarios, with feedback from the instructor. The instructor can provide corrections, modifications, and nuance. For example, in a retail service delivery scenario, a learner could be told that a potential customer enters the store or office articulating his or her needs. For several script variations, the learner would indicate how he/she would respond. It is possible, in this context, to set up student-teacher or student-student role-plays. After each, the instructor can offer comments and suggestions.

As classes explore content at deeper levels, students can benefit from communication in various ways. Some students can engage in direct instructor-student communication. Other students can benefit vicariously through observing the interactions of the instructor and other students. And still other students can interact with other students in discussion about the contents. All of these forms of interaction help take the learners to higher levels of internalization and application of the subject matter (e.g., comprehension, application, analysis, synthesis and evaluation, in Bloom et al's taxonomy (1956); understand, apply, analyze and evaluate in Anderson et al.'s taxonomy (2001); or valuing and organizing on Krathwohl et al.'s taxonomy (1964)). But for all their advantages, two disadvantages of traditional classroom

settings are that, first, students must travel to the classroom site, and, second, for participants to have an opportunity to speak and discuss, there are limitations on the number of participants who can work with a single instructor.

The key advantages of distance learning are that it can avoid these limitations by making education both possible at a distance and more efficient with the instructional resources. The result is a saving in transportation time and cost and in course fees (by better utilizing instructional resources). Distant learning to targeted groups can also permit the instructor to customize content for particular learner groups.

Distance learning in simulated classroom settings can be done by having people remotely participate through videoconference links. For example, as one student group is taught locally, another student group can participate in the same classroom session remotely. The latter group can view a large screen or set of screens; and distant learners can offer queries through a button click, and, when called upon, ask questions through a microphone or by "texting." Alternatively, the Internet can also be used to have the instructor communicate remotely to a number of geographically dispersed students.

For example, "webinar" software allows a speaker to make an oral presentation with slides and video content, and to take questions from remote viewers. As a more elaborate example, software such as Elluminate allows a class of 20 to 60 learners to participate relatively easily. The level of interaction is somewhat limited. The instructor can talk and present PowerPoint slides and observe limited forms of student responses (in the form of icon heads that are effectively nodding "yes" or shaking "no"; students can also raise their hands to address the class). The students who are called on can communicate their questions or comments either through on-screen texting or orally to the group via a microphone-enabled headset.

These various forms of distance learning make possible remote corporate training, but the various technologies limit the range and richness of interactions among the students. Virtualization technology takes this electronically mediated two-way interaction out of a preformatted flat-screen environment into a richer multipurpose 3D environment. The setting may be a virtual classroom, but virtual field trips are also possible. These may include walkthroughs of physical examples, sometimes seen in real museums, such as a functioning human organ like a simulated human heart, a place like a virtual retail store or shopping mall, and any object like a virtual cell or atom. Interaction with the virtual environment can be multifaceted, through texting, oral communication, avatar gestures, and displaying objects that avatars have in their inventory. For instance, the virtual objects can be made to respond to people's requests by enlarging a specific part of the virtual object, revealing more detailed information, giving further instructions, providing answers to frequently-asked questions, etc. In addition, the two-way communication made possible by virtual worlds is particular desirable for such activities as language learning (listening to taped dialogs, practicing speaking, and being corrected), refining sales techniques (role-playing in particular scenarios and receiving constructive suggestions afterward from the instructor), and advertising management (constructing practice advertising campaigns and receiving constructive feedback).

The key advantage of virtual worlds for education is that, while the cost of transportation and of educational materials is largely avoided, there is still richness of interaction with the instructor and among the learners. Anonymity may also be an advantage, because the embarrassment of making a mistake or of initially being awkward trying new things may be reduced. Another advantage is that many of the educational resources are scalable and there may be economies of scale. But even for virtualization technologies, there are still limits on the number of participants who can work with a single instructor. And the instructor

may require special training to fully utilize the potentialities of the virtualization environment. Generally, this is a resource intensive level of engagement, if not in terms of technological assets, then in terms of instructor time. Depending on the effectiveness of the facilitator, this can be a very powerful framework for meeting any level of educational objectives.

Qwaq Inc. is an example of a virtual-world service provider that stresses its technology's ability to integrate with other applications in group situations (involving two-way interactions). This facilitates workgroup collaboration in a simulated virtual operations environment. In a recent application, the U.S. Navy's Naval Undersea Warfare Center is evaluating virtual world technology for training, rapid prototyping, design collaboration, and war gaming. It used Qwaq technology to create a virtual Combat Systems Center. Within the virtual center, crews collaborated with each other, and interacted with applications and data just as they would onboard a submarine. The project leader summed up the usefulness of such a training system: "The virtual Combat Systems Center has the potential to allow us to effectively train crew members around the world without having to transport them to our physical facilities. We now have the ability to replicate our submarine environments in high fidelity and provide virtual access to the applications and data the fleet requires. This means that our sailors and officers could always have access to all of the latest training and technical expertise no matter where they are located." (Qwaq News, 2009)

Education Co-Creation. For this phase, we see the educational process becoming directly active in helping to create value for a learner in attaining a career or life goal. In this case, learning occurs not for its own sake, for a grade, or to please the instructor, but to enhance a career or a life goal of the learner. In principle, such is the case for much primary and secondary education, and we argue that the more motivating forms of such education explicitly recognize this link for students. A key to education co-creation is giving participants effective tools for participation in the creation process and a stake in the outcome.

This activity, already being linked with inherent personal motivations, engenders high involvement, with the learner helping to determine the domain of learning. This approach builds on the concept of value co-creation, which is important in the management literature (Prahalad & Ramaswamy, 2004) and in service science (Vargo & Lusch, 2004). In this process, the participant becomes a co-creator in the experience and takes some responsibility for the experience. This is especially important in a corporate training setting, where developing corporate culture and policies valued by employees can be a significant competitive advantage.

Education co-creation in corporate education can occur when the instructor teaches learners how to improve the current practice that they often use in the course of their careers. This takes scenario-based skill development a step further by improving on the learner's stated current practice. In this way, the instructor takes the role of an onsight expert consultant or counselor for the group. Alternatively, new individual and group activities can be initiated, and counseling services can be provided by the instructor to facilitate this. In this way, the ideas enter directly into the learner's life to improve current practices for the better.

This can occur through the Internet, but is particularly facilitated using virtualization technologies in corporate training. Virtual-delivered corporate education affords the opportunity for distance delivery of expert-consulting or counseling services both in the classroom and on virtual field trips, in one of the following two ways.

First, education co-creation can occur by taking scenario-based skill development a step further. Employees can describe their current practices and the instructor and other students in class can suggest how to improve on those current practices. As with two-way communication, this can be learned through direct interaction with the instructor, vicarious observation of the interaction of a learner and the instructor, and through sharing of ideas between learners.

Second, education co-creation can occur through new desired individual and group vocational activities initiated by the instructor. For example, employees in different functional areas may be combined to form a product design group, because they view and evaluate the product from different perspectives (e.g., marketing, engineering, manufacturing, finance, cost accounting, and customer services). These people could be given a new product development template and the facilitator/instructor would be able to share knowledge through multiple experiences in this process across different industries and for various products or services.

When effectively developed and administered, education co-creation does not have to be significantly more expensive than two-way communication, but learners need to be more invested in the activities. This level of training is also just as scalable as two-way communication. While this has been done with past forms of distance learning, the need for personal interactions makes it easier to assist learners in achieving career or life improvement at a distance using virtualization technologies.

As an example of education co-creation, the I-95 Corridor Coalition (agencies in those states through which I-95 passes) needed a way to train first responders to traffic incidents to shorten response time, clear accidents and congestion more efficiently, and enhance overall safety. They chose the University of Maryland's Center for Advanced Transportation Technology Laboratory to develop a virtual reality training solution. The lab used virtual world technology from Forterra Systems to create a multi-player simulation, in part because the Forterra technology had the ability to easily record simulations, facilitating participants' learning by reviewing performance after completion of the simulation. Participants using this virtual world training environment worked together in simulated accident and congestion scenarios to build a more efficient system, which in turn benefits all the participating members (Forterra, retrieved 2009). No doubt, the training experience improves the performance of all the agencies in the system and contributes to career development of the trainees.

The I-95 Corridor Coalition is interesting as an example of what we feel is a competitive advantage of virtual worlds for corporate training: simulation-based learning. Often the most engaging learning experiences are simulations of real-world (or hypothetical) situations. The problem in the past, however, was that effective simulations in the real world were extremely difficult and expensive, if not impossible, to create. In virtual worlds, however, almost anything can be simulated, and the ease and cost of creating and running such simulations is steadily dropping. (At the same time, simulation-based training presents a challenge for corporate trainers because this approach toward training requires new training skills.)

Community Building. The apex of the hierarchy consists of engagement going beyond relying on the instructor, wherein an ongoing process by learners is facilitated to enhance learning. Teacher-student relationships are limited in scale, and as the number of participants increases, the instructor's available time does not. The key to moving beyond the limits of the teacher-student relationship is to increase the size of the network. It can be preferable if a corporation can foster a process that has a positive influence on the corporate culture. Creating an educational community allows participants to draw on many more resources and communication becomes much more than just two-way. While some sort of central administration or facilitation is possible and often desirable (through on-line community forums and sites), communities cannot be centrally controlled without losing the essence of what gives them value. As they are co-created by their members, they become "owned" by those that create them.

A major advantage to this level of engagement is its ability to escape the scale and scope constraints inherent in the lower levels. As Bob Metcalfe suggested in the early 1980s, the value of the community grows in proportion to the square of the number of participants (known as Metcalfe's Law). In addition, with communities' ability to bring the varied experience and expertise of a diverse organization to bear on training and other challenges, the value can grow even faster.

For example, after a class offering, groups of like-minded employees may wish to maintain periodic (e.g., weekly) communication about their activities for sharing tips and continued learning. This is particularly desirable with companies geographically dispersed throughout the globe, and for companies with different product/service divisions that engage in similar activities where ongoing communication of shared practices can be mutually beneficial.

One of the easiest ways for corporations or other groups to begin using virtual worlds is to use an existing solution that facilitates community building. For example, many companies use designated areas in Linden Lab's Second Life for periodic virtual meetings, training simulations, design collaboration, etc. Thus, in late 2008, IBM's Academy of Technology used Second Life for a Virtual World Conference and Annual Meeting for over 200 participants. IBM designed a virtual conference center in a secure environment within Second Life, with areas for presentations and breakout sessions, as well as a Green Data Center, a library, and areas for informal gathering. One of the barriers to using virtual worlds for meetings is that participants have to learn how to use them (e.g., communication, navigation), so IBM offered pre-conference training on the basics of Second Life (Second Life Grid, retrieved 2009).

Other very popular existing solutions that facilitate community building involve social networking sites such as Facebook, MySpace, and YouTube. Even corporations can use sites such as these to further education through community building by facilitating dissemination of experiences, ideas and opinions, product reviews, digital content (including photos, video, audio, and software), etc. But along with the substantial potential for community building from these solutions come risks to the participants and the corporation, including the loss of privacy together with the possibility that somewhat personal aspects of a person's social self become inappropriately disseminated in the person's business or professional life, or that competing firms gain illicit access to a firm's trade secrets.

Relationship with Existing Learning Theories. Now that we have introduced the hierarchy of engagement for education, we can relate it to four existing learning theories discussed earlier (see Table 2).

First, the hierarchy of objectives models proposed by Bloom et al. (1956), Anderson et al. (2001), and Krathwohl et al. (1964) focus on depicting different cognitive stages at which individual learners internalize educational information (e.g., a learning process progressing from receiving ideas, to understanding, evaluating, applying, and assimilating the ideas). The difference between the older hierarchy of objectives models and our hierarchy of engagement is that the former describe what goes on within a person's mind in the course of the learning process, and the latter describes what goes on between people to stimulate the learning process. The hierarchy of engagement is particularly relevant for describing the effects of interactions in online settings. The two types of

hierarchies are related: in general, we conjecture that increasing levels of interaction (engagement) promote higher-level education objectives.

Second, social presence theory (Short et al. 1976) emphasizes the importance of participants' sense of presence of the other party in two-way communication in order for the communication to be efficient. Because the use of avatars in the immersive 3D virtual environment increases learners' sense of presence, virtual-world-enabled corporate training facilitates two-way communication (so long as the avatars have actual participants behind them and are not "bots".) Third, collaborative learning theory (Johnson & Johnson, 1986) elaborates on shared responsibility of learners and the importance of learners being actively involved in the education process. This bears upon education co-creation in the proposed hierarchy of engagement. Lastly, situated learning theory explains how the community of practice can promote learning, especially unintentional or informal learning (Lave & Wenger, 1991). This is relevant to community building in our hierarchy of engagement, and also to education co-creation. Companies can facilitate the latter two deeper forms of engagement by encouraging employees to increase knowledge, information, and experiences together with their peers and educators, and also to build communities around certain themes and practices in virtual worlds.

Table 2. Relevance of learning theories to proposed hierarchy of engagement

	Hierarchy of objectives	Social presence	Collaborative learning	Situated learning
One-way communication	X			
Two-way communication	X	X		
Education co-creation	X		X	X
Community building	X			X

INFLUENCE OF AVATAR MEDIATION ON LEARNING AND ON TEACHING

We have demonstrated how virtual worlds facilitate all four levels of engagement in our hierarchy and how the hierarchy relates to four existing learning theories. Now we turn to special issues concerning the influence of avatar mediation on learning and teaching.

Class or Individual Instruction. A key issue that instructors must choose is whether they want to have formal class sessions or more individual instruction. Individual one-on-one instruction can be costly in terms of instructor's time, but there is the possibility of having students complete tutorial modules and then meet individually or in groups with the instructor. Instructors using virtual worlds should try different variations. For one class covering materials such as accounting, it may be desirable to have 50% class, 40% tutorials, and 10% direct one-on-one feedback. For marketing, it might be better to have 75% class (alternating between discussion and group presentations), 15% tutorials, and perhaps 10% one-on-one feedback.

Influence of Avatar Mediation on Learning. It should be noted that avatar-mediated communications in corporate training involve varying degrees of anonymity (i.e., reduced awareness of one's self identity). We can distinguish between complete anonymity and partial anonymity in virtual world corporate training. An example of the former is a class in which trainees sign up from outside; an example of the latter would be a class where employees sign up from a company and at times can be expected to meet face-to-face. The implication of anonymity is that it might alter participants' behaviors in the virtual worlds relative to those in the real world.

Previous research on computer mediated communication (CMC) indicates that the state of felt anonymity makes people feel less socially and psychologically inhibited than they normally do in the real world (Kiesler & Sproull, 1992). For example, it is found that anonymous participants in computer-mediated discussions disclose significantly more information about themselves than people who engage in face-to-face discussions (Joinson, 2001). More recently, Messinger et al. (2008) reported the results of a survey among participants of the virtual world Second Life. These results indicate that participants indeed consider themselves to be more outgoing, confident, risk-taking, extroverted, and less inhibited when they interact with others via avatars in virtual worlds than in the real world. This behavioral change in avatar-mediated interaction presents both an opportunity and a threat.

On the positive side, avatar-mediated communications help learners to overcome social and psychological inhibitions. Learners may be more willing to participate in group discussion and share their ideas with others. They may be more likely to say what they think, what first comes to mind, and even candidly offer constructive criticisms about their own companies. In addition, learners tend to be more open to participate in role play in simulated scenarios. Consequently, virtual worlds are particularly conducive to learning processes that include role play and group discussion. It may be desirable to assign people in roles as a presenter and a reviewer, or to have two groups interact, one presenting, and the other critiquing, and then switch roles.

On the negative side, avatar-mediated communications are likely to be more frank when learning objectives are not met or when participants are bored. A particular problem is that it is not really possible to establish true eye-contact with a large group of people. The instructor can see their avatars, but many will be still, and it is not clear whether a particular participant is checking his email or browsing the Internet concurrently with an instructional session. Also some learners are likely to have distractions when they are online attending an instructional session. We encourage instructors to develop a cycle of bringing participants into the discussion. Of course, this will be challenging with classes of more than 50, but we do not encourage classes of more than 30, and even that number may be a challenge.

A second issue is avatar appearance and attire. Research has shown that participants in a virtual world like Second Life will normally make their avatars somewhat more attractive than their real selves, but not inordinately so (Messinger et al., 2008). Also the clothes are likely to be less conservative and more revealing or sexy than in the real world. The instructor has two choices in this regard. In some situations it can be useful to acknowledge this reality and "play with it" with the class. The alternative is to encourage learners to develop and use a business avatar, with suitable body and facial features and attire. This may have attendant risks of appearing over-controlling, so an option (as a tip when learners are giving presentations or engaging in skill-development role-play) is to ask learners to utilize their "business" avatar.

Further issues are training students to avail themselves of the functionality of the world or virtual environment. Chances are for the first such class, it will be necessary to teach the class about certain virtual world features.

Influence of Avatar Mediation on Teaching. A key issue for the instructor is to design the appearance of his or her avatar. Specifically, the instructor needs to decide how attractive and expert-like the instructor's avatar should be. Research has shown that customers purchasing products with moderate levels of involvement react better to avatars that deliver services when those avatars are more attractive (but perhaps not distractingly so). On the other hand, consumers react more positively to expert avatars when they purchase products associated with a high level of involvement (Holzwarth, Janiszewski & Neumann, 2006). Extending this to learning environments, we recommend that the instructor choose an avatar that is attractive, but has some aspects of experience or expertise visible (e.g., an avatar in proper business suit, wearing

Figure 4. First author's avatar

glasses). One interesting feature that the instructor can use in avatar-mediated education delivery is that the instructor has the capability to change dress, appearance, or even use different avatars for different scenarios. This requires a great deal of technical competence to avoid having undue pauses in a class.

Furthermore, the instructor must utilize special methods and techniques to keep a class engaged. For example, the instructor needs to have the skills to display and share multimedia files (e.g., audio files, videos, Word documents, PowerPoint presentations) in the virtual world environment. She might need to develop (and also teach the learners to develop) certain virtual objects for specific training scenarios. Finally, she also needs to develop skills to pass the floor to the students, organize virtual group discussion, group presentations, or role plays.

CONCLUSION

Virtual worlds represent a 3D extension of the Internet combined with social computing functionality. As perhaps the most multifaceted of new media, virtual worlds engender both high potential and low learning cost for companies utilizing them for corporate education.

This chapter describes a four-element hierarchy of progressively deeper levels of educational engagement, involving one-way communication, two-way communication, education co-creation, and community building. This hierarchy, together with the point that the virtual worlds permit multifaceted educational communication across all four elements of the hierarchy, is offered as a conceptual academic contribution.

This chapter goes on to describe current effective practices by which companies achieve all four levels of educational engagement in the hierarchy. One particular area of great potential consists of simulation-based training – an area that has been infeasible for many companies in the past. Virtual worlds make simulations relatively simple and cost effective, and we look forward to corporate trainers increasingly turning to simulations for many types of applications. The description of these practices is intended to assist practitioners. We discuss the above topics after we first provide a background of the historical development of virtual worlds, a discussion of the emergence of distance education, and a short review of relevant past learning theories.

Many issues remain for future consideration. These include continued work developing applications of virtual worlds for education; enhancement of communication technologies; and future research topics concerning education utilizing the new media, including virtual worlds.

Applications. Future applications of virtual worlds for education include (1) improved integration of traditional education with educational techniques that use the new media, including virtual worlds and social networking; (2) increased connectivity between different virtual worlds and forms of social computing; and (3) development of rating metrics of technological capabilities of the various extant worlds, user demographics, and manuals to help firms choose in which worlds to conduct educational activities and enhance community building. Because we are still in the "early days" of virtual worlds, we must continue to develop new best practices to utilize these worlds for each of the four elements of the proposed hierarchy of educational engagement.

Technology. Important issues involve identifying and developing future technologies that will continue to enhance communications and social computing in electronic gaming, online social networking, and virtual worlds. These new technologies should make the linkages more seamless between existing communications forms and between devices (including computers, telephones, cell-phones, televisions, car navigation systems, stereos, home alarm systems, other sensing devices, radios, cameras, camcorders, and musical instruments). Improvements in sensing devices and the non-verbal gesturing capabilities of avatars would also be desirable.

Research. A key research question that requires further examination involves establishing the link between deeper levels of engagement in our proposed hierarchy and educational outcome variables such as concept recognition, understanding, and retention. A second area for future research is to elaborate on ways to best manage each of the four engagement forms of the proposed hierarchy. This would describe which communications media, technologies, social computing sites, and virtual worlds are most amenable to each of the four types of educational engagement. In addition, it would be desirable to further explore the interpersonal implications (among learners and between learners and facilitators) associated with using virtual worlds for corporate learning, including (1) anonymity and employee identity, (2) retaining control over levels of privacy, (3) how corporate culture plays out in a virtual world, and (4) the best way to design and manage instructors' avatars. More generally, research should be done to ascertain how to harness new media generally, what effects various types of new media have on learning behavior, and the new roles of communication technologies in delivery of education.

Lastly, concerning our hierarchy of engagement, an important issue concerns whether the effectiveness of utilizing the proposed hierarchy is universal. We think it would be interesting to consider whether application of our hierarchy of engagement would be equally effective and relevant regardless of various moderating factors including (1) whether the subject matter is complex or simple, (2) whether the students have higher or lower levels of sophistication, educational attainment, and career accomplishment, (3) whether the prevailing culture is collectivistic or individualistic, and (4) whether the prevailing culture is vertical or horizontal in structure.[2]

For complex and subtle subject matter, we conjecture that multiple forms of engagement with students are more effective in achieving educational objectives than using one-way communication. Having some interaction with and testing of new ideas appears to be needed, in our opinion, to put complex ideas into perspective, and a single educational form (such as one-way communication) would be insufficient for achieving standard learning objectives. For students that are sophisticated or have high levels of educational and career accomplishments (regardless of whether the material is complex or simple), we conjecture that utilizing multiple forms of engagement will be relatively more effective in attaining learning objectives than only using one-way communication. These individuals are trained to be critical in their thinking and not to take dogma on faith (this consideration is particularly important when considering the benefits of using virtual worlds for corporate training, where some learners are quite sophisticated and accomplished). For collectivistic and hierarchical cultures, we conjecture that one-way communication is relatively more effective than for individualistic or horizontal cultures. For the latter cultures, we conjecture that one-way communication will be relatively ineffective, and that utilizing a hierarchy of engagement will be much more effective.

Thus, we think a hierarchy of engagement will be particularly effective (1) for complex subject matter, (2) for students that are sophisticated and accomplished, and (3) for individualistic or horizontal cultures. One-way engagement, by contrast, is sufficient and relatively more effective (but not necessarily more effective than using the full hierarchy) when dealing with collectivistic or hierarchical cultures with simpler subject matter and with students that are not particularly sophisticated or accomplished. We hasten to acknowledge that these are just our conjectures. These conjectures need to be tested, and we welcome such inquiry.

Overall, teachers, administrators, and education scholars are still learning how to best teach people in online environments. We are also still learning how well-established educational practices transfer to virtual worlds. Our hope is that the hierarchy of engagement described in this chapter will aid in the future development and application of virtual worlds for corporate education.

ACKNOWLEDGMENT

This research was supported by the Social Sciences and Humanities Research Council of Canada, through its Initiative on the New Economy Research Alliances Program (SSHRC grant 538-02-1013) and by faculty research grants from the University of Alberta School of Retailing and the University of Northern British Columbia. For much help, the authors would like to thank Kristen Smirnov, Kelly Lyons, Michael Bone, and Stephen Perelgut. The work has also significantly benefited from comments of the participants of the 2009 Advanced Research Techniques (ART) Forum in Whistler, B.C., Canada and of the University of Alberta Marketing Seminar.

REFERENCES

Airasian, P. W., Cruikshank, K. A., Mayer, R. E., Pintrich, P. R., Raths, J., & Wittrock, M. C. (2001). *A taxonomy for learning, teaching, and assessing: A revision of Bloom's Taxonomy of Educational Objectives* (Anderson, L. W., & Krathwohl, D. R., Eds.). New York: Longman.

Balkin, J. M., & Noveck, B. S. (Eds.). (2006). *The state of play: Law, games, and virtual worlds.* New York: New York University Press.

Blizzard Entertainment. (2008). *World of Warcraft® surpasses 11 million subscribers worldwide.* Retrieved November 29, 2008, from http://www.blizzard.com/us/press/081028.html

Bloom, B. S. (Ed.). Engelhart, M.D., Furst, E.J., Hill, W.H., & Krathwohl, D.R. (1956). Taxonomy of educational objectives: The classification of educational goals. Handbook 1: Cognitive domain. New York: David McKay.

Boyd, D. M., & Ellison, N. B. (2007). Social network sites: Definition, history, and scholarship. *Journal of Computer-Mediated Communication, 13*(1), 11.

Chaney, B. (2004). *History, theory, and quality indicators of distance education: A literature review.* Retrieved August 28, 2009, from http://ohi.tamu.edu/distanceed.pdf

Driver, E., Jackson, P., Moore, C., & Schooley, C. (2008). *Getting real work done in virtual worlds.* Forrester Research.

Edwards, C. (2006). Another world. *IEEE Engineering and Technology, 9*(1), 28–32. doi:10.1049/et:20060904

Forterra. (date unknown). *Transportation incident management: Using 3D virtual worlds to train first responders.* Retrieved August 13, 2009, from http://www.forterrainc.com/images/stories/pdf/I-95_CaseStudy.pdf

Gokhale, A. A. (1995). Collaborative learning enhances critical thinking. *Journal of Technology Education, 7*(1), 22–30.

Graves, L. (2008). A Second life for higher Ed. *U.S. News & World Report, 144*(2), 49–50.

Herman, A., Coombe, R. J., & Kaye, L. (2006). Your second life? Goodwill and the performativity of intellectual property in online digital gaming. *Cultural Studies, 20*(2/3), 184–210. doi:10.1080/09502380500495684

Herman, L., Horwitzk, J., Kent, S., & Miller, S. (2008). *The history of video games.* Retrieved November 30, 2008, from http://www.gamespot.com/gamespot/features/video/hov/

Holmberg, B. (2003). A theory of distance education based on empathy. In Moore, M., & Anderson, W. G. (Eds.), *Handbook of distance education* (pp. 79–86). Mahwah, NJ: Lawrence Erlbaum Associates.

Holzwarth, M., Janiszewski, C., & Neumann, M. M. (2006). The influence of avatars on online consumer shopping behavior. *Journal of Marketing, 70*(October), 19–36. doi:10.1509/jmkg.70.4.19

Jansz, J., & Martens, L. (2005). Gaming at a LAN event: The social context of playing video games. *New Media & Society, 7*(3), 333–355. doi:10.1177/1461444805052280

Johnson, D. W., Johnson, R. T., & Holubec, E. J. (1993). *Cooperation in the Classroom* (6th ed.). Edina, MN: Interaction Book Company.

Johnson, R. T., & Johnson, D. W. (1986). Action research: Cooperative learning in the science classroom. *Science and Children, 24*, 31–32.

Joinson, A. N. (2001). Self-disclosure in computer-mediated communication: The role of self-awareness and visual anonymity. *European Journal of Social Psychology, 31*(2), 177–192. doi:10.1002/ejsp.36

Keegan, D. (Ed.). (1996). *Foundations of distance education* (3rd ed.). London: Routledge.

Kiesler, S., & Sproull, L. (1992). Group decision making and communication technology. *Organizational Behavior and Human Decision Processes, 52*, 96–123. doi:10.1016/0749-5978(92)90047-B

Krathwohl, D. R., Bloom, B. S., & Masia, B. B. (1964). *Taxonomy of educational objectives: The classification of educational goals. Handbook II: The affective domain*. New York: David McKay.

Lave, J., & Wenger, E. (1991). *Situated learning: Legitimate peripheral participation*. Cambridge, UK: Cambridge University Press.

Messinger, P. R., Ge, X., Stroulia, E., Lyons, K., Smirnov, K., & Bone, M. (2008). On the relationship between my avatar and myself. *Journal of Virtual Worlds Research*, *1*(2), 1–17.

Messinger, P. R., Stroulia, E., Lyons, K., Bone, M., Niu, R., Smirnov, K., & Perelgut, S. (2009). Virtual worlds – past, present, and future: New directions in social computing. *Decision Support Systems*, *47*, 204–228. doi:10.1016/j.dss.2009.02.014

Meyer, K. A. (2002). Quality in distance education: Focus on on-line learning . In Kezar, A. J. (Ed.), *ASHE-ERIC Higher Education Report* (*Vol. 29*, pp. 1–134). San Francisco: Jossey – Bass.

Moore, M. (1990). Background and overview of contemporary American distance education . In Moore, M. (Ed.), *Contemporary issues in American distance education* (pp. xii–xxvi). New York: Pergamon.

Murray, S. (2005). High art/low life: The art of playing grand theft auto. *PAJ a Journal of Performance and Art*, *27*(80), 91–98. doi:10.1162/1520281053850866

News, F. O. X. (2006). *Survey: College kids like IPods better than beer*. Retrieved on March 10, 2008, from http://www.foxnews.com/story/0,2933,198632,00.html

Prahalad, C. K., & Ramaswamy, V. (2004). *The future of competition: Co-creating unique value with customers*. Cambridge, MA: Harvard Business School Press.

Qwaq News. (2009, April 28). *Virtual spaces for real work news room*. Retrieved August 11, 2009, from http://www.qwaq.com/company/press_releases/pr-2009_04_28.php

Second Life Grid. (date unknown). Retrieved August 13, 2009, from http://secondlifegrid.net/casestudies/IBM

Short, J., Williams, E., & Christie, B. (1976). *The social psychology of telecommunications*. London: John Wiley.

Stephenson, N. (1992). *Snow Crash*. New York: Penguin Books.

Vargo, S. L., & Lusch, R. F. (2004). Evolving to a new dominant logic for marketing. *Journal of Marketing*, *68*(January), 1–17. doi:10.1509/jmkg.68.1.1.24036

Watkins, B. L. (1991). A quite radical idea: The invention and elaboration of collegiate correspondence study . In Watkins, B. L., & Wright, S. J. (Eds.), *The foundations of American distance education* (pp. 1–35). Dubuque, Iowa: Kendall/Hunt.

Wenger, E. (1998). *Communities of practice: Learning, meaning and identity*. Cambridge, UK: Cambridge University Press.

KEY TERMS AND DEFINITIONS

Virtual World: A virtual world is a common three-dimensional (3D) or two-dimensional (2D) space where thousands of people can interact simultaneously. Members of a virtual world (through their avatars) can engage in rich interactions with each other: they can exchange messages, objects, and money; they can communicate through voice over a headset and microphone; they can navigate through the world by walking, running, driving vehicles, flying, and teleporting; and they can "experience" the world through a rich variety of interactions with it, including dressing, changing their avatars' shapes, touching things, building and owning things, engaging in quests, doing sports, dancing, hugging, and kissing (for an overview, see Messinger et al. 2009)

Avatar: An avatar is a customizable 3D anthropomorphic digital representation of a virtual world user. In Sanskrit, "avatara" means "incarnation." The use of the term was made popular by Neal Stephenson (1992) in his novel *Snow Crash*.

Social Networking: Social networking is the process of connecting with other individuals or groups to share information or participate in joint activities. As commonly used, this process is moderated by Internet websites, which individuals or groups use to communicate with each other digitally.

Distance Education: Distance education involves the pursuit of a course of study away from the campus of the school providing the instruction. Students typically pursue this course of study from their homes. This is also known as distance learning, correspondence study, home study, independent study, external study, distance instruction, distance teaching and distance education.

Corporate Training: The training of employees to work for a company or corporation, typically involving learning required work skills, company-specific business information, and company processes and values.

Educational Engagement: The process of interacting with another person (a teacher, another student, or an interested layperson) to pursue some form of study or learning activity.

Hierarchy of Objectives: Hierarchy of objectives models describe different objectives (or cognitive attainments) associated with the process of individual learning. According to these models, one must master a lower level of objective before one can move on to achieve the next level of objective.

Social Presence Theory: According to social presence theory, the effectiveness of communication through a medium is principally determined by the degree of social presence (i.e., a person's sense of awareness of the presence of the other party in a communication interaction) that the medium affords to its users (Short, Williams & Christie, 1976). According to this theory, increased sense of presence leads to better interpersonal involvement.

Collaborative Learning Theory: Collaborative learning theory refers to an instruction approach that involves joint effort among students or between students and teachers to achieve an educational goal. It emphasizes the importance of working together and sharing learning responsibilities and experiences, rather than considering the learners as competitors against each other, or viewing the teachers as unilaterally controlling the learning process

Situated Learning Theory: Situated learning theory emphasizes that knowledge is present within the community of practice rather than existing in isolation. The theory emphasizes the importance of learners' interaction with the community that embodies certain beliefs and skills to be acquired and recognizes the important of unintentional learning (versus deliberate learning such as learning through classroom instruction) when newcomers in various occupational groups become engaged with the community of practice through a process referred to as "legitimate peripheral participation" (Lave & Wenger, 1991).

ENDNOTES

[1] Neal Stephenson made this use of the term "avatar" popular in his novel Snow Crash (Stephenson, 1992). The term has since become ubiquitous with the 2009 release of the blockbuster movie "Avatar."

[2] We thank an anonymous referee for suggesting that we acknowledge issues related to culture and education.

Section 4
Connections

Chapter 12
Using Role–Playing And Coaching In Virtual Worlds To Promote Team Transformation

William Ritke-Jones
CyberMations Consulting Group, USA

ABSTRACT

This chapter outlines the need for team members to transform distorted assumptions about team members who are in some way different from them. In our increasingly diverse teams, this transformation is essential. The chapter fully explains transformative learning and how to foster it in role playing and coaching. The chapter argues that a virtual reality is an ideal place to foster transformative learning because it creates a "real" space for teams to interact. This space is safer than a physical space because participants are distant from one another and also because participants can use avatars as representatives of themselves. Having an avatar representative allows participants to switch identities during role play, giving it an advantage over physical space. It also allows for the expression of emotion, neither of which would be as easy in another virtual space. Johnson and Johnson (2006) correctly stated that "small groups almost always contain a diverse selection of individuals, and in order for a team to be successful and effective, diversity must be faced and eventually valued" (p. 444). Johnson and Johnson (2006) defined diversity as differences in culture, gender, skills, and social team membership, among others. In the future, as teams who had been marginalized continue taking their rightful places in organizations and as organizations increasingly establish operations in multiple nations, Johnson and Johnson's remark will ring even truer. This diversity will have positive consequences for some teams because they will enjoy the greater depth of creativity and productivity that Johnson and Johnson (2006) claimed is the result of embracing diversity. Not only will the team as a whole reap the benefits, moreover; the members of the team will gain a greater level of sophistication in working with people different from them, a skill that they can take with them to future teams. Not all teams will embrace their diversity. In fact, most will not, or it will take a long time before team members will be able to work together efficiently and effectively. Those that do not embrace their diversity will likely suffer decreased productivity and morale as well as giving into "fight or flight" impulses that will drive members to either withdraw from the team, doing only what they have to do in

DOI: 10.4018/978-1-61520-619-3.ch012

order to survive, or engage in destructive conflict with other team members. Jones (2007) described what happened when two such teams did not embrace diversity as manifested by gender, culture and skill levels and consequently failed to form the social cohesion necessary for the teams to do their work. Instead, members of each team either stopped communicating with one another, or they engaged in sometimes vicious fighting. The consequence for both teams was a product that lacked creativity and many hard feelings. In many instances, team members fail to embrace their team's diversity because individuals on the team stereotype their peers. Men assign characteristics to women and women assign them to men. Members of different races assign characteristics to each other as do members of different cultures. These stereotypes can lead to prejudice and even bigotry, an act of mental violence towards another. These habits of mind called "distorted assumptions" by Mezirow (1991) can be so ingrained in people that they think that these attitudes are normal and right. Indeed, they may vehemently oppose any accusation of their bigotry, claiming that they are not bigoted in any way, but the behavior that illustrates their "theories-in-use" sharply contradicts their "espoused theories" (Argyris and Schon, 1974). Teams that suffer from members who work from a basis of distorted assumptions generally fall into a hierarchical, punitive structure where democratic collaboration gives way to the more powerful telling the less powerful what to do, what Argyris and Schon (1974) referred to as Model I behavior. The challenge for team trainers is to foster the development of these teams into ones that express Model II behavior, defined by Argyris and Schon (1974) as being "minimally defensive and open to learning." In these teams, "people will tend to help others, have more open discussions, exhibit reciprocity, and feel free to explore different views and express risky ideas (91). To achieve this level of team functioning, the trainer must promote the growth of a Model II mental framework within the individuals of the team. Fundamentally, the transformation of individuals practicing Model I behavior into ones practicing Model II behavior will occur as they become emancipated from "distorted assumptions" (Mezirow, 1991) through critical self-reflection of their "frames of reference," defined by Mezirow (2000) as: the structure of assumptions and expectations through which we filter sense impressions . . . Frames of reference are the results of ways of interpreting experience . . . Many of our most guarded beliefs about ourselves and our world—that we are smart or dumb, good or bad, winners or losers—are inferred from repetitive affective experience outside of awareness (p. 16). Through a process of transformative learning, frames of reference can be changed from those that reflect bigotry, rigid mindedness, prejudice and negative perceptions of self into ones that embrace "respect for others, self-respect, willingness to accept responsibility for the common good, willingness to welcome diversity and [willingness] to approach others with openness" (Cranton, 2001, p. 231). Despite the challenges to teams operating in cyberspace, Ritke-Jones (2008) contended that cyberspace offers a fertile environment for transformative learning in collaborative teams. In this article, I claimed that although racial, cultural, gender, and other status-related power differentials are not extinguished in cyberspace . . . [it] is a good thing because asynchronous communication especially makes it easier to archive, confront, and reflect on assumptions and biases as they act to thwart the team's efforts. Thus, for a person who is committed to her or his personal growth and to the success of a collaborative enterprise, [cyberspace] provides an outstanding tool for transformative learning. This chapter will extend this idea by asserting that a 3-D virtual environment provides an even more fecund environment for transformative learning by offering not only all of the tools of asynchronous communication but also the capacity for role playing with avatars, thus allowing for safe distance but also for personal interaction in real time. Thus, team members have opportunities for reflecting critically on their behaviors and the underlying assumptions dictating those behaviors, an endeavor that could lead to a transformation of personal frames of references to ones more democratic. Consequently, if all team members change, the team itself may grow into one that exhibits Model II characteristics, and this change may promote a more democratic culture in the whole organization.

BACKGROUND

Transformative Learning

By the time people reach adulthood and enter the workforce, they have constructed frames of reference that enable them to interpret and respond to experiences. The assumptions and values of their frames of reference grow from the culture in which they were raised, the social groups in which they operate and their relationships with individuals. When a person has an experience, s/he interprets the experience according to his/her assumptions and responds to the experience as if those assumptions were the only possible way to respond. Consequently, these assumptions are reinforced in a process that Argyris and Schon defined as "self-sealing." Cranton (1994) offers as an example two assembly line workers who face layoffs or retraining. One of these workers has grown up in a family that values education, but the other worker's family scoffed at education. This worker worries that her family will laugh at her if they discover that she is taking courses that will help her to get a professional position, but her and her family's perspective on education could lead her to critical self-reflection, which in turn could lead her to a transformative event. The other worker would likely have no such opportunity because retraining already aligns with her perspective that education is a valuable pursuit.

In another example, Henry has grown up in a family environment that held as an assumption that a certain race was lazy and intellectually and morally inferior. Being around like-minded people in his community, he has joined at least a few social groups that share this assumption. Thus, when he has an experience with one of this race, Lucy, he unconsciously interprets her behavior as fitting the lazy and inferior template, and interestingly, Lucy, if she has been brought up in the same culture, may well seek to play the role of the lazy and stupid one because that is her role in that culture, engaging in what Foucault termed

"self-surveillance," in fact, so that no transgression of these cultural roles may occur. If either Lucy or Henry or both started to question their assumptions, it may also lead to a critical self-reflection, just as in Cranton's example.

We can see this kind of relationship on a large scale with international cultures or on smaller scales with organizational cultures or even small offices. Regardless of the system, people who do not challenge their assumptions and values about themselves and about their roles in the systems in which they operate are imprisoned by them, doomed to continue often interpreting experiences and responding to communicative situations in distorted ways. Good coaches can help these people to emancipate themselves from their "distorted assumptions," defined by Mezirow (1991) as ones "that [lead] the learner to view reality in a way that arbitrarily limits what is included, impedes differentiation, lacks permeability or openness to other ways of seeing, or does not facilitate an integration of experience" (p. 118). According to Mezirow, then, distorted assumptions imprison the mind and disallow empathy or the negotiation of ideas.

Transformative learning events move individuals toward being "more inclusive, discriminating, open, emotionally capable of change, and reflective so that they may generate beliefs and opinions that will prove more true or justified to guide action" (Mezirow, 2001, p. 8). In describing the process of transformative learning, Mezirow outlined ten phases in which a meaning perspective in one's frames of reference undergoes transformation:

- Experiencing a disorienting dilemma
- Undergoing self-examination
- Conducting a critical assessment of internalized role assumptions and feeling a sense of alienation from traditional social expectations
- Relating one's discontent to similar experiences of others or to public

issues—recognizing that one's problem is shared and not exclusively a private matter

- Exploring options for new ways of acting
- Building competence and self-confidence in new roles
- Planning a course of action
- Acquiring knowledge and skills for implementing one's plans
- Making provisional efforts to try new roles and to assess feedback
- Reintegrating into society on the basis of conditions dictated by the new perspective

Henry, for example, may encounter conflict within a team in which he is working with Lucy. He may discover that his assumptions of Lucy's race may be faulty because she appears neither lazy nor intellectually inferior but because he expects Lucy to act according to his template, he continues to treat her as if she conforms to his assumption of her. Others in the team may call Henry on his treatment of Lucy, a disorienting dilemma for Henry, compelling him to examine his assumptions. From there, he would follow the remainder of the sequence, finally integrating into the team, the organization and society with a transformed meaning perspective.

Mezirow (1991) classifies meaning perspectives into three categories: epistemic, sociolinguistic, and psychological. Epistemic meaning perspectives are associated with what we know and how we use that knowledge. Sociolinguistic meaning perspectives reflect social norms, cultural templates, religious beliefs, family background and personal interactions. Finally, psychological meaning perspectives illustrate a person's self-concept as well as her/his inhibitions and anxieties. Meaning perspectives from all three of these categories may affect team collaboration. In Lucy's and Henry's examples, for instance, Henry's sociolinguistic meaning perspectives would impact his ability to collaborate with Lucy, and Lucy's negative self-concept would

also impact her ability to collaborate with Henry. An example of an epistemic meaning perspective impacting a collaborative team could be, for example, members of the team having different ways of processing and disseminating ideas. In this last case, a transformation of meaning perspective would be not a transformation of how one learns but an acceptance that others learn in different ways.

Transforming meaning perspectives requires that one first become aware of a distorted assumption in one of the categories of meaning perspectives often as a result of a disorienting dilemma. Becoming committed to self-examination at this stage, the individual may then engage in critical self-reflection defined by Dewey (1933) as "active, persistent and careful consideration of any belief or supposed form of knowledge in the light of the grounds that support it and the further conclusion it tends" (p. 9) and that Mezirow (1991) called "the process of critically assessing the content, process, or premise of our efforts to interpret and give meaning to an experience (p. 104). Cranton (1994) explained Mezirow's three types of reflection, aligned with the three types of knowledge that Habermas (1984) contended determined how people learn, by positing that in content reflection a person examines a problem, as in an apprentice mechanic wondering what piece of machinery is and how it operates (Crantion, 1994, p. 49). In process reflection a person examines the process by which he solved or is solving a problem, but in premise reflection, the problem itself is challenged. Cranton (1994) elaborated by offering the example of a learner who is uncomfortable in an educational environment. This learner would be engaged in premise reflection if she asks herself, "What is the basis for my belief that I am uncomfortable," and is it valid (p. 50).

Premise reflection, then, may lead to transformative learning in which meaning perspectives may be changed. In the example in the preceding paragraph, for instance, the person engaged in premise reflection may discover that her trepidation originates from other courses that she has taken in which she felt other learners knew more than she. Reflecting on this experience, she may discover that these experiences shadowed later learning opportunities, causing her to believe that everyone else in the course knew more than she, whether they did or not. At this stage, she may explore new ways of acting and continue on in the later stages of transformation until she has evolved a new, more self-confident, meaning perspective that she will bring with her into future learning contexts.

Creating an Environment for Transformative Learning

Mezirow (1991) argued that the "core of transformative learning . . . is the uncovering of distorted assumptions—errors in learning—in each of the three domains of meaning perspectives" (Crantion, 1994, p. 75). To uncover distorted assumptions, a person needs to engage in critical self-reflection or what Brookfield (1987) termed "critical thinking." To promote critical self-reflection, in Mezirow's mind, one needs to undergo a disorienting dilemma, often some negative occurrence that can violently shake one's frames of reference; however, Brookfield felt that a person could also undergo transformation under more positive conditions, such as reading a book. In either instance, the event reflects back to the person his meaning perspective. Working with people on a team project creates a fertile environment for transformative learning, then, if the team has as one of its primary goal personal transformation.

A team can create ideal conditions for discourse that compels one to critically assess and challenge assumptions if the environment is safe and supportive and well facilitated. The environment must meet these conditions because if a person has founded her or his way of doing things or, more deeply, his or her way of interpreting and acting within events, on a meaning perspective or a set of meaning perspectives, s/he will often become

defensive and afraid. To overcome this fear, the learner must feel empowered because "learner empowerment is both a goal of and a condition for transformative learning" (Crantion, 1994, p. 72). To achieve empowerment for its members, the team must develop trust, or individuals on the team must at least feel comfortable that they will not experience negative consequences such as loss of status in the workplace or even of employment. Only then would an individual capable of transformative learning be receptive to techniques designed to promote it. An individual who is sufficiently emotionally and cognitively develop can experience a transformative learning event, that development being defined more thoroughly later in this chapter.

Promoting Transformative Learning

To promote transformative learning, not only does a safe environment have to be created but one as egalitarian as possible, but in a team where some have greater status, an egalitarian environment may be difficult to achieve. Likewise, the facilitator of the team, most likely an educator or consultant, will have power that s/he will have to relinquish. To meet the challenge of creating an egalitarian space, then, the facilitator must not only give up the power of her/his position while maintaining what Cranton (1994) called personal power, the power to connect with learners and invite their trust; s/he must also "ensure freedom from coercion and equal opportunity for participation, and support learner-controlled decision making" (p. 146). Accomplishing this task, the facilitator sows the seeds for equal exchange, the ultimate goal being to promote rational discourse which in turn promotes critical reflection and consequently, perhaps, the transformative process.

In Mezirow's (1991) mind, rational discourse in a team compels each individual to challenge the soundness of his/her frames of reference. He argued that "participation in rational discourse under . . . ideal conditions will help adults become critically reflective of the meaning perspectives and arrive at more developmentally advanced meaning perspectives" (qtd in Cranton, 1994, p. 153). For the conditions to be ideal, as already mentioned, the team must have developed trust if not totally in one another then at least that speaking their minds will not result in negative consequences for them because providing honest feedback to one another in carefully facilitated dialogue fertilizes the soil for critical reflection.

CHAPTER FOCUS

Computer Mediated Communication as a Tool for Promoting Transformative Learning

Other chapters in this book suggest how virtual worlds can be used for reflection on epistemic and sociolinguistic meaning perspectives (see chapters in "Applications" for epistemic learning and chapters in "Connections" for sociolinguistic learning), so this chapter will focus on using the virtual world to foster reflection on psychological meaning perspectives that could lead to transformation. A team collaborating in physical space can certainly take advantage of the virtual world for transformative learning, but since unique challenges impede the formation of social cohesion in teams operating in cyberspace (Jones, 2007; Palloff and Pratt, 1999), transformative learning in a virtual world may be especially valuable for them.

Cyberspace does not erase gender, racial and cultural biases (Hum, 2002; Jones, 2007; Lea and Spears, 1992; Selfe and Selfe, 1994; Smith, 2005) that can impede the formation of trust and stress task performance. Other scholars show that although biases are not erased, electronic environments can empower women, minorities, and others who either lack power or are merely reticent because of the distance cyberspace creates between communicators (Barker & Kemp,

1990; Jones, 2007, Harasim, 1990; Hawisher and Moran, 1993; Thompson, 1990; Ritke-Jones, 2008). This distance can be used to advantage by the facilitator to create a ripe environment for transformative learning because the added distance and anonymity of the online space tends to flatten hierarchies somewhat, thus creating a more egalitarian environment.

In addition, Ritke-Jones (2009) described how a facilitator could have used distance as well as other cyberspace characteristics such as the capacity for easily archiving communications to foment transformative learning opportunities in two diverse teams collaborating in cyberspace on writing projects. Using the conflict engendered by their differences, conflicts that were severe enough to cause team disintegration, Ritke-Jones (2009) contended that by prompting the team members to reflect on their behavior within the team, critical reflection could have been initiated. Accomplished by adopting a coaching demeanor, the facilitator could ask challenging questions during interviews of the team members about communicative events that had been archived during text chat or in threaded discussions. These questioning sessions could occur individually or as team employing a team chat tool, and since team members would have some distance from one another, the power hierarchy may be somewhat flattened, allowing for a more honest discussion, even if more heated.

Cranton (1994) described two models for interviewing that may promote critical reflection presented in Mezirow and Associates (1990). The first of these, the Peters' (1990) Action-Reason-Thematic Technique, she named the simplest and is essentially a strategy for understanding behavior in problem situations. Five steps are involved:

- Identification of the learner's problem as defined by the learner
- Establishment of the time frame of the problem, the beginning and end of the problem, and its possible solution

- Identification and description of specific actions taken to solve the problem, for example, asking the learner, "What did you do?" Or, "What did you do next?"
- Identification and description of reasons for each action taken
- Reduction of actions and reasons to argument themes (or identifying assumptions that guided behavior) (Cranton, 1994, p. 203).

According to Cranton, Peters (1990) claimed that using this technique would lead to an uncovering of assumptions and offered ten directions for using the technique:

- Ask both What did you do? and why did you do it? questions
- Ask open-ended questions to allow the learner to describe his or her experiences and reasoning
- Ask probing questions to reveal the learner's reasoning
- Ask only one question at a time and frame questions based on the context of the interview up to that point
- Avoid learning questions
- Mirror learners' answers to enhance understanding and indicate interest
- Postpone judgment of learners' answers
- Use a conversational tone
- Avoid giving opinions or instructions until an analysis of the assumptions is made
- Always focus on the learner and his or her problem (pp. 322-323, as qtd. in Cranton, 1994, p. 204).

Gould (1990) developed the other model called the Therapeutic Learning Program that Cranton (1994) described. Cranton said that Gould designed this model "to facilitate transformative learning in educational, work and treatment contexts" (Gould, 1990, p. 135 as qtd. in Cranton, 1994, p. 104). Gould proffered seven steps to use questioning to promote critical reflection:

- Identifying and framing the function to be recovered (identifying the conflict, the problem situation, and the stresses involved)
- Clarifying the action intention, that is, determining action as well as the costs and benefits of the action
- Distinguishing realistic dangers from exaggerating fears (looking at the fear response provoked by the intention to act)
- Isolating and exposing fears as predictions confused with memories (in Mezirow's language, separating the sources of underlying assumptions from the consequences of acting on them)
- Explaining the origins of catastrophic predictions (understanding the source of old fears)
- Demonstrating and diminishing self-fulfilling prophecies; developing an awareness of the tendency to continue to act in old ways
- Consolidating new view of reality (Cranton, 1994, p. 204).

Both of these models strive to foster critical reflection and were designed with physical space in mind, but cyberspace may often be a better place for questioning; and a 3-D virtual environment may be better still.

Interviewing in a Virtual World

For interviews to instigate and nurture critical premise reflection, the interviewer must establish a relationship of trust, openness and honesty with the interviewee so that s/he will feel safe. A virtual world may be the perfect place to create such an atmosphere because while the technology distances the two people, it also provides a physical representation of them that allows for the physical expression of emotion, emotion being as important to transformative learning as cognition (Dirkx, 2006; Dirkx, 2001). The expression of emotion through the avatar would require that the participants in the interview identify the avatar as an extension of themselves. In my personal experiences in role-playing games, I infuse my avatars with emotion so much so that when one is injured in combat or is not treated well by another avatar, I take personal issue. In interviews that I conducted with five other players in the game that I played, all reported that their avatars were extensions of themselves and that the emotion that their avatars expressed was their own personal emotion. A more scientific study than the informal one that I conducted should be done to determine whether people infuse their avatars with emotions, but studies such as Blascovich, et. al. (2002) and Messinger, et. al. (2008) supports the notion that people identify their avatars as extensions of themselves.

The expression of emotion through an avatar does require forethought, however, thus disallowing unconscious paralinguistic cues that the interviewer/coach could use to decipher meaning. The interviewer/coach could model expression using the tool provided in a virtual world like Second Life. For instance, if the interviewer/coach wanted to let the interviewee know that s/he was fully engaged in the interviewee's message, s/he might emote, "William listens intently." To express surprise, the coach could emote, "William cocks his eyebrows in surprise." If the interviewee has been working in a virtual world already, s/he may already know how to make such emotes, or the interviewer/coach could commit to just a little bit of training and encouragement to help the person take advantage of this part of the communication tool.

Although the lack of paralinguistic cues limits the interchange, the virtual environment creates distance between the interviewer/coach and the interviewee that could make the interviewee feel safer to explore her/his role in team dysfunction. As the interviewee seeks to respond to challenging questions designed to prompt him/her into self-reflection, s/he may have a greater opportunity to

seriously consider the values and background that s/he brought into the team that may have had a role in team dysfunction or that may be impeding the team's progress. Too, the interviewee may have less trouble confronting and expressing fears and prophecies in the virtual world than in a physical space, especially if the person perceives that s/he must maintain a persona of control, thus ripening the conditions for transformative learning to occur.

The virtual world also flattens power differentials, especially useful when coaching a person who may feel scrutinized by superiors through the interviewer/coach. Whereas in a physical setting the interviewee may steel him or herself, the virtual environment may help the interviewee to take some of her/his defenses down. Besides promoting the efficacy of questioning, this flattening may also assist the interviewer/coach in helping the interviewee develop and test a new plan of behavior because s/he may feel more willing to ask for help and to make mistakes that can be discussed with the coach. Using archived dialogues between the coach and her/him, the interviewee can read and reflect on where s/he deviated from a plan and what lingering habits of thought are responsible. The virtual world becomes a valuable tool, then, for seeing the transformative learning process to its culmination.

Using Role Play in a Virtual World to Promote Transformative Learning

Cranton (1994) claimed that "experiences that encourage learners to take on the roles and hence the perspectives of others can lead to consciousness-raising" (p. 174) and possibly to transformative learning. She cited several sources (Brookfield, 1990; Corey, 1985; Cranton, 1992; Johnson and Johnson, 1982;) to support her contention that role playing is the most productive and most often used strategy to effect consciousness raising. Cranton (1994) also provided several different scenarios for role-playing:

- Two people reverse roles and express views they had previously opposed in a discussion;
- Two people reverse roles they play in real life (for example, a manager and a staff member . . .)
- . . .
- Learners write short autobiographies—of someone else's life . . .
- Learners write down opinions or views that are antithetical to those they hold . . . (p. 175).

Ritke-Jones (2008) speculated how a virtual 3-D environment that allows for the creation of identity could be used for role-playing of the sort the Cranton described. For instance, a person on a team experiencing destructive conflict could easily adopt the identity of another on the team with whom s/he is in conflict by merely signing on as that person's avatar into the virtual world. Then, s/he would attempt to act as s/he believes the other would during discussions, putting forth the opinions that s/he believes the other holds. After the discussion, a team coaching session could be held using archived transcripts of the discussion with the members who swapped identities correcting any misunderstandings that were uncovered by explaining how the other missed the mark in expressing her/his opinions. This exercise would also be instrumental in helping the person see how others perceive him/her, and it would also be useful in revealing distorted assumptions that the person may hold.

To develop empathy for another person on the team, each could write an autobiography as if s/he were someone else and then create that identity in the virtual world, a creation that could include making the avatar look according to how the person perceives the other to look and mannerisms according to how s/he thinks the other would act. In this particular instance, an understanding of another's background and current social groups would be the primary aim. An African-American woman might get a better understanding of a Caucasian man and vice versa; people from different cultures might understand better what being from someone else's culture might be like and so on. Again, it would be necessary for careful facilitation, and each member of the team would need to provide generous and compassionate guidance to one attempting to portray him/her. Some conflict could result from this endeavor regardless of how well it is conducted, but the conflict should not be avoided but embraced as an opportunity to help the two (or more) people understand each other better. Again, the profound opportunity for challenging distorted assumptions using this scenario should not be wasted.

Finally, the virtual world offers a prime opportunity for people to understand the viewpoints of others and to challenge their own distorted assumptions by offering them the chance to role play the viewpoints that they believe someone else holds. Again signing on with the identity of the other person, the team member could create a persuasive argument based on what s/he thinks is the other person's position. The two (or more) would then debate each other in the virtual world based on the perceived other position. This scenario allows for the opportunity to not only clearly understand the other's position but also to challenge notions held that are steeped in rigid thinking and distorted assumptions. Ripe for premise reflection, the person may begin a process of transformation by engaging in this method.

Challenges to Using Virtual Environments for Transformative Learning

The most obvious challenge to transformative learning in a virtual reality is the lack of physical presence because transformative learning depends upon critical discourse whether within a coaching or a role-playing context. In order to be effective, critical discourse must occur between two or more people who are present with each other. Obviously, when people are connected via any kind of technology, they are not physically present. Because the individuals involved in the discourse are represented by an avatar that creates the illusion of physical presence and because the participants are acting within the confines of a virtual space, if not a physical one, a 3-D virtual environment offers a richer environment for transformative learning than any other kind of technology, an important point for teams connected only with technology. In a teleconference, for instance, participants can see and hear each other, but no space exists for them. If participants are using chat or asynchronous communication, they become merely text on the screen to one another unless they have met or share pictures. If they are using voice, they have only disembodies sounds. But in the 3-D world, they communicate with a representative of the other people within a space that they can claim as their own.

Blascovich, et al (2002) remarked that "if a participant believes that he or she is interacting with the representation of a real other, his or her sense of the social presence of that virtual human will be high" (p. 112). In my own experience in role-playing games in virtual worlds over the course of the past six years, I have always had the sense that I was playing with other people. Still, some would argue that the avatar representation of another person is not that person, and in fact, in a virtual world such as Second Life, a person could represent him or herself as anything, such as another person, a giraffe, a cup of instant tea or a beach ball. In the virtual world, people often interact with one another as if they are the avatar and forget that the avatar is merely a representation of another person. Thus, when the OD specialist directs people in creating avatars for themselves in worlds that allow identity creation, s/he should encourage an individual to create those that is an accurate representation of him or herself.

Messinger, et. al (2008) argued that not much encouragement would be necessary in a report of quantitative data illustrating that people create avatars that resemble themselves anyway, except that the avatars are generally more attractive. For the purposes of transformative learning, the more attractive avatar creates a positive situation since it elicits greater empowerment than one would have in a physical environment, helping marginalized people to feel more empowered to participate in critical discourse (Messinger, et al, 2008) and by extension helping those in power positions to recognize when and why they are oppressing others, thus initiating transformation. If a transformation begins in the virtual world, one must nonetheless wonder whether the transformative process will continue in the physical world. Citing Cabiria (2008), Messinger, et. al (2008) argued that it would, claiming that people "find therapeutic benefit by participating in communities in virtual worlds, and then transferring these benefits to their real lives" (p. 5).

Besides these "soft" issues, participants must be comfortable with the technology. To be comfortable with the technology does not merely mean that the participants can navigate physically through the virtual surroundings, nor does it mean just that can converse, although training them how to do those two things plus creating an identity by acquiring "skins," "shapes," hair, clothes, even a walk unique to themselves would be necessary in an environment such as Second Life. As important as being able to accomplish these physical tasks are, if participants have not gained some experience working in a virtual environment, one cannot expect them to be accustomed enough to the environment to immediately engage in transformative learning activities.

People less than 40 who have grown up with social networking and with game playing in virtual worlds may have a much easier time adjusting to transformative work in virtual worlds. Often, these younger people feel as much comfort with conversing over the network as they do face-to-face, and in the case of traditionally disempowered or introverted people, they may feel more comfortable. On the other hand, these same people may be so accustomed to using cyberspace to connect socially that they may have to re-adjust their perspectives so that they can use the technology for work. Older workers may approach the technology as a tool to help them work better, the correct position, or they may approach it as another means by which their managers torture them.

Young or old, the organizational development specialist's primary challenge will be achieve "buy-in" not only from the organization but from the participants, as well. If people are too busy socializing or resent having to use the technology, promoting self-reflection will prove to be a futile effort. If a company has been using a virtual world for meetings, the effort becomes easier because the participants will be accustomed to using the environment. Nevertheless, the OD specialist will need to train them to move, create themselves online, and so forth, so a simple but immersive environment such as Wonderland may be more advantageous than one like Second Life for transformative learning since participants would have fewer and less complicated things to learn. On the other hand, the identity creation and superior collaborative building capabilities of a platform such as Second Life offers advantages that a simpler platform does not. For instance, identity creation creates opportunities for reflection when one is asked why s/he has created him or herself or another in a particular way, thus providing a chance to bring a self-perception or a perception of another to the surface where it can be challenged, and the challenge to premises on which perceptions are founded is the essence of transformative learning.

FUTURE TRENDS

Virtual environments promise tremendous benefits for geographically distributed teams because they offer simulated personal interaction in a virtual space. Having their own space in which to work

and interact socially, even only a virtual space, aids teams to bond emotionally and to build the trust so important to good teamwork. In order for teams to build trust, team members must develop empathy and understanding for one another, and to accomplish that task, often a transformation of perspectives must occur. In promoting transformative learning in teams, virtual environments offer a valuable tool that has not yet been exploited.

A number of reasons exist for virtual environments not yet being exploited for transformative learning. Buy-in for transformative learning in any environment by management team members remains the greatest challenge because team development of this sort can often be seen as a distraction from the team's main mission. Too, distributed teams will more than likely choose technology such as video conferencing software to collaborate. The future for virtual environments in transformative learning, then, rests in its capacity to integrate with other technologies because most organizations are not going to abandon collaborative software that they think works and is easy to use in favor of virtual worlds that require their employees to invest time in learning.

One way to take advantage of virtual environments for transformative learning while still using other tools for collaboration, employees could use the technology that they normally use for collaborating at a distance but for transformative intervention, the OD specialist could have them work within the virtual world. To be effective, the OD specialist could make an initial analysis of the team's dynamics by observing them in their primary collaborative environment by being a participant/observer. Interviews would be helpful, as well, in discovering possible team dysfunctions possibly attributable to the distorted assumptions of one or more team members. The OD specialist could conduct more thorough analysis of the team during exercises that s/he sets up for the team to do in the virtual world. Then, OD specialist could engage in the processes of coaching or role playing in conjunction with coaching with team members. Here again, however, buy-in from the team members would be necessary as would some training with the technology.

Sloodle, discussed at length elsewhere in this book by Peachey and Livingstone, could be an outstanding tool for transformative learning because of the combined potential of role playing and easily archiving communications for later reflection. Also, the asynchronous aspect of Sloodle provides a means of having participants discuss issues within the team at a greater distance than would synchronous discussion. Imagine a scenario, for instance, in which a team is challenging one of its members. The asynchronous environment would allow a safer distance, useful especially if the challenged member ranks higher in the organization than the other team members. The OD specialist would need to skillfully facilitate to both open up the discussion and to prevent destructive attacks. The asynchronous discussion used in combination with role playing and coaching in the virtual world may give the OD specialist a powerful tool for promoting transformative learning, however, so the effort to learn how to facilitate in the virtual world as well as in asynchronous discussions may be worth the effort.

CONCLUSION

This chapter has provided an overview of transformative learning and how virtual worlds can be used as tool to promote transformation in individuals and consequently in teams and organizations. As organizations become more diverse and distributed, people will bring their preconceptions, prejudices and bigotry to their interactions with others. These negative characteristics can poison an organization, turning it into a battleground where people compete for power rather than collaborate to produce high quality services and products. Moreover, even if none of these negative characteristics exists, as organizations become increasingly global, cultural differences

that range from approaching a task to approaching the management of the entire organization will need to be addressed.

The only lasting way to manage diversity is to embrace it, finding ways to promote empathy and understanding among people who at least confuse with one another and who on occasion may actually hate one another. Transformative Learning is the key to foster greater understanding, empathy, and democratic habits of thinking to employees, teams and organizations. Virtual Worlds provide an outstanding tool for the internal or external consultant who wants to promote transformative learning, especially in distributed teams but not necessarily only those. Because it is such a valuable tool, understanding it and how to use it to promote transformative learning should become a high priority learning goal for internal consultants and for external consultants, especially those who work with distributed teams.

REFERENCES

Argyris, C., & Schon, D. (1974). *Theory in practice: Increasing professional effectiveness*. San Francisco: Jossey Bass.

Barker, T., & Kemp, F. (1990). Network Theory: A Postmodern Pedagogy for The Writing Classroom. In Handa, C. (Ed.), *Computers and community: Teaching composition in the twenty-first century* (pp. 1–27).

Blascovich, J., Loomis, J., Beall, A., Swinth, K., Hoyt, C., & Bailenson, J. (2002). Immersive virtual environment technology: A methodological tool for social psychology. *Psychological Inquiry*, *13*(2), 103–104. doi:10.1207/S15327965PLI1302_01

Brookfield, S. (1987). *Developing critical thinkers: Challenging adults to explore alternative ways of thinking and acting*. San Francisco: Jossey-Bass.

Cabiria, J. (2008). Virtual world and real world permeability: Transfer of positive benefits for marginalized gay and lesbian populations. *Journal of Virtual Worlds Research, 1*(1).

Corey, G. (1985). *Theory and practice of team counseling* (2nd ed.). Pacific Grove, CA: Brooks/Cole.

Cranton, P. (1994). *Transformative learning: A guide for educators of adults*. San Francisco: Jossey-Bass.

Cranton, P. (2001). Individual differences and transformative learning. In J. Mezirow & Assoc. (Ed.), Learning as transformation: Critical perspectives on a theory in progress, (pp. 181-204). San Francisco: Jossey-Bass.

Dewey, J. (1933). *How We Think. A restatement of the relation of reflective thinking to the educative process*. Lexington: D.C. Heath and Company.

Dirkx, J. (2001). The power of feeling: Emotion, imagination, and the construction of meaning in adult learning . In Merriam, S. B. (Ed.), *The new update on adult learning theory*. San Francisco: Jossey-Bass.

Dirkx, J. (2006). Engaging emotions in adult learning: A Jungian perspective on emotion and transformative learning. *New Directions for Adult and Continuing Education, 109*, 15–26. doi:10.1002/ace.204

Gould, R. (1990). The therapeutic learning program. In J. Mezirow & Assoc. (Eds.), Fostering critical reflection in adulthood. San Francisco: Jossey-Bass.

Habermas, J. (1984). *The theory of communicative action*. Boston: Beacon Press.

Harasim, L. (1990). Introduction to online education . In Harasim, L. (Ed.), *Online education: Perspectives on a new environment*. New York: Praeger.

Hawisher, G., & Moran, C. (1993, October). Electronic mail and the writing instructor. *College English, 55*(6), 627–643. doi:10.2307/378699

Hum, S. (2002, Summer). Performing gendered identities: A small-team collaboration in a computer-mediated classroom interaction. *Journal of Curriculum Theorizing*.

Johnson, D., & Johnson, F. (1982). *Joining together: Team theory and team skills* (2nd ed.). Englewood Cliffs, NJ: Prentice-Hall.

Johnson, D., & Johnson, F. (2006). *Joining together: Team theory and team skills* (9th ed.). Englewood Cliffs, NJ: Prentice-Hall.

Jones, W. (2007). Why they don't work: factors that impede the development of social cohesion in online collaborative teams. *Pennsylvania Association of Adult and Community Educators Journal of Lifelong Learning, 16*, 37–62.

Lea, M., & Spears, R. (1992). Paralanguage and social perception in computer-mediated communication. *Journal of Organizational Computing, 2*, 321–341. doi:10.1080/10919399209540190

Messinger, P., Ge, X., Stroulia, E., Lyons, K., Smirnov, K., & Bone, M. (2008, November). On the relationship between my avatar and myself. *Virtual Worlds Research: Consumer Behavior in Virtual Worlds, 1*(2), 1–17.

Mezirow, J. & Assoc. (1990). *Fostering critical reflection in adulthood*. San Francisco: Jossey-Bass.

Mezirow, J. (1991). *Transformative dimensions of adult learning*. San Francisco: Jossey-Bass.

Mezirow (2000). Mezirow, J. (2001). Learning to think like an adult: Core concepts of transformation theory. In J. Mezirow & Assoc. (Ed.), *Learning as transformation: Critical perspectives on a theory in progress,* (pp. 3-34). San Francisco: Jossey-Bass.

Palloff, R., & Pratt, K. (1999). *Building learning communities in cyberspace: Effective strategies for the online classroom*. San Francisco: Jossey Bass Publications.

Peters, J. (1990). The action-reason-thematic technique: Spying on the self. In J. Mezirow & Assoc. (Ed.), Fostering critical reflection in adulthood. San Francisco: Jossey-Bass.

Ritke-Jones, W. (2008). Using cyberspace to promote transformative learning experiences and consequently democracy in the workplace . In St. Amant, K., & Zemliansky, P. (Eds.), *Handbook of research on virtual workplaces and the new nature of business practices* (pp. 204–219). Hershey, PA: IGI Global.

Selfe, C., & Selfe, R. (1994). The Politics of the interface: Power and its exercise in electronic contact zones. *College Composition and Communication, 45*(4), 480–501. doi:10.2307/358761

Smith, R. (2005, May). Working with difference in online collaborative teams. *Adult Education Quarterly, 55*(3), 182–199. doi:10.1177/0741713605274627

Thompson, D. (1990, August). Electronic bulletin boards: A timeless place for collaborative writing projects. *Computers and Composition, 7*, 43–53. doi:10.1016/S8755-4615(05)80026-X

KEY TERMS AND DEFINITIONS

Critical Self-Reflection: refers to the reflection on experience that reveals the underlying assumptions, values, and beliefs that compel a person to act as she/he does in a particular situation and to interpret the actions of another in a particular way; thus critical reflection unveils one's "frames of reference" as Mezirow calls them or one's "espoused theories of action" as Argyris and Schon referred to them. Critical reflection is necessary before transformative learning may occur, but critical reflection does not necessarily lead to transformative learning.

Diversity: Refers to the different demographic characteristics that the different members of a team or other group may have. These differences could be cultural, social, age, ethnicity, gender, language, or religious. Diversity could also pertain to different personality characteristics or learning styles that cause individuals to perceive situations or tasks and approach task or problem solution in different ways.

Distorted Assumptions: Are deeply ingrained habits of thought that reflect bigotry, hatred, or merely closed, rigid thinking. These assumptions can cause people to wholly reject the ideas of others and may cause the person holding the distorted assumption to think that others who hold different views are crazy or somehow abnormal.

Frames of Reference: Are the "structures of assumptions and expectations through which we filter sense impressions" (Mezirow, 2001, p. 16). One's frames of reference shape how a person perceives, thinks and feels and provides the framework by which one makes meaning of experiences. Frames of Reference are "composed of two dimensions, a habit of mind and resulting points of view (Mezirow, 2001, p. 17) that determine how we will choose to act in a particular situation and how we will interpret the actions or speech of others.

Meaning Perspectives: Are templates that we begin to acquire during childhood that we use to interpret situations and to choose appropriate responses to a situation. Meaning perspectives are categorized into epistemic, sociolinguistic and psychological and make up the broader frames of reference that become habits of thought.

Model I Behavior: Is behavior that is competitive and hostile. Argyris and Schon approach claiming that this kind of behavior is barbaric and uncivilized. In this behavior, individuals compete to get their own needs and wants satisfied with little thought to the collective good. Those practicing this kind of behavior seek to dominate others.

Model II Behavior: Is behavior that is collaborative and inclusive. Rather than seeking to dominate, people who practice this behavior strive to be democratic, inviting and encouraging weaker voices to be heard. Argyris and Schon imply that this way of behaving illustrates more enlightened and emotionally mature people. When conflict occurs in organizations acting from model II, members of the organization seek to understand and empathize with one another even while stating their individual points of view.

Team: Refers to a group of people who work together toward a common goal. A team usually consists of no more than ten people, and its efforts are collaborative rather than cooperative, meaning that the team must develop a common vision for solving a problem. A common vision can only happen when a collective consciousness develops in the group, and a collective consciousness can only develop when a high level of social cohesion develops within the team.

Transformative Learning: Involves a reframing of assumptions that provide a different perspective on the world. As such, transformative learning leads to "respect for others, self-respect, willingness to accept responsibility for the common good, willingness to welcome diversity and to approach others with openness" (Mezirow, 2001, p. 14). It should be noted that this concept of transformative learning assumes that the aforementioned characteristics are positive, but the pronouncement that these are positive characteristics is a social construct.

Chapter 13
The New Company Water Cooler:
Use of 3D Virtual Immersive Worlds to Promote Networking and Professional Learning in Organizations

Amelia W. Cheney
Appalachian State University, USA

Richard E. Riedl
Appalachian State University, USA

Robert L. Sanders
Appalachian State University, USA

John H. Tashner
Appalachian State University, USA

ABSTRACT

Employees gathered around the water cooler – the image is now a corporate cliché. This type of informal networking allows members of an organization to build – or break – personal and professional relationships in ways not possible in more formal settings or business situations. As companies become larger and more geographically dispersed, these types of opportunities and relationships are increasingly more difficult to create and maintain. Organizations must investigate new means of communications and technology. Three-dimensional (3D) immersive worlds offer a range of possibilities for accomplishing this goal. In this chapter, the authors will highlight their eight year experience using 3D virtual immersive worlds in graduate programs at Appalachian State University. Their experience based on feedback, observation, and survey results suggests that 3D virtual worlds developed for education support deep learning and can help learners make meaning and feel part of a learning community. The chapter will consider ways in which corporate organizations can draw upon the experience of higher education in the design, creation and utilization of virtual worlds to create opportunity for both purposeful and serendipitous interaction.

DOI: 10.4018/978-1-61520-619-3.ch013

INTRODUCTION

Employees gathered around the water cooler – the image is now a corporate cliché. Here, discussions range from baseball to babies to work itself. This type of informal networking allows members of an organization to build – or break -- personal and professional relationships, discuss strategies and plans and to exchange ideas in ways not possible in more formal settings business situations or email. Organizations have traditionally responded to the need for more informal interaction in a number of ways – trust falls and team sports come easily to mind.

As companies become larger and more geographically dispersed and as sections of organizations become more isolated, these types of opportunities for exchanges are increasingly more difficult to create and maintain. Organizations must investigate new means of communications and technology. Three-dimensional (3D) virtual immersive worlds and Web 2.0 tools offer a range of possibilities for accomplishing this goal.

In our own university department we have several graduate preparation programs in education. These separate program areas may represent different sections or departments within an organization in the corporate world. Each program has its own faculty, students and job orientation. For instance, we have one program that develops school management personnel. Another program develops instructional technology specialists, while others provide training for librarians and for higher education instructors and administrators. Each program, though housed within the same organizational structure tends to be isolated in its own silo. While each is tasked with developing experts for specific roles in education, students are afforded few opportunities to work with others who are studying different roles. Thus, they leave their formal training with a deep understanding of their particular role and have to learn ways to work with other roles within the confines of the school environment. This isolation of roles may contribute to the role conflicts that we see occurring in various educational institutions where managers do not really understand the added value that various others bring to the table. We need to create formal and informal learning environments that break down these educational silos while students are in graduate school so that they will enter the workplace with the knowledge and skills necessary to quickly bring relevant and meaningful collaborations to solve the problems quickly and efficiently. 3D immersive worlds and Web 2.0 have provided us the technologies needed to implement these concepts. We have had, like many organizations, some specific successes, and continuing to expand these notions in authentic ways remains our current challenge.

In this chapter, we will highlight our eight-year experience using 3D virtual immersive worlds in graduate education programs at Appalachian State University. In the AET Zone, based on an Active Worlds platform and supplemented by Web 2.0 tools such as VoIP, threaded discussions, wikis, blogs, and podcast technologies, students and faculty work together to create a learning community of practice that includes programs in instructional technology, library science, school administration, higher education and educational leadership. Our experience, based on feedback, observation, and survey results and other research suggests that 3D virtual worlds developed for education support deep learning and can help learners make meaning and feel part of a learning communities that transcends the traditional single classroom experience.

Ways in which corporate organizations can draw upon the experience of higher education in the design, creation and utilization of virtual worlds to create opportunity for both purposeful and serendipitous interaction will be explored in this chapter.

BACKGROUND

Eight years ago the Instructional Technology program at Appalachian State was wrestling with issues of how to move online. The program served middle career teachers throughout western North Carolina with cohort-based courses offered in locations convenient to students; course instructors traveled to those locations. At that time, the faculty of the program used a wide array of online tools to supplement coursework and was well aware of the advantages and disadvantages of each. Appalachian State was using WebCT as its online course management system, and the program instructors were leery of the typical pattern of breaking courses into 'chunks' of content with its attendant readings, quizzes, papers, and discussion board entries. These processes delivered content, but the faculty was not convinced they provided the types of learning experiences they desired.

Courses taught in the Instructional Technology program were (and still are) active explorations of content, issues, questions, and skills that ask students to continuously engage with each other and their instructors to create real world ways to incorporate digital technologies into their classrooms and to support teachers in their efforts to use these technologies in teaching and learning. The Reich College of Education at Appalachian State has adopted a social constructivist framework for teaching and learning. This framework speaks to the development of communities of learners with goals of moving learners from novice to expert and understanding that at any given time any individual in the community may serve as an expert or be a novice. These roles can also shift depending on the topic, skill, issue, or problem being explored. In fact, in a rapidly changing digital world and in the everyday life of schools and school districts, it is not inconceivable that the instructor becomes a novice for some element of the course.

With all of these things in mind, the faculty were reluctant to make the leap from blended or hybrid (face-to-face and online activity used together) to fully online experiences. They did not find any of the online tools available to them through the university that were sufficient to overcome their doubts and questions about providing the full richness of teaching and learning they desired.

While struggling with these questions, they were introduced to 3D virtual worlds by a candidate being interviewed for a position. These early 3D worlds were really chat rooms with objects and avatars presented in 3D perspective and very new on the Internet horizon. Richard Riedl and a group of graduate students decided to look more closely at these environments to see if they might be used for education. They decided to build a course environment over the summer and to try it as a pilot experience in a course the following fall.

Active Worlds (www.activeworlds.com) was chosen for the reason that of the two available 3D worlds available to them at the time, Active Worlds offered free space on their education server. Following this experiment the Instructional Technology faculty revisited the issues they perceived related to going online, discussed the experiences of using Active Worlds, and decided that it was worth trying to move their program into such a platform. Fortunately, they also discovered that they could afford to purchase their own server. More detailed descriptions of the environment are located elsewhere in the literature (Bronack, Riedl & Tashner, 2006; Riedl, Bronack, & Tashner, 2005; Tashner, Bronack, & Riedl, 2005).

In the fall 2002 semester the first course was offered as a blended course using the Instructional Technology Active Worlds 3D immersive world environment. The following spring two more courses were added. These additions provided the first opportunities for 'cross-cohort' activities. Students from geographically separate locations and on different meeting schedules were expected to work together online to accomplish specific tasks.

In subsequent semesters more courses were added and faculty began understanding the potentials and limitations of the 3D environment. Continuing opportunities for formal and informal interactions among students and with faculty were developed. As the success of these pilots became evident, faculty in other programs began to take notice and the conversation was broadened to include cross-program/cross-major tasks that would enrich the learning experiences of all involved.

Many of the lessons learned from the eight years of exploration in virtual worlds may have applications to venues other than higher education. The water cooler metaphor is intentional because many of the lessons learned speak to the strength of informal settings within the formal workplace that help with the development of communications, problem solving partnerships, and other aspects of the training, support, and development of a sense of corporate well being that are necessary for any organization to be successful.

ISSUES, CONTROVERSIES AND PROBLEMS

One of the driving considerations for Appalachian's move to 3D immersive environments was the geographical distance between students – a problem increasingly faced in business and other organizational environments. Online resources have emerged as logical tools to help build and maintain relationships and communication between teams of people separated by time and space. As a result, several pertinent issues have emerged which must be considered:

- What are the best online tools to accomplish organizational goals? Should virtual worlds be considered?
- How can virtual spaces best be used to create and maintain relationships over space and time?

- How can virtual environments be designed to best facilitate different types of tasks and interactions?
- How can organizations build critical mass within virtual spaces to best optimize their potential?

These questions will be considered in this section.

Selection of Online Tools and Consideration of Virtual Worlds

With the myriad of online tools available, a fundamental question exists for any organization: why consider virtual worlds at all? What added value might they present to the organization? The answers to this question depend largely upon the purpose of the tools to be used. If traditional content delivery is the goal, virtual worlds may not be needed, but when the goals are to create community and facilitate communications and meaningful interactions, the scenario changes dramatically.

It is worthy of note that virtual worlds continue to gain momentum at a dramatic rate. Gartner Research predicts that by 2011, over 80% of active Internet users will have some type of virtual presence (2007), and that 70% of organizations will be utilizing private virtual worlds by 2012 (2008). People of all ages are becoming rapidly accustomed to the affordances of 3D environments, and corporations have moved to incorporate this trend into marketing and brand presence endeavors. Despite this, Gartner also notes that nine out of ten corporate forays into virtual spaces fail within 18 months. Why is this so?

"Businesses have learned some hard lessons," said Steve Prentice, vice president and fellow at Gartner. "They need to realize that virtual worlds mark the transition from web pages to web places and a successful virtual presence

starts with people, not physics. Realistic graphics and physical behavior count for little unless the presence is valued by and engaging to a large audience." (2008)

A recent report by the released by the Entertainment Software Association (2008) found that 70 percent of major employers utilize interactive software and games to train employees. Likewise, Nortel is developing a highly interactive 3D immersive business environment characterized by audio and collaborative tools to meet, train employees and to conduct business (2009). IBM also sees added value in the emerging 3D world platforms for business training and educational activities, as well as conducting various aspects of business.

This isn't just about living in Second Life or playing sophisticated games. It's about building platforms where serious business can be conducted, including 3D intranets, private business worlds, application-specific platforms, and tools for business transformation…. We're devising immersive environments for meetings that are more like real life, re-creating real-world events and destinations, and providing cultural and interactive experiences for people who can't make it to the real places. And when it comes to education, we're using 3D models to simplify complex topics, build interactive training modules, and enhance rehearsals and role playing. (Parris, 2007)

Sun Microsystems also sees potential for businesses in 3D immersive worlds as they continue to develop their Wonderland platform. This is uniquely suited for business applications including real timeshared applications and a place for personal and team sharing work (Kronos, 2007). Wilson (2009) has identified eleven immersive virtual world platforms that have the potential to change the ways we work over the next few years. He has categorized these in three distinct groups: those that are currently business ready, those that

are on the radar, and those that are upcoming. Several of the possible uses identified for 3D immersive worlds in business include conferences and exhibitions, product launches, corporate meetings and secure virtual spaces. Interestingly, one 3D immersive world that is placed in the "business ready" section is the Active Worlds platform that we have been using as the platform for the AET Zone. Our experience would add large and small group collaborations, presentations, and education and training. eWeek (2008) introduces a video which explain how some Web 2.0 technologies work for companies:

Increasingly, organizations are using Web 2.0 applications and technology to help aggregate corporate knowledge, simplify the building of repositories of best practices, and enable new levels of collaboration. What's more, managers and workers alike can use Web 2.0 technology to quickly create dashboard-like mashups to assimilate decision-making data from different sources.

Describing the influence of the internet on business in 2001, the *Cluetrain Manifesto* speaks to the changes in business as the internet emerges and matures. It is all about where people and markets meet and it is all about conversations:

. . . the interaction of the market conversation with the conversation of the corporate workforce hardly signals the end of commerce. Instead, this convergence promises a vibrant renewal in which commerce becomes far more naturally integrated into the life of individuals and communities.

Education, like other organizations, is similarly posed toward the change. The AET Zone combines immersive characteristics of a 3D world with collaborative Web 2.0 tools into an environment that provides opportunities for rich interactions across traditional boundaries of roles, location and time.

Use of Virtual Spaces to Maintain Relationships over Space and Time

A primary issue when considering the use of such environments involves ways in which corporations might leverage consideration of issues listed above in virtual spaces and utilizes this knowledge within organizations to build needed relationships and encourage teamwork.

As noted above, a primary difference in the use of 3D virtual spaces from traditional web-based learning management systems lies in the concepts of presence and co-presence. Though definitions vary, presence can be defined as the sense of being somewhere else; co-presence is the sense of being in that somewhere else place with others. Certainly, people feel 'present' in traditional classrooms or training sessions with face-to-face interaction with instructors, but that sense is often limited to the times during which instruction takes place. Through avatars, synchronous and asynchronous communications tools, environments and activities designed to facilitate differing types of tasks and interactions, presence and co-presence can indeed be used to make possible relationships between participants regardless of the geographical locations.

For the creation of relationships and learning communities, this sense of presence and co-presence is a necessity. Our own experience in AET Zone supports research by Rovai (2002) and Tu (2002) which note that these elements are essential both in the creation and maintenance of online communities. The creation of community is, in turn, a key for student learning. Liu et al (2007) report significant relationships between a sense of community and perceived learning engagement, perceived learning, and student satisfaction with online learning experiences.

The element of community is a desirable by-product of feelings of presence within a virtual world. Vygotsky (1978) identified the idea of the community of practice – learning as a social activity. Wenger writes, "Communities of prac-

tice develop around things that matter to people. As a result, their practices reflect the members' own understanding of what is important" (2006). Certainly, this type of community of practice is built in face-to-face interactions throughout the corporate world, but is one that is hard to reproduce in flat, web-based environments.

Shared purpose, trust, support and collaboration are essential elements in development of quality online environments (Shea et al, 2002). In a setting such as AET Zone, these necessities are addressed by offering learners opportunities to participate in projects, discussion and other activities, and to turn interaction into artifacts and ways of knowing into expertise. A well-designed virtual environment will capitalize on presence and co-presence to recognize ways in which all participants, regardless of any type of external hierarchy; can interact in serendipitous ways because of this greater awareness of one another. Both synchronous and asynchronous tools, including discussion boards, blogs, wikis, collaborative writing tools, voice and text chat, are helpful in encouraging these types of encounters. Participants can choose the tools most appropriate to the ways in which they wish to work and communicate to accomplish the necessary tasks.

Design of Virtual Environments to Facilitate Different Types of Tasks and Interactions

The first iteration of the AET Zone, while a radical departure from both traditional face-to-face courses and online courses delivered through standard 2D learning management systems, reflected a structure and format of learning spaces that mirrored the way programs and courses were traditionally organized. A common space for the online program was created, which included portals to course spaces unique to each course offered in the instructional technology program. Once in those course spaces, learners had access to resources and tools relevant to that specific course. Those tools and resources necessary for supporting certain desired tasks and interactions relevant to more than one course were either duplicated across courses or students were encouraged to return to the course spaces where the required tools and resources were located.

As other departmental programs migrated into the AET Zone, it was clear that many of these same tools and resources would be useful to students across program areas. It no longer made sense to have these materials organized by individual courses when a common need for them existed. Learning management systems that organize learners into private course spaces minimize or prevent sharing and communication among students across sections and courses. AET Zone allowed for spaces that were open to all learners registered as citizens of the Zone. The typical organization of learners into distinct sections, courses and programs was neither necessary nor desirable as the AET Zone continued to grow and become a more inclusive learning space. This shift in thinking about the sharing of tools and resources resulted in a similar shift in thinking about how the environment could be redesigned to create common spaces shared by all learners, regardless of program area, to access these tools and resources, and to engage in collaborative tasks and interactions with other students. However, a critical mass of participants must be present in order to fully realize the potential of this presence as a way to encourage and promote engagement in the corporate Community of Practice.

As organizations begin to consider the design of virtual environments, these types of issues are common. How can spaces be designed to promote interaction rather than isolation? What is the most effective way to make tools and resources available to all participants? What are the optimum ways to design spaces to promote engagement and collaboration? A key to all of these considerations is a discussion of developing a critical mass of participants.

Developing Critical Mass within Virtual Spaces

In our initial experience with AET Zone, we found that use of the space and resources was limited to the specific designated tasks that could only be completed in the Zone. It became rapidly apparent, however, that as more users entered the space for purposeful activity, the Zone became a valuable place for serendipitous communication and interaction between participants. The difference was critical mass.

In the case of virtual worlds, critical mass can be defined as the number of participants necessary to create the desired effect. Quite simply, if a user anticipates logging in and being alone in the world, there will be very few reasons to do so. It is the interaction that makes the experience worthwhile; without others with whom to communicate; virtual spaces will likely remain underutilized if at all. It was not until the third semester of use that our learners reached critical mass in AET Zone, interacting in ways not possible with typical web-page based online systems, when the Zone began being used for more and different types of interactions. A deeper sense of presence and co-presence was in evidence.

How then can moderators of purposeful immersive virtual spaces create activities and environments which will encourage frequent and meaningful use?

SOLUTIONS AND RECOMMENDATIONS

After spending more than eight years designing, reflecting upon, and conducting graduate programs in AET Zone, several important elements have emerged as key for effective use of 3D virtual spaces for teaching, learning, and building relationships.

Table 1. Hargardon's (2008) definition of paradigm shift in learning

From:	To:
Consuming	Producing
Authority	Transparency
Expert	Facilitator
Lecture	Hallway
Access to information	Access to people
Learning about	Learning to be
Passive learning	Passionate learning
Presentation	Participation
Publication	Conversation
Formal schooling	Lifelong learning
Supply-push	Demand-pull.

Understanding of Changes in Learning and Relationship-Building

Important implications for corporate interactions emerged as users gradually became more accustomed to Internet-based communications for both work and play. Brown and Adler (2008) discuss the notion of 'social learning', which is based on the premise that understanding is socially constructed through conversations about content and grounded in interactions around problems or actions - that the focus is not on what is being learned but how it is being learned. In a consideration of the ways in which new tools have prompted a paradigm shift in teaching and learning, Hargadon (2008) points to the following factors in this shift:

Our experience has led us to believe that virtual worlds, when designed and implemented to facilitate purposeful as well as serendipitous interaction, promote this shift in ways of learning and interacting. Of particular interest is the shift from the lecture to the hallway – from hierarchical content delivery to more informal interaction between participants in the world. The trends toward participation, toward conversation, and toward access to people are certainly available in virtual worlds in ways not previously possible in computer-mediated tools. Understanding this

paradigm shift is an important factor in the design and utilization of immersive spaces.

Design of Virtual Spaces to Facilitate Interaction

Through continuous, reflective environmental redesign, as mentioned above, the value of these cross-course and cross-program collaborations became evident. Faculty from all program areas now in the AET Zone held common beliefs and values about building Communities of Practice comprised of students and faculty from across these multiple program areas. Tools and resources could be situated in a cross-program 'Commons' area as part of a redesigned AET Zone that would provide universal access to those spaces necessary for collaborative participation in this community to occur. The Commons area was designed around the metaphor image of a town plaza. Spaces (storefronts or buildings) were created to house, facilitate and manage shared dialogue, conversation, reflection, knowledge construction, and knowledge management.

Multiple spaces exist in the AET Zone to facilitate both synchronous and asynchronous dialogue among learners. A space identified as the 'Discussion Depot' offers access to a variety

Figure 1. Students interact in a classroom in the commons area of AET zone

of discussion boards. While most boards available in this space are course specific, several boards exist to support cross program conversations about shared issues and opportunities. Students who enter the depot to participate in these ongoing discussions run into other students doing the same, often resulting in serendipitous interactions with these other students. These synchronous interactions are further supported by a walk over to the 'Chit Chats Coffee House,' another space in the Commons designed for small group meetings. Eight sofas are distributed throughout the coffee house, each linked to a Talking Communities (http://www.talkingcommunities.com) collaboration space that provides text, audio, and video chat capabilities along with whiteboard, desktop sharing, and application sharing functionality.

Students, asked to engage in reflective writing on course projects and activities, find their way to the 'Blog Bar and Grill.' This space offers access to both blogging tools as well as aggregated menus of student blogs. Like the Discussion Depot, students in the bar and grill may find other students also blogging, which often results in rich and powerful discussions between students regarding the themes and issues on which they are reflecting.

Additional spaces in the Commons have been developed to encourage collaborative knowledge construction through the use of wikis and tools such as Google Docs, and Adobe's Buzzword. Learners, working in pairs or small groups, arrange time to use these tools together on a wide variety of projects, ranging in the development of a shared document to the collaborative planning and execution of a multidisciplinary research study. These tools are accessible through 'Wiki World' and the 'Student Center.' Furthermore, the products and artifacts of these collaborative projects can be shared throughout the AET Zone by capitalizing on its ability to serve as a 3D knowledge management space. Remaining spaces in the Commons, the 'Information Gardens,' the 'Theatre' and 'Video Annex,' the 'Training Shoppe,' and 'Spectacles,' are all spaces that function as management tools for the exchange of information and knowledge.

The 3D nature of the AET Zone also provides visual cues to navigate to other resources, which consist of learner produced products, web-based resources, and subscription-based databases. The 'Information Gardens,' built and maintained by librarians from the university library, provides access to the same online resources and services that are offered to our on-campus students. This online library is organized through a garden metaphor that makes finding needed resources easier and

Figure 2. Necessary elements for creation of community in virtual worlds

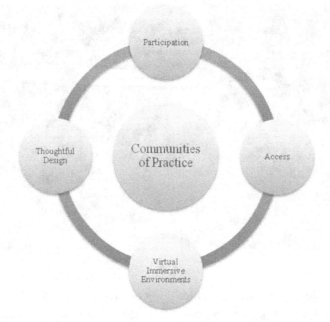

more intuitive. In the Gardens, leisure-reading materials are found in the Zen Garden, scholarly articles can be accessed in the Online Database Garden, and special collections can be found in the Northwoods Collection Garden. Elsewhere in the Commons, videos and podcasts can be located in the Theatre and Annex, respectively.

This design of a virtual space has relevance for companies wishing to develop their own cross-department Communities of Practice for professional development or other collaborative purposes. Companies desiring to engage their employees in similar forms of shared dialogue, reflections, and knowledge construction will want to identify the specific tasks and interactions valued by the organization and identify tools and resources required to facilitate such tasks and interactions. A 3D environment provides an immersive, shared space that provides access to these tools and resources

FUTURE TRENDS

While prognosticating the future of something as large an enterprise as education or business is problematic, several major trends may be noted from future studies research as well as directly from our experiences. Limiting our vision is the traditional tendency for education, and, in some cases, business. We often find ourselves looking backward rather than forward while attempting to preserve and protect the past culture. Society is now expecting education to fulfill an additional role in preparing students for a future that is in constant transition. A significant number of the jobs these students will work in have not yet been invented. Similarly, the corporate world finds itself in need of addressing products and processes that are not always clear to leaders or employees. As Christensen points out in *The Innovator's Dilemma* (2003), corporations often fail to understand new products or processes and their potential, and suffer from isolation and silos of knowledge that may keep them from taking advantage of their own expertise.

We are currently entering a period of experimentation in our educational and business enterprises that we have not seen in several generations. Whether we explore charter schools, new forms of human resource development or online training/education programs, much piloting and exploring is evident. Tomas Frey of the DaVinci Institute suggests that participative bottom-up systems, following the marketplace in online worlds portend the future of education. He cites examples such as Ebay and iTunes as such occurrences (2007). The KnowledgeWorks Foundation (2006) has also extensively researched trends for the future. This has resulted in a production of a "Map of Future Forces Affecting Education". An extensive list of these identified forces includes among others, mediated immersive learning and developing communities of practice that utilize the new collaborative tools in creative and powerful ways. Jarvis (2009) considers the question, "What Would Google Do?" in a book by the same name. In it, he confirms that we are now working in a new world with new rules. From our own experiences working the AET Zone, we find that the newer collaborative tools provide another layer of possibilities for community building, peer to peer instruction and interactions, and collaborations distributed across time and distance.

The Web 2.0 tools that we are currently using, imbedded within the virtual environment, enable students to form task specific groups not only within their cohorts but also across cohorts and indeed beyond the formal educational settings. We see teams of individuals with different roles and responsibilities in educational settings working together to solve real world issues. Unlike the older generations of web-based environments, newer 3D immersive environments have many of collaborative tools built into them. Not only do participants have a sense of presence alluded to above, they also have the capabilities to collaborate synchronously and asynchronously in small groups. Hence, we see a progression toward the development of 3D worlds that are designed specifically for online communication and collaboration. This leads directly to collaborative knowledge creation and authentic learning not possible in other learning environments.

From our perspective, demands for tools for online interaction will continue to increase. As we continue to move further away from the university campus, we notice that more students are interested in enrolling in an online program rather than one that meets face to face. Curiously, many programs report a high attrition rate from their online programs and courses. To the contrary, we find that our online experiences using a 3D learning environment results in increased enrollments rather than attrition. We attribute this to the various communities of practice that we encourage and develop with the use of collaborative tools.

Carr (2008) writes of the changes in our society brought about by the coming cheap, utility-supplied computing or so called "cloud computing". Individual computers will rent software from a central distributer rather than having it reside on the local hard drive. Such changes may be as profound as those brought about by cheap electricity in the beginning of the 20th century. Just as we see the power in controlling media by individuals emerging from that of institutions, we also see the power of learners selecting 'just in time' education rather than years of tangential studies.

We have been reluctant to move into the current tier of high level 3D worlds due to bandwidth requirements. Our student and their schools are not prepared to invest in the high cost of high bandwidth until recently. As the local infrastructure increases, we plan to continue exploring more robust environments for teaching and learning.

As we continue to think about the next steps in our web-based learning environment, we think about the confluence of gaming, 3D worlds and online instruction. Clearly, the new gaming engines that can be easily modified for different content and participant roles provide opportunities for active team development and problem solving. We are currently in the process of moving a successful leadership development activity from a board game to an online experience within a 3D world. The plan is to help people learn basic leadership skills through an online experience while collaborating and working with others – certainly a type of activity which could be useful in the corporate world.

We are also exploring ways to develop augmented reality opportunities for training online. This would allow various role playing participants to receive different information from "chatterbots" (programmed applications that hang out and offer specific information to specific role players as they come by). For instance, a team participant might receive different information than the supervisor. Hence each role character would have privileged information within the group that is trying to solve a problem.

Any time, any place interaction will continue to complement or even replace the need for face-to-face experiences. With this change business and education will be ever more forced to shift focus from a hierarchical model to a learner-centered one. Current employees and students will continue to become as much the producers as consumers of information. In a business context, virtual environments will level the playing field, allowing those participating in virtual worlds to flatten hierarchies and develop meaningful relationships with one another through varied interactions.

Like other consumers, our students have many choices in where and how they study for advanced degrees. That is, they are capable of working with information in new and fundamentally different ways that were not available to previous generations. Not only can they seek, find and collect information, they are able to remix it in new digital formats for presentations, decision making and other higher level applications. Corporate environments are certainly feeling this change, and must respond in ways most productive for their organizations.

CONCLUSION

Benkler (2006) argues that this newly networked economy enables individuals and private groups to be more productive than many traditional formally organized groups. How can business leverage this new type of productivity in virtual worlds? What lessons can corporate organizations learn from the experience of higher education in a 3D virtual environment? The lessons involve not only design considerations, but careful consideration of the way these spaces are used to stimulate interaction and participation. These lessons include:

- Careful consideration of the appropriateness of virtual worlds for desired purposes
- Thoughtful design of virtual environments, which includes activities designed to help reach critical mass and stimulate both purposeful and serendipitous interaction
- Incorporation of tools and artifacts designed to foster a sense of community of practice, including both synchronous and asynchronous opportunities
- A change from hierarchy-driven to participant-driven opportunities – true awareness of a changing organizational paradigm.

With these factors in place, businesses can begin to utilize 3D immersive worlds as tools to build teams, facilitate communication and teamwork, and build true communities like those found in informal face-to-face settings.

REFERENCES

Benkler, Y. (2006). *The Wealth of Networks: How Social Production Transforms Markets and Freedom*. Retrieved May 20, 2008, from http://www.benkler.org/Benkler_Wealth_Of_Networks.pdf

Bronack, S., Riedl, R., & Tashner, J. (2006). Learning in the zone: A social constructivist framework for distance education in a 3D virtual world. *Interactive Learning Environments, 14*(3), 219–232. doi:10.1080/10494820600909157

Brown, J. S., & Adler, R. P. (2008). Minds on fire: Open education, the long tail and learning 2.0. *Educase Review.* Retrieved April 30, 2008, from http://net.educause.edu/ir/library/pdf/ERM0811.pdf

Carr, N. (2008). *The Big Switch: Rewiring the World, from Edison to Google.* New York: W.W. Norton & Co.

Christensen, C. (1997). *The Innvator's Dilemma.* New York: HarperCollins Publishers.

Entertainment Software Association. (2008, June). *Use of video game technology in the workplace increasing.* Retrieved March 15, 2009, http://www.theesa.com/newsroom/release_detail.asp?releaseID=24

eWeek. (2008, October). *Web 2.0: Business Process Enabler.* Retrieved March 15, 2009, from http://www.week.com/c/a/Video/Web-20-Buiness-Process-Enabler/

Frey, T. (2007, March). *The Future of Education.* The DaVinci Institute. Retrieved March 15, 2009, from http://www.davinciinstitute.com/page.php?ID=170

Gartner Research. (2007). *Gartner Says 80 Percent of Active Internet Users will Have a "Second Life" in the Virtual World by the End of 2011.* Retrieved February 15, 2009, from http://www.gartner.com/it/page.jsp?id=503861Jarvis, J. (2009) *What Would Google Do?* New York: HarperCollins Publishers.

Gartner Research. (2008). *Gartner Says 90 Per Cent of Corporate Virtual World Projects Fail Within 18 Months.* Retrieved March 2, 2009, from http://www.gartner.com/it/page.jsp?id=670507

Hargadon, S. (2008). *Web 2.0 is the Future of Education.* Retrieved May 3, 2008, from http://www.stevehargadon.com/2008/03/web-20-is-future-of-education.html

KnowledgeWorks Foundation. (2006). *The 2006-2016 KnowledgeWorks Foundation and the Institute for the Future Map of the Future Forces Affecting Education.* Retrieved March 15, 2009, from http://www.kwfdn.org/map/node.aspx

Kronos, A. (2007, May). *Sun Aims New 3D Environment at Business.* Retrieved March 15, 2009, from http://www.3pointd.com/20070501/sun-aims-new-3d-environment-at-business/

Liu, X., Magjuka, R. J., Bonk, C., & Lee, S. (2007). Does sense of community matter? An examination of participants' perceptions of building learning communities in online courses. *The Quarterly Review of Distance Education, 1*(8), 9–24.

Locke, C., Levine, R., Searls, D., & Weinberger, D. (2001). *The Cluetrain Manifestor: The End of Business as Usual.* New York: Basic Books.

Nortel. (2009, March). *Nortel Teams Up with Virtual Heroes to Deliver 3D Virtual Training Application.* Retrieved March 15, 2009, from http://www2.nortel.com/go/news_detail.jsp?cat_id=-8055&oid=100253197

Parris, C. (2007, May). Do better business in 3D. *Business Week Online.* Captured March 15, 2009, from http://www.businessweek.com/technology/content/may2007/tc20070501_526224.htm?chan=top+news_top+news+index_technology

Riedl, R., Bronack, S., & Tashner, J. (2005, January). *3D web-based worlds for instruction.* The Society for Information and Teacher Education, Phoenix, AZ. Published in the Book of Proceedings.

Rovai, A. (2002). Building sense of community at a distance. *International Review of Research in Open and Distance Learning, 3*(1). Retrieved January 16, 2008, from http://www.irrodl.org/content/v3.1/rovai.html

Shea, P., Li, C. S., Swan, K., & Pickett, A. (2002). Developing learning community in online asynchronous college courses: The role of teaching presence. *Journal of Asynchronous Learning Networks, 9*(4), 59–82.

Tashner, J., Bronack, S., & Riedl, R. (2005, March). Virtual worlds: Further development of web-based teaching. In *Proceedings of Hawaii International Conference on Education*, Honolulu, HI.

Tu, C. H. (2002). The measurement of social presence in an online learning environment. *International Journal on E-Learning, 1*(2), 34-45. Retrieved January 20, 2008, from www.aace.org/dl/files/IJEL/IJEL1234.pdf

Vygotsky, L. S. (1978). *Mind in society: The development of higher psychological processes*. Cambridge, MA: Harvard University Press.

Wenger, E. (1998, June). Communities of Practice: Learning as a Social System. *Systems Thinker*. Retrieved October 16, 2006 from http://www.co-i-l.com/coil/knowledge-garden/cop/lss.shtml

Wilson, N. (2009, January). *11 virtual worlds technologies that will change the way we work*. Retrieved March 15, 2009, from http://cleverzebra.com/virtual-worlds

KEY TERMS AND DEFINITIONS

AET Zone: A three-dimensional virtual, immersive world used by graduate programs in education at Appalachian State University.

Community of Practice: A learning environment based upon social learning theory, in which novices and experts interact to create knowledge and meaning.

Co-Presence: A sense of being in a place with others at a given time.

Presence: A sense of being in a place at a given time.

Social Constructivism: A philosophy which holds that knowledge is created culturally, socially and within communities.

Chapter 14
Team Dynamics in Virtual Spaces:
Challenges for Workforce Training, Human Resource Development, and Adult Development

Martha C. Yopp
University of Idaho, USA

Allen Kitchel
University of Idaho, USA

ABSTRACT

Collaboration within virtual environments is an increasingly important aspect of organizational and workplace activities. "Virtual teams" are intentional groups of highly qualified people brought together in a virtual environment in order to capitalize upon each member's unique attributes. In many instances these people represent different organizations, or branches of an organization, who work together virtually to tackle a specific problem or project. This paper examines issues that "virtual teams" encounter and identifies best practices that can positively contribute to effective and efficient teamwork within the virtual environment. The ideas and practices presented may be of value to organizational leaders, planners, human resource professionals, adult educators, and others involved in workforce training.

INTRODUCTION

The purpose of this chapter is to examine team dynamics in a virtual environment and identify ways to make them successful. Collaboration within virtual environments is an increasingly important aspect of workplace activities. It is up to organizational leaders, planners, human resource professionals, adult educators, and others involved in organizational development to identify and establish best practices that make virtual team work positive and productive.

DOI: 10.4018/978-1-61520-619-3.ch014

BACKGROUND

In the best of circumstances, teambuilding occurs naturally as people work together, form alliances and establish collegial relationships. However, in reality this is often not the case and a more attentive approach is needed. Team members are prone to experience anxiety in the team forming process. They wonder how the team will work together, whether they will be liked and whether they will like the people they are working with. Teambuilding activities can help alleviate some of these feelings by consciously providing shared experience and goals (Brown, Huettner, & James-Tanny, 2007).

When building a team it is important that everyone feels included and welcome. Team members should be involved in initial planning and goal setting. Facilitators should watch for signs of social isolation, encourage participation from everyone and create an environment that promotes active engagement. Early in the process, there should be an open discussion about team expectations, policies, and practices. Both team and individual efforts should be recognized. Some best practices suggested by Brown, Huettner & James-Tanny (2007) include:

- Negotiate goals together
- Document expectations, goals, position descriptions and contact information
- Hold regular team meetings and allow time to check in with each member at the beginning of the meeting
- Provide frequent and timely feedback
- Maintain a positive, constructive attitude even when things go wrong
- Focus on strengths (Brown, et al., 2007). Group success requires members to be willing to share their efforts and accomplishments, and work to meet clearly defined goals (Odgers, 2005). It is important that team members have incentives to participate. Some benefits of being on a team

are experience, recognition, and visibility. The high-energy and motivation created through effective teamwork is contagious and leads to a special synergy whereby employees and administrators attain extraordinary results. Characteristics of effective teams include:

- The members are loyal and committed to one another and the leader.
- The members and leaders have a high degree of confidence and trust in each other.
- The group is eager to help each other develop to reach their full potential.
- The members communicate fully and frankly about everything relative to the team.
- The members feel secure and empowered to make decisions.
- The atmosphere and climate is supportive and risk free, and members put the organization first (Odgers, 2005).

Virtual teams are an important component of many corporate and educational organizations, and have evolved largely because of globalization, technology, and changing demographics (Merriam, Caffarella, & Baumgartner, 2007). Virtual teams are composed of members who are physically located in different places. They conduct most of their work through electronic technology. Team members rarely meet face-to-face and rely primarily on digital forms of communication. Effective communication that leads to a shared understanding of the teams' purpose, goals and objectives is vital for success.

For purposes of this discussion, virtual teams are defined as more than typical groups of people who work together in a virtual environment. Instead, "virtual teams" are defined as intentional groups composed of identified individuals who have special talents/skills/knowledge related to the goals of the team. Teams are brought together for a specific reason and purpose. In many instances these will be groups of people who represent different organizations, or branches of an organization, who work together primarily in a virtual environment to solve a common problem.

Virtual teams are intentional groups of highly qualified people who are brought together in a virtual environment in order to capitalize upon each member's unique attributes. It is rare to find teams where individuals know each other, occupy the same space, work the same hours, belong to and are paid by the same organization, have a common business culture and enjoy a history of working together. Today's teams are an alliance of talented individuals from different organizations, departments, professions, and locations. Teams are made up of people with different backgrounds, languages, cultures and education who are involved in collaborative activities in varying degrees (Thompson & Good, 2005). Shachaf and Hara (2005) write that virtual teams are groups of people who work interdependently with a shared purpose across space, time and organizational boundaries using technology. Davis and Scaffidi (2007) define a virtual team as a collection of individuals who are geographically and/or organizationally dispersed who collaborate via communication and information technologies in order to accomplish a specific goal. Nunamaker, Reinig, and Briggs describe a virtual team as consisting of "a well-defined group of individuals brought together to produce a specific deliverable..." (2009, p. 1).

The virtual aspect of teaming presents a variety of challenges that coalesce on communication and trust. Three of these addressed by Roebuck, Brock, and Moodie (2004) are:

- Lack of face-to-face interaction
- Relationship building
- Accessing and leveraging the unique knowledge and expertise of each member to achieve team goals.

Effective team building must concentrate on how team members relate to each other and how work is implemented and completed. Unfortunately, but not surprising, although virtual teams are popular and widely accepted, communication researchers contend there is no substitute for face-to-face interaction (Pillis & Furumo, 2007). The lack of, or diminished aspect of non-verbal cues, facial expression, and voice inflections can decrease trust and commitment of team members who become reluctant to share ideas and concerns. This can cause mixed or misinterpreted messages which lead to conflict, splintering of unity, and less trust. Loss of trust is fatal to the effectiveness of a virtual team (Pillis & Furumo, 2007). The literature provides us with many definitions and descriptions of virtual teams, and most of them identify trust as one of the essential ingredients for success.

Parker (2007) recognized the need for virtual teams to be made up of adaptive team players who are able to communicate with different types of people, who "subordinate their functional goals to the goals of the team" (p. 3), and who are able to quickly develop trust. Building trust quickly is a challenge for which a solution may be found within the adult and human resource development and training literature.

FACILITATORS OR TEAM LEADERS

Team leaders in a virtual environment can benefit from examining the history of andragogy and guidelines for working well with adults in their quest for success in team development and effectiveness. The work of Malcolm Knowles is well known and provides insights into team development and implementation. Knowles, writing from years of experience, advocates that administrators or facilitators of adults should exhibit some of the following characteristics:

- Have a genuine respect for the capacity of adults to be self-directing
- Derive satisfaction from the accomplishments of others
- Value the experience of others as a resource for accomplishing both work and learning
- Are able and willing to take risks involved in experimenting with new ideas and new approaches
- View failures or set-backs as opportunities to be learned from
- Have a deep commitment to and skill in the involvement of people in organizations and learning processes
- Have faith in the value of education and learning for contributing to the solution of organizational and societal problems
- Are able to establish warm, empathic relationships with people
- Engage as a good listener (Knowles, 1980).

Thompson and Good (2005) address the fact that virtual teams are not always successful in using technology to engage in effective collaboration. The teams frequently get bogged down by technology issues, communication breakdowns, reliance on out-dated work methods, and the absence of strong team motivation. Thompson and Good contend that the adoption of new technology tools without the parallel development of a new culture that supports its use is unrealistic. In effect, successful virtual teams require more than internet technology to be successful. What is needed is a culture of collaboration and cooperative learning capable of developing strategies and techniques which encourage team unity and interaction. Unless members think and act with solidarity, no amount of technology will transform inefficient teams into highly effective and productive units.

In spite of expensive technology, and sometimes because of it, virtual teams are not always successful. In fact, some of the statistics used to measure success are not positive (Thompson & Good, 2005). One problem is that leaders do not readily recognize the evolving and living nature of successful teams. Many leaders treat their teams more like machines than dynamic individuals. They are inclined to control the team and its members rather than looking at them as an evolving entity, capable of creative and innovative thinking.

Rethinking how teams should be nurtured, organized and supported is a first step toward finding effective and suitable ways of improving the productivity of virtual teams. It is important to develop team intelligence, although, superior team intelligence does not necessarily predict how successful a team will be. A distributed intelligence model uses intellectual capabilities in a collective, collaborative and cooperative fashion to support the development of team intelligence. Eventual success requires that team intelligence be supported by team members who are motivated, optimistic, share a set of beliefs and commitment, and who treat each team member as a leader (Thompson & Good, 2005).

Davis and Scaffidi (2007) discuss challenges that virtual teams must overcome. Just as with traditional teams, leaders must build group cohesion, facilitate communication and establish realistic team objectives. Davis and Scaffidi focus on member selection whereby some of the most talented employees, who have the ability, knowledge, and tenacity to enhance team performance, are recruited. They must also be experts in their field. A benefit of virtual teams is that location does not drive member selection. Team leaders choose members based on expertise not geographic proximity. In addition to expertise, interaction style is also important. Personality type impacts group productivity. Research indicated that extroverted personalities are a great addition to virtual teams but that too many extroverted individuals negatively impact productivity. Each team needs balance (David & Scaffidi, 2007).

While team members must possess superior knowledge in their field, they must also be comfortable in a virtual environment. Communication skills are a necessity, as are self-confidence, self-motivation, and self-esteem. Virtual team members must manage their schedules efficiently. They must complete tasks on time and take initiative to communicate with team members when they are having difficulties. This communication will lead to quicker and more effective problem solving and avoid problems that are likely to affect the entire group (Davis & Scaffidi, 2007).

Creating a sense of community within a team helps to strengthen relationships and positively reinforce group performance. Research indicates that face-to-face interaction used strategically at the beginning of a relationship, as well as during key times to establish a shared vision, to overcome anxiety, and build trust is optimal in creating a sense of community. This, however, is not feasible for all virtual teams. Other practices and strategies must be explored and refined so that people may get to know each other and establish commonalities. Personalized electronic interactions are one possibility. Virtual team leaders and members must be encouraged and provided incentives to take advantage of every opportunity to build personal relationships with virtual team members (Davis & Scaffidi, 2007; Odgers, 2005; Parker, 2007).

Stronger personal relationships facilitate more productive work relationships. In order to develop a feeling of community in virtual teams, members must feel motivated and supported by their team, their leader, and the organization. Motivation is positively associated with the perception of the significance of a team member's task. Periodically and over time steps should be taken to recognize each member's contribution. If team members feel they are a vital part of the team and the organization they are more apt to stay focused and engaged. Processes must be developed to create

a sense of team spirit within the group and the organization as a whole. Camaraderie within virtual teams leads to motivation, commitment, and increased productivity, and promotes a shared vision of purpose.

Shachaf and Hara (2005) present an ecological approach to team effectiveness in virtual environments. The authors state that prior studies on virtual teams use a model of input-output process based on traditional, and possibly dated, team effectiveness known as the Systems Approach (Galbraith, 1997). Shachaf and Hara seek to capture the complexity of work groups and information technology through a framework that examines environmental aspects of teamwork (social, cultural, organizational and technological) and then they propose an ecological approach relevant to teaching and learning with virtual teams.

Shachaf & Hara (2005) contend that in traditional teams trust is important, but in virtual teams it is even more important. Team members in virtual teams have to rely on other people, share a purpose and rewards, and trust their information channels. The members in a virtual team have only their shared reliance on each other to guarantee the success of their joint work. Shachaf & Hara also highlight leadership as an important factor for team effectiveness. They report that the leadership role becomes more ambiguous in the virtual team because the leader is not the gatekeeper but rather a negotiator and facilitator. In addition, in virtual teams the leadership/facilitator role may be rotated and shared.

The ecological framework consists of three components: the external environment, the internal environment, and boundaries. In on-line collaborative settings internal environments are particularly important. Team leaders should emphasize building learning communities that foster a sense of belonging through peer-to-peer interaction.

VIRTUAL TEAMS

Parker (2007) writes that in the last decade the world in which virtual teams and team players are asked to perform has changed. Team members are located in multiple locations, and cultural differences are evident. He acknowledges that the bar has been raised for team success. Organizations now expect that teams will function at a high level. There is a greater impatience among management when they observe a breakdown in team progress.

There is recognition that team success requires a support system that draws from a variety of sources. Simply creating teams will not ensure success. There is a need for a total system that includes a supportive management style, performance management processes, reward systems, and a team-based culture. The search is on for new and creative ways of selecting leaders, and appraising and rewarding team members. It follows that the organization must adopt new methods that incentivize teams, recognize outstanding team players, and incorporate performance of a team into the overall employee appraisal process (Parker, 2007).

STRATEGIES AND TECHNIQUES

When team members are identified and asked to serve, the leader or facilitator must make them feel welcome and important. The atmosphere from the beginning should be inclusive, comfortable, safe, inviting, and empowering. Each member must feel that they have been selected to participate in this very important assignment because they have abilities and strengths that will add value to the team.

Nunamaker, Reinig, and Briggs (2009) synthesize their decade long experience with virtual teams into nine principles intended to "help designers, managers, and virtual team members … improve their effectiveness" (p. 116). The nine principles are:

- **Principle 1**: Realign reward structures for virtual teams.
- **Principle 2**: Find new ways to focus attention on task.
- **Principle 3**: Design activities that cause people to get to know each other.
- **Principle 4**: Build a virtual presence.
- **Principle 5**: Agree on standards and terminology.
- **Principle 6**: Leverage anonymity when appropriate.
- **Principle 7**: Be more explicit.
- **Principle 8**: Train teams to self-facilitate.
- **Principle 9**: Embed collaboration into everyday work (Nunamaker, Reinig, & Briggs, 2009).

Nunamaker, Reinig, and Briggs' principles provide a framework that promotes productivity and trust among team members. In global virtual teams, trust is associated with the perception of team members' "integrity, ability, and benevolence" (David & Scaffidi, 2007, p. 9). Building trust is important and incorporating trust building exercises needs to be an integral part of the initial team building process. One way or another trust must be earned through optimism and respect. Helping to build trust may transpire through the effective use of virtual introductions, photographs, autobiographical sketches, and icebreakers. To help develop unity and team spirit the teams might be given names, a logo, and a mission.

If there are three or more members of a team at a common site, one person should be identified as the facilitator and be responsible for making certain the site is set up to maximize team effectiveness. Facilitation responsibilities can be rotated so that each team member serves as the facilitator over a period of time.

The meeting area should be inviting and well suited to the technology being used. Water and possibly light snacks should be available. Every member of the team should be able to hear and be heard. If video is used, every member should be situated so they can see and be seen. The room should be comfortable with respect to heat, air conditioning, lighting, glare, noise reduction, and wiring for laptops or other equipment. A white board, projector, and host computer should be available. The internet in most cases is essential. All too often, when virtual teams come together nobody is in charge and people come and go and sit wherever they want. This is a mistake. Planners and facilitators should take as much time and care setting up a virtual meeting as they would a face-to-face meeting. Agenda and handouts should be available, attendance should be recorded, someone should serve as recorder at each meeting, and a summary should be prepared, circulated, and discussed with the local team prior to the next virtual team meeting.

If there are only one or two members at each site, the lone member, or pair, should be provided incentives for creating a comfortable and hospitable environment. They should have adequate technology support and be encouraged to bring a beverage or light snack. Again, they should take notes which are then typed and maintained as a journal or record at least until the team project is completed and the team is disbanded. This record may be very valuable for the preparation of a final written report.

Team members at different locations are frequently in different time zones. These differences must be recognized and appreciated. If people are being asked to participate during a time that is not part of their normal workday, they should be compensated by receiving extra pay, perks, or compensatory time. If the team meeting is during the normal lunch or dinner hour, some type of catering should be provided or members should be encouraged to bring in food and beverages. Many significant returns can be achieved by paying attention to realistic creature comforts.

Team members must develop a feeling that they are connected with all of the team members – near and far. At each site, members should meet between meetings and have small group discussions about the project and their role in it. They should be a team within a larger team. They should have lunch together periodically and be encouraged to get to know each other at a personal level. They should know each other's names, job description, and a little about their career. They should also be encouraged to share something interesting or unusual about themselves that most people don't know. Members might be divided into pairs or sub-groups to investigate certain aspects of the project and bring that information back prior to the next large meeting.

In the virtual environment, every member of the total team should have a recent headshot photo. These photos, along with a brief autobiographical sketch should be shared and all members should be encouraged to use them in an effort to be able to communicate more effectively with each and every member. At every meeting, members should be asked their thoughts or opinion about something, particularly if they are not a regular contributor to the conversation. Ask them what they think -- get everyone involved. Every member should have one or more assigned responsibilities so that they share ownership in at least part of the larger endeavor. Depending upon how frequently the teams meet, they should be asked to provide an update since the last meeting. This can be personal, professional, cultural, or environmental. This type of informal sharing can build familiarity and foster trust, respect, dedication, and synergism.

Dani, Vurns, Blackhouse, & Kochhar (2006) write extensively about the implications of organizational culture and trust in the working of virtual teams. They emphasize that the working practices in industry are changing, with organizations becoming more knowledge based and focused on core competence, and that they are willing to share their unique competencies in alliances with partner organizations. These alliances are facilitated through the use of virtual networks and the use of globally based teams (Dani, et al., 2006). Team members may or may not know each other so it is important that trusting relationships develop quickly.

Virtual teams represent a new form of organization that offers unprecedented levels of flexibility and responsiveness that has the potential to revolutionize the workplace. Virtual teams cannot be implemented on faith and they do not represent a perfect solution. Peter Druker, as referenced by Dani, et al. (2005), has identified changes in organizations and potential changes likely to emerge over the next few years. The market place is complex and uncertain, and becoming more so. Traditional organization structures and management concepts of the past are no longer viable. Organizations are placing more emphasis upon trust between collaborating individuals, groups and companies. The ability to respond to change requires high levels of agility. Organizations are utilizing improved communication technology to support the increased need for agility (Dani, et al., 2005).

APPRECIATIVE INQUIRY

Periodically, members should be asked what is working well for them. Only after being asked about what is going right, should they be asked what they would like to see improved and what are their recommendations for improvement. This line of reasoning comes from the literature on Appreciative Inquiry (AI), which focuses on what is going right and what is working well (Cooperrider, et al., 2001).

Appreciative Inquiry (AI) is about the search for the best in people, their organizations, and the world around them. It involves the discovery of what gives "life" to a living system when it is most alive, most effective, and most constructively capable in economic, ecological, and human terms (Cooperrider, et al., 2001, p. 7). AI involves asking questions that help heighten positive potential and involves the mobilization of inquiry through crafting "unconditional positive" questions. The task of intervention gives way to imagination and innovation. There is discovery, dream, and design. AI seeks to build a "constructive union among people and what they talk about as past and present achievements, assets, unexplored potentials, innovations, strengths, elevated thoughts, opportunities, high point moments, lived values, traditions, strategic competencies, stories, wisdom, insights into the organizational spirit and visions of valued and possible futures" (Cooperrider, et al., 2001, p. 7). The positive core of organizational life is one of the greatest and largely unrecognized resources in the field of change management. The single most prolific thing a team can do if its aims are to construct a better future is to embrace the positive by appreciating the best of what is and dream what might be (Cooperrider, et al., 2001).

CULTURE

Additional challenges occur with virtual teams whose members reside in different countries, speak different languages, and are of different ages, ethnicity, and religions. Culture and language determines how an individual processes and interprets the environment around them. Cultural differences may also account for misinterpretations during communications. Distance and a lack of nonverbal cues intensify this situation. Cultural differences and cultural values can lead to cultural miscommunication (Davis & Scaffidi, 2007). This chapter does not address cultural miscommunications directly but it recognizes the potential for serious challenges and problems. It is essential that those involved in team building and team effectiveness and trust understand these differences exist and that they seek expert guidance on how to best overcome them.

BIOTEAMING

Virtual teams are a reality in the modern workplace and their success relies in part on ways to ensure that trust, unity, cohesion, and performance are cultivated and rewarded. Thompson and Good (2005) discussed a new paradigm for conceptualizing virtual, networked business teams called *The Bioteaming Manifesto*. They believe that in order to produce cooperative and highly motivated teams, adoption of new technology must be accompanied with the development of a new culture that supports the delivery and interaction methods required by virtual teams.

A Virtual Networked Team should be recognized as a separate entity from its members. It is in itself a super-organism that needs to be nurtured in ways that enhance and support its complex and interconnected nature. The team is a whole that is more than the aggregation of the individual parts (Thompson & Good, 2005).

Bioteaming is a dynamic concept used to enhance team effectiveness. Bioteaming is about building organizational teams that operate on the basis of the natural principles which underpin nature's most successful teams. One key mission of Bioteaming is a review and analysis of scientific literature in search of the common traits of Mother Nature's most effective biological teams. Bioteaming is based on a distributed intelligence model whereby members are able to self-select when to use personal intelligence and critical thinking and when to rely on team intelligence. Team member motivation and optimism are important aspects of, and required for effective Bioteaming. These high performance teams are more successful when they share beliefs by which their behavior and attitude is determined:

- **Belief 1**: Clear and Public Accountability
- **Belief 2**: Trusted Competency
- **Belief 3**: Give and Take
- **Belief 4**: Total Transparency
- **Belief 5**: Shared Glory
- **Belief 6**: Meaningful Mission Value
- **Belief 7**: Outcome Optimism (Thompson & Good, 2005).

High performance team members come to believe that the other team members trust them to do their job without being supervised. This translates into, "I know what you have to do and am confident you can do it – how you do it is your business" (Thompson & Good, 2005, p. 15). High performance team members believe they can ask for help and that, with moderation, asking for help increases their standing within the team. Members expect to be kept informed in an honest and timely manner of any important issues in the project. Team members believe they should be free to express opinions about situations they are not directly responsible for and that these opinions should be highly respected and listened to.

Team members believe they are all in it together and that glory and pain will be shared. They do not believe that the leader will take an unfair portion of the credit for a success or all the blame for a failure. Each team member is equally accountable to the leader and fellow team members. The team members believe that the group's mission is significant, important and meaningful. They believe that if they are successful they will have made a fundamental contribution to their organization. This is not just about business as usual. The task must not seem trivial or unnecessary (Thompson & Good, 2005).

Team members also feel that they are the best people in the organization to succeed in accomplishing the identified task. The members are confident they will succeed in delivering a positive outcome for the project. The teams work better if they develop a deeply shared set of beliefs and a commitment by members to put in the necessary amount of work for the project to succeed. If the team feels trusted, it acquires self-confidence and adopts a meaningful, positive and responsible attitude toward successful completion of the mission (Thompson & Good, 2005).

Bioteaming works as the implementation process for leaders who want to make their virtual business teams more productive. Four action zones have been identified which generate repeating patterns common to all living things. These include:

- Leadership zone
- Connectivity zone
- Execution zone
- Organization zone

In the Leadership Zone every team member is treated as a leader. The rule is to stop controlling and to communicate information not orders. Team members are trained to judge for themselves what they should do in the best interest of the team. Team members achieve accountability through transparency not control.

In the Connectivity Zone team member are synergistically connected with other team members, partners, and networks. Information flows freely. Team members are selected carefully but once they have committed to them they treat them with full transparency and trust. Symbiosis is achieved. Team members cluster and pay attention to the collective networks and relationships of each team member. They are truly a team and not just a group of individuals.

In the Execution Zone team members experiment, cooperate and learn. For a team to be effective it is critical to count on the ability of the team to guarantee a pre-defined set of key tasks in a reliable and systematic fashion. Members take a proactive and responsible interest in anything which might affect the ultimate success of their project whether it is within their defined role or not. Win-win is an outcome not a strategy. Traditional teams believe that analysis is the best way to get things right. These bioteams believe that live controlled experimentation is the best way to get things right. In this environment teams quickly experiment with multiple alternative courses of action to find out what works best. After they

have collected sufficient data they build on and methodically apply the most promising results.

In the Organization Zone teams define their goals and roles in terms of the transformations they intend to make in the people and partners they engage with. In a bioteam environment members select the other members and recognize that the team will change and emerge over time. They keep looking for new and useful team members through the team life span. They tend to seek out part-time members as advisors, experts and allies who can help them just in time as necessary. Members are aware that growth cannot always be managed or controlled. The leaders and members treat their own team like a living thing and watch for and facilitate natural opportunities for growth (Thompson & Good, 2005).

TECHNOLOGY

Many technological tools and resources exist to support the interaction of virtual team members. The chosen applications and technology hardware should depend upon what works best to achieve the team goals and objectives. Uniformly, a digital network is required with appropriate bandwidth and security features. Newer forms of communication tools rely upon computer networks and digital tools, and provide virtual teams powerful forms of interaction. These include innovative technologies such as those used to facilitate interaction between individuals in 3-D virtual worlds, to more common but important means of communication such as the use of email. Within this spectrum lie a plethora of other tools, examples include instant messaging, webinars, shared whiteboards, chat rooms, asynchronous discussion boards, wikis, meeting software, video streaming and web pages. Not mentioning other forms of communication tools available to virtual teams would be remiss. Some of these non-computer based media include interactive video or video conferencing and the use of the telephone bridges. Variety helps keep people interested and engaged, thus consideration should be given to using more than a single communication tool.

Effective engagement in 3-D virtual worlds requires computers with good graphics ability and high-speed internet access. It also requires participants to learn how to navigate and interact within the virtual world which may require more training than other forms of communication. Although, because virtual teams meet regularly and intensively, the benefits of engaging in a virtual world may far exceed the additional investment needed in training. At the other end of the technological sophistication spectrum are telephone bridges, which are relatively inexpensive but do not work well with more than seven or eight people. A webinar combines attributes of a telephone conference call with online digital content and is effective in certain situations. Meeting software, instant messaging and chat rooms allow people using individual video cameras and microphones to see and talk with each other one-on-one or in small groups. Organizations are using Blackboard, social networking sites, and internal blogs to share information. Video can be produced at one or more locations and distributed on demand through collaborative websites or email.

While email may not be the most effective way to facilitate virtual team relationships, it remains a useful tool. Daily or weekly updates sent regularly to all virtual team members contain pertinent business information to keep them updated and connected to each other and the project. To promote personal relationship building, at the end of the update the facilitator and the team members are encouraged to write something that happened to them personally during the week. These personal stories help to develop collegiality and trust within the team (Davis & Scaffidi, 2007).

When working with video conferencing technologies from multiple locations, teams must plan ahead and work smarter rather than harder. At each location there needs to be a facilitator, or at least facilitator guidelines. People should position themselves around the room in such a manner that ensures the greatest likelihood that they can be seen and heard at the remote sites. In many cases one microphone may not be sufficient for the audio needs of the meeting, work with the IT people to obtain sufficient types and quantities of microphones. Have a podium or location, where the camera and the microphone are well situated to capture the speaker. When people are giving a report or discussing important issues they should move to that location so that team members everywhere can see and hear them clearly. It is important that people are able to be seen, distinguished from each other, and heard at remote sites. In video conferences, every member should be expected to be an active participant. This participation requires that they come to the meeting prepared to engage and contribute in some way. The meeting facilitator, as well as team members, should engage with other members and ask for their opinion frequently if they do not volunteer information.

VIRTUAL WORLDS

Virtual worlds are difficult to define in narrow terms (Wilson, 2009). A range of names have been used for them that include virtual social worlds, massively multiplayer online role-playing games, multiplayer online games and 3-D Internet (Krell, 2007). The variance in names indicates the wide array of applications that virtual worlds offer. Virtual worlds are three-dimensional spaces in which users interact with each other through an avatar. Avatars in these spaces are three-dimensional (3-D) representations of the user. They are user created and may appear in any variety of forms, including a realistic human representation, a fanciful embellishment of the human form, or a completely imaginary creation. The three-dimensional environment in which they interact may be fixed, or be open-ended and generated and manipulated by the user.

There are key words that are associated with virtual worlds. They include Business ready, On the radar, and Upcoming. Wilson (2009) identified a number of virtual worlds that are business ready, meaning they are established and organizations are using their services. These business ready virtual worlds include: Active Worlds, OLIVE, Protosphere, Qwaq Forums, Second Life, Web Alive and others (Wilson, 2009). Substantial investment into companies involved with providing virtual world platforms and services is occurring, for example, in the fourth quarter of 2007 more than $425 million was invested into virtual world companies in the United States alone (Tampone, 2008).

Corporations around the world recognize the value of teams working within virtual worlds to hold meetings, conduct training, or build prototypes or simulations in a safe learning environment. Although a variety of virtual world platforms exist, for purposes of this discussion we are going to concentrate on one, that being Second Life. Second Life is not without its critics, but "for inexpensive, non-critical applications Second Life is far ahead of the pack" (Wilson, 2009, p. 13). Despite any flaws, both business and educational organizations use Second Life for meetings, trainings, simulations, conferences and exhibitions. Recommendations from Wilson (2009) are that businesses and educators use second life to get a feel for virtual worlds. He recommends using the platform quietly and privately at first and to be aware of text-chat logging and other security concerns.

SECOND LIFE

Second Life is a virtual world developed by Linden Lab in 2003 that is accessible via the Internet. A free program called the Second Life Viewer enables users, called Residents, to interact with each other through avatars. Residents can explore, meet other residents, socialize, participate in individual and group activities, and create and trade virtual property and services with one another, or travel throughout the world, which residents call a grid. Second Life provides an open-ended environment that can be manipulated and customized and is available for users over age 18. A three dimensional modeling tool is built into the software which allows residents to build virtual objects (Wikipedia, 2009).

In 1999 Linden Lab's founder, Philip Rosedale, developed software that enabled computer users to be fully immersed in a 360-degree virtual world experience. By September, 2008 more than 15 million users had established accounts and Second Life was honored at the 59th Annual Technology & Engineering Emmy Awards for advancing the development of online sites with user-generated content. Second life can take you to a place and event you would otherwise not be able to attend, and put you in contact with people you otherwise would not have any contact with.

There is no charge to create a Second Life account or for making use of the world for any period of time. A premium membership of about $10 per month facilitates access to an increased level of technical support. Avatars may take any form including being made to resemble the person they represent. A single Resident account may have only one avatar at a time, although the appearance of the avatar can change. Avatars can communicate via local chat or global instant messaging. Second Life has an internal currency, the Linden dollar, which can be used to buy, sell, rent or trade land or goods and services with other users. Because of Second Life's rapid growth rate, it has suffered from difficulties related to system instability. Second Life is used as a platform for education by many institutions such as colleges, universities, libraries, and government agencies.

Second Life encourages engagement between users and provides exciting new means for conducting meetings and conferences, conducting focus groups, executing customer research and recruiting, as well as fostering interactive engagement among colleagues and target audiences in an immersive 3-D environment that includes voice, text, video, and other collaborative tools (Second Life Grid, 2009).

With Second Life individuals can publicly communicate with each other in text or 3-D spatial voice chat while private conversations can be held among designated groups or with one-on-one texts and voice channels. It allows keynote speakers to address an entire group while subgroups can maintain communication and share thoughts, ideas and reactions. The platform supports multiple languages and real-time translators are available. Second Life provides a safe and powerful platform for interactive learning experiences whether in a classroom setting or in a dangerous or expensive environment for experimentation. It enables people to learn new languages, rehearse presentations, try out new ideas, practice new skills and functions, and learn without risk of damage or injury.

Second Life brings a new dimension to training events, research, professional certification, and compliance. Trainees can participate in team building activities and training from locations anywhere in the world. Learning and interacting together in 3-D space creates the sense of immersion. This shared experience may improve motivation, training retention and teamwork as a result of heightened sensory engagement and the opportunity for collective activity and communication. Unlike other e-learning technologies, Second Life can bring trainees and their instructors into the same "physical" space where they feel as if they inhabit the same world at the same time. Using Second Life simulations and models avoids the expense of real world training sites.

Corporations and educational institutions of all types choose the secure Second Life Grid software platform to build online 3-D virtual worlds. Business, education, government, and nonprofits create both public and private spaces using the tools and technologies powering Second Life, the largest virtual world community. Many report better col-

laboration, high productivity, reduced costs, and greater innovation. The advantages include:

- Hold meetings without leaving the office using real-time 3-D collaboration
- Construct product and process simulations so participants from all over the world can test new designs and concepts
- Conduct employee training
- Offer seminars and symposia that include distant participants
- Meet with global partners at your virtual headquarters
- Receive product feedback from clients
- Engage different constituencies and raise funds
- Build community (Second Life Grid, 2009).

Although the advantages of using Second Life or other virtual world platforms are intriguing and may far outweigh any disadvantages, those venturing into this arena should be aware of the potential challenges. Some of these include the need for adequate technological equipment and support, a shift in organizational culture, a relatively steep learning curve for users, and the need for designated time to allow users to create their account and the virtual world environment in which the team will meet. One specific example of how the use of virtual worlds can consume a considerable amount of time is seen in the process of creating a user's avatar. A visit into Second Life quickly reveals people's need to represent themselves through their avatar in an attractive manner. Although visual representation is important, the "good looking" avatars typically require a fair amount of time to develop. It is true that user can simply use the default avatar, however, it should be expected that the majority of individuals will want to customize theirs in some kind of appealing manor, and that this customization is likely to consume a considerable amount of time. In some ways this is no different than dressing appropriately for a professional work environment; however, adopters should expect a larger investment of time for this endeavor than required to simply put on a business suite. If an organization adopts the use of virtual world technology, and employs systematic and efficient processes for helping its users overcome these challenges, then they may in fact turn out to be minor in comparison to the rewards.

Planning and building a virtual world can be complicated but Second Life makes the process relatively straightforward. Here is how to do it.

- **Plan Well**. It is important to clearly identify project objectives and goals. Understand what you want to achieve, who you want involved, and the Return on Investment you expect. You need executive support with Virtual World activities if you are to have successful in-world experiences.
- **Understand the Technical Requirements**. Some organizations have strict firewall policies that prevent Second Life from running on business or government computers. It may be necessary to work with the IT department to authorize Second Life into the network. As with all three-dimensional type applications, Second Life runs best on newer computers with advanced graphics cards.
- **Join Second Life.** Go to the join page and register. You need to choose a standard avatar, an in-world name, and provide basic contact information before you can download the Second Life viewer. The Second Life viewer is your Second Life browser.
- **Learn to Work in a Virtual Space**. Once you download the Second Life Viewer, you enter the Second Life environment on Orientation Island. It may look and feel unfamiliar to you. The best resource for beginners is in the Support section.
- **Design Your Avatar**. An avatar is a virtual representation of you. Using your basic avatar you can then change nearly every element from body size to hair color to clothing, and more.
- **Find a Solution Provider**. Second Life has a community of over 300 Solution Providers to help you plan, design, and build a custom environment in Second Life to suit your purposes. To find a Solution Provider search the Solution Provider Directory.
- **Purchase Land**. Purchase land or space where you can build your work or learning space. You buy land from the Land Store.
- **Help**. If you hit a snag the Second Life Knowledgebase and Second Life Wiki have a wealth of information about how to create and run a business in Second Life.

CASE STUDY

Many organizations are using virtual world technology to engage in significant interaction with others and IBM is one of the most prominent. IBM's investment in virtual worlds is significant. They have thousands of employees using several virtual world technologies on a regular basis. IBM is building green virtual data centers as well as running large internal conferences. IBM's Academy of Technology has 300 members within the organization who define the technical agenda for the company.

An example that highlights some of the benefits of the use of virtual worlds is IBM's use of Second Life to conduct a virtual conference. The challenge was to determine how to hold two, multi-day meetings, each for 150-300 IBM employees from dozens of countries, without the need for anyone to travel. The solution was to run a version of Second Life behind IBM's corporate firewall and host the events entirely virtually. Employees participated in conference activities such as keynotes, breakout sessions, poster sessions and networking opportunities.

IBM estimates they saved approximately $250,000 by holding the Virtual Worlds for Business conference virtually. Karen Keeter, a spokesperson for IBM's Digital Convergence group, reports that all the event cost participants was time and much less of it than had they traveled to a physical conference. The Annual General Meeting (AGM) ran for 3 days with 120 poster sessions, social events and over 300 registered attendees for dozens of different countries. It is reported that engagement was high with the conference running 4 hours in the morning and 4 hours in the evening each day. The virtual conference saw over a 100% increase in attendance from prior years. People hung out in the virtual plaza and other social areas where video conference calls and networking took place.

IBM surveyed participants of the conference and asked them how the virtual conference compared to face-to-face conferences on the following four levels: content, presentation style, learning, and networking. The results were surprising and very positive towards the use of virtual worlds. The participants responded as follows: 96% said content was the same or better; 85% said presentation style was the same or better; 78% said learning was the same or better; and 62% said networking was the same or better. These results are impressive.

An Executive Summary of the IBM experience is entitled *A Fifth of the Cost, and No Jet Lag*. The report states that in late 2008 IBM held a Virtual World Conference and an Annual Meeting hosted in a secure Second Life environment with a conference space specially designed by IBM for keynotes, breakout sessions, a simulated Green Data Center, a library, and various areas for community gathering. The participants were offered pre-conference training on the basics of Second Life to make them comfortable communicating and navigating within the environment. IBM estimates the ROI for the Virtual World Conference was roughly $320,000 and the Annual Meeting cost one-fifth the cost of a real world event. Many

IBM staff are reported to have been converted into virtual world advocates. They realized that virtual environments are much more than an interesting gaming environment or social networking tool. Virtual environments have the potential to change the way business is done globally and are worthy of in-depth exploration (Second Life Grid Case Studies, 2009).

CONCLUSION

New and emerging forms of technologies influence the way people interact and work within organizations. Virtual teams are enabled by technologies that allow for the sharing of text, audio, video, and workspaces within a virtual environment. It is important to choose appropriate technologies to support collaborate efforts. In some cases, the use of virtual worlds (e.g., Second Life) may be an appropriate and effective median. In other situations, it may be best to use alternative technologies that have less of a learning curve than those required in virtual worlds, or less of an organizational investment. Virtual team effectiveness and success however, rely on more than just technological tools. The achievement of these teams is dependent upon the types of processes, practices, and incentives that guide their work, that promote a sense of common goals and community, and that nourish individual and group motivation.

REFERENCES

Brown, M. K., Huettner, B., & James-Tanny, C. (2007). *Managing virtual teams*. Plano, TX: Wordware Publishing, Inc.

Cooperrider, D. L., Sorensen, P. F., Yaeger, T. F., & Whitney, D. (2001). *Appreciative inquiry: An emerging direction for organization development*. Champaign, IL [C.]. *Stipes Publishing, L*, L.

Creese, E. L. (2003). Group dynamics and learning in an organization behavior virtual learning community: The case of six virtual peer-learning teams. Melbourne, Australia: UltiBase, RMIT University.

Dani, S. S., Burn, N. D., Backhouse, C. J., & Kochhard, A. K. (2006). The implications of organizational culture and trust in the working of virtual teams. PROC. *IMechE, 220,* Part B: J. Engineering Manufacture.

Davis, D., & Scaffidi, N. (2007). *Leading virtual team*. Paper presented at the annual meeting of the International Communication Association, San Francisco, CA. Retrieved March 1, 2009, from www.allacademic.com

De Pillis, E., & Furumo, K. (2007). Counting the cost of virtual teams. *Communications of the ACM, 50*(12), 93–95. doi:10.1145/1323688.1323714

Galbraith, M. W., Sisco, B. R., & Guglielmino, L. M. (1997). *Administering successful programs for adults. Promoting excellence in adult, community, and continuing education*. Boca Raton, FL: Krieger Publishing Co.

Knowles, M. S. (1980). The modern practice of adult education: From pedagogy to andragogy. New York: Cambridge.

Krell, E. (2007, November). HR challenges in virtual worlds. *HR Magazine*.

Merriam, S. B., Caffarella, S. & Baumgartner (2007). *Learning in adulthood*. San Francisco: Jossey-Bass.

Nunamaker, J. F., Reinig, B. A., & Briggs, R. O. (2009). Principles for effective virtual teamwork. *Communications of the ACM, 52*(4), 113–117. doi:10.1145/1498765.1498797

Odgers, P. (2005). *Administrative office management (13e)*. Mason, OH: Thomson Corporation, South-Western.

Parker, G. (2007). *Teamwork & team meetings: The new reality*. Retrieved October 12, 2008, from http://www.glennparker.com/Freebees/TeamworkandTeamMeetings.html

Roebuck, D. B., Brock, S. J., & Moodie, D. R. (2004). Using a simulation to explore the challenges of communicating in a virtual team. *Business Communication Quarterly, 67*(3), 359–367. doi:10.1177/1080569904268083

Second Life Grid. (2009). Retrieved May 13, 2009, from http://secondlifegrid.net/slfe/corporations-use-virtual-world

Second Life Grid Case Studies. (2009). Retrieved May 15, 2009, from http://secondlifegrid.net/casestudies/IBM

Shachaf, P., & Hara, N. (2005). Team effectiveness in virtual environments: An ecological approach . In Ferris, S. P., & Godar, S. (Eds.), *Teaching and learning with virtual teams* (pp. 83–108). Hershey, PA: Idea Group Publishing.

Tampone, K. (2008, April 18). Companies, colleges use virtual worlds as training tools. *The Central New York Business Journal*.

Thompson, K., (2005). The seven beliefs of high performing teams. *The Bumble Bee, Bioteams Features, *(71).

Thompson, K., & Good, R. (2005, November 9). *The Bioteaming Manifesto: A new paradigm for virtual, networked business teams*. Retrieved November 14, 2008, from http://changethis.com/19.BioteamingManifesto

Wikipedia. (2009). Retrieved April 15, 2009, from http://en.wikipedia.org/wiki/Second_Life

Wilson, N. (2009). *Virtual worlds for business*. Clever Zebra. Retrieved May 2, 2009, from http://cleverzebra.com/book.

KEY TERMS AND DEFINITIONS

Appreciative Inquiry: Appreciative Inquiry (AI) is about the search for the best in people, organizations, and the world around us. It involves the discovery of what is taking place when an organization and its people are most alive, most effective, and the most positive about the future. AI seeks to build a constructive union among people and what they view as past and present achievements, assets, unexplored potentials, innovations, strengths, elevated thoughts, opportunities, high point moments, and lived visions of the future.

Avatars: Avatars are three-dimensional (3-D) virtual representations of the user. They are user created and may appear in a variety of forms including a realistic human representation, a fanciful embellishment of the human form, or an imaginary creation.

Bioteaming: Bioteaming is a dynamic concept used to enhance team effectiveness. Bioteaming is about building organizational teams that operate on the basis of the natural principles which underpin nature's most successful teams.

Second Life: Second Life is a virtual world developed by Linden Lab in 2003 that is accessible via the Internet. Second Life is a free or inexpensive way for people, called residents, to interact with each other through avatars. Residents can explore, meet other residents, socialize, participate in individual and group activities, and create and trade virtual property and services with one another, or travel throughout the world, which is called a grid. Second Life provides an open-ended environment that can be manipulated and customized. Second Life encourages engagement between users and can be adapted for use with a wide variety of audiences.

Team Dynamics: The interaction among and between team members as they engage and work together toward a common objective.

Virtual Environment: A non-physical setting within which individuals interact and work. Virtual environments are typically computer based and rely upon the Internet for functionality.

Virtual Teams: Intentional groups composed of identified individuals who have special talents/skills/knowledge related to the goals of the team. Virtual teams are groups of highly qualified people brought together in a virtual environment in order to capitalize upon each member's unique attributes. Virtual teams are an important component of many corporate and educational organizations and have evolved largely because of globalization, technology, and changing demographics.

Virtual Worlds: Virtual Worlds are three-dimensional online spaces in which users interact with each other through an Avatar. Corporations around the world recognize the value of teams working within Virtual Worlds to hold meetings, conduct training, or build prototypes or simulations in a safe learning environment. A variety of virtual world platforms exist and more are being developed or improved at a rapid rate.

Chapter 15
Virtual Environments and Serious Games:
Teaching Cross–Cultural Communication Skills

K. A. Barrett
Distance Education Consultant, USA

W. Lewis Johnson
Alelo, Inc., USA

ABSTRACT

The Alelo language and culture game-based training has been successfully applied in the K-16 education, government, and military sectors. With increasing globalization of business and widespread use of the Internet, this same approach is applicable for corporate education. The chapter will suggest how virtual environments using cross-cultural simulations that include communicating with virtual avatars could be adopted for corporate use to effectively train and educate employees in cross-cultural communication, as well as other skill sets.

INTRODUCTION

With the globalization of the corporate sector has come the need for employees to know language and culturally appropriate ways of communicating with foreign counterparts. Moreover, shrinking budgets and the increasing need for contact with partners abroad have made it necessary to provide alternatives to standard classroom training for other skills,

such as leadership and technical training. Corporations have been providing face to face training in brick and mortar classrooms for many years. Yet gone are the days when companies could send an employee for a weeks-long training program. Virtual worlds (VW), also referred to as virtual or 3-D environments, provide a less costly alternative to host complex human interactions than face to face simulations. VW are persistent, computer-simulated environments where one or more user(s) interact

DOI: 10.4018/978-1-61520-619-3.ch015

synchronously through avatars, digital representations of themselves (Shaw, 2009). Indeed, avatars can behave like natural humans (Bricken, 1991). Furthermore, through their avatars, users can experience events and activities unknown to them in the real world. Advances in technology have now made it possible for learners to engage in highly interactive instruction via the Web. A new trend is the low-cost delivery of training courses via the Web that use VW to create real-life simulations of situations employees will encounter on the job.

One of the most effective pedagogies underlying these environments is based upon socio-cultural learning theory, which suggests one learns through interacting with virtual avatars in a non-threatening 3D environment. This aspect has been shown to be important to adult learners, who are often intimidated by the live language classroom experience (Johnson, Wang, & Wu, 2007). According to Lave & Wenger (1991), learning is most productive when situated within context in courses that are results-oriented and task-based. The presence of learners in a simulated world where they engage in tasks with other people makes it more likely that learning will transfer back to their place of work.

Virtual environments and socio-cultural theory intersect in the creation of serious games. As Susi, Johannesson, & Backlund, (2007) defines them, serious games are digital games used for purposes other than mere entertainment. Immersive serious games use VW to create safe, yet engaging, virtual environments in which learners can develop a desired set of skills. Studies have shown that a virtual 3D space can be more conducive to learning real-world capabilities than other, more conventional teaching methods (Susi, et. al., 2007). Serious games are especially helpful for military training, as they provide secure areas in which one may develop the skills necessary to carry out dangerous missions. In fact, playing America's Army, the first serious game used for military training, actually improved new recruits' performance on range tests (Zyda, 2005). Because

of the merits of serious games, the serious game industry is only expected to grow over the next several years (Susi et al., 2007).

Based on evidence supporting the use of serious games to teach cross-cultural communication, Alelo has developed courses that are designed to help learners in the military, corporate, and private sectors quickly acquire basic communication skills in foreign languages and cultures. In these courses, immersive, interactive 3D video games simulate real-life communication, allowing users to role play with animated "socially intelligent virtual humans" that recognize the user's speech, intent, gestures and behavior. The virtual agents are used to teach communicative competency and cultural awareness. Cultural protocols involve cultural knowledge, sensitivity and awareness — including non-verbal gestures, etiquette, and norms of politeness — that are critical for successful communication. For example, as part of the military training programs, learners must use their new knowledge of the target language and culture to complete missions including civil affairs, house cordon and search, entry check point, crowd management, team training, and information gathering. If a learner struggles to complete his mission, the virtual agents help him perfect his skills until he reaches the necessary linguistic and cultural level of competency.

Culture and language training is just as relevant for the military world as it is for the corporate world. This common necessity indicates the emergence of a unilateral need for intercultural collaboration skills. In the corporate sector, cross-functional and trans-national teams often must learn to negotiate meaning to achieve project goals. Similarly, in Tactical Dari, servicemembers learn how to work together with the Afghan people to accomplish a project (See Figure 1). No matter the sector, today's global community increasingly requires an efficient method of acquiring cross-cultural communication skills.

Figure 1. Scene from tactical Dari

LITERATURE REVIEW: THEORETICAL FRAMEWORK

Serious Games and Cultural Competency

Serious games offer the opportunity to design learning environments in virtual worlds that are at once engaging and content-rich. Through placing learners at the locus of control (first-person), they are able to become full participants in the simulation, experiencing the results of their decision-making in a safe environment. Simulation and gaming theory is based upon learning theories where behavioral, attitudinal, and cognitive changes due to experience are foremost (Garcâia-Carbonell, Rising, Montero, & Watts, 2001). More contemporary researchers such as Klabbers (2000), differentiate between learning as acquisition and learning as interaction, suggesting that system dynamics plays a role in the design of computer-based interactive learning environments for a wide variety of audiences.

With a world growing smaller each day, cross-cultural considerations also become increasingly important in the design and development of simulation-based learning environments (Morgan, 2000). Elements of cultural competence include: 1) metacultural awareness; attitude toward cultural differences; 2) knowledge of other culture's practices and values; and 3) ability to apply cultural knowledge easily in intercultural interactions (cultural proficiency) (Bhui, Warfa, Edonya, McKenzie, & Bhugra, 2007). Some educators claim that cultural proficiency is achievable only after years of study and experience, analogous with language proficiency (Johnson, 2009). Cultural competence is difficult to achieve for several reasons. For one, culture is pervasive, so many people are not aware of it (e.g, the cultural norms for body language, gesture, and eye contact). Culture courses often present cultural knowledge in abstract terms, making it difficult to understand and apply. Moreover, cultural skills are often learned by trial and error, leaving learners risking embarrassment.

Virtual worlds are an effective method of teaching intercultural competence because they provide learners with multiple, fail safe opportunities to behave and interact with others different from themselves. The consequences of failure are far less than in the real world, where a deal may be lost, or in the case of the military, lives may be lost. As a result, VW, used in the context of serious games, are becoming a commonly-used pedagogical tool. With global virtual teams becoming increasingly commonplace across the corporate sector (Bergiel, Bergiel, & Balsmeierl, 2008; Townsend, DeMarie, & Hendrickson, 1998), the need for intercultural competence becomes crucial for project success.

Serious games allow the learner to interact and engage collaboratively in a constantly changing graphical, three-dimensional virtual environment either with other digital artifacts, avatars, or humans (Dede & Ketelhut, 2005). Simulation and gaming theory is based on the learning theories in which behavioral, attitudinal, and cognitive changes due to experience are foremost (Garcâia-Carbonell et al., 2001). Games may be free-form or rule-based, generating different types of interactive learning environments (Garcâia-Carbonell et al., 2001). The goal of the learning may be to increase skills and knowledge or to modify behaviors.

Klabber's research is supported as well by earlier theories, in particular constructivism and socio-constructivism which assume that knowledge is constructed and socially constructed by learners based upon their interpretations of experiences in the world (Reigeluth, 1999). In multi-player games, skills and knowledge are socially-constructed as part of the game, leading to what some researchers have described as a cognitive apprenticeship approach to instruction (Lave & Wenger, 1991). Post-simulation, participants may debrief their experiences either alone with an instructor or preferably, in a moderated group setting. It is here that the potential for greatest learning can occur (Raybourn, 2004).

E-learning, Serious Games, and Virtual Worlds

E-learning allows businesses to avoid the costs of extra human resources personnel, classroom space, and training time. By switching over to web-based training programs, users are guaranteed convenience, efficiency, and efficacy. Companies like IBM, who saved $200 million in 1999 by moving their training program from the classroom to the computer, have reaped significant economic benefits from educating their employees online (Strother, 2002). This recent phenomenon provides a solution to corporate time pressures and limited resources, and hence has become a popular method of corporate training. Shaw (2009) describes the first corporate immersive, role-playing, team-based, complex learning scenario created in a popular web-based VW called Second Life TM (SL). The goal was to accelerate the process by which project managers successfully applied their knowledge to solve real-world problems.

VWs and serious games share six features (Book, 2004):

1. **Shared Space**: the world allows many users to participate at once.
2. **Graphical User Interface**: the world depicts space visually, with varying styles, including immersive 3D environments.
3. **Immediacy**: interaction takes place in real time.
4. **Interactivity**: the world allows users to alter, develop, build, or submit customized content.
5. **Persistence**: the world's existence continues regardless of whether or not individual users are logged in.
6. **Socialization/Community**: the world allows and encourages the formation of in-world social groups (e.g., guilds, clubs, cliques, housemates, neighborhoods).

With the six features above as a foundation for an immersive game experience, learners in the corporate world would be able to form virtual teams centered around a training topic. Yet serious games here can be considered a customizable solution to an overarching virtual world in which participants learn and interact with one another. Examples of serious games will be presented later in the chapter.

Apart from serious games, there are a number of examples of the use of VWs to educate (e.g., in health care), in particular using Second Life. What makes the Second Life approach different is its ability to call on real-life participants, giving students access to professors or volunteers who act as patients, as well as a range of medical experts who teach or practice at colleges and universities across the country (Lafsky, 2009). Students can interact with the patients and doctors, order tests, diagnose problems, and recommend treatment. One such immersive experience, Heart Murmur Sim, uses real cardiac sounds to train students to listen to a patient's chest and identify heart murmurs. Another program is the Nursing Education Simulation, which requires students to wear a headset with a display, like pilots use, to "monitor" and "use" defibrillators, IV pumps, and medication to treat a virtual patient who is experiencing particular symptoms. Although the use of Second Life to train medical students does not yet offer convincing evidence that it is effective, it offers a richer set of resources, with lower costs, than training in a physical simulated environment (Hendry, 2009).

Despite the lack of evidence in the use of Second Life to effectively train certain students, according to a 2008-2009 study conducted by ThinkBalm, 95% of surveyed organizations that use instructive virtual environments observed successful results. Furthermore, in other studies, evidence has been found to support game-based learning transfer to real-world tasks, such as surgery, piloting, and golf (Tobias & Fletcher, 2007). Enablers of space, place, and landscape in virtual worlds allow for simulations of learning environments that would be impossible in traditional classrooms or with conventional interfaces commonly found in distance education courses. Due to these and similar results favoring instruction in VWs, virtual 3D environments are increasingly being used in the military, government, and higher education to teach cross-cultural communication skills.

Situated Cognition and Virtual Environments

The notion of situated cognition is fundamental to the creation of virtual worlds that are effective learning environments for language and culture. Lave (1988) put forward the idea that learning is situated within activity and occurs through legitimate peripheral participation. Miller and Gildea (1987) showed that when young people learn vocabulary words within the context of every day cognition the gains are rapid and successful. Yet when vocabulary is learned in an abstract way, in other words, taken out of context, learning is slow and many errors are made. People learn languages and their associated ways of thinking best when

they can tie the words and structures of those languages to experiences they have had (Gee, 2004). Activity and situations are integral to cognition and learning (Brown, Collins, & Duguid, 1989). In terms of learning a language and appropriate discourse, Lave and Wenger (Lave & Wenger, 1991) wrote that issues about language might have more to do with legitimacy of participation and with access to peripherality than they do with knowledge transmission. Roth (2001) notes that there are different ways in which cognition is situated, for example, across settings, in group interactions, and embodied in practices.

Socio-Cultural Theory: Relevance to Virtual Environments that Simulate Real-Life

Sociocultural theory informs the design of programs that teach language and culture because it guides the observation and interpretation of people engaged in the activity of teaching, learning, and using foreign languages. The theory is just as applicable for designing instruction in virtual worlds as it is for designing face to face instruction. Sociocultural theories of learning posit that individuals learn by socially interacting and conversing with others. Moreover, sociocultural theory seeks to study the mediated mind in the environments in which people engage in normal living activities (Lantolf & Thorne, 2006). Therefore, game-based environments for educational purposes that employ pedagogical agents, in particular those that teach language, are fertile ground for learning socially appropriate ways of interacting across languages and cultures.

Vygotsky (1978) began what would become the sociocultural movement in education by stating that in order to understand individual psychological development it is necessary to understand the system of social relations in which the individual lives and grows. For Vygotsky (1986), culture and community play a significant role in the early development of a child. He felt that this development is applied primarily to mental development, such as thought, language, reasoning functions and mental processes. Vygotsky observed that these abilities develop through social interactions with significant people in a child's life, including parents and other adults. Through these interactions, children come to learn the habits of mind of their culture, namely speech patterns, written language, and other symbolic knowledge that effects construction of knowledge. Moreover, the specific knowledge gained from these interactions represented the shared knowledge of a culture.

Socio-cultural theory posits that social interaction facilitates the construction of knowledge. This theory of learning and development suggests that learning is also a form of language socialization between individuals. A fundamental principle in sociocultural theory as it relates to language learning is the notion that learners' communicative resources are formed and re-formed in the very activity in which they are used, in other words, linguistically mediated social and intellectual activity (Lantolf & Thorne, 2006). Language and culture are thus inextricably linked, and thus language learning in context is crucial for understanding and practicing appropriate social discourse.

Artificial Intelligence in Education: Agent-based Virtual Learning Environments

Negroponte (1970) was the first to conceive a computerized intelligent agent with his notion of a personal butler or assistant. Agents are increasingly being shown to be valuable for learning (Atkinson, 2002; Johnson, Rickel, & Lester, 2000; Moreno, Mayer, Spires, & Lester, 2001). Although computer agents can never simulate an actual human instructor, agents can better operationalize human aspects of instruction than other methods of computer-based tutoring (Baylor, 2002). Pedagogical agents can respond to learners in a social manner through human-like interactions (Kim & Baylor, 2006). Pedagogical

agents have also been found to be viable and effective with educationally-appropriate personas (Baylor, 2000). In their phenomenological study of human-agent interactions Veletsianos and Miller (2008) described one aspect of the experience of conversing with a pedagogical agent as humanizing the agent somewhere between fantasy and reality.

In VWs, it is important to understand the terminology used regarding "agents." *Agents* are *bots*, and *embodied agents* are agents that have human form. *Conversational agents* are agents capable of conversational dialog with users, while *embodied conversational agents* are embodied, are conversational, and communicate using a combination of verbal and nonverbal communication (body language). It is also necessary to distinguish between bots and avatars in VWs. Embodied agents, a type of bot, are digital models of humans driven by computer algorithms while avatars are digital models driven by real-time humans (Bailenson, Yee, Merget, & Schroeder, 2006). Bots are short for "robot" and are programs that operate as an agent for a user or another program or simulates a human activity. A chatterbot is a program that can simulate talk with a human being. There are also online agents with artificial intelligence, an advanced example of which is A.L.I.C.E. ("Artificial Linguistic Internet Computer Entity") (A.L.I.C.E., 2009). A.L.I.C.E is a chat bot developed in the mid 90s that is capable of holding intelligent conversation, and providing relevant answers to questions. Avatars, on the other hand, are virtual embodiments of users. An avatar is further defined as a user-created digital representation that symbolizes the user's presence in a virtual world (Bailenson et al., 2006).

Intelligent agent technology, and in particular conversational agent technology, offers exciting possibilities for computer and online learning environments, and for overcoming the design challenges mentioned above. Agents can be used to create games that simulate actual human conversation and social interaction, so that the skills acquired in the game transfer more easily to real-life language use. Agents can actively engage learners in language use, making the learners less likely to engage in distracting game activities unrelated to language learning. For example, agents that communicate only in the target language, and not in the learner's native language, can encourage learners to use the target language and discourage them for switching back to their native language.

Conversational signals such as head nods or eye contact further engage the human user. Furthermore, hand gestures and other body language can help visual learners process audio language lessons. Finally, the level of difficulty of conversational interactions with agents can be carefully controlled to provide learners with an optimal level of challenge. For beginning learners, conversational agents can be created that are very tolerant of learner mistakes and hesitations, to reduce the intimidation factor in foreign language dialog. For advanced learners, we can create agents that demand a much higher standard of language fluency, and so help learners to overcome the well-known Plateau Effect in second language learning, where learners progress in their only to the point where they are understandable by native speakers, and no farther.

Alelo uses embodied conversational agents (ECAs), or virtual humans, as intelligent agents to instruct languages to users of their serious games. As defined by Jayfus Doswell (2005), ECAs are 3D bodies in a virtual environment that behave and communicate with human users in a natural fashion. One important attribute of ECAs is their nonverbal communication. Body language can help demonstrate an activity, give directions, or perform customary behavior. For example, an intelligent agent can demonstrate how to greet someone by reaching out his arm to shake a friend's hand. Alternatively, an agent can indicate his disapproval of what a learner said or did by shaking his head and crossing his arms. Where possible, ECAs must also be believable agents,

encompassing several dimensions: personality, affect, social intelligence, and consistent behavior (Pelachaud, Carofiglio, De Carolis, de Rosis, & Poggi, 2002).

For language instruction in serious games, ECAs hold distinct advantages over avatars and bots. An avatar represents a human user in a VW and remains under his control at all times (Cassell & Vilhjalmsson, 1999). Although avatars can perform tasks according to humans' orders, they cannot behave independently. The Alelo VW is a one-user environment without 3rd-party avatars because the focus rests on the learner. All intelligent agents in the virtual environment have been carefully programmed to behave according to the learner's needs. Alelo supports open-ended dialogue relevant to a specific task or situation between ECAs and human users. ECAs differ from bots in that bots perform simple tasks and engage in scripted conversation while ECAs adapt to the virtual circumstances and the learner's behavior. Bots simply do not have the necessary complexity to interact with a language learner who may misspeak and communicate unpredictably in the target language. Alelo chooses to use ECAs because programmers can regulate their actions in response to the needs of the user.

Serious Games in Higher Education and Government: What we know Works and how the Corporate Sector can Benefit

In the Alelo language and culture training courses learners acquire knowledge of foreign language and culture through a combination of interactive lessons and serious games that give trainees concrete contexts in which to develop and apply their skills. The learning environments combine immersive games and interactive instructional materials, and utilize advanced speech recognition and conversational artificial intelligence (AI) capabilities, to give learners opportunities to develop and practice their communication skills.

The immersive games provide extensive levels of engagement, motivation and practice through "free form" storylines with very wide ranges of game-play paths, interactive dialogs and action options. Not all virtual humans are the same; each behaves according to its individual personality, cultural background, emotions and intent, consistent with the storyline and in response to learner actions. The storyline's drama, exploration and elements of surprise include many different opportunities to learn.

Corporations in the 21st century are diverse entities, with cross cultural communication within and across borders an important consideration in virtual teams (Anawati & Craig, 2006). Cross-cultural communication training occurs in a range of different fields. The need for this type of training is most evident in customer service fields, in particular for audiences such as health professionals and first responders. As one example, medical patients have diverse cultural backgrounds, particularly in large urban areas. Yet personnel who interact with these patients are often not provided adequate training in essential medical terminology and phrases in foreign languages, nor are given specialized training to deal with cultural differences (Beach, Price, & Gary, 2005)

Alelo's courses focus on spoken communication, nonverbal communication, and cultural knowledge relevant to face-to-face communication. Three key pedagogic objectives of the approach are to reduce students' frustration and boredom, sustain their motivation even after hours of intense study, and promote the transfer of acquired communication skills to the real world. As a result, learners achieve successes quickly, which builds their self-confidence and maintains their motivation and interest. The courses are designed to provide learners with the specific communication skills that they need for their job, foreign travel, and other interactions across cultures. Adult learners in particular find this performance-based approach very attractive. This highly engaging approach is transferable to the corporate sector,

where learner self-efficacy and motivation are just as central to effective training programs.

Language instruction emphasizes spoken vocabularies and pronunciation, covering grammar and written language only when required. From the first lesson, students learn by listening to and speaking in the foreign language, getting immediate feedback and guidance. The courses tolerate incorrect pronunciation and guide students extensively on how to improve it. Acting as comprehensive cultural tutors, the courses teach practical cultural knowledge, sensitivity and awareness — including non-verbal gestures, etiquette, and norms of politeness — that are critical for successful communication.

Situated Culture Model: A Foundation for Teaching Culture and Communicative Competency

Underlying the instructional design of Alelo's products is a dynamic methodology for identifying and teaching situated culture, that is, the cultural knowledge needed to successfully perform tasks or higher-level projects in a foreign country. Students and learners learn the cultural knowledge they need in order to successfully interact and communicate with people who have grown up in a different linguistic and cultural context. One of the major goals of Alelo products is the acquisition of cultural competence. In addition, learners are trained to be more aware of cultural differences and cultural relativity, also known as meta-cultural awareness. This improved meta-cultural awareness is meant to be a tool kit that learners take with them to the foreign context: once they are living and immersed in a foreign country, this meta-cultural awareness helps them continue to learn culturally appropriate and effective ways of speaking and behaving.

The Situated Culture Methodology (SCM) is used to develop all of our courses (See Figure 2). The methodology is broken down into three major groupings: context, cultural factors, and

Figure 2. Situated culture methodology

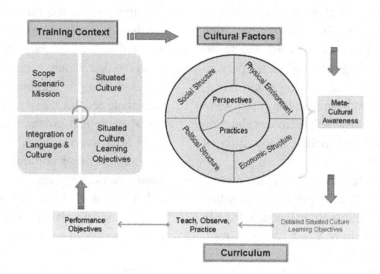

curriculum. All of the groupings are integrated to support learners in reaching performance objectives and in becoming more culturally aware and adaptable.

Instruction in Alelo's courses uses our Situated Culture Model which focuses on tasks the learners are likely to perform, situations in which learners perform those tasks and the culture relevant to those tasks and situations. Learners practice applying culture to tasks and situations. The advantages of this approach are that learners gain a concrete understanding of culture, while getting a shortcut to job-related cultural proficiency.

Intercultural communication and bridging the perceived and implicit gaps between different cultural systems are areas of concern and theoretical interest in many fields. The most prominent and relevant of these fields for the purposes of the Situated Culture Methodology are the areas of medicine and education.

In the field of medicine, one of the major areas of concern is how to train medical caregivers in cultural competence so that they behave appropriately with patients from different backgrounds, avoid potential misunderstandings, and provide effective medical care (Cohen & Goode, 2003). In education, one of the major areas of concern is recognizing the ways that mainstream American education has cultural norms and expectations that may be at odds with the cultural norms and expectations that students have been socialized into at home; these differing behavioral expectations and ways of acquiring and demonstrating knowledge may severely impact student performance at school, where minority or working class students' poor performance may be explained by cultural differences rather than intrinsic intellectual aptitude.

A prominent model for cultural competence among medical caregivers has been developed by Larry Purnell (Purnell, 2005); one assumption of this model is that by increasing one's consciousness of cultural diversity the possibility for healthcare practitioners to provide culturally competent care improves. Purnell's model of cultural competence includes the following components:

- Developing an awareness of one's own culture, existence, sensations, thoughts, and environment without letting them have an undue influence on those from other backgrounds

- Demonstrating knowledge and understanding of the client's culture, health-related needs, and meanings of health and illness
- Accepting and respecting cultural differences
- Not assuming that the healthcare provider's beliefs and values are the same as the client's
- Resisting judgmental attitudes such as "different" is not as good
- Being open to cultural encounters
- Being comfortable with cultural encounters
- Adapting care to be congruent with the client's culture.

VWs offer the opportunity to apply the SCM and these important principles in a safe and immersive virtual environment, where learner feedback can be structured to scaffold the trainee from novice to expert. Studies on the use of simulations in medical schools, both virtual and those that use human patient simulators, have shown that the quality of care given by residents during actual events significantly improved (Wayne et al., 2008).

Immersive Games and Situated Learning: Believable Virtual Environments that Foster Attitudinal and Behavior Change

Using virtual worlds, serious games can simulate situations and tasks so that players learn by doing and can practice without fear of embarrassment. In these environments, games can highlight intercultural differences to promote awareness. Learners are motivated to keep practicing to improve their score. Further, games provide a change of pace (modulate affect) as learners move through the course.

Alelo's curricula incorporate a number of immersive games, in which the learner is given objectives that they must complete by interacting with virtual characters in a virtual world (O'Connor, 2009). These objectives normally reflect realistic tasks they are likely to need to complete in a foreign country: finding a taxi, purchasing something at a market, or completing military missions such as house searches and partner military training. Each task is covered by one "scenario" which connects the immersive game episodes into an overarching storyline.

The basic principle in creating effective serious games is to implement organic feedback/remediation where the learner "wins" by making good choices. The consequences of poor choices appear in the scenario itself. Scenarios are broken down into episodes, i.e., parts of an overall story. Each episode has objectives to be achieved and dialogs that learners need to perform to accomplish these objectives. While engaging in a dialog, learners have multiple options at any point. The development process for episodes is as follows:

- Define basic concept for episodes, connect with learning objectives
- Specify basic path to complete the interaction (good outcome)
- Specify alternative paths (branches) that lead to better/worse outcomes
- Expand interactions based on other common behaviors in the situation, which may lead to more outcomes

Task-based curricula provide learners with contexts that are highly relevant to their missions and daily lives. Virtual world simulations reinforce and let learners transfer their acquired skills to the real world by practicing realistic, extensive inter-personal communication — as opposed to merely repeating uninteresting phrases — at their own pace, as often as they need to, and without embarrassment. (Reigeluth & Schwartz, 1989) model for simulations puts forward a matrix of participation/no participation that determines acquisition and application of knowledge and skills. Using their causal principle variation on their general model, at this stage users will be working with divergent examples, discovering by observation and performance practice strategies that are most effective at achieving positive outcomes in the game.

In terms of engaging learners in conversational interactions in serious games, conversational agents have been used effectively in task-based approaches such as the Tactical Language and Culture Training System where learners converse with Iraqi non-player characters, for example, in order to complete a mission (Johnson, 2007). Agent-based systems offer instructional designers the chance to use virtual characters to motivate and engage learners in new ways.

In the mission games, learners are given a specific task to complete, such as in Tactical Dari where they musts "talk to the locals" in order to find informants and gather critical information for their mission. "Performance before competence" is one of the 16 principles of "good learning" using videogames outlined by (Gee, 2005). While this is the opposite of most traditional instruction, Gee cites in particular the example of language acquisition, in which students can gain competence through reading before actual performance. In Tactical Iraqi, learners man a checkpoint in one scene, and conduct a civil affairs mission in another. If learners do not have all of the requisite skills they are provided hints to enable them to successfully complete the mission – although their game score is less than if they had completed it without hints.

Skillbuilders and Scenarios: From Practice to Practice makes Perfect in a Virtual World

Immersive games provide a practice area for the skills taught in the skillbuilder lessons. The learner is expected to first learn the skills they need to complete a task, and then practice completing the task in an immersive game. To learn the skills they need, the learner will complete approximately

one unit (usually about three to five lessons) of language and culture instruction before entering the first scenario. In some systems, tutor advice is available to learners, specifying which skills are prerequisites for a scenario, and whether or not they have mastered these skills. The scenarios are also dependent on the lessons in a key way: the learner can only use the language that is explicitly taught in the lessons. No prior knowledge of a foreign language is assumed. Figure 3 shows the Skillbuilder and Mission Game components of Tactical French. In the virtual world of the Mission Game, learners practice the linguistic and cultural skills they obtained in the skillbuilders, earning points for correct behavior, and losing points for culturally inappropriate behavior that jeopardizes their mission.

Active Dialogs: Practicing Communication Skills

Active dialogs are essentially scaled-down scenarios. The fundamental purpose of an active dialog is to provide opportunities to practice the specific communicative functions taught in the lesson where it appears (Flowers, 2009). While a scenario normally corresponds to three or four

Figure 3. Main menu of tactical french showing both skillbuilder and mission game components

Figure 4. Scenarios (left) are very similar to active dialogs (right)

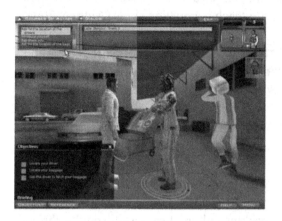

lessons, and can exercise material from all of those lessons, an active dialog corresponds to one skillbuilder lesson, and sometimes only part of a lesson.

As a result of this conceptual distinction, active dialogs are placed directly in the skillbuilder lesson that they are relevant to, while scenarios are separated into the immersive game segment of the system (See Figure 4). In addition, the learner's control is much more limited, the logic is less complex, less advanced language is required, and fewer possible Courses of Action are available in active dialogs. While active dialogs can have good and bad outcomes, they are not a fundamental requirement. Both scenarios and active dialogs contain rich virtual worlds, although scenarios allow for exploration and interaction with multiple characters.

Goals and Purpose of Scenarios and Active Dialogs

The scenarios are a vehicle for practicing and improving language fluency and cultural awareness. The learner should feel comfortable practicing conversational skills in realistic situations. These virtual worlds provide a non-threatening environment where users can slowly improve their oral proficiency. A virtual environment also

means users can safely learn from a cultural faux pas, instead of having such an encounter in the foreign country, where cultural misunderstandings can be deadly. The immersive game environment allows instructors to test learners by putting them in situations where they need to show knowledge of cultural information and/or a foreign language in order to complete the task appropriately.

To complete each active dialog, the learner must speak its character's lines. There are many different things that the learner can say, and the virtual humans in the scenario may respond differently to the learner, depending upon whether or not the learner interacts with the Iraqi characters in culturally appropriate ways. For example, Figure 5 shows a learner talking with a member of a crowd in a crowd-control situation. The menu in the lower left corner of the figure shows the range of different conversational moves that the learner can make. The learner can say a range of things to this character, and express each utterance in a variety of different ways. Furthermore, the learner can speak to multiple virtual humans within the scene. This example shows how in one scene learners obtain many opportunities to practice their spoken dialog skills.

Figure 5. Crowd control scene in tactical Iraqi

EXAMPLES OF IMMERSIVE GAMES AND INTEGRATED SKILLBUILDERS AND THEIR APPLICATION TO CORPORATE TRAINING

In the Alelo courses learners play fun, immersive, interactive 3D video games that simulate real-life communication by role playing with animated socially intelligent virtual humans that recognize learners' intent, speech, gestures and behavior. The Cultural Puppets™ technology used in the courses drives virtual humans to exhibit behavior that is appropriate to the simulation's contexts of storyline, culture, task, user actions, and the personality, emotions and intent specific to each virtual human. User communication towards virtual humans might elicit different responses. If learners speak and behave correctly, the virtual humans become trustful and cooperative, and provide information that learners need to advance. Otherwise, the virtual humans are uncooperative and prevent learners from winning the game. Interactions with virtual humans are also used in training interventions in the corporate sector. In healthcare, virtual humans have been used to train students in motivational interviewing (Villaume, Berger, & Barker, 2006) and in other doctor-patient interactions (Johnsen et al., 2005). In leadership

training, virtual humans in simulations have been used to teach negotiation skills (Aldrich, 2004).

Virtual Cultural Awareness Trainer (VCAT): Teaching Cultural Awareness for the Horn of Africa

The overall objective of the Virtual Cultural Awareness Trainer (VCAT) is to provide cultural awareness training over the Web using a fully embedded social simulation model. Only survival language skills are taught as the focus is on teaching culture. Learners are guided through the program using "metacultural checkpoints" that teach fundamental cultural knowledge and skills that would be needed to become culturally aware in the Horn of Africa, regardless of the country being visited. Learners follow a loose storyline in the game, which consists of task-based lessons appropriate to their rank and mission (e.g., humanitarian assistance), as well as casual games. As learners move through the game, they gain points depending upon successful completion of culturally challenging situations where they must decide upon various courses of action that determine whether or not they are able to achieve a mission objective (See Figure 6).

There is no automatic speech recognition, instead learners must choose the correct action a virtual human must take in order to achieve their

Figure 6. Virtual cultural awareness trainer scenario

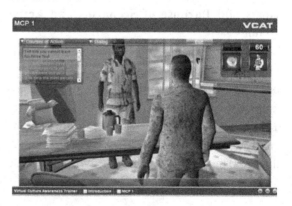

mission objective. Integrated into the game play is a full spectrum of media such as cultural notes with voiceovers, video interviews with cultural experts, and interactive maps, which show the fluidity of tribal migration across national borders, a concept foreign to many American learners.

With corporations challenged to increase cultural competency amongst a globalized and diverse workforce, courses such as the VCAT will become an important adjunct to traditional classroom training. A VCAT type of course that teaches both declarative and procedural knowledge of culture would provide an orientation to new employees being stationed abroad, or finding themselves in daily contact with employees in other countries. Moreover, the increasing diversity of the American workplace calls for an increase in cultural competency. With collaborative teams, including virtual teaming, commonplace throughout the corporate sector, cultural competency skills such as those imparted by the VCAT will increase awareness of differing communicative styles. The result will be more efficient and productive teams.

The Tactical Language & Culture Training Systems

In the Tactical Language and Culture Training Systems extensive levels of engagement, motivation and practice are promoted by providing free form storylines with very wide ranges of game-play paths, interactive dialogs and action options. The storyline's drama, exploration and elements of surprise include opportunities to learn from getting into trouble and trying to gracefully get out of it. For example, in one scene in the Tactical Iraqi course learners can speak perfect Arabic and still offend their virtual Iraqi host by not asking him to enter the house first or by later talking to his wife without observing Iraqi cultural protocols.

Not all virtual humans are the same; each behaves according to its individual personality, emotions and intent, consistent with the storyline

and in response to learner actions. For example, in another Tactical Iraqi scene, the learner's disrespect towards two virtual Iraqis elicits a passive response from one and insults from the other, but learners can fix the problem if they know how to react to the Iraqi's complaints. In a scenario in Tactical French, the agent Laila speaks with the learner, who has arrived at the airport, and they exchange greetings (See Figure 7).

Results from preliminary evaluations of Tactical Language and Culture Training programs have been promising. A Marine unit that trained with Alelo's Tactical Iraqi prior to deploying to Iraqi reported that it had a direct impact on operational effectiveness, so much so that it completed its entire deployment tour without suffering a single combat casualty. Anecdotal evidence showed that Marines knew what to say and how to act culturally appropriately, in several cases diffusing potentially hostile situations. Knowledge of Iraqi language and culture contributed directly to the unit's mission success through enabling Marines to develop rapport with the local populace.

Just as in the military, employees in private sector businesses often find themselves in situations that require acting culturally appropriately to diffuse difficult situations. Customer service is one example where employees are often placed in difficult circumstances where negotiation skills and developing rapport are essential for successful communication and problem resolution. Other examples are managerial and supervisory situations where knowledge of communicative styles and cultural differences can mean the difference between success and failure.

VOICE OF AMERICA'S ENGLISH LEARNING WEBSITE

The English Learning website developed for the Voice of America targets Mandarin and Persian speaking audiences (18-35 year olds) in the countries of China and Iran. The website includes

Figure 7. Tactical french scenario

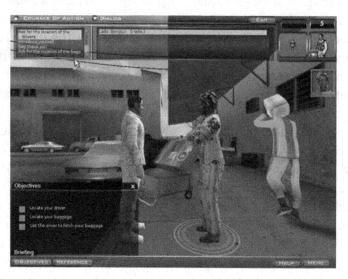

beginning, intermediate and advanced English lessons that convey the American experience through a language-in-culture approach. The material being presented assumes some familiarity with English. Many EFL speakers have had years of English in their formal schooling, yet have poor listening comprehension and speaking skills. In addition, entry into a culture includes knowing both appropriate words and phrases and discourse styles. As such, the curriculum teaches learners how to navigate common situations youth will find in America (e.g., roommates, college life, fast food, dating). Many idioms are presented in each lesson, together with a translation in the learner's native language.

The assumption is that many of the learners will not have a chance to visit America, so the virtual environments created for this curriculum will afford an opportunity to experience a culture very different from their own. Likewise, with corporations spanning the globe and employees often communicating across languages using English, similar learning experiences using virtual environments could be created for employees to teach them EFL skills as well as culturally relevant material. In particular, courses that teach business

travelers how to prepare for travel and possible deployment in a foreign country could benefit from this type of virtual training that focuses on key situations they will encounter, together with survival language skills. In addition, teaching colloquialisms in any language helps to bridge the cultural gap by providing the learner with friendlier discourse options.

FUTURE TRENDS

Increased Access - Serious Games Go Mobile

As the cost of creating virtual environments decreases and technology becomes increasingly available, serious games that teach language and culture will continue to become more widely available across the corporate sector. Future trends are for the serious game environment to expand into the mobile market, making anytime-anywhere training possible. More corporate training departments will use mobile technology as an adjunct or substitute for traditional face to face training, in particular larger companies with workforces in many different countries. The worldwide availability of the iPhone and other mobile devices coupled with an explosion in wireless broadband technology means that visually rich environments such as those found in virtual worlds will become increasingly available. Courses that teach language skills and cultural competency that originally were bound to desktop and laptop computers—or limited to podcasts and videocasts—will be able to be taught at a high level of interactivity on mobile devices.

Another future trend will be avatars that learn and "travel" with you. Learners progress in a training program will be able to be tracked and their program of instruction tailored to meet their performance goals. Employees will be seen as lifelong learners, with their personal avatar guiding them throughout their career.

CONCLUSION

The global reach of business demands the need for cross-cultural communication and with it cultural competency and at least a basic level of language proficiency in the target language. As costs of designing and developing virtual environments decrease they will be able to expand into widespread use among corporations in the private sector. Simulation games are beginning to make inroads into the suite of training offerings. With Web-enabled delivery, employees will have the opportunity to try out new ways of communicating and getting things done in risk-free, contextualized environments.

There are a number of benefits to training programs that incorporate virtual worlds. These include cost savings and greatly increased training design flexibility. With serious games, employees have unique learning opportunities that can include the ability to see different perspectives on situations, as well as receive detailed real time metrics and performance feedback. Virtual worlds also offer the ability to accelerate learning because

of their similarity to on-the-job actual tasks, resulting in increased performance outcomes. Serious games that teach language and culture using virtual worlds hold promise for businesses large and small as people and processes become increasingly transnational and products become globally distributed.

ACKNOWLEDGMENT

The authors wish to acknowledge the contributions of various members of the Alelo team to the work presented here, particular Ellen O'Connor and Michelle Flowers. This work was funded in part by DARPA, USSOCOM, PM TRASYS, and other US government agencies. It reflects the opinions of the authors and not of the US Government.

REFERENCES

Aldrich, C. (2004). *Simulations and the Future of Learning*. San Francisco, CA: Pfeiffer.

A.L.I.C.E. (2009). A.L.I.C.E. Artificial Intelligence Foundation. *The A.L.I.C.E. Project* Retrieved 7/31/09, from http://alice.pandorabots.com/

Anawati, D., & Craig, A. (2006). Behavioral adaptation within cross-cultural virtual teams. *IEEE Transactions on Professional Communication*, *49*(1), 44–56. doi:10.1109/TPC.2006.870459

Atkinson, R. K. (2002). Optimizing Learning from Examples Using Animated Pedagogical Agents. *Journal of Educational Psychology*, *94*(2), 416–427. doi:10.1037/0022-0663.94.2.416

Bailenson, J., Yee, N., Merget, D., & Schroeder, R. (2006). The effect of behavioral realism and form realism of real-time avatar faces on verbal disclosure, nonverbal disclosure, emotion recognition, and copresence in dyadic interaction. *Presence (Cambridge, Mass.)*, *15*(4), 359–372. doi:10.1162/pres.15.4.359

Baylor, A. L. (2000). Beyond Butlers: Intelligent Agents as Mentors. *Journal of Educational Computing Research, 22*(4), 373–382. doi:10.2190/1EBD-G126-TFCY-A3K6

Baylor, A. L. (2002). Agent-Based Learning Environments as a Research Tool for Investigating Teaching and Learning. *Journal of Educational Computing Research, 26*(3), 227–248. doi:10.2190/PH2K-6P09-K8EC-KRDK

Beach, M. C., Price, E. G., & Gary, T. (2005). Cultural Competence: A Systematic Review of Health Care Provider Educational Initiatives. *Medical Care, 43*(4), 356–373. doi:10.1097/01.mlr.0000156861.58905.96

Bergiel, B. J., Bergiel, E. B., & Balsmeierl, P. W. (2008). Nature of virtual teams: a summary of their advantages and disadvantages. *Management Research News, 31*(2), 99–110. doi:10.1108/01409170810846821

Bhui, K., Warfa, N., Edonya, P., McKenzie, K., & Bhugra, D. (2007). Cultural competence in mental health care: a review of model evaluations [Electronic Version]. *BMC Health Services Research 2007*. Retrieved 4/1/09 from http://biomedcentral.com/1472-6963/7/15.

Book, B. (2004). Moving beyond the game: social virtual worlds. *State of Play, 2*, 6–8.

Bricken, M. (1991). Virtual worlds: No interface to design. Cyberspace: first steps, (pp. 363-382).

Brown, J. S., Collins, A., & Duguid, P. (1989). Situated Cognition and the Culture of Learning. *Educational Researcher, 18*(1), 32–42.

Cassell, J., & Vilhjalmsson, H. (1999). Fully embodied conversational avatars: Making communicative behaviors autonomous. *Autonomous Agents and Multi-Agent Systems, 2*(1), 45–64. doi:10.1023/A:1010027123541

Cohen, E., & Goode, T. D. (2003, Summer). *Rational for Cultural Competence in Primary Care*. National Center for Cultural Competence. Retrieved April 1, 2009.

Dede, C., & Ketelhut, D. J. (2005). Designing for Motivation and Usability in a Museum-based Multi-User Virtual Environment. *Retrieved, 10*(1), 2005.

Doswell, J. (2005). *It's virtually pedagogical: pedagogical agents in mixed reality learning environments*.

Flowers, M. (2009). Virtual Cultural Awareness Trainer Preliminary Design Document. Los Angeles, CA: Alelo TLT, LLC.

Garcâia-Carbonell, A., Rising, B., Montero, B., & Watts, F. (2001). Simulation/gaming and the acquisition of communicative competence in another language. *Simulation & Gaming, 32*(4), 481–491. doi:10.1177/104687810103200405

Gee, J. P. (2004). *Situated Language and Learning: A Critique of Tradional Schooling*. New York, NY: Routledge.

Gee, J. P. (2005). *Why are Video Games Good for Learning?* [Electronic Version]. Retrieved 3/10/09 from www.academiccolab.org/resources/documents/Good_Learning.pdf

Hendry, E. R. (2009). Virtual Medical Training Comes to Second Life [Electronic Version]. *The Chronicle of Higher Education*. Retrieved from http://chronicle.com/blogPost/Virtual-Medical-Training-Comes/7277/print

Johnsen, K., Dickerson, R., Raij, A., Lok, B., Jackson, J., Shin, M., et al. (2005). *Experiences in Using Immersive Virtual Characters to Educate Medical Communication Skills*. Paper presented at the IEEE Virtual Reality, Bonn, Germany.

Johnson, W. L. (2007). Serious use of a serious game for language learning. *Artificial Intelligence in Education: Building Technology Rich Learning Contexts that . Work (Reading, Mass.)*, •••, 67.

Johnson, W. L. (2009). *Developing Intercultural Competence through Videogames*. Paper presented at the The Second International Workshop on Intercultural Collaboration.

Johnson, W. L., Rickel, J. W., & Lester, J. C. (2000). Animated pedagogical agents: Face-to-face interaction in interactive learning environments. *International Journal of Artificial Intelligence in Education, 11*(1), 47–78.

Johnson, W. L., Wang, N., & Wu, S. (2007). *Experience with serious games for learning foreign languages and cultures.* Paper presented at the SimTecT 2007, Brisbane, Queensland, Australia.

Kim, Y., & Baylor, A. L. (2006). A Social-Cognitive Framework for Pedagogical Agents as Learning Companions. *Educational Technology Research and Development, 54*(6), 569–596. doi:10.1007/s11423-006-0637-3

Klabbers, J. H. G. (2000). Learning as Acquisition and Learning as Interaction. *Simulation amp Gaming, 31*(3), 380-406.

Lafsky, M. (2009). Can Training in Second Life Teach Doctors to Save Real Lives? [Electronic Version]. *Discover.* Retrieved from http://discovermagazine.com/2009/jul-aug/15-can-medical-students-learn-to-save-real-lives-in-second-life/article_view?b_start:int=0&-C=

Lantolf, J. P., & Thorne, S. L. (2006). *Sociocultural theory and the genesis of second language development*. Oxford, UK: Oxford University Press.

Lave, J. (1988). *Cognition in practice*. New York: Cambridge University Press. doi:10.1017/CBO9780511609268

Lave, J., & Wenger, E. (1991). *Situated learning: legitimate peripheral participation*. New York: Cambridge University Press.

Miller, G. A., & Gildea, P. M. (1987). How children learn words. *Scientific American, 257*(3), 94–99. doi:10.1038/scientificamerican0987-94

Moreno, R., Mayer, R. E., Spires, H. A., & Lester, J. C. (2001). The Case for Social Agency in Computer-based Teaching: Do Students Learn More Deeply When They Interact with Animated Pedagogical Agents? *Cognition and Instruction, 19*(2), 177–213. doi:10.1207/S1532690XCI1902_02

Morgan, K. (2000). Cross-Cultural Considerations for Simulation-Based Learning Environments. *Simulation & Gaming, 31*(4), 491–508. doi:10.1177/104687810003100404

Negroponte, N. (1970). *The architecture machine*. Cambridge, MA: MIT press.

O'Connor, E. (2009). Alelo Immersive Game Process Document. Los Angeles, CA: Alelo TLT, LLC.

Pelachaud, C., Carofiglio, V., De Carolis, B., de Rosis, F., & Poggi, I. (2002). *Embodied contextual agent in information delivering application.*

Purnell, L. (2005). The Purnell Model for Cultural Competence [Electronic Version]. *Journal of Multicultural Nursing & Health*. Retrieved 2/27/09.

Raybourn, E. (2004). (pp. Personal conversation). Albuquerque, New Mexico.

Reigeluth, C. M. (Ed.). (1999). *Instructional-Design Theories and Models (Vol. II)*. Mahwah, NJ: Lawrence Erlbaum Associates, Publishers.

Reigeluth, C. M., & Schwartz, E. (1989). An Instructional Theory for the Design of Computer-based Simulations. *Journal of Computer-Based Education, 16*(1), 1–10.

Roth, W. M. (2001). Situating Cognition. *Journal of the Learning Sciences*, *10*(1/2), 27–61. doi:10.1207/S15327809JLS10-1-2_4

Shaw, B. (2009). *Project Management Rehearsal Studio: A Collaborative Learning Experience in a Virtual World*. Armonk, NY: IBM.

Strother, J. (2002). An assessment of the effectiveness of e-learning in corporate training programs. *International Review of Research in Open and Distance Learning*, *3*(1).

Susi, T., Johannesson, M., & Backlund, P. (2007). Serious games–An overview. *Skövde: University of Skövde* (Technical Report HS-IKI-TR-07-001).

Tobias, S., & Fletcher, J. D. (2007). What Research Has to Say About Designing Computer Games for Learning. *Educational Technology*, *57*(5), 20–29.

Townsend, A. M., DeMarie, S. M., & Hendrickson, A. R. (1998). Virtual teams: Technology and the workplace of the future. *Academy of Management Science*, *12*(3), 17–29.

Veletsianos, G., & Miller, C. (2008). Conversing with Pedagogical Agents: A Phenomenological Exploration of Interacting with Digital Entities. *British Journal of Educational Technology*, *39*(6), 969–986. doi:10.1111/j.1467-8535.2007.00797.x

Villaume, W. A., Berger, B. A., & Barker, B. N. (2006). Learning Motivational Interviewing: Scripting a Virtual Patient. *American Journal of Pharmaceutical Education*, *70*(2).

Vygotsky, L. S. (1978). *Mind in society*. Cambridge, MA: Harvard University Press.

Vygotsky, L. S. (1986). *Thought and Language*. Cambridge, MA: MIT Press.

Wayne, D., Didwania, A., Feinglass, J., Fudala, M., Barsuk, J., & McGaghie, W. (2008). Simulation-Based Education Improves Quality of Care During Cardiac Arrest Team Responses at an Academic Teaching Hospital*. *Chest*, *133*(1), 56. doi:10.1378/chest.07-0131

Zyda, M. (2005). From visual simulation to virtual reality to games. *Computer*, •••, 25–32. doi:10.1109/MC.2005.297

KEY TERMS AND DEFINITIONS

Serious Games: Educational computer games used to teach knowledge and skills.

Virtual Worlds: Persistent, computer simulated environments where participants can interact with one another through avatars.

Intelligent Agents: Computerized entities that use goal-directed behavior to act upon their environment.

Socio-Cultural Theory: Argues that individuals learn by socially interacting and conversing with others.

Cultural Competency: Knowledge of other cultures, including metacultural awareness, and the ability to apply that knowledge and awareness to behave in a culturally appropriate manner.

Mission Game: A virtual, game-based environment where learners apply their new skills and knowledge as they interact with non-player characters to achieve a performance goal and winning outcome.

Task-based Curricula: Aims to improve learning and performance outcomes through engaging learners in contextually relevant activities and tasks.

Section 5
Integrated Technologies

Chapter 16
Corporate Training Goes Virtual:
A Hybrid Approach to Experiential Learning

Natalie T. Wood
Saint Joseph's University, USA

Michael R. Solomon
Saint Joseph's University, USA

Greg W. Marshall
Rollins College, USA

Sarah Lincoln
Saint Joseph's University, USA

ABSTRACT

Eighty million members of the Millennial Generation are knocking at the door of Corporate America. Can traditional "chalk and talk" corporate training techniques adequately address the needs of a generation that views the world through a digital lens? In this chapter, the authors will explore the learning styles of Millennials and how virtual world platforms can mesh with the learning styles of these new workers. They review existing literature on virtual learning and identify the types of conditions that argue for an immersive digital platform as opposed to a traditional face-to-face or distance learning encounter. They conclude by outlining a specific scenario (within the domain of pharmaceutical sales training) that illustrates how corporate educators can deliver both types of learning using a hybrid real/virtual platform.

DOI: 10.4018/978-1-61520-619-3.ch016

PAPER (AND PENCIL) TRAINING IN A DIGITAL WORLD

The Millennial Generation is eagerly knocking at the door of Corporate America. These 80 million members of "Gen Y" are optimistic, confident, multicultural, and goal-oriented. They excel at multitasking, like to collaborate, and enjoy cooperative activities. Most importantly, they are avid social networkers, bloggers, and videogamers. They see the world through a digital lens and often appear to be more comfortable interacting with a colleague's Facebook page or virtual world avatar than conversing in face-to-face situations.

Can traditional "chalk and talk" corporate training techniques adequately address the needs of these new knowledge workers? Can existing training programs accommodate learners who have grown up holding a mouse or joystick rather than a pencil? These "Digital Natives" will change the game for companies, and employers need to anticipate these changes now. Forward-thinking organizations from IBM to the U.S. Army already are experimenting with new 3D immersive learning platforms that synchronize with the dynamic recreational environments in which young people immerse themselves every day.

Virtual environments hold tremendous promise for corporate training, but they are not a panacea. Nor is it likely that they will entirely replace traditional in-person techniques (at least in the near future). To reflect this reality, we advocate a *hybrid approach* to curriculum development that "cherry-picks" the best aspects of each domain and appeals to multiple learning styles. Furthermore, we propose that these factors vary significantly depending upon the type of learning the organization needs to stress. At this point it is important to make a distinction between education and training. The purpose of education is to increase insight and understanding; it teaches the "why." Training on the otherhand increases skills and competence; it teaches employees the "how" of a job (Stack & Lovern, 1995). Whereas both types of instruction can be delivered with the use of 3D immersive environments, the emphasis of this chapter is corporate training.

In this chapter, we will discuss the learning styles of Millennials and explore how virtual world platforms can mesh with the learning styles of these new workers. We also will explore the different types of learning that need to occur in the corporate world, and review attempts others have made to transfer each type of learning to a virtual environment.

In particular, we will emphasize a dichotomy of *content* versus *experience*-based learning. Content-based learning refers to the acquisition of knowledge and mastery of concepts (lectures), while experience-based learning refers to the acquisition of skills, and mastery of interpersonal contingencies (role-playing).

We identify the types of conditions that argue for an immersive digital platform, as opposed to a traditional face-to-face or distance learning encounter. We then develop a specific scenario within the domain of pharmaceutical sales training that illustrates how corporate educators can deliver both types of learning using a hybrid real/virtual platform.

Learning Styles of the Millennial Employee

The emergence of new information and communication technologies has significantly influenced the way we learn, and the way we teach. As Table 1 illustrates, each new generation develops technological innovations that eventually find their way into corporate classrooms.

For the Millennial generation, born after 1982 and raised in a digital world, immersive communications technologies are an integral part of everyday life. By preschool, kids are exposed to the Web and virtual education. By middle school, the Web is a frequent resource for homework assignments. Exposure to the technology increases throughout high school, and for many students, the

Table 1. Generational technologies, teaching and learning styles

Generation	Technologies Available	Dominant Teaching and Learning Styles
Seniors	Vacuum-tube radios, mechanical calculators, 78-rpm records, dial telephones, and party lines.	Classroom instruction. Extensive note taking and studying using rote memorization.
Baby Boomers	Transistor radios, mainframe computers, 33⅓ and 45 rpm records, and the touch-tone telephone	Lecture and workshop based instruction. Strong emphasis on books and manuals which minimizes, but does not eliminate the need for detailed note-taking and extensive studying.
Generation X	CDs, personal computers, and electronic mail	Learning in lecture and classroom settings encouraging exploration, role playing and hands-on experiental learning. The use of video and powerpoint to disseminate information complemented by books and manuals.
Millenials (GenY)	MP3s, cell phones, PDAs, podcasts, wikis, social networking sites, and virtual environments; communication via instant messaging, text messaging, and blogs.	Classroom and online learning using a variety of Web 2.0 technologies (e.g, wikis, podcasts, blogs, virtual environments). Websites containing class notes, reading materials and audio study guides (e.g VangoNotes).

(Adapted from Hartman, Moskal & Dziuban 2005; Laderas-Kilkenny, 2006)

college experience offers podcasts, virtual world simulations, and blogs as standard learning tools. When this generation reaches the workplace the expectation is that technology-based instruction is the norm and not the exception.

To appeal to the learning styles of the younger generation, companies need to evolve their traditional methods of instruction to include new technology. Characteristics of Millennials' learning styles include "…fluency in multiple media and in simulation-based virtual settings, communal learning, a balance among experiential learning, guided mentoring and collection reflection" (Dede, 2005). Individuals who exhibit a Millennial learning style are very accustomed to "multiprocessing" and switching contexts rapidly. They often don't realize that they are carrying out multiple tasks simultaneously (Brown, 2000). Collaborative learning is also key to this generation. They are as comfortable in a group environment as the Baby Boomer generation was with independent study (Howe and Strauss, 2000). They are highly receptive to technology-based pedagogical experiences, and they thrive in online enviroments (Ferrell & Ferrell, 2002).

A childhood filled with interactive video games has created similar expectations regarding interactive educational experiences, and many Millennial learners naturally try to combine their learning and entertainment, finding success in discovery-based learning modules (Brown, 2000). Early exposure to video games has also given this generation of learners a fondess for trial-and-error learning, since winning their favorite game often requires players to try, fail and try again in an environment of suspended reality (Frand, 2000), again reinforcing their learning through discovery. Other characteristics of the Millennial learning style include an overall positive attitude, goal orientation, and a collaborative, team-driven approach (Oblinger, 2008).

A major aspect of the Millennial's experience is never having been "disconnected." That is, through cell phones, instant messaging, Twitter, Facebook, and myriad other modalities, the Millennials are always in touch with someone – on a digital rather than physical channel. As a result, they do not value traditional "face time" when compared to their older siblings. They also have expectations for instaneous access and response that cannot always be provided in traditional settings, often favoring instant or text messaging over the delays associated with emailing (Oblinger, 2008). Hence, trainers who are not Millennials must be careful not to overly interject their own value system into the development of training models for this younger generation. They need to question the blanket assumption that more face-to-face training necessarily translates into more effective learning. In fact, given their proclivity toward all things technological, Millennials can be surprisingly efficient at grasping information on their own through a coached virtual environment. When designing their curricula, non-Millennial trainers must also keep in mind that most Millennial learners do best in a non-linear, parallel congnition environment versus the sequential, linear and structured systems preferred by past generations (Prensky, 2001).

The military has been quick to adapt to this change in learning preferences. In 2002, the U.S. Army launched the computer simulation, *America's Army*. Now in its third edition, this web-based virtual environment allows young people to participate in team-based virtual missions, and explore Army career opportunities in the process. Today, the simulation boasts over 9 million registered players. In addition, the Army's website (www.goarmy.com) is home to Sergeant Star, a 6'3" (in the real world), no nonsense, straight-talking virtual guide. Since his launch in 2006, Sergenat Star has become the face of Army recruiting, engaging visitors and answering more than three million questions from potential recruits ("Army's Sergeant," 2009). Both of these initatives have been very successful in providing career information in an engaging environment, without the need to speak face-to-face with a real recruiter.

Migrating Millennials to Corporate Training

For many industries, human capital is one of the most important sources of competitive advantage

("Corporate Education," 2007). To maximize employee potential and stay ahead in an environment where knowledge becomes obsolete faster than ever, companies need to make significant investments in the training of new employees and periodic retraining where necessary. In 2007, U.S. companies and organizations spent $58.8 billion on employee training; a 4.8% increase over the previous year ("2007 Industry," 2007). In the increasingly complex and hurried corporate workplace, it seems that employees have more to learn, and less time in which to learn it (Musselwhite, 2006). As such, the goal of upper management is to maximize the cost-effectiveness of instruction, while minimizing employee downtime during the training experience.

There is an important caveat that bears mention here. A pervasive attitude in some organizations today, with regard to Millennial workers, is that the firm should not be obligated to match new employees' learning preferences – that is, "Let them mold themselves to our corporate culture and ways." Of course, this rallying cry comes from mostly Boomer and Gen X managers who, as we have seen, grew up with a very different learning model. They therefore assume that the traditional learning styles to which they are accustomed are superior.

We caution organizational leaders not to fall into this self-indulgent trap! The very essence of effective training is that the modalities should be target-driven. Millennials are bright, intuitive, quick learners, and they are used to seeking out information on their own via the Internet. Providing a training platform that fits their comfort level can only prove more efficient than trying to match their "square peg" learning preferences into a firm's "round hole" delivery system.

MATCHING LEARNING OBJECTIVES AND CONTENT DELIVERY

We categorize corporate learning goals as either content-oriented learning (e.g. comprehension of company policies, procedures, and product knowledge), or experience-oriented learning (e.g. the performance of specific manual tasks, or the acquisition of interpersonal skills such as, customer service techniques and sales presentations). Experiential learning is a "process whereby knowledge is created through transformation of experiences" (Kolb, 1994). It is a non-direct teaching style in which the "instructor delegates, consults, and facilitates" (Shields, 1997). The process positions students as active collaborators in their own learning, as opposed to passive recipients of knowledge (Bobbitt, Inks, Kemp & Mayo, 2000; Saunders, 1997).

Whereas organizations often conduct each type of training separately, in some cases, they do combine both learning modalities in the same program. For example, a company might conduct a training exercise where employees learn about its product and service offerings (features, benefits, applications etc.); then they engage in a role-playing exercise where they apply their newly acquired skills.

Within the corporate sector, there are three primary methods of providing both content and experience instruction: classroom/seminar, on-the-job coaching, and electronic learning (e-learning). Classroom-based instruction combined with some on-the-job coaching has been for many decades the standard way to train employees – in 2007, 65% of formal corporate learning took place in a classroom ("2007 Industry," 2007). However, the poor economic climate and heightened concerns about the high environmental costs of employee travel, coupled with the high (direct and indirect) cost associated with classroom-based instruction and a lack of time for detailed on-the-job instruction, has resulted in a movement toward alternative methods of instruction, including computer assisted learning.

COMPUTER ASSISTED LEARNING

Computer assisted learning are self-contained learning materials and resources that can be used at the pace and convenience of the learner. They included stand-alone computer based training programs, materials and exercises, as well those that are accessed through the internet or an intranet, often referred to as "e-learning" ("E-learning," 2005).

E-Learning

E-learning offers numerous advantages over classroom and on-the-job instruction; these include the ability to access training materials regardless of geographic location, a more flexible schedule, access to archived and recorded documents (including transcripts and live discussions), and training materials that can be posted online for convenient access. E-learning can also significantly reduce the amount of time required for training. By moving from a paper-based training program to an e-learning solution, for example, Delta Airlines reduced the duration of a six-hour course, to less than one hour. In addition to enhanced efficiency, the company also found the e-learning method to be more effective, due to a higher level of trainee engagement (Zimmerman, 2001). E-Learning can also contribute directly to the bottom line. By the beginning of the last decade, large corporations such as Unilever were producing an estimated $20 million in additional sales as a result of their e-learning initiatives (Strother, 2002). Finally, and importantly, e-learning directly facilitates assessment through ongoing benchmarking and metrics. Unlike traditional learning platforms in which assessment sometimes feels inflexible and unchanging, e-learning measurement can be ongoing and programmed as a more natural part of the process.

Analysts estimate the 2008 corporate e-learning market at $13.5 billion within the United States, and up to nearly $21 billion worldwide (Womble, 2008). Indeed, self-study e-learning and virtual classroom models now account for 30% of total formal training employers conduct ("2007 Industry," 2007). Popular forms of e-learning include game- based systems, podcasts and vodcasts, virtual communities, E-meetings, virtual learning communities and virtual role playing. We will briefly review each type.

Game-Based Systems

Game-based systems are customizable, individually paced, interactive games. They are particularly popular in the biotech and pharmaceutical industries. Game-based systems are popular for those seeking to learn a foreign language quickly. Programs such as the Tactical Language Training System (TLTS) promote language and cultural skills learning in an interactive, simulated game world where players practice their skills by engaging with non-player characters in a series of different virtual situations. While TLTS was originally developed for military application, its potential in business and general learning is well recognized. The program relies on the concept that the interactive format and the lively narratives and characters serve to sustain user interest in a "fun' way that is not always possible in traditional settings. The game interface allows users to connect and identify with their characters, thereby increasing motivation, reinforcing skills learned and enhancing the overall learning experience (Johnson et al, 2005).

Other language learning systems that incorporate games and virtual worlds have been developed in recent years, but experts caution that these systems cannot fully substitute for real-life cultural and linguistic exposure. Rather, the systems are used to form a "bridging apprenticeship"

(Henderson et al, 2008), which serves to connect classroom theories with the real world context. Students practice their skills in the game world and are then better prepared for their real world tasks. Reports suggest that use of game-based systems format results in a knowledge transfer four times greater, and in knowledge retention ten times greater, than traditional methods. The downside is that unless a company develops its own game, which can be expensive, the ability is limited to customize or tailor these "off-the-shelf" games for specific needs ("Totally Learning," 2008).

Podcasting and Vodcasts

Podcasts and vodcasts (also called vcasts) are prerecorded audio programs (pod) and video clips (vod) that can downloaded from a website to personal computers and portable devices, such as cell phones and MP3 players. These formats give employees the flexibility to download and review material at a time and place convenient to them.

IBM is one organization that is experimenting with these formats; the company finds that employees respond better to a natural, conversational presentation than one that is scripted and formal. Accordingly, the company models its training podcasts after radio programs and its vodcasts imitate television quiz and talk show formats. Some employees are so motivated by these programs that they create and upload their own sales force training content to the IBM intranet. By January 2007, IBM offered more than 2,700 podcasts; its 340,000 employees worldwide collectively downloaded almost a million of these modules (Gronstedt, 2007). However, while podcasts and vodcasts can enhance content-based learning, due to their asymmetrical nature that does not allow for interaction, they are not suitable for experience-based learning.

E-meetings and Virtual Learning Communities

E-Meetings include web based conference calls and webinars. Participants have the ability to interact with each other, and can send and receive information in real time. An e-meeting can cost as little as one fifth of a traditional on-site meeting (Cooney, 2007; "Learning Communities," 2007). They are particularly popular with organizations that span numerous locations and time zones. This format helps to ensure a consistent standard of training, while it allows employees in different geographic locations to share their experiences and practices. The downside is that in cases with large groups of participants, communication with the instructor, and interaction with other participants may be limited to text. Furthermore, it may not be possible for all participants to see each other (via web cameras).

Virtual Learning Communities (VLC) often employ e-meetings to communicate and share information, but they are more comprehensive instruments that can include other tools such as videos, podcasts and other course materials which are posted online. The success of a VLC often relies on the input of a network of people, and it is this communal interaction that further contributes to the learning experience ("Learning communities," 2009). This collaborative model of learning finds a basis in the work of Lave and Wenger (1991) who developed the theory of "communities of practice" to describe the importance that a community has in reinforcing individual behavior and practice. Garrison and Anderson (2003) suggest that a collaborative-networked learning environment that can support a wide range of multimedia technologies will result in active participation and engagement.

Virtual Role Playing

Experience-based learning obviously requires a far greater level of immersion than an organization can achieve with an asymmetrical "lecture" format such as podcasts or in some cases e-meetings where, depending on the size of the group and the method of communication, interaction may be limited. Many companies rely on role-playing exercises to provide this higher level of engagement – particularly when they conduct sales training.

Traditional role-playing typically requires one or more flesh-and-blood actors to play the parts of physicians, consumers or other sales prospects; this is obviously a costly process. The logistical and financial requirements of these exercises are propelling some organizations to explore virtual role-playing environments instead. For more than a decade now virtual role playing has also proved effective in team-building exercises, where it can be difficult to gather all members of a team in one physical location. Virtual world environments provide a setting for team members to practice their group tasks in real time and navigate through the non-verbal and intangible cues of the team relationship in an environment that mimics the actual work process (Rickel & Johnson, 1999). For example, the IP company Global Crossing chose to conduct sales training online on its Web meeting and audio conferencing site. Feedback revealed that the majority of participants found the experience to be helpful. The company estimates that by using virtual technology it was able to save more than four hours of training per day, and approximately $300,000 a year in travel and associated expenses (Kleps, 2006).

Virtual Challenges

Despite all of the potential benefits it offers, e-learning is not without its pitfalls. The most notable shortcoming is that this technique permits only a limited amount of interaction. For example, many online courses only permit communication between the instructors and his students via email or text chatting. These methods can hinder discussion, and fail to offer the participants the opportunity to enhance their verbal and nonverbal communication skills.

There are also cultural differences that may hinder success. Some linguistically diverse regions, such as Canada or the Asia Pacific area, have experienced problems implementing one-size-fits-all e-learning products (Kelly, 2001). Jenny Yan, Director of Motorola University in China, suggests that one of the reasons e-learning has not caught on in China is because Chinese people generally prefer face-to-face communication (Rotwell, 2004). Furthermore, inconsistencies in technology or connection speeds can dilute the experience (Rasmusson, 2000). There is also the complaint that utilizing Web or e-learning systems at home to catch up or avoid missing work can encourage bad habits ("Learning Communities," 2007).

In terms of sales training, the belief is that e-learning technologies should not completely replace live sales training. Many training experts believe that no matter how dynamic, online learning should be used in conjunction with a live instructor and not as a replacement (Agnvall, 2006; The University of Albertay Dundee, 2006; Zimmerman, 2001; Rasmusson, 2000). "Doing simulations just to do a simulation doesn't achieve anything [because] it's not the role playing that's so beneficial," observes one training professional. "The real learning happens in the debriefing session when participants can be introspective about their behavior, and the resulting impact on the process and end product. It's here where they translate the experience into real learning that will stick with them."(Quoted in Musselwhite, 2006, p. 58).

Real, Virtual or Both?

Many organizations are wrestling with the decision to migrate their programs to "new media" formats. This can be a highly-charged issue; it pits the traditionalists who believe nothing can replace the "up close and personal" learning experience against the progressives who are eager to capitalize on the efficiencies a digital system offers.

We propose a simple compromise: A hybrid approach that matches learning objectives with the best delivery system to achieve those objectives. This hybrid model will allow trainers to have their cake and eat it too; they will be able to offer highly engaging experiences, while at the same time maximizing cost-efficiency and ease of assessment.

Table 2 illustrates that the real vs. virtual question is in fact four questions: In each quadrant, trainers need to identify the best match that will optimize content delivery. Our discussion now turns to the lower right quadrant, which represents the "brave new (virtual) world" of corporate Training.

CORPORATE TRAINING'S NEXT STEP: VIRTUAL WORLDS

A *virtual world* is a 3D computer environment that graphically imitates visual spaces and where people are represented on the screen by an animated

Table 2. A hybrid approach to corporate training

	LEARNING OBJECTIVE	
LEARNING FORMAT	Content-Oriented	Experience-Oriented
Physical (in-person) delivery	Classroom lecture	Traditional role-play
Virtual delivery	E-meeting	Virtual world

character/avatar. Virtual worlds include simulations that are played by one individual, or those where players have the ability to interact and work with other players from around the globe (Bainbridge 2007, p.472). Six characteristics define these worlds ("What is," n.d., Wood, 2009).

1. **Graphical user interface**: Virtual worlds use 2D or 3D digital imagery to create realistic environments and user *avatars*. An avatar is an online digital persona that allows the user to navigate the virtual environment and interact with other virtual world participants (Wood, Solomon & Alan, 2008). The avatar often mimics the actual trainee's appearance, but in reality, it can take on virtually any form the user desires. For example, in a role-play exercise one of the avatars can look like a potential customer.

2. **Shared space**: Virtual worlds have the ability accommodate tens of thousands of people in-world, at the same time. Each world is composed of scores of small regions - parcels of virtual real estate, similar to plots of land. Each region can usually host 40-60 avatars simultaneously. Trainees can log in from any location around the world to participate in the training exercise. Being able to see the digital representation of other people creates *telepresence* (the feeling of being there), but even more powerfully a feeling of *co-presence* (the sense of being there together) (Wood, Solomon & Alan, 2008).

3. **Interactivity**: In a virtual world, the user can alter, develop, build, or even submit customized content to the environment. The platform can be easily calibrated to reflect real world environments. A bank employee practicing customer service skills can do so inside a virtual replica of a bank, while a pharmaceutical sales trainee can make a sales call to a virtual doctor's office.

4. **Immediacy**: As in the real world, in a virtual world all interactions take place in real time. There is little to no lag effect. Communication via text messaging or voice chat (typically via Skype or similar means) is instantaneous.

5. **Persistence**: When the last day is over in a physical delivery-training program, typically that is it. However, like the Web a virtual world never closes. It continues regardless of whether an individual trainee user is logged-in or not. These environments are similar to other e-learning technologies in their ability to provide continuous access to course content. This modality fits well into the mind of the Millennial–always connected, always able to access information, operating on his/her own time.

6. **Socialization/Community**: A virtual world is a digital community: a group of individuals that connect and interact online for the purpose of personal and shared goals. They develop vivid and enduring personas, strong connectedness, and a sense of shared community. Whereas many online (and offline) courses employ a variety of popular Web 2.0 technologies such as wikis, blogs and podcasts, they still largely rely on email or text chatting to let teachers and students communicate. Despite this ability, students often feel they are "out there" on their own. In contrast, virtual worlds offer rich visual interfaces, visual representation of each individual (avatars), real-time text, and audio communication. These elements foster an increased sense of community among students that replaces the feeling of isolation many e-learners experience (Childress & Braswell 2006).

Current Virtual World Platforms

Second Life (www.secondlife.com) is the most widely used shared platform in this emerging space. It offers a parallel economy and an open-source model that permits users to retain the content (and IP) they create on their "islands." We can classify Second Life users as follows:

1.   Individuals who enter these worlds to interact and socialize with others.
2.   Entrepreneurs who use Second Life to test-market real world products, or to create and sell (for a profit) virtual items to other Second Life residents.
3.   Not-for-profits that promote their causes to the digital generation.
4.   Educational institutions that use these environments to enhance traditional classroom teaching.
5.   Corporations that employ Second Life as a promotional tool, an alternative product, and service delivery system, or as a platform to conduct training. (Wood, 2009)

IBM is an enthusiastic proponent of Second Life. The company holds several hundred meetings a year on its network of islands. The CEO addressed the company's employees globally in a Second Life event. One of the company's HR programs that it calls Fresh Blue orients new Chinese staff to its corporate culture. It encourages staff to meet senior executives while flying around in a virtual space (Hatch, 2007).

Second Life is a public world; it is accessible to anyone with a computer, internet access and a reasonably sophisticated video card. This capability cuts both ways: While ease of entry promotes diversity of experiences, the open environment also creates security concerns for companies. Startups such as Qwaq Inc., Multiverse Network Inc., and Rivers Run Red are showing off technology that offers companies the equivalent of a private "workspace" -- simulated three-dimensional rooms that allow employees to meet as avatars, view presentations, and conduct other business. Sun Microsystems Inc. built a simulated building called MPK20 that employees of the computer maker can use to collaborate. Sun teams from around the world attend simulated meetings, at

which their avatars may view presentations and videos and hold discussions. One of the project's managers observes, "The biggest value of MPK20 is stimulating the kind of collaboration that comes from chance encounters, like those employees might have in a real hallway" (quoted in Clark, 2008).

Several startup companies now develop private virtual training environments. For example, Forterra Systems (www.forterrainc.com) specializes in creating private secure virtual environments for the military and the health care industry. Tandem Learning (www.tandem-learning.com) offers a similar service to the health care and pharmaceutical industries. ProtonMedia (www.protonmedia.com) also offers custom virtual world courseware for pharmaceutical, medical devices, financial services, and technology industries.

Virtual Opportunities

At this point there is only a small body of published research that examines the use of virtual worlds for instructional purposes. This literature largely originates from the world of academia. In particular, we can find ongoing dialogues in fields including medical and health education (Kamel, Boulos & Hetherington, 2007; Scott, 2007; Skiba, 2007); foreign languages (Svensson, 2003); English composition; education pedagogy ("Real Learning in a Virtual World," 2006); scientific research (Bainbridge, 2007); library services (Swanson, 2007) and business studies (Wood, Wetsch, Solomon & Hudson, 2009; Wood, Solomon & Alan, 2008).

Reports from these fields strongly suggest that the game-based learning opportunites in virtual worlds offer great educational promise (Kamel, Boulos & Hetherington, 2007). For example, the illusion of being physically present with other students (via their avatars) is a positive development for teaching and learning as it facilitates collaboration, promotes greater reflection, and encourages conversation much like one would experience face-to-face, so that learning is once again a shared experience (Cheal, 2007; Kirkup, 2001; Wagner, 2007). Virtual environments thus offer great potential to employ experiential learning techniques in a timely and cost-efficient manner. By immersing students in a virtual environment with others, the learning process is enhanced as learners are challenged to be creative in their problem-solving and to engage in risky decisions; perhaps even behaviors that they may not be comfortable performing in real life. For example, a new pharmaceutical sales trainee who may be intimidated upon encountering a flesh-and-blood (and often time-pressed and curt) physician, may summon the courage to take a more assertive tone during a virtual sales call.

Virtual Challenges

However, like any new technology, virtual world instruction poses challenges. Interestingly, many of these challenges are people-based rather than technology-based. For example, many instructors simply don't understand the technology well enough to know when and how to use it most efficiently. As a result, for some there is a tendency to continue using the same instructional techniques that they have always used. However, studies such as the 2001 ASTD-Masie which explored the learning preferences of over 700 trainees indicated a growing number of corporate trainees actually prefer e-learning to in-classroom training (Strother, 2002). Corporations therefore must find a way to blend the two.

In general, past research supports the notion that most instructors simply teach the way they learned as students; they rely on the instructional techniques with which they are most familiar such as lectures and manuals (Stitt-Gohdes, 2001). Traditional instructors are, not surprisingly, often skeptical of the value and legitimacy of some new technologies, particularly those that at first glance appear more directed toward entertainment than training or education. And, they may be reluctant

to take the risk or expend the effort required to master a new medium, if they believe their current teaching methods achieve results. Indeed, just because something is "new" does not necessarily make it better. In some contexts, the traditional classroon lecture accompanied by Power Point notes may be an efficient way to present factual information and may appeal to learning styles of other generations (e.g. Baby Boomers). All things equal however, this static approach is incongruent with the more immersive learning style of Gen Y (Millennials).

A reluctance to change may or may not be justi-fied. Research indicates the brains of Millennial teenagers seem to develop differently than their Boomer and Gen-X counterparts. In particular, an early exposure to digital technologies enables them to respond quicker to unexpected stimuli as well as endowing them with a different set of cognitive skills. The Millennial mind may therefore be physiologically different from that of parents and older siblings (Prensky, 2001), thus widening the gap of shared experience between these generations even more. Nonetheless, the inexorable generational march means that over time we can also expect younger trainers who will be equally at home with new platforms to enter the scene. The lack of understanding of how the technology works undoubtedly creates a barrier that trainers must overcome. This potentially steep learning curve exists for both the student and the instructor. To help students up the learning curve, instructors need to create "help" resources and hold orientation sessions in-world prior to the beginning of the program.

As all instructors can attest, the first time you conduct a new training course, or employ new technology, the amount of time that you need to dedicate to preparation grows, often exponentially. Lessons need to be well prepared if they are to work properly, and carefully structured exercises are the key to success. Instructors should also resist the temptation to introduce too much too fast. As to how to bring instructors themselves up to a satisfying comfort level with the approach, train-the-trainer programs are essential. These should use the exact same technologies to immerse the instructor as will apply to training the students. It is helpful if some of these master trainers are themselves drawn from the younger generation, as part of being successful in training is to understand the mindset of the trainees, and not just the technology of the delivery.

Some instructors will argue that no matter how well designed the virtual experience it cannot offer the same benefits as a real life experience, primarily because it is not "real." However, assessments of these experiences to date indicate that in virtual worlds "…users seem willing to suspend disbelief and relate to virtual reality as if it were authentic reality" (Nebolsky, Yee, Petrushin & Gershman, 2005, p.33). Furthermore, it appears that workers from all generations are at an increasing rate adopting the Millennial learning preferences (Dede, 2004). The computer programs, technologies, and team interaction that they employ on a daily basis may be behind this shift; but whatever the cause, the growing adoption of this learning style will serve to help facilitate cohesive training programs in a demographically varied corporate world.

A HYBRID SCENARIO: PHARMACEUTICAL SALES TRAINING

In the first year alone a typical pharmaceutical company spends a significant amount of money to train a new sales representative ("Vital train-ing," 2008). Therefore, it should come as no surprise that the pharmaceutical industry is eager to identify ways to reduce training expenses. As one of the early adopters of e-learning, these companies were quick to realize the benefits of nontraditional delivery methods. Capitalizing on recent college graduates desire to balance any time spent on lecture with equal time spent on interactive, technology rich activities these same companies are exploring corporate education in virtual environments (Roberts, 2005). Novartis and Johnson & Johnson are working with virtual world developer Proton Media (www.protonmedia.com) to create virtual training programs, and Glaxo Smith Kline is exploring possibilities in Second Life (Donahue, 2007).

Referring back to Table 2, which showed the four-quadrant hybrid approach to corporate training, let us consider how a pharmaceutical sales firm might implement the chapter's suggestions. First, who are pharmaceutical firms hiring today for sales jobs? The answer: almost exclusively Millennials! And what are the main components of a pharmaceutical rep's job? Among the key roles are:

- Building professional relationships with physicians in order to support the firm's brands and products, and to supply product knowledge and samples
- Calling on pharmacies and drug wholesalers to ensure that the supply chain is operating effectively
- Continually staying on top of new medications of their own and of competitors, as well as new uses of existing medications

Table 3. A hybrid approach to corporate training: the pharmaceutical sales training scenario

LEARNING FORMAT	LEARNING OBJECTIVE	
	Content-Oriented	Experience-Oriented
Physical (in-person) delivery	Classroom lecture *Drug education and training*	Traditional role-play *Detailing preparation*
Virtual delivery	E-meeting *Staying informed about new products*	Virtual world *Modeling sales calls*

- Providing support of customers in their community through special local seminars, and participating in company-sponsored CME (continuing medical education) events on a regional or national basis.

These activities lend themselves well to a hybrid approach to training. However, it is important to keep in mind that not all trainees (in this case pharmaceutical sales representatives) will be Millennials, or even if they are, that they will all embrace virtual worlds with the same level of enthusiasm. As such, it is important for instructors to adopt a cross-generational approach to learning. A hybrid approach does this by offering a variety of delivery styles to appeal to a variety of learning styles. Let us consider how a firm can employ each of the four boxes of the matrix (see Table 3).

1. **Content-Oriented/Physical (In-Person)**: Delivery Gathering representatives together physically for information sharing and networking can be particularly important at three junctures. First, a classroom-style training scenario is probably cost-effective upon initial hire of a representative. It facilitates socialization and enables the new hire to develop a network of mentors and comrades by pulling representatives into a home-office. Second, we recommend this be repeated annually – likely through some sort of annual meeting – in order to maintain a modicum of personal touch, and especially to allow for any new hires during the prior year to interact directly with the old hands. Finally, when the organization launches a major new product or other initiative, there is no substitute for the fanfare and excitement of a good old-fashioned sales meeting rally as a launch vehicle.

2. **Content-Oriented/Virtual Delivery Beyond** the three "main event" scenarios described above, most of the content part of a representative's training should be handled by e-meetings, or simply by Web-driven personal communication and access. In particular, the concept of e-mentoring – an ongoing one-on-one training and development relationship between a newer sales representative and an assigned seasoned mentor representative – is an ideal application. Interestingly, in the long run sometimes the tables are turned in this context such that the most senior representatives that are in need of content retooling, yet are timid about virtual approaches, end up mentored by representatives of midrange experience that are very comfortable with the virtual approach. Retooling very senior representatives can be a real training challenge for pharmaceutical companies both due to their generational reluctance to embrace technology and a general tendency to be locked into sales approaches that made them successful in the past. Overall, traditional face-to-face content mentoring is expensive and cumbersome compared to virtual approaches, thus firms must be facilitative of virtual delivery both in cases of newer and very senior representatives. Pharmaceutical representatives rely heavily on their laptops when they call upon physicians, and physicians rely heavily on the representatives for updates on drug applications and other new developments. Integrating the representatives' content training through virtual approaches that trainers can translated visually saves a lot of time and ensures better accuracy of communication of sensitive drug information.

3. **Experience-Oriented/Physical (In-Person Delivery)**: The first training experience of the representative will be in the initial home-office period referred to above. The content-oriented portion can be delivered – at least in part – through traditional classroom lecture and discussion. The experiential aspect, though, is best delivered through in-

person role-play exercises in which trainers simulate common rep/physician scenarios, and then vary the details so that the new representatives can get used to the sort of nuances they will encounter in the field. The introductory portion of this training is best handled in person, because: (a) much of what is learned is completely new to the representatives, and trouble in the field often arises from nuances; and (b) there's no substitute early in the process for a human sales trainer, who is there to intercede just at the right moment, to assure a novice representative that he/she is going to make it! Notwithstanding their fluency with advanced technology, Millennial learners still view their interaction with committed and expert teachers as highly important to the success of their learning (Roberts, 2005). We recommend that during these initial training days, the firm begin to wean representatives slowly to a virtual world approach, so that at the end of a week or two of initial home office training, representatives are familiar with how it works, and have a schedule for the ongoing training to-come via virtual means. Subsequently, when representatives return for annual sales meetings or sporadic new product launch meetings, it will behoove the firm to reinforce the virtual approach to experiential training by delivering all or most of that type of training by virtual means.

4. **Experience-Oriented/Virtual Delivery Essentially**, all of the ongoing training on experiential aspects of the sales role should be handled virtually. The firm can accomplish this by setting up realistic virtual environment that simulate physicians' offices, pharmacies, informational seminars, and other relevant encounters in which a representative works (see Figure 1). In pharmaceutical sales there is a never-ending stream of reasons why representatives must interact with their clients and channel partners one-on-one.

Figure 1. A virtual role play – physician and pharmaceutical representative

Many of these deal with client education, product usage modification, competitive product clarification, and putting out fires in the channel. The ongoing experience-oriented aspects of pharmaceutical representative sales training require customization, and must be engaging and fresh. A virtual world approach is cost-effective; it also captures representatives "where they live" as Millennials – in technology.

CONCLUSION

As a new breed of worker enters the corporate world, they bring with them a set of expectations about their work environment. One of these expectations relates to the use of technology. The Millenial worker not only excels in the use of technology, but also thrives in technology-based learning environments. To cater to this, corporations the world over need to continue not only to explore how existing technologies, such as wikis and podcasts can be employed, but also how emerging interactive technologies can be utilized to provide a more engaging and robust instructional experience – one that meets the expectations of Millenials. As virtual worlds continue to grow, both in membership numbers and corporate involvement, it is only a matter of time before we see more corporate training being conducted in these environments. Indeed, analysts predict that by 2011, 80 percent of active internet users will be members of at least one virtual world, and by 2012, 70 percent of organizations will establish their own private virtual worlds (Cavall, 2008; "Virtual Great Enters," 2008).

Still, it is unlikely that virutal worlds will totally replace the real world classroom for all forms of training. Instead, a hybrid approach incorporating real and virtual world training is a more realistic goal -- at least in the short term. For those innovative companies that do decide to embrace this new technology, the opportunites it presents and the benefits it affords are virtually endless.

REFERENCES

Agnvall, E. (2006, May). Just-in-Time Training. *HR Magazine, 51*(5), 66-71. Retrieved March 24, 2009, from ABI/INFORM Global database. (Document ID: 1035890651).

Army's Sergeant STAR Repels in to Action. *GoArmy's Virtual Guide takes next step in Human Emulation* (February 2, 2009). Retrieved March 23, 2009, from http://www.nextit.com/SGT_STAR_Animation.ashx

Bainbridge, W. S. (2007). The Scientific Research Potential of Virtual Worlds. *Science, 317*(5837), 472–476. doi:10.1126/science.1146930

Barab, S. (2003). An Introduction to the Special Issue: Designing for Virtual Communities in the Service of Learning. *The Information Society, 19*, 197–201. Retrieved May 23, 2009 from http://www.indiana.edu/~tisj/readers/full-text/19-3%20guest.pdf

Bobbitt, L. M., Inks, S. A., Kemp, K. J., & Mayo, D. T. (2000). Integrating Marketing Courses to Enhance Team-Based Experiential Learning. *Journal of Marketing Education, 22*(1), 15–24. doi:10.1177/0273475300221003

Brown, J.S. (2000). Growing Up Digital. *Change, 32*(2). Retrieved May 26, 2009 from Academic Search Premier database, Document ID: 00091383

Cavall, E. (2008, May 19). *90 Percent of Business-Launched Virtual Worlds Fail.* Retrieved May 19, 2008, from www.wired.com.

Cheal, C. (2007). Second Life: Hype of Hyperlearning. *Horizon, 15*(4), 204–210. doi:10.1108/10748120710836228

Childress, M. D., & Braswell, R. (2006). Using Massively Multiplayer Online Role-Playing Games for Online Learning. *Distance Education, 27*(2), 187–196. doi:10.1080/01587910600789522

Clark, D. (2008, April 3). Virtual World Gets Another Life: Technology Offers Companies Private Workspace. *Wall Street Journal*, B10.

Cooney, B. (2007). Virtual meetings offer solid benefits for investigators. *Pharmaceutical Executive, 16*.

Corporate education: One-to-one training. (2007). *Maclean's,120*(35/36), 75.

Dede, C. (2004). Planning for "Neomillennial" Learning Styles: Implications for Investments in Technology and Faculty. *Harvard Business School.* Retrieved May 23, 2009 from http://www.gse.harvard.edu

Dede, C. (2005). *Planning for Neomillennial Learning-Styles.* Retrieved March 15, 2008, from www.educase.edu: http://www.educase.edu

Donahue, M. (2007, November). Setting up Shop on Second Life. *Pharmaceutical Executive: Consultants Confidential*, 8-10. Retrieved February 28, 2009, from ABI/INFORM Global database, Document ID: 1390552031.

Ferrell, O., & Ferrell, L. (2002). Assessing Instructional Technology in the Classroom. *Marketing Education Review, 12*(3), 19–24.

Frand, J. L. (2000). The Information-Age Mindset: Changes in Students and Implications for Higher Education. *EDUCAUSE Review*. Retrieved May 26, 2009 from http://net.educause.edu/ir/library/pdf/ERM0051.pdf

Garrison, D. R., & Anderson, T. (2003). *E-learning in the 21st century*. New York: Routledge. doi:10.4324/9780203166093

Greats Enters, V. *$1.5 Billion Virtual Goods Market*. (2008, June 9). Retrieved June 9, 2008, from Business Wire: http://www.businesswire.com

Gronstedt, A. (2007). The changing face of workplace learning. *T + D, 61*(1), 20.

Hartman, J., Moskal, P., & Dziuban, C. (2005). *Preparing the Academy of Today for the Learner of Tomorrow*. D. G. Oblinger, & J. L. Oblinger, (Eds.). Retrieved July 15, 2008, from www.educause.edu/educatingthenetgen/

Hatch, S. (2007, February 1). Meetings in Second Life. *Meetings.Net*. Retrieved March 2, 2009 from http://meetingsnet.com/technology/virtual_meeting/meetings_virtual_worlds_real/

Henderson, J., Fishwick, P., Fresh, E., & Futterknecht, F. (2008). An Immersive Learning Simulation Environment for Chinese Culture. *Interservice/Industry Training, Simulation, and Education Conference (I/ITSEC)*. Retrieved May 20, 2009 from http://cero11.cise.ufl.edu/~webmaster/Downloadablecontent/Hendersonetal2008_IITSEC-UF.pdf

Howe, N., & Strauss, W. (2000). *Millennials Rising: The Next Generation*. New York: Vintage Books.

Johnson, W. L., Vilhjalmsson, H., & Marsella, S. (2005). Serious Games for Language Learning: How Much Game, How Much AI? In Looi, C.-K. (Eds.), *Artificial Intelligence in Education* (pp. 306–311). Washington, D.C: IOS Press.

Kamel Boulos, M. N., Wheeler, L., & Hetherington, S. (2007). Second Life: An Overview of the Potential of 3-D Virtual Worlds in Medical and Health Education. *Health Information and Libraries Journal, 24*, 233–245. doi:10.1111/j.1471-1842.2007.00733.x

Kelly, J. (2001, June 6). E-learning on course for strong growth: The internet offers companies a way of delivering training in a flexible and cost-effective manner, writes jim kelly. *Financial Times,* 01.

Kirkup, G. (2001). Teacher or Avatar? Identity Isseus in Computer-Mediated Contexts . In Burge, E. (Ed.), *Using Learning Technologies: International Perspectives on Practice*. London: Routkedge Falmer.

Kleps, K. (2006). Virtual sales training scores a hit. *T + D, 60*(12), 63.

Kolb, D. A. (1994). *Experiential Learning: Experience as the Source of Learning and Development*. Englewood Cliffs, NJ: Prentice Hall.

Laderas-Kilkenny, N. (2006, August 30). *Generational Learning Styles and Methods*. Retrieved July 15, 2008, from Design for Learning, http://nkilkenny.wordpress.com/2006/08/30/generational-learning-styles-and-methods

Lave, J., & Wenger, E. (1991). *Situated learning: Legitimate peripheral participation*. New York: Cambridge University Press.

Learning communities in the workplace: The virtues of going virtual. (2007, November). *Development and Learning in Organizations, 21*(6), 28. Retrieved March 24, 2009, from ABI/INFORM Global database: Document ID: 1341289591.

Musselwhite, C. (2006). University executive education gets real. *T + D, 60*(5), 57.

Nebolsky, C., Yee, N.K., Petrushin, V.A., & Gershman, A. V. (2005). Corporate training in virtual worlds. *Systemics, Cybernetics and Informatics, 2*(6)

Oblinger, D. G. (2008). Boomers, Gen-Xers, and Millennials: Understanding the "New Students". *EDUCAUSE Review.* Retrieved May 26, 2009 from http://net.educause.edu/ir/library/pdf/ERM0342.pdf.

Prensky, M. (2001). Digital Natives, Digital Immigrants, Part II: Do They Really Think Differently? *On the Horizon, 9* (6). Retrieved May 23, 2009 from http://www.marcprensky.com/writing/

Rasmusson, E. (2000). Training goes virtual. *Sales and Marketing Management, 152*(9), 108.

Real Learning in a Virtual World. (2008, March 15). *The Christian Science Monitor.* Retrieved October 5, 2006 from http://www.csmonitor.com

2007Report, I. (2007, November/December). *Training,* (pp. 9-24). Retrieved on February 24, 2009 from http://www.bersinassociates.com/fr3/annualreport.pdf

Rickel, J., & Johnson, W. L. (1999). Virtual Humans for Team Training in Virtual Reality. In *the Proceedings of the Ninth World Conference on AI in Education,* July 1999. Washington, DC: IOS Press.

Roberts, G. R. (2005). Technology and Learning Expectations of the Net Generation. In D. Oblinger & J. Oblinger, (Eds.), *Educating the Net Generation.* Retrieved May 23, 2009 from http://net.educause.edu/ir/library/pdf/pub7101c.pdf

Rothwell, W. J. (2004). Scaling the great wall: Training in china. *Training (New York, N.Y.), 41*(12), 32.

Saunders, P. M. (1997). Experiential Learning, Cases and Simulations in Business. *Business Communication Quarterly, 60*(1), 97–114. doi:10.1177/108056999706000108

Scott, D. (2007). Learning the Second Way. *Medical Education, 335,* 1122–1123.

Shields, P. (1997). Teaching Techniques for Contemporary Marketing Issues. In Varble, Young, & Maliche (Ed.), Marketing Management Association, (pp. 1-5).

Skiba, D. J. (2007). Nursing Education 2.0: Second Life. *Nursing Education Perspectives, 28*(3), 156–157.

Stack, R. T., & Lovern, E. R. (1995). A Lively Learning Agenda. *The Healthcare Forum Journal, 38*(5). Retrieved May 28, 2009 from Proquest Research Library http://www.proquest.umi.com

Stitt-Gohdes, W. L. (2001). Business Education Students' Preferred Learning Styles and Their Teachers' Preferred Instructional Styles: Do they match? *Delta Pi Epsilon Journal, 43*(3), 137–151.

Strother, J. (2002). An Assessment of the Effectiveness of e-learning in Corporate Training Programs. *International Review of Research in Open and Distance Learning, 3*(1). Retrieved May 26, 2009 from http://www.irrodl.org/index.php/irrodl/article/view/83/161

Svensson, P. (2003). Virtual Worlds as Arenas for Language Learning . In Felix, U. (Ed.), *Language Learning Online: Towards Best Practice* (pp. 123–142). Lisse, The Netherlands: Swets and Zeitlinger.

Swanson, K. (2007). Second Life: A Science Library Presence in Virtual Reality. *Science & Technology Libraries, 27*(3), 79–86. doi:10.1300/J122v27n03_06

The University of Albertay Dundee. (2006, May). *Beyond eLearning: practical insights from the USA.* Retrieved March 24, 2009, from http://www.epic.co.uk/content/news/resources/eLearning_mission_report.pdf

Total learning concepts develops interactive game-based learning system to train sales force for leading specialty company. (2008). *Business Wire*. Retrieved February 28, 2009, from ABI/INFORM Dateline database: Document ID: 1499362761.

Vital Training Tools Elevate New Pharmaceutical Sales Reps into Top Performers During Critical First Year. (2008, June 2). *PR Newswire*. Retrieved February 28, 2009, from ABI/INFORM Dateline database: Document ID: 1488244491.

Wagner, M. (2007, September 21). *The Future of Virtual Worlds*. Retrieved October 22, 2007, from Information Week, http://www.informationweek.com

What is a virtual world? (2008, September, 15). In *Virtual Worlds Review* [database online]. Retrieved September 15, 2008 from http://www.virtualworldsreview.com/info/whatis.shtml

Womble, J. (2008). E-learning: The relationship among learner satisfaction, self-efficacy, and usefulness. *The Business Review, Cambridge, 10*(1), 182.

Wood, N. T. (2011). *Marketing in Virtual Worlds, 1e*. Upper Saddle River, NJ: Pearson.

Wood, N. T., Solomon, M. R., & Allan, D. (2008). Welcome to the Matrix: E-learning Gets a Second Life. *Marketing Education Review, 18*(2), 45–53.

Wood, N. T., Wetsch, L. R., Solomon, M. R., & Hudson, K. (2009). From Interactive to Immersive: Advertising Education takes a Virtual Leap of Faith. *Journal of Advertising Education, 13*(1), 64–72.

Zimmerman, E. (2001). Better training is just a click away. *Workforce, 80*(1), 36.

KEY TERMS AND DEFINITIONS

Experiential Learning: Learning as a result of direct experience.

E-Learning: The delivery of education and training through electronic means.

Game-Based Systems: Customizable, individually paced, interactive games.

Pod-Casts: Prerecorded audio casts that can be downloaded to a personal computer or portable electronic device.

Vod-Casts: Prerecorded video clips that can be downloaded to a personal computer or portable electronic device.

Virtual Learning Community: A network of people who interact through online technologies with the purpose of sharing information and enhancing learning.

Virtual Word: A 3D computer mediated environments that graphically imitates virtual spaces and people.

Avatar: An online digital persona.

Chapter 17
Digital Connectionsand Learning Styles

Julie Davis
Clarkson University and Texas Tech University, USA

Letitia Harding
University of the Incarnate Word and Texas Tech University, USA

Deanna Mascle
Morehead State University and Texas Tech University, USA

ABSTRACT

Online or e-learning is increasingly becoming an integral part of education and training programs both in the academic world and in industry. This chapter includes a study which examines the ways in which faculty and students in an online Ph.D. program plan, adapt, and correlate coursework, teaching, study habits, and networking practices to accommodate all types of learning styles and to ensure that students feel part of a community of learners. The findings indicate that distance education should incorporate both synchronous and asynchronous instruction, personal and individual contact, a proper balance between the specific demands of the material to be covered and the learning styles of the students, and a willingness to adjust and modify delivery methods in order to obtain course or training objectives.

INTRODUCTION

The concept of distance education is not new. Indeed, many institutions in myriad countries boast programs of distant learning that go back decades and, in some instances, more than a century. And, until very recently, the distance student was exactly that—more often than not studying alone, enjoying little or no contact with fellow learners. The Open University in the United Kingdom, for example, which admitted its first students in 1971, delivered its early courses through television and radio broadcasts, home experiment kits, set textbooks, and carefully produced study booklets and audiotapes. Students typed assignments (using typewriters and carbon paper), posted them to tutors for grading, and waited for their return. Face-to-face tutorials were occasionally available and some courses mandated attendance at a summer school, but for the most part, students remained isolated. As communications technology has developed, however, distance education has morphed into online or e-learning, and

DOI: 10.4018/978-1-61520-619-3.ch017

today's distance student has an arsenal of tools to aid both learning and communication with faculty and other students.

In the May 2002 editorial of *T.H.E. Journal*, Dr. Sylvia Charp quoted the International Data Corporation's (IDC's) findings that "e-learning will overtake classroom-based instruction as the primary method by 2004" (p. 1). And while IDC's figures have yet to be realized, educational and professional training programs, both in the United States and abroad, are increasingly utilizing online environments to support and deliver classes and programs. According to the National Center for Education Statistics, 56% of all two-year and four-year Title IV-eligible, degree-granting institutions during the 12-month period of 2000-2001 offered distance education courses in various capacities (Tabs 2003). For the 2006-2007 period, that number had increased to 66%. (U.S. Department of Education. Fast Facts). Students enrolled in these programs come from many walks of life and backgrounds, providing challenges to teaching outside the traditional face-to-face environment. In order to provide the best possible educational experience for this disparate body of students, educators must understand and maximize the benefits of the teaching tools available to them. Equally important is the need for students to recognize the innate differences between distance education programs and those offered in a face-to-face environment, and then to assess their own ability to adapt accordingly. Students must also learn to recognize that not all distance education programs are the same – not only do the instructors and content vary but so do the instructional format and technology.

New technologies and the ability to provide programs online are also providing new markets for distance education. Consequently, we are seeing a rise in the number and type of institutions offering students opportunities to participate in programs from remote locations, including war zones in Iraq and Afghanistan. And while this can be extremely alluring to both institutions and

students, as the former can reach new markets and the latter have more convenient and often cheaper choices, the danger is that some schools will rush to adopt the concept without due planning and preparation. The provision of online programs does not mean that everyone is suited to them. Equally, not every program is suited to every individual. Research has proven conclusively, and not surprisingly, that not all students are the same; their life experiences are different, as are their needs and learning styles. It is understood that, as in face-to-face programs, students' learning styles play a significant role in their level of success, but when instructors and students are in the same physical location, problems may be more apparent and, therefore, easier to identify and rectify. And while it is true that it is the students themselves who must assess their own needs and learning styles, and connect with programs whose style, or diversity of styles, fits those needs, little is really known about the relationship between virtual delivery methods of professional and social communication and student learning styles.

In the corporate world, distance education methods and technologies can also be employed to provide cost effective and efficient media for employee education and training. But while students in an education scenario can choose programs that are suited to their learning styles, corporate employees may not be afforded that luxury. Thus it is imperative that employers are cognizant of the diversity of training program formats available to them, and of the various learning styles of their employees.

When people think about using virtual environments for educational purposes, it is often the case that they immediately turn their thoughts to Second Life with its avatars operating in their virtual world. Virtual communities comprise, however, all types of people using a diversity of virtual environments to learn and to network with others. Rheingold (2000) offers a broad overview of the variety of tools that can be utilized for professional and personal education and networking. He describes for example, "an enormously lucrative chat culture in an information system" as a virtual city (231), a Japanese company's use of "an online community devoted to cooperative play" (195), and a youth with severe disabilities whose only connection to the outside world is via his virtual connections (329). The point that Rheingold stresses is that virtual environments are created to facilitate virtual communities. It is the people who are using these environments that are of the utmost importance. Thus, the focus for corporate education must be on the value of a virtual environment to a company's training program and the educational needs and learning styles of its employees, not solely on the virtual environment *per se*.

In this chapter, we proffer the results of an exploratory study to investigate relationships between student learning styles and instructor teaching techniques that explain correlations between the varying virtual delivery methods of professional and social communication and student learning styles. The study also outlines factors influencing the choice of virtual communication methods utilized by the instructors. Finally, it provides some indication of the ways that students within virtual programs obtain knowledge as well as create and sustain a sense of community.

The study was conducted using faculty and students who are currently involved in the online version of Texas Tech University's (TTU) Ph.D. program in Technical Communication and Rhetoric (TC&R). The program is offered in both a face-to-face and online format. Students within the online program bring with them a varied background of corporate and academic experience, which makes the program unique, and offers valuable insight into virtual education and social networking as it pertains to both audiences. This experience includes a number of virtual education and social networking strategies for both educational and social activities. While the study focuses on one program, that program in particular offers a rich source of information about distance education from both the instructor and student perspective. Due to the diverse nature of the students involved in this type of program and environment, this study also provides valuable scope for understanding the use of distance education in corporate environments.

TTU's online TC&R Ph.D. program is a forerunner in its field, and has, since its inception in 2004, enjoyed a high rate of success. This success is demonstrated by the program's high visibility in the field at conferences and in publication, as well as in the quality of its graduates. As a result, TTU's online TC&R program offers an unparalleled opportunity for research into educational strategies that can be applied to other educational settings within academe and in the corporate world, and can be used as a model of a successful virtual education environment.

BACKGROUND

Course Planning

In these days of economic decline, it is easy to understand why many institutions are rushing to enter the world of online education. The cost of travel, declining markets, and dwindling investment portfolios make the enterprise more appealing than ever. There are, however, more than just economic reasons for turning to online options for corporate training. Thrush and Bodary (2000) point out the value of using virtual environments in the training of personnel for dangerous activities, such as the removal of asbestos. They explain that the workers "…were being trained in slide and lecture sessions that had proved very ineffective. The task was both to turn the technical information about asbestos and removal procedures into usable training materials and to make the training more interactive" (317). By using some type of virtual environment "the workers could encounter actual situations … and carry out the functions of wetting the material down, removing it properly in correctly marked disposal bags, putting on and taking off all the gear, and all the other aspects of asbestos removal that make it a difficult, dangerous, and unpleasant job" (318). Regardless of the reasons for turning to online delivery systems, program and course planning must be meticulous to ensure that institutional goals match the delivered model, and that students receive a quality product (Rude, 2005). And while Rude continues by saying that, in her experience, faculty "are eager to teach online courses" (p. 67), institutions must ensure that they are suitably qualified and committed to the task; "(t)hese qualifications are more important than their ability to work with technology" (pp. 72-73). Yet, while people tend to be more concerned about students' needs, over the past decade, the Conference on College Composition and Communication (CCCC) has been developing a set of guidelines to ensure that institutions "pay more attention ... to the needs of online educators" (Blair & Hoy p. 46).

Durrington *et al* (2006) acknowledge that teaching an online course can be "challenging and at times seem overwhelming" (p. 193). Yet they remind instructors that the goals for both online and face-to-face teaching are basically the same (p. 193). Carter & Rickly's (2005) advice to online instructors is to "look further into the future than you would in a face-to-face classroom." (p. 134). Indeed, they feel that preparation is so important that they begin their preparation to-do list with the title "Over-prepare everything." (p. 134). When Eaton (2005) discusses course design, she advises instructors to think about students' traits when designing a course. These include the type of degree being pursued; the ages and genders of students; their workload, both at home and at school; and the projected length of their program (p. 32-33). All of these factors will affect student performance. Moallem (2007) goes further to suggest that instructors should not only attend to the traits mentioned above, but also understand the relationship between instructional design and learning styles (p. 218).

Course Delivery

When people consider delivering an online course, many immediately think about choices of technology, yet one of the first, and most important, duties of online instructors is to consider the ways that they can bridge the gaps between themselves and their students (Carter & Rickly, 2005; Durrington *et al*, 2006). Some strategies offered by Durrington *et al*, such as providing a course syllabus with clear instructions, breaking students into small discussion groups, and offering timely feedback, are important in face-to-face programs, but the authors suggest that for students engaged in online learning, the need is even greater. Using the analogy of the London Underground, Carter & Rickly (2005) point out that gaps exist in both face-to-face and online environments, and while some may need to be bridged to promote effective learning, some "merely need to be minded. Participants need to be mindful, adjust to things observed, and adapt proactively" (p. 125).

Choice of Technology

While few would disagree with Rude (2005) when she cautions that pedagogy is more important to quality than technological tools (p. 69), and Herrington & Tretyakov (2005) state that online learning and technology is "less important" than student interaction (p. 273), there is no doubting the role that technology has played in the ability to offer instructional programs of all types to students who are not physically present in a conventional classroom. Grady & Davis (2005) highlight the workload placed on the instructor who has to deal with issues of what technology to use and how to apply it to his or her course, but much of the literature on this subject offers lists of, or suggestions for, appropriate software and tools that can be utilized in the online classroom (Buckley & Smith, 2008; Moallem, 2007; Rubens & Southard, 2005). Although this type of information is useful, Rubens & Southard lament that little attention has been given to the problems that students might have with technology "assuming that the only students who will succeed in online courses have either the requisite computing experience or the self-motivation to learn the skills they need quickly" (p. 193). This is of immense importance to instructors in corporate training programs who often do not have the time or the opportunity to ensure that all employees have the skills needed to complete training tasks in a virtual training environment. Of course, some tools work more smoothly than others, so Rubens & Southard's advice is repeatedly to test and evaluate technology that will be used in an online class (p. 203). Looking at technological problems from the student's point of view, Carter & Rickly (2005) remind their readers that while a variety of technologies may all work in a given online situation, students may have an "easier time" with some over others (p. 127).

Moallem (2007) emphasizes the connection between instructional materials and learning styles; "the designer's/teacher's challenge is to produce courses or instructional materials that do not have an obvious tilt toward one learning and thinking style" (p. 218). Moreover, Moallem suggests that providing a variety of tools can challenge students to "adjust their strategic approaches to learning in order to achieve expected learning outcomes without impacting their attitude and satisfaction" (p. 238). According to Moallem, "learning styles can be integrated into instruction in online learning environments without compromising the appropriateness of instructional strategies for specific content and learner outcomes" (p. 239).

Teaching Techniques

What is the role of the instructor in an online teaching environment? While some might see it as an easy way to make some extra money for little effort, Rude (2005) warns that an online delivery system must not diminish the role of the instructor (p. 68), and that online courses must be afforded "the same priority for faculty time and energy as onsite courses" (p. 71). Again, Rude cites the TTU model, "the instructor-led, Internet-based course offered on a semester schedule with a synchronous weekly class meeting" as a way to ensure institutional and faculty commitment to the program (69). Faculty members must not only be committed to the program, but they also must be trained for the task (De Simone, 2006).

No matter what methods are used to create an online course, instructors must provide support for their students (Blair & Hoy, 2006; Durrington *et al*, 2006; Grady & Davis, 2005). Blair and Hoy, while pointing out the generally lower student retention rates of online courses, caution that the physical distance between students and their instructors may affect the latter's ability "to show an ethics of care," an issue that might add to student losses. The answer, according to Grady & Davis (2005), is scaffolding that can be linked to learning styles. In such a system, which is used successfully with elementary school children, instructors introduce a concept by modeling, then gradually remove the scaffold, or support, as the student "becomes more competent with the task at hand" (p. 102). As students become increasingly independent, feedback becomes more and more important, and while face-to-face students can attend office hours or walk the hallways in the hope of meeting an instructor, the online student does not have that opportunity. Thus, feedback is vital to student support (Carter & Rickly, 2005; Durrington *et al*, 2006). Some companies might see the use of virtual environments as a way to eliminate or at least minimize the expense of instructors in their training programs. The research cited above, however, indicates that the opposite is true and that instructors must be fully equipped to deal with students' needs and difficulties.

Learning Styles

While research on learning styles is abundant and far-reaching, some scholars agree that the subject is both confusing and unreliable (Lu *et al*, (2007); Santo, 2006). Akdemir & Kosalka's (2008) study into the relationship between teaching strategies and learning styles proved inconclusive. Santo (2006) concedes that it is likely that learning differences do exist, but with the number of different theories proffered, and doubt about whether students' styles can change over time, she suggests that questions surrounding how styles influence learning have yet to be answered (p. 86). When thinking about the way students learn, Santo prefers to use the analogy of an onion with the inner layers representing personality style, the middle layers cognitive style, and the outer layers being influenced by the environment (p. 74).

According to Kolb & Kolb (2005), however, the Kolb Learning Style Inventory (LSI) is unlike others in that it is "based on a comprehensive theory of learning and development," and has been developed around the thinking of "prominent twentieth century scholars who gave experience a central role in their theories of human learning and development" (p. 1). The Kolb LSI comprises the following six propositions:

1. Learning is best conceived as a process, not in terms of outcomes.
2. All learning is relearning.
3. Learning requires the resolution of conflicts between dialectically opposed modes of adaptation to the world.
4. Learning is a holistic process of adaptation to the world.
5. Learning results from synergetic transactions between the person and the environment.
6. Learning is the process of creating knowledge. (Kolb & Kolb (2005) p. 2).

Lu *et al* (2007), using Kolb's LSI, recorded a correlation between learning styles and online behavior (p. 189). Moreover, they also noted "a significant effect of learning styles on reading time and total discussion," e.g., a student with high scores in Concrete Experience oriented toward peers and benefitted from discussion, while one displaying Abstract Conceptualization tendencies learned best in impersonal learning situations. Lu *et al*, however, found no correlation between learning styles and outcomes (pp. 193-194).

Regardless, however, of whether an instructor sees a student as an onion with layers that control learning, or as displaying some type of learning style, the most important aspect of the discussion is the way in which it can inform instructors about the best ways to help their students learn. Nevertheless, most scholars agree that instructors tend to be in some way cognizant of students' learning styles. For example, Eaton (2005) advises learning about students' traits (p. 31), Carter & Rickly (2005) place importance on cognitive space (p. 127), and Buckley & Smith (2008) suggest using multimedia to enhance more traditional teaching strategies and materials, and to offer students a variety of ways in which to learn and interact with content (p. 65).

Social Communication and Sense of Community

The importance of the link between communication styles and social networking has been well documented (Avery *et al*, 2005; Blair & Hoy, 2006; Cho *et al*, 2007; Grady & Davis, 2005). Cho *et al* (2007) found that a social network in a computer-supported collaborative learning community (CSCL) "had a tangible impact on individual performance" (p. 324). Moreover, they suggested that "in order to foster a CSCL community … an appropriate social infrastructure … should also be put in place" (p. 323). This should not be too much of a problem if Grady & Davis (2005) are correct when they reiterate that, "(n)early everything we technical communicators teach is grounded in a strong sense of community" (qtd. on p. 101). Nevertheless, we must not fall into the trap of thinking that all students need, or even want, close contact with their classmates or faculty. According to Blair & Hoy (2006), it is important to recognize that "among our adult learner populations there might be students who thrive as well in private space as they do in public space" (p. 45). Thus, it is just as important to provide opportunities for one-to-one student/instructor interactions in an online program as it is in the face-to-face environment.

Not all types of technology, however, work well for every student. Rubens & Southard (2005) reported students' frustrations with listservs. While some students found that the system provided "a useful interaction style," others listed a host of problems including difficulty joining, overwhelming numbers of messages, and confusion between listserv and other e-mails (p. 198). But the problems are usually outweighed by the gains. In their Global Classroom Project, a learning collaboration between students from Russia and the United States, Herrington & Tretyakov (2005) reported that because "global interaction is more important than ever, students' opportunity to experience online interaction may be more valuable than ever" (p. 273).

Research on student or trainee retention and success has categorically proven that when students feel a sense of community, they are generally more successful in their studies. Vincent Tinto, whose voice on the link between learning communities and retention has resonated throughout the education world for more than three decades, stated in 1997, "The college classroom lies at the center of the educational activity structure of institutions of higher education; the educational encounters that occur therein are a major feature of student educational experience" (p. 599). So, do those words signify that online education, because of its obvious lack of physical classroom space, is an inherently poor choice for students? Programs that are delivered using only asynchronous technology might be, but those, such as TTU's online TC&R Ph.D. program with synchronous class sessions go a very long way toward combating the problem.

Ways of Obtaining Knowledge and Reasons for Choosing Online Courses

A large number of students participating in online educational programs, both academic and corporate, are working adults who do not take kindly to "busy work". Indeed, one of their most pressing requests is that classroom content has real world context (Durrington *et al*, 2006; Grady & Davis, 2005). Grady & Davis further explain that many students are … seeking to improve and enhance their knowledge and skills in order to advance and to make more valuable contributions to their companies" (p. 121). This is also one of the reasons most often cited for students choosing online courses over face-to-face offerings. Eaton (2005) provides an extensive list that includes: fit schedule, participate in distant program, improve skills, save commute, work from home or work, employer pays, retain job, and diverse classmates (35). Blair & Hoy's (2006) findings that online students are often attending courses "for both career change and career advancement" (p. 34) and that face-to-face classes do not always suit working adults (p. 36) support Eaton's (2005) list.

Relationship between Faculty Teaching Styles and Student Learning Styles

To ensure a successful online program, both faculty teaching styles and student learning styles must work together to form a learning environment that is conducive to student satisfaction and success. Based on the results of an online student survey, Eaton (2005) offers advice for faculty that is listed under these headings: respect student's time, be involved, and structure courses carefully (p. 39). Carter & Rickly (2005) suggest that instructors are often missing knowledge (or have information gaps (p. 125) with regard to their students, and so they suggest getting to know the learners and, thus, fill those gaps (p. 137). Feedback is of vital importance to the online student (Carter & Rickly, 2005; Eaton, 2005). Without the ability to meet with faculty face-to-face, students need to hear in a timely manner that their work has been received and to know when it will be returned.

Faculty and students in an online learning environment do not have the same relationship as those in a face-to-face classroom (Blair & Hoy, 2006; Carter & Rickly, 2005; Grady & Davis, 2005; Herrington & Tretyakov, 2005). Often, the differences are overcome by the maturity and self-motivation of the students, but faculty can help by playing the role of coach over teacher (Blair & Hoy, 2006, p. 40), undertaking learner/task analysis (Grady & Davis, 2005, p. 105), and being aware of time differences when developing schedules (Herrington & Tretyakov, 2005, p. 274). One of the most important aspects of online learning is that instructors and students from all types of institutions ensure that they work toward a mutual understanding of the goals and needs of all parties as this educational medium continues to occupy an increasing section of the market.

THE CHALLENGES OF DISTANCE EDUCATION

Today professionals are harnessing technology for many marketing and communications purposes, and yet there are still gaps in our knowledge about how technology can be used for education and professional development. Some innovative programs in the academic world are, however, pushing the boundaries of the definition of "community" through the use of digital connections. This is even more important as the workplace evolves and many workers no longer share physical space even when located within the confines of the same geographic location. Employees often utilize virtual technologies to communicate with one another, for example using Instant Messenger.

Although distance education is growing by leaps and bounds, there is still much that is not known. This holds as true for the lone trainer or educator planning to move a traditional class to a hybrid or online format as it does for the institution moving an entire program into a virtual space. Distance education places different requirements on both instructors and students. Instructors must learn a variety of new technologies in order to select the best tools to deliver and support distance learning for a specific class, particular content, and individual student learning styles. The selection of tools available for virtual education is ever expanding and fads abound. The choice of technology is not the only question facing instructors. Others include: How can educators make the best choices for their program and their students? Is it better to structure a class synchronously or asynchronously? How can personal contact be made between instructor and student as well as student and student? What tools are clunky and cumbersome? What makes students choose one class or one program over another? To what kinds of technology will the instructor have access, and to what kinds of technology will the students have access? What student traits should be considered when planning? How can students be best supported for the most effective learning opportunity? Are there other unforeseen factors that might affect learning? Instructors who are planning distance education programs and courses should consider all these questions and more.

TTU's online TC&R program can provide answers to these questions – or at least the answers with which instructors in that program choose to work. Courses currently taught within the TTU online program use multiple virtual delivery methods including: MOOs, Moodles, Webboards, blogs, and wikis. The MOO serves as the primary tool for synchronous class meetings, small group conferencing, and student get-togethers. While it does not offer the virtual experience of Second Life, students are able to create a profile identity and meet in virtual classrooms or gathering spaces. Communication tools allow students to participate in class discussions, give presentations, upload visuals and data to share with classmates, and even have private conversations (whispering) with neighbors. Other rooms allow students to break out for collaborative group work, and the bar offers a virtual venue for social events. Indeed, the MOO is such a "real" space for students that a group just out of coursework plans regular meetings there for continued support and social gatherings.

Each of these methods offers benefits and hindrances to a variety of users. The students enrolled in the online program are involved in educational institutions and corporations across America, and overseas, allowing our study access to a wealth of information that would otherwise be impossible to obtain. An understanding of the various tools available to instructors and students and how the adult learner navigates within, and comprehends, them can assist educators and provide models with which they can shape their courses. Similarly, these lessons can be applied outside academe in the private sector, as reported by many of the program's students who work in the private sector.

In order to gather more information about the program, students and faculty of TTU's online TC&R program were invited to participate in online surveys. The student survey focused on student learning style and what, if any, advantages or disadvantages students have experienced while using the various virtual tools adopted by the faculty. The faculty survey focused on the instructors' specific selection process of virtual teaching tools. In addition, several students and faculty members participated in follow up interviews to expand upon their survey responses.

Students entering the TTU TC&R program come from a variety of backgrounds. The student participants in this study included more females (70%), than male (30%). The age range of students spanned four decades with 75% of the students falling into either the 36-45 (35%) or 46-55 (40%) demographic. Professionally, the largest group of respondents were those who have worked in a mixture of educational and private sector pro-

fessions (60%). Those private sector professions have included freelance work, self-employment, contract work, small business employment and/or ownership, and corporate work. Twenty percent have only worked in education and 15% have only worked in the private sector. One respondent has also served in the military. All survey respondents were instructors and Ph.D. students at TTU and, as the program has now admitted its fifth cohort, all students are in various stages of their degree plan. Sixty percent of the students responding are still in coursework, while 25% are preparing for comprehensive examinations. The remaining students are working on dissertation proposals (10%) and dissertations (5%).

ONE PROGRAM'S RESPONSE TO THE CHALLENGE

Although instructors are a key component in distance education, the students and their needs remain the focus for how successful a course will be. In addition, those students are a valuable resource when it comes to learning more about what makes a distance program a success — or a failure. It is also informative for instructors to understand what makes students choose a particular program.

Reasons for Choosing This Program

The distance education component was an essential part of most students' decision to apply because it eliminated the need to relocate while pursuing their education, although it was not the only factor in their decision. That the program had a proven traditional component and faculty with a strong reputation in the field was as important as the specific program of study and courses offered. All the students were seeking a particular program that was either unavailable in institutions more geographically convenient or not offering the same level of quality. A member of the newly admitted cohort explains his reasoning succinctly as "quality and availability."

"I looked at programs in my geographic area," said one student, "TTU has the program I want." She said faculty, research, and program emphasis all played a role in her decision. "It is also online, so I can actually do it. I could not have moved to attend a school somewhere else." Another student pointed out another crucial factor that influenced many students' choice to attend. "It's with a reputable and traditional university, as opposed to an online mill that might be questionable in the eyes of potential future employers."

The Distance Learning Experience

A number of students were familiar with distance education before entering the program — as students and/or instructors — but were still worried about true distance learning, as for many their past experience was often encompassed within a more traditional educational program where face-to-face contact was still possible. As one student in the middle of her coursework commented:

My biggest concern going into the program was that an online program might be too isolating, but that concern was dispelled pretty quickly. I found our listserv to be a great way to feel and stay connected with others in the program. It hasn't been the best way to get to know people, but I do feel part of a community.

Many students have found that sense of community in this distance program. Another student who recently finished her coursework reports that she completed her undergraduate degree in the 1980s through distance education and thinks she has enjoyed her current online experience at least as much as her later Master's coursework offered in a face-to-face environment. "I feel that I know my online fellow students better than any with whom I have taken face-to-face courses."

Other students find that this program is also a better educational fit. A student nearing the end of her coursework remarked:

This program works well for the way I learn. Putting my thoughts and questions and answers into words whether in MOO or wiki or blog really helps me think through issues in a way I could not when sitting in a classroom. When I struggle with material in a face-to-face class, I often feel behind the curve and it seems easier to face that uncertainty in an online environment, but I also think the process of sharing digitally helps me process more effectively than a traditional auditory lecture experience could.

Another student at the beginning of her coursework was excited about the potential of online learning and has found her expectations exceeded. When interviewed she shared her enthusiasm:

I have been impressed with how well it works so far. In particular, I feel like I have more interaction with online professors and classmates — inside and outside of class —than I ever did in a traditional classroom situation. I'm not sure if my natural shyness and inhibition disappear online, or if it's because I'm comfortable expressing myself in text, or what. But I like it — even more than I expected to.

A member of the newest cohort stated," My learning and schedule wouldn't work as well in a face-to-face, highly structured, rigid environment."

Many students reported that there are both advantages and disadvantages to a distance education program although the advantages outweigh the disadvantages. One advantage that more than one student pointed out is the ability to easily "record" conversations. As one student preparing for his qualifying exam said: "That means that during the actual exchange I don't have to scramble to take notes and can really just listen."

While technology can bring instructors and students together across great distances and time zones, it does have limitations when it comes to personal contact. Students reported that faculty may be "relegated forever to the instructional mode and it's possible to never be seen as human." Students also cautioned that it might also happen in reverse as "faculty members never see students going about their routine business, so faculty can make the mistake of forgetting that the students have lives, too."

One solution to that problem TTU has chosen to adopt is a May Workshop on campus that brings everyone involved in the program together for two-weeks of face-to-face contact. For many students, this time is key to building personal connections within the program. As one student who recently finished her coursework commented, "The May workshop also makes sure that the students feel that they are part of a community of learners." Another student said that she thinks the "face-to-face time" gives the program real credibility as it clearly links it to the on-site program and to the institution. Echoing her sentiment another student noted, "I felt a connection in the MOO and the e-mail listserv. Then after I met people in person it was easy to maintain those connections electronically."

When the Student is a Teacher

Many of the program's students are also college-level instructors who have a professional interest in the delivery and methods almost as much as the content of the courses. One student remarked:

I was interested to see how a program that relies so heavily on the MOO would work. The online nature of the program also has given me a chance to experience a different approach to online learning from the program where I teach, so it rather fattens my portfolio of expertise.

Others reported the experience has changed their teaching. One said,

I've become much more aware of the value of using discussion forums to make student work and thought 'public' within the context of the course. I'm now using forums for reading responses and getting students to really prep those carefully.... It makes a world of difference to class discussions ... and because students are reading each other, they are helping each other learn.

Another student nearing the end of her course-work reflected that the program has piqued her interest "in experimenting with different methods and technologies" as well as her teaching practice.

Their experience as distance education students has taught these teachers more about the advantages and disadvantages of distance learning as well as its various tools. One student remarked that she saw a great advantage in the wide range of web tools and course management software that can be used to supplement course material as well as to preserve class time for discussion and activities rather than shuffling papers between instructor and students She also noted, however, that those tools come at a price. Preparing materials in the proper file formats and setting up and maintaining course management sites can be time consuming. She further notes that grading online offers similar disadvantages and advantages as it takes longer to grade online "but the comments are richer."

Another advantage is that online discussion "allows more time and thought before communication takes place" as well as "much more meaningful conversations in context than a lecture scenario in a traditional classroom." One student, who also teaches online, noted that distance can also make it more difficult to connect with students. "Students don't always get a sense of my personality and may feel I'm a colder, more unfeeling person than

I really am." She further commented that distance can both help and hinder communication depending on the situation. "I think for some students it is easier to ask for help from an instructor or fellow students they see in person regularly but students also say it is easier to give and receive criticism at a distance."

Student Learning Styles

The largest group of respondents (70%) reported that they have a multi-modal learning style. Visual and textual learners each represent another 10% while auditory and kinesthetic each represent 5%. When asked to describe the way they learn best, 70% reported they like to match the learning method to the occasion or situation; 10% indicated that they find visual aids such as maps, diagrams, charts, and symbols to be useful; 10% said they like to see information displayed as text; and 10% said they prefer concrete personal experiences, examples, and practice.

No respondents believe their learning style has changed as a result of their involvement in the program although their study habits may have changed. This seems to be especially true for those whose learning style includes visual and textual. Many also reported their willingness to use new technology as a study tool and learning aid. While the distance-learning experience has been good for all the respondents, moving from coursework to dissertation work has changed the tenor of the experience for others. One student preparing for his qualifying examination explained that the personal discipline required to work independently at a distance was "brutal".

A number of students who also teach reported that they consider student learning styles when making decisions about presentation in their classrooms. One student who teaches in a variety of formats pointed out that one huge advantage of online instruction is the flexibility it gives students. "My students have loved the online nature of my classes because they can 'go to class' anywhere,

anytime; because they have hugely complex schedules, that flexibility has been important to them." That flexibility is not only in time but also form, she explained. "Because of the way I set up my online sections, they can sort of pick and choose how much "lecture" they want (and how they want it; most of them are available as videos), and they appreciate not being glued to a classroom for time they find they can spend more usefully in other ways."

One student who teaches in traditional classes indicated that he does consider student learning styles as a teacher. His emphasis is mainly on providing a mix of delivery methods. Another student who teaches traditional, hybrid and online classes said, "I provide verbal (text) versions of the 'lecture' information, videos, and assignments that include, as much as possible, at least some kinetic and visual aspects. That way, I'm hoping to reach students with all three of these learning styles."

A student who frequently teaches hybrid classes stated:

I do — though I'm not always 100% successful at supplying what they all need. Online tools are primarily visual. I haven't gone into podcasts yet to help auditory learners, but I do try to provide links to web material that is both visual and auditory (YouTube videos, NPR reports, etc.). I've even linked to a couple of engineering sites that are more kinesthetic, but it's hard to find something for all learners for a single lesson, so I rely on our in-class meetings to respond more to learning styles.

While yet another student who teaches traditional, hybrid, and online classes responded:

Yes, I do and have almost from the beginning. I have students take a self-test at the beginning of every Internet course and that includes a learning styles quiz. Clearly some learning styles benefit more from an Internet class and other learning styles might struggle more. It is not that I ban auditory learners, for example, but I think it is important that they realize that is how they learn and that not all learning styles work as well in an online class. Our institution does offer I-TV classes and those might be a better choice for auditory learners, for example, especially if they already feel they struggle with the particular subject matter.

The Role of an Instructor

An instructor takes on more than just the role of an educator in a distance education course. As the students are not physically located in a classroom setting where the instructor can actually see their nonverbal cues of agreement, boredom or confusion, the instructor must work harder to engage and involve the students. Understanding the teaching tools available to them and maximizing the benefits of such tools is essential to creating a successful learning environment for distance education. The instructors involved in this study use numerous virtual delivery methods in an effort to keep students engaged throughout the semester. According to the instructors surveyed for this study, a balance of synchronous and asynchronous learning is the key to providing a rich and fulfilling classroom experience in a virtual space.

Many of the students surveyed responded that a mix of synchronous and asynchronous virtual delivery methods make for a more effective course. As one student noted, "I think online courses need all three — synchronous space, asynchronous information, and asynchronous collaboration." Another student agreed, "If we relied on any single method, it wouldn't be sufficient, but together the synchronous and asynchronous methods combine to cover a variety of learning styles." A student in the program who also teaches in traditional classrooms stated, "synchronous and asynchronous deliveries are necessary for online

education as much as they are for traditional classroom practice." Another student who also teaches in a traditional classroom said that while the asynchronous elements allow her flexibility "the synchronous class meetings for coursework ensures that students do not ever feel isolated."

Selecting a Delivery Method

Distance education provides instructors various opportunities that traditional face-to-face courses do not. Through the selection of a delivery method for a distance education course, an instructor can lay the groundwork for an effective learning experience. Due to the availability of numerous methods, selecting the right one for a class can be as difficult as teaching the course itself. Instructors are influenced by a number of factors when selecting the appropriate product but most participating in this study report convenience and ease-of-use for students to be the main influence, second only to convenience and ease of use for themselves. Many other, often unknown, factors come into play in a distance education course that need to be taken into account in order to make the experience worthwhile and successful. A student's access to hardware, software, and bandwidth present numerous problems to the teaching process. Additionally, teaching online does not afford an instructor the opportunity to perceive intuitively learning deficiencies within their students as a consequence of various learning styles.

The ability to provide a standardized experience for all students is a difficult factor for distance education courses. Students do not have the same resources and access to hardware or software programs that a student attending a class in a face-to-face environment would. In order to minimize this differential, an instructor must select products that are free, readily available, or subsidized and offered through the institution. Synchronous learning environments put an additional strain on classroom instruction when students have varying bandwidths. Online applications like webinar programs or Second Life, which could otherwise be an option for synchronous learning, function poorly when operated in a low bandwidth situation. This limiting situation is the leading reason for advanced programs such as the one offered by TTU to continue to use software applications written in the 1990s.

Student learning styles are a factor in the decision process but are much harder to use when making the decision for a course method. Instructors clearly have no way of knowing their students' learning styles before a course begins. In an effort to modify a course for learning styles, instructors responding to this study suggested the need to be constantly cognizant of the intended final outcomes and each student's progress throughout the course in order to adjust the methods used. As one instructor explained it, "I like to try to fix problems [in a course] so I tweak delivery methods in the same way we'd tweak the order of assignments, the texts, or the focus of the course."

Synchronous Learning

In order to offer a consistent synchronous experience that spans all courses the TTU online TC&R program supports a MOO (MUD, object oriented) platform for synchronous meetings. Although MOOs are not new and have been around since 1990, the system provides a stable platform that is relatively easy for students and instructors to learn.

Instructors reported that they have used a variety of virtual delivery methods for their classes including the MOO (100%), WebBoard (85%), wikis (80%), blogs (65%), and Moodle (60%). The MOO was ranked as the favorite virtual delivery method with WebBoard, Moodle and wikis closely grouped together, and Facebook as the least favorite. The MOO ranked 3.8 on a 5-point satisfaction scale while Moodle and WebBoard ranked 3.6. Wikis and blogs were 3.1 and 3.0 respectively.

Most students report that while the MOO isn't perfect, it is an effective virtual delivery method

for "real-time interaction between students and faculty." Learning to use the MOO is not challenging, but it does take some getting used to as one student shares.

The MOO sessions were very draining initially. I felt like it was impossible to keep up with the multiple conversations. Since that first class, I've discovered that the pace and quality of the conversation varies from course to course, and with practice, I also find it easier to keep up and contribute.

Students also report that larger classes reduce the effectiveness of the MOO.

Several instructors within the study have also experimented with classes by offering synchronous sessions using Skype (VoIP technology), instant messaging group chat, teleconferencing, and Second Life with varying degrees of success. A student in the program comments:

A couple of classes have experimented with some video delivery, but those are complicated by the time lag: Viewing a video at home through the MOO often results in up to two minutes (but it can be as short as 30 seconds) of delay, and that's hard to get accustomed to and stifles conversation; on the other hand, it's nice to connect a name with a face. I tend to prefer the text-based delivery.

Most instructors noted that the method must fit the content of the course and one specifically states that "complex materials are best taught in an 'easy' platform, one I am comfortable with."

Some students willingly use the MOO but do prefer other forms of communication technology. One said he preferred group chat on Yahoo IM as "it's faster and you can have a personal archive rather than wondering if the MOO's recorder is turned on." Another enjoyed a weekly phone conference used for one of her classes and said it was "the most engaging technology we tried." She said that while she "liked it a lot" and "felt very connected" there were disadvantages such as people talking over each other and the potential for disruptions coming from every participant's location. "I couldn't have the kids within a 20-mile radius of me during class (they caused serious disturbances)."

Other students appreciate the addition of audio for either synchronous or asynchronous instruction and/or discussion. One student said, "All of my classes have used MOO with a live class meeting. Some of the classes used Skype, with podcast replay and podcast lectures which I very much appreciated."

Asynchronous Learning

The asynchronous component to distance education provides students with a collaborative environment to build on their learning outside of the weekly classroom session. This environment also affords students an opportunity to build a virtual community amongst themselves. The selection of an asynchronous tool is where most instructors differ with regard to their methods, with a large majority (50%) selecting WebBoard as a tool of choice. WebBoard's ability to host running threads of conversations, feedback, and readily available user statistics make it an easy choice by which instructors can supplement their synchronous sessions.

Instructors in this study also used blogs (37.5%) and Moodle interfaces (26%) to provide an additional out-of-class experience. Blogs provide a personal reflective journal style account of a students learning throughout the course. This method of asynchronous learning allows students to create blogrolls to other class participants, and to provide feedback to each other through comments. An additional value to using blogs within the virtual classroom is the possibility for use beyond the classroom. Some students, however, prefer the discussion be kept private. "For personal reasons, I really don't want to be "found" on the Web in this program, so I have sort of resented 'open access' options; I'd have preferred to handle those assignments through a password/identification-protected site."

A Moodle, an open source product that is free and downloadable for anyone to use, is much like the WebBoard product. It is an educational course management system that provides instructors the ability to develop a secure site in order for students to participate in forum-based discussions with the ability to maintain and access user statistics. They allow instructors the opportunity to offer additional materials, post events, chat and fully manage a course much like similar but expensive course management software packages.

The instructors in this study reported using wikis (12.5%) on an infrequent basis as a tool for asynchronous communication within the virtual classroom. Although a valuable tool for collaborative work they may not provide the best possible experience for all students, whereas another tool might much as Carter and Rickly remind readers in their 2005 study. Instructors in this study reported wikis to be "difficult for everyone to use," particularly as a "course-sponsored" project, but rather suggest that students use it as a tool for collaboration on smaller group projects.

Connections beyond the Classroom

Face-to-face time with an instructor is impossible in most distance education programs based on the diverse geographic locations of students. But this time is often essential in supplementing a student's learning, as well as helping to form a productive student-instructor relationship.

In a virtual environment, the instructors at TTU have overcome this impasse by reaching out to students through social media avenues readily available. All instructors in the study use e-mail as a regular point of contact with students but many also conduct personal conference sessions within the MOO, leave messages on a WebBoard, participate in IM sessions, and are available for periodic telephone calls at the student's request. This extra level of interaction between the instructor and the student provides a vital link between the two in an environment which can otherwise feel limiting and isolated.

Student respondents reported using a variety of social media to stay connected with other students and faculty in the program including e-mail, Ning, Facebook, MySpace, MOO, WebBoard, Twitter, Blogging, VoIP, and IM. E-mail and IM seem to be the preferred methods of direct contact although a number rely on the student listserv. A number of students mentioned using social networking such as Twitter, Ning, and Facebook to keep up with their peers. Students also use the MOO for social gatherings and discussion groups. One stated "I like e-mail when dealing with large groups: You can quickly get a detailed message to many people, keep a copy of that message, and make sure you've edited/revised that message before sending it out."

Some students like having a variety of tools to stay in touch with their peers. "I love following friends on Twitter and Facebook — those little updates often make me smile, but I use e-mail a lot." Other students, however, are less comfortable with these tools. "I was initially uncomfortable using Yahoo or other chat tools to meet with professors. I'm much more comfortable popping into someone's office for a face-to-face chat. But I'm getting more comfortable with chat — slowly."

Connections outside Academe

Digital connections are already beginning to become commonplace within corporate cultures. A number of students involved in this study report using digital connections both for communication purposes and to extend their professional knowledge. One student reports that his company, an international manufacturer, uses meeting software and video conferencing for remote training, while another student, who telecommutes for a national company, points out that instant messaging and phone conferences allow him to stay in touch and current with his co-workers. "I do not feel any different than I did working in the same office space. We are in frequent contact throughout the day. It is so easy to just ask a question and to get

an immediate answer." A student who conducts intensive training camps for his major international employer has come to realize that the TTU TC&R program model could be used to deliver the same training he conducts onsite at a much lower cost through digital methods while still creating the same user experience . The transfer of knowledge from the TTU program into the workplace has already begun as one student who works for a major international company has brought many of her TC&R social media lessons to her employer to enhance dialogue and communications.

The lessons of the TTU TC&R Ph.D. program have implications not only for training and professional development, but also for collaboration and communication. Ph.D. work is different from other levels of higher education, where often the flow of information is strictly one way – from instructor to student. However, Ph.D. work challenges students to collaborate together and with instructors to pursue and create new knowledge much as team members and colleagues must collaborate in many professions.

FUTURE TRENDS

In the current economic climate, distance education will continue to grow in both the academic world and the private sector. Even though, as noted in the introduction to this chapter, Charp's 2002 prediction about distance education utilization rates has yet to come to pass, the economic strain of the current recession has public and private sectors scrambling to save money through various cost-cutting measures. The ability for an individual to gain advancement through distance education is advantageous not only to employees but also to employers. Distance education internally and external to a corporation has become a viable, cost effective option. (United States Distance Learning Association).

A trend, which began with for-profit institutions such as The University of Phoenix, has now spread into public universities, which have discovered that the value of their recognized names (branding) and their not-for-profit model make them prime candidates to excel in the market. A *Chronicle of Higher Education* article from April of 2007 states that, "By all accounts, demand for online education is expanding." About 3.2 million students took at least one online course during the fall of 2005. This increase represents 39% more than the 2.3 million the previous year, according to the Sloan Consortium, which promotes standards for online learning" (Foster and Carnevale). As technological innovations in education and communication continue to develop, so will the need to study the implications of those developments for education and training.

CONCLUSION

Although learning methods cannot easily be foreseen or addressed ahead of time, the selection of a particular learning method, the combination of synchronous and asynchronous collaboration and information, provides an ideal solution that covers a number of learning styles in different ways. This balance of a consistent real-time interaction teamed with a tool that provides ongoing contact and learning helps to enrich the learning experience for most students and trainees.

All participants within a distance education course or training program are responsible for the final outcomes and the program's success. Students need to be willing to engage and interact in the offered environment while instructors need to be willing to adjust their methods to students or trainees as the course progresses.

The instructors in the TTU TC&R program have collectively taught over 100 courses through distance education. They have had time to experiment and to learn from their successes and failures in a virtual environment. Many suggest avoiding the fad products and instead approaching the selection of a virtual teaching method as critically as the

choice of a textbook. The selection of a method should be soundly based on the goals of a course rather than on an instructor's personal preference. All instructors involved in the study stressed the importance of a balance between synchronous and asynchronous learning in order to promote course objectives and real-time interaction between student and faculty. In the corporate world where employees may not have the same choices as academic students, the responsibility lies with the instructor to ensure that the appropriate tools are chosen to meet the needs of the trainees and to achieve course goals.

Respondents who took part in this study, both faculty and students alike, pointed out that the growth in distance education offerings both for higher education and for corporate training also means that distance education consumers can usually be more selective than in the past. While convenience still rates high in program choice, the quality of the instructors and of the overall program are even more important factors. Reputation and quality matters, and distance education consumers are no longer as willing to simply choose the most convenient option.

REFERENCES

Akdemir, O., & Koszalka, T. A. (2008). Investigating the relationships among instructional strategies and learning styles in online environments. *Computers & Education*, *50*(4), 1451–1461. doi:10.1016/j.compedu.2007.01.004

Avery, C., Civjan, J., & Johri, A. (2005). Assessing student interaction in the global classroom project: Visualizing communication and collaboration patterns . In Cooke, K. C., & Grant-Davie, K. (Eds.), *Online Education: Global Questions, Local Answers* (pp. 245–264). Amityville, NY: Baywood Publishing Company.

Blair, K., & Hoy, C. (2006). Paying attention to adult learners online: The pedagogy and politics of community. *Computers and Composition*, *23*(1), 32–48. doi:10.1016/j.compcom.2005.12.006

Buckley, W., & Smith, A. (2008). Application of multimedia technologies to enhance distance learning. *RE:view*, *39*(2), 57–65. doi:10.3200/REVU.39.2.57-65

Carter, L., & Rickly, B. (2006). Mind the gap: Modeling space in online education . In Cooke, K. C., & Grant-Davie, K. (Eds.), *Online Education: Global Questions, Local Answers* (pp. 31–48). Amityville, NY: Baywood Publishing Company.

Charp, S. (2002). Changes to traditional teaching. *T.H.E. Journal*, *29*(10).

Cho, H., Gay, G., Davidson, B., & Ingraffea, A. (2007). Social networks, communications styles, and learning performance in a CSCL community. *Computers & Education*, *49*(2), 309–329. doi:10.1016/j.compedu.2005.07.003

De Simone, C. (2006). Preparing our teachers for distance education. *College Teaching*, *54*(1), 183–184. doi:10.3200/CTCH.54.1.183-184

Durrington, V. A., Berryill, A., & Swafford, J. (2006). Strategies for enhancing student interactivity in an online environment. *College Teaching*, *54*(1), 190–193. doi:10.3200/CTCH.54.1.190-193

Eaton, A. (2005). Students in the online technical communications classroom . In Cooke, K. C., & Grant-Davie, K. (Eds.), *Online Education: Global Questions, Local Answers* (pp. 31–48). Amityville, NY: Baywood Publishing Company.

Foster, A., & Carnevale, D. (2007, April 27). Distance Education Goes Public. *The Chronicle of Higher Education*. Retrieved from http://chronicle.com/weekly/v53/i34/34a04901.htm

Grady, H. M., & Davis, M. T. (2005). Teaching well online with instructional and procedural scaffolding . In Cooke, K. C., & Grant-Davie, K. (Eds.), *Online Education: Global Questions, Local Answers* (pp. 101–122). Amityville, NY: Baywood Publishing Company.

Herrington, T., & Tretyakov, Y. (2005). The global classroom project: Troublemaking and troubleshooting . In Cooke, K. C., & Grant-Davie, K. (Eds.), *Online Education: Global Questions, Local Answers* (pp. 267–284). Amityville, NY: Baywood Publishing Company.

Kolb, A., & Kolb, D. (2005). *The Kolb Learning Style Inventory – Version 3.1: 2005 technical specifications. LSI Technical Manual* (pp. 1–71). Boston, MA: Hay Resources Direct.

Lu, H., Jia, L., Gong, S., & Clark, B. (2007). The relationship of Kolb learning styles, online learning behaviors and learning outcomes. *Education Technology & Society*, *10*(4), 187–196.

Moallem, M. (2007). Accommodating individual differences in the design of online learning environments: A comparative study. *Journal of Research on Technology in Education*, *40*(2), 217–245.

Rheingold, H. (2000). *The virtual community: Homesteading on the electronic frontier*. Cambridge, MA: The MIT Press.

Rubens, P., & Southard, S. Students' technological difficulties in using Web-based learning environments . In Cooke, K. C., & Grant-Davie, K. (Eds.), *Online Education: Global Questions, Local Answers* (pp. 193–206). Amityville, NY: Baywood Publishing Company.

Rude, C. (2005). *Strategic Planning for online education: Sustaining students, faculty, and programs. Online Education: Global Questions, Local Answers* (pp. 67–85). Amityville, NY: Baywood Publishing Company.

Santo, S. A. (2006). Relationships between learning styles and online learning: Myth or reality? *Performance Improvement Quarterly, 19*(3), 73–88.

Tabs, E. (2003). *Distance education at degree-granting postsecondary institutions: 2000-2001.* (NCES report 2003-017). National Center for Education Statistics. Retrieved November 10, 2008, from http://nces.ed.gov/pubs2003/2003017.pdf

Thrush, E. A., & Bodary, M. (2000). Virtual reality, combat, and communication. *Journal of Business and Technical Communication, 14*(3), 315–327. doi:10.1177/105065190001400304

Tinto, V. (1997). Classrooms as communities: Exploring the educational character of student persistence. *The Journal of Higher Education, 68*(6), 599–623. doi:10.2307/2959965

U. S. Department of Education Institute of Education Sciences. (n.d.). *Fast Facts.* Retrieved March 8, 2009, from http://nces.ed.gov/fastfacts/display.asp?id=80

United States Distance Learning Association (USDLA). (n.d.). *Resources: Research, Statistics and Distance Learning Resources.* Retrieved March 12, 2009, from http://www.usdla.org/html/aboutUs/researchInfo.htm

KEY TERMS AND DEFINITIONS

Blogroll: A list of blogs on a blog, intended to read as a list of recommended reads.

Community: A body, class, or cohort of learners.

Distance Education: An instructional method that replaces the traditional face-to-face classroom experience with alternative (not necessarily online) modes of delivery and student/faculty interaction.

Learning Styles: The different methods and practices that students adopt to aid learning.

Listserv: Electronic mailing list software designed to send messages to multiple users. It allows users to add or remove themselves without the aid of a human.

MOO/MUD: An object-oriented, text-based virtual reality system for multiple users.

Moodle: A free open source course management system.

Online Education: An instructional method that adopts computer technology to provide educational programs to students who cannot, or prefer not to, attend traditionally delivered programs.

Social Networking: A set of practices or techniques used by students to form communities of learners.

WebBoard: A software package designed to assist in the process of online community creation, designed specifically for its robust use of forum and message board use.

Webinar: A Web conference session used to conduct real-time meetings or presentations via the Internet.

Wiki: A collection of Web pages designed to enable community collaboration.

Chapter 18
Intelligent Agents in Education

Mikail Feituri
Università Telematica Guglielmo Marconi, Italy

Federica Funghi
Università Telematica Guglielmo Marconi, Italy

ABSTRACT

Distance learning through information and communication technologies has consistently had a notable impact and influence on the academic and professional world. This is greatly due to the fact that distance learning allows users, especially professionals, to learn at their own pace, according to their availability, in addition to having limited costs. These features are consistent with and support the concept of life long learning. Traditional courses delivered in an E-learning modality can sometimes, however, result in being unstimulating and leaving the student with the impression of being isolated during their learning process. Pedagogical intelligent agents, however, are able to be constantly present in the learner's training environment, interacting verbally and non verbally (gestures and expressions) with users, thus making E-learning much more interactive, interesting and fun. This ongoing interaction and support of the agent, therefore, notably helps reduce the possibility of users feeling excluded during their E-learning course, thus better enhancing their overall learning experience and reinforcing their motivation. This chapter will introduce features and potential of pedagogical agents and will illustrate, with examples, the most common techniques used to design an agent or a "society" of intelligent agents and how to integrate them into a learning environment.

INTRODUCTION

Intelligent agent technology can be considered an interesting approach to meet the challenge of modern educational systems that are greatly influenced by ICT and especially by the development of the Internet. The rapid growth of these technologies allows, on the one hand, the complexity of educational infrastructures to be managed in a more efficient way and on the other, to develop and provide innovative typologies of learning services. More specifically, it is important that these services

DOI: 10.4018/978-1-61520-619-3.ch018

offer a range of features such as personalization, mobility, efficiency and information circulation that helps enhance the approach to working with new technologies. Intelligent agents seem to better provide these kinds of features compared to other existing technologies.

Improvements in user interfaces and intelligent agent technologies have enabled the development of new virtual tutors e.g. pedagogical agents that are able to converse with students in a natural language. Several interesting features characterize this kind of intelligent agent who dynamically responds and adapts to environment variations and facilitates a learning by doing approach. Agents have animated personas that permit them to show how to perform a task while communicating both verbally and non verbally, with facial expressions, gazes and gestures. They are able to interact with a community of students and other agents in order to facilitate team work and group learning. They are capable of learning from human instructors and then consequently teach students what they have learnt.

This chapter will demonstrate how pedagogical intelligent agents can effectively support a user's learning and training process. It will explore the definition of artificial intelligence (AI), its fields of application and provide a summary of the main methods currently used for the knowledge representation in AI.

The following paragraphs will provide a general description of intelligent agents that use one of the specific methods of artificial intelligence and feature a list of the most significant definitions of intelligent agents in order of complexity and properties. These definitions, according to major experts in the field, will classify the different types of agents, but will also demonstrate how all agents share at least one property in common or some similar forms of "intelligence".

The next section will discuss how intelligent agents can interact with the Learning Management System and highlight how intelligent agents or rather virtual tutors assist and support students throughout their learning path.

In conclusion, four examples of pedagogical intelligent agents will be described that clearly demonstrate and represent an effective approach for E-learning. The primary objective of this chapter, therefore, is to invite readers, especially those involved in the E-learning field, to consider the benefits and possibility of incorporating pedagogical intelligent agents into their distance learning courses.

BACKGROUND

A special type of intelligent agent is the "pedagogical agent", an actual virtual tutor who supports the students throughout their learning process within the learning management system. The virtual tutor is a unique intelligent agent due to the following specific features:

- Always visible to the user within the educational milieu.
- Takes on human (or humanoid) forms, usually having a face, hands and arms in order to point out objects to the user or to perform actions.
- Interacts with the user both verbally (by means of language) and non verbally (through gestures and/or facial expressions).
- Moves and interacts directly with the learning milieu and within the milieu itself.

Based on these general definitions, Johnson, Rickel and Lester (2000), pioneers in pedagogical intelligent agent research, describe intelligent agents as, "They increase the bandwidth of communication between students and computers, and they increase the computer's ability to engage and motivate students."

DEFINING ARTIFICIAL INTELLIGENCE

Artificial Intelligence is a computational model that enables to carry out the typical functions and reasoning related to the human mind. Its essential feature is to comprehend the theory and techniques that are needed in order to develop algorithms that allow computers to demonstrate the ability and or intelligent activity, in specific environments.

One of the main issues and challenges concerning artificial intelligence is to formally define synthetic/abstract systems of reasoning, meta-reasoning and the human learning process, in order to develop computational models that can successfully realize and implement these functions.

Two areas of significant current research and development, using artificial intelligence, are:

* Knowledge-based or expert systems
* Robotics

Artificial intelligence systems are used to operate robots or equipment in factories and industrial environments, but there are also artificial intelligence systems that can give expert advice, in certain areas or disciplines, to decision makers. An expert system that is well designed and contains an extensive knowledge base - the facts and rules that experts use in making judgments and decisions - can rival the performance of a human specialist in that discipline.

The Knowledge Representation community follows two different description methods. The first utilizes logic languages to represent explicit knowledge and logic inference to deduce implicit knowledge. The second represents knowledge by means of graph structures, following the approach proposed by Charles Pierce, who, in 1896, seven years after Peano developed what is now the standard notation for first order logic, proposed a graphical notation called "existential graphs". The latter are known today as semantic networks, and, since the time of Peano and Pierce, the Knowledge Representation community has debated the advantages and disadvantages of logic and semantic network approaches. At the beginning of the eighties, logic began to be considered as a unifying language in which it is possible to precisely express semantics of a knowledge base. Furthermore, results about the decidability, tractability and expressiveness of logic formalisms can be applied to non-logic formalisms (such as semantic networks): it is enough to translate the latter into the former.

DEFINITION OF AN INTELLIGENT AGENT

This section provides an analysis of the definitions of agents currently used. We have chosen to focus on some of the most influential definitions of agents that are taken from books either widely used in education or are recognized state-of-the-art surveys. These definitions describe the classification of different types of intelligent agents.

Russell and Norvig (1995) stated that "An agent is anything that can be viewed as perceiving its environment through sensors and acting upon that environment through effectors" (p.33).

To add to this, Maes (1995) describes the important concept of autonomy and the focusing on objectives: "Autonomous agents are computational systems that inhabit some complex dynamic environment, sense and act autonomously in this environment, and by doing so realize a set of goals or tasks for which they are designed" (p.108).

Smith, Cypher and Spohrer (1994) focus instead on the significant concept of persistence in the virtual environment:

"Let us define an agent as a persistent software entity dedicated to a specific purpose. 'Persistent' distinguishes agents from subroutines; agents have their own ideas about how to accomplish tasks, their own agendas. 'Special purpose' distinguishes

Table 1. Agent classification

Property	Definition
Reactive	Responds in a timely fashion to changes in the environment
Autonomous	Exercises control over its own actions
Temporally continuous	Is a continuously running process
Adaptive	Changes its behaviour based on its previous experience
Character	Has a believable "personality" and an emotional state
Flexible	Agent actions are not scripted
Communicative	Communicates with other agents, also including people

them from entire multifunction applications; agents are typically much smaller."

Hayes-Roth (1995) introduces the concept of reasoning before action, therefore, emphasizing the need to develop an agent with at least a minimum amount of "intellectual capacity": "Intelligent agents continuously perform three functions: perception of dynamic conditions in the environment; action to affect conditions in the environment; and reasoning to interpret perceptions, solve problems, draw inferences, and determine actions".

The final definition by Wooldridge and Jennings (1995) describes the communicative capacity that an agent must possess:

"a software-based computer system that enjoys the following properties: autonomy: agents operate without the direct intervention of humans or others, and have some kind of control over their actions and internal state; social ability: agents interact with other agents (and possibly humans) via some kind of agent-communication language; reactivity: agents perceive their environment, (which may be the physical world, a user via a graphical user interface, a collection of other agents, the INTERNET, or perhaps all of these combined), and respond in a timely fashion to changes that occur in it; pro-activeness: agents do not simply act in response to their environment, they are able to exhibit goal-directed behaviour by taking the initiative (p. 2)."

The agent definitions mentioned earlier examine a host of properties of an agent. The table below lists the different properties mentioned above in order to help further classify intelligent agents and define their functions.

This table provides a basis on which different agents can be categorized according to specific features. Every agent, considering our definition, embodies the first four properties and any additional properties added attribute to different categories of agents, such as flexible, or communicative agents, thus automatically establishing a hierarchical classification based on set inclusion. For example, a flexible, communicative agent is considered a subcategory of flexible agents.

PEDAGOGICAL AGENTS AND THEIR IMPACT ON LEARNING

Pedagogical agents are animated computer characters, based on artificial intelligence technology, that are physically embodied and can detect external stimuli such as keyboard input, mouse position, and mouse clicks. The artificial intelligence backend has a behaviour system able to engage human learners in natural instructional dialogues, simulate human emotions and actions, as well as various components tied to learning.

The use of pedagogical agents for learning improvement helps private and public training institutions face topical challenges in the field of education such as the rapid evolution of disciplines, the growing heterogeneity of learners, the undefined boundaries between subjects and the consequent need for trainers to teach both soft and hard skills (Roda, Angehm & Nabeth, 2001). In this framework technology enhanced systems are expected to play an important role by: accelerating the learning process, facilitating access, customising the learning process and supplying a richer learning environment.

Pedagogical agents and conversational agents in particular, address the abovementioned challenges by promoting human-like dialogue, realistic learning environments and representing the role of learning facilitators.

Integration of Agents into Pedagogical Platforms

In order to increase the effectiveness of agents' intervention and support the learning process on a comprehensive level, they should interact directly in the learning environment and not be merely included within an existing learning system.

Pedagogical agents act as teachers in a realistic setting who give lessons by presenting contents and tailoring their instruction on the basis of students' needs, expectations and difficulties. These agents, therefore, are not external factors just included in the learning environment but rather directly impact it and are built accordingly in order to properly adapt to it. Following a systemic approach, agents ensure adaptiveness and adaptability to both the user and the subject and system they belong to. The comprehensive learning environment consists of a Learning Management System (LMS) also referred to as a pedagogical or E-learning platform which is a software system designed and developed to manage computer-based education by delivering courseware and e-tutoring through the Internet. In case the course coordinators consider the intervention of pedagogical agents relevant to advance students' knowledge and skills, the agents must be conceived as a meaningful component

of the LMS and be deeply integrated into other tools and contents. Smith and al. (1999) explain that "The agent acts as a gatekeeper, offering flexible access to the system including on-line help facilities and reference materials as well as synchronous and asynchronous access to human support. As a personable, natural language speaking guide through the course support system, the agent enables ease of use especially for novice users. It provides a simpler interface for a student so that there is no effort wasted in learning how to use the learning tool".

The learning system moderated by the pedagogical agent can be defined as an intelligent learning environment or ILE (Sampson, Karagiannidis & Kinshuk, 2002) "an intelligent learning environment is capable of automatically, dynamically, and continuously adapting to the learning context, which is defined by the learner characteristics, the type of educational material being exchanged". Since ILEs are capable of automatically adapting to the individual learner, they represent promising technologies towards the achievement of personalised learning, an ever growing popular concept which explains that education should not be limited by space and time constraints and should adapt to the continuously changing learner's requirements, abilities, needs or interests.

In this framework, embodied conversational agents, representing realistic players able to perform behaviours with emotive responses and effective pedagogy, can play a fundamental communicative role in learning environments by providing students with contextualized problem-solving advice and creating appealing learning experiences. Agents are conceived to communicate in a human-like manner, portray realistic aspects and execute conversational functions and emotional states, thus improving the quality of communication between humans and computers.

Beneficiaries

Pedagogical agents are able to strengthen student-learning outcomes by exploiting both the auditory and visual channels of the learner.

Their behaviour and actions are particularly suitable for adult learners who generally prefer a level of control over their learning experience and can interact with the agent to focus on a certain content of interest. Thanks to a variety of features, that will be explained hereafter, pedagogical agents allow students to focus on concepts within the context of their applications and orient course content towards direct applications rather than towards theory thus satisfying adult learners who are often goal / relevancy oriented, have concrete, immediate needs and therefore prefer when theory is applied to practical problems. Agents are able to show how knowledge and skills can be applied to solve actual problems and promote the use of participatory techniques (e.g. case studies and problem-solving) thus addressing adult learners' typical problem-oriented approach to learning. Pedagogical agents promote controlled learning which works best when learners already possess significant related knowledge or when the contents do not need to be studied following a particular order. The ultimate feature of interactive animated pedagogical agents, therefore, is its potential to provide individualized instruction for a large number of learners. Many online training programs allow learners to personally schedule when to study material, making it possible to leave and return to the training contents. Learners may also be able to control the sequence of material that is provided, the number of topics covered and the total amount of material covered (DeRouin, Fritsche, & Salas, 2005; Sims & Hedberg, 1995). Learner control is considered one of the main benefits of E-learning paths but when learners are left on their own, they may not be motivated or engaged enough to dedicate adequate time and attention to the learning process. Thus greater flexibility in learning can sometimes lead to such problems.

Many people, for example, are more comfortable with classroom environments because the isolation of a web-based course can often make learning less fulfilling and more anxiety-provoking than classroom training. Students attending E-learning courses need to make many decisions about what to learn and how, and this can result in a high proportion of skipped content or dropout rates. Thus, even if learner control is often publicized as an important advantage of computer based training (Clark & Mayer, 2008; Kraiger & Jerden, 2007), it can have positive or negative effects, depending on the student's choices. It means it is necessary to better understand learner control in order to successfully integrate it into a training path. As discussed in the next section, intelligent agents have the potential to increase engagement and reduce isolation by acting as a tutor or peer.

Although the use of intelligent agents are particularly helpful for adult learners who have a problem/results-oriented learning approach, they can be less useful for younger users. It seems that when dealing with children there is a connection between "pedagogical agent" and "distraction" because children (average age 12 years old) might be too fascinated by the interaction with the animated character and consequently not focus on the subject. Nevertheless, a study conducted with one hundred middle school students found that encouraging results have been gained with the use of an animated pedagogical agent, Herman the Bug, a lifelike agent able to perform various kinds of explanatory behaviours (Lester, Converse, Stone, Kahler & Barlow 1997). In particular the study meant to assess students' perception of agents' affective characteristics and it discovered that the so "called persona effect" – that is the presence of a lifelike character within an interactive learning environment – can positively impact students' perception of their learning experience. Students considered the agents as being very helpful, credible and entertaining. Furthermore this work revealed that combinations of type of advice can boost students' positive perception of the agent and increase their learning performance. One of the main challenges remains the careful identification of the suitable agents' features for particular age groups, domains and learning contexts.

Main Roles and Functionalities of Pedagogical Agents

The main functionalities of pedagogical agents depend on what they can do in terms of guidance, instructions and communication within a learning environment. Pedagogical agents are able to perform the following:

- Adapt, constantly evaluating learners' level of comprehension and adapt the lessons following users' feedback. If needed, the agent can provide further instructions to solve users' difficulties;
- Motivate, encouraging students to interact by asking questions, giving prompt feedback and meaningful examples, as well as interpreting student responses;
- Engage, demonstrating specific features that can be conceived as appealing and attractive trainers;
- Evolve, revising and updating new contents and features.

The abovementioned functionalities allow the pedagogical agent to perform three main roles within an online environment: a facilitator, who supports students in identifying their suitable and personalised learning path according to their progress and preferences, a tutor, who promotes active learning and offers facilities or exercises and an advisor, who displays emotional responsiveness and problem solving skills. By playing the role of facilitator, the pedagogical agent is both reactive by responding to students' queries and proactive by offering suggestions to resources. As a tutor, the pedagogical agent encourages active learning by using interactive and individually paced exercises created to assess users' performance and provide

feedback until the student is able to execute a given task. As an advisor, the pedagogical agent displays a degree of emotional intelligence by offering suggestions to alleviate any frustration which can lead to de-motivation exploiting a repository of typical solutions to common problems (Smith, Affleck, Lees & Branki 1999).

In order to perform these main roles, specific forms of agent-student relations need to be activated. Currently there are no existing agents that are able to support all possible types of interaction, although each type can improve a learning environment without other agents and different combinations will be useful for different kinds of learning environments. The various types of human-computer interactions supported by pedagogical agents can be summarised as follows (Johnson, Lewis, & Rickel, 2000):

- Interactive Demonstrations. The agent can teach students how to execute physical tasks in a given environment by directly demonstrating how to perform the action, indicating the objects linked to the specific task and giving some oral explanations. A real demonstration leads to a better retention than a mere written or verbal description since it combines visual and auditory stimuli. The demonstration become interactive when the users are also active and can interrupt, make questions or finish the task under the agent's monitoring and assistance. The objective of the interactive demonstration is to increase users' understanding of how to undertake particular tasks by encouraging them to make some practice without the feeling of being judged. The comprehension is reinforced by the active role and participation of the users not allowed for instance by videotapes which allow demonstration but do not foresee users' practice and performance.
- Navigational Guidance. In case of a large and complex student work environment,

animated agents can serve as navigational guides, leading students around and preventing them from becoming lost. In case of a 3-D learning environment, the agents can guide the student around the learning setting, showing where relevant objects are located and giving instruction to achieve them. Thanks to the help of navigational guides within 3-D learning environments, students can develop spatial models related to the subject even if they will probably never renter the actual world there represented.

- Gaze and Gesture as Attention Guides. The agent is able to guide student's attention through the most common and natural methods: gaze and deictic gesture. Agents can combine speech, locomotion, and gesture, can move through their environment, point to objects, and refer to them appropriately as they provide problem-solving advice. An agent might include some or all of these capabilities. Furthermore, coherently with the role of a tutor, the agent provides feedback on students' tasks by adding to its verbal feedback the nonverbal communication. Agents can use a nod of approval to show agreement with a student's actions and shakes his head to indicate disapproval. The Adele agent (to be better introduced later) nods or smiles when in agreement with the student's actions whilst presents a look of puzzlement when the student makes an error. Moreover, body language can help indicate to students that they have just committed a very serious error thus making a strong impression on them. The ability to use nonverbal feedback in addition to verbal comments allows conversational agents to provide more varied degrees of feedback than earlier intelligent agents. Concerning the variety of agreement in response to the student's performance, the next paragraph

will introduce the Arianna agent developed by a European team of researchers lead by Università Telematica Guglielmo Marconi. During the assessment of students' performance, Arianna gives feedback by combining verbal and nonverbal communication and processing data through a fuzzy logic system which employs a range of values from true to false as a means to model the uncertainty of natural language. The use of nonverbal communication may play different roles, while some occasions need these types of unobtrusive feedback, other occasions may call for more exaggerated feedback than a verbal comment can offer.

- Conversational Signals. As people employ a wide variety of nonverbal signals to help regulate the conversation during face-to-face dialogues, animated pedagogical agents simulate face-to-face interactions to which people are most accustomed. Some nonverbal signals are closely tied to spoken utterances, and could be used by any animated agent that produces speech output (e.g. pitch accents or a blink of the eyes). Although people can clearly communicate in the absence of these nonverbal signals (e.g. by telephone), communication and collaboration proceed most smoothly when they are available.

- Conveying and Eliciting Emotion. Clark Elliott, Jeff Rickel, and James Lester (1999) explain that animated agents displaying appropriate emotions provide a number of educational benefits to learners. First, agents that appear to care about students' progress may help motivate students to care about their own progress. Second, agents that are sensitive to learners' emotions (e.g., boredom or frustration) can provide feedback that prevents students from losing interest. Third, agents that convey enthusiasm for the subject matter are more likely to evoke the same enthusiasm in learners. Finally, agents that have rich and interesting personalities make learning more enjoyable for the learner. A learner that enjoys interacting with a pedagogical agent may have a more positive perception of the overall learning experience and may consequently opt to spend more time in the learning environment.

- Virtual Team-mates. Complex tasks often require teamwork. To perform effectively in a team, each member is required to play his role and learn to coordinate their actions with their companions. The virtual learning environment offers team members the opportunity to work at different locations, and practice together in realistic situations. In this type of training, animated agents can play the role of instructors for individual students and can also replace missing team members thus allowing students to practice team tasks when some or all human instructors and team-mates are unavailable.

- Adaptive Pedagogical Interactions. Animated pedagogical agents must be capable of other various pedagogical abilities such as: answering questions, generating explanations, asking probing questions and tracking learners' skill levels.

The incorporation of these pedagogical functions in pedagogical agents promotes a kind of pedagogy that is dynamic and adaptive, as opposed to deliberate, sequential, or pre-planned.

ANALYSES OF REALIZED PROJECTS

This section of the chapter analyzes the functions, interfaces and methodologies which were used to realize four virtual agent projects: Steve and Adele (agents developed by the USC Information Sciences Institute's Center for Advanced Research

in Technology for Education), Arianna and Clara (agents realized by the Guglielmo Marconi Open University).

In particular their differ for the role they play within the learning context, the typology of relationship with the student, the backend technology, their rapport with the environment they are incorporated in, the domain of applications.

Agent Steve

Steve (Soar Training Expert For Virtual Environments) is an agent designed and implemented in order to interact with students in a virtual reality system in 3-D. Steve was realized as an application to train navel staff on ships, for example regarding specific operations on American ship engines.

Within the virtual world, students may see Steve inside a 3-D environment, where the agent moves and interacts with devices. Steve is also able to speak with students. The student enters and interacts with the virtual world and with Steve using a system developed by Lockheed Martin and composed of a helmet for 3-D vision and a glove with sensors, in order to interact with virtual world devices.

It is important to highlight that Steve is the prototype of what a pedagogical agent should be especially concerning practical job simulations.

Otherwise the development of a system like Steve needs time, human resources and of course an extensive budget.

Sections below will describe briefly the peculiar features of the system.

Virtual World

It is essential to point out that the reproduction of a learner's working place together with an animated agent embedded in the environment allows great opportunities to teach practical tasks such as repairing tools or conducting maintenance. For example Steve is able to show a student how to manage a High Pressure Air Compressor located in a military ship. During the simulation, Steve first gives an overview of the task objectives and then explains in detail the actions he is performing. A possible comment he would say could be:

"Now I will perform a functional test of the temperature sensors to make sure that all the alarm leds work properly. To do this operation, I press the corresponding button that performs a test. Consequently, all the alarm lights should illuminate."

After this first check, Steve continues to illustrate the most relevant part of the tool that has, in some degree, connections with the task to be performed. For example, once the alarm leds are illuminated, Steve will point out to the lights and say "All the lights are on and work properly."

In a 3-D virtual environment, students are able to "live" in the simulated world and watch the tasks Steve is performing from different viewpoints as if they were in a real working environment . Learners can interrupt the agent to ask questions or even try to finish the task by themselves. In the latter case, Steve checks the student actions and eventually gives some tips or hints just like a real tutor. The agent is also able to dynamically change the sequence or the type of actions that are necessary to complete a task in order to adapt his behaviour in response to different kinds of situations relating to various environment initial states, failure modes or help the student recover from errors.

Navigational Guidance

Due to the fact that a ship is a large and complex environment, providing an animated agent to teach learners where things are located and how to navigate within the environment is a clear advantage. The ship's engine room where Steve lives, is quite complex which is composed of turbines, several platforms and paths in the engines and around them, a control panel and other various engine elements that can be manipulated i.e. valves. While Steve illustrates the tasks to be performed,

he shows the walking paths to the learner as well. Moreover, he demonstrates where relevant tools can be found and how to handle them. Steve is able to find the available short path from his actual position to the location of the next tool necessary to perform the assigned task, thanks to a complete internal representation of the ship.

Gaze and Gestures as Attention Guides

An animated agent is able to focus the student's attention by using gazes and gestures in a natural and humanlike way.

Steve uses such modalities in different contexts for pinpointing objects while he is speaking. He looks at an object just before starting to manipulate or indicate it. He also looks at a tool while a student or another Steve agent is handling it, or looks at an object to check its state. He looks at students or other Steve agents while waiting for them, listening or talking with them. He is also able to visually track a student when he or she is moving in the virtual environment.

Nonverbal Feedback

An essential role of a real tutor is to provide verbal and non verbal feedback on student performances. An animated agent, who simulates a tutor, can also use body language to communicate with the student. Steve shows he is in agreement with a student by a nod of approval or shakes his head to communicate disapproval.

Virtual Teams

In 3-D virtual environments, it is useful to have more than one animated agent because they can substitute the missing members of a team. This allows learners to participate in working groups even if some human trainers or colleagues are missing.

Steve supports this kind of feature where different Steve agents and students can participate

Figure 1. Steve in action in the ship engine room

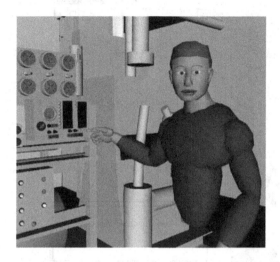

in a working team, where each one is assigned a specific role. Each person sees the other participants with a head and two hands in the virtual environment and is able to represent him or herself with a desired look. In order to avoid confusion, the agents have a distinguishable look, clothes and even a different tone of voice. Moreover, each Steve agent not only has a total internal representation of his tasks but also a representation of other agent tasks. This implies that Steve agents are able to coordinate their tasks both spatially and chronologically in order to successfully complete their assignment in the working group.

Agent Adele

Unlike Steve, the intelligent agent Adele (Agent For Distance Education – Light Edition) was realized in order to be installed on traditional computers with standard interfaces. The reason behind this was so the agent could be distributed more easily and to demonstrate the actual applicability of pedagogical agent technologies, also concerning projects with commercial aims and with smaller development budgets.

Adele is designed to run within the web browser of the trainee's computer and provides educational materials via web. The Adele agent was used to train general practitioners and dentists specializing in curing the elderly.

The following sections will demonstrate the features of Adele, the methodology behind the agent, and examine its differences in respect to agent Steve.

Features

Figure 2 displays an example of the typical functionalities that the Adele agent can provide. The student is presented with a simulated patient in a clinical office visit setting. The student physician is able to perform a variety of actions on the simulated patient, such as asking questions about his or her medical history, performing a physical examination, ordering diagnostic tests, giving a diagnosis and making referrals. Adele monitors student actions together with the patient's state, and provides relative feedback.

If the student clicks a button in the simulation window, Adele turns her head and looks at that direction. She has a pointer that can be used to indicate objects situated in the different windows of the application, which as functionally developed to, in a sense, compensate for the lack of direct object manipulation like in Steve.

Similarities and Differences Compared to Steve

In spite of the differences in the design and the interfaces, Adele's functionalities are pretty similar to Steve's. Although Steve has been developed to support training on the job where Adele provides a more theoretical education offer to medical students, the style of learning and instruction conveyed by each agent, however, is quite similar, especially concerning the acquisition of new competences. For every clinical case, Adele is equipped by a plan that describes the kind of actions to be performed, the correlations between them and the motivations behind them.

Figure 2. Adele suggests to the student to study the subject further

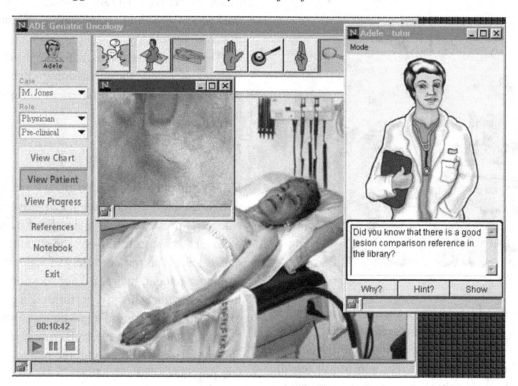

This feature allows Adele to provide hints and explain the actions to be conducted in a comparable way to Steve.

Moreover, Adele is supplied with some external features and training capacities that Steve does not offer. She has a repertoire of facial expressions and body postures that represent emotions, such as surprise and disappointment. This allows Adele to respond to students' actions in a more humanlike way. From a learning viewpoint, more educational pathways have been developed within Adele. Depending on student's actions, Adele may decide to intervene directly or give some advice on what to do e.g. " before ordering a chest X-rays, you should check the condition of the lesion". Or depending on the context and action sequence, Adele can present a pop up quiz asking the student to answer before carrying on, just to make sure that he or she understands the meaning of the data previously collected regarding the patient.

A More Accessible Pedagogical Agent

Adele is based on the autonomous agent paradigm instead of the tutoring intelligent system, this is why the agent shares many similar features to Steve. In the latter case, the distinction from a traditional tutoring system is evident because each Steve agent can operate in a dynamic environment together with the option to have a community of students and / or agents. Adele, therefore, has less interaction capabilities mainly due to its more traditional 2-D Interface. Nevertheless, the agent oriented approach has advantages, even with a more limited interface. For example Adele uses different gazes and gestures, is able to react to student actions and show a variety of facial expressions that gives the impression that she is self aware. Moreover, the agent-based approach made it relatively straightforward to extend Adele from a single-user system to a multi-user collaborative system.

Adele is an excellent example of a system based on pedagogical agents at a reasonable cost, especially compared to Steve. The Adele intelligent engine can easily be integrated into other educational applications with completely different contents which makes the system scalable, efficient and cheap. Moreover, the agent itself can be easily upgraded with new animations in order to enhance the gesture and facial expression repertoire.

Agent Arianna

The Arianna Agent was developed within the Parmenide project, funded by the European Commission, with the aim of building a novel educational and training environment for fire prevention based on intelligent agents. By realizing and testing the agent, the Parmenide project attempted to overcome some of the shortcomings of traditional educational and training programmes for fire prevention for transport staff that will be better explained in the following paragraphs (Mascitti et al. 2008).

The main idea behind this system was to develop an intelligent evaluation path that is of course a complement of the theoretical course provided by a standard E-learning platform.

The Workflow of the Application

During the pilot application each user is advised to carefully listen to all the instructions given by the virtual tutor, who reads a question and the possible answers that are also visually displayed simultaneously by the system. When Arianna has finished reading the question and the possible answers, the user can answer by double-clicking on one of the proposed icons which represents one of the possible answers.

An hourglass will appear, signaling the passing of time and amount of time remaining for the user to answer. Once the question is answered, the virtual tutor will give verbal and non verbal

feedback on the users' response. When giving feedback the virtual tutor will also consider the user's performance on previous answers.

The system will also show the score of each answered question, ranging from very negative to very positive. The user will then have the option to listen to a short didactic pill, relating to the question topic that will explain the correct answer and why the other possible answers are incorrect. If the user answers correctly, he or she should skip the pill. The system will also provide theoretical references to the course subject, allowing the student to immediately find more information on the question topic for further study.

The application ends with the tutor says the user's test results verbally and, then if necessary, gives some advice and suggestions for improvement or further study.

Intelligent Evaluation Paths

Parmenide's proposed didactic model was also developed based on the concept of "emotional learning", which offers learners engaging scenarios with a strong visual stimulus impact through very detailed graphics. The pilot application starts by choosing an important question randomly from the dataset. The application begins with an important question just like in a real exam when a teacher wants to verify if the student is comfortable with the principal topics.

By answering questions, the student acquires a certain level of knowledge depth which measures the degree of the user's knowledge regarding the subject matter, in this case, fire prevention and security. The system defines the user's learning path (total number and type of question) based on the level of his or her knowledge depth. Depending on the quality of the user's answer, the system provides another significant question (if the minimum level of knowledge depth has not already been reached) or any other question.

Arianna behaves like a real teacher who starts to assess students by asking important questions and

Figure 3. Arianna's working space

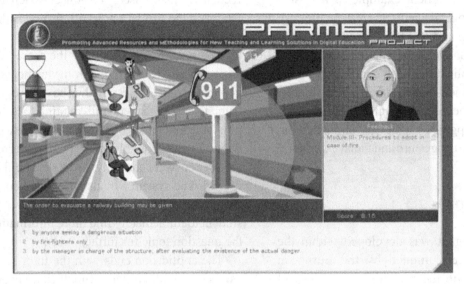

then, depending on the quality of their response, will either formulate more important questions or not. During an examination, a teacher will often ask a student only a few questions if he or she consistently provides satisfactory answers. A similar situation happens during the pilot application, where the student has to answer only a few questions if he or she reaches a good knowledge depth level (ultimately depending on the quality of his or her answers).

The Virtual Teacher's Mind

3 Fuzzy Logic inference systems were implemented to make the Arianna's behavior and the entire system appears more realistic. Fuzzy logic manages reasoning that is approximate rather than precisely deduced from classical predicate logic. Fuzzy logic is used in complex systems often found in the real world (Zadeh 1976). To deal with such complex systems, human beings use approximate, but flexible reasoning. Fuzzy Logic, with its linguistic rules, simulates such human behaviors and translates human natural language syntax into an artificial language suitable for computers.

The First Fuzzy inference engine defines a learning path which depends on the following inputs: importance of the question, difficulty of the question, quickness of the user's response and correct / incorrect answer. These inputs will ultimately infer the user's knowledge depth. The two inputs, importance and difficulty were mentioned earlier. The third input, the quickness of the user's response, is assessed based on the idea that the quicker the student answers a question "correctly", the more the answer will be evaluated as satisfactory. If the student takes more than the maximum time allowed to answer a question, the system will automatically consider the answer wrong, regardless of the answer. The fourth input correct or incorrect answer is self explanatory.

The Second Fuzzy inference engine provides the user's score after each answered question. The inputs are the same as those described in the first FIS, but have different linguistic rules.

The Third Fuzzy inference engine defines the verbal and non verbal tutor behavior which depends on the following inputs:

- The user's Knowledge Depth level if he or she has answered the question correctly or the score if he or she has answered incorrectly.

- Cumulative score (which also depends on previous answers)
- Correct / incorrect answer

From these inputs, the virtual tutor is able to provide verbal and non verbal behaviors (facial expressions).

Verbal and Facial Expressions

More than 100 verbal feedback expressions are stored in the database offering a wide range of response behaviors from very sad to very positive. If the user has answered an important question incorrectly, for example, Arianna will choose a message that will include specific information. In this case a possible feedback message is: This topic is very important, but maybe it is not quite clear yet. What about going back to it? The tutor is able to provide 11 different facial expressions from very worried or sad to very happy. The tutor always shows a neutral expression when reading questions and providing the didactic pills. In the pilot application, the developers tried to avoid any virtual tutor behaviors that can be classified as "unstable" or from a human being viewpoint as "hysterical". This is why the user's performance will be assessed collectively encompassing all answered questions and not just individual ones. In order to achieve this, the user's cumulative score is considered as an input in the third fuzzy engine. For example, if the user has answered two important questions correctly and quickly, but incorrectly to a third question, the tutor will provide a mild negative feedback, both verbal and non verbal, for this last question because it "remembers" the user's good performance regarding the previous important questions.

Agent Clara

The CoachBot project, funded by the European Commission, aims at designing and testing an innovative E-learning methodology for adult education that combines Conversational Agent Technology (chatbot) with an ad hoc designed modular learning path. The pilot e-course addresses a target group of home health care professionals (e.g. medical staff, nurses, etc). The project's innovation consists of the development of a collaborative E-learning environment featuring a "chatbot" or "Virtual Assistant" who interacts with users through a human-like interface. The "Virtual Assistant" acts as a teacher or coach who supports learners "individually" during the modular e-course by providing in-depth information, assessment, case studies, role playing and technical support. The e-course curriculum is based on a personalised approach allowing learners, with help from the Clara agent, to customize their own training path and choose suitable training contents that are relevant to their profession and based on their own specific needs, knowledge and skill requirements.

Clara can be considered as a complete student assistant within an open source E-learning platform and could be easily transplanted from one platform to another.

The virtual agent's main semantic structure is described by the following graph.

All these sections are embedded in the same virtual assistant, so the user does not perceive this segmentation in the dialogue software. Each area is then structured into sub areas that relate to the virtual assistant's different tasks and the course contents it will cover.

Guidance interview

The guidance interview can be considered the first contact between the conversational agent and the student. The user begins to become more familiar with the virtual agent who starts a friendly con-

Figure 4. Virtual agent's conceptual map

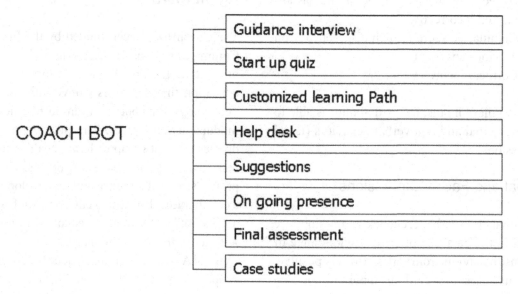

COACH BOT
- Guidance interview
- Start up quiz
- Customized learning Path
- Help desk
- Suggestions
- On going presence
- Final assessment
- Case studies

versation in order to create a sort of empathetic relationship.

The final goal is therefore, to define a professional profile and consequently a learning path that best fits the student's needs.

The conversational agent also asks more general questions concerning the student's expectations and his or her professional ambitions and, in this sense, Clara behaves more like a mentor who tries to understand the user's emotional thoughts and feelings.

Start up Quizzes

After the guidance interview that defines the student's professional profile and consequently his or her learning path, the student is allowed to access the exercise area of the E-learning platform. The system presents the user with as many quizzes as the number of modules foreseen for his or her learning path. These exercises are considered as start up quizzes in order to test the initial knowledge of the student concerning topics presented in the course.

The virtual agent will present the quizzes, their meaning and will comment the results. From the

students' viewpoint, Clara behaves like a teacher who tests their knowledge and assigns the compulsory learning objects to be studied.

Learning Path

The student can find the course module list in the learning path area of the LMS. However, unlike the standard version of the LMS, only modules corresponding to start up quizzes already taken will be shown in the list. Within the module, learning objects are highlighted in two different colors depending if they are compulsory or optional. Also in this case, the standard tracking system has been enhanced in order to allow the virtual agent to memorize, for a particular user, what learning object is compulsory together with the number of times and the duration he or she studied a particular learning object.

This kind of information is useful for the virtual agent to invite a student, after a certain delay of time, to view compulsory learning object. In that sense, Clara is behaving like a tutor.

Help Desk

The goal of the Help Desk area is to provide the user a detailed help on the LMS functionalities or tools.

By using only natural language, the meaning of the different functionalities are well explained by the CoachBot when a student asks for help. This user-friendliness allows learners to concentrate only on learning course contents and allows users who are not experts in using a PC and/or learning management systems (e.g. the elderly or first time users) to effectively use the system.

Clara behaves in this case as a technical tutor.

Suggestions

The virtual agent is able to help the user regarding specific topics featured in the course. The virtual agent area related to course content is called Suggestions. This virtual agent area can be seen as an interactive glossary or a "quick answer teacher" but does not have to substitute the main learning sources that are, and remain, the learning objects. When the user wants more information and deepening, the virtual agent will address her/him to the learning object that talks about the requested content.

Ongoing Presence

In order to keep learners motivated, the CoachBot interacts with each learner throughout the entire course in different ways, providing ongoing verbal feedback concerning their progress. Learners can therefore receive positive feedback when they are proceeding well with the course or be advised if they are studying too slowly or miss some fundamental lessons.

Final Assessment

The aim of the final assessment is to check the student's learning progress after the e-course with the virtual agent's assistance. Ideally, the student should have better results than in the start up quizzes due to the learning objects provided by the e-course. The virtual agent will present the quizzes, provide explanations and comment the student's results.

FUTURE TRENDS

The two main interest areas to focus on in terms of the development of research in the pedagogical intelligent agent field in the future are mobile learning and virtual learning.

Mobile-learning is distance learning through mobile devices that allow users to choose where and when they wish to learn, thanks to their portable feature.

Ally et al (2005) recommends using an intelligent agent for adapting and delivering course materials to mobile devices.

"The m-learning system must be proactive, anticipating what the learner will do next and providing the most appropriate interface for the interaction to enhance motivation and learning".

According to Desmond Keegan (Keegan 2005):

"The mobile-learning system rather than presenting all of the available materials to learners, intelligent systems must be built to develop an initial profile of the learner and present materials that will benefit the specific learner. As the learning system interacts with the learners, it 'learns' about each student and adapts the interface and navigation pattern according to that learner's style and needs".

Another important area to explore is virtual worlds, for example the most renown is Second Life by Linden Lab. Users are represented in the virtual world by their alter ego in the form of an avatar. Different courses have already been developed and adapted into virtual classes where students attend the class at a certain time and place in the virtual world that is conducted by a real teacher who is represented by his/her avatar. In this case, it would be interesting if the teacher was actually a pedagogical intelligent agent that would always be present and available for students independently of when the real teacher was available or online.

CONCLUSION

Various studies have been undertaken in order to measure the effects of Agents on learners. Previous experience revealed that the mere presence of an agent sometimes increases enjoyment. Berry, Butler, and DeRosis (2005) compared the effects of the intervene of animated agent, GRETA, who delivered information about healthful eating to the effects of the same information delivered in plain text or read by a human actor. Results demonstrated that GRETA was rated as more helpful than voice or text only. However, this effect has not been confirmed by other research; for examples, in some case the users have explained that a non-agent activity is more entertaining and enjoyable than the same activity with an agent (Den & van Mulken, 2000).

Similarly, agents may have effects on learning, although these effects are not entirely understood. Some researchers argue that the presence of an agent promotes a higher engagement, which consequently implies users' retention of more contents (Lester & Stone, 1997). Other researchers claim that the agent usually distracts the learner from the course contents, and that simpler instructional design features can accomplish the same goals than an agent is.

The two dialectic positions are accompanied by a diverse and more moderated view on the matter which suggests that the effects of agents are not universal, but depend on the specific features of the agent within a learning environment (Kim & Baylor, 2005). In accordance with this view, researchers have gone over the simple comparison between training with agents and training without, they prefer exploring which specific characteristics may contribute to advance pedagogical agents' effectiveness.

Moreover it is important to acknowledge that in order to successfully design, develop and implement one or more pedagogical intelligent agents in a learning environment ample time and a vast amount of resources, both human and financial are required. This is especially true regarding the prototypic phase. It is therefore crucial to first conduct a cost-benefit analysis to help better evaluate if the work and efforts required to develop an intelligent agent is actually worthwhile and beneficial. It is very difficult to truly define general rules to determine the value and how useful pedagogical intelligent agents are for training organizations, considering that specific training needs and requirements can vary greatly based on different factors and situations. The best possible solution for training organizations whose training needs are not too specific that they require ad hoc development or do not have the resources needed to design and develop complex applications, could be, therefore, to purchase set applications developed by a third party,

This chapter provides merely a brief overview of intelligent agents in education rather than in exhaustive detail. Nevertheless, in spite of some issues mentioned above, it does clarify how well built pedagogical intelligent agents can significantly add value to an E-learning platform, supporting learners more effectively throughout their learning process by providing them with an interface to interact with that will motivate and assist them during the course. In addition, the presence of the agent helps make the course more interesting, engaging and fun, which in turn ultimately enhances and improves the student's overall learning experience.

REFERENCES

Ally, M. (2005, October). An intelligent agent for adapting and delivering electronic course materials to mobile learners. In Proceedings of Mlearn 2005 conference, Cape Town, South Africa.

Baldwin, J. F. (1981). Fuzzy logic and fuzzy reasoning . In Mamdani, E. H., & Gaines, B. R. (Eds.), *Fuzzy Reasoning and Its Applications*. London: Academic Press.

Berry, D. C., Butler, L. T., & DeRosis, F. (2005). Evaluating a realistic agent in an advice-giving task. *International Journal of Human-Computer Studies*, *63*, 304–327. doi:10.1016/j.ijhcs.2005.03.006

Brustoloni, J. C. (1991). *Autonomous Agents: Characterization and Requirement*. Carnegie Mellon Technical Report CMU-CS-91-204. Pittsburgh: Carnegie Mellon University.

Craig, S. D., Gholson, B., & Driscoll, D. (2003). Animated Pedagogical Agents in Multimedia Educational Environments: Effects of Agent Properties, Picture Features, and Redundancy. *Journal of Educational Psychology*, *94*, 95–102.

Johnson, W. L., Lewis, W., & Rickel, J. (2000). Animated Pedagogical Agents: Face-to-Face Interaction in Interactive Learning Environments. *International Journal of Artificial Intelligence in Education*, *11*, 47–78.

Johnson, W. L., & Rickel, J. (1998). Steve: An animated pedagogical agent for procedural training in virtual environments. *SIGART Bulletin, 8*, 16–21. doi:10.1145/272874.272877

Johnson, W. L., Rickel, J., Stiles, R., & Munro, A. (1998). Integrating pedagogical agents into virtual environments. *Presence (Cambridge, Mass.), 7*, 523–546. doi:10.1162/105474698565929

Lepper, M. R., & Chabay, R. W. (1985). Intrinsic motivation and instruction: Conflicting views on the role of motivational processes in computer-based education. *Educational Psychologist*, *20*, 217–230. doi:10.1207/s15326985ep2004_6

Lester, J. C., Converse, S. A., Kahler, S. E., Barlow, S. T., Stone, B. A., & Bhogal, R. S. (1997). The persona effect: Affective impact of animated pedagogical agents. In *Proceedings of CHI '97* (pp. 359-366).

Lester, J. C., Converse, S. A., Stone, B. A., Kahler, S. E., & Barlow, S. T. (1997). Animated pedagogical agents and problem-solving effectiveness: A large-scale empirical evaluation. In *Proceedings of the Eighth World Conference on Artificial Intelligence in Education,* (pp. 23-30). Amsterdam: IOS Press.

Lester, J. C., Stone, B. A., & Stelling, G. D. (1999). Lifelike pedagogical agents for mixed-initiative problem solving in constructivist learning environments. *User Modeling and User-Adapted Interaction*, *9*, 1–44. doi:10.1023/A:1008374607830

Lester, J. C., Voerman, J. L., Towns, S. G., & Callaway, C. B. (1999). Deictic believability: Coordinating gesture, locomotion, and speech in lifelike pedagogical agents. *Applied Artificial Intelligence*, *13*, 383–414. doi:10.1080/088395199117324

Maes, P. (1990). *Designing Autonomous Agents*. Cambridge, MA: MIT Press.

Magoulas, G. D., Papanikolaou, K. A., & Grigoriadou, M. (2001). Neuro-fuzzy Synergism for Planning the Content in a Web-based Course. *Journal of Informatrics*, *25*, 39–48.

Müller, J. P. (1996). *The Design of Intelligent Agents: A Layered Approach*. Berlin: Springer-Verlag.

Nedic, Z., & Nedic, V., & Machotka, J. (2002). Intelligent tutoring System for teaching 1st year engineering. *World Transaction on Engineering and Technology Education, 1*(2).

Nijholt, A. (2004). Where computers disappear, virtual humans appear. *Computers & Graphics, 28*, 467–476. doi:10.1016/j.cag.2004.04.002

Roda, C., Angehrn, A. A., & Nabeth, T. (2001). Applications and Research . In *BotShow 2001*. Paris, France: Conversational Agents for Advanced Learning.

Russell, S. J., & Norvig, P. (1995). *Artificial Intelligence: A Modern Approach*. Englewood Cliffs, NJ: Prentice Hall.

Sampson, D., Karagiannidis, C., & Kinshuk, K. (2002). Personalised learning: educational, technological and standardisation perspective. *Interactive Educational Multimedia, 4*, 24–39.

Shaw, E., Ganeshan, R., Johnson, W. L., & Millar, D. (1999). Building a case for agent-assisted learning as a catalyst for curriculum reform in medical education. In *Proceedings of the Ninth International Conference on Artificial Intelligence in Education*. Amsterdam: IOS Press.

Smith, T., Affleck, G., Lees, B., & Branki, C. (1999). Implementing a generic framework for a web based pedagogical agent. In *ASCILITE99 Conference Proceedings*.

Zadeh, L. (1976). A fuzzy-algorithmic approach to the definition of complex or imprecise concepts. *International Journal of Man-Machine Studies, 8*, 249–291. doi:10.1016/S0020-7373(76)80001-6

Zheleva, M. M., Zhelev, Y., & Mascitti, I. (2008). E-learning, E-Practising and E-Tutoring: an integrated approach. In International Book Series (Ed.), Methodologies and Tools of the Modern (e-) Learning, (pp.84-90).

KEY TERMS AND DEFINITIONS

Artificial Intelligence: Artificial Intelligence generally enables a computer to carry out the typical functions and reasoning related to the human mind. Its essential feature is to comprehend the theory and techniques that are needed in order to develop algorithms that allow computers (typically calculators) to demonstrate the ability and or intelligent activity, in specific environments. One of the main issues and challenges concerning artificial intelligence is to formally define synthetic/abstract systems of reasoning, meta-reasoning and the human learning process, in order to develop computational models that can successfully realize and implement these functions.

Conversational Agent: An autonomous conversational agent is an agent that dialogues according to a specific context and the user's profile. In addition, it follows the rules of face to face interaction which is credible; referring to being capable of expressing emotions and conveying a personality and is multimodal; providing the user with multiple modes of interfacing, not only written, but also using a voice, gestures, posture, facial expressions and glances.

E-Learning: E-learning refers to the concept and possibility of learning using the Internet network and multimedia technologies to transmit information remotely or enabling "distance learning". E-learning is not only limited to school education, but also addresses adult learners, university students, teachers, etc, and is ideal for professional business training, especially for companies with multiple office branches.

Intelligent Agents: An agent is defined as something that is capable of perceiving and understanding its surrounding environment through sensors and by performing actions through actuators. An intelligent or rational agent is a fundamental concept of the artificial intelligence field and can be defined very generically as "something that does the right thing at the right time".

LMS: A Learning Management System (LMS) is software for delivering, tracking and managing training. Most LMSs are web-based to facilitate 'anytime, any place, any pace' access to learning content and administration.

M-Learning: M-learning is the acronym of mobile learning which is learning with the aid of mobile devices such as smartphones, PDAs, digital audio players, voce recorders, pen scanners, etc.

Pedagogical Agents: A special type of intelligent agent is an actual virtual tutor that is available to support students throughout their learning process within a Learning Management System (LMS).

Chapter 19
Blueprint for a Mashup:
Corporate Education in Moodle, Sloodle and Second Life

Anna Peachey
Eygus Ltd, UK

Daniel Livingstone
University of the West of Scotland, UK

Sarah Walshe
Open University, UK

ABSTRACT

In 2005 the Centre for Professional Learning and Development at the Open University (OU) established a pioneering collaboration with Reuters (which in 2008 became Thomson Reuters), working together on The Management Challenge Online (TMCO), a 10-week cohort-based course for First Line Managers. The course is currently delivered in the open source Moodle environment using Flash learning modules, to a model that encourages and supports collaborative participation and deep learning for delegates. This chapter will begin with an introduction to TMCO, providing some context and background to its development, structure and delegate groups. This has been described in detail elsewhere, see Peachey & Walshe (2008), where it was identified that "a Second Life activity programme element for TMCO would offer additional engagement potential for a significant number of participants." The chapter will describe the virtual world Second Life and the course management integration system Sloodle before exploring the motivation and structure for integrating these new tools into the next evolution of TMCO. The chapter will propose an adaptation of an evaluation framework originally proposed by de Freitas & Oliver (2006), creating a tool for evaluating the introduction of virtual world technology into a work based training curriculum, and will outline the proposed Second Life/Moodle/Sloodle activity for TMCO in some detail.

DOI: 10.4018/978-1-61520-619-3.ch019

INTRODUCTION AND BACKGROUND TO TMCO

TMCO was established in partnership between The Open University and Reuters in 2005 in response to a demand for focused, repeatable and adaptable professional development for the First Line Managers that provide the organisational interface between middle/senior managers and frontline staff and customers. These line managers, with a variety of experience and service vested in the company, face considerable challenges managing the needs of many stakeholders, often in circumstances where time and other resources are limited. Their pivotal role in the system requires them to work across a global organisation with all the inherent challenge that implies, and significant emphasis is placed on supporting their professional development in ways that are both meaningful and flexible.

Many models of distance learning conform to an instructional, isolationist model where there is a central focus on the delivery of knowledge from the teacher (expert) to the student (novice), either directly or as mediated through instructional learning material. This form of learning is predicated upon 'facts', making it easy to assess at a distance through automated summative assessment such as multiple choice quizzes and computer marked assignments (CMAs). As noted in Peachey and Walshe (2008), this model is currently employed by The Open University in its regular undergraduate courses, where course material is delivered online and increasingly assessed through the use of CMAs, but blended with tutor support to facilitate the student's self-directed learning and to mark and provide feedback on electronically submitted tutor marked assignments (eTMAs). Despite efforts to engage students with critical analysis and 'knowledge age skills', there remains a tendency for eTMA assessment to advantage information description over ways of thinking and doing, primarily due to the scale of provision

that drives a need for consistency across multiple tutorial groups.

The Centre For Professional Learning And Development (CPLD) provides a commercial facility from within the OU, catering to professional development needs by offering a bespoke service to create and deliver flexible, accessible and personalised learning that can be tailored to the needs of the participant's immediate workplace setting. TMCO was designed and evolved according to pedagogies of social constructivism, see Vygotsky (1934) and later in this chapter, and experiential learning, see Kolb & Fry (1974), providing participants with learning material, enabling them towards the construction of understanding from that material and the application of that understanding in practical experimentation and active workplace experience, and encouraging them to reflect on that experience within the Virtual Learning Environment (VLE). Kolb & Fry (1974) proposed that experiential learning is a cycle of abstract conceptualisation, active experimentation, concrete experience and reflective observation and that a learner may join the cycle at any point – the structure of TMCO strives to recognise the experience that participants bring to the course and to enable them to share that experience constructively. The course has evolved over its lifetime as the course team have incorporated a move from Teletop, the original VLE, into Moodle, and have adapted the course according to the manner in which participants are seen to be gaining most benefit. The pedagogy and evolution is described in detail in Peachey & Walshe (2008) but for the purposes of this chapter we are describing the course as it stands today.

The ten week online Management Challenge begins for a cohort in the week that immediately follows their participation in a three day residential workshop, facilitated by Development Dimensions International (DDI), a third partner. The cohorts of up to 30 participants are loosely grouped by area as EMEA, Americas and Asia, but within that grouping they may be widely

Figure 1. Discussion in moodle

geographically distributed and many continue to move between countries following news stories over the duration of a course.

The TMCO schedule comprises six bespoke, interactive learning modules and nine discussion forums, all delivered within the Moodle VLE. The learning modules, derived from Open University postgraduate management material, cover topics such as Knowing Your Team, Delegating, Recognising Difference and Managing Complexity. The discussion forums support various collaborative activities aimed at drawing out best practice in the workplace. Specifically, for example, the first three forums that correspond to learning modules are designed according to a 'Swap Shop' paradigm, where participants are asked to pose an issue that they need help with in their own immediate workplace and, in return, to respond to another posting with support and advice – see Figure 1: Discussion in Moodle. Alongside the online work, participants are provided with a development tool that personalises their course assignment, enabling them to create a series of work-based

tasks that are based on needs identified in their immediate working environment and to draw on TMCO learning to support and reflect on their execution of these tasks - the Swap Shop topics are drawn on for this End of Course Assignment (ECA). Participants are also supported via email, through teleconferences and by assignment feedback from a coach. The coach will engage with participants individually by email if necessary, but the main role is to guide and facilitate the group to learn from the material and from each other. The coach sends out a group email at the beginning of each week with a summary of the tasks for that week and any appropriate reminders, and will also check the participation records in the VLE and contact anyone who has not been active for more than 10 days. Where appropriate the coach will respond to postings in the forums, but with a focus on encouraging interaction rather than didactic response.

Participants who complete the minimum participation requirements for the course (it is not enough simply to have 'attended'), and who submit a completed ECA in the final week, are recognised by the company as TMCO Graduates and will attend a small local graduation ceremony to mark their achievement.

BACKGROUND TO SECOND LIFE AND SLOODLE

Second Life is a popular 3D virtual world featuring extensive opportunities for dynamic content creation and sharing. The content development tools and scripting languages are sufficiently powerful to allow users to create a richly detailed interactive environment and even to embed their own games in the 3D world (Rymaszewski et al., 2007). Free client software, available for a range of platforms, means that the initial costs of exploring and experimenting with the 3D platform are low, and this along with the freedom to create content has encouraged its use not just for entertainment, but also for a wide variety of educational applications and uses. Second Life can be used quite simply as an enhanced and embodied 'chat room', allowing different users to meet virtually to collaborate, socialise or attend seminars. While such basic objectives can also be achieved with a wide range of other solutions, meeting in the 3D space provides an enhanced sense of presence and is found by many users to be more engaging. Linden Research (2009) reports on this specifically with regard to corporate seminars and conferences held by IBM, and there is a long history of more academic research on 'presence'. Alternatively, more structured learning experiences can also be developed - from simple 3D models to complete immersive simulations. Healthcare and medical training has been one particularly productive and active area in this regard (c.f. Yellowlees & Cook, 2006; Taylor et al. 2009).

A series of reports published by the Eduserv Foundation (Kirriemuir, 2007, 2008, 2009) illustrate the rapid growth in use of Second Life and (to a lesser degree) other virtual worlds in higher and further education in the UK - with the most recent report stating that it now appears that almost all higher education institutions are engaged in some form of virtual world teaching, research or preparation. This growth is mirrored internationally, with endeavours also spreading to other education sectors. With much of the activity driven from the grassroots now increasingly receiving institutional support, use of virtual worlds in formal education settings is set to continue to grow over the coming years (Kelton, 2008).

In the corporate space, the potential of virtual worlds for training and enhancing internal and external communications has been noted in reports by Forrester and IBM amongst others. In 2007, an IBM report (IBM, 2007) considered the role and example of massively-multiplayer online games, such as World of Warcraft, in developing leadership skills, but did not consider the use of such worlds in a business setting. The same year, a Forrester report on virtual worlds (Jackson et al, 2007) warns business strategy leaders to be realistic about short term benefits, but recommends that they start building frameworks for assessing potential business value. Less than a year later, a subsequent report (Driver, 2008) argues that within five years virtual worlds will be as important as the internet for work, noting the rapid growth of virtual worlds as real business tools with potential to reduce costs and improve the work experience. More recently yet, a case study co-authored by Linden Lab, makers of Second Life, and IBM outlines the significant return on investment (ROI) gained from using Second Life to organise and host a global conference for IBM staff (Linden Research, 2009). The report notes that the virtual conference provided many of the benefits that meeting in a traditional conference has over simply video-conferencing a number of presentations, and notes the greater social nature and sense of presence in a virtual world.

In fact, virtual worlds have been used in workplaces to support socialisation and as a platform for delivering training for longer than most people suspect (see, for example, Churchill & Bly, 1999), but it is clear that such use is only now emerging from the fringes, driven by the popularity and flexibility of the likes of Second Life. There are still a number of issues which can limit the acceptance of virtual worlds in the workplace, however. Setting up an environment can be a challenge for those lacking experience, and basic tasks such as navigating the 3D environment and communicating with others can be difficult for the un-initiated, although this is likely to become less of an issue over the coming years (Driver, 2008). A quite separate challenge is that posed by the lack of integration between the 3D training environment and existing web-based systems for supporting training and communication across the enterprise. Whilst effective for a range of role-play activities and simulations, virtual worlds are distinctly lacking at handling long form documents, or providing tools for tracking learner progress, conducting assessment and measuring student performance against learning outcomes. Conversely, these are some of the areas where web-based learning management systems (LMS) such as Moodle, Blackboard, Angel Learning or Desire2Learn excel, and are widely used in both formal education, government and corporate training contexts.

These factors helped motivate the development of SLOODLE - the Simulation-Linked Object Oriented Dynamic Learning Environment - a plugin for the popular open-source Moodle LMS which provides integration with, and teacher and student tools for, Second Life (Kemp & Livingstone, 2006). An alternative, and complementary, description is that SLOODLE is a plugin for Second Life which provides access to a Moodle backend for learner and teacher support.

SLOODLE provides a range of tools and features intended to support teaching and learning in Second Life. Some features are administrative in nature – such as providing a means for identity authentication between the web and 3D environments – matching the online identities of users who will typically have differing user names on the two systems. A virtual drop-box allows students in the virtual world to submit their own digital models and 3D creations and creates corresponding gradebook entries in Moodle recording submission details and allowing facilitators to grade work in the same web-based environment used for other parts of a course.

Other tools aim to support common teaching tasks. A presenter tool simplifies the creation of visual presentations in Second Life, allowing tutors to use a custom Moodle page to easily create presentations which may mix images, web-content and videos that can then be 'streamed' into Second Life. Presentations may be part of some lecture or created as part of a self-paced immersive learning environment. Without the presenter tool, tutors need to manually prepare images for presentation, upload these into Second Life, and then manually add these to some other inworld tool – a lengthy and time consuming process. Simple typographic errors or content changes can result in a requirement to repeat all these tasks.

Remaining tools are more in-line with the underlying social-constructivist pedagogical philosophy of Moodle – supporting different means for student engagement, dialog and reflection. A web-intercom mirrors typed chat between Second Life and a Moodle chatroom. This helps make conversations in Second Life accessible to a wider audience and also allows Moodle to act as a repository for archived conversations. This allows students and facilitators to review dialogue, and has proven valuable for students needing a means to record group decisions, and for those (such as students learning a foreign language) who wish to take time to review and reflect on previous discussions. Finally, a toolbar provides means for enhancing virtual conversations with a range of common gestures and for recording reflections and notes direct from Second Life to their Moodle blog.

In a subsequent section we highlight a few of the SLOODLE tools, highlighting how some of the features it provides can be used to support TMCO. A side benefit of integration that is worth noting briefly is that it can also aid acceptance of the organisational use of virtual worlds - some users of SLOODLE report that as colleagues and students become aware that the 3D environment links to their LMS they accept that it is indeed more than 'just a game', and some barriers to the introduction of Second Life are lowered.

Proposed Structure and Pedagogy for bringing a Course such as TMCO to Second Life

In bringing an established, successful course such as TMCO into a virtual world it is imperative to identify the clear benefit to the participant, and to be certain that we are not 'doing it because we can'. This temptation is often recognised and cautioned against in the field of e-learning generally, for example Graham et al (2000) states 'Students must not feel that e-learning is just an afterthought tacked on, and therefore strong links with the subject aims must be evident'. Put simply, there must be a need before there is a solution. In this section we identify how the need in our case study was recognized and translated into pedagogy before the solution was found, creating a mashup model for the new course proposal.

The development of the course to date has done much to move away from repetitive training that meets an abstract conception of course delivery and instead work towards situating participant's learning in the domain of their practice, taking the theoretical notions from the learning modules and encouraging participants, where relevant, in shared problem-solving of real issues from the workplace. Comments from ECAs have reflected the positive value of this, and the swap shop style of learning in the first half of the course is now well established. However, participants from all three cohort regions have also consistently reflected through ECA comments and email and forum feedback that they would like to see more case

study work in the course, and more opportunity for the role-play that they have valued in the face to face workshops.

As the second half of the course sees an average drop-off in forum participation of up to 75% there is clearly room to change the means by which learning is supported across this area, so we have a scope and subject to be developed. The challenge then becomes how to combine role-play and case study, as the participant's preferred modes of learning, within the context and logistical restrictions of the course.

In pedagogical terms it is apparent that participants are looking for more opportunity to construct meaning from theory. The seminal research positions in this tradition come from Vygotsky's theory of social cognition (1934) and Piaget's developmental theory (1936).

The course team, recognising that social constructivism was already a successful pedagogy within TMCO, returned here to source the next development of the course. Social cognition theory emphasises the significance of societal context in learning, where meaning is socially produced and situationally interpreted. Vygotsky proposed that the ability to construct meaning through systematic organisation of information is initially culturally developed or imposed, but transfers structural organisation into personal meaning by a process that comes from an understanding of everyday concepts mediated by previous social and cultural development. He recognised these everyday, experiential concepts as *spontaneous* and those that are externally imposed through cultural development as non-spontaneous or *scientific*. Cognitive development therefore comes from a dialectical process of shared problem-solving as the learner passes through the Vygotskian zone of proximinal development - a state of transition from needing help to becoming independent in a task - assimilating the scientific into the spontaneous.

The challenge for TMCO is to create conditions where a participant's spontaneous concepts can encounter and ultimately become controlled

347

by the scientific concepts that the course seeks to impose, and to provide the structure for shared problem solving through tutor or peer support (known in the Vygotskian tradition as scaffolding). This practice is established in the swap shop element to the course, which is currently the most successful element, but to repeat the swap shop model in the second half loses freshness and may push participants beyond their willingness and/ or capacity to assist each other with this sort of direct solution. This solution would also ignore the calls for case study and role-play as favoured and familiar modes of learning, and the practice in interpersonal skills that role-play provides. Bailey & Butcher (1983) emphasised that effective interpersonal skills training should develop perceptual, cognitive, and behavioural skills components, and the requests for role-play highlighted an emerging need for greater interaction in the revised course. Simpson & Galbo (1986) define this as '...behaviour in which individuals and groups act upon each other. The essential characteristic is reciprocity in actions and responses in an infinite variety of relationships: verbal and nonverbal, conscious and non-conscious, enduring and casual. Interaction is seen as a continually emerging process, as communication in its most inclusive sense' (p. 38).

Moodle provides the capacity for collaborative work through applications such as the wiki or database, and the database has been adopted into the proposed course for resource building (see Table 2: Proposed Course), but there were no forthcoming solutions that met all the requirements by exploiting the VLE alone.

Laurillard (2002) poses that 'it is legitimate and necessary for teaching to go beyond the specific experience, to offer symbolic representation that allows the learner to use their knowledge in an unfamiliar situation.' Many recent studies have aligned social cognition with the emerging pedagogies of learning in virtual worlds and so the course team began looking towards this relatively new media for an innovative solution.

Second Life was the virtual world of choice as The Open University has an established presence in this environment and so financial investment both in research and direct costs would be kept to a minimum. The lead tutor on TMCO has worked with Open University student groups in Second Life since 2006 (see Bennett & Peachey, 2007), enabling a confidence and familiarity with both the advantages and disadvantages of facilitating learning in this complex setting, and supported the OU Human Resources department in a successful pilot study using inworld role-play for professional development within the university (see Peachey, Broadribb, Carter and Westrapp, 2009).

Second Life offered an obvious solution for the role-play, but as a stand-alone element work was needed to integrate it successfully into the existing course. A solution was proposed that exploited the mashup potential of SLOODLE to integrate Moodle and Second Life, and enabled the role-play to provide material for a case study to be met through a model of social cognition.

The course team's understanding of the course and participant pedagogy, and our experience with Second Life, has led to the changes proposed in Table 1: Course Review / Proposed Course. In order to demonstrate a thorough critical evaluation for this development, the course team looked for an evaluation framework that supported curricula development in virtual world contexts. In 2006 De Freitas & Oliver noted that, 'Currently when tutors are thinking of introducing games- and simulation-based learning into their practice, they are faced with several questions, for example:

Which game or simulation to select for the specific learning context?

Which pedagogic approaches to use to support learning outcomes and activities?

What is the validity of using the chosen game or simulation?'

They posed that at time of writing there was '[...] an over-reliance upon using available methods of evaluating leisure-based games (Kirriemuir & McFarlane, 2004)' leading to problems such

Table 1. Course Review/Proposed Course shows a scheduled review of the course by the lead tutor identifying several areas for change, creating the opportunity to draw in the suggestions for case study and role-play

Week	In Moodle	Reflections on existing course	Recommendations for change
0		Face to Face course, participants are shown screen-shots of Moodle	Face to Face course Participants to see machinima of Second Life, receive instructions for getting online. Resource activity has now become a database of useful resources that transfers from course to course, so any participant can add/access at any time
1	Common Room: Introductions	Difficult to find the balance between not overloading in first week (as with earlier version of course) but maintaining group focus on keeping momentum going and seeing this as continuum from face to face course.	Social event in Second Life to allow socialisation with environment and to provide synchronous point of focus for continuation of group working as cohort. Also provides early opportunity to link avatars to Moodle IDs (for Sloodle) and address any fear factor.
2	Knowing Your Team: Learning module Discussion forum: ECA swap shop	Weeks 2, 3 and 4 are the strongest element of the course at the moment with significant engagement and contribution from the majority of most cohorts.	No change
3	Delegating: Learning module Discussion forum: ECA swap shop		No change
4	Managing Key Relation-ships: Learning module Discussion forum: ECA swap shop		No change
5	ECA Introduction: Template and sample provided Time allowed for develop-ment	Networking calls Although the time in this week is allocated for working on part one of the ECA, many participants see it as a break and don't work on the ECA until the following week when prompted by individual reminders.	Networking calls Exchange forum brought forward into same week as ECA introduction to combat sense of 'week off'. Voting opened on choice for role play topics
6	ECA Exchange: Discussion forum: Exchange of development plans	Most work in this forum occurs during weeks 7 and 8	2 separate Second Life sessions (weeks 6 and 7 to allow flexibility in timing) where participants work in pairs to role-play one to one interviews. Interviews are streamed back into Moodle for reflection in weeks 7 and 8.
7	Recognising Difference: Learning module Discussion forum: Relate a learning outcome to personal experience	This is consistently the least used discussion forum, averaging just 3 or 4 postings during week 7. My requests for feedback indicate that participants find it a useful and relevant module so the issue is not with the module, but perhaps with the loss of momentum following the 'time out' period for working on the ECA. Current discussion – sharing experiences of difference – is clearly not sufficient to draw participants in.	
8	Projecting Yourself: Learning module Discussion forum: Resource gathering activity	Discussion forum for this module is currently a resource gathering exercise, attracting perhaps up to 8 postings in the closing weeks of the course. There continues to be value in sharing additional resources but propose moving this to an editable database within Moodle that runs concurrent to the course and can be accessed/added to at any time. The database can be copied from cohort to cohort and continue to build.	
9	Managing Complexity: Learning module Discussion forum:	Reflective discussion forum asking participants what they will take forward from the course.	

Table 1 continued

Week	In Moodle	Reflections on existing course	Recommendations for change
10	Submit ECA Discussion forum: feedback and farewells	Use of this forum varies considerably depending on the cohort. Any feedback provided usually reflects personal preference and is rarely valuable to the course. Participants often discuss routes for keeping in touch as a group without any significant conclusion.	Instead of feedback on course participants now asked for footprints to leave for next cohort. Participants informed about Facebook group – direct link to be provided in feedback email to those who have submitted ECA.

as 'a mismatch between methods and content, the use of inappropriate terminology and concepts, and the use of approaches not based upon evidence-based research.' De Freitas & Oliver acknowledged the existence of general recommendations about the design of games for learning (e.g, Amory & Seagram, 2003) but argued that these recommendations were not useful to the stakeholders and consumers who wanted to employ such games. They developed a contextual evaluation framework to support educators in evaluating the potential use of games and simulations in their practice, and to promote a critical approach to the use of games and simulations in an educational context. Their checklist is a very practical tool for educators in a school, college or

Table 2. Proposed framework for evaluating the use of virtual world technology in work based training

Context	Learner specification	Pedagogic consideration	Mode of representation (tools for use)	Costs
What are the geographical locations for learners? Will location affect ability to participate in synchronous activities (eg time difference, level of resources, accessibility, technical support) Will learners be given time to access at work or will they be expected to access from home? Does this context affect learning? (e.g. level of resources, accessibility, technical support) How can links be made/reinforced between the course and the workplace? How will the course be promoted to learners? Is participation mandatory?	Who is the learner (eg role within company, business unit etc)? What is their background and learning history? What are the learning styles/preferences? Who is the learner group? How can the learner or group be best supported? In what ways are the groups working together (e.g. singly, partially in groups) and what collaborative approaches could support this? What are the advantages to the learner in participating in the proposed activity/ activities? What are the risks to the learner in participating in the proposed activity/activities?	Which pedagogic models and approaches are being used? Which pedagogic models and approaches might be the most effective? What are the curricula objectives? What are the learning activities? How can the learning activities and outcomes be achieved through existing virtual world technology? How can the learning activities and outcomes be achieved through specially developed software? How can the learning activities and outcomes be integrated with any existing course provision, where relevant? How can briefing/debriefing be used to reinforce learning outcomes?	Which software tools or content would best support the learning activities? What level of fidelity needs to be used to support learning activities and outcomes? What level of immersion is needed to support learning outcomes? What level of realism is needed to achieve learning objectives? How can links be made between the virtual world and reflection upon learning? Can the virtual world be integrated with existing facilities? How can participation be tracked/captured/assessed? What are the security implications for working in this virtual world?	Will existing trainers/ coaches have requisite skills? What are the costs of training the trainers? Will external expertise be needed to set up learning activities, and will this expertise be needed for support on an ongoing basis? Can the training be established in a private space in a publically accessible virtual world, or is a bespoke environment required? What are the costs of establishing a presence in the virtual world? Can space be rented temporarily or is a permanent presence necessary? Do resources need to be purchased or created? Can these be re-used or repurposed from existing resources? What are the costs of establishing multiple user accounts? Will accounts be reused between groups, or should each learner have a new account?

Figure 2. Personalising the avatar

university setting who are considering the merits of embedding a games-based simulation into their curriculum. We have adapted the tool to make it relevant for evaluating the use of virtual world technology in work based training, and present this in Table 2:

A key addition made for this context is the fifth column, costs, which is often a primary consideration when evaluating the introduction of new technology for training and may be particularly difficult to approach for those who are considering a first foray into virtual worlds. We have also taken the opportunity to acknowledge the potential for greater variety in learning contexts in a commercial environment, for example in TMCO participants may be in any country/timezone in the world and may be accessing from work, from home, or from a laptop in the field via satellite connection. Using this adapted tool has enabled the team to apply an objective framework to evaluating the new course proposal and to confirm the validity of the move into virtual worlds.

STUDENT AS AVATAR

According to the proposal for the new course, participants would be allocated their avatar, watch a machinima[1] of some appropriate inworld activity and be talked through the process of the Second Life and Sloodle activity during a dedicated section of the face to face workshop, so that they are prepared for the socialisation activity in the first week of the online course. In this activity they will simply meet inworld and have the opportunity to practice working with an avatar, personalise it should they so wish, and reconnect with colleagues from the workshop. The provided avatars would be wearing generic business apparel, individualised sufficiently that no two avatars in the pool are matching.

The avatars would also have a small selection of clothes and accessories in each inventory, so that participants may personalise their outfits if they so choose, and the environment enables radical individualisation of each avatars bodily characteristics should users wish to experiment, or to reflect aspects of their own appearance – see Figure 2: Personalising the avatar.

Avatars would have names drawn from a variety of nationalities, reflecting the global range of participants, and there would always be sufficient available to enable the correct gender allocation. It is acknowledged that whilst some users view the avatar simply as a tool with which to augment reality, others need to feel engaged and have some sense of ownership of their virtual body in order to mediate comfortably through it. The proposed compromise of providing ready-to-go avatars yet enabling personalisation seeks to meet as many preferences as possible, and as a relatively innovative activity will be monitored closely with feedback sought from early participants.

Wenger (1998) noted, "We define who we are by where we have been and where we are going" (p. 149) and argued that learning has a significant and profound impact on personal identity, as identity is mediated and evolves through our experience of learning. The issue of identity management in virtual worlds is a rapidly emerging field with many complexities far beyond the scope of this chapter but it is clear that there is a necessary triangulation for TMCO participants to manage their developing identity as a learner with their online identity as mediated through the Moodle environment and their identity as an avatar in a virtual world. This should be given due consideration in course planning and management where associated risks should be identified and mitigated for, especially for example in briefing and debriefing from role play activities. Further reading on identity and issues for learners in virtual worlds may be sought with Yee (2006), Robbins (2006), Meadows (2008), Adrian (2008), Ball & Pearce (2008) and Peachey (2010). It is suggested that the subject of how the TMCO participants relate to their avatars and to the management of their identity throughout the course would provide rich scope for a research study independent of general course evaluation.

WORKING IN SECOND LIFE AND THE SLOODLE MASHUP

As noted in the timetable of activities in Table 1: Proposed Course, the proposed use of Second Life within TMCO focuses primarily on two role-play activities, selected from a list of role-play scenarios by the TMCO delegates themselves via an online vote. A number of role-play scenarios have been conceived, the following example is given for illustrative purposes:

John(/Jane) has previously been a happy, outgoing team player but in the last month has started coming in late and leaving early, has missed several key deadlines and seems unhappy and distracted. The team leader has called John in to discuss his behaviour.

If this scenario were then selected by the cohort then pairs of participants would be given the interview to work through, with one of each pair being asked to role play John(/Jane), the other acting as the team leader. A notecard provided

to the student taking on John's role provides the backstory, and different pairs would receive different stories, e.g.:

"You are John. Until recently you have been a productive member of the team, but last week you went for an interview elsewhere, didn't get the job and have been left feeling dissatisfied with your current role at Thomson Reuters"

"You are John. Until recently you have been a productive member of the team, but currently your mother-in-law is very ill and you are managing additional family commitments while your partner is away caring for her."

"You are John. Until recently you have been a productive member of the team, but a recent argument with a co-worker means that you now find it very uncomfortable to be around him in the office"

"You are John. Until recently you have been a productive member of the team, but you are currently concerned that another team worker is receiving more responsibility in delegated work and you haven't felt able to raise this."

The voting would be managed using one of the standard Moodle activities – the aptly named "Choice" activity. This activity, which provides a mechanism for conducting online polls and votes within Moodle is also accessible via Second Life using a corresponding SLOODLE choice tool (see Figure 3: Sloodle Course Choice Tool). This allows users to vote, and to preview the poll results in both Moodle and in Second Life. Providing these alternative interfaces to the poll creates an additional opportunity and introductory virtual world activity for delegates already familiar with Second Life and for those wishing to familiarise

Figure 3. Sloodle course choice tool

Request for increased line management support [2]

Delegation of boring/repetitive jobs [1]

Performance evaluation interview [3]

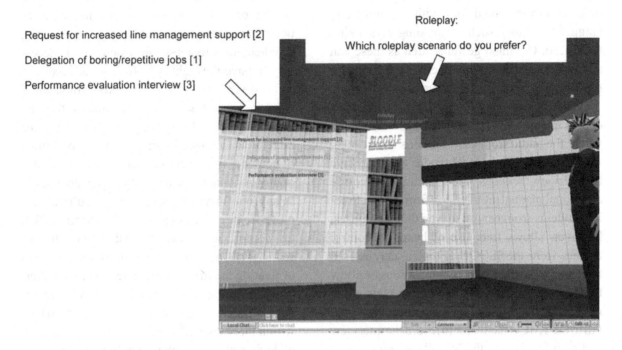

themselves with the 3D environment prior to the role-plays.

With pairs assigned, and suitably briefed, a prepared office setting in Second Life is then used for conducting the interview. There are two distinct communication modes that can be used for role-playing such meetings in Second Life. Integrated Voice-over-IP (VoIP) software allows users to talk to each other, and typed 'chat' communications also allow synchronous conversation. Despite the near universality of voice communications in Second Life, many users still prefer to use typed conversation. In a role-play scenario, especially where participants know each other, typed conversations help enforce a level of anonymity which may support immersion in the role-play. However spoken communication offers access to a wide range of voice cues, and allows more natural communication - especially where participants are slow typists.

Role-play in a virtual recreation of a real world setting, similar to this proposal, has been shown

to be effective in previous work, for example Hudson & Degast-Kennedy (2009). There are several ways in which such a role-play may benefit from integration with Moodle. If the role-play is conducted primarily using typed chat, then the SLOODLE web-intercom can be used to copy all chat to a Moodle chat-room, which can act as an archive of all such interviews. These can later be accessed via the Moodle web-interface and reviewed. The value here is that assessors then have a complete archive for review, allowing them to both grade and to highlight strengths and weaknesses. Students may review their own sessions for reflection. Previously, in a language learning setting, similar review was found to be useful - making typed conversation a valuable part of a course that also included VoIP enabled spoken conversations (Livingstone, Kemp and Edgar, 2008). Usefully, the archive on Moodle lists the student name as recorded on Moodle as well as the avatar name - ensuring that the anonymous avatar chat is correctly associated with the corresponding students. A SLOODLE toolbar can be used by students to provide additional conversational cues, with common body language gestures such as nodding or shaking their head. Common gestures such as these can add to a role-play but are otherwise difficult for users new to Second Life to perform.

When using voice communications, the intercom is unable to archive the dialogue. However, where the audio from such sessions is recorded, it is still possible to use Moodle as an archive of interview sessions, though this will require additional manual intervention from tutors. Freeing students from having to type their responses, however, allows freer use of hands to control avatars. Here, the SLOODLE toolbar may be used to enhance the student communications or allow them to record notes during the interview while remaining engaged in the virtual world. It would fall to the TMCO facilitator to record the interview audio and upload to the Moodle forum – either as simple file upload or using one of a number of audio plugins available for Moodle (such as Audio Recorder or Audioconference module).

Following the role-play in week 6 the facilitator would choose one or two of the role-play discussions for group review and discussion in weeks 7 and 8, with permission from the participants involved. Thus, the virtual world activities – using the SLOODLE tools as required to aid logging and/or to enrich the interactions – are embedded within the larger course context.

CONCLUSION

After critically evaluating the new course proposal, the next step is to pilot the course and to evaluate the participant experience. Evaluations of courses that engage technology often provide more evidence of the functionality of the hardware/software than of the student experience, and the TMCO course team are keen to maintain an appropriate focus in this next piece of work. Laurillard (1994) writes about how technologies can be used to improve learning and reflects on a number of evaluative studies on the implementation of new technology that have, she comments, 'predictable outcomes' - for example it is necessary to have the right specification of hardware and software, and to be sufficiently competent in using it. These findings are so common that she argues they should be regarded as replications rather than findings. Laurillard poses a multitude of potential influences on a student's experience of any given activity with any given technology at any one time, including social, cultural and professional aspects of persuasion, and argues that this complexity of context must be mitigated for so that it can be removed from the equation when evaluating the fundamental question of whether/how a learning technology is improving learning. She defines a number of causal relationships within these contexts, and then presents an array of logistical factors that enable a facilitator to manage as many aspects of the student experience as are within their control. If these conditions are applied with the development for TMCO, then the evaluation should provide a truer measure of the student's engagement with the activity rather than, for example, their misfortune with the technology or inadequate preparation.

TMCO is a successful and established course. It has an average first time completion rate of about 85-90%, which is high given the context and responsibilities of the participant groups. Nearly all who withdraw during their first attempt do so because of extraordinary work commitments taking priority, and are encouraged by their local training champion to come back and complete with a later cohort at a more convenient time. Qualitative reflections from TMCO graduates are generally positive, and cite the collaborative activities and the opportunity to learn from peers as highlights of the course, but note that role-play and case study would be valued as additional learning tools. By looking backwards at what has worked well, and by looking forwards at new opportunities, the course team have identified a restructuring of the course that has the potential to build on existing strengths and engage students more deeply with their learning in an exciting new environment. The team have recognised the danger of adding 'technology for technology's sake' and have strived to apply a critical process of evaluation to the new course proposal, creating a tool that can be applied across the platform for training in virtual worlds.

In the last few years, use of virtual worlds has expanded from niche into a rapidly increasing global commercial market. In 2006 the Open University was one of the first UK universities to have a presence in a virtual world; in 2009 there is only one university in the UK who does not have any form of activity taking place in such an environment. Where academia and front end research leads, the commercial world is quick to follow. Mahaley (2009) comments, 'As learning leaders continue developing people even as budgets are constrained, virtual worlds provide a new locus for learning – always there, as big as you need them to be and right at your fingertips'. We hope that readers will find our experience and reflections to be of practical value in their own circumstances, and will consider the merits of engaging with the huge potential for corporate training in virtual worlds.

REFERENCES

Adrian, A. (2008). No one knows you are a dog: Identity and reputation in virtual worlds. *Computer Law & Security Report, 24*(4), 366–374. doi:10.1016/j.clsr.2008.03.005

Amory, A., & Seagram, R. (2003). Educational game models: conceptualization and evaluation. *South African Journal of Higher Education, 17*(2), 206–217.

Bailey, C. T., & Butcher, D. J. (1983). Interpersonal Skills Training I: The Nature of Skill Acquisition and Its Implications for Training Design and Management. *Management Education and Development, 14*(1), 48–54.

Ball, S., & Pearce, R. (2008). Learning Scenarios and Workspaces with Virtual Worlds: Inclusion Benefits and Barriers of 'Once-Removed' Participation. In *Proceedings of Researching Learning in Virtual Environments, ReLIVE09,* (pp. 17-26), Milton Keynes, UK. Retrieved June 06, 2009 from www.open.ac.uk/relive08

Bennett, B., & Peachey, A. (2007). *Mashing the MUVE: A Mashup Model for Collaborative Learning in Multi-User Virtual Environments.* Paper presented at International Computer Aided Learning 2007, Austria: International Association of Online Engineering

Churchill, E. F., & Bly, S. (1999). Virtual Environments At Work: Ongoing Use Of MUDs In The Workplace. In *Proceedings Of The International Joint Conference On Work Activities Coordination And Collaboration,* (pp. 99-108). San Francisco: ACM.

de Freitas, S., & Oliver, M. (2006). How Can Exploratory Learning With Games And Simulations Within The Curriculum Be Most Effectively Evaluated? *Computers & Education, 46,* 249–263. doi:10.1016/j.compedu.2005.11.007

Driver, E., Jackson, P., Moore, C., Schooley, C., & Barnett, J. (2008). *Getting real work done in virtual worlds.* Los Angeles: Forrester.

Graham, D. McNeil, J. & Pettiford, L. (2000). Untangled Web: Developing Teaching on the Internet, (1st Ed.). London: Pearson Education Limited.

Hudson, K. & Degast-Kennedy. (2009). Canadian border simulation at Loyalist College. *Journal of Virtual Worlds Research, 2*(2).

IBM. (2007). *Virtual World: Real Leaders*. Retrieved June 02, 2009 from www.ibm.com/ibm.gio/media/pdf/ibm_gio_gaming_report.pdf

Jackson, P., de Lussanet, M., Driver, E., Schadler, T., & Menke, L. (2007). *The Real Business Of Virtual Worlds*. Los Angeles: Forrester. Retrieved March 08, 2009 from http://www.forrester.com/Research/Document/Excerpt/0,7211,40701,00.html

Kelton, A. J. (2008). Virtual Worlds? Outlook Good. *Educause Review, 43(5)*, 15-22. Retrieved June 02, 2009 from http://connect.educause.edu/Library/EDUCAUSE+Review/VirtualWorldsOutlookGood/47219

Kemp, J., & Livingstone, D. (2006). Putting a Second Life "Metaverse" Skin on Learning Management Systems. In Livingstone & Kemp (eds.), *Proceedings of the Second Life Education Workshop at SLCC*, San Francisco, August, (pp. 13-18). Retrieved March 08, 2009 from http://www.simteach.com/SLCC06/slcc2006-proceedings.pdf

Kirriemuir, J. (2007). [*"snapshot" of UK Higher and Further Education Developments in Second Life*. Bath, UK: Eduserv Foundation.]. *An update of the*, (July): 2007.

Kirriemuir, J. (2008). *An autumn 2008 "snapshot" of UK Higher and Further Education Developments in Second Life*. Bath, UK: Eduserv Foundation.

Kirriemuir, J. (2009). *The Spring 2009 Snapshot of Virtual World use in UK Higher and Further Education*. Bath, UK: Eduserv Foundation.

Kirriemuir, J., & McFarlane, A. (2004). *Literature review in games and learning. Report 8*. Bristol: Nesta Futurelab.

Kolb, D. A., & Fry, R. (1975). Toward an applied theory of experiential learning . In Cooper, C. (Ed.), *Theories of Group Process*. London: John Wiley.

Laurillard, D. (1994). How can learning technologies improve learning? *Law Technology Journal, 3*(2). Retrieved March 16, 2009 from http://web.archive.org/web/20070322002729/http://www.law.warwick.ac.uk/ltj/3-2j.html

Laurillard, D. (2002). *Rethinking University Teaching* (2nd ed.). London: Routledge Falmer. doi:10.4324/9780203304846

Linden Research, Inc. (2009). *Case Study: How Meeting In Second Life Transformed IBM's Technology Elite Into Virtual World Believers*. San Francisco: Linden Lab. Retrieved March 08, 2009 from http://secondlifegrid.net.s3.amazonaws.com/docs/Second_Life_Case_IBM.pdf

Livingstone, D., Kemp, J., & Edgar, E. (2008). From Multi-User Virtual Environment to 3D Virtual Learning Environment. *ALT-J. 16*(3), 139-150. Retrieved March 08, 2009 from http://www.informaworld.com/10.1080/09687760802526707

Mahaley, S. (2009). A Second Look at Second Life. *Chief Learning Officer, 8*(5), 20-27. Retrieved June 02, 2009 from http://www.clomedia.com/features/2009/May/2622/index.php?pt=a&aid=2622&start=0&page=1

Meadows, M. (2008). *I, Avatar: The Culture and Consequences of Having a Second Life*. Berkley, CA: New Riders.

Peachey, A. (2010). Living in Immaterial Worlds: Who are we when we learn and teach in virtual worlds? In Sheehy, K., Clough, G., & Ferguson, R. (Eds.), *Controversial Issues in Virtual Education: Perspectives on Virtual Worlds*. New York: Nova Science.

Peachey, A., Broadribb, S., Carter, C., & Westrapp, F. (2009). Second Life in The Open University: How the Virtual World Can Facilitate Learning for Students and Staff. In Wankel, C. (Eds.), *Higher Education in Second Life*. New York: Emerald.

Peachey, A., & Walshe, S. (2008). The Management Challenge Online: e-Learning in Practice. *International Journal of Advanced Corporate Learning, 1*(1).

Piaget, J. (1936). *The Origins of Intelligence in Children. M. Cook, (trans)*. Harmondsworth, UK: Penguin.

Robbins, S. (2006). "Image Slippage": Navigating the Dichotomies of an Academic Identity in a Non-academic Virtual World. In *Proceedings of the First Second Life Education Workshop, Part of the 2006 Second Life Community Convention*, August 18th-20th.

Rymaszewski, M., Au, W. J., Wallace, M., Winters, C., Ondrejka, C., & Batsone-Cunningham, B. (2007). *Second Life: The Official Guide*. Mahwah, NJ: John Wiley & Sons.

Simpson, R., & Galbo, J. (1986). Interaction and Learning: Theorizing on the Art of Teaching. *Interchange, 17*(4), 37–51. doi:10.1007/BF01807015

Taylor, D. I., Winter, R., Chan, M., Davies, R., Kinross, J., & Darzi, A. (2009, April 28-30). *Virtual Patient and Medical Device Simulation In Second Life: the Use Of Immersive Virtual Worlds For Learning and Patient Safety*. Paper presented at the MedBiquitous Annual Conference 2009, Baltimore.

Vygotsky, L. (1934). Thought and Language. Trans. & ed. A. Kozulin. Cambridge: MIT Press.

Yee, N. (2006). The Demographics, Motivations and Derived Experiences of Users of Massively-Multiuser Online Graphical Environments. *PRESENCE: Teleoperators and Environments, 15*, 309–329. doi:10.1162/pres.15.3.309

Yellowlees, P. M., & Cook, J. N. (2006). Education About Hallucinations Using an Internet Virtual Reality System: A Qualitative Survey. *Academic Psychiatry, 30*, 534–539. doi:10.1176/appi.ap.30.6.534

ENDNOTE

[1]   Machinima is a film created inworld in a virtual world or game

Compilation of References

2007Report, I. (2007, November/December). *Training*, (pp. 9-24). Retrieved on February 24, 2009 from http://www.bersinassociates.com/fr3/annualreport.pdf

A.L.I.C.E. (2009). A.L.I.C.E. Artificial Intelligence Foundation. *The A.L.I.C.E. Project* Retrieved 7/31/09, from http://alice.pandorabots.com/

Adams, N. (1996). *A study of the effectiveness of using virtual reality to orient line workers in a manufacturing environment*. Unpublished Masters of Arts Thesis, De Paul University, School for New Learning, Chicago, IL.

Adrian, A. (2008). No one knows you are a dog: Identity and reputation in virtual worlds. *Computer Law & Security Report*, *24*(4), 366–374. doi:10.1016/j.clsr.2008.03.005

Agnvall, E. (2006, May). Just-in-Time Training. *HR Magazine*, *51*(5), 66-71. Retrieved March 24, 2009, from ABI/INFORM Global database. (Document ID: 1035890651).

Airasian, P. W., Cruikshank, K. A., Mayer, R. E., Pintrich, P. R., Raths, J., & Wittrock, M. C. (2001). *A taxonomy for learning, teaching, and assessing: A revision of Bloom's Taxonomy of Educational Objectives* (Anderson, L. W., & Krathwohl, D. R., Eds.). New York: Longman.

Akdemir, O., & Koszalka, T. A. (2008). Investigating the relationships among instructional strategies and learning styles in online environments. *Computers & Education*, *50*(4), 1451–1461. doi:10.1016/j.compedu.2007.01.004

Aldrich, C. (2004). *Simulations and the Future of Learning*. San Francisco, CA: Pfeiffer.

Alexander, G. O. (1993). Computing practices in small Arkansas manufacturing. *Arkansas Business and Economic Review*, *26*(2), 20–26.

Ally, M. (2005, October). An intelligent agent for adapting and delivering electronic course materials to mobile learners. In Proceedings of Mlearn 2005 conference, Cape Town, South Africa.

Alverson, D. C., Saiki, S. M., Caudell, T. P., & Summers, K. L. (2005). Distributed immersive virtual reality simulation development for medical education. *J Int Am Med Sci Educ*, *15*, 19–30.

Ambient (2007). *Ambient insight event: the hottest learning technologies for 2007 Jan 18, 2007*. Retrieved from www.ambientinsight.com

Amory, A., & Seagram, R. (2003). Educational game models: conceptualization and evaluation. *South African Journal of Higher Education*, *17*(2), 206–217.

Anawati, D., & Craig, A. (2006). Behavioral adaptation within cross-cultural virtual teams. *IEEE Transactions on Professional Communication*, *49*(1), 44–56. doi:10.1109/TPC.2006.870459

Andersen, A., Hristov, E., & Karimi, H. (2008). *Second Life - New Opportunity for Higher Educational Institutions*. Bachelor Thesis, Business Administration, Jönköping University, Sweden.

Andre, E., Rist, T., & Muller, J. (1999). Employing AI Methods to Control the Behavior of Animated Interface Agents. *Applied Artificial Intellilgence*, (415-48).

Antonacci, D., & Modaress, N. (2008). Envisioning the Educational Possibilities of User-Created Virtual Worlds. *AACE Journal, 16*(2), 115–126.

Applebaum, J. (2008). *10 Steps to Successful Business Writing*. Alexandria, VA: ASTD Press.

Argyris, C., & Schon, D. (1974). *Theory in practice: Increasing professional effectiveness*. San Francisco: Jossey Bass.

Army, U. S. America's Army. (2003). [Multiple platforms] Montreuil-Sous-Bois. France: Ubisoft.

Army's Sergeant STAR Repels in to Action. *GoArmy's Virtual Guide takes next step in Human Emulation* (February 2, 2009). Retrieved March 23, 2009, from http://www.nextit.com/SGT_STAR_Animation.ashx

Athavaley, A. (2007). A job interview you don't have to show up for: Microsoft, Verizon, others use virtual worlds to recruit: dressing avatars for success. *Wall Street Journal*. Retrieved May 7, 2009 from http://online.wsj.com/article/SB118229876637841321.html

Atkinson, R. K. (2002). Optimizing Learning from Examples Using Animated Pedagogical Agents. *Journal of Educational Psychology, 94*(2), 416–427. doi:10.1037/0022-0663.94.2.416

Aukstakalnis, S., & Blatner, D. (1992). *Silicon Mirage: The Art and Science of Virtual Reality*. Peach Pit Press.

Avery, C., Civjan, J., & Johri, A. (2005). Assessing student interaction in the global classroom project: Visualizing communication and collaboration patterns . In Cooke, K. C., & Grant-Davie, K. (Eds.), *Online Education: Global Questions, Local Answers* (pp. 245–264). Amityville, NY: Baywood Publishing Company.

Avouris, N. M., Tselios, N., & Tatakis, E. C. (2001). Development and Evaluation of a Computer-Based Laboratory Teaching Tool. *Computer Applications in Engineering Education, 9*(1), 8–19. doi:10.1002/cae.1001

Azuma, R. T. (2001). Augmented reality: Approaches and technical challenges . In Barfield, W., & Caudell, T. (Eds.), *Fundamentals of Wearable Computers and Augmented Reality* (pp. 27–63). Mahwah, NJ: Lawrence Erlbaum Associates.

Baddeley, A. (1990). *Human Memory: Theory and Practice* (Rev. Ed.). New York: Allyn and Bacon.

Bailenson, J. N. (2006). Transformed Social Interaction in Collaborative Virtual Environments . In Humphreys, L., & Messaris, P. (Eds.), *Digital Media: Transformations in Human Communication* (pp. 255–26). New York: Peter Lang.

Bailenson, J., Yee, N., Merget, D., & Schroeder, R. (2006). The effect of behavioral realism and form realism of real-time avatar faces on verbal disclosure, nonverbal disclosure, emotion recognition, and copresence in dyadic interaction. *Presence (Cambridge, Mass.), 15*(4), 359–372. doi:10.1162/pres.15.4.359

Bailey, C. T., & Butcher, D. J. (1983). Interpersonal Skills Training I: The Nature of Skill Acquisition and Its Implications for Training Design and Management. *Management Education and Development, 14*(1), 48–54.

Bainbridge, W. S. (2007). The Scientific Research Potential of Virtual Worlds. *Science, 317*(5837), 472–476. doi:10.1126/science.1146930

Bal, M., Manesh, H. F., & Hashemipour, M. (2008). Virtual reality-based information requirements analysis tool for CIM system implementation: a case study in die-casting industry. *International Journal of Computer Integrated Manufacturing, 21*(3), 231–244. doi:10.1080/09511920701216246

Baldwin, J. F. (1981). Fuzzy logic and fuzzy reasoning . In Mamdani, E. H., & Gaines, B. R. (Eds.), *Fuzzy Reasoning and Its Applications*. London: Academic Press.

Balkin, J. M., & Noveck, B. S. (Eds.). (2006). *The state of play: Law, games, and virtual worlds*. New York: New York University Press.

Ball, S., & Pearce, R. (2008). Learning Scenarios and Workspaces with Virtual Worlds: Inclusion Benefits and Barriers of 'Once-Removed' Participation. In *Proceedings of Researching Learning in Virtual Environments, ReLIVE09*, (pp. 17-26), Milton Keynes, UK. Retrieved June 06, 2009 from www.open.ac.uk/relive08

Bandura, A. (2001). Social cognitive theory of mass communication . In Bryant, J., & Zillman, D. (Eds.), *Media effects: Advances in theory and research* (2nd ed., pp. 121–153). Hillsdale, NJ: Lawrence Erblbaum.

Banerjee, P., & Zetu, D. (2001). *Virtual manufacturing*. Chichester, UK: John Wiley and sons.

Barab, S. (2003). An Introduction to the Special Issue: Designing for Virtual Communities in the Service of Learning. *The Information Society, 19*, 197–201. Retrieved May 23, 2009 from http://www.indiana.edu/~tisj/readers/full-text/19-3%20guest.pdf

Barab, S., Thomas, M., Dodge, T., Carteaux, R., & Tuzun, H. (2005). Making learning fun: Quest Atlantis: A game without guns. *Educational Technology Research and Development, 53*(1), 86–107. doi:10.1007/BF02504859

Barger-Anderson, R., Domaracki, J. W., Kearney-Vakulick, N., & Kubina, R. M. Jr. (2004). Multiple baseline designs: The use of a single-case experimental design in literacy research. *Reading Improvement, 41*, 217–226.

Barker, T., & Kemp, F. (1990). Network Theory: A Postmodern Pedagogy for The Writing Classroom . In Handa, C. (Ed.), *Computers and community: Teaching composition in the twenty-first century* (pp. 1–27).

Barnett, R. H. (1991). Bringing realism to the classroom: an experimental design project for a lecture setting. *Frontiers in Education Conference, 1991, Twenty-First Annual Conference, 'Engineering Education in a New World Order,' Proceedings*, September 21-24, (pp. 639-641).

Barr, J. (2006).*Amazon Web Services Presentation In Second Life*. Retrieved September 6, 2007 from http://www.jeff-barr.com/?p=571

Barry, A. (in press). *Mirror neurons: How we become what we see.*

Bates, A. W. (2000). *Managing technological change: Strategies for college and university leaders*. San Francisco: Jossey-Bass.

Bates, A. W. (2005). *Technology, E-Learning and Distance Education*. London: Routledge.

Baylor, A. L. (2000). Beyond Butlers: Intelligent Agents as Mentors.*Journal of Educational Computing Research, 22*(4), 373–382. doi:10.2190/1EBD-G126-TFCY-A3K6

Baylor, A. L. (2002). Agent-Based Learning Environments as a Research Tool for Investigating Teaching and Learning. *Journal of Educational Computing Research, 26*(3), 227–248. doi:10.2190/PH2K-6P09-K8EC-KRDK

Beach, M. C., Price, E. G., & Gary, T. (2005). Cultural Competence: A Systematic Review of Health Care Provider Educational Initiatives. *Medical Care, 43*(4), 356–373. doi:10.1097/01.mlr.0000156861.58905.96

Becker, G. S. (1964).*Human Capital*. Chicago: University of Chicago Press.

Becker, L. A. (1999, October 5). *Crosstabs: Measures for nominal data*. Retrieved April 22, 2008 from http://web.uccs.edu/lbecker/SPSS/ctabs1.htm

Benford, S., Greenhalgh, C., Rodden, T., & Pycock, J. (2001). Collaborative virtual environments. *Communications of the ACM, 44*(7), 79–85. doi:10.1145/379300.379322

Benioff, M. (2008, August 1). *Welcome to Web 3.0: Now Your Other Computer is a Data Center*. Retrieved March 16, 2009, from TechcrunchIT http://www.techcrunchit.com/2008/08/01/welcome-to-web-30-now-your-other-computer-is-a-data-center/

Benkler, Y. (2006). *The Wealth of Networks: How Social Production Transforms Markets and Freedom*. Retrieved May 20, 2008, from http://www.benkler.org/Benkler_Wealth_Of_Networks.pdf

Bennett, B., & Peachey, A. (2007). *Mashing the MUVE: A Mashup Model for Collaborative Learning in Multi-User Virtual Environments*. Paper presented at International Computer Aided Learning 2007, Austria: International Association of Online Engineering

Bergiel, B. J., Bergiel, E. B., & Balsmeierl, P. W. (2008). Nature of virtual teams: a summary of their advantages and disadvantages. *Management Research News, 31*(2), 99–110. doi:10.1108/01409170810846821

Berry, D. C., Butler, L. T., & DeRosis, F. (2005). Evaluating a realistic agent in an advice-giving task. *International Journal of Human-Computer Studies, 63*, 304–327. doi:10.1016/j.ijhcs.2005.03.006

Bhui, K., Warfa, N., Edonya, P., McKenzie, K., & Bhugra, D. (2007). Cultural competence in mental health care: a review of model evaluations [Electronic Version]. *BMC Health Services Research 2007.* Retrieved 4/1/09 from http://biomedcentral.com/1472-6963/7/15.

Billo, R. E., Rucker, R., & Paul, B. K. (1994). Three rapid and effective requirements definition modeling tools: evolving technology for manufacturing system investigations. *International Journal of Computer Integrated Manufacturing, 7*(3), 186–199. doi:10.1080/09511929408944608

Blair, K., & Hoy, C. (2006). Paying attention to adult learners online: The pedagogy and politics of community. *Computers and Composition, 23*(1), 32–48. doi:10.1016/j.compcom.2005.12.006

Blascovich, J., Loomis, J., Beall, A., Swinth, K., Hoyt, C., & Bailenson, J. (2002). Immersive virtual environment technology: A methodological tool for social psychology. *Psychological Inquiry, 13*(2), 103–104. doi:10.1207/S15327965PLI1302_01

Blizzard Entertainment. (2008). *World of Warcraft® surpasses 11 million subscribers worldwide.* Retrieved November 29, 2008, from http://www.blizzard.com/us/press/081028.html

Bloom, B. S. (Ed.). Engelhart, M.D., Furst, E.J., Hill, W.H., & Krathwohl, D.R. (1956). Taxonomy of educational objectives: The classification of educational goals. Handbook 1: Cognitive domain. New York: David McKay.

Bobbitt, L. M., Inks, S. A., Kemp, K. J., & Mayo, D. T. (2000). Integrating Marketing Courses to Enhance Team-Based Experiential Learning. *Journal of Marketing Education, 22*(1), 15–24. doi:10.1177/0273475300221003

Bonk, C., & Dennen, V. (2005). Massive multiplayer online gaming: A research framework for military training and education. Office of the Under Secretary of Defense (Personnel and Readiness), Readiness and Training Directorate, Advanced Distributed Learning Initiative, Washington, D.C.

Book, B. (2004). Moving beyond the game: social virtual worlds. *State of Play, 2,* 6–8.

Boyd, D. M., & Ellison, N. B. (2007). Social network sites: Definition, history, and scholarship. *Journal of Computer-Mediated Communication, 13*(1), 11.

Bricken, M. (1991). Virtual worlds: No interface to design. Cyberspace: first steps, (pp. 363-382).

Bricken, M., & Byrne, C. (1992). *Summer students in virtual reality: A pilot study on educational applications of VR technology. Technical Report.* Seattle: University of Washington, Human Interface Technology Laboratory.

Bronack, S. C., Cheney, A. L., Riedl, R. E., & Tashner, J. H. (2008). Designing Virtual Worlds to Facilitate Meaningful Communication. *Technical Communication,* (261-69).

Bronack, S., Riedl, R., & Tashner, J. (2006). Learning in the zone: A social constructivist framework for distance education in a 3D virtual world. *Interactive Learning Environments, 14*(3), 219–232. doi:10.1080/10494820600909157

Brooke, J. (1996). SUS: A "quick and dirty" usability scale . In Jordan, P. W., Thomas, B., Weerdmeester, B. A., & McClelland, A. L. (Eds.), *Usability Evaluation in Industry.* London: Taylor and Francis.

Brookfield, S. (1987). *Developing critical thinkers: Challenging adults to explore alternative ways of thinking and acting.* San Francisco: Jossey-Bass.

Brookfield, S. D. (1992). Developing criteria for formal theory building in adult education. Adult Ed. 42(2), 79-93.

Brown, D. G., Coyne, J. T., & Stripling, R. (2006). Augmented reality for urban skills training. In *Proceedings of the IEEE Conference on Virtual Reality* (March 25 - 29, 2006), (pp. 249-252). Washington, DC: IEEE Computer Society.

Brown, J. S., & Adler, R. P. (2008). Minds on fire: Open education, the long tail and learning 2.0. *Educase Review*. Retrieved April 30, 2008, from http://net.educause.edu/ir/library/pdf/ERM0811.pdf

Brown, J. S., Collins, A., & Duguid, P. (1989). Situated Cognition and the Culture of Learning. *Educational Researcher, 18*(1), 32–42.

Brown, J.S. (2000). Growing Up Digital. *Change, 32*(2). Retrieved May 26, 2009 from Academic Search Premier database, Document ID: 00091383

Brown, M. K., Huettner, B., & James-Tanny, C. (2007). *Managing virtual teams*. Plano, TX: Wordware Publishing, Inc.

Brustoloni, J. C. (1991). *Autonomous Agents: Characterization and Requirement*. Carnegie Mellon Technical Report CMU-CS-91-204. Pittsburgh: Carnegie Mellon University.

Buckley, W., & Smith, A. (2008). Application of multimedia technologies to enhance distance learning. *RE:view, 39*(2), 57–65. doi:10.3200/REVU.39.2.57-65

Burdea, G., & Coiffet, P. (2003). *Virtual reality technology* (2nd ed.). New York: John Wiley and Sons.

Burge, L. (1988). Beyond andragogy: Some explorations for distance learning design. *Journal of Distance Education, 3*(1), 5–23.

Cabiria, J. (2008). Virtual world and real world permeability: Transfer of positive benefits for marginalized gay and lesbian populations. *Journal of Virtual Worlds Research, 1*(1).

Calongne, C. M. (2008). Educational Frontiers: Learning in a Virtual World. *Educause Review Magazine, 43*(5), September/October.

Candy, P. C. (1989). Constructivism and the study of self-direction in adult learning. *Studies in the Education of Adults, 21*, 95–116.

Candy, P. C. (1991). *Self-direction for lifelong learning*. San Francisco: Jossey-Bass.

Cao, J., Crews, J. M., Lin, M., Burgoon, J. K., & Nunamaker, J. F. (2008). An empirical investigation of virtual interaction in supporting learning. *SIGMIS Database, 39*(3), 51–68. doi:10.1145/1390673.1390680

Carlsson, C., & Hagsand, D. (1993). DIVE - multi-user virtual reality system. *VRAIS '93, IEEE Virtual Reality Annual international Symposium*.

Carnevale, A. P. (1991). *America and the new economy: How new competitive standards are radically changing American workplaces*. San Francisco: Jossey-Bass, Inc.

Carpenter, E. (1970). *They became what they beheld*. New York: E.P. Dutton.

Carr, N. (2008). *The Big Switch: Rewiring the World, from Edison to Google*. New York: W.W. Norton & Co.

Carrillo, C. I. P. d. (2004). *Intelligent Agents to Improve Adaptively in a Web-based Learning Environment*. Spain: Doctoral, University of Girona.

Carter, L., & Rickly, B. (2006). Mind the gap: Modeling space in online education . In Cooke, K. C., & Grant-Davie, K. (Eds.), *Online Education: Global Questions, Local Answers* (pp. 31–48). Amityville, NY: Baywood Publishing Company.

Carter, M. (2007). Ways of knowing, doing and writing in the disciplines. *College Composition and Communication, 58*, 385–418.

Casanueva, J., & Blake, E. (2000). *The effects of avatars on co-presence in a collaborative virtual environment*. Rondebosch, South Africa: University of Cape Town, Collaborative Visual Computing Laboratory, Department of Computer Science.

Cassell, J., & Vilhjalmsson, H. (1999). Fully embodied conversational avatars: Making communicative behaviors autonomous. *Autonomous Agents and Multi-Agent Systems, 2*(1), 45–64. doi:10.1023/A:1010027123541

Castronova, E. (2005). *Synthetic Worlds: The Business and Culture of Online Games*. Chicago, IL: University of Chicago Press Publisher.

Cavall, E. (2008, May 19). *90 Percent of Business-Launched Virtual Worlds Fail.* Retrieved May 19, 2008, from www.wired.com.

Cavalli, E. (2008). Man imitates America's Army, saves lives. *Wired.com.* Retrieved November 26, 2008, from http://blog.wired.com/games/2008/01/americas-army-t.html

Census, U. S. (2008). *Small and medium-sized businesses.* U.S. Census Bureau. Retrieved October 13, 2008, from http://www.census.gov/epcd/www/smallbus.html

Cervantes Medina, L. (2004). *Application of a collaborative virtual reality tool and 3D models adaptation to support medical diagnosis of bone injuries.* Unpublished thesis, M.S. Telematics, School of Telematics, University of Colima, Mexico.

Chan, K. K. P., & Lau, R. W. H. (2004). Distributed sound rendering for interactive virtual environments. *IEEE International Conference on Multimedia and Expo,* (pp. 1823-1826).

Chaney, B. (2004). *History, theory, and quality indicators of distance education: A literature review.* Retrieved August 28, 2009, from http://ohi.tamu.edu/distanceed.pdf

Charp, S. (2000). Distance education. *T.H.E. Journal, 27*(9), 10–12.

Charp, S. (2002). Changes to traditional teaching. *T.H.E. Journal, 29*(10).

Chartrand, T., & Bargh, J. (1999). The chameleon effect: The perception-behavior link and social interaction. *Journal of Personality and Social Psychology, 76*(6), 893–910. doi:10.1037/0022-3514.76.6.893

Chau, T. (2005). A Case Study of Wiki-Based Experience Repository at a Medium-sized Software Company. In *Proceedings of the 3rd international conference on Knowledge capture* (pp. 185-186). Banff, Canada: International Conference On Knowledge Capture.

Cheal, C. (2007). Second Life: Hype of Hyperlearning. *Horizon, 15*(4), 204–210. doi:10.1108/10748120710836228

Chee, Y. S. (2001). Invited talk. *International Symposium on Virtual Education 2001*, Busan, South Korea, (pp. 43–54). Symposium Organizing Committee, Dongseo University.

Chetan, S., Vazquez, M., & Chen, F. (1996). Virtual Manufacturing: An Overview. *Computers & Industrial Engineering, 31*(1-2), 79–82. doi:10.1016/0360-8352(96)00083-6

Chickering, A., & Ehrmann, S. C. (1996). Implementing the seven principles: Technology as lever . *AAHE Bulletin, 49*(2), 3–6.

Childress, M. D., & Braswell, R. (2006). Using Massively Multiplayer Online Role-Playing Games for Online Learning. *Distance Education, 27*(2), 187–196. doi:10.1080/01587910600789522

Chittaro, L., & Ranon, R. (2007). Web3-D technologies in learning, education and training: Motivations, issues, opportunities. *Computers & Education,* (49): 3–18. doi:10.1016/j.compedu.2005.06.002

Cho, H., Gay, G., Davidson, B., & Ingraffea, A. (2007). Social networks, communications styles, and learning performance in a CSCL community. *Computers & Education, 49*(2), 309–329. doi:10.1016/j.compedu.2005.07.003

Chodos, D., Naeimi, P., & Stroulia, E. (2009, April). An integrated framework for simulation-based training on video and in a virtual world. *Journal of Virtual Worlds Research, 2*(1).

Choi, A. C. K., Chan, D. S. K., & Yuen, A. M. F. (2002). Application of Virtual Assembly Tools for Improving Product Design. *International Journal of Advanced Manufacturing Technology, 19*, 377–383. doi:10.1007/s001700200027

Christensen, C. (1997). *The Innvator's Dilemma.* New York: HarperCollins Publishers.

Churchill, E. F., & Bly, S. (1999). Virtual Environments At Work: Ongoing Use Of MUDs In The Workplace. In *Proceedings Of The International Joint Conference On Work Activities Coordination And Collaboration,* (pp. 99-108). San Francisco: ACM.

Clark, D. (2008, April 3). Virtual World Gets Another Life: Technology Offers Companies Private Workspace. *Wall Street Journal*, B10.

Coates, J. (2006). Generational Learning Styles. River Falls, WI: LERN books.

Cohen, E., & Goode, T. D. (2003, Summer). *Rational for Cultural Competence in Primary Care*. National Center for Cultural Competence. Retrieved April 1, 2009.

Collison, G., Elbaum, B., Haavind, S., & Tinker, R. (2000). *Facilitating online learning: Effective strategies for moderators*. Madison, WI: Atwood Publishing.

Cooney, B. (2007). Virtual meetings offer solid benefits for investigators. *Pharmaceutical Executive, 16*.

Cooperrider, D. L., Sorensen, P. F., Yaeger, T. F., & Whitney, D. (2001). *Appreciative inquiry: An emerging direction for organization development*. Champaign, IL [C.]. *Stipes Publishing, L*, L.

Corey, G. (1985). *Theory and practice of team counseling* (2nd ed.). Pacific Grove, CA: Brooks/Cole.

Corporate education: One-to-one training. (2007). *Maclean's,120*(35/36), 75.

Council for Programs in Technical and Scientific Communication. (2008). *Research Assessment Project*. Retrieved 3 16, 2009, from Council for Programs in Technical and Scientific Communication: http://www.cptsc.org/research-assess.html

Craig, S. D., Gholson, B., & Driscoll, D. (2003). Animated Pedagogical Agents in Multimedia Educational Environments: Effects of Agent Properties, Picture Features, and Redundancy. *Journal of Educational Psychology, 94*, 95–102.

Cranton, P. (1994). *Transformative learning: A guide for educators of adults*. San Francisco: Jossey-Bass.

Cranton, P. (2001). Individual differences and transformative learning. In J. Mezirow & Assoc. (Ed.), Learning as transformation: Critical perspectives on a theory in progress, (pp. 181-204). San Francisco: Jossey-Bass.

Creese, E. L. (2003). Group dynamics and learning in an organization behavior virtual learning community: The case of six virtual peer-learning teams. Melbourne, Australia: UltiBase, RMIT University.

Cross, K. P. (1981). *Adults as learners*. San Francisco, CA: Jossey.Bass.

Csikszenthihalyi, M. (1990). *Flow: The Psychology of Optimal Experience*. New York: Harper Perennial.

Csikszentmihalyi, M. (1990). *Flow: The Psychology of Optimal Experience*. New York: Harper and Row.

Csikszentmihalyi, M. (1997). *Finding flow*. New York: Basic.

Dani, S. S., Burn, N. D., Backhouse, C. J., & Kochhard, A. K. (2006). The implications of organizational culture and trust in the working of virtual teams. PROC. *IMechE, 220,* Part B: J. Engineering Manufacture.

Davenport, J. (1993). Is there any way out of the andragogy mess? In Thorpe, M., Edwards, R., & Hanson, A. (Eds.), *Culture and Processes of Adult Learning*. London: Routledge.

Davis, D., & Scaffidi, N. (2007). *Leading virtual team*. Paper presented at the annual meeting of the International Communication Association, San Francisco, CA. Retrieved March 1, 2009, from www.allacademic.com

De Freitas, S. (2006). Learning in immersive worlds: A review of game-based learning. *Joint Information Systems Committee (JISC) e-Learning Programme.*

de Freitas, S., & Oliver, M. (2006). How Can Exploratory Learning With Games And Simulations Within The Curriculum Be Most Effectively Evaluated? *Computers & Education, 46*, 249–263. doi:10.1016/j.compedu.2005.11.007

De Pillis, E., & Furumo, K. (2007). Counting the cost of virtual teams. *Communications of the ACM, 50*(12), 93–95. doi:10.1145/1323688.1323714

De Simone, C. (2006). Preparing our teachers for distance education. *College Teaching, 54*(1), 183–184. doi:10.3200/CTCH.54.1.183-184

Dede, C. (2005). *Planning for Neomillennial Learning-Styles*. Retrieved March 15, 2008, from www.educase.edu: http://www.educase.edu

Dede, C. J., Salzman, M., & Bowen Loftin, R. (1996). The development of a virtual world for learning newtonian mechanics. In Multimedia, Hypermedia, and Virtual Reality Models, Systems, and Applications, (LNCS). Heidelberg, Germany: Springer Berlin.

Dede, C., & Ketelhut, D. J. (2005). Designing for Motivation and Usability in a Museum-based Multi-User Virtual Environment. *Retrieved, 10*(1), 2005.

Depince, P., & Chablat, D. (2004). Tools for improving Design and Production . In *CIRP International Design Seminar*. Cairo, Egypt: Virtual Manufacturing.

Dewey, J. (1933). *How We Think. A restatement of the relation of reflective thinking to the educative process.* Lexington: D.C. Heath and Company.

Dewey, J. (1938). *Experience and education.* New York: Collier Books.

Dewey, J. (1963). *Experience and Education.* New York: Collier Books.

Diaz, D. P., & Bontenbal, K. F. (2001, August). Learner Preferences: Developing a learner-centered Environment in the Online or Mediated Classroom. *Ed at a Distance Magazine and Ed Journal, 14*(80), 1–8.

Diaz, D., & Cartnal, R. (•••). (1999). Student learning styles in two classes. *College Teaching, 47*(4), 130–141. doi:10.1080/87567559909595802

Dickey, M. D. (2005). Brave New (Interactive) Worlds: A Review of the Design Affordances and Constraints of Two 3D Virtual Worlds as Interactive Learning Environments. *Interactive Learning Environments, 13*, 121–137. doi:10.1080/10494820500173714

Dickey, M. D. (2005). Three-dimensional virtual worlds and distance learning: Two case studies of Active Worlds as a medium for distance education. *British Journal of Educational Technology, 36*(3), 439–451. doi:10.1111/j.1467-8535.2005.00477.x

Dinov, I. (2007). *Choosing the right test*. Retrieved December 4, 2008, from http://www.socr.ucla.edu/Applets.dir/ChoiceOfTest.html

Dirkx, J. (2001). The power of feeling: Emotion, imagination, and the construction of meaning in adult learning . In Merriam, S. B. (Ed.), *The new update on adult learning theory*. San Francisco: Jossey-Bass.

Dirkx, J. (2006). Engaging emotions in adult learning: A Jungian perspective on emotion and transformative learning. *New Directions for Adult and Continuing Education, 109*, 15–26. doi:10.1002/ace.204

Donahue, M. (2007, November). Setting up Shop on Second Life. *Pharmaceutical Executive: Consultants Confidential*, 8-10. Retrieved February 28, 2009, from ABI/INFORM Global database, Document ID: 1390552031.

Doswell, J. (2005). *It's virtually pedagogical: pedagogical agents in mixed reality learning environments.*

Driver, E., Jackson, P., Moore, C., Schooley, C., & Barnett, J. (2008). *Getting real work done in virtual worlds*. Los Angeles: Forrester.

Durrington, V. A., Berryill, A., & Swafford, J. (2006). Strategies for enhancing student interactivity in an online environment. *College Teaching, 54*(1), 190–193. doi:10.3200/CTCH.54.1.190-193

Eaton, A. (2005). Students in the online technical communications classroom . In Cooke, K. C., & Grant-Davie, K. (Eds.), *Online Education: Global Questions, Local Answers* (pp. 31–48). Amityville, NY: Baywood Publishing Company.

Edwards, C. (2006). Another world. *IEEE Engineering and Technology, 9*(1), 28–32. doi:10.1049/et:20060904

Edwards, S. E., & Schaller, D. T. (2007). The Name of the Game: Museums and Digital Learning Games . In Din, H., & Hecht, P. (Eds.), *The Digital Museum: A Think Guide* (pp. 62–68). Washington, DC: American Association of Museums.

El-Mounayri, H., Aw, D., Wasfy, T., & Wasfy, A. (2005). *Virtual manufacturing for training and education.*

American Society for Engineering Education (ASEE) Conference.

Entertainment Software Association. (2008, June). *Use of video game technology in the workplace increasing.* Retrieved March 15, 2009, http://www.theesa.com/newsroom/release_detail.asp?releaseID=24

Entertainment, B. (2004). *World of Warcraft.* Irvine, CA: Blizzard Entertainment.

Epstein, R. M., & Hundert, E. M. (2002). Defining and assessing professional competence. *Journal of the American Medical Association, 287,* 226–235. doi:10.1001/jama.287.2.226

Esqueda-Machiche, G. (2005). *Development of a collaborative virtual reality environment to teach an engine part assembling (in Spanish).* Unpublished thesis, College of Telematics, University of Colima, Mexico.

European Commission (2003). The new SME definition. User guide and model declaration. *Commission Recommendation 2003/361/EC* as published in the Official Journal of the European Union L 124, p. 36 of 20 May 2003.

eWeek. (2008, October). *Web 2.0: Business Process Enabler.* Retrieved March 15, 2009, from http://www.week.com/c/a/Video/Web-20-Buiness-Process-Enabler/

Falk, J. H., & Dierking, L. D. (2002). *Lessons Without Limit, How Free-Chioce Learning is Transforming Education.* Walnut Creek, CA: AltaMira Press.

Fencott, C. (2005). A methodology of design for virtual environments. In Sanchez-Segura, M. I. (Ed.), *Developing Future Interactive Systems.* Hershey, PA: IGI Global Publishing.

Ferrell, O., & Ferrell, L. (2002). Assessing Instructional Technology in the Classroom. *Marketing Education Review, 12*(3), 19–24.

Fidishun, D. (2000). Andragogy and Technology: Integrating Adult Learning Theory as We Teach with Technology. In *Proceedings Middle Tennessee State University Instructional Technology Conference.*

Flint, T. (1999). *Best Practices in Adult Learning: A CAEL/APQC Benchmarking Study.* New York: Forbes Custom Publishing.

Flowers, M. (2009). Virtual Cultural Awareness Trainer Preliminary Design Document. Los Angeles, CA: Alelo TLT, LLC.

Fogg, B. J. (2003). *Persuasive technology: Using computers to change what we think and do.* Amsterdam: Morgan Kaufmann Publishers.

Forterra. (date unknown). *Transportation incident management: Using 3D virtual worlds to train first responders.* Retrieved August 13, 2009, from http://www.forterrainc.com/images/stories/pdf/I-95_CaseStudy.pdf

Foster, A. L. (2008). What happens in a virtual world has a real-world impact, a scholar finds. *Chronicle of higher education, April 4, 2008.* Retrieved April 21, 2008, from http://chronicle.com/free/v54/i30/30a01402.htm

Foster, A., & Carnevale, D. (2007, April 27). Distance Education Goes Public. *The Chronicle of Higher Education.* Retrieved from http://chronicle.com/weekly/v53/i34/34a04901.htm

Fox, J., & Bailenson, J. (2009). Virtual self-modeling: The effects of vicarious reinforcement and identification on exercise behaviors. *Media Psychology, 12,* 1–25. doi:10.1080/15213260802669474

Francis, G.A., & Tan, H.S. (1999). Virtual reality as a training instrument. *The TEMASEK journal, 7,* 4-15.

Frand, J. L. (2000). The Information-Age Mindset: Changes in Students and Implications for Higher Education. *EDUCAUSE Review.* Retrieved May 26, 2009 from http://net.educause.edu/ir/library/pdf/ERM0051.pdf

Fraser, M., Glover, T., Vaghi, I., Benford, S., Greenhalgh, C., Hindmarsh, J., & Heath, C. (2000). Revealing the realities of collaborative virtual reality. In E. Churchill & M. Reddy, (Eds.) *Proceedings of the Third international Conference on Collaborative Virtual Environments,* San Francisco, CA, (pp. 29-37). New York: ACM.

Freeman, D., Slater, M., Bebbington, P., Garety, P. A., Kuipers, E., & Fowler, D. (2003). Can virtual reality be used to investigate persecutory ideation? *The Journal of Nervous and Mental Disease, 191*(8). doi:10.1097/01. nmd.0000082212.83842.fe

Freire, P. (1986). *Pedagogy of the Oppressed.* New York: Continuum.

Frey, T. (2007, March). *The Future of Education.* The DaVinci Institute. Retrieved March 15, 2009, from http:// www.davinciinstitute.com/page.php?ID=170

Friedman, T. L. (2006).The World Is Flat [Updated and Expanded]: A Brief History of the Twenty-first Century. New York: Farrar, Straus and Giroux.

Gagne, R. M., Wager, W. W., Golas, K. C., Keller, J. M., & Russell, J. D. (2005). *Principles of instructional design* (5th ed.). Belmont, CA: Wadsworth/Thomson Learning.

Galbraith, M. W., Sisco, B. R., & Guglielmino, L. M. (1997). *Administering successful programs for adults. Promoting excellence in adult, community, and continuing education.* Boca Raton, FL: Krieger Publishing Co.

Galloway, A. R. (2006). *Gaming: Essays on algorithmic culture.* Minneapolis: University of Minnesota Press.

Garcâia-Carbonell, A., Rising, B., Montero, B., & Watts, F. (2001). Simulation/gaming and the acquisition of communicative competence in another language. *Simulation & Gaming, 32*(4), 481–491. doi:10.1177/104687810103200405

Garcia-Ruiz, M. A., & Alvarez-Cardenas, O. (2005). Application of virtual reality in collaborative Work of small and medium businesses (in Spanish). In *Sixth International Congress of Computer Science*, Colima Institute of Technology, Colima, Mexico.

Garcia-Ruiz, M. A., Edwards, A., Aquino-Santos, R., & El-Seoud, S. A. (2008). Collaborating and learning a second language in a Wireless Virtual Reality Environment. *IJMLO Int. J. Mobile Learning and Organisation, 2*(4), 369–377. doi:10.1504/IJMLO.2008.020689

Gardner, H. (1991). *The Unschooled Mind: How Children Think And How Schools Should Teach.* New York: Basic Books.

Garrison, D. R., & Anderson, T. (2003). *E-learning in the 21st century.* New York: Routledge. doi:10.4324/9780203166093

Gartner Inc. (2007). Retrieved November 29, 2007, from http://www.gartner.com/it/page.jsp?id=503861

Gartner Research. (2007). *Gartner Says 80 Percent of Active Internet Users will Have a "Second Life" in the Virtual World by the End of 2011.* Retrieved February 15, 2009, from http://www.gartner.com/it/page. jsp?id=503861Jarvis, J. (2009) *What Would Google Do?* New York: HarperCollins Publishers.

Gartner Research. (2008). *Gartner Says 90 Per Cent of Corporate Virtual World Projects Fail Within 18 Months.* Retrieved March 2, 2009, from http://www.gartner.com/ it/page.jsp?id=670507

Gasperini, J. (2000). The Role of Ambiguity in Multimedia Experience . In Jacobson, R. (Ed.), *Information Design* (pp. 301–316). Cambridge, MA: MIT Press.

Gee, J. P. (2004). *Situated Language and Learning: A Critique of Tradional Schooling.* New York, NY: Routledge.

Gee, J. P. (2005). *Why are Video Games Good for Learning?* [Electronic Version]. Retrieved 3/10/09 from www. academiccolab.org/resources/documents/Good_Learning.pdf

Gee, J. P. (2007). *What Video Games Have to Teach Us about Learning and Literacy.* New York: Palgrave.

Gee, J. P. (2009, April). Games, learning, and 21st century survival skills. *Journal of Virtual Worlds Research, 2*(1).

Gerbaud, S., & Arnaldi, B. (2008). Scenario sharing in a collaborative virtual environment for training. In *Proceeding of the 2008 ACM symposium on virtual reality software and technology,* (pp. 109-112).

Gibbons, H., & Wentworth, G. (2001). Andrological and pedagogical training differences for online instructors. *Online Journal of Distance Learning Administration, 4*(3), 1–5.

Gogala, S. (2005). Chosen Pedagogic Essays. Ljubljana, Slovenia: Drustvo 2000.

Gokhale, A. A. (1995). Collaborative learning enhances critical thinking. *Journal of Technology Education, 7*(1), 22–30.

Gould, R. (1990). The therapeutic learning program. In J. Mezirow & Assoc. (Eds.), Fostering critical reflection in adulthood. San Francisco: Jossey-Bass.

Grady, H. M., & Davis, M. T. (2005). Teaching well online with instructional and procedural scaffolding . In Cooke, K. C., & Grant-Davie, K. (Eds.), *Online Education: Global Questions, Local Answers* (pp. 101–122). Amityville, NY: Baywood Publishing Company.

Graham, D. McNeil, J. & Pettiford, L. (2000). Untangled Web: Developing Teaching on the Internet, (1st Ed.). London: Pearson Education Limited.

Grant, M. R., & Dickson, V. J. (2008). Matrix on Virtual Teaching: a Competency-based Model for Faculty Development. In *Adult Education Research, (AERC), Conference Proceedings*, University of Missouri St. Louis, St. Louis, Missouri.

Grant, M. R., & Thornton, H. R. (2007). Best practices in undergraduate adult-centered online learning: Mechanisms for course design and delivery. *MERLOT Journal of Online Learning and Teaching, 3*(4), 346–456.

Graves, L. (2008). A Second life for higher Ed. *U.S. News & World Report, 144*(2), 49–50.

Greats Enters, V. *$1.5 Billion Virtual Goods Market.* (2008, June 9). Retrieved June 9, 2008, from Business Wire: http://www.businesswire.com

Green, T. B. (1992). *Performance and MotivationStrategies for Today's Workforce: A Guide to Expectancy Theory Applications*. London: Quorum Books.

Gronstedt, A. (2007). Second Life produces real training results. *T + D Magazine*, August.

Gronstedt, A. (2007). The changing face of workplace learning. *T + D, 61*(1), 20.

Gronstedt, A. (2008). Making Learning Fun and Social. *E-learning Magazine*. Retrieved May 10, 2009 from www.gronstedtgroup.com/pdf/ELearningMagazine.pdf

Guasch, T., Espasa, A., & Alvarez, I. M. (2008). A transnational study of Teachers' ICT competencies in online learning environments in Higher Education . In *How do we learn? Where do we learn?*Lisboa: EDEN.

Gutierrez, M., Vexo, F., & Thalmann, D. (2004). The mobile animator: interactive character animation in collaborative virtual environment. In Proceedings of Virtual Reality conference, (pp. 125-284).

Gutwin, C., Benford, S., Dyck, J., Fraser, M., Vaghi, I., & Greenhalgh, C. (2004). Revealing delay in collaborative environments. In *Proceedings of the SIGCHI Conference on Human Factors in Computing Systems,* Vienna, Austria, April 24 - 29, *CHI '04* (pp. 503-510). New York: ACM.

Habermas, J. (1984). *The theory of communicative action.* Boston: Beacon Press.

Hamburg, I., & Engert, S. (2007). Competency-based training in SMEs: The role of e-learning and e-competence. *Paper presented at Web-based Education (WBE 2007)*, Chamonix, France.

Hansen, J. A., & Barnett, M., MaKinster, J. G., & Keating, T. (2004). The impact of three-dimensional computational modeling on student understanding of astronomy concepts: a qualitative analysis. *International Journal of Science Education, 26*(13), 1555–1575. doi:10.1080/09500690420001673766

Harasim, L. (1990). Introduction to online education . In Harasim, L. (Ed.), *Online education: Perspectives on a new environment.* New York: Praeger.

Hargadon, S. (2008). *Web 2.0 is the Future of Education.* Retrieved May 3, 2008, from http://www.stevehargadon.com/2008/03/web-20-is-future-of-education.html

Hart, K. (2009, March 5). D.C. Tech Chief Tapped for White House Slot. *The Washington Post*. Retrieved March 16, 2009, from http://www.washingtonpost.com/wp-dyn/content/article/2009/03/05/AR2009030501060.html

Hartman, J., Moskal, P., & Dziuban, C. (2005). *Preparing the Academy of Today for the Learner of Tomorrow.* D. G. Oblinger, & J. L. Oblinger, (Eds.). Retrieved July 15, 2008, from www.educause.edu/educatingthenetgen/

Hashemipour, M., Manesh, H. F., & Bal, M. (in press). A modular virtual reality system for engineering laboratory education. *Computer Applications in Engineering Education.*

Hatch, S. (2007, February 1). Meetings in Second Life. *Meetings.Net.* Retrieved March 2, 2009 from http://meetingsnet.com/technology/virtual_meeting/meetings_virtual_worlds_real/

Havenstein, H. (2007, September 7). IT is a Key Barrier to Corporate Web 2.0 Adoption, Users Say. *Computerworld.* Retrieved July 16, 2009, from http://www.computerworld.com/s/article/9034898/IT_is_a_key_barrier_to_corporate_Web_2.0_adoption_users_say

Hawisher, G., & Moran, C. (1993, October). Electronic mail and the writing instructor. *College English, 55*(6), 627–643. doi:10.2307/378699

Heeter, C. (1992). The Subjective Experience of Presence. In Presence: Teleoperators and Virtual Environments (pp. 262–271). Being There.Presence

Henderson, J., Fishwick, P., Fresh, E., & Futterknecht, F. (2008). An Immersive Learning Simulation Environment for Chinese Culture. *Interservice/Industry Training, Simulation, and Education Conference (I/ITSEC).* Retrieved May 20, 2009 from http://cero11.cise.ufl.edu/~webmaster/Downloadablecontent/Henderson-etal2008_IITSEC-UF.pdf

Hendry, E. R. (2009). Virtual Medical Training Comes to Second Life [Electronic Version]. *The Chronicle of Higher Education.* Retrieved from http://chronicle.com/blogPost/Virtual-Medical-Training-Comes/7277/print

Herman, A., Coombe, R. J., & Kaye, L. (2006). Your second life? Goodwill and the performativity of intellectual property in online digital gaming. *Cultural Studies, 20*(2/3), 184–210. doi:10.1080/09502380500495684

Herman, L., Horwitzk, J., Kent, S., & Miller, S. (2008). *The history of video games.* Retrieved November 30, 2008, from http://www.gamespot.com/gamespot/features/video/hov/

Herrington, T., & Tretyakov, Y. (2005). The global classroom project: Troublemaking and troubleshooting . In Cooke, K. C., & Grant-Davie, K. (Eds.), *Online Education: Global Questions, Local Answers* (pp. 267–284). Amityville, NY: Baywood Publishing Company.

Holmberg, B. (2003). A theory of distance education based on empathy . In Moore, M., & Anderson, W. G. (Eds.), *Handbook of distance education* (pp. 79–86). Mahwah, NJ: Lawrence Erlbaum Associates.

Holt, R. (2000). *Examining Video Game Immersion as a Flow State.* Bachelor Thesis, Department of Psychology, Brock University, Canada.

Holzwarth, M., Janiszewski, C., & Neumann, M. M. (2006). The influence of avatars on online consumer shopping behavior. *Journal of Marketing, 70*(October), 19–36. doi:10.1509/jmkg.70.4.19

Howe, N., & Strauss, W. (2000). *Millennials Rising: The Next Generation.* New York: Vintage Books.

Howes, M. (1990). *The Psychology of Human Cognition: Mainstream and Genevan Traditions.* New York: Pergamon Press.

http://www.kzero.co.uk/blog/?p=854, (n.d.).

http://www.pscoe.gov.sg/repository/open/2/522/Training.htm, (n.d.).

http://www.virtualworldsnews.com/2009/02/ibm-saves-320000-with-second-life-meeting.html, (n.d.).

http://www.websitemagazine.com/content/blogs/posts/articles/second_life_metaverse.aspx (n.d.).

Hudson, K., & deGast-Kennedy, K. (2009). Canadian border simulation at Loyalist College. *Journal of Virtual Worlds Research, 2*(1).

Hudson, K., & Nowosielski, L. (2009, April). *Canadian border simulation.* Poster session presented at the Federal Consortium on Virtual Worlds Conference, National Defense University, Washington, DC.

Hudson, K., Wood, N., Wetsch, L., & Solomon, M. (2009). From interactive to immersive: Advertising education takes a virtual leap of faith. *Journal of advertising education, 13*(1).

Hum, S. (2002, Summer). Performing gendered identities: A small-team collaboration in a computer-mediated classroom interaction. *Journal of Curriculum Theorizing.*

IBM. (2007). *Virtual World: Real Leaders.* Retrieved June 02, 2009 from www.ibm.com/ibm.gio/media/pdf/ibm_gio_gaming_report.pdf

Inc, A. H. G. (2008). *Second Life Training Simulations.* Retrieved May 7, 2009 from http://second-life-e-learning.ahg.com/second_life_training_simulations.htm

Inhelder, B., & Piaget, J. (1958). *The Growth of Logical Thinking from Childhood to Adolescence.* New York: Basic Books. doi:10.1037/10034-000

InSTEDD. (2008). *InStedd.* Retrieved 3 16, 2009, from InStedd: Innovative Support to Emergencies, Diseases, and Disasters http://www.instedd.org

Iqbal, M., & Hashmi, M. S. J. (2001). Design and analysis of a virtual factory layout. *Journal of Materials Processing Technology, 118,* 403–410. doi:10.1016/S0924-0136(01)00908-6

ISO 9241-11 (1998). Ergonomic requirements for office work with visual display terminals (VDTs) – Part 11: Guidance on Usability. *International Organization for Standardization.*

Iwata, K., Onosato, M., Keramoto, K., & Osaki, S. (1997). Virtual manufacturing systems as advanced information infrastructure for integrated manufacturing resources and activities. *Ann. CIRP, 46*(1), 335–338. doi:10.1016/S0007-8506(07)60837-3

Iwata, K., Onosato, M., Teramoto, K., & Osaki, S. A. (1995). Modeling and Simulation Architecture for Virtual Manufacturing System. *Annals CIRP, 44,* 399–402. doi:10.1016/S0007-8506(07)62350-6

Jackson, P., de Lussanet, M., Driver, E., Schadler, T., & Menke, L. (2007). *The Real Business Of Virtual Worlds.* Los Angeles: Forrester. Retrieved March 08, 2009

from http://www.forrester.com/Research/Document/Excerpt/0,7211,40701,00.html

Jain, S., Choong, N. F., Aye, K. M., & Luo, M. (2001). Virtual Factory: An Integrated Approach to Manufacturing Systems Modeling. *International Journal of Operations & Production Management, 21*(5-6), 594–608. doi:10.1108/01443570110390354

Jansz, J., & Martens, L. (2005). Gaming at a LAN event: The social context of playing video games. *New Media & Society, 7*(3), 333–355. doi:10.1177/1461444805052280

Jarvis, P. (1987). *Adult Learning in the Social Context.* London: Croom Helm.

Johnsen, K., Dickerson, R., Raij, A., Lok, B., Jackson, J., Shin, M., et al. (2005). *Experiences in Using Immersive Virtual Characters to Educate Medical Communication Skills.* Paper presented at the IEEE Virtual Reality, Bonn, Germany.

Johnson, D. W., Johnson, R. T., & Holubec, E. J. (1993). *Cooperation in the Classroom* (6th ed.). Edina, MN: Interaction Book Company.

Johnson, D., & Johnson, F. (1982). *Joining together: Team theory and team skills* (2nd ed.). Englewood Cliffs, NJ: Prentice-Hall.

Johnson, D., & Johnson, F. (2006). *Joining together: Team theory and team skills* (9th ed.). Englewood Cliffs, NJ: Prentice-Hall.

Johnson, R. T., & Johnson, D. W. (1986). Action research: Cooperative learning in the science classroom. *Science and Children, 24,* 31–32.

Johnson, W. L. (2007). Serious use of a serious game for language learning. *Artificial Intelligence in Education: Building Technology Rich Learning Contexts that . Work (Reading, Mass.),* 67.

Johnson, W. L. (2009). *Developing Intercultural Competence through Videogames.* Paper presented at the The Second International Workshop on Intercultural Collaboration.

Johnson, W. L., & Rickel, J. (1998). Steve: An animated pedagogical agent for procedural training in virtual environments. *SIGART Bulletin*, *8*, 16–21. doi:10.1145/272874.272877

Johnson, W. L., Lewis, W., & Rickel, J. (2000). Animated Pedagogical Agents: Face-to-Face Interaction in Interactive Learning Environments. *International Journal of Artificial Intelligence in Education*, *11*, 47–78.

Johnson, W. L., Rickel, J., Stiles, R., & Munro, A. (1998). Integrating pedagogical agents into virtual environments. *Presence (Cambridge, Mass.)*, *7*, 523–546. doi:10.1162/105474698565929

Johnson, W. L., Vilhjalmsson, H., & Marsella, S. (2005). Serious Games for Language Learning: How Much Game, How Much AI? In Looi, C.-K. (Eds.), *Artificial Intelligence in Education* (pp. 306–311). Washington, D.C: IOS Press.

Johnson, W. L., Wang, N., & Wu, S. (2007). *Experience with serious games for learning foreign languages and cultures.* Paper presented at the SimTecT 2007, Brisbane, Queensland, Australia.

Johnson-Eilola, J. (2004). Relocating the Value of Work: Technical Communication in a Post-Industrial Age . In Selber, J. J.-E. (Ed.), *Central Works in Technical Communication* (pp. 175–194). New York: Oxford University Press.

Joinson, A. N. (2001). Self-disclosure in computer-mediated communication: The role of self-awareness and visual anonymity. *European Journal of Social Psychology*, *31*(2), 177–192. doi:10.1002/ejsp.36

Jonassen, D., Mayes, T., & McAleese, R. (1993). A Manifesto for a Constructivist Approach to Technology in Higher Education . In Duffy, T., Jonassen, D., & Lowyck, J. (Eds.), *Designing constructivist learning environments*. Heidelberg, FRG: Springer-Verlag.

Jones, J. G. (2004). 3-D on-line distributed learning environments: An old concept with a new twist. In R. Ferdig & C. Crawford (Eds.), *Proceedings of the Society for Information Technology and Teacher Education International Conference,* (pp. 507–512), Atlanta, GA.

Jones, W. (2007). Why they don't work: factors that impede the development of social cohesion in online collaborative teams. *Pennsylvania Association of Adult and Community Educators Journal of Lifelong Learning, 16*, 37–62.

Jordan, P. W. (2000). *Designing Pleasurable Products*. New York: Taylor and Francis.

Kalyuga, S. (2007). Enhancing Instructional Efficiency of Interactive E-learning Environments: A Cognitive Load Perspective. *Educational Psychology Review*, 387–399. doi:10.1007/s10648-007-9051-6

Kamel Boulos, M. N., Wheeler, L., & Hetherington, S. (2007). Second Life: An Overview of the Potential of 3-D Virtual Worlds in Medical and Health Education. *Health Information and Libraries Journal*, *24*, 233–245. doi:10.1111/j.1471-1842.2007.00733.x

Kaslow, N. J., Borden, K. A., Collins, F. L. Jr, Forrest, L., Illfelder-Kaye, J., Nelson, P., & Rallo, J. S. (2004). Competencies Conference: Future Directions in Education and Credentialing in Professional Psychology. *Journal of Clinical Psychology, 60*, 699–712. doi:10.1002/jclp.20016

Kaur, K., Sutcliffe, A., & Maiden, N. (1998). Improving interaction with virtual environments. In proceedings of IEEE Colloquium on The 3D Interface for the Information Worker (Digest No. 1998/437), London.

Kearsley, G. (2000). *Online education: Learning and teaching in cyberspace*. Belmont, CA: Wadsworth.

Keegan, D. (Ed.). (1996). *Foundations of distance education* (3rd ed.). London: Routledge.

Kelly, J. (2001, June 6). E-learning on course for strong growth: The internet offers companies a way of delivering training in a flexible and cost-effective manner, writes jim kelly. *Financial Times,* 01.

Kelton, A. J. (2008). Virtual Worlds? Outlook Good. *Educause Review, 43*(5), 15-22. Retrieved June 02, 2009 from http://connect.educause.edu/Library/EDUCAUSE+Review/VirtualWorldsOutlook-Good/47219

Kemp, J., & Livingstone, D. (2006). Putting a Second Life "Metaverse" Skin on Learning Management

Systems. In Livingstone & Kemp (eds.), *Proceedings of the Second Life Education Workshop at SLCC*, San Francisco, August, (pp. 13-18). Retrieved March 08, 2009 from http://www.simteach.com/SLCC06/slcc2006-proceedings.pdf

Kerka, S. (1998). *Competency-based education and training: Myths and realities*. ERIC/ACVE. Retrieved March 06, 2009, from http://www.calpro-online.org/eric/textonly/docgen.asp?tbl=mr&ID=65

Ketelhut, D. J., Dede, C., Clarke, J., & Nelson, B. (2006). *A multi-user virtual environment for building higher order inquiry skills in science*. Paper presented at the American Educational Research Association, San Francisco, CA.

Kiesler, S., & Sproull, L. (1992). Group decision making and communication technology. *Organizational Behavior and Human Decision Processes*, *52*, 96–123. doi:10.1016/0749-5978(92)90047-B

Kim, P. (2006). Effects of 3-D virtual reality of plate tectonics on fifth grade students' achievement and attitude toward science. *Interactive Learning Environments*, *14*(1), 25–34. doi:10.1080/10494820600697687

Kim, Y., & Baylor, A. L. (2006). A Social-Cognitive Framework for Pedagogical Agents as Learning Companions. *Educational Technology Research and Development*, *54*(6), 569–596. doi:10.1007/s11423-006-0637-3

Kinneavy, J. L. (1986). Kairos: A neglected concept in classical rhetoric . In Stephenson, H. (Ed.), *Forecasting opportunity: Kairos, production and writing*. Lanham, MD: UP of America.

Kirkup, G. (2001). Teacher or Avatar? Identity Isseus in Computer-Mediated Contexts . In Burge, E. (Ed.), *Using Learning Technologies: International Perspectives on Practice*. London: Routkedge Falmer.

Kirriemuir, J. (2007). [*"snapshot" of UK Higher and Further Education Developments in Second Life*. Bath, UK: Eduserv Foundation.]. *An update of the*, (July): 2007.

Kirriemuir, J. (2008). *An autumn 2008 "snapshot" of UK Higher and Further Education Developments in Second Life*. Bath, UK: Eduserv Foundation.

Kirriemuir, J. (2009). *The Spring 2009 Snapshot of Virtual World use in UK Higher and Further Education*. Bath, UK: Eduserv Foundation.

Kirriemuir, J., & McFarlane, A. (2004). *Literature review in games and learning. Report 8*. Bristol: Nesta Futurelab.

Klabbers, J. H. G. (2000). Learning as Acquisition and Learning as Interaction. *Simulation amp Gaming, 31*(3), 380-406.

Kleps, K. (2006). Virtual sales training scores a hit. *T + D, 60*(12), 63.

KnowledgeWorks Foundation. (2006). *The 2006-2016 KnowledgeWorks Foundation and the Institute for the Future Map of the Future Forces Affecting Education*. Retrieved March 15, 2009, from http://www.kwfdn.org/map/node.aspx

Knowles, M. (1975). *Self-directed learning*. Chicago: Follet.

Knowles, M. (1980). *The modern practice of adult education* (2nd ed.). New York: Cambridge Books.

Knowles, M. (1984). *The adult learner: A neglected species* (3rd ed.). Houston, TX: Gulf Publishing.

Koh, S. H., Zhou, H., Tan, H. S., & Tan, K. C. (2002). Virtual Environments for Manufacturing & Training (VEMAT). *Distance Learning and the Internet: Human Capacity Development (DLI 2002) Canberra and Sydney Conference. Association of Pacific Rim Universities (APRU)*. Singapore.

Kolb, A., & Kolb, D. (2005). *The Kolb Learning Style Inventory – Version 3.1: 2005 technical specifications. LSI Technical Manual* (pp. 1–71). Boston, MA: Hay Resources Direct.

Kolb, D. (1984). *Experimental Learning (Experience as The Source of Learning and Development)*. Upper Saddle River, NJ: Prentice-Hall.

Kolb, D. A. (1994). *Experiential Learning: Experience as the Source of Learning and Development*. Englewood Cliffs, NJ: Prentice Hall.

Kolb, D. A., & Fry, R. (1975). Toward an applied theory of experiential learning . In Cooper, C. (Ed.), *Theories of Group Process*. London: John Wiley.

Koplowitz, R. (2007). *Web 2.0 Social Computing Dresses Up For Business*. Cambridge, MA: Forrester.

Korves, B., & Loftus, M. (2000). Designing an Immersive Virtual Reality Interface for layout Planning. *Journal of Materials Processing Technology, 107*, 425–430. doi:10.1016/S0924-0136(00)00717-2

Krashen, S. D. (1982). *Principles and practices in second language acquisition*. New York: Prentice-Hall, Prentice Hall International.

Krashen, S. D. (1988). *Second language acquisition and second language learning*. New York: Prentice-Hall.

Krathwohl, D. R., Bloom, B. S., & Masia, B. B. (1964). *Taxonomy of educational objectives: The classification of educational goals. Handbook II: The affective domain*. New York: David McKay.

Krell, E. (2007, November). HR challenges in virtual worlds. *HR Magazine*.

Kress, G. (2004). *Literacy in the New Media Age*. London: Routledge.

Kress, G., & Van Leeuwen, T. (2001). *Multimodal Discourse: The Modes and Media of contemporary communication*. New York: Hodder Arnold.

Kronos, A. (2007, May). *Sun Aims New 3D Environment at Business*. Retrieved March 15, 2009, from http://www.3pointd.com/20070501/sun-aims-new-3d-environment-at-business/

Kumar, A. (2008). *Mobile broadcasting with WiMAX: Principles, technology, and applications*. Boston: Focal Press.

Kuznik, L. (2007). *Interactive Learning Environments and Children's Museums - Theoretical Model and It's Planning*. Unpublished Doctoral Dissertation, University of Ljubljana, Slovenia.

Lacefield, R. (1999). *Adult Education in Practice: Teaching Methods and Course Structure*. Tripod Education Tipsheets.

Laderas-Kilkenny, N. (2006, August 30). *Generational Learning Styles and Methods*. Retrieved July 15, 2008, from Design for Learning, http://nkilkenny.wordpress.com/2006/08/30/generational-learning-styles-and-methods

Lafsky, M. (2009). Can Training in Second Life Teach Doctors to Save Real Lives? [Electronic Version]. *Discover*. Retrieved from http://discovermagazine.com/2009/jul-aug/15-can-medical-students-learn-to-save-real-lives-in-second-life/article_view?b_start:int=0&-C=

Lancaster, C., & Stillman, D. (2003). *When Generations Collide: Who they are, Why they collide, How to Solve the Generational Puzzle at Work*. New York: HarperCollins.

Lang, J. M. (2009). When published research on teaching doesn't help you, why not use your own classroom as a laboratory? *Chronicle of Higher Education (March)*. Retrieved May 7, 2009 from http://chronicle.com/jobs/news/2009/03/2009033101c.htm

Lankshear, C., & Knobel, M. (2005). *Digital literacies: policy, pedagogy and research considerations for education*. Paper presented at Opening Plenary Address: ITU Conference, Oslo, Norway, October 20, 2005. Retrieved from http://www.geocities.com/c.lankshear/Oslo.pdf

Lanshear, C., & Knobel, M. (2004). *New Literacies: Changing Knowledge and Classroom Learning*. Berkshire, UK: Open University Press.

Lantolf, J. P., & Thorne, S. L. (2006). *Sociocultural theory and the genesis of second language development*. Oxford, UK: Oxford University Press.

Lauria, R. (2000). Understanding the tactile nature of electric sensibility in virtual environments. *Spark Online, 15*. Retrieved March 9, 2009 from http://www.spark-online.com/december00/print-friendly/lauria.htm

Laurillard, D. (1994). How can learning technologies improve learning? *Law Technology Journal, 3*(2). Retrieved March 16, 2009 from http://web.archive.org/web/20070322002729/http://www.law.warwick.ac.uk/ltj/3-2j.html

Laurillard, D. (2002). *Rethinking University Teaching* (2nd ed.). London: Routledge Falmer. doi:10.4324/9780203304846

Lave, J. (1988). *Cognition in practice*. New York: Cambridge University Press. doi:10.1017/CBO9780511609268

Lave, J., & Wenger, E. (1991). *Situated learning: legitimate peripheral participation*. New York: Cambridge University Press.

Lawler, P. A., & King, K. P. (2000). *Planning for effective faculty development: Using adult learning strategies*. Malabar, FL: Krieger Pub Co.

Lea, M., & Spears, R. (1992). Paralanguage and social perception in computer-mediated communication. *Journal of Organizational Computing, 2*, 321–341. doi:10.1080/10919399209540190

Learning communities in the workplace: The virtues of going virtual. (2007, November). *Development and Learning in Organizations, 21*(6), 28. Retrieved March 24, 2009, from ABI/INFORM Global database: Document ID: 1341289591.

Lee, G. B., Cheung, f., & Li, J. G. (2001). Application of virtual manufacturing in material processing. *Journal of Materials Processing Technology, 113*, 416–423. doi:10.1016/S0924-0136(01)00668-9

Lepper, M. R., & Chabay, R. W. (1985). Intrinsic motivation and instruction: Conflicting views on the role of motivational processes in computer-based education. *Educational Psychologist, 20*, 217–230. doi:10.1207/s15326985ep2004_6

Lester, J. C., Converse, S. A., Stone, B. A., Kahler, S. E., & Barlow, S. T. (1997). Animated pedagogical agents and problem-solving effectiveness: A large-scale empirical evaluation. In *Proceedings of the Eighth World Conference on Artificial Intelligence in Education,* (pp. 23-30). Amsterdam: IOS Press.

Lester, J. C., Stone, B. A., & Stelling, G. D. (1999). Lifelike pedagogical agents for mixed-initiative problem solving in constructivist learning environments. *User Modeling and User-Adapted Interaction, 9*, 1–44. doi:10.1023/A:1008374607830

Lester, J. C., Voerman, J. L., Towns, S. G., & Callaway, C. B. (1999). Deictic believability: Coordinating gesture, locomotion, and speech in lifelike pedagogical agents. *Applied Artificial Intelligence, 13*, 383–414. doi:10.1080/088395199117324

Lim, S., & Reeves, B. (2006, June 16). *Being in the game: Effects of avatar choice and point of view on arousal responses during play*. Paper presented at the annual meeting of the International Communication Association, Dresden International Congress Centre, Dresden, Germany.

Lin, E., Minis, I., Nau, D. S., & Regli, W. C. (1997). *The institute for System Research*. CIM Lab, University of Maryland.

Lin, M.-H., & Fu, L.-C. (2001). A Virtual Factory Based Approach to On-line Simulation and Scheduling for an FMS and a Case Study. *Journal of Intelligent Manufacturing, 12*(3), 269–279. doi:10.1023/A:1011201009821

Linden Research, Inc. (2009). *Case Study: How Meeting In Second Life Transformed IBM's Technology Elite Into Virtual World Believers*. San Francisco: Linden Lab. Retrieved March 08, 2009 from http://secondlifegrid.net.s3.amazonaws.com/docs/Second_Life_Case_IBM.pdf

Linden, A. (2009). *Second life lives behind a firewall*. Retrieved May 31, 2009, from https://blogs.secondlife.com/community/workinginworld/blog/2009/04/01/second-life-lives-behind-a-firewall

Liu, X., Magjuka, R. J., Bonk, C., & Lee, S. (2007). Does sense of community matter? An examination of participants' perceptions of building learning communities in online courses. *The Quarterly Review of Distance Education, 1*(8), 9–24.

Livingstone, D., Kemp, J., & Edgar, E. (2008). From Multi-User Virtual Environment to 3D Virtual Learning Environment. *ALT-J. 16*(3), 139-150. Retrieved March 08, 2009 from http://www.informaworld.com/10.1080/09687760802526707

Locke, C., Levine, R., Searls, D., & Weinberger, D. (2001). *The Cluetrain Manifestor: The End of Business as Usual*. New York: Basic Books.

Lohr, S. (2008). Free the Avatars. *The New York Times.* Retrieved October 15, 2008 from http://www.nytimes.com

Lu, H., Jia, L., Gong, S., & Clark, B. (2007). The relationship of Kolb learning styles, online learning behaviors and learning outcomes. *Education Technology & Society, 10*(4), 187–196.

Lucia, A. D., & Lepinsinger, R. (1999). *The art and science of competency models.* San Francisco, CA: Jossey-Bass/Pfeiffer.

Lycos. (2009, March). *Lycos.* Retrieved March 2009, from Lycos: http://lycos.com

MacFarlane, S., Sim, G., & Horton, M. (2005). Assessing usability and fun in educational software. In *Proceedings of the Conference on interaction Design and Children IDC '05*, Boulder, CO.

Maes, P. (1990). *Designing Autonomous Agents.* Cambridge, MA: MIT Press.

Magoulas, G. D., Papanikolaou, K. A., & Grigoriadou, M. (2001). Neuro-fuzzy Synergism for Planning the Content in a Web-based Course. *Journal of Informatrics, 25,* 39–48.

Mahaley, S. (2009). A Second Look at Second Life. *Chief Learning Officer, 8*(5), 20-27. Retrieved June 02, 2009 from http://www.clomedia.com/features/2009/May/2622/index.php?pt=a&aid=2622&start=0&page=1

Malaby, T. M. (2007). Contriving constraints: The gameness of Second Life and the persistence of scarcity. *Innovations: Technology, Governance, Globalization, 2*(3), 62–67. doi:10.1162/itgg.2007.2.3.62

Malone, T. W., & Lepper, M. R. (1987). Making Learning Fun: A Taxonomy of Intrinsic Motivations for Learning . In Snow, R. E., & Farr, M. J. (Eds.), *Aptitude, Learning and Instruction III: Conative and Affective Process Analyses* (pp. 223–250). Hillsdale, NJ: Lawrence Erlbaum Associates.

Manesh, H. F., & Hashemipour, M. (2007). A New Software Development Tools with Virtual Reality for Computer Integrated Manufacturing Requirements Analysis. *Journal of Passenger Cars Mechanical Systems-SAE Transaction,* 908-917.

Manetta, C., & Blade, R. (1995). Glossary of virtual reality terminology. *International Journal of Virtual Reality, 1*(2), 35–39.

Marinov, V. (2000). *What Virtual Manufacturing is? Part II: The Space of Virtual Manufacturing.* Turkey: Bosphorus University.

Markel, M. (1998). Testing visual-based modules for teaching writing. *Technical Communication,* (47-76).

Marketing Executives Research Group. (2008). *Beyond Wikipedia: Wikis as Workplace Tools.* New York: E-Marketer.

Maropoulos, P. G. (2003). Digital Enterprise Technology. *International Journal of Computer Integrated Manufacturing, 16*(7-8), 465–466. doi:10.1080/0951192031000115778

Mascarenhas, B., Baveja, A., & Jamil, M. (1998). Dynamics of core competencies in leading multinational companies. *California Management Review, 40*(4), 117–132.

McLuhan, E., & Zingrone, F. (Eds.). (1995). *The essential McLuhan.* Toronto: Anansi Press.

Meadows, M. (2008). *I, Avatar: The Culture and Consequences of Having a Second Life.* Berkley, CA: New Riders.

Merriam, S. B., & Caffarella, R. S. (1999). *Learning in adulthood* (2nd ed.). San Francisco: Jossey-Bass.

Messinger, P. R., Ge, X., Stroulia, E., Lyons, K., Smirnov, K., & Bone, M. (2008). On the relationship between my avatar and myself. *Journal of Virtual Worlds Research, 1*(2), 1–17.

Messinger, P. R., Stroulia, E., Lyons, K., Bone, M., Niu, R., Smirnov, K., & Perelgut, S. (2009). Virtual worlds – past, present, and future: New directions in social computing. *Decision Support Systems, 47,* 204–228. doi:10.1016/j.dss.2009.02.014

Messinger, P., Ge, X., Stroulia, E., Lyons, K., Smirnov, K., & Bone, M. (2008, November). On the relationship between my avatar and myself. *Virtual Worlds Research: Consumer Behavior in Virtual Worlds, 1*(2), 1–17.

Methods of virtual reality. (2008). Wikipedia. Retrieved February 10, 2008, from http://en.wikipedia.org/wiki/Methods_of_virtual_reality

Meyer, K. A. (2002). Quality in distance education: Focus on on-line learning . In Kezar, A. J. (Ed.), *ASHE-ERIC Higher Education Report* (*Vol. 29*, pp. 1–134). San Francisco: Jossey – Bass.

Mezirow (2000). Mezirow, J. (2001). Learning to think like an adult: Core concepts of transformation theory. In J. Mezirow & Assoc. (Ed.), *Learning as transformation: Critical perspectives on a theory in progress,* (pp. 3-34). San Francisco: Jossey-Bass.

Mezirow, J. & Assoc. (1990). *Fostering critical reflection in adulthood.* San Francisco: Jossey-Bass.

Mezirow, J. (1991). *Transformative Dimensions of Adult Learning.* San Francisco: Jossey Bass.

Miller, G. A., & Gildea, P. M. (1987). How children learn words. *Scientific American, 257*(3), 94–99. doi:10.1038/scientificamerican0987-94

Miller, P. (2008, February 26). *Sir Tim Berners-Lee: Semantic Web is Open for Business.* Retrieved July 19, 2009, from ZDNet: http://blogs.zdnet.com/semantic-web/?p=105

Minks, G. (2008, September 15). *Can Second Life be used as a reliable Corporate Training Tool?* Retrieved July 18, 2009, from Adventures in Corporate Education: http://gminks.edublogs.org/2008/09/15/can-second-life-be-used-as-a-reliable-corporate-training-tool/

Mitham, N. (2008, April). *Virtual Worlds by The Numbers: Today and The Future.* Paper presented on Virtual Worlds Expo 2008, New York.

Moallem, M. (2007). Accommodating individual differences in the design of online learning environments: A comparative study. *Journal of Research on Technology in Education, 40*(2), 217–245.

Moore, A. H., Moore, J. F., & Fowler, S. B. (2005). Faculty Development for the Net Generation. In Oblinger &

Oblinger, (Eds.), *Educating the Net Generation.* Retrieved November 28, 2008 from http://www.educause.edu/PreparingtheAcademyofTodayfortheLearnerofTomorrow/6062

Moore, M. (1990). Background and overview of contemporary American distance education . In Moore, M. (Ed.), *Contemporary issues in American distance education* (pp. xii–xxvi). New York: Pergamon.

Moore, M. G., & Kearsley, G. (1996). *Distance education: A systems view.* Belmont, CA: Wadsworth.

Moreno, R., Mayer, R. E., Spires, H. A., & Lester, J. C. (2001). The Case for Social Agency in Computer-based Teaching: Do Students Learn More Deeply When They Interact with Animated Pedagogical Agents? *Cognition and Instruction, 19*(2), 177–213. doi:10.1207/S1532690XCI1902_02

Morgan, K. (2000). Cross-Cultural Considerations for Simulation-Based Learning Environments. *Simulation & Gaming, 31*(4), 491–508. doi:10.1177/104687810003100404

Mujber, T. S., Szecsi, T., & Hashmi, M. S. J. (2004). Virtual reality applications in manufacturing process simulation. *Journal of Materials Processing Technology, 155/156,* 1834–1838. doi:10.1016/j.jmatprotec.2004.04.401

Müller, J. P. (1996). *The Design of Intelligent Agents: A Layered Approach.* Berlin: Springer-Verlag.

Mullins, R., Duan, Y., Hamblin, D., Burrell, P., Jin, H., Jerzy, G., Ewa, Z., Billewicz, A. (2007). A web based intelligent training system for SMEs. *Electronic Journal of e-Learning, 5*(1), 39 – 48.

Murray, S. (2005). High art/low life: The art of playing grand theft auto. *PAJ a Journal of Performance and Art, 27*(80), 91–98. doi:10.1162/1520281053850866

Musselwhite, C. (2006). University executive education gets real. *T + D, 60*(5), 57.

Nah, Y. (1999). Can a self-director learner be independent, autonomous and interdependent: Implications for practice. *Adult Learning, 1*(1), 18–25.

Nakamura, J., & Csikszentmihalyi, M. (2002). The concept of flow . In Snyder, C. R., & Lopez, S. J. (Eds.), *Handbook of Positive Psychology* (pp. 89–105). Cambridge, UK: Oxford University Press.

National Center for Education Statistics. (2005). *Projections of education statistics to 2014 (NCES 2005-074)*. Washington, DC: U.S. Government Printing Office.

Neal, D. (2007). *Harnessing Web 2.0: Enterprise Strategies for Living on the Web. Leading Edge Forum Executive Programme*. Falls Church, VA: Computer Sciences Corporation.

Nebolsky, C., Yee, N. K., Petrushin, V. A., & Gershman, A. V. (2003). Corporate Training in Virtual Worlds. In *The 3rd International Conference on Advanced Learning Technologies,* (pp. 412-420). Riga, Latvia: IEEE Computer Society Press.

Nebolsky, C., Yee, N.K., Petrushin, V.A., & Gershman, A. V. (2005). Corporate training in virtual worlds. *Systemics, Cybernetics and Informatics, 2*(6)

Nedic, Z., & Nedic, V., & Machotka, J. (2002). Intelligent tutoring System for teaching 1st year engineering. *World Transaction on Engineering and Technology Education, 1*(2).

Negroponte, N. (1970). *The architecture machine*. Cambridge, MA: MIT press.

Neumann, U., & Majoros, A. (1998). Cognitive, performance, and systems issues for augmented reality applications in manufacturing and maintenance. In *Proceedings of Virtual Reality Annual International Symposium (VRAIS),* (pp. pp 4-11). Washington, DC: IEEE.

New London Group. (1996). A pedagogy of multiliteracies: Designing social futures. *Harvard Educational Review, 66,* 60–92.

NewDilligence. *The Collaborative Internet: Usage Trends, End User Attitudes and IT Impact*. San Francisco: NewDilligence.

Newitz, A. (2007). Your Second Life is Ready. *Popsci. com*. Retrieved May 6, 2009 from http://www.popsci.com/scitech/article/2006-09/your-second-life-ready

Newlin, M., & Wang, A. (2002). Integrating technology and pedagogy: Web instruction and seven principles of undergraduate education. *Teaching of Psychology, 29*(4), 325–330. doi:10.1207/S15328023TOP2904_15

News, F. O. X. (2006). *Survey: College kids like IPods better than beer*. Retrieved on March 10, 2008, from http://www.foxnews.com/story/0,2933,198632,00.html

Nielsen, J., & Landauer, T. K. (1993). A mathematical model of the finding of usability problems. In *Proceedings of ACM INTERCHI'93 Conference,* (pp. 206-213), Amsterdam, The Netherlands, Norman, D. (1998). *The invisible computer*. Cambridge, MA: The MIT Press.

Nijholt, A. (2004). Where computers disappear, virtual humans appear. *Computers & Graphics, 28,* 467–476. doi:10.1016/j.cag.2004.04.002

Norman, D. A. (2002). *The design of everyday things*. New York: Basic Books.

Norman, D. A. (2004). *Emotional Design: Why We Love (or hate) Everyday Things*. New York: Basic Books.

Normand, V., Babski, C., Benford, S., Bullock, A., Carion, S., & Farcet, N. (1999). The COVEN project: exploring applicative, technical and usage dimensions of collaborative virtual environments. *Presence (Cambridge, Mass.), 8*(2), 218–236. doi:10.1162/105474699566189

Nortel. (2009, March). *Nortel Teams Up with Virtual Heroes to Deliver 3D Virtual Training Application*. Retrieved March 15, 2009, from http://www2.nortel.com/go/news_detail.jsp?cat_id=-8055&oid=100253197

Nunamaker, J. F., Reinig, B. A., & Briggs, R. O. (2009). Principles for effective virtual teamwork. *Communications of the ACM, 52*(4), 113–117. doi:10.1145/1498765.1498797

O'Connor, E. (2009). Alelo Immersive Game Process Document. Los Angeles, CA: Alelo TLT, LLC.

O'Reilly, T. (2005, September 30). *What is Web 2.0: Design Patterns and Business Models for the Next Generation of Software*. Retrieved March 8, 2009, from O'Reilly Media http://www.oreillynet.com/pub/a/oreilly/tim/news/2005/09/30/what-is-web-20.html

Oblinger, D. G. (2003). Boomers, Gen-X'ers, and Millennials: Understanding the 'New Students. *EDUCAUSE Review, 38*(4), 37–47.

Odgers, P. (2005). *Administrative office management (13e)*. Mason, OH: Thomson Corporation, Southwestern.

Olka, K. (2007). Technical Communicators as Teachers: Creating E-Learning that Matters. *Intercom, 24*(4).

Olwal, A., & Hollerer, T. (2005). POLAR: Portable, optical see-through, low-cost augmented reality. In *Proceedings of VRST 2005 (ACM Symposium on Virtual Reality and Software Technology)*, Monterey, CA, Nov 7-9, (pp. 227-230).

Ong, S. K., & Mannan, M. A. (2004). Virtual reality simulations and animations in a web-based interactive manufacturing engineering module. *Computers & Education, 43*(4), 361–382.

Onosato, M., & Iwata, K. (1993). Development of a Virtual Manufacturing System by Integrating Product Models and Factory Models. *Annals of the CIRP, 42*(1), 475–478. doi:10.1016/S0007-8506(07)62489-5

Osimo, D. (2008). *Web 2.0 in Government: Why and How?* Seville, Spain: Joint Research Centre of the European Commission.

Palloff, R. M., & Pratt, K. (2001). *Lessons from the cyberspace classroom: The realities of online teaching.* San Francisco: Jossey-Bass.

Palloff, R., & Pratt, K. (1999). *Building learning communities in cyberspace: Effective strategies for the online classroom.* San Francisco: Jossey Bass Publications.

Pan, Z., Cheok, A. D., Yang, H., Zhu, J., & Shi, J. (2006). Virtual reality and mixed reality for virtual learning environments. *Computers & Graphics, 1*(30), 20–28. doi:10.1016/j.cag.2005.10.004

Park, S., & Catrambone, R. (2007). Social Facilitation Effects of Virtual Humans. *Human Factors: The Journal of the Human Factors and Ergonomics Society,* 1054-1060.

Parker, G. (2007). *Teamwork & team meetings: The new reality.* Retrieved October 12, 2008, from http://www.glennparker.com/Freebees/TeamworkandTeamMeetings.html

Parris, C. (2007, May). Do better business in 3D. *Business Week Online.* Captured March 15, 2009, from http://www.businessweek.com/technology/content/may2007/tc20070501_526224.htm?chan=top+news_top+news+index_technology

Parry, S. R. (1996). The Quest for Competencies. *Training (New York, N.Y.),* (July): 48–56.

Paton, R., Peters, G., Storey, J., & Taylor, S. (2005b). *Handbook of Corporate University Development: Managing Strategic Learning Initiatives in Public and Private Domains.* London: Gower.

Peachey, A. (2010). Living in Immaterial Worlds: Who are we when we learn and teach in virtual worlds? In Sheehy, K., Clough, G., & Ferguson, R. (Eds.), *Controversial Issues in Virtual Education: Perspectives on Virtual Worlds.* New York: Nova Science.

Peachey, A., & Walshe, S. (2008). The Management Challenge Online: e-Learning in Practice. *International Journal of Advanced Corporate Learning, 1*(1).

Peachey, A., Broadribb, S., Carter, C., & Westrapp, F. (2009). Second Life in The Open University: How the Virtual World Can Facilitate Learning for Students and Staff. In Wankel, C. (Eds.), *Higher Education in Second Life.* New York: Emerald.

Pelachaud, C., Carofiglio, V., De Carolis, B., de Rosis, F., & Poggi, I. (2002). *Embodied contextual agent in information delivering application.*

Peng, Q., Hall, F. R., & Lister, P. M. (2000). Application and evaluation of VR-based CAPP system. *Journal of Materials Processing Technology, 107*(1-3), 153–159. doi:10.1016/S0924-0136(00)00677-4

Peters, J. (1990). The action-reason-thematic technique: Spying on the self. In J. Mezirow & Assoc. (Ed.), *Fostering critical reflection in adulthood.* San Francisco: Jossey-Bass.

Phipps, R., & Merisotis, J. (2000). *Quality on the line: Benchmarks for success in Internet-based distance education.* Washington, DC: The Institute for Higher Education Policy. Retrieved July 2, 2003, from http://www.ihep.com/Pubs/PDF/Quality.pdf

Piaget, J. (1936). *The Origins of Intelligence in Children. M. Cook, (trans).* Harmondsworth, UK: Penguin.

Piaget, J., & Inhelder, B. (1990). Psychology of Children. Novi Sad, Serbia: Dobra vest.

Prahalad, C. K., & Ramaswamy, V. (2004). *The future of competition: Co-creating unique value with customers.* Cambridge, MA: Harvard Business School Press.

Prashant, C., Palvia, A., Shailendra, C., Palviab, P. C., & Palvia, S. C. (1999). An examination of the IT satisfaction of small-business users. *Information & Management, 35,* 127–137. doi:10.1016/S0378-7206(98)00086-X

Prasolova-Førland, E. (2008). Analyzing place metaphors in 3D educational collaborative virtual environments. *Computers in Human Behavior, 24,* 185–204. doi:10.1016/j.chb.2007.01.009

Pratt, D. (1993). Andragogy after twenty-five years. In *An Update on Adult Learning Theory . New Directions for Adult and Continuing Education, 57,* 15–24. doi:10.1002/ace.36719935704

Prensky, M. (2001). Digital Natives, Digital Immigrants, Part II: Do They Really Think Differently? *On the Horizon, 9* (6). Retrieved May 23, 2009 from http://www.marcprensky.com/writing/

Purnell, L. (2005). The Purnell Model for Cultural Competence [Electronic Version]. *Journal of Multicultural Nursing & Health.* Retrieved 2/27/09.

Qwaq News. (2009, April 28). *Virtual spaces for real work news room.* Retrieved August 11, 2009, from http://www.qwaq.com/company/press_releases/pr-2009_04_28.php

Rasmusson, E. (2000). Training goes virtual. *Sales and Marketing Management, 152*(9), 108.

Raybourn, E. (2004). (pp. Personal conversation). Albuquerque, New Mexico.

Real Learning in a Virtual World. (2008, March 15). *The Christian Science Monitor.* Retrieved October 5, 2006 from http://www.csmonitor.com

Reich, R. (1991). *The Work of Nations: Preparing Ourselves for 21st Century Capitalism.* New York: A.A. Knopf.

Reigeluth, C. M. (Ed.). (1999). *Instructional-Design Theories and Models (Vol. II).* Mahwah, NJ: Lawrence Erlbaum Associates, Publishers.

Reigeluth, C. M., & Schwartz, E. (1989). An Instructional Theory for the Design of Computer-based Simulations. *Journal of Computer-Based Education, 16*(1), 1–10.

Reinhold, S. D. (2006). Concepts for Extending Wiki Systems tov extend collaborative learning . In *Z. e. Pan, Edutainment 2006* (pp. 755–767). Berlin: Springer-Verlag.

Remley, D. (2010). *Second Life literacies: Critiquing writing technologies of Second Life.* Computers and Composition Online.

Review, H. B. online version. (2006). *Avatar - based marketing.* Retrieved April 12, 2009 from http://harvardbusinessonline.hbsp.harvard.edu/hbsp/hbr/articles/article.jsp?articleID=R0606B

Rheingold, H. (2000). *The virtual community: Homesteading on the electronic frontier.* Cambridge, MA: The MIT Press.

Rickel, J., & Johnson, W. L. (1999). Virtual Humans for Team Training in Virtual Reality. In *the Proceedings of the Ninth World Conference on AI in Education,* July 1999. Washington, DC: IOS Press.

Riedl, R., Bronack, S., & Tashner, J. (2005, January). *3D web-based worlds for instruction.* The Society for Information and Teacher Education, Phoenix, AZ. Published in the Book of Proceedings.

Ritke-Jones, W. (2008). Using cyberspace to promote transformative learning experiences and consequently democracy in the workplace . In St. Amant, K., & Zemliansky, P. (Eds.), *Handbook of research on virtual workplaces and the new nature of business practices* (pp. 204–219). Hershey, PA: IGI Global.

Robbins, S. (2006). "Image Slippage": Navigating the Dichotomies of an Academic Identity in a Non-academic Virtual World. In *Proceedings of the First Second Life Education Workshop, Part of the 2006 Second Life Community Convention*, August 18th-20th.

Roberts, G. R. (2005). Technology and Learning Expectations of the Net Generation. In D. Oblinger & J. Oblinger, (Eds.), *Educating the Net Generation.* Retrieved May 23, 2009 from http://net.educause.edu/ir/library/pdf/pub7101c.pdf

Robertson, D (2002). *Andragogy in color.* US Department of Education, ERIC document Reproduction Service No.EADU 9020.

Roda, C., Angehrn, A. A., & Nabeth, T. (2001). Applications and Research . In *BotShow 2001*. Paris, France: Conversational Agents for Advanced Learning.

Rodolfa, E. R., Bent, R. J., Eisman, E., Nelson, P. D., Rehm, L., & Ritchie, P. (2005). A cube model for competency development: Implications for psychology educators and regulators. *Professional Psychology, Research and Practice, 36*, 347–354. doi:10.1037/0735-7028.36.4.347

Roebuck, D. B., Brock, S. J., & Moodie, D. R. (2004). Using a simulation to explore the challenges of communicating in a virtual team. *Business Communication Quarterly, 67*(3), 359–367. doi:10.1177/1080569904268083

Rogers, C. (1967). The facilitation of significant learning. In L. Siegel, (Ed.) Instructions: Some Contemporary Viewpoints, (pp. 37-54). San Francisco, CA: Chandler.

Rogers, C. R. (1969). *Freedom to learn.* Columbus, OH: Merrill.

Rooks, B. (1999). The reality of virtual reality. *Assembly Automation, 19*(3), 203–208. doi:10.1108/01445159910280065

Rosenberg, M. J. (2001). *E-learning: Strategies for delivering knowledge in the digital age.* New York: McGraw Hill.

Roth, W. M. (2001). Situating Cognition. *Journal of the Learning Sciences, 10*(1/2), 27–61. doi:10.1207/S15327809JLS10-1-2_4

Rothfarb, J. R., & Doherty, P. (2007). Creating Museum Content and Community in Second Life . In Trant, J., & Bearman, D. (Eds.), *Museums and the Web 2007.* Toronto, Canada: Archives & Museum Informatics.

Rothwell, W. J. (2004). Scaling the great wall: Training in china. *Training (New York, N.Y.), 41*(12), 32.

Roussos, M., Johnson, A. E., Leigh, J., Barnes, C. R., Vasilakis, C. A., & Moher, T. G. (1997). The NICE project: Narrative, immersive, constructionist/collaborative environments for learning in virtual reality. In *Proceedings of ED-MEDIA/ED-TELECOM*, (pp. 917-922).

Rovai, A. (2002). Building sense of community at a distance. *International Review of Research in Open and Distance Learning, 3*(1). Retrieved January 16, 2008, from http://www.irrodl.org/content/v3.1/rovai.html

Rubens, P., & Southard, S.Students' technological difficulties in using Web-based learning environments . In Cooke, K. C., & Grant-Davie, K. (Eds.), *Online Education: Global Questions, Local Answers* (pp. 193–206). Amityville, NY: Baywood Publishing Company.

Rude, C. (2005). *Strategic Planning for online education: Sustaining students, faculty, and programs. Online Education: Global Questions, Local Answers* (pp. 67–85). Amityville, NY: Baywood Publishing Company.

Russell, S. J., & Norvig, P. (1995). *Artificial Intelligence: A Modern Approach.* Englewood Cliffs, NJ: Prentice Hall.

Rymaszewski, M., Au, W. J., Wallace, M., Winters, C., Ondrejka, C., & Batsone-Cunningham, B. (2007). *Second Life: The Official Guide.* Mahwah, NJ: John Wiley & Sons.

Saadoun, M., & Sandoval, V. (1999). *Virtual Manufacturing and its implication, Virtual reality and Prototyping.* France: Laval.

Sampson, D., Karagiannidis, C., & Kinshuk, K. (2002).

Personalised learning: educational, technological and standardisation perspective. *Interactive Educational Multimedia, 4,* 24–39.

Santo, S. A. (2006). Relationships between learning styles and online learning: Myth or reality? *Performance Improvement Quarterly, 19*(3), 73–88.

Saunders, P. M. (1997). Experiential Learning, Cases and Simulations in Business. *Business Communication Quarterly, 60*(1), 97–114. doi:10.1177/108056999706000108

SBA. (2008). *Bureau of Labor Statistics. Technical report.* Washington, D.C.: United States Department of Labor.

Schaefer, D., Borgmann, C., & Scheffter, D. (2001). *Factory Planning and the Potential of Virtual Reality.*

Scheiter, K., & Gerjets, P. (2007). Learner Control in Hypermedia Environments. *Educational Psychology Review,* 285–307. doi:10.1007/s10648-007-9046-3

Schleich, J.F., Corney, W.J., Boe, W.J. (1990). Microcomputer implementation in small business: Current status and success factors. *Journal of Microcomputer System Management,* 2 - 10.

Schroeder, R. (2006). Being There and the Future of Connected Presence. *Journal of Teleoperators and Virtual Environments, 15*(4), 438–454. doi:10.1162/pres.15.4.438

Scott, D. (2007). Learning the Second Way. *Medical Education, 335,* 1122–1123.

Screven, C. (2000). Information Design in Informal Settings: Museums and Other Public Spaces . In Jacobson, R. (Ed.), *Information Design* (pp. 131–192). Cambridge, MA: MIT Press.

Scroeder, R. (2008). Defining virtual worlds and virtual environments. *Journal of Virtual Worlds Research, 1*(1).

Second Life Grid Case Studies. (2009). Retrieved May 15, 2009, from http://secondlifegrid.net/casestudies/IBM

Selfe, C. (2004). Toward a new media text: Taking up the challenges of visual literacy . In Wysocki, A. F., Johnson-Eilola, J., Selfe, C., & Sirc, G. (Eds.), *Writing*

New Media: Theory and Applications for Expanding the Teaching of Composition (pp. 67–110). Logan, UT: Utah State Press.

Selfe, C., & Selfe, R. (1994). The Politics of the interface: Power and its exercise in electronic contact zones. *College Composition and Communication, 45*(4), 480–501. doi:10.2307/358761

Senge, P. (2006). *The Fifth Discipline.* New York: Doubleday.

Shachaf, P., & Hara, N. (2005). Team effectiveness in virtual environments: An ecological approach . In Ferris, S. P., & Godar, S. (Eds.), *Teaching and learning with virtual teams* (pp. 83–108). Hershey, PA: Idea Group Publishing.

Shaw, B. (2009). *Project Management Rehearsal Studio: A Collaborative Learning Experience in a Virtual World.* Armonk, NY: IBM.

Shaw, E., Ganeshan, R., Johnson, W. L., & Millar, D. (1999). Building a case for agent-assisted learning as a catalyst for curriculum reform in medical education. In *Proceedings of the Ninth International Conference on Artificial Intelligence in Education.* Amsterdam: IOS Press.

Shea, P., Li, C. S., Swan, K., & Pickett, A. (2002). Developing learning community in online asynchronous college courses: The role of teaching presence. *Journal of Asynchronous Learning Networks, 9*(4), 59–82.

Shedroff, N. (2001). *Experience Design 1.* Indianapolis, IN: New Riders.

Sherman, B., & Judkins, P. (1992). *Glimpses of Heaven, Visions of Hell: Virtual Reality and its implications.* London: Hodder and Stoughton.

Sherman, W. R., & Craig, A. B. (2003). *Understanding virtual reality.* San Francisco, CA: Morgan Kauffman.

Shieh, D. (2009, January 26). 'Social Bookmarking' Site for Higher Education Makes Debut. *The Chronicle of Higher Education.* Retrieved March 16, 2009, from http://chronicle.com/free/2009/01/10124n.htm

Shields, P. (1997). Teaching Techniques for Contemporary Marketing Issues. In Varble, Young, & Maliche (Ed.), Marketing Management Association, (pp. 1-5).

Shipman, C., & Kay, K. (2009). *Womenomics: Write Your Own Rules for Success*. New York: HarperCollins.

Shirky, C. (2008). *Here Comes Everybody*. New York: Penguin Press.

Shneiderman, B., & Plaisant, C. (2004). *Designing the user interface: Strategies for effective human-computer interaction* (4th ed.). Boston: Addison-Wesley.

Short, J., Williams, E., & Christie, B. (1976). *The social psychology of telecommunications*. London: John Wiley.

Siegel, D. (1997). *Creating Killer Websites: The Art of Third Generation Site Design*. Indianapolis, IN: Hayden Books.

Siemans, G. (2005). *Connectivisim: Learning as Network Creation*. Retrieved November 28, from, http://elearnspace.org/Articles/networks.htm

Simpson, R., & Galbo, J. (1986). Interaction and Learning: Theorizing on the Art of Teaching. *Interchange*, *17*(4), 37–51. doi:10.1007/BF01807015

Skiba, D. J. (2007). Nursing Education 2.0: Second Life. *Nursing Education Perspectives*, *28*(3), 156–157.

Skiba, D. J., & Barton, A. J. (2006). Adapting your teaching to accommodate the net generation of learners. *Online Journal of Issues in Nursing*, *11*(2), 15.

Sloan Consortium. (2005). *Growing by degrees: Online education in the United States*. Retrieved January 10, 2007 from, http://www.sloan-c.org/resources/growing_by_degrees.pdf

Smith, M. K. (1999). *Andragogy, the encyclopedia of informal education*. Retrieved April 30, 2008 from, http://www.infed.org/lifelonglearning/b-andra.htm

Smith, M. K. (2002). Malcolm Knowles, informal adult education, self-direction and andragogy. *The encyclopedia of informal education*. Retrieved April 30, 2008 from http://www.infed.org/thinkers/et-knowl.htm

Smith, R. (2005, May). Working with difference in online collaborative teams. *Adult Education Quarterly*, *55*(3), 182–199. doi:10.1177/0741713605274627

Smith, T. C. (2005). Fifty one competencies for online instruction. *The Journal of Online Educators*, *2*(2), 1–18.

Smith, T., Affleck, G., Lees, B., & Branki, C. (1999). Implementing a generic framework for a web based pedagogical agent. In *ASCILITE99 Conference Proceedings*.

Spector, J. M., & Anderson, T. M. (Eds.). (2000). *Integrated and holistic perspectives on learning, instruction and technology: Understanding complexity*. Dordrecht: Kluwer Academic Press.

Spector, J. M., & de la Teja, I. (2001) Competencies for Online Teaching. *Eric Digest*. Retrieved March 01, 2009 from, http://ericit.org/digests/EDO-IR-2001-09.shtml

Spencer, B. (1998). *The purposes of adult education*. Toronto: Thompson Educational Publishing, Inc. *Spingner-Littles, D & Anderson, C.E. (1999). Constructivism: A paradigm for older learners. Educational Gerontology*, *25*(3), 203–209.

Srivastava, S. C. (2005). Managing core competence of the organization. *Vikalpa . The Journal for Decision Makers*, *30*(4), 49–63.

St. Clair, R. (2003). Myths and realities, andragogy revisited: theory for the 21st Century? *Clearinghouse on Adult Career and Vocational Education*. ERIC document Reproduction Service No. ED 99-CO-0013.

Stack, R. T., & Lovern, E. R. (1995). A Lively Learning Agenda. *The Healthcare Forum Journal*, *38*(5). Retrieved May 28, 2009 from Proquest Research Library http://www.proquest.umi.com

Stana, R. (2008). Border patrol: Costs and challenges related to training new agents. *Testimony before the subcommittee on management, investigations, and oversight, Committee on Homeland Security, House of Representatives*. Retrieved from http://www.gao.gov/cgi-bin/getrpt?GAO-07-997T

Stanney, K. M. (Ed.). (2002). *Handbook of virtual environments: Design, implementation, and applications.* Mahwah, NJ: Lawrence Erlbaum.

Steed, A., & Frecon, E. (2005). Construction of collaborative virtual environments . In Sanchez-Segura, M. (Ed.), *Developing Future Interactive Systems*. Hershey, PA: Idea Group.

Stephenson, N. (1992). *Snow Crash*. New York: Penguin Books.

Stitt-Gohdes, W. L. (2001). Business Education Students' Preferred Learning Styles and Their Teachers' Preferred Instructional Styles: Do they match? *Delta Pi Epsilon Journal, 43*(3), 137–151.

Strother, J. (2002). An Assessment of the Effectiveness of e-learning in Corporate Training Programs. *International Review of Research in Open and Distance Learning, 3*(1). Retrieved May 26, 2009 from http://www.irrodl.org/index.php/irrodl/article/view/83/161

Strother, J. (2002). An assessment of the effectiveness of e-learning in corporate training programs. *International Review of Research in Open and Distance Learning, 3*(1).

Sunrise. (2008). *Sunrise Company*. Retrieved from http://www.sunrisevr.com

Susi, T., Johannesson, M., & Backlund, P. (2007). Serious games–An overview. *Skövde: University of Skövde* (Technical Report HS-IKI-TR-07-001).

Svensson, P. (2003). Virtual Worlds as Arenas for Language Learning . In Felix, U. (Ed.), *Language Learning Online: Towards Best Practice* (pp. 123–142). Lisse, The Netherlands: Swets and Zeitlinger.

Swain, J. J. (2001). Power Tools for Visualization and Decision - Making. ORMS Today. Retrieved May 7, 2009, from http://www.lionhrtpub.com/orms/surveys/Simulation/Simulation.html

Swanson, K. (2007). Second Life: A Science Library Presence in Virtual Reality. *Science & Technology Libraries, 27*(3), 79–86. doi:10.1300/J122v27n03_06

Sweller, J. (1988). Cognitive load during problem solving: Effects on learning. *Cognitive Science*, 257–285.

Tabs, E. (2003). *Distance education at degree-granting postsecondary institutions: 2000-2001.* (NCES report 2003-017). National Center for Education Statistics. Retrieved November 10, 2008, from http://nces.ed.gov/pubs2003/2003017.pdf

Tait, A. (1998). *Dimension International Desktop Virtual Reality*. IEEE Colloquium Series.

Tampone, K. (2008, April 18). Companies, colleges use virtual worlds as training tools. *The Central New York Business Journal.*

Tan, s., & Francis, G. A. (1997). *Virtual reality as a training instrument, THEC project*. Temasek Polytechnic.

Tapias Garcia, H. (2005). Technological capacities: A strategic element of competency. In Spanish. Revista Facultad de Ingenieria de la Universidad de Antioquia, 033.

Tapscott, D., & Williams, A. (2006). *Wikinomics: How Mass Collaboration Changes Everything*. New York: Portfolio.

Tashner, J., Bronack, S., & Riedl, R. (2005, March). Virtual worlds: Further development of web-based teaching. In *Proceedings of Hawaii International Conference on Education*, Honolulu, HI.

Taylor, D. I., Winter, R., Chan, M., Davies, R., Kinross, J., & Darzi, A. (2009, April 28-30). *Virtual Patient and Medical Device Simulation In Second Life: the Use Of Immersive Virtual Worlds For Learning and Patient Safety*. Paper presented at the MedBiquitous Annual Conference 2009, Baltimore.

Teece, D. J., Pisano, G., & Shuen, A. (1997). Dynamic capabilities and strategic management. *Strategic Management Journal, 18*(7), 509–533. doi:10.1002/(SICI)1097-0266(199708)18:7<509::AID-SMJ882>3.0.CO;2-Z

Tennant, M. (1996). *Psychology and adult learning*. London: Routledge.

Terdiman, D. (2006). Newsmaker: Reuters' Second Life Reporter Talks Shop. Retrieved April 5, 2009 from http://www.news.com/Reuters-Second-Life-reporter-talks-shop/2008-1043_3-6129335.html

The Chartered Institute of Personnel and Development. (2007, July 1). *Virtual worlds and learning: using Second Life at Duke Corporate Education*. The Chartered Institute of Personnel and Development. Retrieved July 18, 2009, from http://www.cipd.co.uk/helpingpeople-learn/_Teedce.htm

The State of Delaware. (2009, January 21). *State of Delaware: The Official website of the first state*. Retrieved March 16, 2009, from State of Delaware: The Official website of the first state http://www.delaware.gov

The University of Albertay Dundee. (2006, May). *Beyond eLearning: practical insights from the USA*. Retrieved March 24, 2009, from http://www.epic.co.uk/content/news/resources/eLearning_mission_report.pdf

Theil, S. (2008). Tune in tomorrow. *Newsweek*, August 18-25 issue.

Thompson, D. (1990, August). Electronic bulletin boards: A timeless place for collaborative writing projects. *Computers and Composition*, 7, 43–53. doi:10.1016/S8755-4615(05)80026-X

Thompson, K., & Good, R. (2005, November 9). *The Bioteaming Manifesto: A new paradigm for virtual, networked business teams*. Retrieved November 14, 2008, from http://changethis.com/19.BioteamingManifesto

Thompson, K., (2005). The seven beliefs of high performing teams. *The Bumble Bee, Bioteams Features*, (71).

Thrush, E. A., & Bodary, M. (2000). Virtual reality, combat, and communication. *Journal of Business and Technical Communication*, *14*(3), 315–327. doi:10.1177/105065190001400304

Tinto, V. (1997). Classrooms as communities: Exploring the educational character of student persistence. *The Journal of Higher Education*, *68*(6), 599–623. doi:10.2307/2959965

Tisdell, E., J. (1993). Feminism and adult learning: power, pedagogy and praxis. *New Directions for Adult and Continuing Education*, 7, 91–103. doi:10.1002/ace.36719935711

Tobias, S., & Fletcher, J. D. (2007). What Research Has to Say About Designing Computer Games for Learning. *Educational Technology*, *57*(5), 20–29.

Toro-Troconis, M., Mellstrom, U., Partridge, M., Meeran, K., Barrett, M., & Higham, J. (2008). Designing game-based learning activities for virtual patients in Second Life. *Journal of cyber therapy & rehabilitation, 1*(3).

Total learning concepts develops interactive game-based learning system to train sales force for leading specialty company. (2008). *Business Wire*. Retrieved February 28, 2009, from ABI/INFORM Dateline database: Document ID: 1499362761.

Towns, S. (2008, July 9). *Vivek Kundra, CTO of Washington, D.C., Focuses on Project Management*. Retrieved March 16, 2009, from Public CIO http://www.govtech.com/pcio/articles/375806

Townsend, A. M., DeMarie, S. M., & Hendrickson, A. R. (1998). Virtual teams: Technology and the workplace of the future. *Academy of Management Science*, *12*(3), 17–29.

Tromp, J. G., Steed, A., & Wilson, J. R. (2003). Systematic usability evaluation and design issues for collaborative virtual environments. *Presence (Cambridge, Mass.)*, *12*(3). doi:10.1162/105474603765879512

Tu, C. H. (2002). The measurement of social presence in an online learning environment. *International Journal on E-Learning, 1*(2), 34-45. Retrieved January 20, 2008, from www.aace.org/dl/files/IJEL/IJEL1234.pdf

U. S. Department of Education Institute of Education Sciences. (n.d.). *Fast Facts*. Retrieved March 8, 2009, from http://nces.ed.gov/fastfacts/display.asp?id=80

United States Distance Learning Association (USDLA). (n.d.). *Resources: Research, Statistics and Distance Learning Resources*. Retrieved March 12, 2009, from http://www.usdla.org/html/aboutUs/researchInfo.htm

US Department of Defense. (2008). Retrieved from http://www.defenselink.mil

USDL. (2008, June). *News, Bureau of Labor Statistics.* United States Department of Labor, Washington, D.C. Retrieved February 15, 2008, from http://www.bls.gov/news.release/pdf.nlsoy.pdf van Wyck, E., de Villiers, R. (2008). Usability Context Analysis for Virtual Reality Training in South African Mines. In *Proceedings of SAICSIT*, Wilderness, South Africa. New York: ACM.

Valve Corporation. (2004). *Counter-Strike Source.* Bellevue, WA: Valve. [Microsoft Windows]

Vargo, S. L., & Lusch, R. F. (2004). Evolving to a new dominant logic for marketing. *Journal of Marketing, 68*(January), 1–17. doi:10.1509/jmkg.68.1.1.24036

Varvel, V. E. (2007). Master Online Teacher Competencies. *Online Journal of Distance Learning Administration, 10*(1). Retrieved on March 3, 2009 from http://www.westga.edu/%7Edistance/ojdla/spring101/varvel101.htm

Veletsianos, G., & Miller, C. (2008). Conversing with Pedagogical Agents: A Phenomenological Exploration of Interacting with Digital Entities. *British Journal of Educational Technology, 39*(6), 969–986. doi:10.1111/j.1467-8535.2007.00797.x

Villaume, W. A., Berger, B. A., & Barker, B. N. (2006). Learning Motivational Interviewing: Scripting a Virtual Patient. *American Journal of Pharmaceutical Education, 70*(2).

Vince, J. (2004). *Introduction to virtual reality.* London: Springer.

Virtual Manufacturing User Workshop. (1994, 12-13 July). Technical report, Lawrence Associates Inc.

Vital Training Tools Elevate New Pharmaceutical Sales Reps into Top Performers During Critical First Year. (2008, June 2). *PR Newswire.* Retrieved February 28, 2009, from ABI/INFORM Dateline database: Document ID: 1488244491.

Vygotsky, L. (1934). Thought and Language. Trans. & ed. A. Kozulin. Cambridge: MIT Press.

Vygotsky, L. (1978). *Mind in Society: The development of higher psychological processes.* Cambridge, MA: Harvard University Press.

Vygotsky, L. S. (1977). Thinking and Talking. Belgrade, Serbia: Nolit.

Vygotsky, L. S. (1986). *Thought and Language.* Cambridge, MA: MIT Press.

Wagner, M. (2007, September 21). *The Future of Virtual Worlds.* Retrieved October 22, 2007, from Information Week, http://www.informationweek.com

Wang, Q. H., & Li, J. R. (2004). A desktop VR prototype for industrial training applications. *Virtual reality, 7*(43-4), 187-197.

Wark, M. (2007). *Gamer theory.* Cambridge, MA: Harvard University Press.

Watkins, B. L. (1991). A quite radical idea: The invention and elaboration of collegiate correspondence study . In Watkins, B. L., & Wright, S. J. (Eds.), *The foundations of American distance education* (pp. 1–35). Dubuque, Iowa: Kendall/Hunt.

Wayne, D., Didwania, A., Feinglass, J., Fudala, M., Barsuk, J., & McGaghie, W. (2008). Simulation-Based Education Improves Quality of Care During Cardiac Arrest Team Responses at an Academic Teaching Hospital*. *Chest, 133*(1), 56. doi:10.1378/chest.07-0131

Wei, C., & Chen, S. (2002). VR-based teleautonomous system for AGV path guidance. In *Seventh International conference on control, automation, robotics and vision (ICARCV'02)*, Singapore.

Weigel, V. (2000). E-l5earning and the tradeoff between richness and reach in higher education. *Change, 33*(5), 10–15. doi:10.1080/00091380009605735

Wenger, E. (1998). *Communities of practice: Learning, meaning and identity.* Cambridge, UK: Cambridge University Press.

Weyrish, M., & Drew, P. (1999). An interactive environment for virtual manufacturing: the virtual workbench. *Computers in Industry, 38*, 5–15. doi:10.1016/S0166-3615(98)00104-3

What is a virtual world? (2008, September, 15). In *Virtual Worlds Review* [database online]. Retrieved September 15, 2008 from http://www.virtualworldsreview.com/info/whatis.shtml

Wiendahl, H. P., & Fiebig, T. H. (2003). Virtual factory design: A new tool for a co-operative planning approach. *International Journal of Computer Integrated Manufacturing, 16*(7-8), 535–540. doi:10.1080/0951192031000115868

Wierzbicki, I., & Margolf, K. (2002). Affordable Virtual Reality Content as a Marketing Instrument in Small and Middle businesses. In *proceedings of EUROPRIX, The Scholars Conference.*

Wikipedia. (2009). Retrieved April 15, 2009, from http://en.wikipedia.org/wiki/Second_Life

Wilkes, C. W., & Burnham, B. R. (1991). Adult learner motivations and electronics distance education. *American Journal of Distance Education, 5*(1), 43–50. doi:10.1080/08923649109526731

Wilson, N. (2009). *Virtual worlds for business.* Clever Zebra. Retrieved May 2, 2009, from http://cleverzebra.com/book.

Winn, W. (1993). *A conceptual basis for educational applications of virtual reality.* Human Interface Technology Laboratory, University of Washington. Retrieved September 28, 2007, from http://www.hitl.washington.edu/publications/r-93-9/

Witmer, B. G., & Singer, M. J. (1998). Measuring Presence in Virtual Environments: A Presence Questionnaire. *Presence (Cambridge, Mass.),*225–240. doi:10.1162/105474698565686

Witte, S. P. (1992). Context, text, intertext: Toward a constructivist semiotic of writing. *Written Communication, 9,* 237–308. doi:10.1177/0741088392009002003

Wittrock, M. C. (1974). A generative model of mathematics learning. *Journal for Research in Mathematics Education, 5*(4), 181–196. doi:10.2307/748845

Wittrock, M. C. (1990). Generative processes of comprehension. *Educational Psychologist, 24*(4), 345–376. doi:10.1207/s15326985ep2404_2

Womble, J. (2008). E-learning: The relationship among learner satisfaction, self-efficacy, and usefulness. *The Business Review, Cambridge, 10*(1), 182.

Wonacott, M. E. (2000).Web-Based Training and Constructivism. In Brief: Fact Facts for Policy and Practice No. 2. Columbus, OH: National Dissemination Center for Career and Technical Education, the Ohio State University (ED 447 257).

Wood, N. T. (2011). *Marketing in Virtual Worlds, 1e.* Upper Saddle River, NJ: Pearson.

Wood, N. T., Solomon, M. R., & Allan, D. (2008). Welcome to the Matrix: E-learning Gets a Second Life. *Marketing Education Review, 18*(2), 45–53.

Wood, N. T., Wetsch, L. R., Solomon, M. R., & Hudson, K. (2009). From Interactive to Immersive: Advertising Education takes a Virtual Leap of Faith. *Journal of Advertising Education, 13*(1), 64–72.

Wooldridge, M. (1999). Intelligent agents . In Weiss, G. (Ed.), *Multiagent Systems* (pp. 25–77). London: The MIT Press.

Wurman, R. S. (2000). Information Anxiety 2, (2nd Ed.). Indianapolis, IN: Que.

Xa, D., & Wang, H. (2006). Intelligent agent supported personalization for virtual learning environments. *Decision Support Systems, 42,* 825–843. doi:10.1016/j.dss.2005.05.033

Xu, Z. J., Zhao, Z. X., & Baines, R. W. (2000). Constructing Virtual Environments for Manufacturing Simulation. *International Journal of Production Research, 38*(17), 4171–4191. doi:10.1080/00207540050205000

Yahaya, R. A., Euler, T., & Godat, M. (2004). Enhancement of learning in decision making and negotiation within virtual reality environment . In McWilliam, E., Danby, S., & Knight, J. (Eds.), *Performing educational research: Theories, methods and practices.* Queensland, Australia: Postpressed Flaxton.

Yahoo. (2009, March). *Yahoo!* Retrieved March 2009, from Yahoo!: http://www.yahoo.com

Yao, Y., Li, J., Lee, W. B., Cheung, C. F., & Yuan, Z. (2002). VMMC: a test-bed for machining. *Computers in Industry, 47*, 255–268. doi:10.1016/S0166-3615(01)00153-1

Yee, N. (2006). The Demographics, Motivations and Derived Experiences of Users of Massively-Multiuser Online Graphical Environments. *PRESENCE: Teleoperators and Environments, 15*, 309–329. doi:10.1162/pres.15.3.309

Yee, N., & Bailenson, J. (in press). The difference between being and seeing: The relative contribution of self perception and priming to behavioral changes via digital self-representation. *Media Psychology.*

Yee, N., Bailenson, J., & Ducheneaut, N. (2009). The proteus effect: Implications of transformed digital self-representation on online and offline behavior. *Communication Research, 36*(3), 285–311. doi:10.1177/0093650208330254

Yellowlees, P. M., & Cook, J. N. (2006). Education About Hallucinations Using an Internet Virtual Reality System: A Qualitative Survey. *Academic Psychiatry, 30*, 534–539. doi:10.1176/appi.ap.30.6.534

Youngblut, C. (1998). *Educational uses of virtual reality technology. Technical report, IDA Document D-2128.* Alexandria, VA: Institute for Defense Analyses.

Youngblut, C., (1997). Educational uses of Virtual reality technology. *VR in the schools, 3*(1), 1-4

Youtube. (2009, 3 16). Retrieved 3 16, 2009, from Youtube: http://www.youtube.com

Zadeh, L. (1976). A fuzzy-algorithmic approach to the definition of complex or imprecise concepts. *International Journal of Man-Machine Studies, 8*, 249–291. doi:10.1016/S0020-7373(76)80001-6

Zaharias, P. A. (2006). Usability evaluation method for e-learning: Focus on motivation and learning. In *Proceedings of CHI 2006*, Montreal, Canada. New York: ACM.

Zaharias, P. A. (2004). Usability and e-learning: The road towards integration. *eLearn Magazine*, (6).

Zappen, J., & Geisler, C. (2009). Designing the Total User Experience: Implications for Research and Program Development. *Programmatic Perspectives, 1*(1), 3–28.

Zappen, J., Harrison, T. M., & Watson, D. (2008). A New Paradigm for Designing E-Government: Web 2.0 and Experience design. *The Proceedings of the 9th Annual International Digital Government Research Conference* (pp. 17-27). Montreal, Canada: 9th Annual International Digital Government Research Conference.

Zhang, Z. C.-H. (2008). Bringing web 2.0 to bioinformatics. *Briefings in Bioinformatics, 10*(1), 1–10. doi:10.1093/bib/bbn041

Zheleva, M. M., Zhelev, Y., & Mascitti, I. (2008). E-learning, E-Practising and E-Tutoring: an integrated approach. In International Book Series (Ed.), Methodologies and Tools of the Modern (e-) Learning, (pp.84-90)

Zimmer, L. (2006). Thomson NetG Second Life Corporate Training Campus. *Business Communicators of Second Life.* Retrieved May 6, 2009 from http://freshtakes.typepad.com/sl_communicators/2006/09/thomson_netg_se.html

Zimmerman, E. (2001). Better training is just a click away. *Workforce, 80*(1), 36.

Zyda, M. (2005). From visual simulation to virtual reality to games. *Computer*, 25–32. doi:10.1109/MC.2005.297

About the Contributors

William Ritke-Jones is the President and Principal of CyberMations Consulting Group in Boston, MA. CyberMations designs, develops and implements organizational and team growth initiatives as well as distance learning programs for corporations. These initiatives transform people, teams and organizations into those that are high-functioning, collaborative and democratic and that can reach their highest creative and productive potential. Ritke-Jones has designed online learning programs that integrate a variety of tools for eight years. Much of his work and research on education has been on education in virtual realities. This work started when he was the co-wizard of Oak MOO at Indiana University of Pennsylvania from 2001-2003 and continues with his research on designing corporate education in virtual worlds.

* * *

Kerrin Barrett has over 20 years varied experience in designing, developing, and implementing courses for a wide variety of audiences in the public, private, and international sectors. In 2008, she obtained her Ph.D. from the University of New Mexico in Organizational Learning and Instructional Technology, with a research focus at the intersection of distance education, culture and language learning. She holds an Ed.M. in Technology in Education from the Harvard Graduate School of Education. Throughout Dr. Barrett's career she has collaborated closely with customers to design innovative courses that leverage technology while considering culture and issues of access. Dr. Barrett has broad experience in instructional design and in the integration of technology into education projects that span cultures. Since 1999, Dr. Barrett has focused her applied research on online course design that leverages synchronous communication for language and culture learning. In her most recent position, Dr. Barrett was Director of the Content Design and Development team at Alelo.

Dr. Amelia W. Cheney is an Assistant Professor in the Department of Leadership and Educational Studies at Appalachian State University, where she teaches in and serves as program coordinator for the Instructional Technology program. She holds a B.A. in English and a M.A.Ed in Secondary Education from Wake Forest University, and an Ed.D. in Educational Leadership from Appalachian State. Prior to joining the faculty, she worked for more than thirteen years in K-12 education, including teaching and serving as Chief Technology Officer in two school districts. She is a Board member of the North Carolina Technology in Education Society, and a member of the Technology Committee of the Carolinas Virtual Worlds Consortium. Dr. Cheney's current research is focused on social constructivism in virtual worlds along with the creation of relationships in these types of environments.

Julie M. Davis is a Ph.D. student in Texas Tech University's technical Communication and Rhetoric program. She serves as Director of Web Development at Clarkson University in Potsdam, NY where she also teaches as an adjunct instructor in the Communication & Media Department. She has taught photography painting & drawing, digital imagery, digital studio I and II and 2-D digital design. Her primary research interests include social networking, mobile technology, and the impact of online education.

Arthur Edwards is a Senior Professor/Researcher at the College of Telematics of the University of Colima, Mexico, where his primary interest is Computer Assisted Language Learning, multimedia applications, collaborative learning environments, educational information systems, virtual reality applications and wireless and mobile learning systems.

Samir Abou El-Seoud received his BSc degree in Physics, Electronics and Mathematics from Cairo University in 1967, his Higher Diplom in Computing from Technical University of Darmstadt (TUD) / Germany in 1975 and his Doctor of Science in Computing (Dr. rer-nat.) from the same University (TUD) in 1979. His research interests is focusing on Computer Aided Learning, Parallel Algorithms, Numerical Scientific Computations and Computational Fluid Mechanics. Professor El-Seoud helds different academic positions at TUD Germany. Letest Full-Professor in 1987. Outside Germany Professor El-Seoud spent different years as a Full-Professor of Computer Science at SQU – Oman and Qatar University and acted as a Head of Computer Science for many years. Professor El-Seoud joined Princess Sumaya University for Technology (PSUT) in 2004. Currently, he is the Chairman of the Computer Science Dept. at PSUT

Mikail Feituri has a master degree in electronic engineering from Università La Sapienza of Rome. Actually, he is the technical coordinator of the international project department at Università Telematica Guglielmo Marconi in Rome. Under this role, he is in charge of research on new methodology and technology in distance learning such as mobile learning and artificial intelligence applied to E-Learning. He is also responsible for the technical coordination from design to the final release of products or services specified under the project proposals. He is author or co-author of several publications and participates as a presenter in many conferences, including: INTED, IADIS, EUCEN, EDEN, Online EDUCA, EARLY. He also is involved as a reviewer for the International Journal of Learning.

Federica Funghi is graduated in "Educational Sciences" from the Università degli Studi di Perugia (2002), with a specialization as "Expert of Training Processes". She works as a Project Manager for European funded projects at Università Telematica "Guglielmo Marconi" and she deals with planning and management of European funded projects focusing on the application of ICT in education and training. Presently she coordinates various European transnational projects concerning the use and experimentation of innovative e-learning platforms and social software. She is responsible for managerial and contracting activities, organization of meetings with partners and workshops with stakeholders, participation in national and international conferences.

Miguel A. Garcia-Ruiz graduated in Computer Systems engineering and obtained his MSc in Computer Science from the University of Colima, Mexico. He received his PhD in Computer Science and Artificial Intelligence from the University of Sussex, England. Miguel has been a visiting professor at the University of Ontario Institute of Technology, Canada. Miguel is currently an Assistant Professor at the University of Colima, where teaches CS courses and do research mainly on virtual reality. He has published more than twenty scientific papers and chapters, including a book, and has directed a video documentary about an introduction to virtual reality.

Dr. Xin Ge got her Ph.D. in Marketing from the University of Alberta. She is an assistant professor of Marketing at the University of Northern British Columbia, School of Business. Her research interests include consumer judgments and decision making, consumer information processing, constructive consumer preferences, and consumer behavior in the virtual worlds. Xin's research has been recently published in *Journal of Retailing, Journal of Virtual Worlds Research,* and *Canadian Journal of Administrative Sciences.*

Mary Rose Grant, Ph.D. Mary Rose is the Chair of the Liberal Arts Program and Director of Faculty Development for the School for Professional Studies (SPS) at Saint Louis University. She is an Assistant Professor, teaching biology and other life science courses online and in the traditional classroom. She has a BS in Medical Technology from Saint Louis University and a MS in Microbiology-Parasitology/Public Health from the University of North Carolina, as well as an MS and Specialist Degree in Education and doctorate in Higher Ed Leadership and Administration from Southern Illinois University. Dr. Grant is responsible for curriculum development and oversight, as well as the professional development of SPS faculty using a model she designed and implemented. She spearheaded the development and implementation of Distance Learning and International Study for the School. She regularly presents seminars and workshops on teaching, learning and assessment in both traditional and virtual settings.

Letitia Harding is a full time instructor at the University of the Incarnate Word in San Antonio, Texas teaching courses in Composition, World Literature, Rhetorical Theory, and Integrated Language Arts. She is involved in both the student success and learning community programs within the university. Letitia is currently pursuing a doctorate in Technical Communication and Rhetoric with Texas Tech University. Her research interests include the rhetoric of science writing, visual rhetoric, and the relationship between discourse, power and knowledge. Before emigrating from the United Kingdom to the United States, Letitia served as an Air Traffic Control Officer in the Royal Air Force. She now calls San Antonio home.

Ken Hudson is Managing Director of the Virtual World Design Centre, Loyalist College, where he creates virtual world environments and experiences for business, education, and government. He has collaborated with dozens of organizations using virtual worlds including Harvard and Brown Universities, U.S Department of State, and CBSA. In 2008, Ken's work was recognized with the Colleges Ontario Innovation Award and the Orion Learning Award of Merit. Ken is also a freelance brand and digital media strategist, who worked on the recent California earthquake alternative reality game "After Shock," which was featured in both TIME and WIRED magazines. He was educated at University of Toronto and the Institute for the Psychological Study of the Arts. He is a Senior Fellow, sLAB, Ontario College of Art and Design, Toronto

W. Lewis Johnson co-founded Alelo while he was director of the Center for Advanced Research in Technology for Education (CARTE) at the Information Sciences Institute of the University of Southern California, where he was the principal investigator of the original Tactical Language project. He is currently Chief Scientist and President of Alelo, where he leads several research projects investigating the rapid acquisition of proficiency in language and culture. He also continues to be active in research focusing on the successful adoption of interactive learning environments and in the field of artificial intelligence. His work on Tactical Language won DARPA's Significant Technical Achievement Award in 2005. Dr. Johnson is past president of the International Artificial Intelligence in Education Society, and past chair of the ACM Special Interest Group for Artificial Intelligence. He holds a B.A. in linguistics from Princeton University and a Ph.D. in computer science from Yale University.

Christopher Keesey is focused and committed to improving design and delivery of learning experiences for professionals and practitioners in industry and higher education. Keesey is The Project Manager for Ohio University Without Boundaries(OUWB). Through OUWB Keesey has worked with multiple industry and NGO clients including Sogeti Netherlands (a division of Cap Gemini), Arthur D. Little, World Education, The U.S. State Department, Academy for Educational Development (AED), Chemonics International Inc., The Doctors Company and many others. Along with serving current clients and students, Keesey led Ohio University in 2006 to becoming one of the first universities globally to develop and support a fully functioning 3-D virtual campus in Second Life. Keesey also consults industry clients independently on the design and implementation of innovative solutions for development and delivery of technologically mediated learning experiences. Solutions range from more traditional e-learning initiatives to high-end games, simulations and holistic, fully functioning virtual campuses

Dr. Allen Kitchel is an Assistant Professor of Business and Marketing Teacher Education at the University of Idaho. He teaches business and marketing education methods, research, student organization supervision and leadership, and information technology. Prior to teaching at the post-secondary level, he taught accounting, business law, marketing, and business technology subjects at the secondary level. He has been working within virtual environments and teaching online courses for approximately a decade. His research interest include online/virtual learning, best practice models for online pedagogy, program and curriculum development in business and marketing education, and educational technology adoption by teachers. Dr. Kitchel earned his Ph.D. from the University of Idaho with an emphasis in assessment and educational technology.

Lea Kuznik was born in 1975 in Ljubljana, Slovenia. Graduated in 1999, master's degree in 2004 and doctor's degree in 2007 at University of Ljubljana, Faculty of Arts, Department of Ethnology and Cultural Anthropology. She is an assistant for Slovene Ethnology. She has been taking interests on museology, children's museums and interactive learning environments, pedagogical and psychological theories of learning and play and developmental theories of children for years. Her doctoral thesis "Interactive Learning Environments and Children's Museums: Theoretical Model and It's Planning" presents first scientific research on children's museums in Slovenia. Her research is focused on up-to date technologies, virtual worlds, virtual museums, and possibilities for learning in virtual learning environments especially in educational virtual worlds. Her recent research project was designing an interactive learning environment for families in a shopping centre.

Sarah R. Lincoln graduated *summa cum laude* with a degree in English from Saint Joseph's University in Philadelphia in 2007, where she was also inducted into the Phi Beta Kappa society. She earned a master's degree in International Marketing from Saint Joseph's two years later while interning at both the university's Office of the President and the Global Interdependence Center, a respected Philadelphia nonprofit. She is also a member of the Alpha Epsilon Lambda Graduate Honor Society.Sarah has developed a strong background in research, writing and communications and is fluent in Italian. She is currently pursuing opportunities in international commerce and affairs.

Dr. Daniel Livingstone lectures in Computer Science at the University of the West of Scotland, specialising in Computer Game Technology and Virtual Worlds, teaching classes from Real Time 3D software development with OpenGL through to Collaborative Virtual Environments. Daniel is an active researcher in the educational applications of multi-user virtual environments. His first experiences of MUVE's led to him becoming a wizard in an LPMUD – despite which he managed to graduate from the University in Strathclyde with a degree in Computer and Electronic Systems. This was followed by a Masters in Artificial Intelligence from the University of Essex and then a PhD in the computer modelling of the evolution of language and languages at the University of Paisley (now University of the West of Scotland) – since when his active research interests have taken him back to virtualworlds. In recent years, Daniel co-chaired the Second Life Education Workshops in 2006 and 2007, and founded the Massively Multi-Learner series of workshops for the HEA-ICS in the UK, and recently completed co-editing a volume on Researching Education and Learning in Virtual Environments (RE-LIVE) to be published in 2010 by Springer. He is a co-founder of the open-source SLOODLE project - the world's first project attempting to formally integrate multi-user virtual environments with web-based virtual learning environments. Dr. Livingstone was the lead-investigator in the EDUSERV funded project "Online Learning In Virtual Environments with SLOODLE", a US$240,000 project to further develop the SLOODLE software and community. This two-year grant awarded in 2007 is now nearing completion, and has seen SLOODLE grow from an idea into a tool that has been used by dozens of educators around the globe, with class sizes ranging from less than ten students to classes of hundreds. Dr. Livingstone's research interests also include Artificial Intelligence in games and the use of handheld devices for game based learning. Dr. Livingstone's alter egos include Buddy Sprocket (Second Life,Home) and dlivingstone (MetaPlace).

Glenn E. Mayhew is Professor of Marketing at Aoyama Gakuin University. He has also served as Associate Dean of the Graduate School of Management at the International University of Japan, and as Assistant Professor of Marketing at Washington University. He holds a Ph.D. from the University of California, Berkeley, and an M.B.A. from the University of Chicago. His research interests include virtual worlds, e-commerce, pricing and customer lifetime value.

Hamed Farahani Manesh is a research assistant in the Department of Mechanical Engineering at Eastern Mediterranean University (EMU), N. Cyprus. He received a Master's Degree in Information Systems and another Master's Degree in Mechanical Engineering from EMU. Currently, he is involved in a research group, which carries out research and development activities for industry-oriented projects of intelligent manufacturing systems, automation, networked manufacturing, virtual environment in modeling and simulations of agile and de-centralized manufacturing control, holonic manufacturing, and virtual reality based laboratory education. He is member of ASME and SAE

Greg W. Marshall (Ph.D., Oklahoma State University) is the Charles Harwood Professor of Marketing and Strategy in the Crummer Graduate School of Business at Rollins College, Winter Park, Florida. Greg is the Editor of the *Journal of Marketing Theory and Practice*, former *Editor of the Journal of Personal Selling & Sales Management*, and presently serves on the editorial review boards of the *Journal of the Academy of Marketing Science, Industrial Marketing Management*, and *Journal of Business Research*. He is co-author of four textbooks and has published over 40 refereed journal articles. Prior to entering academe, Greg held management positions with Warner-Lambert, Mennen, and Target Corporation. He is a Distinguished Fellow and President-Elect of the Academy of Marketing Science, Past President of the American Marketing Association Academic Division, and a Fellow and Past-President of the Society for Marketing Advances.

Miguel Vargas Martin is an Associate Professor at the University of Ontario Institute of Technology (Oshawa, Canada), and Chief Technology Officer of Hoper Inc., an Oshawa-based research and development company that offers innovative Web tools. He is a licensed Professional Engineer in Ontario, Canada. He holds a Ph.D. in Computer Science (Carleton University, Canada), a Master's degree in Electrical Engineering (CINVESTAV, Mexico), and a Bachelor of Computer Science (UAA, Mexico). His current research interests include computer forensics, mitigation of denial-of-service attacks, security and human computer interaction, hidden communication channels, and Web modeling and optimization.

Deanna Mascle is a Ph.D. student in Texas Tech University's Technical Communication and Rhetoric program. She is the site director for the Morehead Writing Project and a full-time English instructor at Morehead State University in Kentucky teaching courses in composition, creative writing, technical communication, and rhetoric and writing theory and pedagogy. Her primary research interests include collaboration and negotiation in writing and education, digital pedagogy, and the connection between writing self efficacy and transfer.

Paul R. Messinger is Associate Professor of Marketing at the University of Alberta School of Business and IBM Faculty Fellow in the Centre for Advanced Studies program at the IBM Toronto Laboratory. He recently served as Principle Investigator of the Research Alliance "Harnessing the Web-Interaction Cycle for Canadian Competitiveness" for the Social Science and Humanities Research Council of Canada and as Founding Director of the University of Albert School of Retailing. Paul currently serves on the Editorial Board of the journal *Marketing Science* and as guest editor for a special issue on eService for the *Canadian Journal of Administrative Sciences*. Paul's research focuses on e-commerce, 3D mediated virtual worlds, service science, emerging retail formats, dynamic pricing, and recommendation systems; his publication outlets include *Marketing Science, Journal of Retailing, Journal of Economic Dynamics and Control, Journal of Virtual Worlds Research, Journal of Business Research*, and *Journal of Retailing and Consumer Services*. For more details, see *http://www.business.ualberta.ca/pmessinger/*

Run H. Niu is an assistant professor of Operations Management at Webster University School of Business and Technology, St. Louis, Missouri, USA. She received her Ph.D. degree in Management Science from the University of Alberta School of Business. Her research interests include decision problems on the interfaces of operations and marketing, operations and Supply chain Management, business and education applications of virtual worlds such as Second Life, and Word-of-Mouth and referral rewards management in retailing.

Anna Peachey is a Teaching Fellow, Centre for Open Learning in Mathematics, Science, Computers and Technology (COLMSCT) at The Open University Anna is Director of Innovations at Eygus Ltd, the company responsible for coordinating the Open University UK presence in virtual worlds. She was Academic and Organising Chair of Researching Learning in Virtual Environments 08 (www.open. ac.uk/relive08) and is an editorial board member of the International Journal for Advanced Corporate Learning, the International Journal of Virtual and Personal Learning Environments and the forthcoming journal Impact, The Journal of Applied Research in Workplace E-Learning. Anna is currently researching identity and community in virtual worlds with COLMSCT, and has worked with students around the world using online and distance learning since 1995.

Dirk Remley is a lecturer at Kent State University, where he teaches business writing and technical writing courses. Dirk's research interests include business writing and technical writing pedagogies as well as digital literacy learning and workplace and community literacies. Dirk has published articles in the *Community Literacy Journal*, *Across The Disciplines* and *Computers and Composition Online,* and he has made several presentations at national conferences including Computers and Writing and Conference on College Composition and Communication.

Dr. Richard E. Riedl is Chairman of the Leadership and Educational Studies Department and Professor of Education specializing in Instruction Technology at Appalachian State University in North Carolina. He has a Ph.D. in Curriculum and Instruction from Arizona State University and has taught at Clarke College in Iowa, the University of Alaska Fairbanks, and Appalachian State. He first began offering online classes in Alaska in 1987 using a combination of phone conferencing and modem-based computer systems. He joined Appalachian State in 1989. More than eight years ago he and his colleagues in the Instructional Technology program, seeking the most effective online learning environment possible, began working with an early 3D virtual world from Activeworlds and, with this successful experience, moved their entire master's degree program into this environment, now called AET Zone.

William Ritke-Jones is the President and Principal of CyberMations Consulting Group in Boston, MA. CyberMations designs, develops and implements organizational and team growth initiatives as well as distance learning programs for corporations. These initiatives transform people, teams and organizations into those that are high-functioning, collaborative and democratic and that can reach their highest creative and productive potential. Ritke-Jones has designed online learning programs that integrate a variety of tools for eight years. Much of his work and research on education has been on education in virtual realities. This work started when he was the co-wizard of Oak MOO at Indiana University of Pennsylvania from 2001-2003 and continues with his research on designing corporate education in virtual worlds.

Sarah "Intellagirl" Robbins (M.A., University of Indianapolis) is a Ph.D. candidate at Ball State University in Rhetoric and Composition. Her dissertation, "A Faceted Classification of Virtual World Communication Mechanics," which she hopes to finish by December 2009, is a study of 75 virtual worlds. Sarah, along with her husband Mark W. Bell, is the coauthor of *Second Life for Dummies*. She currently holds a position with Kelley Executive Partners at the Kelley School of Business at Indiana University as the Director of Emerging Technologies where she also teaches courses and workshops on social media and marketing. Sarah regularly consults with universities to assist the integration of virtual worlds and social media into pedagogy. Her Web site is www.sarahrobbins.com.

Dr. Robert L. Sanders is an Associate Professor in the Department of Leadership and Educational Studies at Appalachian State University, where he teaches in and serves as the program director for the library science program. Prior to this position, Dr. Sanders worked professionally as a teacher, media specialist, administrator, and instructional technologist. He is the past president of the Ohio Distance Learning Association and the League of Worlds, an international virtual world collaborative, and is currently a Fellow with the Carolinas Virtual World Consortium, a collaborative research and development effort between Appalachian State University and Clemson University focused 3D immersive learning environments for teaching and learning. Dr. Sanders' current research is focused on the use of Action Learning pedagogy in these 3D virtual worlds and the symbiotic relationship that exists in the convergence of these two phenomena as it relates to our understanding of teaching and learning in virtual worlds.

Raúl Aquino Santos graduated from the University of Colima with a BE in Electrical Engineering, received his MS degree in Telecommunications from the Centre for Scientific Research and Higher Education in Ensenada, Mexico in 1990. He holds a PhD from the Department of Electrical and Electronic Engineering of the University of Sheffield, England. Since 2005, he has been with the College of Telematics, at the University of Colima, where he is currently a Research-Professor in telecommunications networks. His current research interests include wireless and sensor networks.

Dr. Dirk Schaefer is an Assistant Professor at the George W. Woodruff School of Mechanical Engineering at Georgia Institute of Technology. Prior to joining Georgia Tech, Dr. Schaefer was a Lecturer in the School of Engineering at Durham University, UK. During his time at Durham, he earned a Postgraduate Certificate in "Teaching and Learning in Higher Education" (PG-Cert). He joined Durham from a Senior Research Associate position at the University of Stuttgart, Germany, where he earned his Ph.D. in Computer Science. Dr. Schaefer started his career as an apprentice Toolmaker with one of Germany's leading metal forming companies, where he specialized in CNC machining and the manufacture of compound tool sets for knuckle joint presses. On completion of his apprenticeship he went on to obtain an Advanced Technical College Certificate in Mechanical Engineering and followed this with a Masters degree in Mathematics from the University of Duisburg, Germany. Prior to working in academia Dr. Schaefer gained experience as a Software Engineer in the area of CAD system development. Dr. Schaefer has published around 80 papers in journals, books and conference proceedings on Computer-Aided Engineering and Design as well as Engineering Education. Dr. Schaefer is a registered professional European Engineer (**Eur Ing**), a Chartered Engineer (**CEng**), a Chartered IT-Professional (**CITP**) and a Fellow of the Higher Education Academy (**FHEA**) in the UK.

Michael R. Solomon, Ph.D. is Professor of Marketing and Director of the Center for Consumer Research in the Haub School of Business at Saint Joseph's University in Philadelphia. He also is Professor of Consumer Behaviour at the Manchester School of Business, The University of Manchester, U.K His research interests include consumer behavior and lifestyle issues, branding strategy, and marketing applications of virtual world platforms. Prof. Solomon has been recognized as one of the fifteen most widely-cited scholars in the academic behavioral sciences/fashion literature, and as one of the ten most productive scholars in the field of advertising and marketing communications. His textbook, *Consumer Behavior: Buying, Having, and Being,* is the most widely-used in the world. His latest book, *The Truth about What Customers Want* , was published in October 2008 by FT (*Financial Times*) Press.

Eleni Stroulia is a Professor and iCORE Industrial Research Chair on Service Systems Management with the Department of Computing Science at the University of Alberta. She holds M.Sc. and Ph.D. degrees from Georgia Institute of Technology. Her research addresses industrially relevant software-engineering problems with automated methods, based on artificial-intelligence techniques. Her team has produced automated methods for migrating legacy interfaces to web-based front ends, and for analyzing and supporting the design evolution of object-oriented software. More recently, she has been working on the development, composition, run-time monitoring and adaptation of service-oriented applications, and on examining the role of web 2.0 tools and virtual worlds in offering innovative health-care services. She was the program co-chair for the Canadian AI in 2001, WCRE in 2003 and 2004, CASCON 2006 and ICPC 2007 and the general chair of ICSM 2009.

Dr. Debi Switzer is a Professor of Education at Clemson University. She teaches educational psychology courses, including learning and motivation theory, measurement, and research methods. She spent the first nine years of her career as a secondary mathematics and computer science teacher. She received her Ph.D. in educational psychology (Quantitative and Evaluative Research Methodology) from the University of Illinois Urbana. She has been at Clemson University since 1990. In 2000 she was named a Distinguished Professor by the South Carolina Commission on Higher Education, and in 2003 she received the Prince Award for Innovation in Teaching presented by the Clemson University student government. She has given college teaching effectiveness workshops to faculty for over a decade. She served as a consulting editor for the Journal of Educational Research for two terms. In research projects she has collaborated with faculty in engineering, psychology, education, recreation, counseling, public health, and business, supplying expertise in assessment and experimental design. In 2000, she received the Harold E. Mitzel Award for Meritorious Contribution to Educational Practice Through Research. Currently she has funded grants with faculty in engineering, computer science, communication, and biology. Her interests in motivation, assessment, and research design include the instructional benefits of virtual worlds, improving retention in STEM majors, and the use of electronic portfolios for program evaluation.

Dr. John H. Tashner is a Professor in the Instructional Technology program at Appalachian State University with 30+ years experience in university teaching. Prior to this, John served in various roles as a central office school administrator, an assistant principal, and a public school science teacher. He received his BS in Biology and an MS in Science Education, both from Old Dominion University. He earned his Ed.D. in Curriculum and Instruction from the University of Virginia in 1973. For the past eight years John has been exploring with his colleagues the efficacies of 3D immersive worlds for on-line teaching and learning. Together with the other program faculty, the entire IT graduate program at ASU has been moved into a 3D immersive world environment. Current research interests involve the continued development and study of viable pedagogies that result in deep learning for use in online 3D immersive worlds for education.

Natalie T. Wood, Ph.D. is Assistant Professor of Marketing, and Assistant Director of the Center for Consumer Research in the Haub School of Business at Saint Joseph's University in Philadelphia.

Her research on avatars and virtual worlds has been published in journals such as *Marketing Education Review*, *International Journal of Internet Marketing and Advertising*, *Journal of Website Promotion*, and *Journal of Advertising Education*. She is also an advisory editor for the *Journal of Virtual Worlds Research*.

Dr. Marty Yopp is a professor in Adult and Organizational Learning at the University of Idaho Boise Center. She has been teaching and advising graduate students in adult education and human resource development for more than a decade. She has developed and taught graduate students using a virtual format and has participated in and planned virtual meetings. Dr. Yopp earned her Ed.D. from George Washington University in Washington, DC in higher education with an emphasis in human resource development and adult education. She is a past-president of the Idaho Liflong Learning Association and a member of the Treasure Valley Chapter of ASTD.

Pavel Zemliansky is an associate professor in the School of Writing, Rhetoric, and Technical Communication, where he also coordinates the graduate program in technical and scientific communication. Dr. Zemliansky teaches courses in writing, rhetoric, and technical communication. He has published books, book chapters, and journal articles in the fields of rhetoric and composition as well as technical communication. His latest books is The Handbook of Research on Virtual Workplaces and the New Nature of Business Practices, which he co-edited with Kirk St. Amant in 2008 and which was published by IGI-Global.

Index